SEA OF STORMS

LAWRENCE STONE LECTURES

Sponsored by:

The Shelby Cullom Davis Center for Historical Studies and Princeton University Press

2012

A list of titles in this series appears at the back of the book.

SEA OF STORMS

∿∿∿

A History of Hurricanes in the Greater Caribbean
from Columbus to Katrina

Stuart B. Schwartz

PRINCETON UNIVERSITY PRESS
PRINCETON AND OXFORD

Published by Princeton University Press, 41 William Street, Princeton, New Jersey 08540

In the United Kingdom: Princeton University Press, 6 Oxford Street, Woodstock, Oxfordshire OX20 1TW

press.princeton.edu

Jacket Art: detail of engraving from "Plenas" series © Lorenzo Homar. Reproduction authorized by Susan Homar Damm and Laura Homar Damm.

ISBN 978-0-691-15756-6

Library of Congress Control Number: 2014950430

British Library Cataloging-in-Publication Data is available

This book has been composed in Palatino Lt Std

Printed on acid-free paper. ∞

Printed in the United States of America

1 3 5 7 9 10 8 6 4 2

to don Victor and doña Seti

for the past

to Ali and Lee

for the present

to Leo and Mae

for their future

to María

forever

Contents

ⓥⓥⓥ

Preface

◌◌◌◌

In the summer of 1986, I took my dog-eared copy of Fernand Braudel's *The Mediterranean and the Mediterranean World* off the shelf and began to reread it. During much of the period from the mid-1960s to the mid-1980s I had been researching and writing a book about the history of sugar plantations and slavery in Brazil. During that time I had read extensively in some of the wonderful and innovative books published in that period about slavery, race relations, plantation systems, and colonial societies not only in Brazil and Spanish America, but in North America and the Caribbean as well. As I finished my book on Brazilian sugar, I began to consider beginning a new project on the Caribbean, but I wanted to branch out and to explore some dimension other than slavery that might provide a unifying theme for my studies. The Caribbean seemed broadly analogous to the Mediterranean, and so I turned to Braudel's book, an old friend, for inspiration. This great book is filled with provocative ideas, some that have withstood the test of time better than others, but its focus on the sea itself, its islands and surrounding mainlands, peninsulas, mountain ranges, and the coasts that gave the Mediterranean its shape had been at its time an exciting way to reconceptualize the history of a region. By downplaying political change and by disregarding the division of that sea into Christian and Muslim spheres, or into histories confined by national or cultural boundaries, Braudel had sought the elements that had defined the region as a whole, and that had often resulted in shared behaviors, beliefs, and actions transcending national, religious, and other cultural divisions.

As I read on through that summer, it was clear that geography and environment, or what Braudel called "climate," set the parameters of culture, politics, and history in that ancient sea where bread, olives, and the vine had created a shared civilization. While Braudel writing in the late

1940s had a rather static idea of climate as an unchanging physical context for human action which today's environmental historians would question, his turn toward the relation of human activity to the physical world, an interest he shared with a number of his postwar French colleagues, was a major historiographical breakthrough.[1] Braudel, Leroy Ladurie, and the other French scholars had not been alone in this approach. As a Latin Americanist by training, I already knew of a remarkable early environmental history *avant la lettre* by the Chilean scholar Benjamín Vicuña Mackenna on the climate of Chile done in 1877, and I reread that too.[2] As I thought about my project and read more widely about the Caribbean, it seemed to me that there were few places better suited to Braudel's approach than the circum-Caribbean region, and perhaps fewer still that might profit more from a history in which the linguistic, political, and cultural boundaries that have created separate peoples and separate historiographies might be overcome. Here were hundreds of islands scattered by ancient tectonic movements in a chain extending some 2,500 miles (4,000 km), between the coastal regions of two great continents, joined together by the isthmus of Central America and Mexico, what Pablo Neruda called "the sweet waist of America." These territories, divided by the languages and cultures of their colonial settlers, where each had developed its own local or creole linguistic variations, were divided geographically as well into continental and insular nations each with its own history and identity; there were many reasons for separate treatment. As the Jamaican historian Neville Hall once noted about the strand of "pearls" that made up the island Caribbean: "The pearls, unstrung by nature, have defied each successive effort of political artifice, whether by Caribs, Spaniards, other European colonizers or post-colonial polities, to be re-strung on a single enduring chain and held together by some unifying informing principle."[3]

But at the same time, the commonalities were clear. From Charleston to Cartagena or Veracruz to Bridgetown, similar vegetation, similar landscapes, similar rhythms of life, and similar products had made the Caribbean societies sisters in experience and sibling rivals for survival. All had in some way or to some degree experienced European colonization, destruction of indigenous populations, African slavery, plantation regimes, the creation of multiracial societies, waves of African, Asian, and European immigrants, the legacies of race and the struggle for independence, experiments with political forms and sometimes authoritarian rule in a search for viable political and economic outcomes that in the postmodern world have sometimes brought the surreal solutions of offshore banking, drug trading, or sexual tourism. Perhaps it would be an overreach to see here a cultural unity parallel to the Braudel's Mediterranean civilization of bread, wine, and olives in the Caribbean's plantains, salt cod, and rum so common on the tables of this American sea, but there are many commonalities born of time, experience, and place. Among these, the geography of the region has exerted a tremendous influence, and the shared environmental conditions and hazards—earthquakes, volcanoes, tsunamis, droughts, epidemic diseases—have created a certain "transnational" unity of experience. Of these common challenges, none has been greater, more frequent, or more characteristic than the cyclonic storms, the hurricanes of the North Atlantic.

And so I began to think about using hurricanes and the ways societies of the Greater Caribbean understood them and responded to them as a kind of meta-narrative, a general organizing theme that would allow me to examine the past of the region over the long course of its history. Other such general themes have been used in the past. Slavery, war, plantations, migration, and colonialism have all provided "transnational" meta-narratives, or ways of telling the region's history, and my intention is not to replace them, but rather to use an element of natural history as a leitmotif that provides yet another useful tool for viewing the history of the region, and as an element that in a variety of ways has influenced all these other themes as well. But beneath my somewhat naïve intention lurks two epistemological problems. First, hurricanes seem to be classic examples of acts of God, phenomena outside of history, beyond human control, and perhaps more deserving of theological or scientific explanations than historical analysis. At the same time, there is also the danger of falling into the trap of geographic or environmental determinism that has snared many scholars, in which everything is described in terms of environmental limits by using geography or climate as an independent variable, making everything else dependent. I have tried to be aware of that pitfall and to be careful not to ascribe too much to environment, or to deemphasize human influence in shaping it or its effects. Climate and geography set limits and created possibilities; societies continually tested those boundaries or reshaped them, and it was human agency that exploited or missed opportunities in the process. This book seeks to explore why and how that happened across a broad region in which, despite considerable cultural and historical differences, the same environmental threat produced responses that were similar, but that were always constrained by local politics and social realities.

In this study I have accepted the widely held position that natural disasters are never simply natural, but are also the result of human actions, policies, and attitudes taken or held before, during, and after the event. In this study of hurricanes, the storms themselves are not the protagonists here as they are in the work of meteorologists who have done such wonderful research in reconstructing the dimensions, intensity, and track of past storms.[4] I have learned much from that field, but my objectives are different. My focus is on the societies affected by the storms, how peoples and governments responded to them, and how, over time, cultures perceived or understood their nature and meaning. So while atmospheric phenomena are at the heart of this study, and there are elements here drawn from the major approaches of environmental history such as a concern with the physical properties and scientific understanding of hurricanes, or how changing understandings of Nature, science, and God shaped human responses to the storms, the principal focus of this study is on how the hurricanes shaped social and political life, and how in turn social and political patterns in the Greater Caribbean influenced the impact of the storms.[5] Given the geography and history of the region, this book is by necessity transnational and comparative. The hurricanes have no respect for political and cultural boundaries, and so much of this story is about how different peoples and states confronted the same natural hazards, and often the same storm, with different policies and results, but at times also sought similar solutions to their common challenges, and even collaborated in their responses despite religious or political differences.

Hurricanes are one kind of potential catastrophe in a region that is subject to many physical hazards, and in some ways it makes little sense to separate hurricanes from a more general consideration of natural disasters. Individual volcanic events like the 1902 eruption of Mount Pelée on Martinique that killed 30,000 people have historically been more deadly than most hurricanes, and over the course of the centuries the greatest killer of all has been disease, which has decimated indigenous populations, exacted a morbid tribute from forced African immigrants, and killed Europeans who arrived in the region at a mortality rate about four times that suffered by Africans.[6] Still, of all the hazards that humans confront in the region, none is more characteristic than the hurricanes, destructive forces in themselves, but also the triggers of other calamities. Even in the eighteenth century, there was recognition that the hurricanes' destruction of shelter and crops weakened populations and made them more vulnerable to famine, epidemics, or other threats.

Early modern observers also perceived a certain unity of misfortunes. They believed that hurricanes, shortages, droughts, and sickness were interrelated hazards, and that along with the piracy, warfare, imperial rivalries, and early forms of ethnic cleansing, they were characteristic of the region. The combination of these hazards sometimes led to fatalism and a view of the region as a dystopia, but that negative view was balanced to some extent by the possibilities of wealth and power that the region could provide. John Fowler, writing in 1781 from the rubble of the worst hurricane in the region's history, argued that just as men of the best hearts and greatest talents are moved by violent passions, Caribbean islands, which have the richest soils and most abundant products, were subject to more hurricanes and earthquakes than the rest of the world. The region's disasters, for Fowler, were thus evidence of its singular potential and advantages.[7]

While it is true that a distinction between natural events over which humanity has no control, and those like war or economic collapse that are the result of human actions or decisions, has often been made, there have always been those who have argued that to the victims it makes little difference in which realm—nature or culture—the origins of their misery lay. In fact, the argument about the validity of that distinction itself lies at the heart of government responses to natural disasters, and in the very origins of the welfare state or what the French called the *état providence*. Moreover, since the mid-twentieth century, with the rise of environmental concerns, a case has been made for extensive human influences on climatic conditions, which further blurs any distinction between anthropogenic and natural catastrophes.

Hurricanes are violent cyclonic storms, usually but not always accompanied by very heavy rainfall. In the North Atlantic, they often form in the area where the prevailing northeasterly trade winds meet southeasterly winds rising from south of the equator and their meeting creates atmospheric instability. In the summer months, warm moisture is pulled into the unstable air in these low-pressure cells that form over tropical or subtropical waters, and as the winds begin to swirl in a counterclockwise rotation, convection causes the moisture to rise rapidly. With favorable atmospheric conditions and temperature, the storm will intensify around the relatively calm "eye." Often accompanied by thunderstorms and torrential rain, the winds can reach above 175 miles per hour and the storm's diameter can cover areas of 300–500 miles or even more. The destructive potential of an intense hurricane is frightening.

Cyclonic storms take place across the globe, in the northern and southern Pacific, the Indian Ocean, and the North Atlantic; the latter is home to only about eleven percent of the annual global occurrence of hurricanes, but that region, much of what I have called here the Greater Caribbean, is of particular interest to me because of the interconnected past of colonial settlements, plantation economies, and slavery, and then its subsequent history of independence, decolonization, and the hegemony of the United States. This circum- (or Greater) Caribbean region lies physically and conceptually at the core of an Atlantic world defined in the early modern era by that history of conquest, settlement slavery, and plantations, and the weight of its past still burdens much of this region.

Different scholars have made various attempts to define the boundaries of this Greater Caribbean, which in this study also includes the Gulf of Mexico and the southeastern United States. If we take a compass and place its point at Bridgetown, the capital and major city of Barbados, we can then create a great circle that roughly encompasses the principal locales that formed this Atlantic world. Dakar in Senegal lies 2,800 miles to the east and Mexico City 2,700 miles to the west (fig. 0.1). To the south the

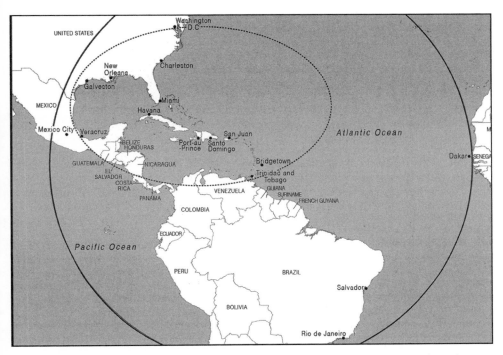

FIGURE 0.1 The Greater Caribbean and the principal zone of hurricane strikes (Map by Santiago Muñoz Arbalaez)

great port of Rio de Janeiro is also about 2,700 miles distant, and Salvador, the colonial capital of Brazil and a major terminus of the slave trade, about 430 miles closer to Barbados. To the north, the Chesapeake Bay marks the northern boundary of the slave and tobacco economy. Washington, DC is some 2,000 miles from Bridgetown. Certainly slaves labored and plantations and haciendas flourished in the lands beyond the limits of this great circle, and the colonial authorities in Madrid, London, Amsterdam, Copenhagen, and Paris all lived beyond the circle's perimeter, but in a way, Barbados was a geographic center of an Atlantic world defined by a brutally consistent history.[8]

Where this book departs from others that have used an Atlantic history approach and that have emphasized a comparative and interconnected history is in extending the chronological coverage into and beyond the twentieth century by showing not only the continuities and interconnections of the early modern era, but also those created within the Atlantic world by technology, science, ideology, finance, and other forms of modernity.[9] In that sense, I am also following Braudel by looking at the *longue durée,* although I am aware that this scope creates its own challenges of focus and coverage.

Within the circle that defines the Greater Caribbean is the much more restricted Atlantic hurricane zone; Barbados lies close to its southern edge. While tropical depressions that become hurricanes form in the broad expanse of the Atlantic and have always been a danger to maritime commerce and sailors' lives, my interest in these pages is focused primarily on the effects of these storms over land and societies. Surely, hurricanes, conceived and born always over warm oceanic water, underline the predominance of the sea in the life of the Greater Caribbean, but their impact is not felt equally throughout the region. Hurricanes are not random phenomena. Atmospheric conditions and physics limit their movement. For example, they rarely move directly west across the Atlantic above 20°N latitude to strike the coasts of the southeastern United States because the relatively stationary high pressure zone over Bermuda deflects them southward or northward back into the Atlantic.[10] Barbados lies about 13° north of the equator, and so it is infrequently visited by hurricanes, which are uncommon at that latitude, and never form closer than 5° from the equator, since for geophysical reasons the rotational movement of cyclonic storms is impeded by the so-called Coriolis effect in which the earth's rotation at the latitude of the equator impedes the characteristic circulatory wind pattern of the hurricanes. Thus, islands south of Barbados such as Trinidad, Tobago, and Curaçao have rarely been affected by the storms, nor are the rimlands of Venezuela, the Guianas, and Colombia, even though they all have played an important role within the Greater Caribbean region and shared many of its other attributes. Still further to the south, coastal Brazil, another great American plantation-slavery complex that through much of its history was the Caribbean's rival, and sometimes its model, has also been exempted from the visits of the hurricanes and the challenges they present. Thus it does not play a major role in this study, although in many ways its history paralleled that of the Caribbean islands and the southern United States.

The focus of this book is not the hurricanes themselves, but how people, governments, and societies have responded to them. I take up this story from the time that Europeans first arrived in the Caribbean in 1492, but modern meteorological and oceanographic studies indicate that hurricanes had visited the North Atlantic for many millennia before the Pleistocene epoch, when *Homo sapiens* arose as a species, and long before peoples inhabited the Americas. While, of course, these natural phenomena were not "disasters" so long as human lives were not at risk, the subfield of paleotempestology (the study of ancient storms and weather) and hundreds of modern post-hurricane studies have shown that the great storms have tremendous effects on flora and fauna, water resources and landscapes, coral reefs, nesting sites, and species survival.[11] Studies show that cyclonic storms have a differential impact on mainlands and islands, or between large islands and small islands. They also demonstrate that the distribution of heat and moisture from the tropics northward is an essential element of a hurricane's function, and how that process has produced long-term effects on the formation of continents and islands and on their inhabitants. Much contemporary research on hurricanes deals with these environmental and ecological processes.[12] From the modern study of hurricanes, I have taken one of its advances and used it somewhat anachronistically. The Saffir-Simpson Hurricane Scale, developed in the early 1970s by Herbert Saffir, an engineer, and Bob Simpson, a meteorologist, created categories of hurricanes ranked from 1 to 5 based on the velocity of their sustained winds and their barometric pressure (fig. 0.2).[13] This scale then facilitates estimates of the height of accompanying storm surges and associated property and environmental damage. Storms of Category 3 and above (winds 111–130 miles per hour and barometric pressure from 27.90 to 28.46 inches (945–964 millibars) are considered major. Prior to the use of this scale it was difficult to speak comparatively about hurricanes and their effects, although people have always (if inaccurately) done so. Reports from governors and observers in the seventeenth and eighteenth centuries often made reference to the memory of elderly residents who might say that a particular storm was "worse that the hurricane of '99," or "more frightening than the one of '28." That kind of anecdotal accounting along with records of losses and deaths was all that governments and so-

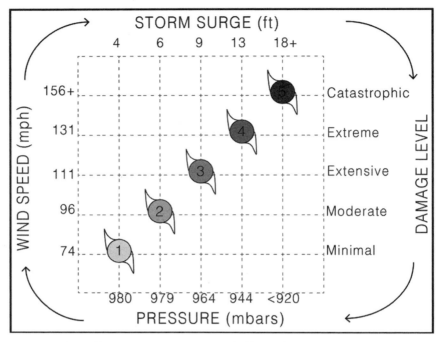

FIGURE 0.2 The Saffir-Simpson Hurricane Scale (design by R. L. Shepard)

cieties could depend on to gauge a storm's effects. The Saffir-Simpson scale now allows for easier comparisons across time, and I have used the scale to give estimates of hurricane intensity and impacts.[14]

Much of the history of the interaction of cyclonic storms and human agency in any of the world's seas where they occur might emphasize the same themes of destruction and response: the theories of the storms' origins, government responsibility, the important impact of scientific knowledge and technology and of communication systems in lessening the storms' impact. But, as I have suggested above, the history of hurricanes in the Greater Caribbean cannot be adequately told without reference to two peculiar historical conditions that provide continuities and interconnections: the reality of slavery and its legacy of racial prejudice and, in the twentieth century, the political, technological, and economic hegemony of the United States. Both of these phenomena cast long, and at times quite distinct, shadows over the whole region and its history of dealing with natural calamities. As this book will demonstrate, social and racial distinctions patterned societal response even long after slavery had been eliminated as an institution, and the issue of race, even as in the nineteenth century and in contemporary times it shades into vocabularies of class, has never been far from the way in which governments and peoples of the Greater Caribbean have met the storms. This study will reveal a remarkable continuity in the arguments for and against governmental aid to the victims of disaster over the last five centuries. Finally, the United States, by its military and political expansion into the Caribbean after 1898, its foreign policy objectives in the Cold War, and through its advocacy of certain forms of capitalism joined with its ability to impose its preferences on international institutions, has also influenced the way in which the whole region has faced hurricanes and other disasters.

Writing a history of interaction between an environmental phenomenon and various societies over the course of more than five centuries imposes certain methods and limitations. Since in modern times the average number of hurricanes per year in the region is about eight, we can roughly gauge that since Columbus's arrival the region has experienced some 4,000 to 5,000 hurricane-level storms. A hurricane-by-hurricane approach is thus clearly not possible. Moreover, even if it was, the repetition of descriptions of the storms' characteristics and tracks and the sad accounting of the rising water, violent winds, flying roofs, broken homes, and broken hearts would be numbing. So I have throughout this book looked for the storms in each period that could be used to illustrate the predominant thinking about natural phenomena at the time, or which because of the availability of sources about them make it possible to recapture social and political strategies in meeting their threat. Hurricanes that were clearly linked to social or political change or which elicited governmental policies that underlined existing realities or transformed societies have often been chosen as my examples. That strategy has tended to sharpen my focus on particularly deadly or costly storms, which were usually the ones that generated more sources and more government concern, but these "great" storms are somewhat atypical, and so I have tried to balance my account at various places by more general discussions of societal responses under less calamitous circumstances.

With a chronological scope of over five centuries, and across a region of many cultures and nations, I realize that I have sometimes skimmed too briefly over important subthemes like the histories of meteorology, communication technologies, or the insurance industry, and I have only scratched the surface of other well-developed fields related to my study. Since Pitirim Sorokin's study of calamities was first published in 1942, social scientists have developed an extensive literature on disaster and risk, from micro-level studies of individual floods or earthquakes to broad studies of disaster as an aspect of the postmodern world.[15] A whole separate field of disaster management policy and economics has also developed, with its own publications and conferences, and with authors and readers from public, nongovernmental, and international relief institutions. I have learned from both these fields, but have not always found them helpful for understanding other eras and other cultures. My objective has been to write a history that reflects how changing concepts of divine providence and nature patterned the perception of the great storms, and with it, the concept of how to deal with them. I wish to explore how changing attitudes about the role of charity, community, and the function of government altered the way in which states and peoples responded to natural calamities; and how political and intellectual transformations eventually produced a perception of natural phenomena as part of an environment over which humans bore some responsibility.

There has long existed a historiography of hurricanes. The earliest studies were produced in the nineteenth century by scholars who intuitively understood that establishing a record of the storms and their characteristics might help define patterns that could be useful in predicting future hurricanes. Later, meteorologists began using historical sources to advance their understanding of the characteristics of these storms as part of the physical world. By the twentieth century many histories had appeared, some of them detailed studies of individual storms, and others the hurricane histories of individual islands, countries, or states, sometimes with a focus more regional and antiquarian than analytical, but usually presenting a wealth of local information. Many of them appear in the footnotes on the following pages. In the last twenty years, a number of books and articles have appeared in a new social and political history of hurricanes and of other natural disasters that have provided excellent models for this book, and covered in detail events and questions that I have only presented here in a summary fashion. Matthew Mulcahy's in-depth study of hurricanes in the British West Indies, Charles Walker's study of the 1746 Lima earthquake, John McNeil's *Mosquito Empires*, Geoffrey Parker's *Global Crisis*, Louis Pérez's and Sherry Johnson's detailed volumes on hurricanes in Cuba, Erik Larson's book on the great Galveston disaster, and Raymond Arsenault's overview article of U.S. hurricane policy are all part of an innovative historiography that has brought environmental, social, cultural, and political history together in a new way.[16] I hope this book will carry their work forward and that through this study of past calamities we may gain a better understanding of how to deal with the social and political dimensions of environmental challenge in the future.

Acknowledgments

⊙⊙⊙⊙

$\mathbf{A}$lthough my interest in hurricanes had begun in the 1980s and I had published an article on Puerto Rico's San Ciriaco hurricane in 1992, and continued to collect archival sources and bibliography, other projects kept me from writing this book. An invitation from the Shelby Cullum Davis Center at Princeton University to present the Lawrence Stone Lectures in 2012 gave me an opportunity to return to this subject and to concentrate my attention on the materials that I had gathered over the years. Those three lectures, entitled "Providence Politics and the Wind: Hurricanes in the Shaping of Caribbean Societies," examined only the early modern period. The present volume includes that material, but extends the chronological coverage from the nineteenth into the twenty-first century. I am grateful to the Davis Center and its directors Daniel Rodgers and Philip Nord for the honor of their invitation, and appreciative to those who attended the talks for the excellent discussion, criticism, and suggestions that resulted. I would like to note here a special thanks for the questions and suggestions that I received from Jeremy Adelman, Arcadio Díaz Quiñoes, Anthony Grafton, Caley Horan, Michael Barany, and William Jordan. I also owe a special debt of thanks to the late David Ludlum (1910–1996), a former Princeton history major, army meteorologist, and long-time resident of the Princeton community. An important historian of American weather, he was willing to meet with me on a number of occasions when I was just beginning this project while a fellow at the Institute for Advanced Study in 1984. He gave me some direction, good advice, and a copy of his *Early American Hurricanes,* and took an interest in this project at its origins. I think he would have been pleased to see its publication and to hold in his hands this book that he did so much to shape. I also wish to thank Stanley J. Stein, my former professor, who also raised interesting questions at my lectures, and, as he has always done, forced me to question my sources and my assumptions.

I have sometimes reminded graduate students of Marcel Proust's warning that "books are the work of solitude and the children of silence." Historians spend much of their time poring over documents in archives or engaged in solitary study of a text. But, in truth, writing a book like this one often becomes a collaborative effort. First of all, like all historians I owe a special debt of thanks to the directors and staff of the various archives and libraries in Europe, the United States, and the Caribbean where I carried out the research for this book. Their help, guidance, and professionalism have been indispensable to my work. Then over the years of travel, archives, conferences, lunches, and correspondence, I have benefited and learned a great deal from many friends and colleagues. They have shared their work with me, provided archival and bibliographical tips, sometimes generously shared their own research findings, helped me resolve difficult questions, and responded to what must have seemed to them sometimes irritating and persistent inquiries. Their friendship, patience, encouragement, suggestions, criticism, and caveats make the office of historian a pleasurable cooperative experience, and make the lonely work of an historian seem more bearable. Here in the United States, Greg Grandin, Francisco Scarano, Matthew Mulcahy, Matthew Restall, Robin Derby, Jorge Cañizares-Esguerra, Philip Morgan, Rebecca Scott, Lillian Guerra, J. R. McNeil, Louis Perez, Sherry Johnson, Raymond Arsenault, Wim Klooster, Charles Walker, Carla Rahn Phillips, Alan Isaacman, David Ryden, Russell Menard, and the late Teresita Martínez, have all given me help and encouragement and caught some of the more egregious errors. Alejandro de la Fuente and Laurent Dubois were exceptionally generous, providing me with their research notes and allowing me to use and cite them. Judge José Cabranes of the United States Court of Appeals kindly shared with me the story of his family's sad association with the San Ciriaco hurricane of 1899, and took a continuing interest in this project as it developed.

Scholars and friends who live and work in the Caribbean have made a major contribution to my work, and I have great benefited from the help and advice of Roberto Cassá, Aldair Rodrigues, Genaro Rodríguez Morel,

Manolo Rodriguez, Pedro San Miguel, Fernando Picó, Gervasio Luís García, Francisco Moscoso, Reinaldo Funes Monzote, Richard and Sally Price, James Robertson, and Terencia Joseph. I particularly appreciate the support of Humberto Garcia Muñiz and his colleagues at the Institute of Caribbean Studies of the University of Puerto Rico for providing me an institutional affiliation and inviting me to share my work in their lecture series. I also greatly profited during my work at the Centro de Investigaciones Historicas at the University of Puerto Rico from the support and help of its director and my friend, María Dolores "Lolita" Luque, the editorial help of Miriam Lugo, and the generosity other members of the staff. The Official Historian of Puerto Rico and old classmate of mine, Luís E. González Valés, has continually provided support to this project and supplied me with the invaluable reeditions of historical texts sponsored by his office. Various colleagues and friends in Europe also gave me archival tips and pointed me in the right direction or saved me from at least some serious errors. These included José Piqueras, Fernando Bouza Alvarez, Jean-Fédéric Schaub, Bethany Arram, Diana Paton, and Gad Heuman.

As a teacher as well as a scholar I have also benefited from my contact with students.

At the University of Puerto Rico and the Catedra Jaime Cortesão of the University of São Paulo, where I taught courses related to the theme of this book, students challenged my conceptualizations and pointed me toward new materials. I have also had the good fortune to teach for many years at universities with excellent graduate programs, and a number of students and former students have helped me in many ways. Luis González, Arlene Díaz, Casey King, Elena Pelus, Tatiana Seijas, Ingrid Castañeda, Jennifer Lambe, and Michael Bustamante have read chapters or provided suggestions or leads to documents. Santiago Muñoz Arbalaez has helped with the preparation of the maps. I owe a special debt to Taylor Jardno, who has tried unsuccessfully to keep me digitally up to date, and who helped with editorial preparation of the book. I have had the benefit of research assistance from Catherine Arnold at Yale, Ramonita Vega Lugo in San Juan, Jonas Pedersen in Copenhagen, and Roseanne Baars in the Netherlands. Lectures and seminars at a number of institutions and various academic symposia and conferences allowed me to present early ver-sions of some of the chapters printed here, and profit from the comments and discussions of colleagues and students. These included presentations at New York University, UCLA, Columbia, Indiana University, Harvard University, Universidad de Puerto Rico, Universidad Madre y Maestra in Santo Domingo, Universidade Federal de Rio de Janeiro, Universidade Federal de Minas Gerais, and the Universitat Jaume I, as well as papers at the meeting of the American Historical Association and at the Third Allen Morris Conference on Florida and the Atlantic World of Florida State University (2004).

I owe thanks to many colleagues at Yale. Roberto González-Echevarría shared his extensive knowledge of the Caribbean and his memories of a Cuban boyhood. Rolena Adorno pointed me toward some colonial sources, while Aníbal González and Priscilla Meléndez brought hurricane references in contemporary Caribbean literature to my attention and provided encouragement and support. My history colleagues Edward Rugemer, Paul Freedman, Gilbert Joseph, Jennifer Klein, Carlos Eire, Francesca Trivellato, Alan Mikhail, Steve Pincus, Andy Horowitz, and Jay Gitlin all gave me the benefit of their knowledge and command of historiographies about which I had much to learn. My colleague Jay Winter shared the proofs of his new book on human rights, which was particularly helpful. The process of preparing the book for publication was made less burdensome than usual by Brigitta van Rheinberg, my editor at Princeton University Press, whose encouragement and patience helped me at every stage of publication.

On a personal level, my children Alison Bird and Lee Schwartz have always been patient and encouraging, offering suggestions and advice on digital challenges and resources, and taking an interest in the project while building their own families. Finally and most importantly, I should confess that my passion for the Caribbean owes a great deal to my marriage to María Jordán, a native of Puerto Rico, a scholar in her own right, and an excellent source of information on hurricanes, politics, popular culture, and much else about the Caribbean. From her, her siblings, and especially her parents, doña Divina Arroyo de Jordán and the late don Victór Jordán Hernández, I learned much about the history of the storms and about life and politics in their shadow. I hope they will find that these pages reflect in some way their perceptions and wisdom. María has also been an excellent reader, and occasionally a translator and interpreter of texts. When, in 2012, far from the Greater Caribbean, we were forced from our home in Connecticut by Hurricane Sandy, her experience and knowledge of hurricanes guided us through that difficult time. She has made this book possible in many ways, and the long hours spent in its research and writing it have passed all too quickly with her at my side.

Stuart B. Schwartz

Guilford, Connecticut, 2014

SEA OF STORMS

CHAPTER 1

⟨⟩⟨⟩⟨⟩

Storms and Gods in a Spanish Sea

The worst storms of all the world's seas are
those of these islands and coasts.
—*Bartolomé de Las Casas (1561)*

San Miguel, arcangel	Saint Michael, Archangel
Principe general	The Prince over all
libranos de los rayos	Save us from the lightning bolts
del tremendo temporal	of the great storm

—*Traditional prayer, rural Puerto Rico*

The wind began on Thursday, the last day of August 1552, and by Friday it had become a storm of powerful winds and heavy rain. The residents New Spain's port of Veracruz were already accustomed to the *nortes*, strong north winds, brought by the cold fronts of November and December that could reach a force of 80 miles per hour along the coast and in the bay, but this was different. By Friday night it had become a violent tempest blowing from the north, and then shifting, as one observer later testified, "from all the other points of the compass" (*de todos vientos de la aguja*)—the telltale phrase for an early modern description of a hurricane. The rain had become a deluge, and by Friday night the Huitzilapan and San Juan rivers bordering the city were threatening to overflow their banks. The town, set in the flatlands adjoining the rivers, was in danger. Hernán Cortés's original settlement of Veracruz in 1519 had been created on the mosquito-infested sands near the coast. It had lacked good water, and was too far from any indigenous towns that could provide it food. He had moved it nearer to an Indian town, but that site also had proven un-satisfactory, and in 1524–25 it had been moved again to the confluence of the two rivers.[1] The local Totonac peoples lived in the hills rising behind the coast, where they were protected from the *nortes* and flooding in the lowlands. The Spaniards had chosen poorly. The Totonacs could have warned them of the dangers of the region. Not far to the north in the up-lands lay their great ceremonial center dedicated to Tajín, God of the Storms, the same deity that the Maya called Hurakan.

At ten o'clock on Saturday morning a sea surge swept onto the island of San Juan de Ulúa, just offshore, where a large fortress had been built to guard the harbor. Throughout the city and in the nearby countryside, trees were uprooted and houses began to crumble and collapse. Father Bar-tolomé Romero, vicar of the principal church, later testified that the wind and water were so bad that neither he nor the other priests could reach the church to say mass. The river water began to flow through streets and plazas with considerable force, isolating people in their homes and send-ing many to the roofs as the waters rose.

In the harbor there was havoc. Veracruz was New Spain's principal port, and it had become the terminus for the convoy system that had been established by the Spanish crown to transfer the silver of Mexico to Spain, and in return to deliver wine, textiles, and emigrants to New Spain.[2] The protecting fort at San Juan de Ulúa could do nothing for the ships in the roadstead. Five of the large merchant vessels or *naos* sunk, four others were demasted, and many service boats, and small vessels in the coastal trade from Yucatan, Tabasco, and Campeche, or that came in from Cuba or Hispaniola, also sank. Houses and merchant warehouses were flooded and the docks swept away or damaged. Many of the sailors from the ships took refuge on the island of San Juan itself, in a large house in front of the anchorage, and although four or five drowned, the majority were able to survive the sea surge that swept over the docks with such force that it dismantled the seawall and carried some of its stones to another nearby island. Elsewhere on the island, when the winds shifted direction, a house that served as an inn where ten or twelve blacks and whites had sought refuge was swept into the sea with the loss of all except one man left cling-ing to a tree for two hours before he swam to safety. Fifty or sixty Spaniards reached the upper floor of another large house and hung on to safety. Some slaves survived by holding onto the wreckage of houses. A church bell was loosened and carried by the wind to the shore. It was a disaster that "in the memory of people had not been seen for a long time in these parts."[3]

In the midst of disaster, who could offer help? By nine or ten o'clock on Saturday morning, the mayor and aldermen of the town had mounted their horses and were circulating through the streets warning the residents to get their families and property to high ground because of the rising water that they warned would rise to a level higher than it had in the serious flooding the city had suffered in the previous year. Many people fled on horseback to the surrounding hills. By Saturday night the water was in some places well above a man's height, and houses of adobe were disintegrating. Now barrels and casks of wine, bottles of vinegar and olive oil, and crates of merchandise flowed through the streets and were swept into the sea. Father Romero later testified that by Saturday night he saw the *alcalde* Martín Díaz and some helpers in a boat, moving about the city rescuing those residents who had stayed in their homes, taking the women and children who had fled to the roofs and were pitifully crying for God's mercy to save them from such a death. A young man named Juan Romero circulated with two of his slaves in a canoe, taking the ill and infirm, men, women, and children, to high ground from a large house near the church. The canoe sometimes tipped, and the passengers' money and jewels were lost in the righting of the vessel.

It was a flooded city: wreckage and refuse floating everywhere, shattered homes and broken lives, commerce disrupted, the bloated corpses of animals and people decaying or washing up on shore for days after, the smell of rot and death, and soon, sickness and a shortage of water and food. These were the images of a sixteenth-century Katrina—but they were set in a social, political, and conceptual frame that made an understanding of this catastrophe a moment for reflection on human sin and moral failure as the cause of God's anger. That interpretation would change over time from a providentialist view to one that by the eighteenth century emphasized the normal risks of the natural world, and thus no longer made humans the cause of their own suffering. Explanations would then shift again in the late twentieth century to an emphasis on climatic change that once again placed the onus for natural disasters on human error, but this time on human decisions and policies, not on sin or moral failures.[4]

From his house Father Romero had seen the trees felled and the houses flattened; hour by hour he watched the river rise and eventually overflow its banks, flooding streets and plazas and causing great waves in the streets. He awaited an opportunity to swim to the church in order to rescue the Holy Sacrament, but it was impossible. After the storm had passed he was able to enter the sanctuary, now filled with mud and debris, but he could later report that the water had not risen to the level of the golden tabernacle where the Eucharist was kept, and thus it had not been necessary for him to carry it to the hills. He believed that its presence in the church had stopped the rising water and, in fact, explained why the whole city had not been lost. "God," he said, "was served to punish us all by the loss of our possessions and homes, and to leave us our lives so we could do penance for our sins." Society's relation to nature was not direct but mediated through God's will. The turbulence and disorder of nature had mirrored the disorder of society caused by sin, and departure from virtue provided the moral origin of the storm.[5] Other Catholic interpretations of catastrophe were also possible. The forces of evil and the Devil might also be responsible for such harm, and thus the need for the protection of the saints, public prayers, and processions to reassure and protect the faithful.[6]

Spanish officials and settlers were by this time no strangers to the natural disasters of the New World. They had already acquired sixty years of experience of earthquakes, droughts, epidemics, floods, and hurricanes. In some way, their explanations of these phenomena were consistently providential, and even abnormalities of natural phenomena like earthquakes were still considered normal within divine purpose. But despite their acceptance of God's will as a primary cause, there was always a practical and a political aspect to their perceptions and to their responses as well. In this case, the Veracruz hurricane of 1552, we know the details of the disaster because the viceroy of New Spain, don Luis de Velasco, and the members of the *audiencia* or High Court that served as his council, asked to be informed of the damage suffered so that the king, Charles I, could decide what steps to take. The mayor (*alcalde mayor*) of Veracruz, García de Escalante Alvarado, responded to the request by providing a report supported by testimony from various witnesses. They made clear that the municipal government and courageous town residents had been the first responders, warning the residents of the danger and carrying some to safety. Now the royal government would provide help. In the months following the storm, the viceroy took steps to assure that the people of the Veracruz region would be provided for by assigning a number of Indian communities in the region of Puebla, which had also suffered from the storm, to supply food.[7] Escalante Alvarado pleaded to have the city relocated away from its dangerous location between the river and the sea, but that fourth and final move of Veracruz was not made until 1599, and even then, the city and its port remained, like everything else in this region, under the shadow of the great storms, the characteristic hazard of the Caribbean.

Gods of the Wind

If at first the Spaniards, and then the other Europeans, basically saw in these great American storms a supernatural power, they differed very little in that regard from the native peoples of the region. For the latter, the great storms were part of the annual cycle of life. They respected their power and often deified it, but they also sought practical ways to adjust their lives to the storms. Examples were many. The Calusas of southwest Florida planted rows of trees to serve as windbreaks to protect their villages from hurricanes. On the islands of the Greater Antilles—Cuba, Jamaica, Hispaniola, and Puerto Rico—the Taino people preferred root crops like yucca, malanga, and yautia because of their resistance to windstorm damage. The Maya of Yucatan generally avoided building their cities on the coast because they understood that such locations were vulnerable to the winds and to ocean surges that accompanied the storms. Archaeologists who work on Mesoamerica have suggested that such aspects of life as field management and crop selection, urban layouts and

drainage systems, house construction, forest usage and maintenance, warfare, migration, trade, and cultural shifts or interruptions like the Maya
abandonment of some of the Classic cities (c. 200–1000 CE) all have been
influenced by hurricanes and other natural calamities.[8] It was from the
inhabitants of the islands, the Taíno of the Greater Antilles and the Caribs
who inhabited the smaller islands of the Lesser Antilles, that the Europeans first learned of the storms, but they subsequently also tapped into the
knowledge and understanding of the peoples who occupied the Mexican
Gulf Coast and of the Maya speakers of the Yucatan peninsula and northern Central America. All of the Mesoamerican peoples believed that wind,
water, and fire were the essential elements in the cycles destruction by
which they marked the passage of time. so the gods of rain and wind—
Tlaloc and Ehcatl (a form of Quetzalcoatl) for the Nahuatl speakers of the
Mexican highlands; Tajín for the Totonacs of Veracruz; and Chaak and
Hurakán for the Maya—played a predominant role in the cosmogony and
cosmology of these peoples. In the *Popul Vuh,* the origin myth of the Qui-
ché Maya, Hurakán, "heart of the heavens," god of wind, storm, and fire,
was one of the creator gods in the cycle of destruction and creation of the
universe. Sculptures from the Totonac ruins at El Tajín and the Maya cities
of Uxmal and Copan as well as pre-contact and post-conquest picto-
graphic codices make clear the importance and destructive power of such
gods. The Mesoamerican religions recognized a duality of forces so that
the gods of wind could in their benevolent form bring rains for the crops,
but in their malevolent aspects were destroyers of homes and *milpas,* bear-
ers of misery and death.[9] Even among the Maya of contemporary Quintana Roo there is still a belief that hurricanes represent a struggle between
benign and malevolent aspects of Chaak as part of a cosmic battle that can
bring the destruction of floods, tidal surges, and high winds, but can also
renew the earth and bring life-giving waters.[10]

A great deal of confusion clouds the etymology of the word "huracán,"
by which the Spanish came to know the storms and from which the English "hurricane," French "ouragan," Dutch "orkaan," and Danish "ork-
anen" all derive. Was it just coincidence that the Taíno word "hurakan"
and the Maya "Huracán" were so similar, or was this the result of linguistic ties, or affinities, or cultural contact? Perhaps the Spanish "huracán"

simply postdates the contact with Mesoamerica and was applied after the fact by chroniclers who were writing about earlier contacts on the islands. We know that the term does not appear in Fray Ramón Pane's descriptions of Taíno culture from the 1490s, and is first used in Fernández de Oviedo's *Historia natural* in 1526. Columbus's journal employs the term, but the original of that document disappeared long ago, and the version that finally appeared in print was not published until the mid-sixteenth century, long after the conquest of Mexico had taken place. Thus, there is the possibility of a later post-Mesoamerican contact interpolation of the term.[11] It is also possible that the etymology of "huracán" is not Amerindian at all. The word does not appear in the original 1611 edition of Sebastian de Covarrubias's great dictionary, the first vernacular dictionary of Spanish, but a later edition of 1674 claimed that the etymology could be traced to the Spanish verb *horadar* (to penetrate) because the water seemed to almost penetrate the ships that were sunk, causing a "horacán." An eighteenth-century Spanish dictionary ascribed the origins of the word to the Latin term *ventus furens* (violent wind), which was then hispanized as "furacan" or "furacano"—the form in which Columbus first used it.[12]

Whatever the origins of the term, however, the Native American peoples who had migrated to the islands from the South American continent had learned to structure their lives to the seasonality, frequency, and power of the storms. The Taínos of the large islands marked time in their communal ceremonial dances or *arreitos* by singing of the great deeds of their ancestors and chiefs and by remembering the occasions of the great hurricanes. Ramón Pané, the Augustinian friar who accompanied Columbus's second voyage in 1492 and who became the first European to write about the indigenous peoples of the Greater Antilles, reported that the Taíno saw the winds as the force of the *cemi* or deity Guabancex, the mistress of the winds, who was accompanied by her two assistants, Guataubá, the herald who produced hurricane-force winds, and Coatrisquie, who caused the accompanying flooding.[13] The power of these *cemis* was widely feared. The island people dreaded them because of their effect on agriculture and because of the devastation they caused, but the Taíno also came to know the storms and to recognize their seasonality and the signs by which their coming could be anticipated.

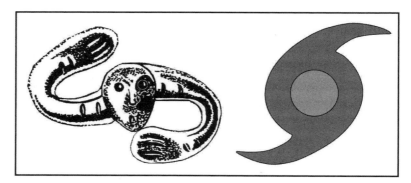

FIGURE 1.1 The curving arms of the Taino *zemi* on a Cuban ceramic seem to indicate a recognition of the rotation of the hurricane winds, just as does the modern meteorological symbol for a hurricane. (Original drawing of *zemi* appeared in Fernando Ortiz, *El huracán, su mitología y sus símbolos*, Mexico City: Fondo de Cultura Económica, 1947)

The Taíno saw the great storms as a dangerous but creative cosmic force in the formation of their world. In their cosmology these winds in the past had separated the Virgin Islands and the Bahamas from Cuba, and their force continued to shape the contours of the island world. As was pointed out by the Cuban scholar Fernando Ortiz in the 1940s, perhaps the most remarkable and most impressive evidence of Taíno familiarity with the hurricanes is the archaeological evidence from eastern Cuba of ceramic images of a round face with spiraling arms pointing in opposite directions, which suggests that the Taíno perceived the circulatory nature of the hurricane winds around an eye (the face of the image; fig. 1.1), a fact that would not be established by Western science until the mid-nineteenth century.[14]

The power and danger of the storms was no less important to the other major group of the island Caribbean, the Caribs of the Lesser Antilles. They also recognized the destructive nature of the storms and believed that evil spirits or *maboyas* were responsible for them. They too feared the storms, but recognized their seasonal nature and integrated them into rhythm of their year, and especially into their cycle of vengeance and war against their archenemies, the Taíno. Each year when the constellation of Ursa Minor, also known as the Little Dipper, appeared in the Caribbean sky following the summer solstice, it signaled to the Caribs the approach of their raiding season. They called this constellation "the canoe of the heron," and its return each year around the middle of June signaled the opening of the season when, following the stormy months of July, August, and early September, their own canoes were launched. The Carib raids against the Taíno for women, food, and captives, and later against the Europeans, were carried out principally from late September to December.[15] These patterns continued for almost a century after the European arrival in the islands. Carib raids against Puerto Rico persisted until the early seventeenth century despite Spanish counterattacks against the Carib home islands of Dominica and Guadeloupe.[16] The Spaniards saw the Caribs as the quintessential "savages," and the term "Carib" became a juridical more than an ethnic designation, since their purported cannibalism and savagery justified enslavement according to Spanish law. At the same time, the Spaniards, and later the French and English, were impressed by their nautical skills and knowledge. The Carib ability to navigate three or four hundred miles by using the shape of the clouds, the direction of the wind, the color of the sky, and their knowledge of the stars, all drew admiration. A French observer, known only as Anonymous of Carpentras, claimed that their navigation showed an almost incredible knowledge of the sun and the stars. His compatriot Jacques Bouton called their familiarity with the skies a marvel, and found their ability to predict bad weather and storms uncanny.[17]

These indigenous epistemologies and understandings, a kind of local knowledge, became part of a cultural transfer, the transmission of objects, language, and knowledge that formed one side of the development of the distinctly American "conquest culture," which was created in the first century of European occupation of the Caribbean. To some extent this interchange was made possible, or perhaps acceptable, because Europeans also had a long tradition of popular practices and beliefs that combined aspects of religion and astrology with a knowledge of the physical world and the signs that revealed it. Although often called "superstitious" by authorities, these popular beliefs remained, nevertheless, a powerful force in shaping a worldview, and Europeans in the Caribbean quickly incorporated into that cosmology what they learned from the native peoples of the region.

Early European Observations

Columbus was undoubtedly a skilled mariner, but he was also a very lucky one. About ninety percent of all tropical storms in the Atlantic form between the latitudes of 10° North and 35° North. Yet in September 1492, at the height of the hurricane season, Columbus voyaged uneventfully from the Canary Islands to his landfall in the Bahamas with good weather, sailing as he did along the predominant track of the great Atlantic hurricanes. While historians are unsure if in fact Columbus during his first decade in the Caribbean actually experienced any storm with what today we could define as hurricane force winds, it is clear that by1498 he had weathered some heavy squalls or tropical depressions and had learned enough about the island seas and their winds to sense a tropical storm's approach.[18]

In July 1502, Columbus was making his fourth and final voyage from Spain when he stopped at the harbor of Santo Domingo, by now the main Spanish port in the Caribbean, to outfit an additional ship before continuing on to explore the mainland to the west. What Columbus found in Santo Domingo at that moment was a Spanish fleet of thirty ships preparing to weigh anchor for a voyage to Seville under the command of Francisco de Bobadilla, the royal investigator who had previously sent him back to Spain in chains in 1500 when complaints about Columbus's rule had caused a rebellion. The fleet was loaded with the gold that had been extracted by the forced labor of the Taíno Indians. The governor, Nicolás de Ovando, appointed to assert royal control and to undercut the concessions originally made to Columbus, was on bad terms with him and so refused his ships shelter in the port despite the fact that Columbus warned him that the southeasterly swell of the water, high cirrus clouds, and hazy atmosphere all signaled an impending storm. Ovando ignored Columbus's advice to hold the Spanish fleet in port for a few days, and some of the sailors and pilots even ridiculed him for his prophetic pretensions.[19] The fleet sailed. Columbus's own small flotilla rode out the storm in a protected bay, but the governor's fleet was caught unprepared two days out of port. About twenty vessels went down with all hands; six others sank, with a few survivors reaching shore; and only three or four ships remained afloat. Of these, only the ship carrying the gold that was Columbus's personal portion as Admiral of the Ocean Sea continued on to Spain. That stroke of luck, and Columbus's apparent ability to read the signs of the hurricane, caused rumors that he was a magician in concert with the Devil and that he had actually called down the storm upon his enemy.[20] His later chroniclers, his son Fernando and the Dominican priest Father Bartolomé de Las Casas, both reported that Columbus believed that a providential hand had saved his own treasure while Bobadilla's fleet, five hundred sailors, and the rest of the gold had gone to the bottom.

In this first European account of a Caribbean hurricane, we find intertwined three elements that often appear in the early observations about hurricanes: description of a violent natural hazard, explanations based on providential or diabolic intervention, and the use of theoretical knowledge and practical experience to understand and survive the storms. The tension between theology, theory, and experience in the face of nature both fascinated and baffled European observers during the following three centuries. The first Europeans in the Caribbean naturally turned to their previous experiences as a guide. While waterspouts and tornados were not unknown in the Mediterranean and North Atlantic, and had been commented upon by ancient natural philosophers and cosmographers, hurricanes were virtually unknown and thus an entirely new phenomenon for which theories of natural philosophy, astrology, and meteorology, as well as previous practical experience, had left Europeans essentially unprepared. First for the Spaniards and then for the other Europeans who sojourned in the Caribbean over the course of the next two centuries, the great storms challenged the idea that the world and its physical interactions were fully known and explained by classical authorities. Like so much of nature in the New World, the hurricanes seemed an anomaly, and their devastating power, be it natural, diabolical, or divine, demanded the attention of natural philosophers and theologians, as well as mariners, colonists, and kings.

In the sixteenth century, Spanish humanists and theologians sought to reconcile the existence of hurricanes within a framework of Aristotelian and Augustinian authority. In Aristotle's *Meteorologica* and the works of classical geographers like Pliny there was no reference to nonnatural explanations, and so when Christian authors like Aquinas commented on these texts they rarely went beyond a general statement of God's power over all things.[21] But, unlike many things observed in the Americas but unknown in Europe, hurricanes, despite zealous attempts, were not easily reconciled with the existing classical and biblical interpretations of the cosmos.[22] Moreover, the struggle between learned natural philosophers and theologians that developed over the storms and the vagaries of natural phenomena in general was never simply a conflict of religious belief and theories of the natural world, or just another episode in a transition from a medieval to a modern and more "scientific" explanation of nature. It also involved a shared conversation with alternative popular beliefs and practices that, while often defined by church authorities as "superstitious," nevertheless allowed for experience and for alternative systems of knowledge to enter into the discussion. These alternative beliefs and lore about wind and weather, often in combination with prayers, rites, relics, and liturgies of the Church, provided a certain sense that men and women were not entirely powerless in the face of natural phenomena.[23] Finally, in the Caribbean, the existence of indigenous cosmologies and knowledge of the great storms also required the Europeans to consider and to incorporate indigenous understandings and experience, despite the fact that Europeans generally dismissed the indigenous peoples and their culture as inferior.

In Spain, interest in the natural phenomena of the New World had been slow to develop. Despite the flurry of excitement after Columbus's first voyage and the rapid circulation of printed letters and newsletters across Europe, the Spanish monarchs, Isabella of Castile (d. 1504) and Ferdinand of Aragon (d. 1516), did not demonstrate much official interest in the peculiarities of the new lands during their reigns. Although early explorers, mariners, missionaries, and local officials had shown a curiosity about the geography, people, and nature of the New World, the rulers had not, and, according to Antonello Gerbi's study, the character and peculiarities of the New World appear to have generated little royal concern or learned interest in the first decades after the voyage of 1492. Other early Spanish expeditions, for example, were not required to submit reports (*relaciones*) of the lands and seas visited. The only account in print of Columbus's exploits available to Spaniards was Peter Martyr de Anglería's *Decades*, part of which was published in Latin in 1516, a fuller version in 1530; it was not republished again. (It was finally translated into Spanish in 1892.) Elsewhere in Europe, from Antwerp to Venice, many editions in both Latin and the vernacular languages had appeared.[24]

This royal disinterest changed with the appointment by King Charles I (r. 1516–1556) of the humanist Gonzalo Fernández de Oviedo as chronicler of the Indies in 1532, and the king's command that all officials in the Indies should submit reports to him. Perhaps it was the conquests of Guatemala and Peru that generated this change in official policy, but the crown's interest in the nature of the Indies and of its inhabitants was clearly renewed by the 1540s.[25] This curiosity, like so much of Spanish science in this period, was practical rather than philosophical, as the empire of Charles I sought to "see like a state," that is, to inventory, categorize, and control the new territories and their peoples.[26]

After the first two decades of the sixteenth century cosmographers, historians, and natural philosophers began to write about the New World. In their desire to describe its conditions, attractions, and dangers, these authors collected, commented upon, and codified the observations of captains like Columbus and other early mariners who had sailed in the Caribbean during the hurricane season.[27] Mention of the great storms became a feature in many of the early Spanish descriptions of the Indies in general, and the Caribbean in particular.[28] The first book on the Indies, Martin Fernandez de Enciso's *Suma de geographia* (Seville, 1519), included a discussion of the violence of the storms and a warning that failure to understand the hurricanes had already resulted in the loss of many ships.[29] Enciso, a lawyer, had settled for a while in Santo Domingo and had been to Panama and had seen or, at least, heard of the storms' dangers.[30] Father Bartolomé de Las Casas, who as both a settler and later as a priest also knew the islands well, said in his *Historia de las Indias* (1561) that the "worst storms of all the world's seas are those of these islands and coasts"; and he noted in his narrative various occasions when the storms had determined historical events.[31]

These early observers tried to reconcile their experience with the theological and natural interpretations of the storms. Oviedo had first arrived in Santo Domingo in 1514; he participated in the conquest of Panama as well, and would eventually cross the Atlantic six times. Around 1524 he began to compose a natural history as part of a more general history.[32] He had personally seen the destruction of the great storms, and he understood the importance of their impact, reporting, for example, that the site of the city of Santo Domingo had been moved after a devastating hurricane in 1504, and the new site was hit again in 1508 and 1509. [33] Oviedo wrote with eyewitness experience, "I have seen thick forests of very large trees torn down for the space of a league and a half and a quarter of a league wide. It was a terrible thing to see and was so frightening that without doubt it seemed to the Indians to be the work of the Devil." Oviedo himself seemed to agree. He said that the Devil "was an old astrologer" who knows what the weather would be and how nature rules things; by his control of the sun and the rain he could bring plenty or famine. But Oviedo offered his Christian readers a preternatural ray of hope. He informed them that wherever the Eucharist had been placed, "the hurricanes and great storms were no longer as frequent or as dangerous as they had formerly been."[34] Here he was repeating an earlier remark of Peter Martyr, and this tale of the Eucharist's power became a commonplace in sixteenth-century Spanish accounts.[35] The stories were an attempt to demonstrate that the savage novelty of the New World could be dominated and brought under the control of religion. Spanish settlers widely held that opinion, and it was supported at times by the clergy, as we saw in the opening vignette of this chapter, when Father Romero argued that the host had saved Veracruz from total destruction.[36] In fact, the idea that the Eucharist might have power to transform the great storms was nothing new in Europe. In a fusion of Catholic belief and what some theologians complained of as "peasant superstition," priests in rural communities had often taken saintly relics and the Holy Sacrament from churches into the fields to divert storms. Various synods sought to prohibit such practices, but the miraculous power of the host that in the priests' hands could transform bread into flesh was often called upon to transform violent storms or hail into soft and life-giving rain.[37] Spanish colonists brought these practices to the New World as well.

Oviedo and other early commentators demonstrated a strong empirical tendency born of their own experience, or based on first-hand accounts

FIGURE 1.2 "The horrible and unheard-of storm" is one of the earliest European images of a hurricane. The foundering ships and fleeing Spaniards and Native Americans emphasize human helplessness in the face of these storms. (From Johann Feyerabend and Theodor de Bry, *Americae pars quarta*, Frankfurt am Main, 1594; courtesy of the John Carter Brown Library at Brown University)

they had collected. They then sought to explain these observations by references both to classical natural history and to theology.[38] But while there were plenty of classical and biblical references to drought, floods, earthquakes, or other catastrophes and disasters, the great hurricanes, with their extreme velocity, rotating winds, great size, and seasonal regularity, were novel phenomena for which traditional authorities or Mediterranean precedents could provide little guidance, and so early observers, while not abandoning theological or classical explanations, looked to their own experience or turned to a rich European tradition of popular weather lore and beliefs, and even depended on the local knowledge of the native peoples of the region. In that sense the hurricanes provided an occasion and a pathway for a knowledge that crossed cultural and ethnic boundaries.

Early European images of hurricanes (fig. 1.2) and almost all of the descriptions made by Spanish eyewitnesses revealed the awe and terror that the violence of these tempests inspired. Around 1566, for example, Fray Diego de Landa, Bishop of Yucatan, reported:

> One winter night, there came at about six in the evening a storm that grew into a hurricane of the four winds. This storm blew down all the fully grown trees, causing great slaughter of all kinds of game; and it knocked down the tall houses, which, being thatched and having fires within for the cold, caught fire and burned a great many people, while some who escaped being burnt were crippled by blows from [falling] timbers. The hurricane lasted until noon the next day, when they saw that those who lived in small houses had escaped, among them the newly married couples, whose custom was to build huts in front of the homes of their fathers or fathers-in-law where they lived for their first years [of marriage]. In this way, the land lost the name it had borne, that "of the turkeys and the deer," and was left so treeless that today's trees, all grown of one size, look as if they were planted together. Thus to view the land from certain high points, it looks as if it were all trimmed with a pair of shears.[39]

The mariners knew the storms and their dangers. Juan Escalante de Mendoza, who mastered many ships in Spain's transatlantic commerce or "Indies run" and finally rose to be captain general of the New Spain fleet, devoted a long section in his 1575 guide to mariners to the origin of the storms and their dangers. He called them "a fury of loose contrary wind, like a whirlwind, conceived and gathered between islands and nearby lands and created by great extremes of heat and humidity," an observation that correctly suggested the circulatory nature of the storms and the importance of warm temperature and humidity in generating them. His account was filled with the steps that needed to be taken aboard ship before and during the storm; how the captain must show no fear and encourage his crew, and how he must supervise all without rest during the hurricane. He also reported the signs to look for—the stage of the moon, the behavior of the fish, or the flight of birds. He was careful to mention that "the things that are to come, you know, sir, only God our Lord knows, and none can know them unless it is revealed by His divine goodness."[40] Prediction of the weather always treaded dangerously close to the Church's disapproval of divination.

But while navigators naturally demonstrated a practical concern for the storms and their characteristics, Spain's theologians and men of letters also took an interest in these novel and dangerous phenomena[41] None of these early writers was more informative than Tomás López Medel. A high court judge, López Medel had served in the *audiencias* (appellate courts) of Santo Domingo, Guatemala, and New Granada (modern Colombia) in the 1540s and '50s, and he knew the Indies well. Influenced by the writings of Las Casas in defense of the native peoples and by his own humanistic readings, López Medel became an ardent believer in Spain's civilizing mission and a critic of Spanish exploitation of the Indians. On return to Spain from service in America, he entered the clergy, and was then nominated (but did not serve) as bishop of Guatemala. Around 1570, probably in response to an effort by the Board of Trade in Seville to collect geographical information on the Indies, he prepared his *Of the Three Elements: Treatise on Nature and Man in the New World.*[42] This was a study of the climate's effect on humans and of environmental characteristics of the Indies. Chapter 5 of book 1, on the "breezes and winds," gave special if brief attention to what he called *"buracanes,"* which he referred to as a "meeting and dispute of varied and contrary winds."[43] This recognizes the distinctive "indistinctiveness" of the winds' direction, and their swirling (which was later learned to be a circular rotation), distinguishing them from the steady direction of other winds. It was, in effect, a precocious perception that preceded the rotational theory of the hurricanes by three centuries. López Medel, like Las Casas and Oviedo, had personally seen the force of a hurricane, having lived through the 1551 blast that struck Yucatan and Veracruz.[44] He joined that personal observation with what he had learned from others to report the "monstrous" and "incredible" results of the hurricanes; of fully loaded ships driven far inland, barrels filled with iron carried through the air, and of a bell in Veracruz weighing over three *arrobas* (seventy-five pounds) that had been carried almost two miles by the force of the wind. "Surely," he said, "we suffer many travails when these winds and the furies of Nature occur."[45]

In López Medel's brief treatment two aspects of the hurricanes appear that were common to many of these early descriptions: their great potential for devastation, and the way in which indigenous inhabitants of America could read the signs of their approach. Like Oviedo, López Medel suggested that the hurricanes had been more intense and frequent when the Indians lived in the darkness of their idolatry than after the Spaniards had brought the Eucharist to Hispaniola; but he also noted that while the native residents on the islands lived in terror of the great storms, "practice and experience" had taught them how to read the signs of their approach. Similarly, Peter Martyr noted that the low-built thatched roof huts or *bohíos* of the Indians seemed to survive the force of the winds better than Spanish-built houses; and it probably did not take the Spanish long to realize that the root crops preferred by the Taíno were well adapted to a hurricane-prone environment, a lesson that later was learned by slaves and slave-owners throughout the region.

The Spaniards first, and later the other Europeans who came to the Caribbean, regularly noted that the native peoples had deified the storms and feared them, but also understood their potential and their seasonality; and, most interesting to the Europeans, they seemed to be able to read the signs of their coming. This problem of prediction in the age before the invention of the barometer and thermometer preoccupied European observers, most of whom, like López Medel, came to believe that the native peoples had developed some system that made prediction possible.

Divination and prognostication were dangerous activities in sixteenth-century Europe, where so-called judicial astrology, the foretelling of human events based on the movement of stars or planets, was condemned for its presumption of predetermining God's will. Augustine had argued that knowledge of the future was solely an attribute of God, and that without divine inspiration, it was a power beyond human ken. True prophecy was possible only with revelation. The Devil might by his astuteness be able to predict some things and derive some fragments of the future, but he did not have real prophetic power. From the thirteenth century forward bishops and inquisitors had campaigned against astrologers who went beyond the accepted limit of suggesting that heavenly bodies might influence nature or human affairs to propose instead that such movements determined outcomes. Similarly, there was an attempt to suppress and discredit seers and diviners, palm readers, conjurers, and magicians, whose prognostications were considered superstitious or fraudulent, and, when occasionally correct, simply accidental.[46] A papal bull of 1586 had condemned all divination, although there was always some leeway conceded to observations with practical application to navigation, medicine, or agriculture. Church authorities tended to be lenient and corrective toward excesses in these practices, unless there seemed to be an implicit diabolical pact in such activity.[47]

But despite the suspect and contentious nature of various forms of divination, reading the signs of weather was a ubiquitous and at times necessary skill in agrarian societies, as the publication and consumption of a myriad of European almanacs confirm. In Spain, as elsewhere in Europe, people noted the shape of a cloud, a shift in the breeze, the taste of water, the movement of animals, and the flight of birds. Sometimes these observations were integrated into *refraneros*, books of short and catchy sayings that were considered depositories of popular wisdom. These were often collected and organized by learned humanists. The Marqués de Santillana's (1398–1458) *Refranes que dicen las viejas atras del fuego (Sayings of Old Ladies around the Fire)*, first published in 1508, was one of the most important, but there were many, and they were widely popular.[48] So too were the chronographies, books that combined astrology, astronomy, meteorology, and history and were used as guides to knowing the best days to take certain medicines, or how to read the signs that could inform you if it would be a cold winter, or if it would rain tomorrow. The *Chronographia o repertorio de tiempos (Chronography or Repertory of the Weather)* of Jerónimo de Chávez (1523–74) went through thirty-nine editions before the 500-page edition of 1588. Chávez's widely read book was no threat to orthodoxy. It was filled with references to Ptolemy, Aristotle, and other classical authorities, and carried a letter of presentation and approval from Philip II.

At the same time, however, a whole range of more suspect popular practices persisted. In Spain, for example, observations of the weather on certain days of the year were used to make predictions called *cabañuelas*. Those made on each of the first twelve days of the year were used to predict the weather in each of the following twelve months. Particular saints' days were used as forecasters of the weather and were conveyed as well in sayings like "A clear St. Vincent's day, a good harvest; a bad St. Vincent's day, no harvest" (*"San Vincente claro, pan harto; San Vincente oscuro, pan ninguno"*). In addition to these widely practiced customs, a kind of popular astrology observed the stages of the moon and other astral activity. Synods tried to prohibit this "wisdom," and treatises of theologians condemned it as superstition, but these traditions were deeply ingrained in Spain as elsewhere in Europe, and they easily crossed the Atlantic. The rural folk of Cuba maintained various forms of *cabañuelas* well into the twentieth century.[49]

Such traditions also easily crossed the supposed divide between learned and popular cultures. A prophetic and millenarian strain of Christian thought accepted that these popular epistemologies might themselves be divinely inspired.[50] Columbus late in life presented himself as a simple mariner whose project, scoffed at by learned men, had been born of his observations and experience inspired by the Holy Spirit. He insisted: "In my own experience, I have met a simple villager who could explain the sky and stars and their movements better than those who paid their money to learn those things. I also believe that the Holy Spirit reveals future events not only in rational beings, but also discloses them to us in signs in the sky, in the atmosphere, and in animals, whenever it pleases him." God revealed his plan through both scripture and experience, even to the humble, in fact to all mankind. "I believe that the Holy Spirit works among Christians, Jews, and Moslems, and among all men of every faith."[51]

While Europeans sought to avoid the harm and devastation caused by bad weather, they also accepted that calamity might be divine punishment for the failure to live as good Christians, a possibility made clear by Aquinas, and confirmed at the Council of Trent in 1551. These demonstrations of God's will might have been welcomed as a purging of sin, but they rarely were, and there existed, in fact, sound scholastic arguments based on Aristotelian distinctions between primary and secondary causes that could justify attempts to avoid their effects. In addition, there was the simple common sense of survival strategies.[52] Still, the hurricanes had a useful purpose in the culture of fear that served an early modern concern with salvation.[53] Different interpretations of the storms were possible. Oviedo had suggested that hurricanes had diminished after the Spaniards had brought the Eucharist to the New World, but Father Bartolomé de Las Casas, the defender of the Indians and critic of Spanish excesses, reported that the Indians claimed that in former times the hurricanes were uncommon, and had increased since the Spanish arrival in the Indies. He suggested the cause of this could be found in the new and many sins of the Spaniards.[54] The divine intention of natural calamity was generally accepted, and rarely did a governor, royal official, or cleric report the effects of a hurricane or other natural disaster without mentioning God's purpose.[55] An anonymous tract reporting a hurricane that struck Santo Domingo in 1680 called the winds the "executive ministers of divine justice," and noted the "just disgust that our faults always motivate" in God.[56] But despite the humility and resignation implied by such statements, the population of the Spanish Caribbean still turned hopefully to traditional remedies and protections.

What is noticeable in these early conjectures about the cause and meaning of the storms is that the early Spanish observers and commentators rarely depended on the learned approaches of natural history or divination, that is, on the texts of the classical world, or the complex systems of astrology or cabala, to explain the origins of the storms, or to suggest methods to combat them. They returned instead to the widely shared popular ideas and sympathetic practices of the agrarian society from which they came. For example, in Spain, one of the traditional ways to respond to the threat of dangerous storms was the ringing of church bells or the firing of artillery, practices based on the theory that the sound would create heat that could dissipate the clouds.[57] Saint Barbara, patroness of artillerymen, was in fact considered a protector against storms.[58] This theory perhaps lay behind the concern in the Caribbean expressed by many of the early commentators over the presence or absence of thunder during hurricanes, and may explain the origins of the Cuban *guajiro* (peasant) belief that thunder during a hurricane meant that it would soon end.[59] Oviedo had warned that absence of thunder in a storm was the worst possible sign, and in early Hispaniola, unlike Spain, thunder and lightning were welcomed because they presaged the end of the storm.[60]

Key in the traditional response to the dangers of weather was the use of prayers, processions, rogations, relics, and the Eucharist.[61] The prayer against storms, *Ad repelendas tempestates*, was made part of the liturgy in Cuba for the months of September and October and in Puerto Rico in August and September, reflecting local perceptions of when the storms were most likely. The 1645 synod of San Juan, Puerto Rico noted that under pressure from the laity some priests had actually removed the Blessed Sacrament from its monstrance and even exposed it outside the church to ward off the great storms. This was prohibited, and the synod urged the use of approved prayers and exorcisms instead. But the traditional practices were deeply rooted, and so as a concession, the synod permitted them in cases of emergency or extreme urgency, "so that the people could be brought to the Church to ask God, Our Lord, for his mercy and that he might relieve them of the danger and straits of their situation."[62]

Even such concessions could not keep the laity from turning to other, less approved, traditional technologies of defense against dangerous storms. Palm fronds brought to churches to be blessed on Palm Sunday were brought back to homes and placed on porches and in windows to ward off catastrophes. Sometimes they were burned in hopes that the smoke would rise and break up threatening clouds, a tradition that was still alive in rural Cuba and Puerto Rico at the beginning of the twentieth century.[63] The old mariners' practice of untying any unnecessary knots on ships' ropes as a way of bringing wind to the sails was adapted to the situation so the tying or untying of knots was thought of as a way to bind up or unleash the winds. The sailors prayed, "Saint Lawrence, Saint Lawrence, tie up the dog and release the winds."[64] The knotted cord that bound the robes of the Franciscans, the missionary order so important in the early phases of Spanish settlement, was thought be especially powerful as a force against the hurricanes, and the Feast of Saint Francis in October was thought to be an especially important day of devotion, occurring as it did during the hurricane season.[65] On the Caribbean islands, many of these beliefs and practices were eventually combined or overlaid with African ideas or concepts for the control of natural forces.[66]

Prediction then was simply an extension of the beliefs and practices of protection, drawn from the same union of authorized religion and a bundle of folk practices of different origins. For protection, the people sought the intervention of various saints, as in these two examples:

> Saint Barbara, the maiden,
> free us from the lightning and sparks;
> like you saved Jonah from the belly of the whale.

> Saint Isidore, the farmer,
> drive away the rain
> and give us the sun.[67]

The early colonists and their descendants also turned to amulets like horseshoes or tortoise shells, and other "superstitious" practices that sometime caused the discomfort of the clergy. Thus there was clerical ambivalence about popular forms of weather prediction and protection in the early Caribbean where prognosis of the coming of a hurricane was truly a life and death matter. There were also similar objections to the borrowing or use by Europeans of indigenous knowledge or beliefs about the storms. While for most of the early European observers the native peoples of the Caribbean represented savagery and idolatry, there was recognition of an indigenous epistemology that might be beneficial, if also potentially dangerous. Various authors seemed to admire the Indians' ability to read the signs and sought to learn from them, but in 1550, an investigation (*residencia*) of the governor of Puerto Rico revealed that he had ordered an Indian punished as a sorcerer for predicting the arrival of a hurricane.[68] It is also curious that the humanist Oviedo in his description of the indigenous perception of the storms linked their knowledge to the influence of indigenous shamans in league with the Devil, and by doing so tied the understanding of the new storms to traditional causes of ill.

English and French observers in their Caribbean colonies in the next century also believed that there was an Indian method of predicting the storms. "The Indians are so skillful that they know two or three or four days beforehand of the coming of it," wrote John Taylor in his *New and Strange News from St. Cristophers, of a tempestuous Spirit which is called by the Indians a Hurricano* (1638).[69] As in the Spanish islands, the skill of indigenous peoples at reading meteorological signs could also be turned against them. The English and French sometimes saw in Carib powers of observation and prediction clear evidence of their pact with the Devil. Early French missionaries had at first dismissed such predictions as false prophecies, but when they turned out to be accurate, they claimed that only through contact with the Devil had they been possible.[70] Such accusations sometimes were used to justify the expulsion of the Indians from particular islands, but this way of thinking could be shortsighted. The elimination of native populations during the European conquest increased European vulnerability. On St. Christopher, after the Caribs had been removed from the island, English colonists had to send to neighboring Dominica, where some Indians still resided, so that they could be brought back to provide storm warnings. A ship captain named Langford reported that settlers on both French and English islands were accustomed to seek word from the Caribs on Dominica and St. Vincent about the immanence of storms, and they were rarely wrong in their predictions.[71]

Some European observers sought to record the signs the Indians used. The Spanish Augustinian Father Iñigo Abbad y Lasierra, in his 1788 account of Puerto Rico, noted that the Indians had read certain signs as forewarnings of a hurricane's approach: a red sun, a strong odor from the sea, the rapid change of the breeze from east to west.[72] Not every European observer was convinced of the Indian's abilities at prediction. Father Jean Baptiste du Tertre, a Jesuit who wrote from experience in the French islands in the mid-seventeenth century, noted that many settlers believed that the Indians could foretell the arrival of the storms, but that in fact, since the storms came in the same period each year, it was natural that sometimes their predictions were correct, even though they had no special knowledge in this matter.

By the mid-seventeenth century, the reading of natural signs was no longer a skill reserved to the indigenous peoples of the islands or to the mariners. It had become a local or creole knowledge, a necessary skill practiced by all. Over time, colonist observations and mariner experience were joined with the clues learned from the indigenous peoples and developed into a kind of local wisdom on each island of the signs to look for. Indians had watched the behavior of certain birds and fish, and the colonists learned from them. Father Jean-Baptiste Labat, a French Dominican, in his description of the French islands in the seventeenth century, noted that on the approach of a hurricane, the birds had certain uneasiness and flew away from the coast and toward the houses. Even today in the U.S. Gulf states and in the Bahamas the flight of the frigate birds inland is taken as a sign of impending storm.[73] Elsewhere other signs were read. "When the crickets, cicadas, toads and frogs disappear, hurricane for sure" is a saying in Puerto Rico.[74] Settlers also observed the habits of the nonnative species, the familiar animals they brought to the islands. López Medel spoke with amazement about how the cattle could sense the storms' arrival; the animals

> [m]any hours before the storm arrives feel and predict it. It is a marvelous thing how they foresee it, coming down from the heights to the lowlands and going to places where from past experiences they know they will be safer. And the instinct of these animals is so precise that the men and residents of those islands take warning from them to predict and understand that which is coming.[75]

In this observation López Medel was following the long-practiced techniques of observation that had become part of the common wisdom shared and exchanged between the learned authors of the chronographies and the residents of the towns and villages of Spain. Those techniques were now transported and adapted to a new environment and a new danger.

The popular wisdom of every Caribbean island and coastal community includes recognition of "signs" that are said to tell of the approach of the hurricanes, such as a particularly good harvest of avocados on Puerto Rico, clams burrowing deep in the sea floor on the Texas Gulf coast, or the roosting of chickens on the island of Nevis. Such signs are given credence alongside the modern predictors of barometer readings, aerial photographs, and computer simulations.[76] Fernando Ortiz, the great Cuban polymath, wrote: "A clap of thunder and the roosting of hens are the Cuban peasants' infallible barometer."[77]

While local knowledge turned toward the immediate challenge of how to anticipate the coming of the storms and how to survive them, scientific interest in Spain itself concentrated on the practical problems that the hurricanes presented to commerce and communication. The Board of

Trade (*Casa de Contratacción*), which established a clearinghouse of information and charts and school for mariners and pilots in the Indies trade, took note of the winds in the Atlantic and the Caribbean and tried to codify that knowledge. In 1573, Philip II ordered each town, village, and city to provide information about its population, topography, and economic activities so that an inventory of information about the Indies could be prepared. The instructions included a section on hydrography and a specific question about the occurrence of hurricanes. In this same period, Juan López de Velasco, the official chronicler and cosmographer of the Board of Trade, published in 1570 his *Geography and Universal Description of the Indies*. This treatise, based on reports collected from all over the Indies, constituted a sort of compendium of Spanish knowledge about the geography and character of their empire. It noted, "the storms called hurricanes [are] the greatest that are known at sea."[78] López de Velasco's objective was practical, with warnings to mariners of the seasonal dangers.[79] But, despite the concrete and scientific line of his discussion, López de Velasco could also not resist noting the seeming "wondrous" power of the storms.

DESCRIBING THE STORMS

The novelty of the hurricanes and their irregular occurrence on any one island made consistent observation difficult and created insecurity about the exact nature of the storms. This confusion about their characteristics was intensified by the general use of the term "huracán" in Spanish, and then by the use of its equivalents in other European languages for any large and destructive storm. Many variations of the word were put to use; some thirty-eight have been counted in English alone, before the common forms were settled on.[80] By the seventeenth century it was not uncommon to find the term used to describe storms that caused destruction anywhere in the Atlantic world. A Spanish reference to a Madrid storm (probably a tornado) in 1622 that lasted no more than a few minutes called it a *huracán*.[81] The term "hurricane" became an adjective to describe any destructive wind or torrential rain.

In the Caribbean itself, where the full brunt of true hurricanes was most commonly felt, they were often associated with another all too frequent threat, earthquakes. For most Europeans the level of destruction of the winds was beyond common experience, and so an assumption was made that the winds must be accompanied by tremors of the earth to explain the devastation that resulted; but undergirding that belief there was also a long-standing theoretical basis in Aristotle's *Meteorology*, which said that winds were the strongest force in nature, and that vaporous winds moving beneath the surface of the earth were the cause of quakes and tremors.[82] This concept survived well into the eighteenth century, and even though the Aristotelian view is no longer held, there are still seismologists who are seeking to establish a direct association between hurricanes and earthquakes.[83]

Part of the problem was simply one of terminology. In fact, in Spanish the terms hurricane (*huracán*) and earthquake (*terremoto*) were at times used interchangeably. A description of a frightening hurricane in 1624 noted a "tumult of rigorous thunder and lightning with very great earthquakes of hurricanes of air."[84] The playwright Calderón de la Barca used the terms "tempest "(*tempestad*) and "earthquake" (*terremoto*) interchangeably to describe a Mediterranean storm in his play *The Prince of Fez* (1668). In the early modern Hispanic world, "a hurricane was an earthquake in the air, and an earthquake was a hurricane beneath the ground."[85]

But the confusion of terminology does not provide a satisfactory explanation of the misperception of the sometimes-simultaneous occurrence of earthquakes and hurricanes. Many early accounts of the storms, especially by people who lived through them, suggest that winds and earthquakes were simultaneous, and such claims were made as well in the eighteenth and nineteenth centuries. The original disbelief that winds alone could cause such destruction may have been partly responsible, but there was also a basis in Aristotelian meteorology, which, as mentioned above, argued that winds moving beneath the earth's surface were the cause of seismic activity. A belief that electricity had something to do with earthquakes that became popular in the eighteenth century made their association with hurricanes often accompanied by thunder and lightning also seem natural.[86] Later English observers were no less prone than the Spanish commentators to report their coincidence. Major Dalling, governor of Jamaica, while reporting on the devastation caused by the great storm of 1780, noted that the winds had been accompanied by the shocks of earthquakes.[87] The historian Bryan Edwards reported a tremendous hurricane that struck St. Lucia in 1788 during which an earthquake killed several hundred inhabitants.[88] In 1848, Robert Hermann Schomburgk, the able Prussian historian and naturalist in the service of Great Britain, listed eight such coincidences between 1722 and 1821, in various parts of the Caribbean, but recognized that the English meteorologist William Reid had challenged the association of the two phenomena. As with so much about the hurricanes, Schomburgk could say, "they are covered with a veil which man has in vain attempted to remove."[89]

Even more important to observers than the possible association of hurricanes and earthquakes was hurricane frequency and whether certain islands or regions of the Caribbean were exempt or less likely to receive their blows. Oviedo had reported that Indians claimed that prior to the Spanish arrival the hurricanes had been infrequent; and he had also told the story of how the host seemed to protect Santo Domingo after its placement in the churches there. While we may have doubts about his explanations, his observations about the changing frequency of the hurricanes may have been accurate. We now know that Atlantic hurricane frequency is linked to the ENSO (El Niño Southern Oscillation) cycle of warming (El Niño) and cooling (La Niña) of the waters in the Pacific. During an El Niño phase, warm equatorial waters of the Pacific extend further to the east and winds blow easterly toward South America, causing great rains to fall on its Pacific coast, which tends to decrease hurricane activity and precipitation in the Atlantic basin, thus causing droughts. During a La Niña phase, the opposite is true: the warm waters do not extend eastward, the winds blow toward Asia, and tropical storms increase in the Atlantic.[90] Hurricanes can take place during either phase or during neutral periods, but La Niña conditions increase their frequency. Important studies have established weather records back to the sixteenth century, and other anecdotal information may provide some clues to general patterns. Perhaps Oviedo's informants were correct. It is possible that the decades prior to Columbus's arrival had been an El Niño period of low hurricane frequency, while the period from 1498 to 1510 or so saw an increase in hurricane activity characteristic of a La Niña episode. This was then followed by another El Niño that coincided with the post-1510 stabilization of the Church and the increased activity of the missionaries, which would seem to support Oviedo's perception of the Holy Sacrament's protective powers. Overall, the principal study of the cycles suggests that periods of increased hurricane activity characterized the years around 1530, 1550, and 1570, during Spain's virtually exclusive control of the Caribbean region. The following period, from the 1590s to the early 1640s, when the English, French, and Dutch began to establish their own settlements, was one of less hurricane activity, a factor that probably facilitated their successful development of plantation agriculture.[91]

These climatic cycles were, of course, unknown at the time. The irregularity of the hurricanes promoted an insecurity and unease. Settlers hoped to be spared the dangers of the storms and sought islands or coasts that were exempt from their visits. Those hopes were often frustrated. Commentators noted that there were sometimes long periods when storms were absent. The English, after taking Jamaica in 1655, were fortunate, and came to believe that unlike Nevis, St. Christopher, or Montserrat, for some reason their island was exempt from the storms—that is, until it was hit by one in 1712, and then again by a major blast in 1722. Barbados too enjoyed a reputation as a safe haven for a while, until a disastrous hurricane in 1675 proved that opinion wrong. By the seventeenth century Europeans had begun to recognize that the islands closest to the northern coast of South America and that coast itself were relatively free from the "dreadful visitations" of hurricanes. The little volcanic island of Grenada, toward the southern end of the Lesser Antilles chain, had that reputation, as did Tobago, near the coast of Venezuela; its promoter, John Poyntz, wrote that this being the southernmost island, "no hurricane has hitherto invaded as ever was heard [of] by any of the inhabitants."[92] We now know that, in fact, those islands and coasts lying south of 12° N latitude benefited from the protection provided by the "Coriolis effect" in which the earth's rotation creates a force that impedes the rotational movement of the winds of a hurricane as it approaches the equator, and thus greatly lessens but does not entirely eliminate the threat of a hurricane strike at these low latitudes.

DANGERS, PROVIDENCE, AND REASON

European inhabitants of the Caribbean came to accept the hurricanes often as one of the inescapable dangers of living or doing business in the region. They quickly incorporated them into a worldview of dangers that included droughts, famines, epidemics, pirates, foreign rivals, poor market prices, and slave revolts as well as earthquakes, tsunamis, and volcanoes. Christian providentialism and a theological acceptance of God's anger because of sin were widely held, at least by those in authority, as the framework in which the great storms were best understood. The cathedral chapter of Santo Domingo, concerned that the tithes supporting the clergy had been greatly reduced by various calamities, wrote in 1600 that God had shown his displeasure by "awarding this land many trials and tribulations." Beginning from the time that Francis Drake had robbed and burned the city, it listed fleets lost at sea, a pestilence that had carried off half of the slaves, three hurricanes that destroyed crops, sugar mills, and homes, and various "other plagues" such as the packs of dogs that so reduced the livestock that former pasture was returning to wilderness.[93] A Jesuit annual letter from the same island reported that the destruction to cacao trees and commerce caused by a 1663 hurricane was due to the greed of merchants and planters who had failed to pay the tithe owed to the Church. Divine justice, said its author, was revealed by a nature out of balance. As hunger was a sign of the earth's infertility, the gathering of wind into great storms demonstrated an instability of air that also bespoke the anger of God.[94]

Nevertheless, noticeably absent in the Hispanic Early Caribbean was the development of an extensive literature of despair and self-criticism so typical of the continental colonies of Peru and Mexico, where catastrophes, especially earthquakes and volcanic activity, generated a culture of fear and eschatological anguish richly conveyed through a variety of literary and artistic means.[95] The apocalyptic sermons and memorials that followed the Santiago de Chile earthquake of 1647, the Lima quake of 1746, and the great 1755 earthquake of Lisbon have virtually no parallel in the Caribbean, where there is little evidence that hurricanes became a central element in a discourse of culpability.[96] The jurist and legal authority Juan de Solórzano Pereira, in his *De indiarum iure* (1628), recognized the great potential of the New World, and believed in Spain's providential role in revealing its lands and peoples, but warned of its many potential dangers, especially its earthquakes and volcanoes. His neostoicism, however, led him to believe that humankind should see all natural phenomena as part of a providential design and should be more concerned with what will happen after death rather than what caused the natural disasters. Perhaps due to his personal experience as a judge in Peru, he was far more concerned with seismic activity and eruptions; he never mentions hurricanes.[97]

Even in the Caribbean itself, ecclesiastical attention to hurricanes was relatively slight. With the exception of the condemnation by the San Juan synod of 1645 of the exposure of the Eucharist to ward off storms, neither it nor the synod of Santiago de Cuba of 1681 devoted any particular attention to the challenges of the storms, or to their theological implications. It is true that to some extent the lack of printing in the Hispanic Caribbean before the nineteenth century may obscure such sentiments from the modern researcher. No flurry of published sermons and popular broadsides developed in the Hispanic Caribbean around the storms. But the absence of such a literature probably had causes that are deeper than the lack of a well-developed printing industry, a popular readership, or the constraints on publication and reading enforced by the Church. The very periodicity and seasonality of the hurricanes undercut explanations that their cause could be found principally in human failure and divine justice. If anomalies in nature supposedly reflected the disorder of society that called for correction, the hurricanes that came to the region each year in the same season seemed to challenge such reasoning. Their regularity, seasonality, and seemingly random appearance in various places within the region made moral interpretations of the storms difficult. At the same time, their seasonal predictability differentiated hurricanes from other kinds of "natural hazards" even though their effects were still awesome and frightening. They were simply too frequent and too random to fit into that "moral cosmos" of destructive tempests, calves with two heads, deformed babies, epidemics, and recurrent catastrophes as divine punishments by which early modern societies sought to explain their world.[98] Since, for Catholic believers, natural disasters might be the result of diabolical or evil action, in the Hispanic and French Caribbean populations turned to the traditional religious protections of benedictions, prayer, processions, and the interventions of the Virgin or the saints to protect them from the vagaries of nature. Providentialist interpretations surely existed and were sometimes applied to interpret individual storms, but it was usually the successive strikes of storms in a single year or multiple strikes within a few years that moved people to consider their sins or those of their society as the principal cause of catastrophe.

The Spanish understanding of the hurricanes remained a mixture of Aristotelian natural explanations, systematic observation, and religious beliefs. These approaches existed simultaneously both in learned discourse and in the day-to-day lives of everyone who entered the world of the Greater Caribbean. When, in 1699, Diego Martínez de Arce, a Mexico City merchant, revealed to Inquisitors his dream about a destructive *juracan,* he used the image of the storm as a depiction of life's insecurities.[99] Sailors, planters, slaves, governors, and housewives all sought to learn the signs of the storms, and get to higher ground or find shelter in anticipation of a hurricane's arrival. At the same time, they turned to the traditional religious remedies and protections like the preternatural power of the host to divert the winds, or the power of a cross tossed into the sea to calm the raging waves. Following a storm they might offer thanks and express contrition as did the crew of a Spanish galleon that survived a hurricane en route from Havana to Seville in 1622, when it celebrated a mass in honor of Our Lady of Carmen, a patroness of mariners and protector against tempests.[100] With the arrival of the other European settlements in the seventeenth century, it became clear that this fusion of secular and religious responses cut across religious and denominational divisions. God could send the winds to punish or admonish, or he could raise his hand to protect against their blast. The questions for all the inhabitants of the Greater Caribbean were not only which action God would take, and why, or if other forces, natural or malevolent, might be involved, but what peoples and governments could do each year, morally and materially, when the sea warmed, and the winds of August again began to swirl.

Melancholy Occasions:
Hurricanes in a Colonial World

A storm of wind and severe sickness have altered our
condition greatly for the worse . . . and lest the Negroes
should take advantage of the disorder to rise, I ordered
all the houses to put out the lights and kept the constables
on watch in the town. . . . This was not the end of our
misfortunes. The place was sickly before, but I believe
these southerly and westerly winds blowing off the
swampy parts of the continent have increased the
sickness which now rages among us.
—*Governor Francis Russell of Barbados*
to the Lords of Trade (1694)

The general dread in the months of August, September, and
October of this expected calamity . . . make the imagination
look for a deluge in every cloud, and expect a tempest at
the daily commencement of the breeze.
—*William Beckford (1780)*

Between 1492 and 1550 Spain extended its control over the large islands of the Caribbean, completing the conquest of Hispaniola, Cuba,
Jamaica, and Puerto Rico, exploring, raiding, and slaving, but not occupying the Bahamas (the so-called "useless islands") and the Lesser Antilles
(fig. 2.1). New Spain (Mexico) was brought under Spanish control in the
1520s and 1530s, for the most part. Yucatan took longer, but by the 1540s,

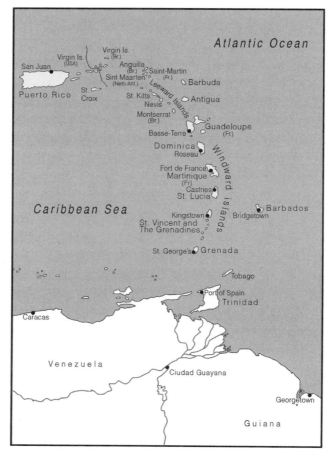

FIGURE 2.1 The Lesser Antilles (Map by Santiago Muñoz Arbalaez)

despite pockets of Maya resistance, it too had been conquered, as had large areas of northern Mexico. To the north, Florida was explored from Puerto Rico in 1513, and competing attempts by the French to establish a colony there were destroyed in 1565 when Spain established a fortified port at St. Augustine in order to guard the northern flank of its maritime return route to Europe.

By 1570, the foundations of the Spanish empire in America had been created. In the Greater Antilles, an early gold-hunting phase on Española and Puerto Rico had passed rather rapidly as the streams had played out, and as warfare, social disruption caused by imposed labor requirements, and epidemic disease decimated the indigenous population. Spanish cities were created at Santo Domingo, San Juan de Puerto Rico, Santiago de Cuba, and, after 1519, Havana, on Cuba's north coast. Smaller towns were scattered over the large islands. In the 1540s, sugar mills or *ingenios* were functioning on Hispaniola and Puerto Rico, and by the 1590s, on Cuba as well. African slaves began to arrive on these islands as laborers in the Spanish settlements, and a regular trade in African slaves developed in the 1550s. The mainland conquests of Mexico and Peru became the heart of Spain's imperial ambitions and of its American empire between 1520 and 1540, and the earlier Caribbean settlements now became a region of secondary imperial concern. The Spanish Caribbean economy shifted primarily to livestock and small-scale subsistence farming, except for a reduced sector of export agriculture based on slave-worked sugar estates and a few other commodities like tobacco and ginger. The islands and the continental ports on the Caribbean, however, maintained their importance as the links and pressure points by which Spain sustained its ties to America, and through which its trade flowed across the Atlantic.

The Spanish Caribbean served as a proving ground for the techniques and violence of empire, and as a crucible where the patterns of cultural fusion, miscegenation, and imperial control were forged. It remained important as the portal to the Indies, but the islands became the hindquarters of empire; poorer, less populated, more vulnerable than the richer and better-defended vice-regal centers of Mexico and Peru. The dispersed nature of the island settlements, the disappearance of much of the indigenous population on the main islands, and at the same time, the continuing hostility and raiding by the Caribs from the Lesser Antilles, created a sense of insecurity and vulnerability among the Spanish colonists. Isolation and violence became persistent themes: isolation because of the distance from the homeland, the precariousness of communication, and, with the exception of a few main ports, the infrequent arrival of news and goods; violence born from the conquest and elimination of the Taíno, the continuing war with the Caribs, the growing numbers of enslaved Africans, and the pockets of resistance that resulted when these slaves escaped and became runaway maroons. Violence was also increasing after the 1540s with the incursions and competition of European freebooters and, eventually, from foreign rivals who began in the mid-seventeenth century to create their own colonies and to threaten the major Spanish settlements. In a sense, commerce, plantations, slavery, and imperial rivalries provide the great themes by which the region's history are best told, but underlying all of them was the environmental and ecological context of danger and vulnerability in which the hurricanes were a central element.

Living with the Winds

Throughout this period of conquest and settlement, the hurricanes were a constant and dangerous limiting factor, a presence that shaped Spanish and, later, other European actions and strategies. Much of the early history of the Spanish conquest and some of its quintessential stories and characters were influenced by the great storms. Take, for example, the case of two castaways, Gerónimo de Aguilar and Gonzalo Guerrero, both of whom had been on an expedition with Balboa to Panama in 1510. Sailing from Panama in 1511, their ships were caught in a hurricane, and Aguilar and Guerrero were among the survivors taken prisoner by the Yucatec Maya. Eight years after his enslavement Aguilar was to play a crucial role as translator when he joined the Cortés expedition that arrived in Yucatan in 1519. Guerrero, however, married a Maya woman and rose to a position of authority among his captors. He refused the opportunity to return, and subsequently died leading Maya resistance against his conquering compatriots. Further to the north, another castaway, Álvar Núñez Cabeza de Vaca, traversed the Gulf Coast and the American Southwest on foot, and left a detailed account of the peoples and places visited, and of the tempest that had initiated his travails.[1] His journey had begun in 1528 when he was a member of the Pánfilo de Narváez expedition to Florida: a hurricane had cast him up on the Texas coast.

The storms not only shaped individual destinies, they also shaped the general environment. In Puerto Rico, a series of hurricanes in 1530 had left the island hungry, defenseless, and subject to attacks from the Caribs of the Lesser Antilles, whose own economy had also been disrupted by the storms. A Carib raid slaughtered what few cattle remained after the storms and killed or captured some thirty Spaniards as well as Indians and black slaves, who were taken back to the Carib settlement on Dominica.[2] One of the responses of the remaining settlers was to bring domestic dogs to the island to serve as sentries, to protect against raids and to help control the cattle. Over time these dogs or *jívaros* became feral and a threat to livestock and to the rural population, remaining so into the eighteenth century. They were an indirect effect of the ecological changes that the hurricanes produced.

Over the course of the struggle for political and military mastery of the region, the hurricanes continually influenced tactics and outcomes. Administrative and military correspondence first of Spain and subsequently of all the European nations involved in the region is filled with references to the hurricane season. One English governor of St. Christopher noted the "annual apprehension of hurricanes," and recognized the dangers of these storms to navigation and to military or naval operations.[3] The effects of hurricanes on military affairs and political decisions could be easily multiplied. For example, the Spanish decision not to settle Bermuda created an opportunity for England. The Earl of Northampton, anxious to promote support for the settlement of Bermuda, told his king in 1612 that the Spaniards had left the Bermudas unsettled because the hurricanes made them fear to adventure in these "devil islands" (*damoniorum insulam*), but the amber and seed pearls that English merchants had extracted "the devils of the Bermudas love not better to retain than the angels of Castile do to recover."[4] On the east coast of Florida, a French attack from their outpost at Fort Caroline (near modern-day Jacksonville) against Spanish St. Augustine was disrupted in 1565 by a hurricane, and the resulting losses so tipped the struggle for the region in favor of Spain that France's claims to the region were mostly abandoned.[5]

The storms played no national favorites. In 1666, Lord Willoughby, governor of English Barbados, operating with a fleet of 17 sail and 2,000 soldiers, was caught by a violent hurricane off French Guadeloupe with the loss of almost the whole fleet and all the troops, losing his own life in the disaster. The storm was known long after as Lord Willoughby's hurricane. The French remembered it as well. A fund was subsequently created by the French crown to have a *Te Deum* chanted each year on August 15, the Feast of the Assumption, to celebrate this victory given by the wind to French arms.[6]

Hurricanes were annual events and thus a regular feature in the historical process: constant enough to demand concern and require planning, but so unpredictable in their specific locations or in their occurrence in any one location that their threat and impact always defied such calculation. Spain, as the first imperial power in the region, and the Spaniards, as the first settlers and administrators, learned to live with the storms and to adjust the rhythms of agriculture, navigation, and commerce to their patterns.[7] Later imperial powers and peoples followed suit, looking to Spanish experience and knowledge as a guide, but adding to it their own observations, experiences, and cultural interpretations.

From a Spanish imperial point of view, the key influence of the hurricanes was their impact on the routes and patterns of transatlantic commerce. The discovery of silver mines in Mexico and Peru in the 1540s and the increasing commerce between Seville and the Indies moved Spain to establish a convoy system, or *flotas;* this system, established by the 1550s, provided a more secure system of transport by limiting contraband and offering protection against corsairs and foreign rivals. Fleets sailed from Seville, eventually dividing into two groups in the Caribbean, with one group heading for Veracruz and its port of San Juan de Ulúa, the other sailing for Nombre de Dios (later shifted to the more salutary port of Portobelo) in Tierra Firme (as Panama was then known) for the trade in silver coming up the Pacific coast from Peru. After 1555, it became the custom to dispatch two separate fleets, the first sailing in April for New Spain and the second heading in August for Panama and then refitting and the well-fortified port of Cartegena on the South American coast. This pattern risked sailing in the hurricane season, but avoided the pestilential summer conditions in the Caribbean ports like Veracruz and Portobelo.[8] The Tierra Firme fleet was able to arrive in the Caribbean during the hurricane season because it was operating south of the latitudes where the hurricanes were common. The plan was always for the ships sailing to Panama and those headed toward Mexico to meet up in Havana in the following spring, where they would then take on supplies, water, and goods from the Caribbean, such as hides, sugar, and ginger, before returning under the protection of heavily armed galleons that also carried the king's share of the treasure. The system was regulated by seasonal weather on both sides of the Atlantic: the ships had to sail for Europe before July and the onset of the hurricanes and to avoid winter storms on the Andalucian coast.[9] Their route was to pass through the channel between Florida and the Bahamas and then, picking up the Gulf Stream, to sail northward to the latitude of the Carolinas before heading east, favored by winds and currents. Delays at both ends of the voyage were common.

Failure to leave Havana on time was, as one commander put it in 1630, to "tempt God," by placing fleets at risk to losses in the storms. But the very regularity and predictability of the system also made the fleets vulnerable to corsairs and foreign rivals, who could lay in wait off the Florida Keys or the Bahamas, knowing just when and where the silver-laden fleet would appear.[10] Losses to corsairs or rivals were usually of individual ships, whereas the destruction caused by hurricanes at sea were more generalized, but together these maritime risks sometimes produced disastrous results not only for ships and men, but for Spanish policy as well. The second decade of the seventeenth century was particularly bad. In 1622, a large part of the New Spain fleet, including three galleons with 1.5 million pesos of silver, was lost to a storm. In 1624 three more galleons were lost, along with over a million pesos belonging to private individuals and about another half million belonging to the Royal Treasury. The New Spain fleet left Veracruz too late in 1631 and was caught by a hurricane, losing its flagship and all its silver off Campeche. And all this to say nothing of the singular event when the Dutch captured a whole fleet off Matanzas, Cuba, in 1628.[11] With these disruptions of trade and the flow of silver to the royal treasury, it was difficult for Spain to finance its domestic commitments, its foreign policy, and its imperial responsibilities.

Meanwhile, in the Caribbean, the Indies run (*carrera de Indies*) shaped the settlements. The structure of this fleet system made Havana the key to the New World. The city, with its docks and its ship building and repair industry, became not only a staging area and service center for the fleets, but also a bustling major center of inter-colonial trade. It attracted commerce and contraband from those areas of the Caribbean that the strictly controlled Spanish mercantilist system excluded from direct trade with Spain. In the sixteenth century, almost two-thirds of the ships entering Havana harbor were from other ports in the Indies, and only a third from Seville, the Canary Islands, or Africa. By the 1590s, about a hundred ships a year were sailing from Havana for Seville, most of them leaving in July and August before the height of the hurricane season.[12] The pilots and captains knew the storms well. Juan Escalante de Mendoza, in his mariner's guide to the sailing routes of the Indies, warned that the "signs of the hurricanes were different than those of other general storms that take place in the seas and lands of Spain, Flanders, and the East." His treatise provided the details of how to read the signs and how to prepare the ships and men for the worst of all the storms at sea.

While from the vantage point of the royal council in Madrid or the merchant guild in Seville, the principal threat of the hurricanes was always the disruption of Atlantic commerce and of the flow of silver and gold to the king's coffers, in the Indies, their threat was a constant feature of customary life. On the islands, the storms produced a general pattern of damage, varying according to the violence and the duration of the storm, but with enough common characteristics so that populations and institutions knew what to expect. The storms generally came in the late summer just as the harvest of sugar and of a number of other crops had ended. Thus there was always a danger of heavy losses after a year of investment and labor. The felling of maize fields was always a risk. Root crops like yucca had better resistance to the wind and water, but too much moisture rotted them in the ground. Not only were current crops lost, but the seeds for the next year were also vulnerable. In 1546, the judge Alonso López de Cerrato wrote from Santo Domingo that the island had never been so prosperous when it was struck by three hurricanes that left no trees, sugarcane, yucca, maize, or shacks (*bohíos*) standing.[13] A violent 1692 hurricane that struck western Cuba destroyed all the seed and plantings of "plantains, yucca, and maize on which this republic singularly feeds itself." Havana was without food, and the governor ordered rural property owners to clear the roads at their own expense so supplies could be conveyed from elsewhere on the island; and both slaves and their masters were subject to punishment or fines for failure to enlist in government work gangs.[14] The hunger that closely followed the winds and rains were less of a problem in the large islands of Cuba, Jamaica, and Hispaniola, where a hurricane might not affect the whole island. On small islands, however, real starvation set in, especially when overconcentration on export crops had already placed foodstuffs in short supply even under normal circumstances.

The destruction of crops was often followed by infestations of insects and other pests. In 1580 the city council of San Juan complained that "for our sins God is served most years to give us storms and worms that destroy our supplies, and our misery and tribulations do not stop there, since each year we are persecuted by the Carib Indians from Dominica and other neighboring islands."[15]

In the aftermath of a hurricane, the physical effects were clearly visible. The salt water driven by the storm winds often stripped trees of their leaves or blackened those that remained. Observers sometimes commented that the areas stripped by the hurricanes looked as though they had been burnt over, and English commentators spoke of areas that had been "blasted." In Bermuda, "the Blast" became a synonym for "Hurricane."

During a hurricane, the coastal storm surge and rising rivers were the principal killers, inundating towns and drowning livestock. The high winds destroyed buildings and brought down trees. Following the storms, roads were impassable and bridges destroyed or damaged, making recovery slow and difficult. Potable water sources were often fouled by brackish water from the storm, and food became a major problem. In the first days after a hurricane, there were plantains, guanabana, and other edible fruits that had fallen to the ground, but these soon were consumed or rotted, and then hunger set in. People turned to emergency foods like roots of plants not usually eaten that were grated and then made into bread or soup. What followed next were various kinds of sickness. Following a hurricane of 1685 in Puerto Rico, for example, about 900 people perished from disease in what the bishop called a "deadly plague" that included measles, smallpox, and typhus.[16] Mosquitoes, flies, and other arthropods reproduced in great numbers. Both floodwater and still-water species of mosquitoes flourished in water-soaked fields and pools of standing water after hurricanes struck. The lack of food weakened populations. The Benedictine Fray Iñigo Abbad y Laserra wrote that what followed the Puerto Rican hurricane of 1772 was "hunger, misery, sickness, and death." This was an apt and generally applicable description for the aftermath of all major Caribbean hurricanes at least until the late nineteenth century.

By the late eighteenth century, some observers had come to realize that within the larger ecological framework hurricanes might have a positive effect. Fray Abbad y Lasierra observed that large harvests often followed hurricanes, and he believed that the "violent agitations turned over the bosom of the land and prepared its fecundity." The Jamaican historian Edward Long agreed that the hurricanes "fertilize the earth, purge the atmosphere from malignant vapors, and bring with them a healthful season."[17] "Better hurricane than no cane" was a planter truism on some islands. The problem, however, was that generally only the large planters had the resources to benefit from the restorative effects of the storms. For the vast majority of the population the immediate effects on food, housing, and health outweighed any future benefit. Writing at the end of the eighteenth century, the French Martinique-born jurist Moreau de Saint-Méry wrote that anyone personally exposed to the terrors of the hurricanes could only with difficulty be convinced of their utility within "the admirable order with which the universe is governed." A man of his era, he believed that only the enlightened philosopher might understand that without the hurricanes the Antilles would be uninhabitable due to the insects that covered their ground and filled the air.[18] But the vast majority of people saw only the destructive effects of the storms and feared them.

SPAIN'S IMPERIAL RIVALS

By the early seventeenth century, Spain's exclusive territorial control in the Caribbean had been broken by its European rivals and competitors. No longer satisfied to raid Spanish shipping and ports or to engage in profitable if prohibited commerce, the English, French, and Dutch began to make inroads into what had become a Spanish sea. English-Spanish hostilities in the last decades of the sixteenth century had sometimes led to major assaults by the English like that on Puerto Rico in 1598, and to a steady stream of income for the English from raiding and mounting defensive costs for Spain.

Raiding and privateering also had their costs, and eventually treaty terms gave English merchants access to American products and whetted appetites for more. Royal patents for settlement were first sought by merchant companies and then by often-absentee aristocratic patrons attracted by profits and power. English settlements in Virginia and Bermuda at the beginning of the seventeenth century were followed by colonization of St. Christopher in 1623 (shared with the French), Barbados in 1627, and, shortly thereafter, Nevis, Antigua, and Montserrat. A major expedition to take Santo Domingo as part of Cromwell's "Western Design" failed in 1655 due to a spirited defense by local troops, but sparsely populated and poorly defended Jamaica was captured from Spain in that year. Unlike most of the other English Caribbean settlements, Jamaica was, therefore, a royal enterprise from its origins. For the most part, the English settlements had been sponsored by lord proprietors or companies, and not until the mid-seventeenth century, and especially after the Restoration of royal government, did the state begin to impose its authority and control over their economy and society.[19]

In the English colonies, representative assemblies had been created that had expanded local rule during the English Revolution after 1642. Their power varied considerably from colony to colony, and the assemblies, which represented the planter interests, were often at loggerheads with the appointed governors. With the restoration of Charles II in 1660 the assemblies accepted the king's authority to tax and the imposition of exclusive trade policies in return for a guaranteed market for their products.[20]

A similar process of slowly increasing royal control also occurred in the areas occupied by France. French freebooters and traders had been regularly raiding and smuggling in the region since the 1540s, often watering, provisioning, and resting on the small islands like St. Christopher, Montserrat, or, further south, St. Lucia or Tobago. With little state support, French colonization began on a small scale with the island of St. Christopher (St. Kitts) in 1627, followed from the 1630s to 1650s by settlements on

the mountainous islands like Martinique, Guadeloupe, and Marie Galante
and some of the smaller, flatter limestone islands like St. Barthélemy, St.
Martin, and Grenada. The French often found more resistance from the
Caribs, who occupied these islands, than from the Spaniards, who had essentially abandoned them in preference for the Greater Antilles and, even
more, Peru and Mexico. French freebooters occupied Tortuga off the
northwestern coast of Hispaniola in 1625 and were operating relatively
freely on the western end of that larger island by mid-century. In 1697, as
part of treaty negotiations, western Hispaniola was formally ceded to
France, becoming its colony of St. Domingue (the modern nation of Haiti).
Some of these French settlement efforts were partly state-sponsored affairs, others the projects of freelance captains and agents, but the general
policy in the early seventeenth century was to use chartered companies or
to make seigneurial grants in order to develop these colonies with little
direct state involvement or risk. Ventures like the Compagnie de Saint
Christophe and the Compagnie des Isles de l'Amerique, whose efforts
were motivated by hoped-for profits from tobacco, cotton, or indigo planting, were granted extensive powers of justice, administration, and trade.
They depended on merchant capital and the support of gentlemen adven-
turers and courtiers who saw opportunities for profit and power. Governors of these early settlements were usually the powerful agents of the
companies or proprietors. The French ministers Richelieu (1624–42) and
Mazarin (1642–61) took little direct interest in these colonies, but sometimes used the companies as their agents.[21]

Not until the reign of Louis XIV and his minister Colbert in the 1660s
did a process of centralization and the presence of royal control become
apparent in the French West Indies, but even then centralization was
something of a myth.[22] The crown maintained control by collaborating
with local mercantile and planter interests on the islands as part of a "negotiated empire," insisting that they trade exclusively with France and
when possible using French ships, but in reality the crown lacked either
the will or the means to enforce a policy of exclusion. Nevertheless, as the
islands began to produce sugar and other cash crops, the local governments as well as the French crown benefited by earned taxes. By the 1670s,
the king had established a governor general at Martinique to handle mili-

tary affairs, and after 1714 a second such office was created in St. Domingue, the two dividing their rule geographically. Civil affairs and financial matters were controlled by intendants who governed with a council that had some local representation. For the most part, this was at least a theoretically centralized system controlled by the officers of the crown. The desire first by the companies and then by the crown to control trade, set the prices for commodities, regulate currency values, eliminate contraband, and tax the settlers provoked a series of revolts by the whites in the French islands, beginning in 1660s and erupting sporadically thereafter (Martinique, 1717; St. Domingue, 1722 and 1768). These revolts represented a set of colonial interests and a desire for some degree of autonomy in the face of a central authority often hampered by the divided authority of the governors and intendants.

A transition from individual initiative to company control had also characterized Dutch activity in Caribbean. The powerful Dutch West India Company was founded in 1621; its commercial and military objectives were both part of the struggle of the United Provinces of the Netherlands against the rule of Hapsburg Spain. The Company's primary efforts were concentrated at first on its conquest of northeastern Brazil (1624–54), but there was also interest in the Caribbean. In the 1630s, the Dutch settled the southern group of Curaçao, Bonaire, and Aruba off the coast of Venezuela. These islands proved to have little agricultural potential, but were well positioned for contraband trade with the Spanish mainland. In addition, in the 1630s the Dutch also made settlements on St. Martin, and on volcanic Saba and St. Eustatius, small islands in the Leeward chain (see fig. 2.1).[23] In its development of these colonies, the Dutch West India Company played a central role, appointing the governors, supplying men and materials, and, when capital was short, sometimes delegating political power to individual merchants.[24] More given to extractive industries like salt collection than to plantation agriculture, and employing its extensive shipping capacity to supply provisions and slaves to other countries' colonies, the Dutch Caribbean outposts became free ports, and the Dutch island settlements remained small, but with a commercial impact on the region much greater than their size, especially in times of war.[25] Edmund Burke's remarks in the House of Commons in 1781 about St. Eustatius might have applied to the Dutch West Indies as a whole: it had no defense, it had no military organization, it had a mixed population of all the nations, and its utility to all was its best defense; "It had risen like another Tyre, upon the waves, to communicate to all countries and climates, the conveniences and necessities of life."[26]

Except for the Dutch settlements on the mainland in Suriname, which sought to create a Brazil-like sugar plantation economy, local colonial interests as expressed by a planter class were less pursued than in the French and Spanish islands. With the decreasing role of the West India Company (it failed in 1674 and was reorganized in that year) and the nonexclusive trading policies of Holland, there was less demand for local autonomy in the Dutch islands than in the French and British colonies.

Finally, the Danish crown, also using the Danish West Indies and Guinea Company as a developer, occupied St. Thomas (1671), St. John (1717), and St. Croix (1733) in the Virgin Islands. The Danes then developed small plantation colonies on these islands, especially on St. Croix, which had forty square miles well suited for sugar agriculture. For the most part, the Danish islands remained heavily dependent on the company's ability to provide slaves and supplies until the crown took direct control of the islands in 1754.[27]

It should be noted that a strict division of the Greater Caribbean along national lines would be deceptive. Some islands were settled and shared by more than one power; St. Martin and St. Christopher, for example, were settled by both the French and the Dutch, and St. Barthélemy was held for a while by Sweden. Tobago, Trinidad, and the mainland areas of Louisiana, Florida, and Belize all changed hands as a result of military operations and in the treaty negotiations that followed them. Other areas in which one European nationality predominated had sizable populations of other nationalities: such was the case, for example, with the predominantly Dutch island of Saba, or the Danish islands of St. Thomas and St. John. Sovereignty, language, and culture did not always coincide in the region.

The general pattern on most islands that had the necessary soil and climatic conditions was a transformation from subsistence farming to the establishment of plantation agriculture of sugar, tobacco, coffee, indigo, cacao, and other export crops. This was a process usually accompanied by a concentration of land in the hands of a few powerful landlords as subsistence plots and the small holdings of poor farmers and former indentured laborers were replaced by larger estates that employed considerable numbers of African slaves. Barbados and the English Windward islands like St. Lucia and St. Vincent imported 277,000 Africans prior to 1700, and by that date ninety percent of the value of those islands' production was in sugar.[28] There were 27,000 black slaves in the French West Indies by 1700; in the following century about a million Africans were imported. In that next century, slavery and the plantation system flourished throughout the region. By about 1815, the British West Indies had a total population of 877,000, of which about seven percent where whites, eight percent were free colored, and 85 percent were slaves. Whites were, in fact, a small minority on most islands; the exceptions were places where plantations were slow to develop or did not take hold, like the small islands of the Bahamas that lacked the proper soils, or the large island of Cuba, where much of the economic activity involved supplying the maritime connections to Europe.

For our purposes there are four points to emphasize. First, the large scale, export-oriented plantation agriculture of the islands tended to concentrate populations near the coast or on lowlands, often near rivers and streams that could provide waterpower or facilitate transportation. Large population centers developed in the major ports, the essential centers of commercial activity. All of this put the island populations at an increased risk of loss in the face of the hazards of wind, tide, and flood that usually resulted from hurricanes. Efforts were sometimes made to build protective dikes, breaker walls, or levees or to improve harbor facilities, but given the nature of economic activity, there was little that could be done to lessen vulnerability.

Second, while the hurricanes intensified or facilitated the transition from subsistence or small-scale farming to slave-based plantations that characterized many islands and some mainland colonies like Carolina, they also increased the vulnerability in those societies. In the wake of hurricane destruction large planters who had capital or access to credit were better able to recover and rebuild, and they often bought up properties of their less well-positioned neighbors. [29] Over time the profitability of plantation agriculture led in places like Barbados and some of the Lesser Antilles to such a concentration in the staple crop that the islands became particularly vulnerable to food shortages and starvation when hurricanes disrupted normal lines of supply. This was especially true on the small islands dominated by monoculture. Spanish, English, French, and Danish imperial systems all sought to institute forms of *"l'exclusif"*: exclusive colonial trade with the mother country, prohibition of trade with other European nations or their colonies, limits on trade with foreigners, and often, even restrictions on trade with other colonies within their own system. While exceptions, exemptions, and licenses often broke these exclusions, such mercantilist measures lay at the heart of the imperial systems. They were the context for the continuous response of the colonies: contraband, smuggling, tax avoidance, and general noncompliance or resistance.

Within this context, hurricanes laid bare the limitations of exclusive trade policies and the desire for the people of the region to circumvent them. Administrators of all the empires tried to comply with the restrictive policies, but realized their limitations. Hunger and necessity forced defiance of imperial restrictions on trade with foreigners and fueled the continual tendency toward contraband trade in the region, especially when food prices soared following a storm.[30] Each of the empires tried when possible to supply their Caribbean colonies from the mother country and from mainland parts of the empire. New Spain sent food, materials, and a subsidy in silver to Cuba and Puerto Rico, and sometimes food could also be obtained in New Granada or Venezuela. New England and ports like Philadelphia and Charleston maintained regular and essential commerce with the British islands, supplying lumber, flour, and salt fish, and Canada and Louisiana played a similar role for the French colonies, but warfare, political problems, and climatic conditions meant these ties were not always secure or dependable. In 1700, the French intendant of Martinique, François Roger Robert, faced with a hurricane's destruction of all available food, and unable to feed the troops and slaves on the island, complained that the delayed arrival of flour and funds from the previous year "was extremely distressing given the present circumstances."[31] Similarly, a royal officer in Martinique complained that after a hurricane of 1713 had destroyed the sugarcane, foodstuffs, and cacao, that the island was threatened by famine, and that the soldiers and slaves on the island had only enough to survive for two weeks. He pleaded for a "prompt delivery," but knew that France was far away.[32] As with natural disasters today, the poorest sectors of the population suffered the worst impact, and as the island societies became increasingly dependent on slave labor, it was the slaves who bore the brunt of the damage and faced the aftermath with the fewest resources.

Third, there was the continual impact of slavery on social arrangements which added to the potential impact of the hurricanes. These were precarious societies in which neither whites nor blacks could maintain demographic growth without importation in the face of high levels of mortality because of disease, the conditions of work, and the hazards of everyday life. The social composition of the islands, with a large and restive slave population and much smaller numbers of whites and free people of color, created anxiety and instability, which in turn generated repression and resistance. This apprehension and disquiet inherent in slave-owning societies was intensified in moments of stress such as military operations, or in the aftermath of natural calamities. Hurricanes were often such moments of increased tensions, and fears of looting, a breakdown of authority, or slave revolt were not uncommon following a storm, but at the same time, the slave populations were often the most debilitated by the shortage of food and the diseases that followed the hurricanes.

Finally, in the English, French, Dutch, and Danish settlements, the mercantile or proprietary nature of the early settlements and their governance tended to weaken the sense of community, reciprocity, or *noblesse oblige* that might be set in motion by natural disaster or other dangers. This is not to say that shared risks were not perceived, nor that cooperative responses such as attacks against hostile Caribs were impossible, for they certainly were, and sometimes were collaboratively mounted by settlers of different nationalities. Still, a diminished sense of national concern and of state responsibility to the settlers in the face of natural disaster was an attitude that was slow to develop and only began to emerge in the eighteenth century.

FACING THE STORMS

By the second decade of the seventeenth century, when Spain's rivals began their own settlements in the Caribbean, there was already over a century of Hispanic experience with the hazards and risks of the region, an experience that other Europeans drew upon. In addition, the mariners, captains, and merchants of these countries also gained their own familiarity with the storms. A mix of observation, theory, and religiosity informed the perceptions and interpretations of the British, French, and Dutch observers and commentators, just as it had the Spanish. All of the European settlements were forced to confront the same phenomena, and the nature of environment and geography often demanded similar responses from all governments and populations in the face of thses dangers, responses that determined the choices that governments and populations could make in the face of these dangers.[33] The shared context of imperial and military objectives and an economy based on slave-produced export agriculture also created a similarity of methods and goals, although political and cultural differences resulted in variations. The shared hurricane hazard was always indifferent to political or cultural differences, a reality that, as we shall see, eventually created a community of experience and often of interest from place to place that cut across imperial rivalries or political divisions (fig. 2.2).

The Dutch had been trading and raiding in the Caribbean since the middle of the sixteenth century, and like the Spanish and other European mariners, they sought to understand the hurricanes and develop strategies to survive them. The Dutch were eager observers of the natural phenomena of the New World and understood that their success against Spain depended on their ability to survive the risks involved in commerce and warfare in the Atlantic. They turned to Spanish experience as a guide and read what they could, but also depended on observation, hearsay, and rumor. By the seventeenth century commentators, navigators, and travelers were making the storms well known to Dutch readers. Joannes de Laet, in his *Description of the West Indies*, wrote that the stages of the moon had a direct influence on the hurricane's formation.[34] Dierick Ruyters's *Torch of Seamanship* of 1623 accurately noted the changing direc-

FIGURE 2.2 "Hurricane strikes land" demonstrates that the power and terror of the hurricanes continued to characterize European respresentations of the great storms into the eighteenth century. (From Peter van der Aa, *Naaukeurige versamel-ing der gedenk-waardigeste zee en land-reysen na Ost en West-Indien*, Leiden, 1707; courtesy of the John Carter Brown Library at Brown University)

tion of the winds, but mixed that observation with fantasy about the fre-quency of hurricanes.

In the olden days, when the Spaniards first came to the West Indies, there was a hurricane, of which some say, having heard this from the savages, that it tends to occur in leap years, though others say every seven years, although it is certain that the hurricane appeared once every seven years, but it is becoming ever less frequent: so that nowa-days it does not occur before sixteen years have passed. People don't become aware of this hurricane before it reaches them, and it disappears on the same hour that it arrives, so that it lasts 24 hours; it starts with rain, thunder, and lightning, and winds from all quarters of the world, so that the winds have circumnavigated the entire compass in 24 hours, with such an incredible storm, that trees that span six and seven fathoms

are utterly uprooted, and in past times even had such force that entire
Spanish ships have been blown landwards beyond forest and trees. [35]

Later in the century, descriptions became less centered on the wondrous,
but remained impressed by the storms' destructiveness. By the 1660s, the
dangers of the storms were known well enough so that advertisements to
attract colonists to Surinam emphasized that colony was "more fertile
than other lands in this region, and moreover free of the dangerous storms
called 'hurricanes' (*Orcanen*) which are all too common in this region."[36]
The Dutch had originally believed that Curaçao was also free of the hurricane threat, but a destructive October storm in 1681 dashed those hopes.
Geerhardt Brant wrote in 1687 about the storms' power, noting that the
hurricane

> destroys entire forests, tears rocks from the mountains, and throws them
> into the valleys, wrecks buildings, and destroys the fields; and agitates
> the sea to such an extent that she seems to mingle with the skies and
> heavens: crushes the ships on the coasts as if they were driftwood, or
> throws them about in the middle of the sea until they burst and sink.
> These hurricanes, that generally occur in the months of July, August, or
> September, and used to come every seventh year, have now been expe-
> rienced for some time twice or even three times a year.[37]

The seven-year interval was a myth picked up by the early French observers as well. Father Du Tertre, in his *Histoire général des Antilles (1667–
71)*, claimed that only after the European settlement had the storms become more frequent. He had probably derived this idea from earlier
Spanish writers, but the French quickly acquired their own knowledge of
the hurricanes. Guadeloupe, Martinique, and nearby Antigua were at a
latitude (16–17° North) that made them particularly susceptible to the
Cape Verde storms, which form in the eastern Atlantic near the Cape Verde
islands (15.1°N and 23.6°W) and then increase in energy and destructive
power as they move westward across the open ocean. The French islands
were hit in 1635, the first year of their settlement. Guadeloupe averaged a
strike every ten years or so in the seventeenth century. Along with Martinique and St. Christopher, it was badly hammered again in August 1666,

at which time an English fleet attacking the island under the command of Lord Willoughby was caught and lost. Between 1699 and 1720, four heavy storms battered the island, and it then suffered other intense periods between 1738 and 1742 (four strikes) and 1765 and 1767 (three strikes). Martinique also was often hit, suffering hurricanes in 1680 and 1695, with great loss of life and damage to shipping in its harbors, and then was periodically visited by the storms in the eighteenth century.

Early French comments about the storms often noted that the information about them had been acquired from the Carib inhabitants of the islands. In the seventeenth-century works of Catholic Fathers Du Tertre and Labat and the probably-Huguenot Rochefort, the hurricanes appear as a feature of life in the islands and a sign of God's power and justice, but all of these authors also expressed a curiosity about the specific nature and natural causes of the storms. Labat, for example, noted the calm before the storm, the cloud formations, the movement of birds, and the rising of the sea level as signs of a storm's approach, and noted from his personal experience on Guadeloupe the damage that a hurricane could cause.[38] The Abbé Raynal, in his popular and widely translated history of European settlement, described the terror caused by hurricanes, which seemed to portend "the last struggles of expiring nature," and he recognized that the Indians had a special knowledge about them. He warned that to ignore "the ideas and even prejudices of savage nations about times and seasons" would be an act of imprudence.[39] Private correspondence from settlers in the French islands as elsewhere often reflected the danger and destruction of the storms, but treated them as a normal quotidian risk. Madame Rouaudières wrote from her estate in 1775 in Saint Domingue about the "cruel hurricane" that had caused so much harm, and complained in the following year that the trees had neither fruits nor flowers.[40] In 1785, she wrote again that the hurricane of that year had not been particularly strong, and, unlike the storms of 1772 and 1775, had only damaged homes and crops. In 1788 she could sigh with relief and offer thanks to God that the "terrible hurricane" of October 16–17 that had caused the rivers to flood had not done more damage to her property. In the agricultural colonial world that she inhabited, the hurricanes could be terrible, but they were the cost of doing business.[41]

We are perhaps best informed about the English perceptions and methods of confronting the hurricanes because of the excellent recent research
of Matthew Mulcahy, and because the English documentary record is particularly well preserved and organized. Seventeenth-century English accounts are full of the same awe and dread in the face of the hurricanes that
are found in the early Spanish reports and chronicles. While the English
settlers found the heat, insects, and general environment of the tropics to
be unpleasant, the hurricane seemed a singular symbol of the primitive
barbarism of the region and its people, as Shakespeare's *Tempest* made
clear to London audiences. William Smith told the readers of his *A Natural
History of* Nevis (1745) not to look for "Paradise in the East or West Indies
because of their earthquakes, excessive heat, mosquitos, and hurricanes."[42]
The dangers to navigation and settlement differentiated the colonies of
New England from the Caribbean and Carolina (and to some extent Virginia), which were those most at risk. The storms of England were but
zephyrs in comparison, said William Beckford in his *History of Jamaica*. He
saw the hurricanes and earthquakes as the worst of "the turmoils of nature that intimidate the inhabitants of the torrid zone."[43] A "Caribbee"
storm became the measure of violent nature and of a tempest anywhere in
the colonies, and its destructive power was constantly noted by all who
survived it. Ralph Payne, governor of Antigua, having witnessed the disastrous effects of a 1772 hurricane that struck the island, bemoaned, "the
miserable circumstances which attended an ever memorable unhappy
Tempest during the time of its existence and the melancholy effects which
it has left upon the whole country are such as might provoke the keenest
sensibility from the most obdurate heart."[44] Such laments, although usually in a less literary tone, were constantly repeated by all who experienced these storms.

Like the Spaniards before them (whose descriptions the English read
when they could), early colonists also looked to the indigenous inhabitants for information about the arrival of the storms, and by the 1680s they
were well informed about their seasonality and the signs that suggested
their arrival. As the Caribbean island colonies and Carolina moved increasingly to sugar, tobacco, rice, and other staples based on slave labor,
planters and merchants accepted the risk of the hurricanes as a price of

doing business, but kept a watchful eye on the storms, their correspondence replete with anxious references to the hurricane season and its possible effects.[45] They learned how to lower their risk, avoiding shipping during the season, insuring their cargoes or spreading them out among a number of vessels, encouraging their slaves to plant root crops, and avoiding the purchase of new slaves until after the storm season had passed. Sugar planters learned how to benefit from price fluctuations when hurricanes hit other islands and, as we shall see, how to use damage to their own properties as a justification for tax exemption in their petitions.[46]

Colonists and their governors learned from experience the challenges the storms posed. The well-documented experiences of Barbados in the mid-1670s are illustrative. The island suffered two storms, one in 1674 and another more destructive one in 1675, that the governor estimated had caused over £200,000 of damage to churches, houses, and sugar mills. He found response to the hurricanes particularly difficult because it took from six to eight months at least to get an answer from London to his appeals, and for the five months of the hurricane season there was hardly a ship to carry them.[47] At that time the island was still making the transition from small, free-owned economy to a plantation system, and it had a population of about 23,000 whites and over 40,000 black slaves when the hurricane of 1675 arrived. The storm altered the face of the country. The extensive damage could not be met in the usual way by bringing in supplies from New England, since those colonies had been disrupted by the savage destruction of native peoples called King Philip's War, and were unable to send food and lumber. The Barbados sugar crop was entirely lost, and creditors were demanding repayment. Unable to rebuild or to obtain credit until the next crop, many small farmers and small-scale planters abandoned the island and left for smaller islands like Nevis or Antigua, or for Tobago and other islands thought not to be visited by hurricanes.[48] This outflow of whites altered the racial balance on the island; by 1780, there were only 22,000 whites left on the island, mostly artisans, managers, and small farmers, and by 1815 that number had diminished to fewer than 16,000.[49]

Similar patterns could be found in the Leeward Islands of Antigua, Montserrat, Nevis, and St. Christopher. In 1670 settlers on Antigua expressed a desire to move to Carolina as a way to be free of the "terrible hurry canes that doth everie yeare destroy their houses and crops." Montserrat, where many Irish migrants had settled, took a heavy blow in 1733, with only six of its thirty-six sugar mills left standing and three-quarters of all the buildings on the island destroyed; the island then suffered again for years later when another hurricane put its main port, Plymouth, under water. Its productivity never fully recovered.[50] The small island of Nevis, dominated by an inactive volcanic cone, was covered with a verdant forest, with rich soil. Although its estates tended to be smaller on the average than those of other islands, by 1680 it had become a major sugar producer. However, planters found that its susceptibility to hurricanes and especially to droughts made it a risky place to grow sugar; over time, these, as well as erosion, soil depletion, and foreign attack, all limited its success as a sugar island.[51]

Even while residents in the colonies were learning to dread the "awful visitations," both in the colonies and in England attention was turned to interpretations of the origins and character of the hurricanes. Providential explanations were never lacking, nor was there ever a lack of those who saw God's judgment as the cause of the storms and other disasters. Exactly whose sins—colonists, Indians, dissenters, or the government—were responsible for divine wrath was usually a matter of some dispute. Most of the British islands established days of prayer at the beginning of the hurricane season and of thanks at its end, and even libertines and free thinkers often joined the services. Robert Carter, a Chesapeake tobacco planter, recognized God's mercy, which had spared his fields, family, and slaves.[52] Few would have disagreed with the author of an account of the 1772 St. Christopher hurricane that "in vain are all our schemes if the hand of Providence interferes to blast our hopes."[53] That same storm moved the young Alexander Hamilton, a young man on Danish St. Croix, to write to the island's gazette an impassioned letter in the language of the Great Awakening calling for compassion and charity in the wake of the hurricane's destruction.

While religious sentiments and pious language were common, and particularly severe storms sometimes generated apocalyptic sermons and tracts, the piety cannot be taken at face value. The anonymous author of

The New History of Jamaica noted that the days of prayer against earthquakes (June 7) and hurricanes (August 28) were devoutly kept but were the only two so honored during the year, and that Sunday was like any other day in Jamaica.[54] This was a world where the Church of England was weak, the clergy often distracted and negligent of its duties, and church attendance very low. The Jamaican Peter Marsden, writing in the 1780s of empty pews, lamented that "the planters seem to have no religion at all." [55] Hurricanes seemed to renew religious sentiments—at least momentarily. "We tremble in the face of danger, and then, and perhaps but then, call on Him for succor who can alone protect us," wrote the anonymous author of the extensive 1772 account of a hurricane on St. Christopher and Nevis; he added, "in prosperous security we forget the Author of our happiness and enjoy His gifts as if they arose spontaneous from ourselves."[56]

More physical explanations of hurricanes were already appearing by the mid-seventeenth century in works like Ralph Bohun's curious *Discourse on the Origins and Properties of the Wind* (1671), which brought Aristotelian, astrological, and practical knowledge together in a curious mixture of accurate observation, myth, and mistake.[57] Natural philosophers looked to the stages of the moon, the influence of the sun on humidity in the atmosphere, or the clash of easterly and westerly winds for their physical explanations of hurricanes. Especially in the eighteenth century, as such inquiries continued, and as new scientific tools like the barometer became available, natural explanations became more common. As historian Matthew Mulcahy has underlined, hurricanes remained, in the British mind, acts of God, but were seen as part of a more general providence and not as punishments for specific sins. In any given year there might be as few as one or two hurricanes in the North Atlantic that made a landfall on an occupied island or coast, or as many as ten or twelve. Unless especially destructive or in some way anomalous, hurricanes were just too frequent to be seen as outside the natural order.[58] In the British Caribbean as elsewhere in the region, they came to be seen as a dreadful, potentially ruinous, or deadly danger, but part of an environment that could also generate great wealth for some. Whatever European perceptions and understandings of the hurricanes and other phenomena of nature, their effects created a series of hazards that governments and peoples in the colonial Americas had to confront.

THE POLITICS OF DISASTER

In each of the colonial regimes social and economic contexts shaped the nature of local expectations and governmental actions For the most part, in all the colonies, little attention was given by the home government to preventative actions before a hurricane's strike, and in the wake of a storm residents mostly depended on help from neighbors or local authorities. This pattern persisted throughout the seventeenth and much of the eighteenth century in the French, English, and Dutch colonies. The situation in the Spanish settlements was different. There, the colonists and colonial administrators had been the first to face the hazards and to seek ways to mitigate their effects. They perceived life in the Caribbean as one of "continuous tribulations, losses, and calamities," as the city councilors of Santo Domingo put it in 1630, when they complained of a hurricane that destroyed much of their city and then saw what little remained of their crop stolen by enemies at sea.[59] Their response was the usual one in the Spanish colonies: a petition for the active intervention of the king.

Spain had a long tradition of municipal organization and administrative autonomy which had been developed during the reconquest of Spain from the Muslims in the later Middle Ages and which was then increasingly controlled and subverted in the sixteenth century by royal government. The tradition of municipal government and a certain autonomy had been extended to the New World. The town councils or *cabildos* exercised jurisdiction over most aspects of local government and were the logical first responders to community crisis. The *cabildo* of Havana, for example, after the hurricane of 1557, ordered the rebuilding of the city slaughterhouse and the clearing of the roads to Matanzas, Batabanó, and Guanajay, the principal routes on which cattle and foodstuffs arrived in the city. In 1588, a similar order was passed to assure the supply of cattle to the city from Bayamo, while the royal governor contacted Veracruz for flour and Hispaniola for manioc-based *casabe* bread.[60] Both municipal and royal government could intervene directly. A terrible hurricane in 1692 destroyed over half of the sugar mills and much of the cane in western Cuba. It left most of the poor in Havana without shelter or food. Governor Manzaneda issued orders requiring the owners of sugar mills, ranchers, and merchants to pay for the opening of roads, and ordered all slaves who worked on the city streets and in the port to report for work details.[61] Such responses for the common good were sometimes resented but were viewed as the governor's and local government's prime responsibility. Town councils were particularly astute in appealing to geopolitical considerations by asking for royal funds to repair fortifications or government buildings damaged by storms as a way of assuring the crown's favorable response to their requests.[62]

The city councils and the royal governors were the first line of defense in the face of disaster and were usually the first institutions to respond, but they often did so to protect elite interests. The councils were not egalitarian institutions, but were dominated by men of property and power, and so they were hardly representative of society as a whole. Town councilors saw disasters not only as difficult challenges, but also as moments to gain advantage. There was always a natural tendency for them to see their own interests as if these were the same as those of the broader society. As early as 1515, the city council of San Juan noted the destruction caused by a hurricane and the subsequent deaths of many Indians due to hunger and sickness in the aftermath. The city's elite needed laborers and so the council asked the crown to release from prison those Indians who had failed to supply their tribute quota of gold, arguing that imprisoned Indians would be of no use to the crown and a valuable asset for the colonists at this time of labor shortage.[63] In 1531, the crown responded positively to a request from the San Juan town council to suspend for two years all debts owed on the island because of the damages caused by storms and hurricanes.[64] Apparently unsatisfied, the council repeated its request in 1534, asking for the same privileges that had been extended to its counterpart of Santo Domingo, complaining that the island was losing population because the gold had played out and the settlers were being lured to the new and wealthier conquests like Peru. Such migration and the abandonment of settled areas were, they argued, contrary to the king's interests. This economic downturn merited *mercedes,* that is, royal concessions, such as government support for the supply of black slaves, debt moratoria, and tax relief. Petitioners often returned to these justifications based on the damages they had suffered from calamities and the service they were rendering to the crown. In 1546, a royal magistrate, Licenciado Cerrato, wrote from Santo Domingo that hurricanes, rebellious slaves, and new taxes were indeed damaging the island's economy and holding back its growth. He advocated concessions to the colonists but warned that if they could get away with it, the colonists would not pay a penny.[65]

Like other Europeans, Spaniards viewed hurricanes and other natural phenomena as demonstrations of providence and divine punishment or warning; but even while accepting their providential origin or design, residents in the Indies did not hesitate to seek assistance, nor to turn such challenges to their advantage. The settlers believed that the list of problems that merited such relief and the beneficence of the monarch could be easily expanded to include Carib raids, attacks by the French, Dutch, or English, droughts, slave rebellions, floods, or even falling prices for the products of the islands. Bad weather, and especially the hurricanes, or what were often called "storms of water and all the winds" (*tormentas de agua y todos los vientos*), came to be seen as simply another one of the many risks of residence in the islands, and one in which the crown could and should act.[66] A good example of this attitude was provided in 1546 in Puerto Rico, when the earlier reports of depopulation due to the lack of gold and the lure of other areas were repeated, but now expanding the causes to include the continuing Carib attacks on the island and the devastation caused by hurricanes.[67] In the same vein, the city councilors of Santo Domingo wrote to the crown in June 1555 complaining of French attacks, the lack of foodstuffs caused by a shortage of slaves, and the "many" hurricanes and storms. They asked that certain "liberties" be extended to the islands: the permission to conduct commerce, that is to raid (*rescate*) on the South American coast for Indian slaves, and particularly, to be excused from tax obligations.[68] Later that year, at the end of August, Santo Domingo was struck by a hurricane that lasted for twenty hours, causing tremendous damage to sugar mills, farms, and livestock. The storm also sank many ships carrying hides and sugar to Spain, as well as those engaged in inter-island traffic. The town needed to be rebuilt, and the solution suggested by the town council was that the king take into consideration the "great labors and losses that the residents had suffered." The council claimed that the appropriate royal action was to assist and favor the colonists by extending tax exemptions and privileges.[69] Such pleas became a constant feature in the Spanish island settlements. The Franciscan Fray Hernando de Contreras wrote from the town of Yaguana on Hispaniola in 1592 that if the sales tax and certain limitations on trade were not reduced, the town, which had been ravaged by corsairs and by hurricanes, would never recover. The residents here were loyal vassals, he argued, and were thus worthy of royal beneficence.[70]

Just how hurricane destruction might be turned to advantage can be seen in a similar and more specific argument made in 1615 on behalf of the governor and the *cabildo* by Captain Francisco Negrete, the representative of Puerto Rico in Madrid. He suggested measures to help the island recover from a series of disasters including an English attack in 1598, the falling prices of sugar and ginger, losses at sea, and, most of all, a hurricane on September 17, 1615. This storm had been reported by the island's governor Felipe de Veumont as being preceded by an earthquake on September 8 which "God had permitted because of our sins" that was followed by the great storm that ravaged the island, ruining agriculture, destroying the cane fields and sugar works, and resulting in general hunger.[71] The San Juan councilors now pleaded for royal consideration, noting that the island was "exhausted and leveled" and that royal clemency and self-interest in stimulating agriculture to increase revenues as well as evangelistic responsibilities all required the king to act with beneficence toward the colonies. Among the concessions to the colonists that the council requested were, first, a twenty-year reduction of the export tax to no more than two percent on all goods sent to Seville, just as had been conceded to the island of Hispaniola in 1598, and second, a subsidy to the sugar planters of 20,000 ducats, to be given in tools and in currency drawn from the treasury of Mexico, just as 40,000 had been conceded to the resident settlers of Havana in 1600. Then followed a series of requests basically designed to help the planter class on the island: a four-year exemption on debt foreclosures; a ten-year extension of all concessions already made; the right to bring in 200 black slaves without passing through Seville first; the right to impose taxes on the import of wine and of slaves to pay for the rebuilding of the city; and even the construction of a convent for the more than 150 daughters and granddaughters of the conquerors of the island.[72] The crown responded favorably to most of the fiscal requests. The islanders' supplication was framed in language designed to appeal to the king's sense of responsibility as "a Christian father" who should not let this "first vine of the Holy Evangel wither," and also reminding him of the harm Spain's enemies could do if they occupied the island. A Dutch attack on the city in 1625 and another storm in 1626 led to requests for even further tax reductions.[73] In 1644 the bishop of Puerto Rico, Damian López de Haro, wrote that despite the island's fertility, much was lacking, especially after another hurricane in 1642. The overall result of these continual concessions in response to the hurricanes was a shortfall of funds for other responsibilities. The bishop felt this personally, since it affected his income. He wrote that the hurricane had "sterilized" the land, and that "everything that is lacking has been blamed on the storm, and this has become a storm of trouble for me because that included the tithe as well."[74] He noted in a letter to the king that the dangers to the bishoprics of the islands were "corsairs, Caribs, and caimans as well as the waters and winds," that is, the hurricanes.[75]

To what extent did the rulers of Spain believe that they bore any responsibility to the inhabitants of the colonies in the wake of catastrophe? Like all of the early modern governments of Western Europe, the Spanish rulers gave primary consideration to the maintenance of order and to the resources that allowed the country to wage war. As a Catholic nation, and one whose very claim to the Indies derived from its compact with Rome to spread the universal church to the heathen, Spanish rulers took seriously their obligations of proselytization and Christian charity. However, the crown placed those functions in the hands of the Church and various ecclesiastical institutions like the missionary orders and lay confraternities. It is noticeable that many of the requests for relief coming from the Indies based their pleas on their own misery and losses, with calls for Christian charity, but still couched these requests in practical language. They stressed the need to strengthen and rebuild after a storm in order to save the colony and its commerce from foreign threat, or social upheavals, such as an uprisings of slaves or Indians.

Charity, in fact, was an issue of considerable theological and theoretical debate in Spain, as in the rest of Europe. Humanists and theologians like Juan Luis Vives (1492–1540) believed that ignoring the needy placed the whole of society in danger, and that distinctions between the real or deserving poor and those who were simply lazy had to be made for social stability and moral order. These claims caught the attention of both Church and state.[76] In these debates, a particular allowance was often made for the "accidental poor," those who needed charity due to plague, fire, or natural disaster through no fault of their own. To lay claim to that status was usually the principal strategy of those who suffered the hurricanes.

Through their governors, the Hapsburg kings of Spain seemed to take direct control of the Indies, responding both to appeals to their patriarchal responsibilities and to the warnings about the fragility of Spanish control after disaster. The crown was willing to take steps that supported the relief of the colonies. The institutions of the Church were sometimes mobilized to provide help to stricken areas, but the idea of offering tax exemptions, relief from debt payments, and a supply of relatively cheap slaves and building materials became a common royal response to the storms in a Spanish sea. The crown needed the island elites to develop the colonies and to serve as a bulwark against foreign incursions, and was thus willing to underwrite relief efforts. This was done as a matter of state policy and as a demonstration of Christian paternalism.

Spain's competitors in the region did not initially respond in a similar way to the impact of disaster on the colonial settlements, but evinced a diminished sense of obligation in response to calamity, at least in the early stages of colonial development. The French kings under the influence of their principal ministers, the cardinals Richelieu and Mazarin, had given minimal attention to the colonies and were reluctant to assume fiscal or other responsibilities even in the wake of disaster. After the move toward more government centralization in France in the 1660s, this attitude toward the colonies began to change, perhaps influenced by the state's negotiated rule through collaboration with powerful merchant and local interests.[77] By the 1720s, there was increasing evidence of a willingness to provide aid to struggling colonists in the form of exemptions. In 1728, cacao planters on Martinique were granted an exemption from the capitation tax for the four-year period of 1727–30 because a disease of the plants had ruined their operations. By 1741, similar consideration was extended to other colonial sufferers of the hurricanes. A royal ordinance granted a tax relief of 90,000 *livres* to the residents of Guadeloupe and 7,000 to those of the nearby island of Marie Galante because of the damages they received in a hurricane of September 1740.[78]

Such changes and concessions accompanied the growing production of the colonies and tended to balance the repression of contraband and violation of the policies of exclusion. They served as a royal incentive to the productive capacity and stability of the colonial settlements. These policies begun in the late seventeenth century had become normal by the mid-eighteenth century in the French colonies. A royal ordinance in 1766 allowed settlers on Martinique to seek food from foreign sources until supplies from France could arrive, and in 1768 Louis XV himself sent beef and flour to hurricane survivors on the island.[79]

A similar process took place in the British colonies. Early colonization under proprietary or company auspices reduced the settler expectation of royal assistance and diminished any sense of direct responsibility by the crown. In the 1650s and 1660s the West Indian economy became a growing concern in England, as restrictive Navigation Acts were put into place to control trade and increase revenues. The relationship between these colonies and England changed somewhat after the Restoration, when royal control was established in most of the American colonies. Despite some resistance, the planters and their assemblies were generally willing to accept trade restrictions and taxes in return for an assured and protected market in Great Britain. King and Parliament demonstrated an increasing concern for the colonies, but even then there was a reluctance to make concessions that might diminish royal revenue or control, or that might jeopardize the balance of interests in the colonies.

A case in point was the island of Nevis, which suffered a French attack and a hurricane in 1707–08 that left the island a shambles. London was willing to send £103,000 for the victims of the French incursions as well as building materials for the storm victims, with specific instructions for egalitarian distribution to help the recovery. Queen Anne noted the "charitable purpose" of this aid and her "compassion to the distressed estate of our subjects in Nevis and St. Christopher who the depredations of the enemy and the late hurricane have almost reduced to ye utmost extremity."[80] The planters, hoping to be relieved of their mortgage obligations and foreclosure for debt, however, wanted more, but the governor was opposed to the planter request to have the court of law suspended for three years. This request was strenuously opposed by the merchant creditors, who saw it as an attempt by the planters, using their influence in England and on the island, to escape their obligations. Governor Daniel Parke agreed and refused to close the court, a policy that won him congratulations from the Lords of Trade, the Colonial council in London. Requests such as had been made by the planters were nothing new. In 1684, after the island had suffered two hurricanes and a drought, planters had also requested a forgiveness of their debt, but had met with similar opposition from the governor.[81] What had been common practice in the Spanish empire from the early sixteenth century was slow to be adopted in the British Empire, and did not become the norm until the mideighteenth century.

The complication of local versus royal interests took many forms in the wake of catastrophe. The kind of political stress that hurricanes could create is made clear from accounts of the aftermath of the storm that struck Charleston in 1752. The South Carolina coastal lowlands area was no stranger to hurricanes, having been blasted in 1686, 1700, and 1728. The burgeoning rice plantation economy had been hit especially hard by the storms. Planters realized that a late summer storm before the harvest had been completed could be disastrous. The 1752 hurricane brought high winds and destructive tides to the city and surrounding areas, where there was tremendous crop loss and the death of cattle and slaves. There were hopes in Charleston that help from England would be forthcoming. Parliament had, in fact, generously sent £20,000 after a major fire had destroyed the town in 1740, but that aid was something of an anomaly. Both the royal governor, James Glen, and the Commons House of Assembly, South Carolina's representative body, sought to respond in the aftermath of the hurricane, but it soon became apparent that their interests and points of view were at odds, and that divergence quickly brought them to confrontation over the particular questions of response. The governor, for example, hoped to arrange for food supplies to be brought from other colonies by government action, and the Commons House of Assembly argued that private merchants should make the arrangements for supply. The loss of revenue caused by the rice crop's ruin, the destruction of timber, and a loss of confidence in the colony's fiscal status caused a crisis a credit crisis in the colony that made any effort at rebuilding and repair difficult. That led to a direct confrontation between the Commons House of Assembly and the governor over the expensive rebuilding of the city's fortifications, which had been severely damaged in the hurricane. The assembly assumed that this was the king's responsibility, while the governor asked the assembly to bear the burden. These struggles eventually came down to a confrontation between royal prerogative and local power.[82]

While George II and Parliament had shown themselves willing in extraordinary circumstances to become directly involved in relief efforts, the English had long depended on charity briefs, that is, relief efforts authorized by the crown and organized by parish churches to provide for those in need. These were used to respond to all manner of calamity from droughts and fires to earthquakes and epidemics. While a generally popular practice, charity briefs in the Caribbean sometimes had limited effectiveness, because on smaller islands like Nevis, Antigua, or St. Vincent, few people were left unscathed after the passage of a hurricane, and thus few could contribute to a general relief effort. Governors on the Caribbean islands, nevertheless, issued the briefs. In addition, at times private individuals or religious groups like the Quakers organized such efforts, and by the later eighteenth-century private subscriptions organized by individuals or organizations had also become popular. But until that period, generally relief efforts for the Caribbean mounted in England or in North America were of little effect due to the distances involved and the difficulty of sending money or supplies in a timely fashion. Moreover, the plight of the Caribbean colonies and their inhabitants was, until midcentury, not a matter of great concern in England or elsewhere in the empire. That situation would change as the sugar economy began to grow rapidly.

The Dutch case is even starker. The Netherlands had developed one of the most advanced system of charitable institutions, and a network of civic welfare far in advance of most contemporary European countries. For the aged, the infirm, and the poor there was an impressive array of institutions, and although hampered by confessional rivalries between the Reformed Church, Lutherans, Mennonites, and other tolerated churches, they were usually a source of civic pride.[83] But in the case of natural disaster in the West Indies, a similar concern by state authorities for the distressed was lacking. The West India Company seemed unable or unwilling to provide much help to colonists unless such actions had direct benefits to the company. The company had in other circumstances offered easy money to planters in Dutch Brazil in order to buy the slaves and equipment needed to start sugar production, but in the 1640s it had begun to squeeze its debtors, and by doing so had set off the rebellion that eventually led to its loss of that colony. It is difficult to find any evidence of a policy of relief in the wake of calamity in the Caribbean colonies, either by the first West India Company or, after its bankruptcy in 1674, by its successor. Whether this was a matter of the company's policies or of the power of commercial interests to resist any attempt to provide relief from debt, there is no evidence of state attempts to provide disaster relief. In this case, we have a remarkable document from the planters on Saba, the tiny (five square miles) mountainous Dutch island in the Leeward group. The island had, like its neighbors, suffered from a disastrous hurricane on August 31, 1772.[84] One hundred and twenty-four of the residents, as well as the governor, council, church, state, and burghers wrote an appeal to the Dutch West India Company, merchants, and "other Christian Gentlemen and citizens of the city of Amsterdam." Their petition pleaded their distress at having lost 140 of the 180 houses on the island, as well as all their crops, furniture, clothing, and wealth, and having suffered as well the leveling of their church. Since all the neighboring islands had also suffered from the storms and could provide no help, the petitioners turned to

you our European friends, who by your situation are happily exempted from these devastating judgments, humbly beseeching you to take our distressed ruined circumstances into mature consideration, and to do with all convenient speed what Humanity and Christianity will dictate to you for our relief on so melancholy an occasion; not only in helping us to build a house for God's public worship, but for the relief of numbers of families among us which are reduced to begging and the most heart affecting wretchedness.

Significantly, the appeal was not for aid from the West India Company or the government, but rather for charitable contributions to be deposited with Nicholas Doekscheer, a merchant of Amsterdam who as agent for the island would turn the funds over to the governor and council of the island.[85] The Netherlands government was absent, the residents on their own.

A hurricane on St. Martin in 1792 further revealed government policy. The storm had left much rubble in the streets, and the governor and council warned residents that if they did not remove it in the next ten days, the government would do so at their expense.[86] Citizens, not the government, were responsible. Throughout the eighteenth and nineteenth centuries voluntary charitable contributions and sometimes-generous donations from the crown remained the principal Dutch response to the distress of its West Indian islands. Not until 1913 was a permanent fund established in the Netherlands for relief of the Dutch Antilles.[87]

Whatever the attitude of rulers and governments toward the sufferers of calamities in the colonies, the hurricanes were a moment of terror that placed tremendous stress on the communities at risk. These were communities split by social and racial distinction, divisions between freeholders and indentured servants, small farmers, shopkeepers, and plantation owners, whites and colored, and above all, slave and free. Concerns for material damage and loss, death, disease, and famine, civil disturbance and the disruption of public order were often foremost in the minds of administrators and preoccupied their correspondence, but some observers who had lived in the Caribbean colonies believed that natural disasters also had the capacity to bring their communities together, elicit heroism and sacrifice, and provide opportunities to rebuild anew for the common good. The Jamaican historian Bryan Edwards wrote that a "hurricane arrests the vengeance of men and by exciting the softer affections disposes them to acts of fraternity."[88] The Martinique-born creole intellectual, jurist, and traveler Médéric Louis Élie de Moreau de St.-Méry, who knew the hurricanes well, wrote, about the recovery from a tempest, "Everyone is employed in reparation, and reestablishment; all are busy; . . . beneficence everywhere exercises its healing and affectionate empire. The time at last arrives when the hurricane and its effects exist no more, except in memory, till another comes to renew the disastrous scene; but hope, the first, the last, the supreme good of man, fills up the happy interval."[89]

Such hopes of communal solidarity, however, were either naïve or disingenuous. Moreau de St.-Méry did not question if the slaves would join in these efforts. This man of the Enlightenment, member of the Philosophical Society of Philadelphia, supporter of the French Revolution, and student of the climate and character of his region and of all the natural sciences, was also a slave-owner and defender of the racial inequalities that were the region's heritage. The contradictions were not subtle. Social divisions had always shaped the responses to hurricanes. By the mid-eighteenth century social, political, and scientific changes were under way that altered the ways in which the storms would be perceived, understood, and combated, and how they would shape and be shaped by the social and political realities of the places over which they passed.

CHAPTER 3

⊙⊙⊙⊙

War, Reform, and Disaster

It is observable that men of the best hearts and greatest
talents are agitated by the most violent passions, and so it is
that the West Indies islands, which boast of the richest soil
and the most valued productions are more subject to
hurricanes and earthquakes than any other part of the world.
—*John Fowler (1781)*

These are scenes to awaken sensibility and make the
moralist exclaim with indignation, "Cursed be your
isles and cursed your institutions!"
—*Hector Macneill (1788)*

The themes that characterize the Greater Caribbean in the eighteenth
century are well known. The various European empires and states
had staked out their claims in the region in the previous century, and each
sought to create profitable colonies. Prior to the 1720s, only the Spanish
colonies and their silver were valuable enough to merit the investment in
major expenditures for defense or state involvement in development.[1]
That situation changed considerably as a result of the expansion of the
sugar economy in the Caribbean and the related explosion of the African
slave trade to these colonies. Sugar (and to a lesser degree, tobacco, indigo,
cacao, coffee, and cotton), slavery, and the commerce they engendered
transformed the region and initiated a different imperial attitude toward
it. What followed was a century of almost continual imperial rivalry and
conflict that carried forward the struggles of the Nine Years' War (1688–97)

and the War of the Spanish Succession (1700–15). All these wars had been motivated by European dynastic and territorial considerations, but often with major colonial effects in terms of territories and trade. The growing power of France, now, after 1715, closely allied with the new Bourbon dynasty of Spain, was increasingly opposed by alliances promoted by England in what would amount to a hundred-year struggle for world hegemony that lasted until the end of the Napoleonic Wars, around 1815. These struggles for empire and commerce, enacted by a growing proficiency and professionalization of militaries, and facilitated as well as justified by the increasing wealth and importance of the colonies, resulted in the consolidation of the imperial states that organized fiscal and commercial policy to support their war-making capacity. From Boston to Caracas, and from Pointe à Pitre to Buenos Aires, the demands of the state and the economic and social realities that underlay them resulted in a revolutionary restiveness in the colonies. Motivations and causes varied, but the issues of commerce, local rights, slavery, and the various meanings of freedom and liberty were all involved. All these processes and events were shaped by environmental conditions like disease, weather, and seismic activity as well as by their social and cultural contexts.

Of course, the hurricanes continued throughout the period, each July bringing the rising temperatures in the Atlantic that served as the motor of evaporation, setting the wind rotation in motion. For the Caribbean region in the period 1700 to 1740, meteorologist José Carlos Millás's catalogue lists forty-one hurricanes, which spared no imperial system. Jamaica suffered hits in 1711, 1712, and 1722.[2] Hurricanes battered the Danish West Indies in 1718 and 1738. Guadeloupe received blows in 1713, 1714, and 1738 and Martinique in 1713 and 1725. Nevis and the English Windwards were particularly badly harmed by a hurricane of 1733, Puerto Rico in 1730, 1738, and 1739, and Martinique, St. Kitts, Antigua, and Guadeloupe in 1740. The French outpost at New Orleans, built in the Mississippi floodplain between the river and Lake Ponchartrain, was an open invitation to hurricane damage. Always susceptible to flooding, the city was badly damaged in 1722, and then again in 1732.[3] This litany is only a sampling of the storms before mid-century, and the later periods of the mid 1760s and 1780s were even worse.

Local and imperial governments responded to the hurricanes in the traditional ways, turning primarily to religious institutions to provide relief
to sufferers, sometimes seeking to restrict liabilities by prohibiting building close to the coast, requiring planters to grow enough provisions for
their slaves, or prohibiting price gouging after storms, and insisting that
planters and merchants pay for cleanup on roadways and bridges.

But while experience had taught governments and residents what to
expect and what measures might be useful for recovery, the islands and
lands of the region had been transformed by the expansion of sugar in
ways that made them even more vulnerable to the effects of the great
storms. On islands like Barbados and Nevis, for example, the tropical forests had been cleared to make way for the cane fields, and the voracious
mouths of the furnaces that heated the kettles where the cane juice was
clarified swallowed tremendous quantities of firewood. It took only a few
decades to strip the lumber and firewood on Barbados forcing the inhabitants to send to St. Lucia and other islands for supplies, and more importantly, to depend on New England. On the smaller islands nothing could
withstand the march of the plantations and cultivation. St. Christopher,
only about 68 square miles, had, by 1775, 44,000 acres in plantations, or
virtually the whole island. This economic process was also supported by
an English belief that clearing and husbandry were the markers of civilization, the taming of wild nature.[4] In Cuba, where about two-thirds of the
island had been covered by tropical forests, the process of clearing had
begun at the end of the previous century and intensified after 1720, even
though the Spanish navy sought to save the forests for its shipbuilding
needs. From modest beginnings around Havana, the sugar mills began to
spring up in Matanzas and Santa Clara, transforming the agriculture and
landscape in those regions, but in truth, Cuba's great era of deforestation
lay in the next century.[5] On Martinique, there were 456 sugar mills in operation by 1742, and St. Domingue thrived as its almost 500,000 slaves
supplied forty percent of Europe's sugar and twenty percent of its coffee.[6]
By 1760, the Caribbean region as a whole was exporting over 165,000 tons
of sugar, with the French and British islands leading the way.

As sugarcane marched, island landscapes were transformed. Observers like the Jamaican creole historian Bryan Edwards, the long-time resi-

dent Edward Long, and the planter William Beckford, sometimes waxed eloquently about the bucolic or pastoral tropical scenes of well-ordered cane fields and the gangs of industrious slaves of which they all approved. "It is hardly possible to conceive of any vegetation more beautiful and more congenial to the painter's eye than that which universally prevails throughout every part of that romantic island," wrote Beckford in his celebration of sugar's progress after his thirteen-year residence in Jamaica.[7] But the expansion of sugar, settlement, and slavery had created new vulnerabilities. Erosion intensified, and ecological balances were altered, making the effects of the hurricanes and other tropical storms and of the periodic droughts even more dramatic.[8]

Of course, there were different effects on different crops. Sugar, a hardy perennial grass, survived the storms better than most crops so long as the cane was only flattened and the roots not torn up. In fact, many planters came to believe that subsequent harvests were improved by occasional hurricanes. Tree crops did less well. Plantain walks or groves suffered badly even in relatively light winds. In Puerto Rico the term *huracán platanero* (plantain hurricane) was used to describe minor storms. Cacao groves also were at risk, and the difficulty and virtual abandonment of cacao cultivation on the French islands seems to have been a result of the trees' susceptibility to the storms. Later, in the nineteenth and twentieth centuries, coffee in Cuba and Puerto Rico would also prove particularly vulnerable, in the latter case not because of the damage to the coffee plants, but to the trees that shaded them. Given the crop's resilience, hurricanes helped to tighten sugar's hold in the region.

The process of agricultural development altered the ecological balance on many islands. A few voices were raised against deforestation in hopes of maintaining climatic equilibrium, but they had little impact on the process.[9] The cleared fields, the pastures opened for grazing cattle and horses, ditches, and canals, all created environments in which varieties of mosquitoes capable of transmitting malaria, yellow fever, and dengue could flourish, especially following the rainy season. Hurricane flooding often resulted in a great mortality of livestock that essentially eliminated cattle, a preferred target for certain types of mosquitos, which then turned to the human populations instead.

Population had grown as the region's economy grew. By 1780, the British West Indies, which was annually exporting sugar and rum valued at almost £4 million, had a population of over half a million people, of which fewer than 50,000 were whites; over eighty percent of the blacks and mulattoes were enslaved.[10] A similar pattern existed in the French Antilles. The growth of population and wealth created new vulnerabilities to hurricanes, earthquakes, fires, and disease. The concentration of populations in port cities put them at risk for storm surges and tsunamis, and created rich disease environments for smallpox, yellow fever, and malaria.[11] Housing the homeless after storms often resulted in overcrowding and an increase in a variety of illnesses. The building of sugar mills near rivers that provided cheap transportation and waterpower for the mills made people and property in these areas more liable to damage. The expansion of merchant shipping that accompanied the economic growth of the region put vessels and cargoes at risk, and the expansion of military operations during the century placed men and ships at the mercy of the storms, sometimes with disastrous results. Buildings, bridges, and infrastructure in general were vulnerable. We lack hard data about the levels of loss, but the economic impact of disasters was surely increasing over time. Especially on the smaller islands, sugar and other export crops had pushed subsistence agriculture to the margins and made those places dependent on food supply from external sources, even though on a number of islands slaves were encouraged to grow food on their own subsistence plots. Vulnerability to shortage and hunger was a reality. Hurricanes were a natural phenomenon; what made them disasters was the patterns of settlement, economic activity, and other human action.

War and governmental reform dominated the Atlantic world throughout the century. After the War of the Spanish Succession, the new Bourbon dynasty in Spain, equipped with French models, French advisors, and a French alliance began to rebuild its navy and reorder its bureaucratic structures both at home and in its colonies. In 1717, its Board of Trade and merchant guild (*consulado*) was moved to Cadiz and the old system of annual fleets that was clearly in disarray was, after 1720, replaced by the sailing of individual ships, first as a wartime measure and then, despite the complaints of the merchant guilds and other monopoly interests, as standard practice. In part this change was made possible by the reduced threat of pirates as the French, Dutch, and English acquired their own American colonies, and now had their own good reasons to suppress rather than encourage piracy as they had done in the previous century. Moreover wartime alliances and post war concessions had allowed for French and English commercial penetration of the Spanish empire. England as a result of the treaty arrangements ending the War of the Spanish Succession had also won the *asiento*, the contract to supply slaves to the Spanish empire along with the right to do some trading legally with it. This arrangement was ended in 1740, and the rupture resulted in the War of Jenkins Ear (1739–48) during which England took Puerto Bello, but mounted unsuccessful attacks against Cartagena, St. Augustine, and Santiago de Cuba. Subsequently, slave supply and commercial control of exports and imports to the Spanish colonies was placed in the hands of a state-sponsored monopoly the *Real Compañia Gaditana* to the displeasure of the residents in the colonies. Spain, in this period, improved its finances and its relative international strength through a variety of pragmatic military, fiscal, and commercial measures. It created a monopoly on tobacco, which had become a major export from Cuba, and the reinvigoration of the Mexican mining industry was perhaps its greatest accomplishment. The greater revenues from silver, the increased income from taxation of its European and colonial populations, and the expansion of its commerce all demonstrated Spain's ability to achieve reforms and to think creatively about the nature and character of government. This was especially true during the reign of Charles III (1759–1788) when some of the most important reforms were introduced. Spain's exponents of the Enlightenment were often pragmatic and utilitarian bureaucrats who applied a more rational approach to the problems of state and society and were willing to assume a regalist approach, limiting the power of any group or institution like the Church that seemed to hinder royal authority.

The reforms were all instituted under the shadows of war. The Seven Years' War (1756–63), during which the British had occupied Havana for a year and after which France ceded New France to Britain and Louisiana to Spain, set the stage for further rounds in the global struggle for hegemony between England and France. The American Revolution (1775–82) and the

wars of the French Revolution and Napoleon (1792–1815) were the culmi-
nation of that struggle. The English and French states became vast war-
making machines whose victories, defeats, and treaty negotiations often
altered political life in the North Atlantic as islands and ports were taken,
lost, and bartered, and as sovereignty and populations were traded or exchanged. The force of strong mercantilist policies and a powerful central-
izing state were combined at least ideologically even when there was considerable negotiation between imperial governments and local magnates
or governing institutions that sought to lessen the control of the mother
country.

How did natural calamity figure into this world of state building, regal-
ism, and reform? It has been suggested that these early modern states
were essentially created by and for war. In the eighteenth century three-
quarters of the French monarchy's budget was spent on military affairs,
almost ninety percent of Denmark's, and over eighty percent of the Dutch
Republic's; but recent research on Great Britain indicates that it devoted a
surprising portion of its budget to public improvements and activities that
could be broadly characterized as social improvement or welfare.[12] Even
in Spain there was a concern with "public happiness" and improvement,
a concern used sometimes to justify the growing authority of the king,
but also reflecting the intellectual currents of Enlightenment thought.[13]
Whether its origins lay in traditional ideas of paternalism, in a growing
sense of nationalism, or in a progressive idea of improvement and innova-
tion, this concern for social amelioration could be directed toward the distresses caused by calamity both in the homelands and in the colonies. But
governmental initiatives and local expectations always depended on the
political objectives that states could achieve by benevolence as well as on
the social contexts in which such measures were embedded.

Studying the Storms and Counting the Losses

If the age of Enlightenment brought changes to the political and economic
spheres that directly affected contexts in which hurricanes occurred and
the ability of societies to deal with the impact of the storms, in the area of

perception and understanding there were also important changes. By the late seventeenth century, regular observation and measurement of natural phenomena had gained many advocates. The Royal Society of London, after its foundation in 1660, became a major advocate of such activities, and it sought to gather information from the Americas as well as from England. A governor sent to Jamaica in 1670, for example, received a list of questions about hurricanes about which the society hoped to gather information. This was also a period in which the thermometer and the barometer began to come into use. The latter, invented by Evangelista Torricelli around 1644, had originally been an instrument only for the scientifically curious, but by the 1720s it was found in many homes across England. Theories about what exactly the falling or rising mercury measured abounded, but increasingly it was realized that a drop in barometric pressure indicated stormy weather, and thus the barometric readings were thought to be useful as a gauge of climatic conditions. This was a theme of great interest, given a generalized belief that climate directly influenced personal health and a society's civilizational capacity, and, of course, that good weather was essential for agriculture. The increasing popularity of the barometer in Great Britain also paralleled the practice of keeping weather records or diaries. These were often obsessively detailed, often daily recording of weather observations, sometimes including barometer and thermometer readings taken at various times during the day.[14] Their objective was scientific observation.

As the Caribbean colonies became more important to England economically and as a number of hurricanes suffered by Barbados and the other islands of the Lesser Antilles in the 1670s caught the attention of the English reading public, interest in hurricanes and how to prepare for them grew. The first barometers arrived in Barbados in 1677, and by 1680 they were in the hands of Colonel William Sharpe, an important sugar planter and former speaker of the Barbados House of Assembly who eventually became acting governor of the island (1714–15). He began to keep a diary of his observations in April 1680, and when the island was hit in August by a storm that subsequently devastated Martinique and then damaged Santo Domingo, Sharpe was able to report his observations to the Royal Society. These were the first barometer readings of a tropical depression.[15]

Observation and measurement of weather and climate continued to fascinate physicians interested in their relation to disease and personal health. They also preoccupied those thinkers like Montesquieu who sought to link national characteristics to aspects of climate, or like the Scottish historian William Robertson who believed nature could be domesticated and transformed as the colonists had done in the New World. By the mid-eighteenth century, men of curiosity and learning like Benjamin Franklin and future president of Yale Ezra Stiles were keeping detailed daily weather logs.

The idea that observation and measurement of the weather might be a useful exercise was not limited to the English-speaking world. Similar developments had taken place in France and in the French islands. Jean-Baptiste Mathieu Thibault de Chanvalon (1732–1788), born in Martinique but educated in France, developed an interest in biology, botany, and the natural sciences. On returning to Martinique in 1751 in an administrative role, he began keeping a meticulous journal of climatic conditions and measurements. A disastrous hurricane in 1756 that took his house and destroyed many of his natural history collections and notes moved him to return to France. There he published his observations in *Voyage à la Martinique* (1756), which included aspects of weather and natural history, but he was obviously pained by the experience of the loss of the notes and observations: "I can not speak of hurricanes without reviving a bitter memory and one full of regrets."[16] Although subsequently vilified and imprisoned for his role in a colonization scheme in Cayenne, his reputation was eventually restored, as was recognition of his role in the origins of scientific meteorology in the Antilles. Following in Chanvalon's footsteps, Alexandre de Moreau de Jonnés (1778–1870), a military officer, administrator, early statistician, and polymath, wrote his *Histoire physique de Antilles françaises* (1822) with a long section devoted to the hurricanes and storm surges (*raz de mare*) and their causes. Not everyone was convinced of the utility of weather measurement. The most important scientific association in the French Caribbean, the *Cercle des Philadelphes*, founded at Cap François in Saint Domingue in the 1780s, deliberately avoided meteorological measurement, explaining that this activity seemed to have no positive application, "no power to control, no ability to prevent or to remedy." In a land where the hurricanes threatened, their power seem to overwhelm such human efforts, but even so, advocates of meteorological observation like the Royal Academy of Sciences in Paris and men like the editor of the *Affiches Américaines* in Port au Prince continued to believe that the results would be beneficial.[17] On the Danish islands, a mission worker kept a four-month daily listing of temperatures at St. Croix, and the Moravian Christian Oldendorp in his 1768 description of his order's activities included a discussion of climate and weather.[18] Meanwhile there were similar developments in the Spanish empire. In Cuba, beginning in 1782, advocates of science were suggesting such observations, and by 1791 the *Papel Periódico de La Habana* was regularly publishing the weekly wind, barometer, and thermometer readings. In 1794, it also published readings taken during a hurricane in Havana that year. This weather reporting was a tradition that continued and expanded in the early nineteenth century.[19]

The development of scientific interest in hurricanes could not be separated from the social and economic context of the region. It is no surprise that most of those people moved by desire for a more scientific observation and who viewed themselves as part of a movement of scientific progress were either Europeans with long experience in the West Indies or creole whites drawn from the upper echelons of colonial societies. Almost all those Enlightenment figures who began the scientific observation of hurricanes were closely linked to the maintenance of slavery. Sharpe was a planter and a defender of planter interests; Thibault de Chanvelon, as a member of the Academy of Bordeaux and corresponding member of the Academy of Sciences of Paris, presented papers on the barometer as well as on the slave trade. A defender of slavery, he believed "the whites were born to rule the slaves," and that the Antilles could only thrive with slavery. His belief extended to supporting the use of castration as the punishment for runaways.[20]

There is no clearer example of this union of the passion for enlightened scientific inquiry and for defense of slavery than the diary of Thomas Thistlewood (1721–86), overseer of a sugar plantation and later a small land owner in western Jamaica near Savanna la Mar from 1750 until his death.[21] Born in England, Thistlewood had arrived in Jamaica as a young man with good background as a surveyor and had broad interests in horticulture, botany, and the natural sciences. He read widely and was curious about the world around him. His skills and interests made him successful and sought out; but what makes him of greatest historical significance was his compulsive record keeping. His diary, which eventually filled 14,000 pages, included thousands of pages of daily weather observations, with temperature and barometer readings. His weather records were careful and meticulous and naturally included important information about a number of hurricanes that struck Westmoreland parish and western Jamaica or passed close to it. He revealed the same meticulous care for detail in recording his constant brutality and cruelty to the slaves under his control; the floggings, beatings, and imposed humiliations were carefully reported, along with detailed descriptions of places, positions, and circumstances of his sexual exploitation of slave women. He represented the racial domination and violence in the slave economy that characterized the region, and that many of the "natural philosophers" of his era in all the Caribbean colonies shared to some degree.[22] Meteorology as well as cartography, botany, astronomy, and other natural sciences had developed in a close association with colonialism, which in the context of the early modern Circum-Caribbean always implied slavery. Of course, there were anti-slavery voices among the scientifically curious of the age as well, Franklin and Stiles among them, but the practical application of science to avoid or diminish natural threats appealed in a direct manner to the interests of the planters and merchants of the region who benefited most from the existing social arrangements.

The application of scientific observation and measurement was increasingly employed by governments in defense of mercantilist and regalist objectives. By mid-century, and especially in the aftermath of the Seven Years' War, all of the empires understood that the struggle for hegemony would continue, and all sought to strengthen their position. Reform and "scientific measurement" became tools to achieve that goal. The taking of censuses became common as a way of knowing the potential supply of military recruits and taxable resources. Statistics became a tool of empire. Government agents prepared censuses, lists, rolls of enlistments, maps and cadastral surveys, and annual accounts of exports, imports, and production for states that saw the world in terms of needs and potential. In a similar way, these same techniques and tools were increasingly applied to post-disaster situations. Such lists and accounts of losses had been erratically prepared before, but increasingly after 1750 they became the rule following disasters. Governors gathered information town by town, or parish by parish, and local officials were required to provide information on churches and houses destroyed, mortalities, injuries, and livestock and crop losses. The results, summarized or tabulated, were then used to guide governmental response to calls for assistance or relief. Losses and misery were to be calculated, and the statistics became "frozen tears."[23] Many examples are in the colonial archives, their results compiled in tabular form or attached to governors' reports. We see them in the wake of the Cuban storm of 1768, in the property by property accounting of the St. Christopher losses in 1777, and in the detailed tables of the damages suffered in the Puerto Rico hurricane of 1825.

Calamity made accounting difficult. In the wake of a hurricane's destruction, populations, the indigent, the homeless, and especially the slaves became more mobile and less "legible" to the state, and thus more dangerous. Little wonder then that fears and rumors of looting or revolt or reports of slave disobedience often followed hurricanes. Guards were posted following the Barbados storm of 1694,[24] and Jamaica asked for and received arms after the terrible storm of 1722. There were, indeed, reasons to be afraid. Hurricanes in 1766 produced a small slave rebellion at Savanna la Mar in Jamaica and a larger one on Grenada.[25] On Danish St. John in the Virgin Islands a July hurricane, followed by a plague of insects and another storm, contributed to a slave revolt in November 1733.[26] To stop looting after a hurricane in the 1770s Danish authorities prohibited slaves from selling anything but fruits, and imposed a curfew.[27] Beneath all such measures lay the fears of a slave society. Hurricanes, by disrupting order and undermining security, revealed a vision of a possible future to be avoided at all costs.

While disaster accountancy served the interest of the state, it could also be appropriated or manipulated by local residents. Everywhere communities and individuals that had suffered calamities created narratives to gain them aid for their loss and suffering. This can be seen in the anony-

mous *Account of the Late Dreadful Hurricane*, which described the damage
suffered by St. Christopher and Nevis on August 31, 1772.[28] Probably prepared by the editor of the *St. Christopher and Caribbean General Gazette*, and
dedicated to the governor of the Leewards, Ralph Payne, "to whose zeal
in service of the King, and regard for the people committed to his care, we
owe our deliverance from a quick approaching famine,"[29] the account proceeded parish by parish to report fatalities and material losses, and clearly
in hopes of compensation, estimating the values of the latter. A typical
entry reads like this one from St. George parish:

> Gilbert Fane Fleming, esq.—Shadwell.
>
> Sick house down, and some other buildings slightly hurt; but the
> crop has suffered considerably. Some pieces of canes washed quite
> away and beds of sand left in their place; so that it looked upon sixty
> hogsheads at least are lost. All the Negro houses are blown away.[30]

Some entries provided details of heroism or of miseries suffered, and others were revealing of the storm's differing impact on slave and free. In St.
Thomas parish, for example, Lord Romney's plantation lost several buildings and sheds; cattle, horses, and mules; and most of the houses of the
slaves. In the report it was not the misery of the slaves that demanded attention, but rather the implications of their situation for the estate. The
entry noted:

> All the negro grounds torn up, and the country provisions destroyed
> which on this estate is of the utmost importance, as the negroes, amount-
> ing to between four and five hundred, mostly supported themselves
> from their own grounds, whereas now the estate has those negroes to
> feed, which must be attended with a prodigious expense; the crop in-
> jured near 200 hogsheads.[31]

Clearly help was needed. The author of the tract warned, "The melancholy evils flowing from this event will be felt when we shall cease to remember them, and posterity becomes acquainted with our mishap by experiment, unless frugality and industry coincide to avert impending
danger." He celebrated the charitable contribution of a St. Christopher na-

tive now resident in South Carolina who immediately sent £75 to help the unfortunates in his homeland, and the author also congratulated the governor's swift appeals to the continental colonies for supplies. Those efforts resulted in a proclamation on October, 9, 1772, in which the lieutenant governor of Pennsylvania made the situation in Antigua, Nevis, and the other Leewards known to the people in his colony, and in which he encouraged merchants and traders to send ships and goods to the stricken region in order to combat a "hurricane, more violent and dreadful than perhaps ever before in the memory of man, and . . . unparalleled in its effects by any recorded in the annals of history."[32] Noteworthy here is the fact that the assembly of Antigua had worked with Governor Payne to seek help from other colonies in order to avoid famine, but the expectation of assistance was to be from private contributions and a mobilization of the commercial sector from the continental colonies rather than by direct royal or parliamentary intervention.

Colonists tended to evaluate the government's effectiveness and its competency by the actions and efforts of its closest representative. The celebration of Governor Payne's efforts, at St. Christopher and Nevis, like those of the creole-born governor De Ceul of Martinique, or the tireless labors of Antonio Garro y Bolívar, the *alcalde* of Havana who went out in the middle of the hurricane of 1752 and "who despite his distinguished birth and rank of nobility was attentive to the humble, and dedicated his hours of repose (*siesta*) to giving justice to country folk," revealed how governmental response could be personified and how it was viewed.[33]

Disasters created both crisis and opportunity. Individuals and groups always sought relief and aid in times of distress, but in such moments, they also saw opportunities to seek advantage. Natural disasters could lay bare the fissures and competing interests within societies. The 1766 storm in Martinique moved French merchants to simply suspend their activities rather than to offer credit or better terms to the settlers with whom they usually did business.[34] British merchants learned how to take advantage of price fluctuations between islands when storms struck some and not others. Manipulation of markets was common. Merchants and planters sought to negotiate their relationship with governments. The detailed 1722 report and appeal from St. Christopher mentioned above reflected the strategy of the sufferers, but in the reformist and activist attitudes of colonial officers of the period, there was a recognition that justifiable petitions for aid or exemption always needed to be balanced against the requirements of the state. As Alejandro Ramírez, the brilliant intendant of Puerto Rico, reported after that island was struck by a series of storms between 1813 and 1816, it was necessary to deal with the "anguished cultivator and the ruined merchants with the benignity that the sovereign desires," but there was also a need to balance the relief for their losses against the demands of the budget, especially for the payment of the troops. Ramírez knew Puerto Rico, and he knew the effect of the hurricanes, and like other observers, he believed that the storms rejuvenated agriculture. This same idea could also be found in non-Hispanic authors of the period who, like the Abbé Raynal, claimed that in nature dissolution was necessary for regeneration so that a hurricane was "the source of partial evil and of general good."[35] Ramírez noted that beneficial reinvigoration had to be taken into account in any calculation of relief offered to compensate for immediate losses.

> It is a common observation that these violent agitations [hurricanes] contribute to the fertility of these lands, and that the accident of loss of the fruits is then followed by more abundant harvests. The very destruction of the plants serves to promote their more abundant reproduction. But at some time the towns that have suffered will ask for relief and deferments in the payment of their taxes, pointing to their losses in order to lower these in the following year. I will have to balance that which should be granted for such a just and well-known reason and that which should be continuously required.[36]

Fiscal needs, political calculations, and the desire to project an image of benevolence tempered government responses.

MERCANTILISM AND CALAMITIES

By mid-century, all of the Greater Caribbean colonies that lived beneath the shadow of the great storms, with perhaps the exclusion of the Dutch islands, where a policy of free trade flourished, were confronted by the contradictions of mercantilist policies that sought to preserve commerce primarily within the framework of each empire, and the tremendous pressures within sectors of these colonies to engage in contraband, and to seek better terms of trade outside the limitations imposed by monopolies or state-controlled markets. Those contradictions had the potential to undermine political stability and loyalty and to begin to create regional ties of mutual support beyond the limitations of place or nation. Each of the empires and each of the colonies responded to this challenge within the context of their institutions and abilities.

A good example of the problem of maintaining exclusivist trade policies in an area of environmental hazards can be seen in the actions of the municipal council of San Juan de Puerto Rico in confronting a series of hurricanes between 1738 and 1740. The island at that time was still sparsely populated and its inhabitants were mostly employed in small-scale agriculture, livestock raising, and contraband.[37] On August 30, 1738, the island was severely damaged by a powerful hurricane. The San Juan city council responded in an attempt to relieve the "public necessities that this republic suffered after the total loss of its agricultural products."[38] It took the usual measures repairing a damaged bridge, clearing rubble, and prohibiting jobbers from buying up food in the countryside and profiting from the scarcity. As usually happened in the storms, fruit-bearing trees, especially those with plantains on which the poor and slaves depended, had been felled or stripped of their fruits. For a few days, until they rotted and spoiled, there was enough to eat, but then the hunger began, even though the governor and the city council had collected and equitably distributed the felled fruits, damaged maize and rice, and other available food. Once this was gone, there was no relief possible for rich or poor. Departing from the usually formal and bureaucratic language of its sessions, the council minutes stated,

> All are reduced to a piece of meat when they can get it, without vegetables or greens or other foods to eat it with, and from this fathers abandon their families, mothers have nothing to pacify their children, nor to sustain themselves, nor anyone to turn their eyes toward for the least relief,

since money (which they don't have) is not lacking but there is nothing
that can be done with it; and finally we will die from hunger if we do not
seek in foreign [non-Spanish] islands some flour to partially sustain the
efforts of the republic.[39]

The council petitioned the governor to act despite the laws prohibiting
trade with foreigners, asking that he immediately send out ships to foreign islands, explaining that "in such cases we must look to natural law,
which is to conserve human life and to avoid by this means the introduction of sickness caused by the making of bread from noxious tree roots and
other wild grasses known to be dangerous to health."[40] Five months later,
the city council was still confronting the scarcity caused by the "never
before seen" violent storm and still seeking permission to look for supplies on foreign islands, and to allow an English ship that had some to sell
to be allowed to do so.[41]

The situation worsened when the island was hit by another storm in
late August of 1739, once again destroying crops and arboreal fruits, but
also drowning large numbers of livestock. The hungry population turned
to the emergency roots. Sickness followed, and to make things worse, an
infestation of worms, perhaps resulting from all the pools of water left by
the rains, destroyed the seedbeds for the next year's crops. The governor,
short on money because the annual subsidy from Mexico had not arrived,
took funds from the royal treasury to meet the emergency. In September of
the following year another hurricane once again damaged crops and
drowned large number of cattle.[42] The cumulative effect of the sequential
storms was to leave the government in a precarious situation, trying to
balance its responsibilities and costs of defense and security with those of
assuring the economic and physical well-being of the island's population.

CLIMATIC CHALLENGES AT THE CENTURY'S END

Natural hazards were and had always been an endemic risk in the region,
but the potential for catastrophic results was increased by the intersection
of the historical process and a shift in climatic conditions. It would appear

that such a change took place in the mid-1760s as an intensive cycle of El Niño/La Niña events beginning with the 1766 hurricane season increased the frequency and intensity of storms and heavy rains in the North Atlantic that then alternated with extended periods of drought. The periods of drought produced poor harvests and worsened conditions of erosion; this in turn made the region vulnerable to flooding when the rains returned. These conditions were suffered not only on the islands themselves, but also by the mainland colonies of the region as well. Mexico, for example, suffered a number of agrarian crises in the 1770s and a particularly bad one in 1785.[43] Since the mainland colonies had always served as a dependable source of foodstuffs when the island colonies were in need, the islands suffered doubly. This cycle of storms and droughts, perhaps marking the closing of the Little Ice Age and a global rise in temperatures, lasted for a period of four decades and created an ecological situation that demanded new kinds of societal and governmental responses from all the imperial powers in the region.[44]

The fifteen hurricane landfalls of 1766 hit the colonies of every empire in the region. Martinique alone suffered a thousand casualties and lost eighty ships, and all of the French islands felt some impact. With France having lost New France to Britain and ceded Louisiana to Spain at the end of the Seven Years' War, the traditional sources of food supply for the French islands were gone. Both the French crown and local officials moved to allow a trade with foreigners in flour, salt meat, and other foods despite the loud complaints of the merchants who controlled that commerce. Spain had already begun to loosen its system of exclusive trade in 1765, and after Cuba was struck twice, Santo Domingo once, and Puerto Rico three times in 1766, Spain, as a temporary measure, lifted restrictions on trade with foreigners in times of necessity. Another hurricane crossed western Cuba in 1768, causing considerable damage in the area of Havana.[45] Shortages on these islands and their inability to procure supplies from the traditional intra-imperial colonies that had changed hands in war or, in the Spanish case, due to droughts or bad harvests in New Spain, forced the empires to loosen restrictions. Merchants in Charleston, Philadelphia, and New York celebrated their good fortune as these new markets opened, drawing the continental British colonies and the non-British Caribbean together. After 1768 the empires tended to return to their former restrictive policies, but 1772 was another year of heavy hurricane activity, with nine major storms that ripped through the region, making it difficult to maintain the exclusivist arrangements.[46] During the remainder of the century and then into the turbulent revolutionary first decades of the next one, the Spanish crown continued to struggle with the desire to improve commercial control over its colonies and the need to respond positively and efficiently to the crises caused by the continuing series of disastrous climatic events. Partly in response to this situation the Spanish crown, now interested in generating a larger proportion of its revenues from the empire, reduced its trade restrictions in 1778, extending the reductions to New Spain in 1789.

In the cycle of storm activity, drought, and war in the last decades of the century, all of the imperial states, rather than depending on charitable institutions, began to take more direct responsibility and a greater role in the response to calamities. In the British Greater Caribbean, the process of assistance or public relief, as historian Matthew Mulcahy has described, went from sympathy to policy.[47] The charitable donations by individuals and relief efforts organized by church authorities, what we could anachronistically call "faith-based initiatives," were the usual methods of response to disasters. After mid-century, private subscription campaigns were commonly mounted and organized by committees to relieve those who suffered loss in the Caribbean. Not without accusations of corruption and high administrative costs, subscriptions became a usual and effective method to provide charity to disaster victims in the colonies. The growing number of newspapers and gazettes made their travails common knowledge in an English-speaking community now fully aware of the commercial and economic importance of the West Indies and the southern continental colonies. In 1785, the pietist Moravian brethren on St. Croix in the Danish West Indies decided to publish an account of the losses suffered by that island as a way of raising funds for their missionary work among the slaves. They took this measure following the example of missionaries on Jamaica and Barbados, who had done the same after a hurricane in 1782 that had successfully brought public donations for the losses those islands had sustained.[48]

In the British Isles, appeals for assistance emphasizing charitable feelings and sympathy for their compatriots across the sea were directed principally toward private contributions, but on rare occasions king and Parliament could act directly. An early example of such action was in response to the great Charleston fire of 1740. Charleston, the main port of the Carolinas, was at first met with the usual forms of charitable benevolence, but then received a grant from Parliament of £20,000 as a result of direct appeals from the colony.[49] The Carolinas had in the immediate past suffered a smallpox outbreak as well as the Stono slave rebellion (1739), and was under threat of a Spanish invasion as part of the War of Jenkins' Ear, which had begun in 1739. The king and Parliament had a definite political and strategic interest in responding to appeals for benevolence. The British colonists, by emphasizing those interests in their appeals, were following a time-honored strategy that Spanish colonial sufferers had been using for two centuries, and that previous British appeals had attempted without success. But in 1740 the context was favorable for the grant, which Parliament voted. Its debates about how to distinguish vagrant or lazy individuals from those truly harmed by the fire in many ways echoed the earlier Renaissance disputes about poverty and charity and foreshadowed the coming debates about the responsibility of the state for individual or community catastrophe. The continual threat of hurricanes in the North Atlantic almost guaranteed that the issue would arise again; how king and Parliament would respond depended on the political and ideological context. By the 1770s, the fact that the continental colonies were in rebellion weighed heavily in the calculations of George III and Parliament on how the island colonies would be treated, and what concessions or aid they might receive in times of need in order to preserve their loyalty.

A similar tendency of government action to respond to crisis situations could be seen in the Caribbean imperial outposts of other nations as well. Following the late August hurricane of 1772, the governor general of the Danish West Indies set a limit on local food prices, removed all taxes on building materials, distributed food to whites, and imposed a curfew on blacks to stop looting and pilfering. In 1785, after another hurricane, the governor general and council removed all taxes on food.[50] It was a policy Denmark continued into the twentieth century.

Although French approaches to these problems had developed in the same direction, the institutional situation in the French Atlantic was somewhat distinct. The French islands lacked the autonomous colonial assemblies of the British colonies, and the municipal organization and local government of Spanish America. Thus, it was the governors and intendants who, depending on their personalities and allegiances, became vectors for colonial interests and spokesmen for local concerns.[51] The French monarchy, often taken by historians as the model of the absolutist early modern state, turned to established precedents. From the late Middle Ages it had confronted the traditional calamities of famine, plague, and war by restricting the mobility of the population, distributing food, controlling prices, and using police powers, but natural disasters tended to be more local or regional and were not a major concern. There were exceptions: as early as 1481, a royal exemption from taxes was granted to Claremont (Auvergne) following an earthquake; but such concessions were rare.[52] Localized threats and natural disasters were generally left to the immediate authorities and to local resources. The state was perceived to have little responsibility, and intervention was limited, intermittent, and irregular. When royal assistance was forthcoming, it usually resulted from the effectiveness of local officials to influence central authority or from the pressure and influence exerted by members of the local nobility.[53] This approach to disaster response lasted well into the seventeenth century.

Beginning in the 1660s, under Louis XIV, state interventions in crises of public health, famine, and plague demonstrated an increasing willingness to take action, although still often depending on local authority and sometimes limited by it. Different means were used to supply assistance. Between 1691 and 1716 the crown sought to grant indemnities to those who suffered losses from bad weather in Languedoc, and during the famine of 1693–94, the state intervened to feed Paris by importing flour and fixing prices despite opposition from local powers.[54] The French no longer depended only on procession, prayer, and exorcism, or on the too often stingy and delayed personal beneficence of the king to confront disaster. The state was becoming more efficient and more prepared to take direct action.[55] This change could also be seen in the colonies where the major settlements were continually battered by the elements. A tremendous hurricane struck Martinique in 1680 and another caused considerable damage to shipping and to Fort St. Pierre in 1694. Guadeloupe suffered six hurricanes between 1713 and 1742.[56] Administrative reports of the damages emphasized the destruction of crops and sugar mills, the loss of shipping, and shortages of food for the slaves and troops on the islands. Food on the French islands had always been a problem, and as sugar flourished and the slave population expanded, the problem grew worse. Requirements to plant proportionally for each slave were often ignored, supplies of food from France were irregular and expensive, and thus contraband was common. The hurricanes destroyed crops, ruined seeds, and were often followed by the intrusion of pests that made recovery more difficult. Following the 1723 storm, slaves on Guadeloupe were dying at a rate of twenty a day and the *habitants* feared an uprising by their starving bondsmen.[57] Recovery was difficult. The hurricanes had destroyed shipping capacity to bring in materials and food, and merchants were reluctant to send commodities, since debtors were liable to default. New measures were needed. In 1738, the governor of Guadeloupe petitioned the governor general on Martinique to permit five years of direct commerce with foreigners, that is, to break the restrictions that limited trade to France. Trade with New England or with the Dutch free port at St. Eustatius would bring flour, salt fish, livestock, and lumber that could be exchanged for molasses or rum. Further storms in 1752 and 1753 brought a new wave of similar permits so that this response to calamity of increasing open trade became routine.[58] Also important is that in 1740, Governor Gabriel de Clieu of Guadeloupe asked for a two-year exemption from the capitation tax for the residents on the island.[59] This resort to tax relief, a practice used by the Spanish crown since the sixteenth century, and a measure that had been used occasionally in France itself and sparingly in the colonies as a response to natural disaster, was, while still passive, a recognition that the state had some responsibility to respond to an *accident du ciel*. An *État protecteur* was slowly emerging in the mid-eighteenth century.

FIGURE 3.1 "Ouragan aux Antilles," by Nicholas de Launay, first appeared in the 1780 edition of Abbé Raynal's popular history of colonization and commerce in the East and West Indies. Images like this naturalized these storms as a dread but regular aspect of life in the Caribbean. (From Guillaume Thomas François Raynal, *Histoire philosophique et politique des établissements et du commerces des européens dans les deux Indies*, Geneva, 1783; courtesy of the John Carter Brown Library at Brown University)

The "Great" and Other Hurricanes of 1780

In the decade of the 1780s, the impact of climatic conditions on war, reform, slavery, and politics became a matter of considerable public interest. Another intense cycle of ENSO (El Niño-Southern Oscillation) events made this decade one of the most meteorologically active and destructive on record, and the social and political context of the North Atlantic intensified the storm- and drought-related effects they produced (fig. 3.1). The hurricane season of 1780 was particularly deadly, and it would never be forgotten. In that year, at least eight major storms made landfalls in the Caribbean and on the Gulf Coast, affecting colonies of all the European empires. The American Revolution was already fully under way. France and Spain had entered the war (respectively in 1778 and 1779) on the side of the rebellious colonies, and the Circum-Caribbean was on a wartime footing, awash with troops and ships. The season started out with a rare hurricane in June that struck Puerto Rico and Santo Domingo, and was then followed by smaller storms that struck Louisiana and St. Christopher in late August, but these were only the heralds of the destruction that was to follow. Three of the subsequent hurricanes of that year (shown here in fig. 3.2) resulted in over one thousand direct fatalities, but the "great hurricane" of October 10–16 was the most deadly to have ever battered the region, causing a minimum of 22,000 deaths and probably as many as 30,000. It would always be remembered, said the Jamaican historian William Beckford, as a "visitation that descends but once in a century, and that served as a scourge to correct the vanity, to humble the pride, and to chastise the imprudence and arrogance of man."[60] All indications from its trajectory and the violence of its impacts suggest that it was one of the large "Cape Verde" hurricanes that start as winds sweep off the African savanna and then form as tropical depressions in the Atlantic about the latitude of the Cape Verde islands. These storms then sweep across the Atlantic, gaining size and power in their traverse, and tend to form some of the largest and most powerful hurricanes in the North Atlantic.[61]

The great storm announced its presence when it slammed into Barbados on October 10, leaving hardly a house in Bridgetown or tree on the island standing. Preceded by heavy rains, the winds, which may have

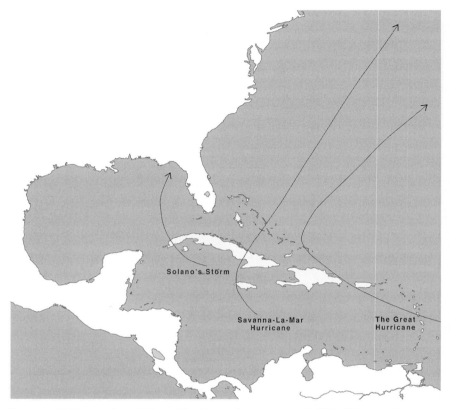

FIGURE 3.2 The paths of three Caribbean hurricanes of 1780 (Map by Santiago Muñoz Arbalaez)

reached 200 miles per hour, destroyed the Government House, and the governor and his family were forced during the night to seek shelter under a cannon. About twenty-five ships in the harbor slipped anchor in an attempt to get to sea, but many were lost. Fortifications were ruined, most churches and sugar mills damaged, and 4,500 people killed. Whole families were destroyed in the "universal destruction." Major General Vaughan, commander-in-chief of the Leewards, wrote to London to report the situation, forwarding a letter from Governor Cunningham of Barbados: "The strongest colours could not paint to your Lordship the miseries of the inhabitants; on the one hand, the ground covered with the mangled bodies of their friends and relations, and on the others, reputable families wandering through the ruins, seeking for food and shelter: in short, imagination can form but a faint idea of the horrors of this dreadful scene."[62] The image of the misery of the respectable families shocked the readers of the London publications that carried news of the storm, but more extensive if less newsworthy was the burden borne by the slaves of the island, left without shelter or food. As Governor Cunningham put it, "The depopulation of the negroes and the cattle, especially the horned kind, is very great, which must, more especially in these times, be a cause of great distress to the planters." Together the number of whites and blacks that perished, he thought, must exceed some thousands, but he found solace that "fortunately few people of consequence were amongst that number."[63] In fact, at least 2,000 slaves died from immediate causes, and the size of the slave population between 1780 and 1781 diminished by 5,000, indicating subsequent deaths from disease, lack of food, and as a result of injury suffered in the storm.[64]

The storm swung northward, moving up the chain of the Lesser Antilles. The eye of the storm had probably passed to the northeast of Barbados, and its trajectory carried it northward to St. Lucia, St. Vincent, and Martinique, bringing havoc in its winds. All indications suggest that, in terms of modern measurement, this was a Category 5 storm. Shipping everywhere in the area was devastated. At Grenada, nineteen Dutch vessels were sunk; at Guadeloupe one French frigate was lifted onto the beach and another, the *Junon*, was smashed to pieces on the coast of St. Vincent. Only sixteen of the 600 houses of Kingston, St. Vincent, were left standing, and at St. Lucia 6,000 people lost their lives.[65]

The French colonies and shipping fared no better. A fleet of 52 sails, which was in the Caribbean in support of the continental rebels on the mainland, was caught in the waters at Fort Royal, Martinique. A number of ships foundered, and the rest made for sea, where they were battered by the winds; only seven survived, and some 4,000 men were drowned. The city of St. Pierre, farther up the coast to the north, was destroyed, mostly by a sea surge that rose to 25 feet and took away 150 houses near the harbor. The hospital where some 1,600 sick and wounded from the fleet were being treated collapsed. Also destroyed was the convent of Saint Esprit and all of the almost 100 sisters and novices killed. The fishing villages of Le Prêcheur and Le Carbet on the western shore were inundated by a sea swell, the fishermen losing all their nets and boats, complicating the ability to feed the hungry island population. In all, perhaps 9,000 people on Martinique were killed, and estimates of damages were calculated as 1,700,000 *louis d'or.* The merchant firm of Beaujon and Son on St. Eustatius wrote to a correspondent in Amsterdam about the horror of the sea surge at Martinique:

> All has to make way for this dangerous force, no occasion, no time, is left to store the tiniest thing, people flee, people scream, people try to save their lives by running through thousands of dangers, even the miser must abandon his treasures and fear nothing but death; the tender mother runs dauntlessly through all dangers, to take in her arms her precious offspring, and with her loving heart tries to flee and secure their salvation. The neighbors who lived close by came to the rescue of these miserable people, they tried to reach them, cast ropes, fetched ladders, and saved the lives of these unfortunates.[66]

As the hurricane moved northward, it caused extensive damage in Guadeloupe. Basse-Terre was leveled and over 6,000 enslaved and free people were killed. The plantations were ruined, the cane in the fields knocked down, and in the governor's estimate some 8,000 slaves worth 320,000 *louis d'or* were lost. It would take, he said, "as long as the siege of Troy" to return the island to its condition before the storm. The little Dutch island of St. Eustatius, which was thriving as an emporium of free trade during the American Revolution, took the brunt of the winds particularly hard; a number of ships sank, and there were between 4,000 and 5,000 deaths. Survivors were given shelter in forts and churches. Whites were buried on land, but slaves, because of the high numbers of dead, were disposed of at sea.[67] The island then suffered a further indignity in 1781 when it was captured by a British fleet and all goods private and public seized. The fleet commander Admiral Rodney, who thought the island a polyglot cesspool, even ordered the destruction of the town at Fort Orange and the use of its roofs and building materials to repair the hurricane damage in Barbados.[68] Admiral Rodney's particularly hostile attitude toward the Dutch outpost may have also been influenced by his own losses, since his fleet had been caught by the storm at St. Lucia, losing eight of its twelve ships and hundreds of men.

Gales and high seas were experienced elsewhere in the island chain, and the storm then veered slightly westward, passing over the Mona Channel and hitting Cabo Rojo, in western Puerto Rico, and eastern Santo Domingo, where years later it was remembered as the San Antonio hurricane or "the tragic storm of the year of 'eighty." It then curved northward, missing Bermuda but damaging shipping in the area, and finally moving off into the North Atlantic.[69]

Bracketing the great hurricane (10–16 October) two other storms had struck further to the west. A major hurricane of tremendous strength (October 1–6) that eventually killed over 3,000 people had hit the little port of Savanna la Mar, passing over Montego Bay, and then slamming into Santiago de Cuba in eastern Cuba. It then caught two British fleets, one operating off Florida and the other off Virginia while engaged in military operations in support of the campaigns against the colonial rebels.

Meanwhile another tropical depression (October 15–22) in the Gulf of Mexico had reached hurricane velocities and passed close to Pinar del Rio in western Cuba on October 16, then moving northeast. Spain, also fighting the British in support of the continental colonies, had successfully attacked and taken Mobile in 1779, and was planning further operations in the Gulf. As this storm moved northward it overtook a Spanish fleet of over 60 sail with 4,000 troops en route under Admiral Solano to attack Pensacola in British-held West Florida. The ships were damaged and scattered, 2,000 men died, and Solano abandoned the project. Solano's Storm, as this hurricane was called, had been a disaster for Spanish plans. The bad weather continued into November, further disrupting British naval operations off the mid-Atlantic coast.

The Savanna la Mar storm in Jamaica had destroyed houses and sugar works, leveled cane fields, and almost totally destroyed the plantain walks.[70] Governor Dalling called it "the most terrible hurricane ever felt in this country." He convoked a meeting of Kingston merchants and raised from them £10,000 of relief for the affected areas while he sent out ships to other islands looking for foodstuffs. His report to London emphasized the material destruction to all buildings and the "pitiable situation" of the population left without clothing, shelter, or food. Losses in Westmoreland parish (where Savanna la Mar was located) alone were set at £950,000. Dalling emphasized to London that the "devastation is immense," and he stressed the "distresses of the poor inhabitants who now look up to their most gracious Sovereign in their timely calamitous situation for some alleviation of their very great sufferings."[71] A decade later, the historian Bryan Edwards compared the destruction of Savanna la Mar by the sea surge as a catastrophe "even more terrible" than the 1692 earthquake that leveled Port Royal.[72] Jamaican sugar production, which had been steadily increasing since 1750, was disrupted by the 1780 storm and by those that followed over the next five years.[73]

Together Jamaica and Barbados, the two principal jewels in Britain's tropical crown, had suffered tremendous losses in property and human life. Appeals by individuals and by royal officials like Dalling emphasized the misery of the population and the threat of famine or even starvation. As was common, subscription funds were created and thousands of pounds were raised from private donors in various cities in Great Britain. Most importantly, Parliament also responded with a bill authorizing a grant of "benevolence" of £80,000 for Barbados and £40,000 for Jamaica. This was an extraordinary measure and a far greater amount than had ever been authorized in the few previous colonial emergencies like the 1740 Charleston fire. It was an action probably motivated by the desire to keep the island colonies loyal, since wartime measures like a trade embargo with the rebellious continental colonies had caused considerable discontent, and the island assemblies were also concerned about their own security because of the wartime threat from their French neighbors. Paternalism, patriotism, and policy had moved the king and Parliament to authorize the relief. Given their assured market for sugar in Great Britain and the ever-present threat of slave rebellion, the chances that the island colonies might have joined the rebellion had always been slim, but the hurricanes of 1780 had created an opportunity and a need to demonstrate the benevolence of the king and the advantages of loyalty.[74]

The other imperial powers responded to the crisis in a similar if less generous fashion. In France, subscription lists were set up in the banks of Paris and Nantes so that people could make donations, while the king and council voted a million crowns to be given to the islands' inhabitants as a "gift from the nation."[75] The Marquis de Bouillé, governor on Martinique, wrote a circular letter to commandants and priests in the parishes to gather information to aid in distributing relief, and he estimated that Martinique alone would need 1,200 barrels of flour and 600 to 700 of salt meat, to say nothing of the similar needs of Dominica and St. Vincent.[76] As Bouillé and the intendant, the Marquis de Peynier, jointly reported to Paris, "In this dreadful circumstance, it was absolutely necessary to distribute relief to the victims." The precedents of 1766 and 1768 were used as a guide as tax exemptions were sought on the islands. The planters were particularly anxious for help. After the hurricane of 1756 they had begun to depend on agents in the major ports to handle their sales and purchases, and after the hurricane of 1766, these agents began to advance credit to them at rates above the usual five percent. Following the 1780 storm the agents also began to demand five percent of the gross sales as well. These arrangements put both the sugar planters and the growing number of coffee planters in a precarious position, and any further loss of crop to weather or other cause would rapidly place them into debt or foreclosure.[77] Tax relief was a possible and traditional response. Two officials on Martinique, assigned to evaluate which quarters on the island should be excused from the capitation tax of 1781, decided that it was too difficult to evaluate and verify individual losses. They recommended an island-wide exemption because of "the general distress, aggravated by the war, which is such that despite the general relief provided since the hurricane, [we] are forced daily to deliver relief to those families who have no means to provide for themselves." Other administrators were reluctant to see the loss of revenue that such an exemption implied.[78]

The Spanish government, after the storms of 1780, followed its usual policy of permitting the purchase of foodstuffs from foreigners, especially now from its allies in North America, but it continued to restrict the extent to which tax exemptions were granted.[79] Much of Spain's post-storm activity was directed to the recovery from military losses and the continua-

tion of its campaigns in the Gulf.[80] The August hurricane that had struck
New Orleans did extensive damage, sinking all the shipping at the mouth
of the Mississippi and destroying crops. The region had suffered a hurricane almost exactly a year before, and the residents of the province were
exasperated by "war, two hurricanes, inundation, contagion, a summer
more rainy and a winter more rigorous than had been previously known."
The *cabildo* and the intendant appealed to Madrid on their behalf and the
crown promised aid, albeit through a circular letter that, while expressing
Charles IV's sympathy for his distressed subjects, reminded residents that
"all countries have their inconveniences" and that they still owed loyalty
to the king.[81] In response to this storm and to the others in the remainder
of the decade, Spain expressed concerns similar these and turned toward
the traditional responses. Continued droughts in Puerto Rico, parts of
Cuba, and New Spain worsened conditions following the hurricanes that
continued in this decade. Droughts, the lack of flour, and bad harvests
filled Spanish correspondence through the 1780s.[82] Despite a royal order
in November 1787 prohibiting further foreign purchases, the governor of
Puerto Rico with support of the town council of San Juan authorized ships
to seek food at Danish St. Thomas and French Guadeloupe.[83] Foreign ships
under the cover of emergency stops caused by hurricanes or war continued to make port on the Spanish islands, where they often found welcome. Unlike Great Britain, neither Spain nor France sent large sums of
monetary relief. There was no question yet in their colonies that loyalty to
king and country might be shaken by calamity or political events. Those
possibilities lay in the coming decade.

The granting of relief or aid by the homelands to the colonies revealed
policy decisions tempered by humanitarian sentiments and religious understandings, but hurricanes had the potential not only to destroy the material bases on which social divisions rested, but also to underscore and
intensify those divisions, and sometimes, even to enable their enactment
as well. For example, Parliament had authorized relief funds for Jamaica
and Barbados, but how those monies were to be awarded was left to a
committee in London, and then to local officials in the colonies. In Jamaica
there were many complaints in the stricken parishes of Hanover, St. James,
and Westmoreland that the money sent to rehabilitate the island had been

given primarily to the large proprietors, and its award had basically ignored the plight of smallholders, shopkeepers, and artisans. Overall, planters received about half of all relief funds. The shopkeepers of Savanna la Mar claimed that "Persons of rank, figure, and fortune" had received a share disproportionate to their losses, and argued that they had lost everything—houses, slaves, apparel, furniture and money—and that the planters had the wherewithal to recover on their own. Eventually a market in discounted shares of Parliamentary relief funds developed that allowed further profit and speculation.[84] The non-planter population felt that the government's largesse had simply reinforced their own disadvantage.[85] Free people of color felt particularly neglected and pointed out their militia service and loyalty as meriting consideration, asking why their color should keep them from receiving Britain's generosity. They, however, were excluded as a class. So too were petitioners who because of age, gender, or religion were not thought worthy by the Jamaica commissioners assigned to make the appropriations.[86]

In Barbados, privately raised aid from Ireland arrived first and quickly provoked a dispute between the governor, his council, and the island's assembly over how the funds should be used and who should be the principal recipients. The dispute became even more intense when the Parliamentary funds began to arrive in 1781. Factions developed: some advocated using the money to pay down the island's debt; the governor wanted to use the funds for defensive fortifications that had been damaged in the storm, since taxation seemed out of the question; and other factions in the assembly wanted either a general distribution, or awards made on the basis of need or loss. The disputes, difficulties, and delays in this first major funding of disaster relief previewed the subsequent history of such distributions of disaster relief.

The social distinctions of island societies and the hierarchies of race were underlined in the post-hurricane period of recovery in many ways besides the distribution of relief funds. In Barbados, almost all the Anglican churches had been destroyed or damaged by the 1780 hurricane, and to refinance their rebuilding, parish vestries created a system of selling or renting out pews. By the 1820s many of these pews had been rented out to less wealthy whites and to some free people of color, which led to disputes about their right to sit in the white areas of the church. This "pew rent" controversy centered on the question of whether the pews had become the property of individual whites who could then rent them to whomever they wished, or whether they belonged to the "white community." In the era of abolition and emancipation, the customary practices of exclusion and segregation were increasingly questioned, and it has been suggested that prior to 1780 these practices had not, in fact, been formalized. The hurricane had in effect created a moment of instability that elicited new techniques to divide whites and blacks, and these became a point of controversy as the issue of slavery as racial separation was questioned.[87]

But above all, the storms had occurred in societies where the vast majority of the population was enslaved, and the long-standing fears of the outnumbered white populations were brought sharply into focus. On all the islands the immediate fear was famine. In the French islands, the lack of foodstuffs placed the slave population at risk and thus was a threat to the recovery of the planters and of agricultural production in general. But the lack of food also threatened to make the slaves unmanageable and defiant. Security and control of the slaves on these islands depended to a large extent on the *maréchaussée,* the constabulary. It was composed in large part of people of color, and on the militia, which, while under white command, also depended on the participation of free people of color. Nevertheless, the official French correspondence was relatively quiet about the possibility of slave unrest in the wake of catastrophe.

In the Spanish islands, where, unlike the French and British islands, the proportion of slaves in the population was still relatively small in the 1780s, fears of slave rebellion were absent in the post-disaster correspondence. That lack of fear changed in the following decade as the opening of the slave trade to foreigners in 1789 and the resulting tripling of slave imports to Cuba over the levels of the 1780s began to change both the demography of slavery in the Spanish islands and the preoccupation with the possibilities of revolt.

On the British islands, the fear of insurrection was palpable.[88] Food shortages in the summer, the "hungry time," were normal, but the hurricanes had created a real crisis of subsistence.[89] The situation was already difficult prior to the storms of 1780 because as a wartime measure trade with the continental colonies, the traditional source of food and building materials, had been suspended.[90] The trade in slaves declined in the period after 1776, raising prices and causing planter concerns; and with the reduced supply of food for their slaves, they feared for their prospects. Slaves on some islands went hungry. On Antigua about twenty percent of the slaves died between 1779 and 1781.[91] Governors and planters throughout the island assemblies quarreled over policy and its enactment; little wonder that London thus saw disaster relief as an important tool for helping itself and the colonies, and for maintaining the loyalty of the islands while the continent was aflame in insurrection. Given the demographics of the islands, and the predominance of slaves, there was probably little chance that the creole planters would have contemplated joining the northern colonies.

What haunted the islanders' dreams especially was the specter of slave revolt in the aftermath of the storms. Jamaica had experienced a serious revolt, Tacky's Rebellion, in 1760, when about a hundred slaves had risen and killed a number of whites. Thomas Thistlewood reported white insecurity because of their precarious situation and because almost all arms and ammunition had been destroyed or lay under the debris. He claimed that following the Jamaica storm slaves immediately were thought to be "turbulent," "daring," and "very impudent."[92] William Beckford, who lived through the storm, reported that when the winds had destroyed the flimsy slave quarters, the "unhappy negroes" had sought refuge in the planters' homes, adding to the confusion, "lamenting by anticipation the loss of their wives and children." Immediately after the hurricane, they had begun to drink and loot, but Beckford ascribed this behavior to the bad example of whites and to the breakdown of civil order.[93] Similar breakdown was also reported in Barbados, where looting took place in heavily damaged Bridgetown—although reports of the time made no distinction between looters and storm victims simply trying to survive the lack of food, shelter, and water. In both western Jamaica and Barbados immediate steps were taken to restore order. In Jamaica, the governor in Kingston sent to Savanna la Mar and even dispatched a warship as a show of force.[94] In Bridgetown, Barbados, fear of slave unrest was joined to the concern that about a thousand prisoners of war being held there might take advantage of the situation. Patrols were set up on the streets of Bridgetown and the presence of British troops helped to restore order. There may have been a rise in slave flight or marronage in mountainous Jamaica, where escape was easier, but on none of the islands did any kind of major organized rebellion follow the storms of 1780. Despite the vulnerability of slave society, the slaves themselves remained the most at risk, and their immediate concern was simply survival. Moreover, at probably no time since the end of the Seven Years' War in 1763 were Caribbean societies more heavily armed, their militias better organized and more on guard, than in 1780, after France and Spain had joined the conflict on the side of the North American rebels and now threatened the British Caribbean colonies.

The decade of the 1780s brought continuing destruction from hurricanes. Jamaica, which had enjoyed a long period free from hurricanes prior to 1780, was damaged again in 1781, and then in 1784, 1785, and 1786 as well. St. Croix suffered damages of over 2.5 million Danish *rigsdalers* in 1785, and Guadeloupe, Barbados, Santo Domingo, and Puerto Rico were also battered in that year. The year 1787 was another year of high incidence, with storms striking from the Leewards to the coast of Honduras and the Yucatan peninsula. Little Dominica was struck by three separate storms in that year. The pattern continued until 1789.

The hurricanes of 1780 and those that followed during the rest of the decade carried a lesson for slave societies. What exactly that lesson taught, and to whom, remained a matter of conjecture. The difficult conditions created by the storms had laid bare the misery of slavery, and while some planters and the West India lobby in London argued that bad living conditions for the slaves were the direct result of the damage and shortages created by the storms, criticism of the conditions of slaves in general increased. In 1784, the Jamaica Assembly began to discuss revision of all laws on slavery, and then passed the Consolidation Act that punished sadistic treatment and provided better medical care and subsistence for slaves. By the 1790s, a movement in England for the abolition of the slave trade and another more conservative movement in England and the West Indies for reform or the amelioration of slave conditions were under way.[95]

Were the horrendous condition of slaves a structural situation inherent in slavery itself, or were the conditions the product of calamities and wartime policies? Literatures of attack and defense developed on both sides of the issue, in which reference to the exacerbation of slave conditions as a result of the storms began to play an important role. In that context, some of the observations about the impact of the hurricanes on slave life come into focus. Hector Macneill was a defender of slavery who had earlier lived in Jamaica and then returned in 1788. He thought that conditions for slaves had much improved since he had originally lived there. Although he spoke out against mistreatment and was even willing to see the slave trade end, he believed blacks to be ignorant, lazy, and incapable of controlling their basic appetites. Macneill conceded that Africans and their descendants might have some positive qualities. He waxed eloquent on the singing of the slave girls in the sugar mills at night that "smoothed my pillow and lulled me into slumber," for "after all a good ear and an African are inseparable," but he remained firm that "as for any plans for emancipating the Negroes and converting them into hired servants, you may respond on it that nothing on earth can be more completely chimerical, nor any system more productive of general mischief."[96] The present misery of Jamaican slaves Macneill blamed squarely on the conditions caused by the storms. The West India hurricane was a destroyer. It was not just the loss of life and property that made the hurricane so terrible, but the planters' inability to provide food or care to the starving, sick, and infirm slaves who pleaded for help. It was the hurricanes and not slavery itself that bore the responsibility for the decrease in the slave population.

> These are scenes to awaken sensibility and make the moralist exclaim with indignation, "Cursed be your isles and cursed your institutions!"— so in the warmth of the moment I might say; but let not calamities be construed as cruelty, nor inevitable destruction be confounded with neglect. Throw up your West India possessions and abolish your African commerce in God's name! But throw not decrease of the helpless West India bondsman on the inhumanity of his master alone.[97]

A year later, William Dickson, former secretary to the governor of Barbados and an advocate of gradual abolition, published his *Letters on Slav-*

ery, which took a much more favorable position on the idea of emancipation and on the suitability of freedom for the slaves. Dickson used the 1780
storm as a demonstration that whites had nothing to fear. The 1780 hurricane had left the whites in dire straits, trying to reclaim their property,
bury their dead, and reconstruct their families. The few troops on the island were in no condition to act, and most of the firearms lay buried beneath the rubble. Still, the slaves had "remained peaceably with their
owners and showed no signs of a spirit of mutiny." Thousands of slaves
had perished in the disaster but, argued Dickson, replacing them with
more slaves was not the answer. He offered a comparison to make his
point. In 1783, an earthquake in Sicily and Naples had killed many people,
but the king of Naples had not replaced them by dragging people against
their will to exile in a distant land. Such population recovery had to be
made with justice and humanity, and slavery, unfortunately, offered neither.[98] The "great" killer hurricane of 1780, its siblings of that year, and its
cousins of the rest of the decade exposed the fracture lines and social divisions of Caribbean societies, and became an element themselves along
with war, commerce, politics, and race in the shaping of social values and
governmental policies.

By the 1780s, after three hundred years of confronting the hurricanes,
governments had increasingly if irregularly moved to take direct action in
response to the recurring calamities they caused; but what had been the
collective effect of these calamities on the social attitudes and the mental
world of the men and women who lived in their shadow? Disasters had
the potential to destroy societies by rending their social fabric and so damaging the institutions and authority that maintained order that chaos in
the struggle for survival was the immediate result. But disasters also had
the capacity to dissipate normal distinctions of class, position, and race,
revealing in commonly shared vulnerability at least a temporary equality
and need to cooperate in the interest of survival. The distinction between
the two results was not always clear. Time also played a part. Cooperation
for the common good might characterize the immediate response by people after a destructive hurricane, but if food and materials remained scarce
and help was not available for an extended period or was not awarded
fairly, then competition and hostility were a likely outcome. The decade of

the 1780s drove that point home. It also made it clear that social cooperation in societies structured by great disparities in wealth and rights and
divided by race, class, and civil status was particularly difficult.

By the last decade in the century the storms of the 1780s could be read
in a variety of ways. Early opponents of the slave trade who had by 1787
organized in London saw them as signs of God's displeasure, not with the
sinful extravagances and excesses of colonial life, but with the sin of trans-
porting and selling slaves, the very essence of that society. But perhaps the
most poignant story of the storms was told in Jamaica itself, not by the
slaveowners but by the slaves. It was said that in the mountains of Westmoreland parish, a young, energetic man of great abilities named Plato
had escaped slavery and formed a band of intrepid maroons that controlled the roads and raided plantations. He was greatly feared because of
his military skills, his leadership, and because he was a powerful practitio-
ner of *obeah,* the African system of beliefs maintained by the slaves. No one
could capture him, and because of his supernatural powers no one would
risk betraying him, but eventually he was captured and sentenced to execution in the town of Montego Bay. He faced the sentence calmly, but
warned his jailer that he would place a curse on him. Plato also threatened
the court that a great tempest would come and the sea would rise to seek
retribution for his death. He was executed in 1780. The jailer, although he
left Jamaica, was plagued by dreams and visions, and eventually wasted
away. Later that year the hurricane of October devastated the island and
the sea inundated Savanna la Mar. Thirty years later, the *duppy* or ghost of
Plato was said to still stalk the Moreland Mountains and the area of Montego Bay.[99] The story may be apocryphal, but it at least provides a window
onto the slaves' own narratives of survival, resistance, and divine intervention in the face of hurricanes. The Jamaica hurricane of 1780 had become Plato's storm.

Finally, we may ask: what was the long-term effect of the hurricanes
and other risks on the character and ways of thinking of the men and
women who lived in their shadow? Of course, there were all sorts of people involved: penal exiles, indentured servants, managers and bookkeep-
ers, small farmers and mariners; but the quintessential figures were the
planters and their families who controlled the land, the laborers, and the

local institutions. Defenders of the planter class saw them as men of action, risk-takers, willing to brave the hazards of the tropics in order to make their fortunes. Upwardly mobile, they were seen as courageous and enterprising builders of empire and of their own fortunes. The worst dangers that confronted them might even be a symbol of the settlers' and the region's potential. John Fowler, in his compilation of documents on the "great hurricane," argued for the quality of both the men and islands: "It is observable that men of the best hearts and greatest talents are agitated by the most violent passions, and so it is that the West Indies islands, which boast of the richest soil and the most valued productions, are more subject to hurricanes and earthquakes than any other part of the world."[100] England, with its temperate climate, might happily be free of the "war of the elements," but she was still subject to the evils of perfidy and ambition—the West Indies had no singular predominance in that regard. In competition with this positive and entrepreneurial image was the view of the planters as morally deficient, hard-driving, heartless men, who lived hard and died young; who often returned to Europe as absentees to live off the sweat of their slaves by the mismanagement and abuses of their attorneys and managers. These criticisms were made not only of the planters of the British colonies, but of the whites of other areas as well.[101] The *Considerations* (1776) of Hilliard d'Auberteuil offered a critique of the residents of the French islands in many ways similar to those made of the inhabitants of the British islands.[102] Of course, this line of criticism intensified as the humanitarian agitation for abolition of the slave trade and demands for better treatment and emancipation grew in the later eighteenth century.

But in the forming of a creole mentality, what role did the risk of hurricanes and vulnerability to them play? Fatalism and depression were never far off when years of work and capital accumulation could be lost in a moment. Charles Leslie wrote that the Jamaicans were "careless of futurity."[103] Thomas Thistlewood described his depression after the Jamaican hurricanes of 1780–81 had cost him £1,000 and moved him to place his estate and slaves for sale. He was in shock: "The external face of the earth so altered that I scarce know where I am." He compared the barren tree trunks stripped of leaves and branches to the mountains of Wales in the winter season.[104] He wrote in his diary of his discomfort and nerves and spoke of a neighbor whose dreams of storms kept him from sleeping.[105] He found no buyers, and shortly recovered his enthusiasm and became a respected member of Jamaican society. But the long-term effects on outlook are difficult to gauge. Some observers tried to do so. Jean-Baptiste Leblond, a French physician and naturalist who lived in the Antilles from age nineteen, noted the precarious nature of life under the threat of hurricanes that could in a moment bring all one's efforts to ruin. That possibility bred fatalism and a colonial disregard for constant labor:

> We do not share the continuously fresh pleasures of Europe's cities, and the idle, monotonous life brings with it heedlessness. Meanwhile we want to enjoy ourselves; we surrender ourselves to shameful debauchery; a passion for gaming drags us into the towns . . . where we ruin ourselves, where we give way to exorbitant expenditures, and where we neglect to attend to our dwellings and agriculture.

Under such risk, Leblond believed, the creoles became improvident and the French-born settlers became absentees. And if the colonists' estates survived the storms, then war could break out and the inability to ship products would reduce prices to nothing and make any imported provisions and goods very costly.[106] The result, suggested Leblond, was a colonial mentality of risk, profligacy, dissolution, and fatalism.

Such evaluations of creole fatalism and a sense of vulnerability tend to concentrate only on the planters and the white settlers. It is far more difficult to know how the threat of the climate and the storms was perceived by the vast numbers of slaves and the population of free people of color and *petite blancs* who certainly suffered from the heat and storms, the droughts, disease, and the shortages of food and shelter. They had to create their own meaning out of these risks. But by the end of the eighteenth century and with the turmoil of American independence, the French Revolution, and the Haitian slave rebellion, their principal concern had become the acquisition of rights or of freedom. The hurricanes now passed over societies that were marked not so much by fatalism as by the sentiments revolutionary change.

CHAPTER 4

Calamity, Slavery, Community, and Revolution

God rewards and punishes in His kingdom . . .
and we in ours.
—*Creole defender of Venezuelan independence*

God is not in the wind.
—*A Jamaican saying*

He would not consider as enemies men who had so barely
escaped in a contention with the force of the elements; but
they having, in common with his own people, been
partakers of the same danger, were in a manner entitled to
every comfort and relief which could be given in a season
of such universal calamity and distress.
—*Marquis de Bouillé (1780)*

The years from the hurricane-prone decade of the 1780s and the creation of the United States (1783) to the independence of most of Latin America by 1825 and the emancipation of slaves in the British Empire in 1834 witnessed tremendous social and political upheavals in the Greater Caribbean. The French Revolution (1789–96), the Haitian Revolution (1791–1804), the Napoleonic Wars (1799–1815), and a series of slave revolts, conspiracies, and maroon wars throughout the region disrupted commerce, altered sovereignties, and sometimes changed social relations. The growing movement in Europe for the end of the slave trade and the abolition of slavery itself, beginning about 1787 and achieving some success with the Danish (1803), British (1808), and Dutch (1818) terminations of the legal trade, all contributed to the transformation of many of these societies. Of course, the ripples of the intellectual and political effects of the revolutionary era were felt far beyond the Caribbean, but the multiracial and slave-based nature of its societies made them particularly susceptible to the intellectual arguments of revolutionary change, to the implied message of equality and the end of servitude, and to the Haitian example of direct action against slavery. At the same time, in reaction to those potential political changes, governments and local elites sought ways to insure stability, loyalty, and political continuity. Environmental factors did not determine the movements for change or the reactions to them, but at various junctures they did have effects, and even more importantly, political and social changes or the threat of them altered the way in which Caribbean societies and their metropolitan governments responded to natural disasters.[1] War and catastrophes had the potential to be either destabilizing crises or moments when governments could demonstrate their effectiveness and concern.

Response to Climate in a Time of Change

This era of revolutionary change was also marked by droughts, floods, earthquakes, and climatic and meteorological phenomena that provoked and facilitated social unrest and dislocation. After the frequent and violent storms of the hurricane seasons of the 1780s, the next decade brought some relief. Modern research has demonstrated that since 1750 (and probably before) there have been alternating periods of ten to twenty years with more and less activity of tropical cyclones.[2] This is probably tied to the ENSO phenomenon, although while El Niño conditions diminish the frequency and size of North Atlantic hurricanes, they do not preclude their formation nor reduce their possible size and destructive impact.[3] Thus there were hurricanes in the last decade of the eighteenth and first years of the nineteenth centuries, although in general they did not have the cumulative impact of the terrible '80s.

There is considerable evidence that a series of El Niño events that constituted a "mega-Niño" took place between 1788 and 1796, with worldwide environmental effects. Temperate North America and Europe had unseasonal high winter temperatures and other meteorological anomalies. Droughts and crop failures in France in 1787–89 created agricultural stress and disruption that contributed to popular discontent as bread and other food prices rose. South Asia suffered extreme droughts and crop failures. Droughts and famines also took place in the hurricane-prone zones of the North Atlantic. Mexico suffered first from a frost and then a widespread famine in 1785–86, and then grappled with reduced maize crops through the 1790s. Caribbean islands endured similar conditions. Antigua, Barbuda, St. Vincent, and Montserrat were all badly affected, leading planters to seek relief from their tax obligations.[4] Meanwhile, North America experienced a series of very hot summers and mild winters often with heavy rains and high temperatures, conditions that provoked other problems like the serious yellow fever outbreak in Philadelphia in 1793.

The early years of the nineteenth century brought new climatic challenges. These were some of the coldest years in European history, including 1816, "the year without a summer," a situation due in part to a number of volcanic eruptions that had filled the atmosphere with so much ash that temperatures fell well below the mean. As a result, harvests failed and prices rose in much of Western Europe and North America.[5] The Greater Caribbean region also suffered climatic effects in this period, in addition to events like a volcanic eruption on Guadeloupe in 1799, the devastating Caracas earthquake of 1812, and the eruption of Mount Soufrière on St. Vincent in that same year.

In this period of political and social turmoil, revolutionary change, and constitutional crises, responses to recurring natural disaster became an art of statecraft. Parliament's generous answer to the hurricanes of 1780s had underlined a new, more interventionist governmental attitude, and the political effects of such policies were not lost on imperial governments nor on their officials. Parliament had made its bequest as a wartime measure, expecting to win support from the major sugar islands and to quiet the grumbling of the West India merchants and absentees planters at home who were concerned about the lack of protection on the islands. It also hoped to satisfy the island assemblies concerned about disastrous failed military campaigns and distressed by their loss of commerce with the rebellious continental colonies. On Barbados, factions soon began to argue over how the relief funds were to be used and whether they should be distributed to everyone, or only to those who had lost the most. This became a bitter quarrel between the governor and his council and the assembly that tied up the funds for almost two years; and when they were finally distributed, costs and expenses were deducted from the total, with half of the monies used to reduce the island's deficit, so that only one-half of the £20,000 was actually given to victims of the hurricane. In Jamaica, a joint committee of the council and the assembly distributed the funds in the western parishes most affected based on petitions, but there were soon bitter complaints about the fairness of the distribution, which favored the large planters and excluded the poor, workmen, and freed persons of color. As Matthew Mulcahy has argued, in these slave societies free status and whiteness were not sufficient to create a sense of equality strong enough to eliminate the divisions of class interest.[6] The planters did not speak for all the free men and women in these societies. The hurricanes had revealed the fracture lines, and while the Parliament and the king had calculated correctly that a demonstration of paternalistic concern was a useful political tool in a moment of crisis, they had learned a lesson that distributing a bounty in the wake of disaster, no matter the sincerity of humanitarian intent, was no simple matter. It was a lesson that all the other governments of the region would learn as well.

The French had since the 1760s been taking a more direct role in responding to the problems created by natural disasters in the colonies, rebuilding churches and hospitals, repairing fortifications and barracks, providing tax relief to those affected, and supplying foodstuffs or loosening trade restrictions to make sure shortages were avoided. Administrators had stopped the import of foreign flour as soon as the immediate crisis was avoided, and returned to a policy of exclusive trade with France. The president of the Council of Martinique, M. de Penier, reported in 1768 that tax collectors would be sensitive to those who had suffered losses in the large hurricane of 1766. Further, he said, the opening of a few ports (one on St. Lucia and another on St. Domingue) where the other French islands could purchase foreign goods that France had never provided had functioned so well that this "first step on the path to free trade" might have opened the government's eyes, "and cause it seriously to consider whether the prosperity of the colonies demanded that we try a system other than a strictly prohibitive one." This desire for more open trade was the colonial dream, and the hurricanes and other catastrophes had opened the door to its realization, but de Penier understood that its pursuit had to be framed in the language of loyalty. As he told the Council,

> The public calamities that we have continually before our eyes and that we recall now with the keenest sorrow, have only become supportable to us through the confidence that we have always had in the paternal sentiments of the best of kings and in the testimonials that he has given of his sensibility to the news of Martinique's disasters, proofs that he desired to make public and that do not allow us to doubt that he will quickly grant us the relief of which we have need; we wait for it eagerly. . . .[7]

The ability to provide relief was presumed to be a royal attribute, but the French, like the British, discovered, following the tremendous losses of 1780, that distributing relief in a manner both effective and fair was no easy matter, given the competing interests of various sectors of society and the fiscal limitations of government. That led to a mixed response in which some state aid was given as a gift, and some as an advance to be repaid in the future. Another hurricane in August of 1788 that killed almost 400 people on Martinique and caused considerable destruction of crops elicited a similar response that sought to balance the interests of state, the merchant suppliers, and the island population. The governor sent out emergency supplies of food to parishes threatened by starvation and an ordinance allowed foreign goods to be imported, but limits on the amount of flour that could be imported were set. The governor had only about 6,000 barrels of flour on hand, but expected with what was en route and with the harvest of manioc that he would not have to open the ports fully to foreign trade to bring in flour. Salt cod, a primary staple of the slaves, was another story. The governor lifted the duties on its import because a famine among the slaves would lead to the loss of the colony, but he assured Paris that once the crisis had passed, the former duties would be reimposed. He emphasized, "we will do everything possible to avoid opening the ports to foreign commerce in order not to harm that of France."[8]

Guadeloupe was mostly spared from hurricanes between 1785 and 1809, although it suffered three in that latter year. Martinique saw four hurricanes in 1809 and another in 1816, Louisiana one in 1812, and Guadeloupe was hit in 1821, 1824, and by a violent storm in July 1825 that caused widespread damage to property and shipping.[9] Responses generally followed the established patterns. But in the decade of the 1790s and the first decades of the nineteenth century, the bloody political upheavals of St. Domingue and in the other French colonies, and the British intervention or occupation of the French islands preoccupied residents and French administrators more than the risks of natural disasters.

Spain continued to control the larger islands of the Greater Antilles. While Santo Domingo became caught up in the struggle for independence that was being waged on the western, French part of the island, and was eventually invaded and controlled by non-Spanish forces, Cuba and Puerto Rico became in this period the staging areas for royalist opposition to the movements for independence in the Spanish mainland colonies. They also became major sources of Spain's revenues, as both islands experienced a new agricultural expansion that marked their shift to intensive plantation agriculture. In Cuba, relatively effective administrators in America, directed by reformist ministers in Madrid, made concessions to island residents to facilitate land tenure, exploit forest resources, and allow easier access to slave imports. A dynamic creole elite seized these opportunities and initiated a vigorous expansion of the sugar industry accompanied by the growth in slave imports. In 1792, Cuba had a population of 272,000, of which 84,000 (31%) were enslaved. By 1827, the total population had reached over 700,000, of which about 287,000 (41%) were slaves.[10] Cuban sugar exports rose from 15,000 tons in1790 to 55,000 in 1820 and 105,000 in 1830.[11] In Puerto Rico, a similar process took place on a reduced scale. In both cases, the elimination of St. Domingue as a producer of tropical commodities opened the market for expansion.

The Spanish islands continued to be visited by the great storms, but during this period of agricultural expansion and economic growth, government officials sought to insure the continued profitability of the islands and the revenue stream their taxes provided to the state, and to solidify the loyalty of the islands in the face of the revolutionary movements in the Spanish empire. Thus the hurricanes took on a heightened political importance. Although an English attempt to take San Juan in 1797 had caused a disruption of the economy, Puerto Rico did not suffer a major hurricane between 1788 and 1804, and during that period it benefited from a number of reforms and concessions that stimulated agricultural production and trade.[12] The revolutionary turmoil in the Caribbean brought to the island immigrants from St. Domingue, Louisiana, and northern South America who were attracted by its seeming stability and by the effective government of its intendant Alejandro Ramírez (1813–15). Hurricanes in 1804, 1806, two in 1809, and two in 1812 caused the usual damages and flooding, but the island continued to flourish due to the expansion of sugar, coffee, and tobacco agriculture in the wake of the destruction of St. Domingue as a French colony. The island population grew rapidly, and by 1807 had reached 183,000. By 1815, in recognition of the island's economic importance and of the necessity to maintain its loyalty, the Spanish crown issued a *cédula de gracias* that codified the new, more lenient policies of immigration, freer trade, slave imports from foreign sources, and tax reforms.[13] The result was further growth, especially in the areas of Ponce on the south coast and Mayaguez to the west, where new sugar plantations were set up. Puerto Rican sugar production doubled from 1820 to 1830 and then again by 1835. During the movements for independence in South America and Mexico, Cuba and Puerto Rico took on a new importance in Spanish imperial calculations, as governors were encouraged to develop the islands and to insure their loyalty by suppressing any revolutionary tendencies or conspiracies.

The improvement of the economy was not made without resistance and complaint. The Spanish government under Charles IV (1788–1808) was far less responsive to the needs of the colonial populations in the face of hurricane damage than it had been in the previous decades under Charles III. Western Cuba, hit by hurricanes in 1791, 1792, and 1794, found the governor Luis de Las Casas unsympathetic to the plight of the general population. Victims in need of food and shelter objected to the governor's demand of compulsory labor from slave and free on roads and bridges, and he was slow to resolve the shortages of food. Unhelpful and demanding in terms of disaster response, the governor showed himself far more sympathetic to the interests of the sugar sector and its representative Havana *cabildo* by granting tax exemptions and other privileges. Popular dissent intensified especially in Santiago de Cuba, and by 1796, shortly after another hurricane, complaints against the governor finally moved the crown to replace him.[14]

The dismissal of the Cuban governor should be seen within the context of response to disaster as a political strategy. In the midst of the revolutionary turmoil of the period, there had been a noticeable change in the efficiency and in the administrative language of dealing with calamity. The Spanish islands, despite some stirrings for independence, had remained loyal to Spain, their elites fearful of Haitian-style slave insurrections and anxious to seize the market advantage that the elimination of St. Domingue had created. Moreover, the use of the Spanish islands of the Greater Antilles as staging areas for the royal troop movements in the effort to suppress the South American revolutions had made any local attempts at independence very difficult. No wonder that Simón Bolívar would write in exasperation in 1822, "Before us we have the rich and beautiful Spanish islands [Cuba and Puerto Rico] that will never be more than enemies."[15] Cuba and Puerto Rico now became crucial to the Spanish economy, and both islands experienced a period of economic growth fostered by imperial policies and concessions under the direction of governors whose principal objectives was to develop the colonies and maintain their loyalty. During the revolutionary upheavals in Spanish America between 1807 and 1825, the opening of trade with neutral powers, especially the United States, had that goal. This policy, along with an increase in the slave trade during the period 1790–1810, generated an agricultural boom, especially in Cuba. Reformers and planters on that island were anxious to make this situation permanent, and their leaders sought that goal through opposition to any limitation on the slave trade and by support of royal opposition to the Spanish Constitution of 1812 as a way of securing concessions from the crown. Captains-general in Cuba sought ways to emphasize the advantages of loyalty, and above all, the increasing importance of slavery to the economy. Effective disaster relief was also an element in that program.

Puerto Rico provides another example of reforms designed to solidify Spain's rule. The government on that island was placed in the hands of Miguel de la Torre (1822–37), a hard-nosed soldier who had commanded royalist forces in the struggles against Bolívar's revolution in Venezuela. He took office during a restorationist rejection of the liberal Spanish constitution of 1812, and his principal concern was to suppress any separatist or liberal tendencies that threatened Spanish rule on the island. Liberal ideas had been expressed during the first two decades of the century by the island's elites, but in the post-Napoleonic restoration of Spanish absolutism, de la Torre was given the task of repression. As governor, using almost dictatorial powers, he strengthened the garrisons, instituted a number of administrative changes, introduced urban reforms like gas lighting on the streets of San Juan, and promoted the agricultural expansion of the island. He was also long remembered for a "bread and circuses" policy, which he called *"baile, botella, y baraja"* (dancing, the bottle, and the deck of cards), aimed at distracting Puerto Ricans from politics. But de la Torre was also a perceptive and astute administrator who understood the utility of demonstrating efficiency in the face of disaster as a political strategy. A September 1824 "furious" storm in Puerto Rico moved the governor to report the miserable situation of a number of towns and villages. The council noted that their response should make clear to the governor that "His Majesty is very sensitive about the damages, and hopes that his zeal will dry the tears of those unhappy vassals who have suffered and who are so valued by the King, our Lord."[16] The July Santa Ana storm the following year moved Governor de la Torre and the intendant of Puerto Rico to meet in order to consider the damages and to express the "paternal desires of His Majesty to promote the well-being and felicity of the inhabitants of the island." In each of thirty towns, a committee was formed by the military commandant, the *alcalde, and* four prominent citizens to determine if taxes should be suspended for a year. In the meanwhile, authorization for trade in foodstuffs with non-Spanish islands was granted and a directive went out to stop profiteering and price gouging. De la Torre sent out a circular to every municipality ordering shelters to be constructed to protect the homeless from disease and the weather, government buildings and barracks to be repaired, and churches to be cleaned and renovated so that the faithful could meet in pious reunion. Most importantly, he ordered that each resident be required to plant at least a *cuerda* (about an acre) of fruits or root crops to feed their families, and more if labor was available.[17] The municipal committees submitted reports that were then quantified in an accounting of losses, detailing town by town the deaths, injuries, houses destroyed, acreage of each crop affected, and animal losses down to the level of individual chickens. Such inventories had occasionally been done in the late eighteenth century, but never with the precision of de la Torre's government following the 1825 storm.[18] De la Torre clearly demonstrated through his actions and attention to detail how an efficient response could turn a disaster into a positive example of government's competency.

The 1825 Santa Ana hurricane, whose violence was considered previously unknown in Puerto Rico's history, presented Spanish representatives of the crown the opportunity to demonstrate the benevolence and efficiency of the crown, and thus the advantages of loyalty. Miguel de la Torre appealed for help to neighboring Cuba, emphasizing the extent of the damages, the inability of Puerto Rico's destitute population to pay for the recovery, and the degree to which the revolutionary insurgents in the recently liberated parts of Spanish America must have taken some pleasure in this situation.[19] In response, Francisco Dionisio Vives, governor of Cuba, called on the inhabitants of that island to go beyond a "sterile compassion" in order to demonstrate their "generous charity." He promoted a collection of funds from the inhabitants of that island. In November 1825 he wrote to Governor de la Torre about the desire of the Cubans to aid "our brothers." Despite their generous inclination, Vives was forced to point out that Trinidad, Santa Clara, and other Cuban towns had been so damaged by another hurricane in late September that they lacked the resources to send aid.[20] Noticeable in the post-storm documents was the use of words like "honor," "loyalty," and "patriotism" to stimulate the population to activity. But like the British and French, Spanish administrators were also reluctant to provide assistance to those victims of the storm they deemed undeserving. They warned against "vagrants and almoners [*limosneros*] whose motive of soliciting the charity of neighbors is laziness."[21] These questions of how to deliver assistance and to whom accompanied the growing concern of states struggling with the political, moral, and practical issues inherent in these policies.

Finally, we should note that there was now another political actor in the region: the United States of America. As early as 1790, Congress had at times sought to grant assistance or relief by the distribution of funds, usually in the form of direct relief to private individuals. Victims of fire, piracy, or other kinds of loss received relief, and occasionally so too did victims of war, rebellion, or natural disaster. Refugees from the Haitian Revolution received congressional aide, and in 1812 Congress, at the time seeking to consolidate relations with South America and sympathetic to emerging republicanism in the Americas, sent relief to the victims of the terrible earthquake in Caracas, in the "sacred cause of distant and oppressed humanity."[22] But from the beginning such actions stirred debate between Jeffersonian Republicans seeking to limit congressional power in making such awards and Hamiltonians supporting a looser interpretation of constitutional power to provide for the general welfare. Debates centered on the applicability of precedent, and the extent to which appeals satisfied the implicit requirement that the cause of the disaster was sudden and unforeseeable and the petitioner was morally blameless.[23] By the 1830s a general consensus seems to have been reached that precedents justified limited relief efforts, but until the Civil War, appropriations for such grants were slight. After 1865 that situation would change considerably. The focus of these early U.S. debates on the wisdom and justification of governmental relief and its political and moral basis was sharpened by the debates' placement within broader discussions of constitutionality and the role of government in general. These arguments about the role of government in responding to catastrophe raised questions that all of the Caribbean imperial powers had long been confronting.

A DISASTER COMMUNITY

Despite the geographical and political fragmentation of the Greater Caribbean region and the imperial rivalries and hostilities that had characterized its history up to this point, political boundaries had become porous as islands had been conquered and surrendered and populations had been moved or expelled. Migrations, both forced and voluntary, had become a characteristic of the region, and sovereignties were often fragile and indefinite. Some islands, like St. Thomas, Dominica, St. Eustatius, and Trinidad, became polyglot. Cutting across political and geographic fragmentation was the relative ease with which people could cross boundaries and the many reasons they had to do so. Contraband trade lay at the heart of this, but those seeking personal, political, or religious freedom, land, or opportunity were also involved.[24] Maritime marronage became endemic as slaves sought freedom by fleeing to colonies where the difference of sovereignty and religion would protect them against arrest or return. Information circulated widely through the region and across political divisions, carried by ship captains, the international, multiracial community of mariners, merchants, and military men. Crop and weather conditions on rival islands, the presence or absence of fleets, changes in policy or trade regulations, and the status of slave insurrections, all were matters of interest and sometimes of profit, loss, or survival throughout the region. Information circulated widely, the gazettes and newsletters of other colonies were read when possible, and rumor and hearsay about imperial policies or local conditions filled the taverns of every port. Despite political division and inter-colony competition, similarities born from slavery, of social and racial structures, and from economic potential created a sense of common destiny, if not exactly of community.

Hurricanes and other disasters had over time created a sense of common threat and shared dependency within the empires, but also between the colonies of all of the empires. The tradition of seeking food and materials from other colonies following hurricanes, earthquakes, and other calamities, despite the imperial restrictions on trade with foreigners, had become common throughout the region. Even during periods of war, information was gathered from neighboring islands, and the same bonds and shared interests that had developed out of contrabanding and illegal trade were fostered by the common threat of hurricanes. Information was shared and gathered from enemies even during hostilities. John Fowler's extensive compilation of reports of the 1780 hurricanes in Jamaica and Barbados, for example, was accompanied by information about the damages suffered in the French and Dutch islands. A French report of the damages of 1780 expressed concern for the destruction done to the islands of "our enemy" (*nos ennemis*).[25] In 1815, the intendant of Puerto Rico reported the news from Swedish St. Bartholomew, where a hurricane had sunk over seventy ships.[26] A small ship from St. Thomas arrived in Fajardo, Puerto Rico, in September 1819 with news of a hurricane that had sunk or beached almost a hundred ships in the principal bay of St. Thomas. The mayor of Fajardo forwarded to the governor in San Juan a detailed description of the character of the storm, the direction of the winds, and the losses suffered.[27] Such information was vital for preparation prior to a storm's arrival, but knowledge of hurricane strikes and their effects could also be essential in the post-disaster stage, when it was important to know where food and materials might be obtained, or how disasters on competitor islands might influence commodity prices.

Like contraband, the shared environmental risks created certain sympathy and bond that undercut cultural, religious, and political differences. A famous incident took place during the great hurricane of 1780 when two British men-of-war were driven ashore at Martinique. All of the officers were lost and only thirty-one seamen of the two crews survived, but they were treated gallantly by the French governor of Martinique, the Marquis of Bouillé (fig. 4.1), who sent them back to Barbados under a flag of truce, with a message that

> he would not consider as enemies men who had so barely escaped in a contention with the force of the elements; but they having, in common with his own people, been partakers of the same danger, were in a manner entitled to every comfort and relief which could be given in a season of such universal calamity and distress, and he only lamented that their number was so small and that none of the officers had been saved.

FIGURE 4.1 "In a common catastrophe, all men are brothers." Portrait of the Marquis of Bouillé, Governor of Martinique, who treated his British enemies with magnanimity after they had suffered from a common enemy: the force of nature. (Lithograph by François Delpech after Henri Grévedon; Print Collection, Miriam and Ira D. Wallach Division of Art, Prints, and Lithographs, New York Public Library)

Bouillé justified his kindness by telling his superiors that "in a common catastrophe, all men are brothers."[28] The magnanimous act was duly noted and later celebrated after the war when Bouillé was feted in England by the West India interests and was honored by the Chamber of Commerce of Glasgow, which presented him a set of matched pistols in recognition of his "humanity and generosity."[29]

The Spaniards had assumed much the same attitude. In Bridgetown, Barbados, the storm of 1780 had destroyed the prison building holding 800 Spanish prisoners of war. The immediate fear was that these men would join the island's slaves, who had already begun to loot damaged properties. A British troop was organized to meet the threat, but their fears of internal danger were allayed when they were assisted by the prisoner of war don Pedro de Santiago, a captain of the regiment of Aragon, who organized the Spanish prisoners to help in the relief efforts and the control of the rebellious slaves. A later commentator wrote, "let it be remembered with gratitude, that laying aside all national animosity in that season of calamity, they omitted no service or labor for the relief of the distressed inhabitants and preservation of the public order."[30]

Perhaps no better example of the idea of a community of interest is found than in the letter Captain Sir Thomas Cochrane sent from St. John's Newfoundland along with one hundred pesos to his "amigo" Miguel de la Torre y Pando, Count of Torrepando, governor of Puerto Rico. The letter was in response to news of the Santa Ana hurricane on the island that had killed 379 people, destroyed 6,883 homes, and ruined almost 6,000 *cuerdas* of coffee. Cochrane was at this moment governor of Newfoundland, having arrived from the Antilles only six weeks before. He courteously inquired about Torrepando's wife and family and noted that since the political news from Spain was bad, he was happy that his friend was not there. The reports of a recent hurricane had reached him, and thus Cochrane sent a hundred pesos to be distributed to the poor of various communities who had suffered in the hurricane. Torrepando set up committees in the affected eastern part of the island. In Caguas, the poor recipients, most of them widows, signed receipts for the four pesos they received; in Yabucoa, six men and six women, and in Patillas, a similar number, including two freed persons, received help.[31] Such demonstrations of sympathy and affinity expressed at the individual level between royal administrators reinforced the feeling of shared risk and common cause in the face of calamity. This was a sentiment that would flourish during the following century as the science of meteorology tackled the challenge of understanding and predicting the storms.

GOVERNMENTS AND PROVIDENCE

By the early nineteenth century governments in the main had reached the conclusion that for political, moral, and humanitarian reasons the state bore some responsibility to the victims of disaster, at least when the sufferers were faultless and bore no responsibility for their plight. To some extent, this attitude had grown in the eighteenth century as a sense that nature itself might be separated from divine intention developed. Still, the idea that natural disasters might be providential in their origins remained widely accepted in a Christian worldview in which history would be played out between the deluge of Noah's ark and the coming apocalype.[32] Everyone sought to protect themselves, to lessen their material vulnerabilities and risks, but despite such pragmatic considerations, governments and peoples still tried to understand and explain these dangers in theological or moral terms. Catholics accepted the possibility that the Devil or other malignant forces might be involved in disrupting the natural order, and thus seeking the protection of the saints or divine intervention was a common response to these threats. Protestant theology that viewed natural phenomena as expressions of God's "infinite might" left little room for diabolical intervention or the evil action of witches, but the idea that a violent sea, tremendous winds, or other fearsome aspects of nature might be the work of evil forces was never entirely absent from popular thinking about the natural world.[33] Although individuals saw catastrophes as divine punishments for their personal failings, by the eighteenth century the idea of natural phenomena as part of an orderly universe within a general providence came to dominate Protestant theology. Despite the growth of more materialist or "scientific" interpretations during the course of that century, in both the Catholic and Protestant worlds, providentialist interpretations of catastrophes as both warnings and punishments continued, as they do today, parallel to less theological interpretations.[34]

The beliefs that natural phenomena were part of a general providence and a divinely ordered universe and that catastrophe was God's punishment were not contradictory. By the late eighteenth century, as interpretations of destructive natural phenomena shifted increasingly toward a view that these were aspects of the natural functioning of the universe, observers like the Jamaican planter, naturalist, and historian Bryan Edwards, in his *History . . . of the British Colonies the West Indies* (1793), was still willing to concede that even the simple Taíno, "terrified at the judgments of the Almighty," had been able to recognize God's power in the storms."[35] "Public judgments," divine warnings, or castigations could inspire awe and wonder and merited a country's attention, since private sins would be weighed at the gates of heaven, but the sins of a kingdom or a society would be punished by God only in this world. The Latitudinarian minister John Tillotson wrote that God might stay his hand, "till the iniquities of a Nation be full, but sooner or later they have reason to expect his vengeance."[36]

The role of God in natural disaster became a central issue in the philosophical and theological debates of Enlightenment thinkers across a spectrum, from those who believed all aspects of nature were the result of divine intention, to those who believed that the laws of nature functioned without God's direction.[37] Most people held to an intermediate position, and so in the Caribbean world while the character and seasonality of the hurricanes raised doubts about any particular divine purpose, few people, Catholic, Protestant, or Jew, were willing to ignore providence entirely, and those who suffered and survived the storms found their doubts diminished and their faith renewed by the experience.

Many islands reserved certain days for prayers, fasting, or thanksgiving during the hurricane season. On Cuba and Puerto Rico the prayer for protection from storms became part of the liturgy. The English on St. Christopher beginning in 1683 fasted on alternate Fridays from August to October; on Nevis it was the last Friday of the month from July to September, with October 3 celebrated as a day of Thanksgiving if the season passed without incident.[38] On St. Lucia, residents sang the *Miserere mei Deus* during the months of danger and a *Te Deum* at the close of the season.[39] The commander of the Dutch part of Sint Maarten (St. Martin) in 1749 ordered a day of prayer in thanks for being spared military attack and to ask God "to continue to save us from storms and tempests with his mercy in these months of hurricanes."[40] Such prayer days became regular. A governor's order of July, 1793 noted that "the most dangerous time of year approaches, and we must fear the punishing hand of the Lord for good reasons, because of our great sins and iniquities."[41] The *Gazette Officiale de la Guadeloupe,* after describing the damages caused by a severe hurricane in 1825, ended its report noting: "We finish this distressing narration of our island's disasters by expressing the shared sentiments of respect for the Sovereign-Arbiter of all things that these disasters inspire.

Thus we say, the same blow struck country and city, the houses, palaces, the Tabernacle, young and old, rich and poor; painful proof by which providence wished to recognize our submission to its decrees."[42]

On Danish St. Croix and St. Thomas special prayers were offered on June 25 at the beginning of the season, and then again on October 25 at its end.[43] After a great storm in 1772, The *Royal Danish American Gazette* on St. Croix editorialized about the universal threat and response to the storms: "A few such events would ruin us in temporals but help us in spirituals, and make us fit for the kingdom of Heaven; for the Turk, the Jew, the Atheist, the Protestant, and the Papist would join in unanimous prayer to appease the Lord of Hurricanes."[44] Over time, the relative balance between a "natural" or theological interpretation of the storms changed, but even when the hurricanes were perceived as aspects of nature rather than divine punishment or diabolical action, God's intervention was called upon as a protective force.[45] In the Danish West Indies, after a hurricane in 1837 destroyed the synagogue and Jewish cemeteries on St. Thomas, the congregation added to the liturgy the hymn "O Hurricane," written by its leader Dutch-born Benjamin Cohen Carillon. It was sung as part of the service into the 1960s.[46]

We will then look on Him above
Whose arm alone can save.
The life, that he in endless love
His human creatures gave.
Nay, Hurricane, we do not fear
Nor tremble for our lot;
One greater yet than thee is here,
'Tis Israel's unit [unique] God.

The hand of God could send the winds or stop them. The Spanish Catholics had been the first in the Caribbean to ponder the relation of these winds to God's design, or if he would use his power to send the winds or to protect against them. The people of other nations and faiths who followed them were no less concerned.

During this period of revolutionary turmoil and military campaigns in the Caribbean it was not surprising that natural conditions often became part of a braided history that joined providence, nature, and politics together. The March 26, 1812 earthquake in Caracas is a case in point. The quake destroyed almost all buildings and fortification and killed some 2,000 just in Caracas (though contemporary reports cited the death toll at 10,000 in Caracas with another 15,000 fatalities in the port of La Guaira). It was not lost on the public that the quake had occurred on Holy Thursday two years after of Bolívar's break with Spain on April 19, 1810. This was taken by many people to be a clear sign of divine displeasure. A report that reached Puerto Rico claimed that the leaders of the revolution in Caracas feared that they might become victims of a mob seeking retribution against those who had provoked God's anger.[47] A story circulated that in the midst of the ruins Bolívar had said, "If Nature opposes us, we will fight against her and make her obey us." Following the Caracas quake the pro-Spanish clergy, led by the archbishop of Caracas, Narciso Coll y Prat, mounted a campaign to demonstrate that multiple sins including disloyalty and disbelief had brought this judgment upon the colony. He recognized that there were laws of nature, but he emphasized that God had not surrendered control of them despite what "false philosophers" and naturalists might argue. The response of the defenders of the revolutionary government was to point out that many natural disasters had happened in America long before the revolution for independence, so it could not be held responsible. Moreover, they argued that God would not be angered by people restoring their God-given rights to a freedom that had been taken from them. As one anonymous defender put it, "This has nothing to do with new governments or old, with kings or republics. . . . God rewards and punishes in His kingdom, and we in ours."[48] Such attitudes of secular rationalism had become more common but were often set in an overarching discourse of divine justice that seemed to still offer the best explanation of the incredible power of natural phenomena.

While from the pulpits of different creeds societies received a message that often emphasized shared danger and common responsibility, a large part of their populations, the enslaved, felt itself excluded and had little incentive to join in communal action in the face of catastrophe. They too had turned to divine sources of protection from the elements. Some had sought solace and relief in the church. James Ramsay, a reforming missionary in the West Indies, wrote that slaves became more attracted to baptism following natural disasters, and he noted an improvement in their morality and behavior following these catastrophes, but he had little to say about the religious alternatives also available to slaves. In their practice of various forms of African-based religion they found different sources of comfort and help. The Yoruba-speaking Lucumi slaves of Cuba, for example, prayed to Chango, the guardian spirit (*orisha*) of storms and lightning, and in deference to him would not smoke during a storm. Oyá, their warrior spirit of the winds, became a powerful force in *Santeria,* the Afro-Hispanic religion maintained in Cuba. Similar dieties were called on in *voudon* in the French Antilles and in *obeah* in Jamaica and other West Indian islands to provide protection from the storms, or, as we saw in the case of Plato in Jamaica in 1780, to bring destruction on the oppressors.[49]

THE GREAT HURRICANE OF 1831

If the turbulent decades of the Circum-Caribbean from 1790 to 1840 could be characterized by a single change it would surely be the transformation of its labor system. The violent end to slavery in St. Domingue, finally resulting in the creation of an independent Haiti in 1804, the growth and intensification of slavery as export agriculture in the Spanish colonies of Cuba and Puerto Rico, and the abolition of the slave trade followed by the emancipation of slaves in the British West Indies, overshadowed all other events. The concepts of property rights and human rights lay at the heart of the issue of slavery. The "great slave question" had been an issue in the American Revolution and had plagued the signers of the Constitution, and it was, from a different perspective, the principal concern in the Haitian Revolution and an issue during the revolutionary fervor in the other French Caribbean colonies. During this period political change and revolutionary ideologies provoked slave unrest and expectations all over the circum-Caribbean region. Beginning in the 1780s and intensifying in the following decades, from Bahia, Brazil, to Coro, Venezuela, to Barbados (1816), Demerara (1823), Jamaica (1831), and Virginia (1831), slave uprisings tested the limits and strength of the institution. At the same time, the abolitionist movement, missionary activity, and slave rebelliousness were creating a transnational community of proslavery interests that sought to maintain the institution or to control any changes within it.[50]

The hurricane of 1831 arrived at a particularly significant moment in the eastern Caribbean, where the British islands were in the midst of the transition that had been set in motion first by the Leeward Islands' Act of Amelioration of 1798 limiting brutality in the treatment of slaves, followed by the abolition of the slave trade in 1807.[51] Both of these measures had origins in the activities of abolitionists in Parliament, but also were a response to the rise in slave rebelliousness in the 1790s, and to a growing anti-slavery sentiment of free traders who could observe that as British exports were doubling, the slave-based West Indies were absorbing a declining percentage of them. As Britain became the dominant maritime nation and the hub of world finance and commerce, the power of the West Indies interests in Parliament and their ability to protect the institution of slavery declined. Philanthropy increasingly joined hands with economy in the attack on slavery.[52]

The West Indian planters and merchants, now under attack, fought an effective rearguard action against the rising sentiments for emancipation, using a policy of amelioration or improvement of slave conditions as an alternative to emancipation. They resisted by seeking to limit the activities and effects of various missionary campaigns among the slaves, opposing petitions for more rights from free colored populations, and by combating the rising expectations of the slaves themselves. The distractions of the Napoleonic Wars had kept Parliament from moving rapidly; but amelioration gradually became official policy of the British government, and pressures for emancipation were growing through the 1820s. Colonial assemblies sought ways to obstruct or slow down the movement to emancipation, pointing to the Demerara slave revolt of 1823 and the Jamaica revolts of 1816 and 1831 as warnings against further liberalization of the slave system.[53] When the Whigs, led by an abolitionist as Lord Chancellor, won control of Parliament in 1830, however, it was clear that the movement for emancipation had gained the upper hand. Planters in Barbados were among those most reluctant to relinquish the institution of slavery. In March 1831, delegates from the British West India colonies met at

Bridgetown, Barbados, to draw up a protest claiming that they had acquired slave property legally and had been encouraged to do so, and that Great Britain had long benefited from their employment of slaves. Thus, any move to limit or injure their property without full compensation was the height of injustice. Moreover, what they had done for the slaves was to provide them relative comfort and raise them from barbarism to the "advantages of civilized life."[54] What was finally worked out in 1833 was gradual emancipation in which the slave-owners would receive £20 million compensation, and slaves who became legally free would be required to serve in a status of apprenticeship from 1834 to 1838.

While Barbados had enjoyed long periods free from hurricanes, and at times was even thought safe from their visits, the hurricane of 1780 had demonstrated that it was not entirely exempt from danger. On August 10–11, 1831, the island was struck by a tremendous storm. Probably a Category 4 hurricane by today's standards, it leveled the island, killing some 1,500 people, injuring thousands more, and causing more than $7 million of property damage, leaving the island desolate, looking to some as though it had been burnt by a great fire, while to others, the usually verdant island, now stripped of all its foliage, looked like Europe in the dead of winter.[55] An anonymous chronicler of Barbados's destruction estimated that "Calamitous as were the many eruptions of nature by which this island has suffered, the aggregate destruction produced by them was probably unequal to that effected by the storm of August 1831."[56] The storm then proceeded westward, striking St. Vincent the following day and damaging virtually every sugar estate on that island.[57] It then swept north, causing damage to Les Cayes, Haiti, then striking Santiago de Cuba and Matanzas before moving into the Gulf of Mexico. Very high tides piled up along the Gulf Coast west of Mobile, damaging wharves and shipping; at New Orleans, shipping suffered, the Customs house was unroofed, and some areas were flooded by the rising waters of Lake Pontchartrain.[58]

The great hurricane of 1831 had struck the eastern Caribbean at a moment when the slave-owning class felt particularly vulnerable and under increasing threat by emancipationists. As Charles Shepard of St. Vincent wrote: "the pressure of the times is severe, the future prospects are gloomy, the days of West Indian prosperity are probably terminated."[59] Depression among the planters and increasing recalcitrance among the slaves was common. Some planters flirted with secessionist fantasies, but strategies now centered not on obstruction to emancipation but how to set its terms, and especially on the question of compensation. These plans played themselves somewhat differently on the two islands most affected by the storm: St. Vincent and Barbados.

St. Vincent, a volcanic island dominated by Mount Soufrière, had developed late as a sugar producer, and only after the English had acquired it from France in 1763 did it begin to take on the character of a classic plantation colony. The local Caribs were killed or expelled in a series of battles in the 1770s and then again 1795–97. Large numbers of African slaves were imported, with the slave population reaching eighty percent of the island's total population by 1831. Additionally, despite St. Vincent's diminutive size of just over 150 square miles, it had also become by 1831 the third largest sugar producer of the British West Indies, behind only Jamaica and Trinidad.[60] The 1831 hurricane damaged ninety-two of the ninety-six sugar estates on the island, destroyed many houses, and caused some 20 ships to founder or run aground. In the short run there were the usual immediate effects on the island. Sugar production and exports dropped by as much as a third over the next two years, shortages of food were experienced, and outbreaks of disease were reported. The question that most preoccupied the planters, however, was the reaction of the slave population. On two St. Vincent estates, where reduced work schedules had been instituted by resident masters, the slaves had demonstrated a willingness to cooperate in the post-storm recovery. According to the owner of the plantation Colonaire Vale, "the slaves behaved like so many Heroes of Antiquity."[61] This situation may not have been typical, because between sixty and eighty percent of St. Vincent's estate owners were absentee, and managers were usually reluctant to reduce labor demands. Still, the collaboration of the slaves remains impressive, given the fact that there were few troops or constabulary on the island who could control uncooperative or rebellious slaves.

In Barbados conditions were horrible. The threat of starvation hung over the island, and food prices were reported to be 200 times their 1830 level.[62] Governor Lyon acted immediately to put the troops and militia

FIGURE 4.2 Commemorative medallion, Barbados Hurricane of 1831. Struck by Governor Lyons, the medal commemorates the generous aid sent by "our sister isles and other friendly shores." (Courtesy of the Victoria Museum, Melbourne, Australia)

into the streets to maintain order, freeze prices to prevent profiteering, authorize cleanup of the streets and roads, and appoint commissioners across the island to keep the slave population under control. He dispatched a ship to Bermuda to ask for a ship-of-war to carry his dispatches to England and also communicated with other governors at Trinidad, Demerara, Grenada, and St. Vincent. In a gracious gesture he asked the Barbados Assembly to use his salary for charitable purposes; they declined his offer, but took a number of measures: setting construction wages, establishing a relief committee, and taking steps to repair the seven island churches destroyed by the storm. Aid came in from other British colonies such as Antigua and Grenada, but also from foreign sources like St. Thomas which raised $1,715 raised by subscription. Meanwhile, the assembly's agent in London, James Mayers, using the previous example of 1780, actively petitioned the government for relief from duties on sugar, the dispatch of supplies and lumber, and a grant from Parliament. [63] The aid received was eventually commemorated in a medal struck in thanks for the generosity shown the island (fig. 4.2).

As in St. Vincent, slavery was a major concern, but the dimension of the problem on Barbados was greater: its land area was about twenty percent greater than St. Vincent's, but it was much more populous; and although the proportion of the population enslaved was nearly about the same (80 percent) on the two islands, Barbados had a far greater density of slaves.

Evidence seems to suggest that the storm had been more intense on Barbados and that differences in topography and population distribution were the main causes of the distinct impacts. The August storm killed over a thousand slaves and caused over £1.6 million in property loss on Barbados. Parliament was moved to send a grant of £50,000 and to suspend the 4.5% sales tax. The Barbadian planter class were already under pressure and fearful that emancipation would ruin their livelihood. The 1831 storm seemed to confirm their concerns. The reluctance of the enslaved population to join in the recovery efforts, the incidence of looting, and the image of a labor force willing to stand by with arms folded, all seemed to confirm the standard planter claims that emancipation was a dangerous fool's errand, and that African peoples were simply unprepared for the assumption of freedom and all it represented. For the planters, the storm had revealed what emancipation might bring in the future: a surly black population unwilling to labor for the common good. The disaster of freedom and emancipation was revealed in life after the storm, and not even the £500,000 loan offered to the islands by Parliament could alleviate the sense that an era was ending. It was "the overthrow of the tropical labor regime."[64]

Fortunately for historians, an anonymous *Account of the Fatal Hurricane, by which Barbados suffered in August 1831* was published a few months after the storm. The author was most likely Samuel Hyde, a creole who later became owner and editor of *The West Indian*, a Barbados newspaper. Like many disaster accounts, Hyde's provides a moving description of the terrors of the storm encased in the expected references to providence and divine judgment as well as an accounting of the damages and injuries suffered. But his book is extraordinary in his description of the rain, wind, lightning, and noise of the storm, the level of detail and personal anecdote he provides in his parish-by-parish report of the damages suffered and the physical effects of the storm on people, property, and landscape. It is also filled with personal stories and observations, details of victim's circumstances, and his own editorial comments on social relations.

Out of the details of sad deaths and miraculous incidents of survival, Hyde builds a narrative of shared catastrophe and communal response. The governor and royal officers are praised for their efforts, the loss of the barracks lamented and efforts of the troops to help others celebrated, the clergy of various denominations honored for their charity and leadership, and the details of the damage to each of their churches painfully given. Even the hundred or so Jews on the island, who, "as a body, are not excelled in responsibility and honorable character in any part of the world," were carefully included, the damages to their synagogue and its "beautiful garden" duly noted, and the death of two of its elderly members detailed. Hyde took the opportunity of the death of Miss Lealtad to remark on her benevolence, since her will left large sums to the philanthropies of her "own nation," but also to a Christian charity on the island.[65] So esteemed was this woman that despite the state of the roads, she was brought from her home at Fontebelle to Bridgetown and buried with all the ceremonies, "peculiar to their religion." This emphasis on common suffering and common challenge to all segments of Barbadian society is even more clear in Hyde's description of the exertions and loyalty of the 35th Regiment:

> The British soldier, with the coloured inhabitant, or black negro, were emulating each other for the general good:—officer and private soldier, black man, coloured, and white man, all were mixed together, and although with heavy hearts, knowing their ruin, yet firmness and resignation were evident on every countenance. In so general a desolation none confined their thought to individual afflictions, but all united in promoting the general welfare.[66]

This vision of a utopia of good will produced by catastrophe was a partial one. Hyde's account noted that some looting had occurred and that access to wine and spirits in the rubble had increased disorder and violence.

While it is not difficult to recover the arguments and opinions of the planters, merchants, and the free population in general in the face of natural disaster and the crisis of the slave system, it is far more difficult to find evidence of slave attitudes and perception, but this account does give some sense of this as well. Although at various points Hyde celebrated heroic action and examples of loyalty among the slaves, it is clear that the slaves constituted the segment of Barbadian society least willing to see their situation through the prism of communal risk. What we learn about

slaves in Hyde's volume is surely filtered through his eyes, but in his account we at least can gain some view of how the slaves on Barbados reacted to the storm and how those in authority sought to use the storm to
maintain the cohesion of society and the stability of the slave system.

Governor Lyon had reported that immediately following the storm the
slaves who were "naturally inclined to be idle, and in some instances re-
fractory," had generated a rebellious spirit on some estates and that had
led to some looting as well. Hyde's account provides some detail on how
the potential for rebellion was suppressed. Reports had come in from estates in the leeward or western parishes of buildings plundered, some
fields raided for food, and general insubordination. A small force of regu-
lars and militia was gathered at Speightstown, led by Sir Reynold Alleyne,
whose sugar estate at Cabbage Tree Hall had been badly damaged. They
marched to Spring Hall and other plantations where order had broken
down. At each estate Alleyne ordered the yard surrounded and then
launched a discourse, "at once firm and conciliatory," stating that he came
as a friend, not an enemy, and that it was painful to have left his family on
a Sunday and so soon after the storm, "which had involved in one common distress both the master and the slave," and that he had been consoled that his own servants had acted in such a "melancholy event with
due obedience and attention." His principal message was the necessary
unity of slave and master in the face of catastrophe.

> He endeavored to impress on their minds that the uproar of the ele-
> ments could not sever the tie that existed between them and their own-
> ers, but that it ought if possible to have united them more strongly, and
> that on every occasion it was the interest of all to make one general effort
> for the preservation of property.

On some estates slaves reacted to this appeal to common circumstances in
the face of calamity with skepticism. Hyde reported that at Spring Hall
and Spring Garden plantations the discourse was met with "unbecoming
and insolent language," and the threat of resistance. Outspoken resisters
were seized and flogged, and at Broomfield, Pleasant Hall, and Spring
Garden estates, "looted" goods—almost all food or butchered livestock,
but some gunpowder as well—were recovered from the slave quarters. At

the Spring estate, slaves refused to be controlled, and a small force was dispatched to subdue them. Some slaves resisted, and one slave was shot after striking a soldier.[67] The following day a slave from that estate tried to convince slaves at labor at a neighboring plantation to stop their work, but he was turned over to the driver and flogged.

We cannot know whether the appeals to common cause or the demonstration of force and punishment produced the "salutary effect" that seemed to bring the slaves back to obedience, or what had caused their resistance in the first place. How had they perceived the storm at this moment when expectations of freedom were in the air? At Three Houses plantation in St. Philip parish, a two-headed calf had been born immediately after the hurricane abated; according to Hyde, this event caused the slaves to fear that the whole course of nature had been disrupted and the world was coming to an end. This kind of apocalyptic or millenarian fervor appeared elsewhere in the slave cabins. At Pleasant Hall a slave told his companions that Jesus had appeared to him twice during the storm and had consoled him by saying that the end had not yet arrived, and that He was coming to do something for them. The man exhorted the others on the estate to refuse to work, but he was seized, and for his insubordination and blasphemy received fifty lashes.[68] Subordination was reestablished and expectations subsided. One slave arrested in St. Peter parish lamented that "this should be the last time he would believe anything about freedom."

In fact, freedom was not far off, even though in Barbados itself the assembly did its best to slow the process. In 1831 local and imperial pressure forced Barbados to accept a bill designed to eliminate the distinctions between whites and free people of color, and acceptance of Paliament's grant of £50,000 following the hurricane had made the planter class once more dependent on London and less able to mount resistance.[69] Still, even when resigned to emancipation, the planters hoped to control the population, and on an island like Barbados where there was little free land available after emancipation, that hope was reasonable.

In April 1832, Governor Lyon opened the assembly with praise for the patience and strength that the people of Barbados had shown in face of the calamities with which God had scourged the island. He had taken consolation in their efforts in which "all selfish consideration had been lost in one general disposition to assist each other, and their duty had been well and zealously performed."[70] He praised the clergy for its humanitarian efforts, and recognized the efforts of the Lord Bishop and the assistance of foreign and British colonies. The Governor predicted, "In the future pages of history these acts of benevolence will be recorded, bearing proud testimony for these Western islands, in which the rich man's offering and the poor man's mite were alike destined for one blessed work of charity." The governor, like Hyde, painted here a picture of a *disaster utopia*, a time when in the face of catastrophe the divisions of society had been eliminated in the common task of rebuilding, and a spirit of goodwill had characterized all social relations.[71] His remarks underlined a community of interest and sympathy in the "Western Islands," as well as a community on Barbados. But noticeably absent from his remarks was any mention of the island's servile population, many of whom had remained unconvinced that the storm called them to communal effort. In fact, the absence of any mention of the slaves in the governor's remarks about the hurricane was more than compensated for by his reference to the order in council on the amelioration of the condition of slaves that required the assembly's attention.

The assembly formally responded, thanking the governor for his many and continual efforts during the catastrophe and for his leadership, but denouncing the amelioration order as "unfair, unconstitutional, and unjust," because it placed oppressive limitations and requirements on the masters and made no provisions for the "contumacious conduct of the slave toward his master."[72] Such complaints, in fact, delayed the enforcement of this legislation, but despite dogged recalcitrance, the West India planters could not stop the march toward emancipation in 1834. What they did accomplish, however, was assuring their compensation for the loss of slave property and securing a period of required apprenticeship of the former slaves until 1838. The 1831 hurricane on Barbados, St. Vincent, and Grenada had been a mirror that revealed to the planters a vision of what they most feared, a slave population not subject to their command. They and the government hurried to impose order and used the storm to reaffirm the existence of an imagined community, one that they would control. The slaves looked into the shattered glass of that same mirror and saw no common cause. Instead, they caught a fleeting glimpse of a future in which they would exercise control not only of their labor, but of their lives.[73]

STORM TRACKERS AND THE END
OF EARLY MODERN HURRICANES

It is not simply a curious coincidence that 1831, the year of the "great hurricane," was also the year that a major advance in the understanding and analysis of hurricanes was set in motion and the early modern era of the hurricanes came to a close. The weather watchers and meteorologists of the previous century had in a Baconian fashion gathered a great amount of data, often by compulsive and fastidious recording of weather, barometer readings, rainfall, or other meteorological phenomena. Some of these storm watchers had by experience, study, and intuition begun to unravel the structure of the tropical storms. The mariner William Dampier in the late seventeenth century and Benjamin Franklin in the eighteenth century had by different paths come to realize that hurricanes were *whirlwinds,* that is, storms in which the winds moved in a circular fashion in a manner analogous to a whirlpool. Observers continued to gather information, and a community of mariners, curious observers, and scientists began to theorize on the formation and characteristics of hurricanes and their Pacific cousin, the typhoon. William C. Redfield (fig. 4.3), a young harness-maker from Middletown, Connecticut, observed that a hurricane in September 1821 had blown trees down in one direction, but forty miles away, trees had fallen in an opposite direction. Redfield's notes suggested that the winds had moved in a circular pattern. He also came to understand that the hurricane's winds revolved around an axis, and that the trajectory and velocity of the storm's path was independent of the speed of the storm's winds themselves.[74] In a chance meeting, a Yale scientist encouraged Redfield to publish his observations and ideas, and after gathering more observations, despite his self-depreciation as an amateur, he did publish an article in 1831 in the *American Journal of Science.* In that same year, in the aftermath of the horrendous blow suffered by the Windwards, the British crown dispatched Lieutenant Colonel William Reid, an able officer of the

FIGURE 4.3 William Redfield (Image in public domain at Wikipedia Commons)

Royal Engineers, to assist in the rebuilding of damaged government buildings on Barbados. Reid had served with distinction in the Napoleonic Wars
and took this new assignment with enthusiasm and with a curiosity about
the storms themselves. He remained in Barbados for the next two and half
years, collecting information about past hurricanes and beginning to develop a theory about their formation and structure. In 1838, after returning
to England, he published *An Attempt to Develop the Law of Storms*, a book
that would have a major impact on the subsequent study of tropical storms.
Although Reid subsequently served as governor of Bermuda, and later of
Malta, receiving a knighthood in 1851, his book set in motion a process of
discovery and debate that made his stay in Barbados the cornerstone of his
career and an important advance in the understanding of hurricanes.[75]

By the 1840s, these two early pioneers of hurricane science were corresponding. Redfield by this time had received an honorary master's degree
from Yale University, and in 1848 he became president of the American

Association for the Advancement of Science. Together, Redfield and Reid began to identify, if not always also to explain, certain aspects of the storms, including their seasonality, and their rotation: counterclockwise in the northern hemisphere and clockwise in the southern. Meanwhile, in 1848 Henry Piddington, a former ship captain in the Indian Ocean and who later would become a judge in marine courts, published *The Sailor's Horn-Book for the Law of Storms*, a practical mariners guide on how to survive the storms, which also demonstrated some understanding of the formation and characteristics of hurricanes.

Redfield's ideas were not without critics. A long and bitter controversy developed between Redfield and the Philadelphia-based teacher and scientist James Pollard Espy, whose research had concentrated on the effect on convection and the importance of rising heat in the development of clouds and rain, and thus of storms. The dispute, which was scientific but at times also bitterly personal, was essentially between the approach of data-based deductive reasoning in science, as represented by Redfield, and the more theoretical approach of Espy that gathered data basically to confirm one's theories. Robert Hare of the University of Pennsylvania, who believed that electricity was an important influence on storm formation, also joined this meteorological dispute. The debate extended through the 1840s, carried out in scientific journals, in American lyceums, and in European lecture halls where Espy found ready listeners, and, especially in France, admirers. In truth, both Espy and Redfield had identified basic physical characteristics of the hurricanes, but neither one had fully grasped the complexity of their formation. For example, it was not until much later that Espy, through the work of William Ferrel, a Tennessee schoolteacher, became aware of ideas of the French mathematician Gustave-Gaspard Coriolis on the effect of the earth's rotation on winds. It was because of that rotation that winds created by the flow of air from high pressure to low pressure took a circular path, and thus why hurricanes exist at all. Espy never fully accepted that idea or the importance of the so-called Coriolis force.[76]

Redfield's interests expanded in other directions, and he became fascinated by ancient fishes and did important work in that field as well; but he always maintained his interest in storms. His later work established the

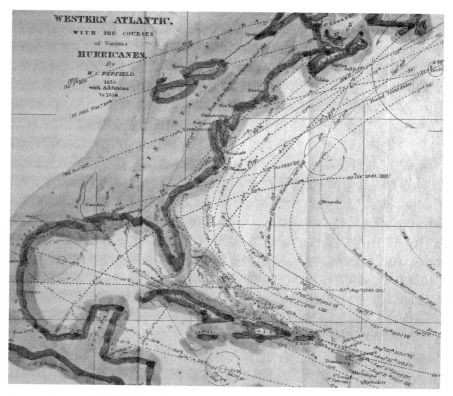

Figure 4.4 Redfield's Map of Hurricane Tracks, 1835–54 (In *Blount's American Coastal Pilot*, 17th ed., New York, 1857; map in the author's possession)

long trajectory of tropical storms and the physical similarity of Atlantic and Pacific hurricanes. He and later his son continued to gather meteorological information.[77] Although he died in 1857, his map tracking hurricane paths was incorporated into a popular coastal guide for American mariners as can be seen in figure 4.4. Espy, his old adversary, retired in the same year as Redfield's death and then occupied his remaining years with essays about theology rather than science. Noticeably, however, in the Redfield-Espy dispute providence and sin had played virtually no role in their explanation of the storms. A meteorological turning point had been reached by this generation of observers and scientists.

Curiously, in this same period a technological advance was also made that marked the end of the early modern hurricane era. In 1832, Samuel

Morse, the Massachusetts-born federalist painter, had a chance encounter with a Yale professor interested in electric magnetism. Morse began to experiment with the idea of using electric magnetism for communication across wires in what came to be known as the telegraph. Others in England were also at work on this idea, and during the 1830s and 1840s competing systems were developed, patents were sought, and a brisk competition developed.[78] With support in Congress, Morse was able to send his first telegraph message in 1844. Ironically, it was the virulently anti-Catholic and pro-slavery Morse who in 1858 personally introduced the telegraph to the Caribbean while visiting his daughter, who had married a planter in Puerto Rico. Morse set up a telegraph line from his son-in-law's hacienda to the town of Arroyo, a small distance of about a mile. The speed of the telegraph in communicating information was a practical advantage that clearly had limitless utility. Its use in the Crimean War (1853–56) and the U.S. Civil War (1861–65) made that clear, and governments in the North Atlantic began to see the advantages of early warning in confronting the hurricanes. The challenge was how to lay down underwater cables to make this possible, and a virtual commercial war developed between competing companies, won to a large extent by a number of British and American firms which laid the cables that began to link the Caribbean islands to Europe and North America.[79]

The early modern era of the hurricanes had ended, and those who now lived or sailed beneath the skies of the North Atlantic had new ways to see the storms, to understand their physical properties, to communicate their progress, and therefore to prepare for their arrival or avoid their worst consequences. Prayer and contrition were still employed in the face of the great storms, states and churches still mobilized charitable impulses to diminish their effects. On Barbados, Governor Lyon had proclaimed October 7 as a day of humiliation and thanksgiving to God, who "in the midst of judgment was pleased to remember Mercy and to stay the fury of the Hurricane."[80] In 1857, the year of Redfield's death and Espy's retirement, the Jesuits of Havana established a weather observatory in their school, the Colegio de Belén, a year after the Spanish government itself had created a chair of meteorology and an observatory on the island. The Jesuits, whose theology emphasized a search for God in everything, and who

sought to reconcile science and God, figured prominently in the next generation of hurricane observers.[81] How the great storms fit into a divine
plan remained a matter of conscience and pulpit, but individuals and nations now had a different way to see the hurricanes, and increasingly
looked to a burgeoning international community of science for help in
confronting them.

CHAPTER 5

Freedom, Sovereignty, and Disasters

Relief for some involves injustices for others.
—*Francisco Moreda y Prieto, Governor of Puerto Rico (1837)*

Many who are not losers by the Hurricane and who were
content to eke out existence in a hovel rather than to labor
for an honest livelihood, rush forward now with a
specious tale of woe and succeed in imposing on
those who are unacquainted with their true position
and the real extent of their loss.
—*Sir Arthur Rumbold, President, British Virgin Islands (1866)*

The torrents of water that have fallen, the hurricanes of
1870, have not been enough to wash away the blood that
inundates Cuba, nor to put out the fires that devour it.
—*Manuel Fernández de Castro (1871)*

With emancipation in the British West Indies in 1834 and the abolition of slavery in the French Antilles in 1848, the plantation system
and slavery in the North Atlantic became concentrated in the U.S. southern states and the Spanish islands of the Caribbean. In the British and
French West Indies the transition to free labor had followed a number of
different trajectories influenced by political conditions, land availability,
and world market prices. In Haiti, the revolutionary destruction of the
plantation economies of the Old Regime, the former association of sugar,
coffee, and other plantation crops with servitude, and the wide availabil-

ity of land, led to the creation of a peasantry with little interest in working as agricultural laborers. On Martinique and Guadeloupe, emancipation in 1848 led to a period of decline in sugar production in the short term, but there was limited access to land for the former slaves, and that work force plus additional indentured workers contracted in Africa had together by the 1860s returned production to pre-emancipation levels. On some islands of the British West Indies, like Barbados, St. Kitts, and Antigua, the dearth of unoccupied land virtually prohibited ex-slaves from withdrawing completely from plantation labor, and thus production continued to expand using them as wage laborers. Later, when world demand for sugar declined and population grew, emigration offered an alternative. Jamaica, St. Lucia, and Grenada, islands that had more land available, witnessed a decline in sugar production and the rise of peasantries. On those islands, sugar planters found their diminishing returns made them unable to afford the importation of Asian or other contract laborers.[1]

Disasters and the Spanish Caribbean Boom

The contraction of agricultural production in much of the non-Hispanic Caribbean now opened the door wider for a process of economic expansion that had already begun in Cuba and Puerto Rico in the 1820s. In Puerto Rico, the opening of the ports and easing of restrictions on land acquisition contributed to agricultural growth. The island's foreign trade increased over 2,000 percent between 1814 and 1854.[2] Coffee thrived in the central highlands, mostly using salaried workers. Sugar production now boomed in the areas of Ponce and Guayama on the southern coast and Mayaguez to the west. Puerto Rican sugar production leaped from just over one thousand tons in 1814, to fourteen thousand in 1830, and forty thousand tons in 1840; it continued expanding rapidly thereafter.[3] This expansion was accompanied and made possible by the doubling of the slave population on the island, much of it concentrated in the sugar-growing coastal areas. By 1850, the island had some 50,000 slaves and had surpassed Jamaica as a sugar producer.[4] Its sugar found ready markets in the United States and Great Britain. Even as the sugar economy expanded and its demand for laborers changed the island's demography, the slaves never constituted more than twelve percent of the population, and as pressures against the slave trade mounted, legislation forcing free rural workers and peasants into contract labor by requiring them register for work permits partially resolved the demand for workers in agriculture.[5] When the abolition of slavery finally came in Puerto Rico in 1873, slaves made up only five percent of the population.

In Cuba, a similar process of agricultural expansion and an increase of slavery had taken place but on an even larger scale. Here and in the cotton South was the heart of the "second slavery," the expansion of slavery in the capitalist development of plantation agriculture by integrating slavery with modern technology like the cotton gin and steam-driven sugar mills, and by producing commodities like cotton and sugar for mass consumption. The western areas of that island had developed flourishing tobacco and coffee establishments in the late eighteenth and early nineteenth centuries. By 1840, Cuba was exporting over 27,000 tons of coffee a year, three-quarters of it produced in that region, where the beautifully managed *cafetales*, shaded by fruit trees and palms, and interspersed with farms of food crops, had spread across the countryside. Tobacco *vegas* were also found in western Cuba, especially in Pinar de Río, where by 1840 they made up about five percent of the acreage under cultivation. Sugar estates had expanded, helped by the elimination of Haiti as a competitor, the introduction of new technologies like steam engines and railroads, and the post-emancipation problems of Jamaica and other British islands. Until the 1840s this agricultural expansion was roughly balanced between the major crops of coffee and sugar, with tobacco and cacao playing a lesser role. Cuba's economy, unhindered by the independence wars of the mainland Spanish colonies and benefiting from the social and political dislocations of its Caribbean competitors, expanded, urged on by creole proprietor advocates willing, in the words of historian Louis Pérez Jr. to "accept the security of colonialism over the uncertainty of independence."[6] Much of this expansion had been made possible by the growth of slavery. By 1841, Cuba had a slave population of about 437,000, concentrated to a large extent in the western agricultural zones. The increasing pressure on Spain from Great Britain to end the slave trade as well as a growing fear of slave rebellion created a sense of unease and insecurity among the property-owning classes in the midst of their success. Nevertheless, although the African slave trade ended in 1867, and new sources of labor like the importation of Chinese were developed, the defenders of slavery continued their campaign. Too much of their position and their success depended on it.

Political instability and foreign invasions plagued the Dominican Republic, which became independent in1844. Its economic development suffered from these conditions, and it fell considerably behind the remaining Spanish islands of Cuba and Puerto Rico, which had become important, wealth-producing, slave-based colonial possessions. By 1868 Cuba alone was satisfying forty percent of the world market demand for sugar. Through this period, the slave-owning planters had watched with self-interest the progress of slavery in the United States and tended to see parallels to their own situation. Their sympathies at first lay with the Confederacy, but gradually began to shift during the U.S. Civil War as the South's fortunes waned. Politically, the planter class was not foolish. After 1864 they could see that slavery in the South was doomed; and in their own context they could see that it was losing ground to Spanish and creole abolitionists, to the political pressure from Great Britain, and to political activists on the island that had linked emancipation to political independence.[7] The 1850s had seen the growth of annexationist sentiments seeking union with the slave-owning United States among the planter class and its allies in Cuba, but that idea lost ground during the U.S. Civil War. By 1865, Cuba, Puerto Rico, and Brazil were left as the last slaveholding regimes in the Americas.

By the mid-1860s, two processes had been set in motion that eventually brought an end to the slave economy, and ultimately to the colonial regime as well: the growth of an abolitionist movement in Spain and its colonies; and an increasing dissatisfaction with Spain's colonial rule—its administrative failures, its restrictions on commerce, and its suppression of dissidence. Sugar and slavery had created great fortunes in Cuba and for Spain, but the colonies felt disadvantaged in the process, and resented the fact that they did not enjoy the same political rights as their continental brethren. Further, Cubans paid taxes at much higher tax rates than did Spaniards. Restrictions on imports of Caribbean sugar in order to favor producers in Andalucía and excise laws favoring Spanish imports were both enforced to the benefit of Spain and the disadvantage of merchants and producers in the colonies.[8] The colonial economy nevertheless boomed. In 1866, Cuba alone collected almost 27 million pesos in revenue.

In Cuba, a policy of accommodation with colonial interests under reformist governors (1859–66) had moderated creole complaints to some extent, but governors in Puerto Rico had been more heavy-handed, controlling the press, prohibiting public political debate and discussion of abolition, and exiling leading liberal spokesmen like the French-educated physician Ramón Emeterio Betances, and the lawyer and municipal official Segundo Ruiz Belvis. Matters in the colonies were coming to a head. In 1867, the year slave trade to Cuba ended, an abolitionist party was created in Spain. Emancipation increasingly became a topic that attracted liberal intellectuals in the islands as well as in Spain. In Puerto Rico, Betances, who along with others had been agitating for abolition, was for the second time expelled from the island. While residing in neighboring Saint Thomas he issued a manifesto closely linking abolition to other political rights and demanding policies more favorable to Antillian interests. In this context of political unrest and agitation, as the question of slavery was being attacked and defended and the role of government widely discussed, nature again intervened and revealed the fragility of government and the colonial regime.

During this period of economic expansion, the storms of hurricane seasons had not ceased, and while their effects were sometimes locally disastrous, they had not slowed the economic growth of the Hispanic colonies. Eastern and central Puerto Rico had suffered a stinging blow in 1825 that killed or injured over 1,500 people and thousands of livestock, and caused major food shortages. Another hurricane in August 1837 caused major damage in San Juan's harbor and surrounding areas, while an 1846 hurricane crossed the center of the island from Ponce to Aguadilla. Cuba, too, had its share, with localized storms striking Cienfuegos in 1832, Trinidad, on the south coast, in 1837, and Havana, Matanzas, and the north coast in 1842. A long drought through much of 1844 ruined agriculture and killed livestock, but was followed on the night of October 2, 1844, by a devastating hurricane that swept across the island. This San Francisco de Asis hurricane sank dozens of ships in Havana harbor and flooded city streets. The winds, gusting to over 150 miles per hour, caused some urban structures to collapse, obliterating thousands of rural houses and *bohios* (shacks). Rising rivers, blasting winds, and saltwater spray destroyed all manner of plants, from food crops to coffee bushes, sugarcane, and tobacco plants. The badly battered island was only beginning to recover when on October 10, 1846, much of the same region was struck again. This time the blow was more intense and deadly; the barometer fell to a record 27.70 inches at Havana, and the storm surge in some places reached 30 feet in height. The hurricane left six hundred dead, thousands injured, tens of thousands homeless;[9] it was, said the U.S. consul, "the most calamitous and unparalleled in the history of the Island."[10]

This time the hurricane had followed weeks of drenching rains that had saturated fields and raised river levels, so that the effects of flooding and of crop spoilage after the storm were extreme. *Ingenios*, farms, slave quarters, *bohios*, and even small towns perished. While tobacco production suffered in the short term, that industry soon recovered and expanded, and by the 1850s, a number of growers had begun to set up factories to produce their own cigars. Sugar also experienced short-term decline after the first storm, the harvest of 1845 being only half the size of the preceding year. Considerable losses in capital equipment and slaves forced some mills to go out of business. But in the long run, both the tobacco and sugar sectors recovered strongly.

The coffee estates had borne the brunt of the two storms, with coffee plants uprooted, shade trees destroyed, and food crops to feed the slaves gone. Capital invested after the hurricane of 1844 was lost again in 1846, and falling world prices for coffee made recovery difficult. Coffee production plummeted from over 70 million pounds per year in the 1820s to less than 20 million by the 1860s. Coffee estates were sold off or turned to cattle ranches, food crop farms, or sugar estates. Many of the slaves on the Cuban *cafetales* were sold to sugar mills at just the moment when British pressure and abolitionist sentiments were mounting against the slave trade. Slave imports to Cuba fell from over twenty thousand a year in the late 1830s to about three thousand in the late 1840s. Coffee's loss became sugar's profit. Just when new technologies in sugar making and railroads were facilitating the rapid expansion of sugar on the island and demand for labor was growing, the wreckage of the Cuban coffee economy was providing a work force, which the declining slave trade was unable to supply. Between 30,000 and 50,000 slaves were moved from coffee to sugar estates. The coffee planters found that the value of their slaves had risen sharply as the pressures against the slave trade and the booming Atlantic market for sugar had combined to their advantage, so that selling them off was the best strategy.

The hurricanes of 1844 and 1846 speeded the process of sugar's gaining dominance of the Cuban economy, moving capital and people into that sector and undercutting the former balance on which the economy had been built. But that transformation came at a social cost. The heavy labor requirements of sugar cultivation and the drive for expansion had resulted in worsening labor conditions and high mortality on the plantations. It also resulted in increasing slave resistance. Resistance, runaways, and occasional uprisings on individual estates reinforced planter insecurities, and when in March 1844 an alleged slave conspiracy, known as the revolt of "La Escalera," was "discovered," repression was widespread and brutal. The high mortality of slaves in the sugar industry, the repression, the deaths caused by the hurricanes, and the weakened condition of the Cuban slave population in their aftermath, all resulted in the decline of that population by 25 percent between 1841 and 1846. But despite these losses, the cane fields captured more and more territory, especially near Havana and in Matanzas. By the 1860s, Cuba was producing over a million tons annually. Sugar had become the island's principal export and made up of three-quarters of Cuba's export value.

The responses to the storms of the 1830s and 1840s had demonstrated the principles on which the Spanish government based its actions, the techniques and institutions upon which it depended, and both its desire and its ability to meet the challenge of natural calamity. How did those in control of the government view that challenge?

From a slightly earlier storm we have a rather remarkable response, written by the governor of Puerto Rico following the heavy damages caused by the hurricane "de los Angeles" of August 2–3, 1837. The storm had sunk much of the shipping in San Juan's harbor. Although it killed only a few people, it ruined what had promised to be a particularly good harvest: almost all of the plantains were destroyed, and the rice and corn harvests also suffered. The governor, Don Francisco Moreda y Prieto, a military officer of high rank who had succeeded the Count of Torrepando (who, as we saw in the previous chapter, had taken important steps to maintain the islanders' loyalty), had assumed his position only in January of that year. Moreda was confronted with a difficult situation. In an open and extensive letter to the "Inhabitants of Puerto Rico," he revealed his frustrations at the challenges caused by the storm that had smashed the hopes of so many. Petitions for tax relief had been the islanders' principal proposal, but the governor, while expressing his sympathies, argued that governments needed to be prepared for such eventualities well before they took place, insisting on better constructions and building codes and putting aside funds for relief. Emergency measures like those requested, he argued, often caused more problems in the long run than they immediately resolved; as he stated, "Effective relief for some involves injustices for others." He argued that the income of the government in normal years barely met expenses, and to reduce it would leave important obligations on behalf of society like the defense of the island, the maintenance of its government, and even its religious obligations unattended. Obligations needed to be fulfilled for the good of all, and "to dedicate ourselves with a new spirit, and to grasp anew the plow in order to oblige our common mother to yield with a prodigious hand that which the furious storm has stolen, is what prudence, the only policy that remains for us to do, calls on us to do."[11]

The governor called for the usual generous humanitarian and charitable impulses, emphasizing that avoiding deaths, diseases, and population loss was in everyone's interest. He ordered a charity board (*junta de beneficiencia*) to be set up in each municipality to meet local needs and to report to the central government. In other words, well-to-do individuals were to sacrifice in order to relieve those affected, and in this way were to act "as calls for, the charity of our holy Religion, the most respectable social principles, and the best understanding of individual interest."[12] Governor Moreda's response seems to have been made with sincerity and careful thought, but his emphasis on traditional charitable impulses and social responsibility and his unwillingness, justified or not, to reduce government revenues by offering tax relief, or to ask the metropolitan government to assume direct responsibility, was not lost on the critics of colonial government. Spain's failure to provide aid, to sufficiently repair roads, bridges, and infrastructure, or to respond adequately to the appeals of the creole propertied classes, contributed to a growing sense of exasperation. Moreover, Moreda's insistence that government could not assume this burden was ironic. The 1822 Law of Charity (*Ley de Beneficiencia*) in Spain and subsequent legislation throughout the century had essentially recognized and advocated an increase in public control of most forms of social assistance; and while a model of public-private cooperation was legally supported and Church participation encouraged, the sequestration of Church properties and growing state control of Church and private institutions like hospitals, orphanages, asylums, and the like signaled state assumption of social welfare. This process was mostly driven in Spain itself by concerns for the "social question" and the rise of a working class, but its implications for government responsibility in the colonies in the face of natural calamity was not lost on colonial administrators or on the peoples of the islands.[13]

The traditional sources of relief had stepped forward after the Cuban hurricanes of 1844 and 1846. The governor had turned to the usual supports: piety, charity, and institutions on the local level. Havana had suffered badly in 1846, especially the poorer neighborhoods (*extramuros*), where 2,800 homes had been brought down or damaged. Even in the heart of the city, almost every government building had suffered some injury, a few churches were wrecked, and 331 houses inside the city walls damaged. Government and church authorities turned to traditional responses. The archbishop ordered a *Te Deum* to offer thanks that so many persons survived. The governor set up patrols to stop looters and then ordered all able-bodied white and colored men to help repair the port facilities. Commissaries in each neighborhood received small amounts to be distributed to the needy, but relief was sought primarily through voluntary contributions to a relief committee or *junta de socorro* created for that purpose. The editor of the newspaper *El Faro Industrial*, in a special issue made the usual

references to "a test of Divine Providence" and the need for Christian resignation, as he tried to capture the horror of the storm whose ferocity was,
he felt, beyond the imagination of Europeans: "Those who have not seen
these American storms can form no idea of them. In no way are they like
the tempests of Europe."[14] He then carefully listed all the losses and deaths
in the city, noted the nature of the damage to each, estimating the losses to
sugar alone would be two million pesos. But he also used this pamphlet to
detail the many examples of heroism and generosity in the face of the
storm, acts that demonstrated, he felt, the quality of the people of Cuba.
Absent from his compendium of losses was comment or criticism of the
government's actions save for a remark that they had taken the "steps that
the situation demanded."[15] Quietly, a shift was taking place in which the
government was assuming a predominant role in organizing all aspects of
social assistance and the editor had chosen not to question its actions.

But the truth was that Madrid was too far away to provide help
promptly, and the enormity of the task seemed to be beyond Spain's capacity to pay. As usual, appeals were made for charitable donations from
nobles, convents, and various associations in Spain and its other colonies.
Under the urging of the Havana municipal council, prices were fixed,
ports opened, and duties on imports temporarily lifted, but an attempt to
get a moratorium on foreclosure of rural estates for debt was blocked by
the appeals court (*audiencia*), which was afraid to disrupt the credit market. Many of the emergency measures that seemed to make sense on Cuba
were subsequently denied by Madrid. Colonial administrators rejected
any measures that limited the metropole's ability to collect revenue from
taxes, tariffs, or duties. A sense of rejection and disregard in the colonies
was growing, and the calamities made it deeper.[16]

By the 1860s there was a new economic and political context in which
these resentments and frustrations flourished. The Civil War in the United
States was closely watched in the slaveholding regimes of Cuba and
Puerto Rico. Spain itself took advantage of the United States' distraction
to reoccupy its former colony of Santo Domingo, now the Dominican Republic. As the Civil War began to swing in favor of the Union, a growing
number of Cuban and Puerto Rican intellectuals and activists expressed
strong abolitionist sentiments, and their desires for emancipation became

increasingly linked to sentiments for more colonial autonomy or even independence.

On Their Own: The British West Indies
and the Other Antilles

The middle decades of the nineteenth century was a time of hope frustrated or betrayed for the hundreds of thousands of former slaves in the British West Indies. Having been emancipated between 1834 and 1838, they were now expecting to receive the rights of free men and women. The sugar industry went into decline in many areas, and the abandonment of the plantations in some islands and mainland colonies by many of the former slaves led to the import of indentured South Asians or Africans and to restrictive legislation that sought to force laborers and peasants back into the export sector of local economies. Suffrage was deeply restricted in all these colonies. In Jamaica, where access to unused lands was made legally difficult and where poll taxes basically disenfranchised the mostly poor black population, frustration caused by royal rejection of appeals and by the unsympathetic rule of the governor eventually led to a major protest, the so-called Morant Bay rebellion of 1865, in which hundreds of people were killed, with hundreds more summarily executed in the brutal repression that followed. While some critics rose to seek justice for the rebels, the Liberal governments that controlled Parliament in the later 1860s proved to be no more sympathetic to the West Indian colonies than the Tories had been.[17] Ethnocentrism and attitudes toward race clearly played a role in imperial policies in the West Indies, as they did in Ireland and India as well.[18] To some extent, by mid-century, the West Indies were on their own in terms of receiving much governmental subsidy or attention, and British interest was shifting to the empire in India, and then, by the 1870s, to the rush for African colonies, as the European powers began to paint the map of Africa in the colors of colonial expansion.[19]

   This political and social context helps us to understand the response of the British government to the continuing challenge of natural disasters in its North Atlantic colonies. We can use two examples, a hurricane that struck rarely affected Tobago in 1847, and another that roared through the Bahamas in 1866. In both cases, detailed government reports were prepared following the storms, and their composition is revealing of the strategies and principles of governmental response.

Tobago, lying at 11.9°N latitude, was too close to the equator to be in the usual hurricane path. The little island of about 115 square miles, heavily forested and hilly, had passed back and forth repeatedly between European rivals—Spaniards, English, Dutch, French, and even Courlanders (Latvians)—until in 1803, when Great Britain took control. Tobago was through most of its early history "in a state of inbetweenity," in the words of historian Eric Williams.[20] Some sugar, cotton, and indigo had been produced there, and by the later eighteenth century there were about 12,000 people on the island, most of them slaves. Revolts and threats of revolts had been common after 1770. Following emancipation in 1834, a period of apprenticeship had passed calmly, until in 1838 it was ended throughout the British colonies and freedom granted to all former slaves. Tobago had administratively become part of the Windward Islands in 1833 and was no longer a separate colony, being governed by a lieutenant governor under the orders from the governor general in Barbados.

Although the island had been struck by a hurricane in 1790, the common opinion was that the island was not at risk from hurricanes, and as a result, building construction was done with no attention to that possibility. The storm came at night on October 10, 1847, and only the frequent lightning allowed people to look for shelter. The wind, moving southwest to northeast, brought down twenty-six sugar mills and damaged another thirty-three; only ten sugar works were left in condition to operate. Many estate houses were ruined as well, to say nothing of hundreds of worker's houses felled by the winds. In the main town of Scarborough, the governor and his family sought shelter in the basement when the winds broke windows and doors at Government House. [21] The barracks roof caved in; and the West India regiment would be placed under canvas after the storm, although care was taken to send the regiment of white troops to Trinidad to avoid further problems of disease.

Only about thirty persons were killed by the storm or the aftermath, but damage was estimated to be as high as £150,000. It was a major blow, since the island's sugar planters, faced with problems of labor shortage and control in the post-emancipation period, were already struggling to compete with the slave-grown sugar of Cuba and Brazil. By 1846 perhaps a third of the work force had deserted full-time plantation labor in the Windward Islands of Grenada, St. Vincent, St. Lucia, and Tobago. The Tobago storm intensified this process of withdrawal.[22]

Lieutenant Governor Lawrence Graeme, the island's senior official, acted quickly, informing the assembly of his willingness, "as far as his humble means will admit," to help the sufferers and the poorer classes, and to assure the peace and security of the island. A proclamation was issued against looting and scavenging and a careful accounting was made of all property losses. The assembly, noting that "it pleased Almighty God, in dispensations of His providence to afflict this island with the visitation of a hurricane," remarked on the loss and misery of all classes and pleaded for Queen Victoria's "gracious consideration." The lieutenant governor continually remarked on the good will and cheerfulness of the population in responding to the disaster, but his correspondence suggests that his words may have been more hortatory than descriptive. An act calling for summary justice and flogging for male looters and hard labor for female looters, passed by the assembly and enacted by the Lieutenant Governor Graeme on October 20, noted that "many idle and disorderly persons are found roving about the country refusing to work, and whose object is evidently to avail themselves of the present opportunity to plunder."[23] But what most concerned him was getting the sugar estates back to operation. He suggested that the storm's destruction might demand that a number of the ruined estates consolidate and begin operating together—in other words, the restructuring of sugar works into central factories as was taking place in Cuba; but he realized that such decisions would have to be made in England.

The queen responded to the disaster with an immediate grant of £5,000 for the destitute, but Parliament was reluctant to offer further aid. When by March 1848 local officials had made a careful accounting of all losses, both the lieutenant governor and Parliament questioned the validity of the estimates. Parliament decided that "the distress or destitution among the poorer classes of the population of Tobago, consequent upon the hurricane, had not been of such urgent nature to call for any immediate and extreme measures or their relief, or to enable them to reconstruct their dwellings": the funds already provided were sufficient. As for the planters, relief would be offered in the form of a loan, as had been recently done with the victims of an earthquake on Antigua, Nevis, and Montserrat in 1843. In this case, the loan of £50,000 at four percent was secured against the island's revenues, and was to be distributed to individuals as needed.[24]

Tobago struggled to repay this debt, and a portion of the funds and interest still remained unpaid in the 1860s. The hurricane had simply exacerbated a situation of decline that had begun with the end of slavery, and the effects of emancipation and the declining world market price for sugar had left marks that no degree of cheerfulness or positive attitude could erase.[25] Tobago's sugar production had fallen by 47.5% between the period of 1824–33 and 1839–46, that is, before and after emancipation, and even as of 1880 it was still only about two-thirds of what it had been before emancipation.[26]

The attitude of the British government was, of course, determined by far more than the race of its West Indian subjects. The Tobago storm was contemporaneous with the great Irish potato famine (1845–47), which resulted in the death or migration of two and half million Irish. During the famine, a tremendous debate erupted when the initial governmental response was that the fears of famine had been exaggerated. Some members of Parliament believed that local institutions or the market should handle the problem and thus opposed relief of the poor and starving population. Other critics argued that the Irish, profligate, besotted, and lazy by nature, would only become worse if given something for nothing. One Oxford professor saw the hand of God in the famine, a painful but necessary Malthusian solution to the Irish problem. The Irish writer John Mitchell's statement that "the Almighty indeed sent the potato blight, but the English created the Famine," which eventually contributed to his trial and exile, was an early recognition of human action in creating disasters out of ecological crises. The potato famine caused the division of political parties, the fall of the Conservative government of Robert Peel, bitter debate in Parliament, and the 1848 uprising in Ireland.[27] The West Indian hurricanes and other disasters like earthquakes and volcanic eruptions never reached the same magnitude of loss, nor did they cause a political impact in London as far-reaching, but in both the West Indies and in Ireland attitudes toward the peasantry or the indigent, whether based on poverty or color or on both, contributed to policies that left the victims without support.

Such attitudes of distrust of the laboring and peasant populations became particularly important in the British West Indies in the middle decades of the nineteenth century because of the difficult economic situation faced by these colonies after emancipation. Tobago's situation after the hurricane of 1847 was not singular, and most of the other British colonies faced the similar challenge of declining production and trade with few resources for emergencies. This condition made the colonies dependent on assistance and relief from the home government, but administrative attitudes against providing such aid often interfered with the response to natural disasters.

A good example of this situation is provided by a considerable hurricane that swept through the Bahamas and the neighboring Turks and Caicos islands in October 1866. Neither of these island groups had developed plantation agriculture to any extent, and they depended primarily on salvaging operations and often illegal commerce. The Bahamas had experienced something of a boom during the North's blockade of southern shipping in the U.S. Civil War. British neutrality during the war and the Bahamas' proximity to the southern United States had stimulated an active contraband trade, and the economy of the islands had flourished through the 1860s, avoiding many of the problems of the former British plantation colonies.

In late September 1866 a large hurricane that had traversed the Atlantic and had developed into a Category 4 storm reached the Lesser Antilles, striking St. Thomas in the Virgin Islands on September 28 and then battering the Turks and Caicos and the southern Bahamas on the following day. The eye of the storm reached Nassau, the main town of the Bahamas, located on the north shore of the island of New Providence, on October 1, causing great damage, and winds remained strong until the following day. By October 3 the storm had left the Bahamas and curved northward into the Atlantic.

The few settlements in the islands were all damaged, but Nassau took the major blow. Its gaily painted two-story buildings, surrounded by fruit trees and flowers, were battered, as were the barracks, hotels, and warehouses near the docks, and even the four-storied Royal Victoria Hotel, the largest building in the British West Indies, which overlooked the town and the sea from a hillside. "Pretty" and "neat," the usual adjectives used to describe Nassau, were now replaced by far more lugubrious descriptions of what Governor Rawson called "a general and wide-spread calamity." It looked, said the governor, as if "a bombardment could hardly have inflicted greater mischief." [28] At Nassau almost a hundred vessels sank, another 140 were damaged, and over a thousand people were left homeless. The outer islands of Inagua, Exuma, Eleuthera, and Long Island had all suffered as well, especially their poorer inhabitants, who were now faced with starvation. On Long Island, for example, cotton plantings had been badly damaged and almost every building destroyed; to make things worse, all the palmetto leaves, which were used for roofing, had been stripped from the trees, and it was feared that it would take five or six months until more would be available. Governor Rawson took the usual steps, trying to meet the immediate threat of hunger, sending to Cuba for seed corn, and setting up a relief committee in Nassau with branch committees in neighborhoods and elsewhere in the islands. By November 17, he was able to report that self-help, charity, kindness, and a positive attitude had improved conditions. But not everything had gone smoothly, and on Exuma, an island not badly damaged by the storm, but whose fields had suffered from a long drought, there was a near riot when the local justice of the peace claimed that the relief supplies were not really necessary. Local islanders threatened to lynch him if he did not distribute the supplies quickly and equitably, which he subsequently did.

But what is most striking in the government response to the Bahamas storm was the insistent reluctance to assume primary responsibility to provide individual relief. Governor Rawson emphasized that people had to be disabused of the idea that the hurricane might provide an excuse for "protracted destitution without any effort on their part to supply their own wants and to restore their dwellings." Instead, he encouraged them to give up the idea of charitable relief and depend on independence and self-help. All were encouraged to return to work, and those who had the means, credit, or friends were told to repair their own dwellings as soon as possible. They were exhorted to follow the example of nature, "which hastens with redoubled energy to the work of restoration, having a confident trust in the beneficial designs of Providence, and a firm conviction that resignation, cheerfulness, and industry are the materials with which a people may not only repair temporary losses, but build up a more durable edifice of private alliance and public prosperity."[29] These were again hortatory urgings of a governor who clearly distrusted the character or inclinations of his population, and sought make sure that government's role in relief was to be limited. Rawson's reference to providence implicitly excused the government for its lack of preparation before the storm and its responsibility afterwards. His emphasis on self-help, neighborly sympathy, and the return to work studiously avoided any reference to post-emancipation social and racial divisions on the islands.

Those same attitudes of distrust were made even more explicit the following year when a hurricane that struck the Danish West Indies and Puerto Rico also battered the British Virgin Islands. From Tortola, Sir Arthur Rumbold, the assembly's president who served as the chief officer of the islands, reported that of the 123 houses in the main settlement of Road Town, half had been totally destroyed, as well as all the public buildings, all but two of the sugar mills, and almost all the dwellings of the rural population. After noting similar losses on other islands in the group and expressing his sympathy for the losses, he reminded his superior that

> Everyone acquainted with the West Indies must know what gross fabrications the negro will make when he entertains the hope of gaining bread without exertion: Many who are not losers by the Hurricane and who were content to eke out existence in a hovel rather than to labor for an honest livelihood, rush forward now with a specious tale of woe and succeed in imposing on those who are unacquainted with their true position and the real extent of their loss.[30]

The social dimension of the British government response to natural disaster in the post-emancipation period could be made no clearer, and this was an attitude that persisted throughout the rest of the century. A case in point is provided in the Windward Islands. St. Lucia, St. Vincent, and Barbados were struck by a heavy hurricane in 1898. Each of these islands sought help from the British colonial government.[31] St. Lucia, unlike Barbados and St. Vincent, where white planters still dominated the economy, had most of its 25,000 acres under cultivation by about 6,000 peasant proprietors, who possessed few resources for recovery.[32] The people on St. Lucia had already been buffeted by a hurricane four years earlier; and while the 1898 storm was not as destructive on St. Lucia as on St. Vincent, it completely destroyed St. Lucia's cocoa crop, which had been developed as a response to the worsening market for sugar. Emergency supplies and most of the funds raised by charity went to St. Vincent. The governor (who resided in Grenada) told the St. Lucians that "like heaven, the Government helps those who help themselves," and urged them to "manfully" return to work.[33] Worst of all was London's refusal to provide a requested loan of £60,000 to St. Lucia, while it responded favorably to the loan requests from Barbados and St. Vincent. The British government demonstrated no trust in the peasantry, and no desire to have its position strengthened on St. Lucia or in the West India colonies in general, which had by now become a financial burden.

During the mid-nineteenth century, especially after emancipation, similar conditions and policies could also be found in the Dutch and French Antilles.[34] The Dutch tried a number of administrative reforms, and eventually placed their West India colonies directly under the crown and created a colonial ministry in 1834. In 1845 the six Caribbean islands held by Holland were designated as the colony of the Netherlands Antilles. The abolition of slavery in 1863 in all the Dutch colonies was a major change, and especially affected the slave-based plantation colony of Surinam in northern South America; but in truth, the Dutch West Indian colonies had already diminished in importance as the Dutch East Indian colonies had become more profitable. In fact, the Netherlands Antilles had become a financial burden. The Dutch maintained a rigid policy that each colony should be self-supporting. Thus expenditure in relief of its population was viewed as an added expense in an already losing proposition. This attitude had characterized Dutch policy since the beginning of the early modern era, and it continued through the nineteenth century.

An 1819 hurricane that struck the Leeward Islands of St. Maarten, Saba, and St. Eustatius provides an informative example of the policy and its effects.[35] The storm caused an almost complete loss of sugar revenues and thus income from export taxes. It forced the government to lower administrative costs and rebuilding efforts so drastically that it took decades to recover; church construction was slow, fortifications on St. Maarten crumbled and decayed, and unattended overgrown ruins marred the appearance of Philipsburg, its capital city, for years. The colonies could do little for themselves. The annual subsidy from the Netherlands for St. Maarten of 31,000 *florins* amounted to only about two percent of the losses suffered on the island from the 1819 hurricane, which killed eighty people and destroyed or damaged almost every house on the island.[36] The metropolis was unwilling, and the islands unable, to do much in the face of such calamities.

The French Antilles followed a different administrative path for their West Indian colonies. After the fall of Napoleon, the Antilles were made part of France, and in 1833, its male citizens were given the right to vote. In 1848 that right was extended to all free males. While further powers were also nominally ceded to colonial assemblies, in effect, the French government maintained tight control and sought consistently to protect the rights of the planter class. It was also in 1848 that Paris abolished slavery, although slave rebellions in Guadeloupe and Martinique in expectation of abolition had already essentially ended the institution. The flight of former slaves from plantation agriculture on Martinique and Guadeloupe moved planters and the government to introduce sharecropping arrangements and to employ repressive systems of labor enlistment, or to a search for new immigrants to do plantation labor. Abandonment of the plantations caused considerable economic disruption. It took two decades before pre-emancipation levels of production were again reached. France maintained centralized control over the Antilles; its governors protected the interests of the *békés,* the large planters and makers of rum who still controlled three-quarters of the cultivated lands. But colonial government struggled financially to maintain the islands. At moments of crisis in the face of continuous natural calamities, that burden became painfully apparent to island residents.

Like all the European nations, France depended on public charitable subscriptions to meet the needs of the people on the hard-hit islands, along with direct aid from the government when available. The acts of the General Council of Guadeloupe in the 1860s, for example, contain many references to the use of charitable funds to support orphanages or hospices for the victims of an 1865 hurricane and the cholera epidemic that followed. Some of those funds were set up as an annuity to support those institutions long after the storm. In a council session of 1868, the government explained that budget deficits were to a large extent due to "events of *force majeure*," to "angers of Heaven and Earth" ("*les colères du ciel et de la terre*"), and to the droughts, floods, hurricanes, and cholera; but it also recognized a transformation in the basic arrangement of government that made the colonies primarily responsible for their own expenses.

The French Antilles suffered from the storms throughout the century, with the 1880s and early 1890s being particularly bad decades.[37] An especially heavy blow was felt in 1891 when Martinique was struck by a tremendous storm that killed between 700 and 1,000 people and injured a thousand more. The storm also ruined agriculture and sunk or damaged all the shipping in the harbors of St. Pierre and Fort de France. This storm focused France's attention on the vulnerability of the islands. In 1892 Henri Monet published a book describing the storm in order to raise money for the victims. In it the author provided a detailed chronology of 67 recorded hurricanes that had struck the island between 1657 and 1858: more or less, one every three years. How was it possible, he asked, for a population to live and prosper under such a formidable sun and a climate so terrible?[38] Island sugar exports declined about forty percent after the storm. A commission arrived to evaluate the losses, and eventually three million *francs* were extended as an interest-free loan to be paid in ten years. But a third of this money went to the island government to balance its budget, and the governor made clear that the help going to the island was to be invested in agriculture and industry that promoted the common good, not to relieve individual losses. As an agricultural inspector wrote to the governor, "Martinique only lives from sugarcane, that is from the sugar industry and the industries that derive from it."[39]

For all the colonial powers, with the decline of the value of Caribbean colonies and with the transformation of their populations from slaves to citizens, the cost of maintaining these colonies in the face of recurring disaster-related expenses loomed large, and that calculation was often based to some extent on prejudicial perceptions of the inherent qualities and abilities of the populations—white creoles, people of mixed origins (*métis*), and the ex-slaves and their descendants. Race and class often played a role in government attitudes and policies. Thus each calamity provoked a social assessment, and each became a potential social disaster as much as a natural one. For those in Europe who saw the colonial financial costs too high in the North Atlantic, the surrender or transference of sovereignty became one possible solution. For those countries in the Americas with brighter political hopes or financial prospects, or for those with expanding geopolitical ambitions, the acquisition of independence or of sovereignty over areas in the Greater Caribbean seemed like worthy goals. But those calculations and hopes always had to consider the physical hazards that the region presented.

We should note that within the region, the sense of common danger and the expression of humanitarian and charitable sentiments that crossed national or cultural boundaries in the face of natural calamity had persisted since the eighteenth century. In response to the 1866 Bahamas and Turks hurricane, a special fund had been created in Spanish Puerto Rico to gather and administer charitable donations for the neighboring islands.[40] Following the hurricane and earthquakes in 1867, the Danish islands of St. John and St. Thomas received donations totaling almost $14,000 from British Guiana, Trinidad, and Jamaica, as well as funds from Dutch Surinam, French Guadeloupe, the United States, and Venezuela, and even another $2,000 from their sister island of St. Croix.[41] This charitable impulse and recognition of common threat, often across religious, linguistic, and national boundaries, tempered political rivalries.

But even in terms of charity, race continued to determine actions. In 1866, a tremendous fire, a veritable "hurricane of flames" as it was called in a sympathetic New Orleans creole newspaper, burned Port au Prince, capital of Haiti, causing the destruction of half of its buildings and putting

9,000 people in the street.[42] Although the great slave rebellion brought independence to that nation in 1804, and the United States and Britain had traded with Haiti, the United States basically sought politically to isolate the black republic, and only in 1862 did it establish diplomatic recognition. While Haiti continued to be a symbol of freedom to the African American populations of the Greater Caribbean region, it generated fear among and was rejected by many of the region's whites, by the colonial powers, and by its neighbors where slavery persisted. No major international effort of relief seems to have been mounted following the fire. Coverage of the great fire, even in the *New York Times*, not only emphasized the failure of the government in a moment of emergency, but placed much of the blame on the "wild" behavior of the Haitians themselves, claiming that they had done nothing for the common good, and had stood idly by or looted and sacked in the confusion, or perhaps had even started the fire intentionally.[43] These were same sorts of accusations made, as we have seen, in governmental reports after catastrophes elsewhere in the region during this period. It was a circular argument: the ex-slaves and their descendants who had not been given a place in the community were now assumed to have no attachments to it, and their presumed failure to have communal sentiments could thus be used as a justification for now giving them no place in it.

SOVEREIGNTIES BENEATH THE WINDS

The active hurricane season of 1867 produced nine storms, the last of which was the late October storm that buffeted the Virgin Islands and Puerto Rico. The termination of the U.S. Civil War in 1865 had defined a shift in the social and political context of the North Atlantic: slavery was ended in North America, and with the war's end the United States now felt less constrained in the pursuit of its strategic and economic interests.

During the war, the United States had begun to consider the acquisition of the Danish West Indies. At first, their elimination as a friendly port of call for Confederate raiders had been a consideration, but in 1865 Secretary of State William Seward began to consider their purchase for other strategic and commercial advantages.[44] Denmark, at first uninterested, changed opinion during its war with Prussia in 1864, and in 1866 there was an exchange of notes and proposals with the United States. A price was agreed upon and a treaty drawn up. Negotiations slowed when the Danes insisted on a vote of approval by residents of the islands, and by late September 1867 Seward, having spent considerable political capital on the purchase of Alaska earlier that year, was urging the Danes to act, since the mood in the United States was now negative, and Congress now seemed "to value dollars more and dominion less." By late October 1867 the Danes were in the process of conducting their plebiscite in the islands in preparation for the signing of a treaty. U.S. officials had already come to see the Danish colonies as useful and strategic islands on the main shipping routes and keys for control of entry into the Caribbean. Vice Admiral David Porter had written to Secretary of State Seward that St. Thomas was a "small Gibraltar," and that its harbor and that of St. John were the best in the region. St. Thomas, he thought, was the keystone to the arch of the West Indies, and perhaps in the spirit of Reconstruction, he reminded Seward that the "inhabitants are mostly colored, but they are extremely well-educated. Nearly all the clerks in the stores are colored." It was a "most hospitable place and people."[45] He did not mention that there had been a bloody slave revolt in the 1730s, that slavery had been abolished in these islands in 1848 only after a plan for gradual emancipation had provoked a major slave uprising, or that the predominant language among former slaves and their descendants was a creole English.[46] While St. Croix had been a plantation outpost, St. Thomas thrived from commerce. Neighboring Puerto Rico had long benefited from trade with St. Thomas, as European goods could be obtained cheaply there. The Puerto Ricans considered St. Thomas their Gibraltar not for its strategic position, but for its role as a port of free trade and a window on world commerce, just as the British fortress in the Mediterranean had served that function for Spain. The negotiations were in progress when the winds interrupted.

The "frightful" hurricane that struck little St. Thomas on the October 29 was the worst that had battered the Danish West Indies since 1837 (fig. 5.1). Probably a Category 3 hurricane by today's standards, with winds reaching 125 miles per hour, this storm, the ninth of the active 1867 season,

FIGURE 5.1 St. Thomas in the hurricane of 1867 (From *Frank Leslie's Illustrated Newspaper*, December 7, 1867; courtesy of History Miami, of the Southern Florida Historical Museum)

left hardly a house with a roof. More than 600 people perished, and in the harbor sixty to eighty vessels sank or were blown ashore, with considerable loss of life. The captain and crew of the Spanish frigate *Nuñez de Balboa*, which happened to be in port when the storm arrived, acted heroically to save the injured and drowning in the harbor. The islands were devastated. There had been an outbreak of cholera on the Danish islands earlier in the year, and a serious fire had also threatened St. Thomas in 1866, so the hurricane exacerbated an already precarious situation; but matters became far worse when, on November 18, both St. Thomas and St. John as well as the more distant sister island of St. Croix were rocked by a series of tremors and two great seismic shocks ten minutes apart that then produced tsunamis in the main harbors, causing tremendous damage to shipping and great harm to the cities and their residents. The quake, centered in the fault in the Anegada Passage that lies between the Virgin Islands and the Lesser Antilles and forms the only deep water passage between the Atlantic Ocean and the Caribbean Sea, had been especially deadly in St. Thomas, where, after an 1832 fire had destroyed much of Charlotte Amalie, the port and main city, a royal order had required building with stone or brick. Ironically, during the earthquake many people were killed by falling stone and brick. Caught between fire and earthquake, two of the great Caribbean threats, the islanders now paid the price.[47] On St. John, the poor population all over the island had suffered greatly from both the hurricane and the earthquake, but the main town had also suffered badly, and the tsunami had brought a wave of twenty to thirty feet that wreaked havoc in the harbor. At St. Croix, the American naval vessel *Monongahela*, which had accompanied the negotiators, was pushed ashore and grounded. It took six months to get her back to sea.

The negotiations between Denmark and the United States had progressed to the signing of a treaty in which the United States agreed to purchase St. Thomas and St. John, but St. Croix was not included. The Danes had insisted on a vote in the islands, and the U.S. representatives had emphasized the requirement of Senate confirmation of any treaty. The merchant community and planters had seen great advantages in the change of government, and voted in favor of the sale; the black population, however, did not support the sale, because of their concerns, bolstered by rumors, that the United States might allow slavery, abolished by the Danish in 1848, to return to the islands. Newspapers on the islands published doggerel poems, putative letters, and song lyrics in the local creole patois about "buddy Thammas" (St. Thomas), "buddy Johnny" (St. John), and "sissy Shanna" (St. Croix), and problems of leaving St. Croix out of the treaty. The Danish king announced the proposed cession of the islands on October 25, 1867, in language that showed his desire for its approval. But the disruption caused by the hurricane that struck on October 29 and the following earthquake, tsunami, and 481 aftershocks greatly delayed diplomatic progress into 1869 and 1870. The administration of President Grant, more interested in acquiring territory in the Dominican Republic, was less willing to act, and when the treaty failed support by a senate committee, it was, in effect, dead. There were resignations in the Danish government, and it was a considerable embarrassment for the Danish throne, which had prepared its subjects in the islands for the separation, and which now found itself a reluctant ruler. Denmark's willingness to sell the islands, a concession the royal chamberlain Edward Carstensen had encouraged the islanders to accept, had, in the words of one observer, "broke that mystic spell which enables a man or a few men in one hemisphere to exercise control over whole communities in another. It was one of those acts which in their nature are irreversible."[48]

Although many in the United States criticized Grant's lack of interest in the islands and the American bad faith, others had lost interest in more tropical—and multiracial—possessions, and there were plenty who saw the project as the expensive purchase of calamities—hurricanes, earthquakes, and tidal waves. Congressional and popular criticism found literary voice in the caustic verses of Bret Harte, America's most famous author of the day. In his somewhat hyperbolic poem *St. Thomas: A Geographical Survey*, he mocked the idea that these were the "isles of Eden, where no ill is."[49]

> So the mountains shook and thundered,
> And the Hurricane came sweeping,
> And the people stared and wondered
> As the sea came on them leaping:
> Each according to his promise,
> Made things lively in St. Thomas.
> Till one morn, when Mr. Seward
> Cast his weather eye to leeward,
> There was not an inch of dry land
> Left to mark his recent island.
> Not a flagstaff or a sentry,
> Not a wharf or port of entry,—
> Only—to cut matters shorter—
> Just a patch of muddy water
> In the open ocean lying,
> And a gull above it flying.

The United States was to buy the Danish West Indies—all three islands—and rename them the U.S. Virgin Islands in 1917.

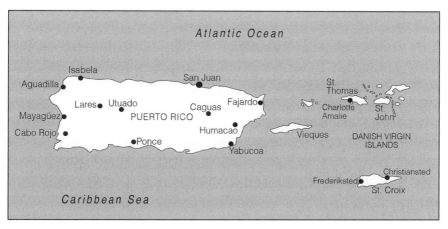

FIGURE 5.2 Puerto Rico and the Virgin Islands (Map by Santiago Muñoz Arbalaez)

St. Thomas lay just forty miles to the east of Crab Island (Vieques) and Puerto Rico (see fig. 5.2). They too had suffered the blows of the late October hurricane and the November quake of 1867. In fact, 1867 had already been a year of bad weather over much of Puerto Rico. The island's agriculture had suffered in 1865 and 1866 and hopes were riding high for better harvests of sugar and coffee in 1867, but the rainy season brought drenching downpours in September and a major storm on October 10 that inundated most of the southern districts of the island.[50] Elderly residents in Ponce, in Peñuelas, and in the central highlands could not recall the rivers ever rising so rapidly and so high.[51] Communication across the island collapsed.[52] In Ponce, the area of the port was cut off from the center of town, and in Guayanilla and San Germán streets flooded and contact with other towns became impossible. Local governments had few resources to meet the crisis; treasuries were bare, and the recent Spanish adventure to reoccupy the Dominican Republic (1861–65) had been a costly failure that left the royal coffers depleted. Locally, taxes had gone unpaid because no one had the funds to pay them. Money to provide relief, or to rebuild the ruined roads and bridges and begin the reconstruction of homes and towns, was difficult to find at the municipal, provincial, or royal levels. On the night of October 29, the feast of San Narciso, the large and intense hurricane that had struck St. Thomas moved in from the east, this time catching the north coast of Puerto Rico, but with a path wide enough to bring heavy rains over much of the island. Rivers already swollen, fields already flooded, and trees already weakened could not withstand the water and wind. Official reports listed 211 deaths and 762 injured in the storm. Losses were particularly heavy in subsistence and export agriculture. Of the estimated 13 million *escudos* in damages on the island, over 10 million were in food crops and coffee, rum, sugar, cotton, and tobacco.[53] This hurricane of San Narciso and the subsequent earthquakes that damaged 168 buildings in the capital alone made 1867 the year of "the storm and the tremors" ("*el temporal y los temblores*").[54]

The year 1867 would be remembered as much for its political ramifications as for its material losses. The problems that the San Narciso hurricane revealed had been developing for years. Few people perceived the danger inherent in the failure of government more clearly than the men assigned to the public works department who had been struggling in the 1860s to improve and repair the infrastructure of roads, bridges, and docks in the face of environmental challenges and a lack of funds. Traditionally, in the Spanish colonies the state had joined with municipal governments to pay for roads and bridges, but now, in the mid-1860s, lack of funds and credit had caused a paralysis in public works. As Miguel de Campos, a Spanish official, wrote in a report just before the storm, "the prestige of the administration and of the peaceful conservation of the established regime" depended on better public works.[55] Puerto Rico, unable to pay for its needs, had reached an unsustainable situation. Over the previous decade only about three percent of the 60 million *escudos* spent by the government had gone to public works, and the people of the island could plainly see the failure of government. Campos emphasized that there were no roads, agriculture and commerce were impeded, and "work was scarce for a working class that was pushed toward misery, and after that perhaps to vice and crime." There was peril here. Carlos de Rojas, another official reporting on public works to his superior ten days before the San Narciso hurricane struck, believed that the worsening situation could bring this "peaceful and tranquil society to the edge of principles never before seen and which Your Excellency would never wish to encounter."

The common folk, what Rojas called "the proletarian class," driven by misery, might be carried to crimes and sin unless sound religious principles and models could be established for them. He felt that only the Church could provide a firm basis for moral life, but there was little money available to maintain its dignity or repair the houses of worship that had also suffered from rains and winds.[56]

Others observers saw the implications of the situation not in religious, but in political terms. The San Narciso storm had underlined the failures of the past. The few public works that the state had created at the cost of much time and notable sacrifice by the municipalities were inadequate. As the engineer José Lianhes reported to the colonial government, "this province has come to an awful and unsustainable situation that the recent calamities have made worse, but the general ill dates from long before."[57] He suggested various projects that would improve communication between the towns and employ the thousands of rural workers who faced misery, and who without work might "surrender to the corrupters of public order or attempt to violate the laws that secure the rights of property."[58] Lianhes was a realist and he warned that appeals to charity or to the patriotism of those with the means to help, the usual recourse in these situations, would only help a little. What was needed was decisive government action to leave public works as permanent and memorable evidence of Spain's efforts to benefit the country. His appeal for over 4 million pesos for docks, lighthouses, lights, roads, telegraph, and civil constructions was beyond the possibility of the government at the moment, but his perception of the political costs of failure was a theme that was taken up by others as well. In April 1868, Miguel de Campos wrote from Puerto Rico to the chief engineer in the Department of Public Works at the Overseas Ministry in Madrid that the efforts to improve the material life of the colonies, while welcomed, had in Puerto Rico been "completely null." The reputation of the government suffered from the delays of months and years to improve the infrastructure, and now the "majority of the inhabitants believe in the immorality of an administration that they see as foreign and hostile."[59] He added that on an island blessed by nature but which, despite its dense population, produced little and remained poor, taxes were seen as excessive, and did not seem to be applied even minimally to what was needed.

One man who sensed the potential threat of political impacts of the San Narciso storm and the subsequent November earthquakes was Vicente Fontán y Mera, a Spanish official with literary ambitions who was serving as inspector of education on the island. Following the hurricane he published *La memorable noche de San Narciso,* a long description of the hurricane and the following earthquakes, filled with details of the losses, and including the usual town-by-town accounting of the lives lost, the property destroyed, and the cost of the damages. Fontán y Mera's style was florid, and he had an irritating fondness for the exclamation point as a literary device, but what most distinguished his account was his attempt as a loyal Spaniard to emphasize the maternal responsibility of the queen and the noble sentiments of the Spanish people for its "brothers" in the Caribbean in a time of crisis. Fontán y Mera called attention to the needs of the island while celebrating heroic actions by Spanish garrison troops during the crisis. He noted with pride the warm welcome given to the Spanish warship *Nuñez de Balboa,* whose captain and crew had acted so heroically in its rescue efforts during the hurricane in St. Thomas. But as witness to the tremendous damage and losses caused by the hurricane and the earthquakes, he wanted also to document in detail the distress of Puerto Rico and to plead on its behalf. [60] He was critical of the government's order to force tax collectors to insist on prompt payment of taxes, and of its comments that the "news of losses had been exaggerated and that many towns had not suffered at all." With the treasury bare, the government had seen little alternative to an insistence on the taxes, but Fontán y Mera noted that the conditions on the island even before the storm had been poor and that they were now disastrous:

> In these almost deserted fields where the proletarian multitude circulates, protected from the scorching sun of day and the rains of night by only a humble hut, it is here where we can investigate not only the [immediate] losses but also the extended effects of the calamity; if we understand as a public calamity the complete lack of the primary and only food of the poor class.[61]

His remedy for the future was the creation of an agricultural bank to provide credit, but in the meanwhile, the government was also responsible to make the wealthy meet their responsibilities and to offer a "protect-ing hand" to those who did not have the resources to meet this crisis. Hidden in his account is a suggestion that the government's inability or failure was leading to a political questioning of the colonial arrangement, but as a loyal Spaniard, he had no sympathy for radical change. As he sug-gested, "The day of 29 October had also provided an occasion to satisfy puerile complaints and to sing out dithyrambs." What did hate and ru-mors between the government and the country provide? What good was political revolution produced by radical reform of the laws? "Delirious radicalism," he said, would destroy industry, commerce, and credit. The greatest truth for Fontán y Mera was that order was the key to all progress and prosperity. Puerto Rico had all it needed to reach its material perfec-tion, and in a time of crisis, love of country and a sentiment of nationality were positive qualities that could help it reach that goal. Fontán y Mera and the officials who had reported on public works had seen the implica-tions of political failure in the face of catastrophe.

The following year brought slow recovery, but radical political action was already under way. One area that had suffered badly in the unpleas-ant and destructive weather of 1867 had been the central highlands on the islands. The town of Lares was nestled in the cordillera. Watered by fast-flowing rivers, it produced cotton and coffee that were exported through the little north coast port of Aguadilla. Under normal conditions the roads were difficult: it took from ten to twelve days for a cart drawn by eight oxen to make a round trip between Lares and the port. The heavy rains and the hurricane of 1867 had made the situation worse, driving up the price of imports and lowering the value of the local products. A *quintal* of salt cod cost 5 *escudos* in Aguadilla but 7 *escudos* by the time it reached the rural workers, while coffee was valued twenty percent lower in Lares than at the port. The poor roads, emblematic of the larger lack of infrastructure, were the key. They caused "the ruin of many, the disheartening of others, and the terror and fright of all."[62] A report from Lares made in November 1867 to petition the government's attention explained that in the past the roads had been maintained by contributions from landowners and mer-chants, with the work done by prisoners and vagrants; but that was no longer possible, and the working population, now faced with hunger, and

after the coffee harvest without work, might be carried by the hopeless-
ness of their situation to theft despite their "just and loyal hearts." The
least the government could do was to repair the impassable roads and
bridges, which at the same time would create jobs for the rural workers.

These conditions in the Puerto Rican highlands provided the context for
the first political movement for independence on the island. The uprising
in Lares on the night of September 23, 1868, originated in a number of dissatisfactions. The large coffee planters who supported the movement were
whites, mostly native-born, heavily indebted to the local merchants, who
were mostly Spaniards or Corsicans. The workers on the coffee estates
who joined them had been forced by government labor legislation into
dependent status and disadvantageous contract arrangements.[63] Moreover, some of the participants held strong abolitionist sentiments, and
deep resentments against the heavy hand of political repression. But it was
clear that the precarious infrastructure in Puerto Rico and the inability of
the government—municipal, provincial, and imperial—to deal with its
challenges had created a situation that had led these sectors of the population to exasperation.[64] No one should have been surprised. The short-lived
uprising at Lares, in which a thousand men seized the town, had not been
caused by the flooding and rains, the storm of San Narciso, or the earthquakes alone. But each natural calamity had placed more stress on Spain's
resources and its ability to respond to any challenge, natural or political.
Loyal Spaniards like Fontán y Mera and Lianhes had given warnings, but
even when the revolt of Lares broke out, the immediate interpretation of
events was that the populace, upset by the floods and earthquakes, had
been misled by disloyal discontents. The creole landowners, intellectuals,
and small merchants who led the revolt failed in their attempt to bring
other communities into the uprising, and it was ended quickly, the leadership imprisoned or fleeing into exile.[65] Despite plans and intentions, there
was no general uprising of the island. The reasons for this were many, but
the inability of Betances to sail to Puerto Rico from his exile in Saint Thomas
(where he had barely escaped the earthquake) with the arms he had gathered certainly contributed to the defeat.[66]

Two weeks after the uprising, on October 8, 1868, Governor Julian José
Pavia, addressed an open letter to the people of Puerto Rico in which he

made clear his perception of the importance of the natural disasters and the government's response in the origins of the rebellion.

> From the moment I took command of this island I have been constantly occupied in following the orders of Her Majesty the Queen to alleviate the calamities of the natural events that have accumulated over this part of the Monarchy. You have been able to see that day and night I have dedicated myself to relieve your pains and to bring consolation to all areas, and to reanimate your spirits that were exhausted by the many misfortunes that you have suffered, including the drought that you have withstood in the last months.[67]

The governor believed that the disloyal men behind the rebellion had used this "special and transitory situation" for their own purposes. This explanation ignored the government's past failures, but still, it is fair to point out that the very situation of hunger and economic dislocation caused by the environmental disasters of 1867 which had contributed to the exasperation and revolutionary sentiments of the conspirators had also created an atmosphere of subsistence insecurity. The floods, hurricane, and earthquakes of 1867 were followed in 1868, as the governor noted, by a difficult drought. A protracted campaign in the countryside would have been particularly difficult at that moment. Revolution had to wait. Betances later wrote in frustration from exile, "the year 1869 has flown by like a dream, and yet we are still slaves." He urged that the least his countrymen should do to restore their honor and dignity was to free the Africans, "the slaves of the slaves." [68]

From the pro-Spanish point of view the natural disasters of 1867 could be taken as a sign from God in defense of the colonial regime. In collaboration with a Spanish naval officer, José Pérez Moris, a journalist and one of the leaders of the pro-Spanish Conservative Party, published in 1872 a still useful detailed account of the Lares rebellion. Condemnatory of his separatist political rivals, his account also played on the racial fears that lay beneath the debates on abolition, suggesting that Betances had planned to land 3,000 armed blacks to lead the rebellion.[69] Pérez Moris was sure that the hand of God had interrupted the plans of the rebels. He argued that the rebellion had originally been scheduled for June 24, 1867, the feast day of San Juan, a day of particular symbolic importance in Puerto Rico, which had originally been named San Juan Bautista, but had then been moved to October 10, the feast day of Santa Isabel. He claimed that the earthquake had disrupted the conspirators' plans, but we know that the earthquake did not happen until November. If natural events were responsible for the delay, they were the torrential rains of early October and the San Narciso hurricane of that month. Pérez Moris may simply have been chronologically confused, but perhaps he was trying to make another point. He reported that some of the leaders of the rebellion had met with Betances in St. Thomas in late 1867, and one of them remembered the 1812 earthquake that had shattered Caracas at the beginning of Bolívar's campaign for independence. Were the quakes of St. Thomas and Puerto Rico, like that of Caracas, "a providential warning that Heaven would punish the rebellion against Spain as a blasphemy, and perhaps sink the island into the Atlantic"?[70] Pérez Moris had no doubt that if God had not shaken the whole island of Puerto Rico, the separatist movement would have erupted in 1867, most likely with a different outcome. Perhaps he, like many, found it easier to see the hand of God in the violent but sporadic earthquakes than in the more common rains and winds of October, but his remarks about the timing of the rebellion and the context of conditions on the island merit consideration. Pérez Moris believed that the rebels of Lares had been encouraged in their hopes for success when they had witnessed the arrival in 1865 of the weakened and disheartened Spanish forces that had been defeated on Santo Domingo "if not by bullets, by the climate" (*"si no por balas, por el clima"*). In a way, he was suggesting a similar explanation for the failure at Lares: the climate had intervened.

Betances, still in exile, drew a different lesson from nature's wrath. He and his wife had barely escaped injury when their house in exile had collapsed, but he noted in a letter to a friend in April 1868 that not only had St. Thomas trembled, but "Puerto Rico also had shaken out the tyrants." He commented on the destruction he experienced in St. Thomas, the tsunami wave that followed the quake rising like a white mountain threatening to swallow the city, and of the people falling to their knees pleading for mercy and pardon for their sins. He wrote, "St. Thomas still trembles, and Puerto Rico shakes to see its sons insensitive to [their] slavery."[71] The

New York Times, like the governor of Puerto Rico, believed that it had been nature that had caused the upheaval. In November 1868, it reported from Puerto Rico, "crops are in a flourishing condition, and prosperity is returning to the island. Political agitation has subsided and the whole population is tranquil."[72]

The century wore on. Spain had undergone a revolution in 1868, and under a Liberal ministry it made adjustments. More representation was conceded to Puerto Rico in the Spanish legislature between 1868 and 1874. The Moret Law of 1870 began the process of abolition. By 1873 slavery had been abolished in Puerto Rico.

In Cuba, the revolt begun in October 1868 eventually spread, dragging on for a decade, but finally concessions were made on a number of issues that brought a truce in 1878. Promises made by both loyalists and rebels to slaves who had joined either side now led to increasing slave expectations and resistance. A compulsory apprenticeship system replaced slavery in Cuba in 1880 until it too was eliminated in 1886. There were administrative changes, political concessions, and a loosening of some of the most repressive civil laws, and then renewed political repression in the 1880s. War and the question of sovereignty would emerge again before the century ended, but this time in the context of the new imperial ambitions of the United States.

GOVERNMENTS, TECHNOLOGY, AND SCIENCE

The last three decades of the nineteenth century witnessed the end of slavery in the Spanish colonies and the last stages of the struggle for independence in those colonies, culminating in what became the Spanish-American War. The period after 1870 also presented a number of seasons of high storm frequency that seem to have come immediately before or after an El Niño event in the Pacific, including 1878–79, 1887, and 1894.[73] These storm-filled years, as well as others without climatic anomalies, presented challenges to all the countries of the Greater Caribbean, but they were now able to draw on institutions, customs, and policies that had, in some cases, developed over a long period of time. Moreover, in some ways, the very trajectory of technological and scientific advances that had in many places transformed agriculture during the century were now being applied to the understanding and analyses of the tropical storms and to the means of mitigating their impact on peoples and governments.

In the case of Spain, the nineteenth-century hurricanes and other disasters revealed the Spanish institutional strategies of response and relief at the royal, colonial, and local levels. The ruler was expected to demonstrate deep personal sympathy for his or her subjects. After the Cuban hurricanes of the 1840s, the queen, the queen mother, and various ministries had all made donations.[74] In 1867, Queen Isabel II created a *junta*, to be presided over by her husband, the Duke of Cádiz, with the purpose of starting a charitable subscription to provide relief to sufferers of the disasters in Puerto Rico and in the Philippines, which had also been devastated by a typhoon in that year.[75] Such efforts may have demonstrated sincere sympathy, but as the overseas minister in Spain explained in similar circumstances in 1884 when Cuba and the Philippines were the victims of hurricanes and a general relief committee had been created, whatever the profound sentiments of the royal family, the government, or the Spanish people, it was simply impossible for the treasury to meet "so many public calamities."[76] Thus voluntary charity was still the first line of defense. Subscription lists were mounted by many sectors of society: by various government offices, the bankers, the journalists, the National Bank, elite private clubs like the Casino Español, and various voluntary associations. Following an 1882 hurricane in Pinar del Río, Cuba, that devastated the tobacco-growing district of Vuelta Abajo, the Havana press carried detailed notices of collective contributions of money, goods, or services from the bakers guild, the tobacco warehouse workers, the professors of the university, the Centro Gallego private club, and the white coachmen of Havana, as well as individual donations, like the promise by the owner of the *La Belleza* cigar factory to turn over two percent of his profits for the month of September to the poor of Vuelta Abajo. Members of the royal family, ministers, public officials, and prominent citizens of society were expected to head the lists of contributors and play a demonstrable role in the theater of collective responsibility. This was a custom that explains the personal contributions made by various government offices and departments and by the royal Lancer Regiment after the Cuban storm of 1846, and by members of the Puerto Rican office of Public Works, who gave according to their relative rank following the 1867 hurricane.[77] The Church and religious institutions also played a role of consolation and charity, offering *Te Deum* services, organizing charitable subscriptions, housing those displaced by the storms, and exhorting everyone to contribute to the relief of victims. Following the 1882 Cuban hurricanes, Don Ramon Fernández de Piérola, the bishop of Havana, set up a charitable fund and made the first donation of 2,000 pesos himself, reminding his flock that they should use this calamity (*desgracia*) to make themselves better, and "to find in their own misfortune a wellspring of new prosperity."[78] Such charity was, of course, a traditional role for the Church, but by the mid-nineteenth century secular civil society now played a much larger role in these activities than it had in the previous century.

To respond to calamities, all kinds of charitable events were scheduled. In Havana, the journalists organized a literary reading in 1882 to help the victims of hurricanes. The firemen collected alms for them during the procession of Saint Teresa. In San Juan, the Ladies and Gentlemen of the Casino and Artistic Literary Circle scheduled a "lyrical-dramatic" performance in the city's theater, to be presided over by the governor to raise funds for the 1862 hurricanes victims.[79] Sometimes the governor sought to coordinate such efforts and to administer the donations centrally and to have the municipal relief efforts report to his office, but central government tended to concentrate on imposing price regulations to stop exploitation of the shortages of food and building materials, to prohibit looting and maintain order, and to provide tax relief and distribute funds made available as loans or relief.

In truth, the primary responsibility for response was at the local municipal level. Here in the town councils that constituted local government organized response, collected information on losses, and petitioned, cajoled, or pleaded for help from the colonial government and, through it, from Madrid. Municipal archives are replete with documentation gathered after each storm from every neighborhood, recording the losses and calculating the value of everything from great sugar *centrales* and town churches to individual hens and pigs. It was also at this municipal level that the charity committees were organized. By the 1830s, these *juntas* had become standard practice in the Spanish Antilles. Following the Cuban hurricanes of the 1840s, Governor O'Donnell created a *junta de socorro* to coordinate relief efforts, and it worked in conjunction with committees created at the local level. In Puerto Rico, following the 1867 hurricane, a relief committee (*junta de beneficiencia*) was created in Ponce, "with the objective to incite the never doubted charity of the people of Ponce to remedy the pressing needs of the unfortunate of this jurisdiction." In this case, the forms the *junta* had printed on blue paper to gather information about losses and needs made no mention of the queen, or of Spain; this was seen as a community matter. The contributions the *junta* received, varying from one peso to 250 pesos, seem to indicate a broad social spectrum of participation across class lines.[80] Relief efforts also reflected a recognition of class distinctions. Following the Puerto Rico hurricane of 1876, for example, the community of Manatí catalogued 1,200 people or families in need of aid, listing not only the needs of each, but also their economic categories: middling, poor, broke (*insolvente*), distressed (*angustiosa*), and well off (*desahogada*). The *junta de beneficiencia* then received hundreds of personal petitions for aid. Similar accountings and petitions were made in other communities as well.[81]

While the *juntas* were normally composed of a mayor, other municipal officials, prominent citizens, and a senior cleric, efforts were made to mobilize other sectors of society as well. In charity and response to personal distress and public disaster, women had an important role in soliciting and distributing relief funds, but they did not hold positions of authority. After the 1876 San Felipe (September 13) hurricane in Puerto Rico, a women's charity committee was created in the town of Caguas that corresponded with the municipal *junta* under the mayor's control.[82] Following that same storm, the charity committee in Ponce sent out forms to women asking for "The generous aid and the valuable influence that the Ladies, angels of charity, have always known how to exert on the hearts of the father, the husband, the brother, the man, that is, those who are never deaf to the pleas of their beloved women." The request went on to ask for women themselves to contribute "according to the dictates of their generosity for such a philanthropic and humanitarian objective."[83] In Havana, following two 1882 hurricanes a month apart that struck Pinar del Río province, a women's committee that had been formed to celebrate the centennial of Saint Teresa of Avila decided to maintain its organization to help the stricken province, a decision applauded in the local press.[84] A ladies' *junta de damas* was created under the presidency of the Marquesa de Victoria de las Tunas, wife of the governor of the island at that time. She petitioned the throne directly for help and received a telegraph communication from "her friend" Isabel II in response.[85] This feminization of charity had deep roots in Spanish society, and it was effectively and continually mobilized throughout the nineteenth century.

Despite a discourse that emphasized self-sufficiency, the system, dependent to a large extent on personal or collective charitable contributions, still became highly bureaucratized. At the local level, it also depended on the funds available for "emergencies and disasters" in municipal budgets, and those were usually sparse or almost nonexistent. Often following the hurricanes, rural populations migrated to the nearest town seeking relief, and this placed an added burden on municipal resources. The towns, said Vicente Fontán y Mera in his description of the San Narciso hurricane, could not perform the "miracle of the loaves and fishes," and therein lay the problem.[86]

Response to calamity was an occasion on which a colonial regime or any government could justify its existence, its efficacy, and its ability to protect its subjects or citizens. In the nineteenth century, as separatist and autonomist forces and sentiments grew in the Spanish Caribbean colonies, the government and the journalists it influenced or controlled continually used the press and official pronouncements after natural disasters to emphasize the sympathy of Spain for the colonies, Spanish generosity, and the heroic actions of Spanish officials and garrisons stationed in the Antilles. Pamphlets recording the storms used these images and stories for political advantage. Like the heroic actions of the sailors of the *Núñez de Balboa* in the harbor of St. Thomas in 1867, tales of heroism or kindness conveyed a message of national unity. Journalists celebrated the tireless efforts to save storm victims by Policarpo García of the Watchmen's Brigade of San Germán in 1867, or the risks taken by three members of the Guardia Civil who not only helped those left homeless in the Cuban storms of 1882, but took money from their pockets to feed them, as examples to emulate and admire. [87] The pro-Spanish journalists and chroniclers of the disasters returned to the themes of unity and reciprocity of "the Great Spanish Nationality." Leopoldo Carvajal, member of the Cuban elite and a colonel in Spain's Cuban military auxiliaries or Volunteers, wrote in 1882, "The island [of Cuba] is Spain, blood of its blood, bone of its bones, and its brothers across the ocean have demonstrated this so many times, they have felt these horrible convulsions that Providence in its high and inscrutable plan has sent."[88] Cubans had helped Spain in times of crisis; now it was Spain's turn. The Marquis of La Habana, president of the Spanish commission on colonial disaster relief, insisted in 1884 that since their "affected brethren [in the colonies] have always generously responded to public disasters in the provinces of the peninsula, we cannot remain indifferent to theirs."[89]

But distant Spain had neither the funds nor the ability to meet the needs of the colonies, and the reluctance of government on occasion to suspend taxes or offer loans at easy credit, or to use surpluses in the colonies rather than at home, had been wedded in the minds of many people to the other dissatisfactions with empire. Two hurricanes battered western Cuba in October 1870, sweeping over the area of Matanzas and leaving some 800 people dead in their wake. Manuel Fernández de Castro, a Spanish mining engineer and student of hurricanes who was resident in Cuba, writing about these storms and the nature of hurricanes in general, remembered with nostalgia how in the midst of war in 1780, Bouillé, the French governor of Martinique, had treated his captured English hurricane survivors with magnanimity and compassion. In that case nature's violent passion had diminished the animosities of men. But in 1868, both in the abortive attempt at Lares in Puerto Rico and in the now expanding uprising in Cuba that would last for a decade, the frustrations with colonial rule had erupted anew. The violence of nature had not cooled human passion: not in Europe between the Prussians and the French in 1870, and not in Cuba. Fernández de Castro lamented that "the torrents of water that have fallen, the hurricanes of 1870, have not been enough to wash away the blood that inundates Cuba, nor to put out the fires that devour it."[90]

Like Spain, the other imperial governments of the North Atlantic continued their traditions of response through the middle decades of the nineteenth century, but just as new technologies like steam and the railroad had transformed the agricultural basis of these societies, new technological advances were also beginning to alter the way in which governments and peoples could react to the threat of the storms. Barometers and thermometers introduced in the eighteenth century had become relatively common instruments for those interested in predicting bad weather. Anemometers (devices to measure wind velocity) in the form of a wheel with cups to catch the wind had been around as a concept since the Renaissance, but they had been reinvented by the late 1840s and were coming into use in the American settlements in the following decades.

To some extent the diffusion of meteorological technologies and information continued to be a collaborative effort between interested private individuals and governments. The work of the early Anglophone meteorologists like Reid, Redfield, Espy, and Piddington now found new Hispanic parallels in the work of men like the Cuban-born Andrés Poëy (1825–1919; fig. 5.3a). The son of Felipe Poëy, the most important Cuban naturalist of his era, the young Andrés was raised and educated in France where, in the National Library in Paris, be began his life's work of carefully cataloguing all works relating to the features, frequency, and track of the Caribbean hurricanes. Poëy returned to Havana in 1845 and became an important meteorologist and first director of the government observatory in Havana. Although a leading figure, he was actually part of a strong Cuban meteorological tradition that had developed since the 1830s, whose results were sometimes reported in local newspapers. [91] His *Bibliographie cyclonique,* based on his cataloguing work, was published in 1866, and included over a thousand items.[92] It initiated research on hurricane chronology and frequency, which has flourished as scholars seek to reveal the patterns of hurricane occurrence by examining the historical record. This work continues today in HURDAT (North Atlantic Hurricane Database) and the analyses based on it.

The hurricane chronologists and those who were gathering measurements of barometric pressures, wind velocity, rainfall, and temperatures

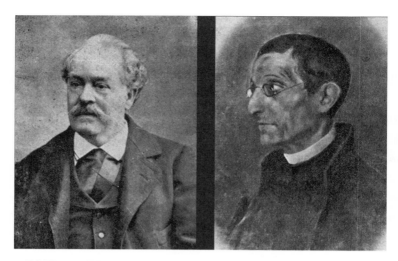

FIGURE 5.3 Pioneer Hispanic meteorologists (*left*) Andrés Poëy and (*right*) Father Benito Vines (Portraits from Carlos M. Trelles, *Biblioteca científica cubana*, Matanzas, Cuba: Juan de Oliver, 1918, 1:161, 166)

were part of a collaborative effort between amateurs and government agents that traversed national boundaries. A good case in point is that of Eugene Suquiet, a French planter resident in Juana Díaz, Puerto Rico, who was a member of the French Meteorological Society. In 1876 Suquiet donated a barometer to the Office of Public Works on the island, "in the name of science." In addition, he presented a long study of the San Felipe hurricane, which included his careful recording of wind, thermometer, and barometer readings as well as his own general discussion of the origins and character of hurricanes. The officers of the Spanish government expressed their thanks for his gracious gift and report, but by that time, a strong tradition in meteorology had already established independently in the Spanish islands.[93]

Growing out of the previous century's academies of scientific interest, the creation of a weather observatory in 1857 at the Jesuit Colegio de Belén in Havana marked an important moment in the development of meteorology in the region. The Jesuits eventually had some thirty of these observatories in different parts of the world, usually linked to chairs of mathematics in their schools, which they believed to be useful in their missionary and educational goals. The Havana Observatory, at the time the tallest building in its part of central Havana, flourished under a series of Jesuit directors, especially after the arrival of the Catalan Benito Vines in 1870 (fig. 5.3b). From that time until his death in 1893, Vines was the most knowledgeable and proficient student of the hurricanes of the North Atlantic. His publications were widely read and translated. *Practical Hints in Regard to West Indian Hurricanes* was a translation of his work published and distributed by the U.S. Army Signal Service which in 1870 had been given the task of establishing a weather service. In 1875 Vines published the first hurricane forecast warning, and in that decade, he began to establish a network of observatories in the Caribbean region to share information so that populations and governments could prepare for oncoming storms. The Vines network and that of the U.S. Signal Service were cooperating by 1880, although only intermittently because of a lack of congressional funding. As historian Raymond Arsenault has pointed out, reluctance to pay for overseas meteorological stations limited American weather prediction and not until a disaster like the hurricane of September 1875 that destroyed Indianola, Texas (see chapter 6) did it become apparent how much they were needed. Even then, federal reluctance to assume responsibility to protect citizens was a major impediment—a reluctance, it must be admitted, that was shared with other nations. Vines's work and his system of observatories and weather stations were mostly financed by shipping companies and telegraph services, and government support everywhere for such efforts were slight. Only in 1890, after a series of destructive winter storms, did the United States finally create a Weather Bureau as part of the Department of Agriculture.[94]

Much of the progress in forecasting and the networking had been made possible by technical advances in communications, and thus in the ability of governments to mitigate hurricane dangers by providing an early warning system. After 1830, the use of steamships began to considerably diminish the sailing time across the ocean, and between New World ports.[95] But chief among the improvements and advances in communication were the telegraph and the oceanic cables that made intercontinental telegraphy possible. By the 1850s, major American cities were being linked by the cables. In 1861, the first transcontinental message was sent, and in 1866 the first transatlantic cable line was laid. There was considerable commercial competition between European companies to lay the transatlantic cables, and not until the 1870s were the cables linking major islands with Washington and Europe effectively in place.[96] Even then, they were used more in post-disaster recovery than in conveying warnings of approaching storms, at least until the late 1880s. The first use of the telegraph for communication following a hurricane was probably a message of condolence sent by Queen Isabella II of Spain to the people of Puerto Rico following the San Narciso hurricane in 1867. By the mid-1870s such communications had become normal between Madrid and its colonies. In September 1888, for example, the governor of Puerto Rico requested an immediate loan *"por via telegrafica"* to help restore Ponce after a September hurricane in the hopes that it would stimulate "the zeal and patriotism of all."

The telegraph had the potential to transform the Greater Caribbean region, diminish its isolation, improve its communications, and lessen its vulnerabilities, especially to the hurricanes. It was a revolutionary technology for its time and the people of the age recognized it as such. It was not incongruous that in St. Thomas in 1867, the ship which Betances had loaded with munitions, and on which he had pinned his revolutionary hopes for Puerto Rico, was named *El Telegrafo*.

CHANGING VIEWS OF NATURE AND RISK

The steamship, the telegraph, and soon the telephone were transforming vulnerabilities, and through the nineteenth century there were many who believed that the natural world was being brought under human control, although the great destructive forces of nature—hurricanes, volcanoes, and earthquakes—tempered such hopes and convictions.[97] As the century moved toward its close, another change, an alteration in perspective, had also become apparent in the description and reporting of the Atlantic tropical storms. Providential language could still be found following devastating storms, and references to *"le colère du ciel"* ("the wrath of heaven") or "the hand of God" were still common enough then, as they are today. The bishop of Havana could still admonish his flock in 1882 that a belief in divine providence was the best basis for morality and society and in the midst of catastrophe, it was best to commit their souls to becoming better Christians.[98] Nevertheless, the discourse of science had overshadowed the proclivity to explain climatic conditions or natural cataclysms as resulting from human sin and error. Those providential interpretations of disaster had always had a certain theological inconsistency, since heavenly reward was to be granted individually, but God's wrath was delivered collectively on the sinful and the innocent alike. Then too, the inconsistency of various interpreters and prophets concerning whose sins, or which sins, were responsible for a particular earthquake or flood also had weakened the force of providential explanations. From the time of Spinoza in the seventeenth century, nature as the physical universe governed by its own regularities or laws had been gaining ground as an explanation for these events, but the processes and laws of nature did not simply replace providential interpretations of catastrophes. The two interpretations were able to coexist, as they still do today, and "scientists" (a term first used in 1833) were able to work without much reference to or concern for the question of first cause or divine intention.[99]

Analytical curiosity about hurricanes, earthquakes, tsunamis, and other violent aspects of the physical world had increasingly separated from theological and philosophical explanations of ultimate causes and human frailties. Even in the works of Jesuit Father Vines and his clerical predecessors at the Havana Observatory, for example, questions of divine intention or cause were not raised, and their writings were devoted to measuring and analyzing natural phenomena, and then applying that knowledge to the benefit of those who might have been affected. In their work, or in Edouard Fortier's reaction to the devastating Martinique hurricane of 1891, the focus of attention had shifted to nature and the hazards of the physical world. Fortier's account of the losses and his stories of mothers and innocent children killed by the storm questioned the traditional providential interpretations. His remark that long after the barometer we read today no longer exists, the birds will still give the sailor warning of a storm's approach, reflected a humility about man's efforts and powers before the forces of nature. This shift to an emphasis that the laws and hazards of nature were beyond human control, and perhaps were not employed as instruments of divine purpose, in effect, lifted responsibility for natural disaster from the shoulders of a sinful society and exculpated the victims from any accountability. By doing so, it also diminished the role of saints or relics as a prophylactic barrier against misfortune, or the utility of religion in general against the common threats of nature. Simultaneously, if implicitly, it underlined the responsibility of the state for the well-being of nature's "blameless victims."[100] True, inherent moral deficiencies or negative habits like sloth associated with a particular race could be used to deny assistance, as had been done after the mid-century storms in the British West Indies, but by the century's close the hazards of nature had become the principal lens through which such events were viewed.

Most western governments, moved by self-interest, the promotion of specific interest groups, and survival, had long felt some responsibility to provide to their members protection against calamities.[101] This was the origin of the "protector state" (*état protecteur*).[102] The question by the late nineteenth century was to what extent government was responsible for the "risks" of life; to what extent were these "risks," that is, hazards with a probability and previsibility, to be borne individually or collectively? This concept of risk and its transformation into a commodity grew out of maritime experience with loss, and by the late nineteenth century as capitalism surged, the hurricane, like any unpredictable storm, became a metaphor easily accommodated to the character of life in general. Risk and uncertainty became the only certainties in modern life.[103] The defraying of risks by various kinds of protective policies or insurance lay at the origins of the welfare state, or what the French call the "providential state" (*état providence*), and some have argued, at the very origins of the modern world.[104] It was not coincidental that the French Law on Workplace Accidents of 1898, which abandoned the concept of culpability for one of presumed risk in any workplace, has been taken as the beginning of the modern welfare state. But as we have seen, natural calamities had already been moving a number of the North Atlantic states—slowly and intermittently to be sure—in that direction for some time. What lay a century in the future was the notion that human actions, especially through technological and scientific accomplishments, might indeed influence nature or, as it would be called, the environment, and change the planet's ecological balances and climate. If that was the case, then humans would again bear the responsibility for natural disasters: because of their policies, actions, or inactions, rather than because of their spiritual or moral failings.

꩜꩜

CHAPTER 6

Nature and Politics at the Century's Turn

It is doubtful if any land or district populated by nearly a
million souls has, in modern times, been so devastated or
overwhelmed as was Puerto Rico in one day August last.
—*Gen. George Davis, 1900*

We drove hundreds of Negroes at the bayonet point to
assist in the work of burning and loading the dead
on barges for sea burial.
—*Major Lloyd R. D. Fayling, Galveston, 1902*

Nations [will] come together in true humanity, which will
know but one deadly foe—blind dead nature.
—*Rosa Luxemburg on Martinique, 1902*

The mid-nineteenth-century advances in communication brought
about by the telegraph now made possible the dream of the weather
watchers: simultaneous observations over widely separated distances and
the creation of synoptic weather maps. These visions seemed to promise
predictability. States could see the utility for agriculture, maritime commerce, and war that such a promise implied.[1]

The idea of sharing meteorological information had developed in the
1840s. In 1853 a ten-nation conference on maritime meteorology, attended
mostly by naval officers, was convened in Brussels. In 1854, due in part
to the work and urgings of Colonel William Reid, after his stay in Barbados and his publication in 1838 of the *Law of Storms*, Great Britain created

a Meteorological Office.[2] In the United States as early as 1849 the Smithsonian Institution in Washington, DC, was providing weather instruments to telegraph companies and collecting reports of observations and mapping them, with the intention of forecasting storms. By 1860, some 500 observation stations were reporting to it, but the Civil War interrupted further development. It was in 1870 that Congress finally created a national weather service as part of the Army Signal Division of Telegrams and Reports for the Benefit of Commerce. This arrangement underscored the close association of telegraphy with meteorological observation and the perception that the ability to predict weather had commercial and security implications of national interest.[3] For the next twenty years, the U.S. Weather Service would remain under military control; only in 1890 did the newly created Weather Bureau within the Department of Agriculture assume the responsibility of meteorological observation and reporting. From mid-century to the 1890s, the main focus of the U.S. Weather Service and Bureau had been on the commercial routes in the Great Lakes, the conditions on the eastern seaboard, and on the possibilities of flooding in the Mississippi basin. There were some early attempts to receive weather reports from Jamaica and from Havana, where, as was noted in the previous chapter, Padre Vines had taken over the Jesuit observatory at Belén in 1870 and had created a network of volunteer observers and telegraph communications that extended over Cuba and eventually incorporated reports from other islands.[4] The Jesuits had also established an observatory in Manila in 1865, which began to create a number of substations to collect weather data useful for agriculture and commerce. In 1897, the Manila observatory and its substations came under the direction of Father José Algué, who played a role in the Pacific very similar to that of Father Vines in the North Atlantic, as organizer of an extensive system of data collection, and as a leading theoretician on tropical storms. Father Algué's *Baguios ó ciclones Filipinos: Un estudio teórico-práctico* (1896), translated as *Cyclones of the Far East*, became a standard reference work.[5] The key to the developing science of meteorology in this period was observation and data collection in the search for patterns that by inference and analogy allowed for forecasting. Theorizing still involved little physics.[6]

The advantages of sharing weather data led in 1873 to the creation of the International Meteorological Organization, one of the earliest examples of global scientific information sharing. This internationalist project faced problems in standardizing measurements and observations among its members as well as problems caused by different national goals and resources and by jealousies and competition. The area of the Greater Caribbean provides a case in point. Despite efforts by the U.S. Weather Bureau to incorporate the developing Hispano-Cuban meteorological system, in the 1870s, politics and finances intervened and the lack of congressional support and appropriations limited integration of information. It was only after a series of damaging winter storms in 1886–87, and the deadly Johnstown, Pennsylvania flood of 1889 that killed 2,209 people and caused $17 million in damages, that complaints rose to a level that demanded congressional action. It was then that the Weather Bureau became a civilian agency. During the 1890s, a series of damaging hurricane seasons in the United States, especially that of 1893, made the insufficiency of the national warning system clear, and even the expansion of observation stations including fifty in Florida did not offer much consolation to endangered coastal populations. The hurricane that devastated the Florida west coast town of Cedar Key in 1896 caught Washington's attention; and the mounting pressure for war against Spain made the integration of Caribbean observations a necessity for military operations, as it already had been for the security of life, property, and commerce in the United States. In 1898, President McKinley, who it was famously rumored feared the hurricanes more than the Spanish navy, ordered the Weather Bureau to set up a warning system for hurricanes in the West Indies.[7] The forecasting post that it established in Kingston, Jamaica was moved to Havana in 1899 after the Spanish-American War, and then to Washington, DC in 1900, the last change made under the cloud of a horrendous disaster on the Gulf coast of Texas. In fact, the years around the turn of the century were marked by a number of catastrophic events that revealed the tension between governmental policies and capabilities and made clear the limitations that social divisions placed on the implementation of disaster programs.

San Ciriaco and the "Empire of Hunger"

On August 8, 1899, with Cuba and Puerto Rico now under American military occupation, an intense hurricane struck the island of Puerto Rico. It was one of the classic Cape Verdean hurricanes, forming in the mid-Atlantic at the latitude of the Cape Verde islands about August 2, moving westward into the Leewards, striking Guadeloupe, St. Kitts, and St. Thomas, and reaching Puerto Rico on August 8 as a Category 4 storm. Its diameter was only about sixty miles; but it moved slowly, thus causing extensive damage. The eye took six hours to diagonally traverse the ninety-mile-long island, making landfall near Humacao on the southeastern shore and then leaving the island near Aguadilla on the northwestern coast. The capital of San Juan was outside the main area of damage, but the devastation elsewhere, especially in the central highland coffee-producing areas and in the southeast, was horrendous. Figure 6.1 shows the effects of the wind on Humacao, where substantial buildings were turned to rubble. Winds of over 85 miles an hour were recorded many places, and in Humacao, Ponce, and Mayaguez (see fig. 5.2) winds of 100 or even 140 miles per hour were reported. Even worse were the rains that continued long after the winds subsided. At Humacao, twenty-three inches fell in twenty-four hours, and other communities reported similar accumulations. The rivers rose and left their courses, causing widespread and deadly flooding.[8] In Ponce, the island's second largest city, five hundred people died, mostly from drowning, and many of them were children or the poor. [9] The city streets flooded, the municipal buildings were badly damaged, and the area near the port, also subject to a heavy storm surge, was cut off, its businesses destroyed. Fifteen ships in the harbor ran aground. The food stored in warehouses near the port was ruined. The coffee crop from the surrounding area was almost entirely lost. Towns in the immediate vicinity suffered similarly. Roads were under water, communications cut, all wires down. Hunger threatened Ponce, and within days there were concerns about sanitation and the conditions of public health. After leaving Puerto Rico the storm moved up the U.S. Atlantic coast, battering North Carolina and eventually curving across the Atlantic

Figure 6.1 Ruins of Humacao after San Ciriaco (Courtesy of the Photographic Collections, Archivo General de Puerto Rico)

and striking the Azores. The system maintained coherence as a tropical storm for twenty-eight days, becoming longest-lasting hurricane–tropical storm on record.[10]

While Puerto Rico had not suffered a major hurricane since 1876, there had been a series of more localized storms in the 1880s and 1890s, and the islanders were certainly not novices in dealing them. But the violence of this storm and the destruction it wrought was unusual. In Ponce, the reaction to the hurricane's devastation was not fatalism, but anger. Although the U.S. Weather Bureau had predicted the storm's arrival, and Puerto Rico itself had just established its own Weather Bureau in October 1898, Ponce's residents believed that the municipal government had not duly warned them. Despite immediate attempts to secure aid from the military government in San Juan, two days following the storm a crowd of a thousand people formed outside the town hall to denounce the negligence of the mayor (*alcalde*), Luis Porrata Doria, and call for his dismissal. [11] Although dispersed by the U.S. Fifth Cavalry stationed in the area, the crowd obtained its objective.[12] The military presence provided some resources, but everywhere on the island, the municipal governments were the first line of recovery and relief, and the military commanders in each district quickly learned to turn to them for help even though their funds were meager.

The political fate of the island and the question of its sovereignty were still undecided, and the island's future depended in some ways on how the United States and the people of Puerto Rico confronted the usual post-hurricane challenges. Loyalties and sovereignty were still being defined following the war, and they were now further tested by the storm. We can see the political crosscurrents and personal anguish that this situation created in the story of one death. José López Peláez and his wife had migrated to Puerto Rico from Asturias, Spain about 1885, and he had taken a post as a customs agent in the region of Humacao. López Peláez and his family were residing in the little port of Punta Santiago, near Humacao, when the San Ciriaco storm struck the island. The customs house at Punta Santiago was the only substantial building with stone or masonry walls in the town and was the logical place to seek protection from the storm, but now a new flag, the Stars and Stripes, flew over the building. López Pelaez, having lost his job, and upset by the loss of the war and the change of sovereignty, refused to find shelter under the new flag. He and his wife died in the storm.[13] In all, over 3,000 people lost their lives, making this the deadliest hurricane in the island's history, and in the ten months following the storm when food was scarce, the mortality rate ran considerably higher than in previous years.[14] Estimates of the total damage were calculated at first at $20 million and later raised. Even today, the San Ciriaco hurricane is the yardstick by which Puerto Ricans measure any storm's impact or destructive potential.[15]

When the storm struck in early August, the island had been under American control for almost exactly a year. Under General George W. Davis, the military governor (May 9, 1899–May 1, 1900), Puerto Rico had already been divided into military districts, and a very energetic program of cataloguing the island's human and economic resources was under way.[16] Davis used the existing military structure for information gathering to report on damage and losses all over the island. In addition, he turned for help and information to the infrastructure of municipal government and local charity boards that the Spanish had developed on the island. An efficient administrator, Davis introduced trial by jury and extended *habeas corpus* in Puerto Rico. He was more sensitive to cultural differences than his short-term predecessors, who had banned cockfighting, altered laws on divorce, and tampered with church-state relations. He was a man with a number of elitist prejudices to be sure, but he was willing to deal with local leaders, and was sensitive to the island's politics; and Davis himself was, like most of the population, a Roman Catholic.[17] In San Juan, he set up a Board of Charities, headed by Major John Hoff and staffed by U.S. military doctors and clergy, but then had local relief committees appointed in each town.[18] In addition, he created an advisory board on insular policies with nine Puerto Rican civilian members to make recommendations on hurricane relief.[19]

Damage reports from the military were arriving within a week of the storm, with estimates of 250,000 people without food or housing; and within three months municipal reports from the entire island were arriving in San Juan with particulars on losses.[20] With considerable variability in detail and care, each municipality had gathered estimates and claims. Total property losses were estimated at just under 36 million pesos, of which over half were suffered by coffee agriculture. Sugar sector losses were only about 3.2 million pesos, and urban property damage was calculated at $7,345,000 or over 21.6 million pesos.[21] Utuado, in the heart of the coffee region, was the municipality hit the hardest, and Ponce followed a distant second. The *Boletin Mercantil* in a special edition reported: "There only remains of this Antillean isle, once so celebrated for its beauty and fecundity, heaps of rubble spread everywhere, which represent a history full of tears, death, and misfortune for its inhabitants."[22]

For the next decade, Puerto Rican authors used the images of debris and destruction, of hunger, migration, and the abandonment of traditional homes, to write about their country. In their novels, Puerto Rican authors used the San Ciriaco hurricane to describe the social dislocation in the countryside, where, in the words of Ramón Juliá Marín, "hunger had established its empire," as a context for addressing the inequalities and suffering of the island's population.[23] In some ways, the impact and disruption of the San Ciriaco hurricane was greater than that of the war and American occupation of the island, and it marked the consciousness of all those who lived through it.[24]

The sixty-nine municipal governments on the island, in existence since the sixteenth century, were really the only civilian institutions that could be mobilized to meet the disaster. They had been reformed in 1870 by the Spanish government, but U.S. officials complained of their venality and incompetence, and worst of all, most were virtually bankrupt. Moreover, the municipal elections that were held throughout the island beginning in July 1899 were often accompanied by violence as scores were settled, with supporters of the old regime and members of the Liberal and Republican parties struggled for control. Despite all this, the municipal councils represented dominant local interests and they did their best to benefit those interests in the wake of the crisis. The town council of Ponce mobilized the support of other towns to make a general request to General Davis for a bond issue of 25–30 million pesos to finance rebuilding, and also sought a loosening of trade restriction with the United States as well as a moratorium on state and municipal taxes for the last two years. The council of Mayagüez made a similar proposal, and within a month many towns had joined in the effort. A month after the storm, some 58 petitions for tax relief had been submitted by mayors, town councils, and interested private citizens.[25]

The question of how best to provide tax relief soon developed. Some advocates felt that tax relief should be extended to all, since it was very difficult to document the value of individual property losses; further, wealthy individuals and the big coffee planters were more likely to meet the requirements, while less wealthy but deserving petitioners would be discouraged from applying. Others believed that only those personally harmed should receive such relief, and that no encouragement of idleness should be promoted by a general policy extended to all. In that school was Caetano Coll y Toste, the civil secretary and Davis's principal Puerto Rican advisor. The coffee planters particularly objected to his hardline intransigence on relief and compensation, and one editorial satirically pointed out that the day of San Caetano, his patron saint, was August 7 and the hurricane had appeared on August 8, the day of San Ciriaco, suggesting that Puerto Rico had suffered calamities back to back.[26]

Despite the hardline position of Coll y Toste, Davis's advisory board felt that with 25,000 farms and almost 35,000 homes and urban properties, proof of loss was too difficult to gather. Davis followed their advice and granted remission of taxes in his General Order 138. It took years for areas like Mayagüez, where coffee planters had been hit particularly hard hit, to pay off their tax debt.[27] In addition, the board encouraged the rebuilding of roads and bridges, an activity that was sorely needed and welcomed by local interests; the military government encouraged these efforts, since the performance of useful "honest labor" was an acceptable way to distribute relief to the indigent inhabitants of the island.

DISASTER AS THEATER

Both General Davis in San Juan and President McKinley in Washington understood that the disaster was an opportunity to demonstrate to the Puerto Ricans the efficiency and charity of the new government. Faced with complete destitution, the *New York Times* reported, "unless immediate and effective relief is given, these unfortunate people will perish of famine." A presidential appeal went out to the "humanity and patriotism" of the American people, noting that: "the inhabitants of Puerto Rico have freely and gladly submitted themselves to the guardianship of the United States and have voluntarily surrendered the protection of Spain, confidently relying upon the more generous and beneficent treatment at our hands. The highest considerations of honor and good faith unite with the promptings of humanity to require from the United States a generous response to the demand of Puerto Rican distress."[28]

Davis had provided army rations to the destitute and homeless almost immediately, and continued to do so. There was no congressional appropriation for relief. Washington sent relief supplies totaling only about $200,000, but it also began to coordinate an enormous program of private donations, calling on the mayors of all cities over 150,000 population to organize this effort.[29] The New York relief committee created by the State Merchants Association was chosen as the central collection agency for the nation. Its chairman, Governor Theodore Roosevelt, understood quite clearly the political advantages that generosity at this moment could produce when he wrote: "I appeal to all patriotic citizens to show the suffering people of our new possessions that the extension of our flag over their

territory is to be of immediate material as well as moral benefit to them."[30]
American politicians and military leaders had used this theme, the bless-
ings of enlightened civilization, from the beginning of the war with Spain,
and in fact, in the Indian campaigns through the three preceding decades.
It filled the correspondence of General Davis, Governor Roosevelt, Secretary of State Elihu Root, and the Bureau of Insular Affairs that adminis-
tered Cuba, Puerto Rico, and the Philippines.[31] The charitable efforts were
sincere; humble people from all over the Unites States donated money,
food, and supplies, as did companies, institutions, and voluntary organizations. General Davis himself donated part of his salary. But the political
ramifications were never forgotten in this period when the sovereignty
and political future of the possessions remained still undecided. For
months, the *New York Times* ran columns on the Puerto Rican disaster with
long lists of the contributors and their donations in money or goods. These
columns often appeared next to articles describing bloody U.S. military
operations against the Philippine insurgents, thus giving American readers an opportunity to see a benign and humanitarian face of U.S. expan-
sionism rather than only one of suppression.[32]

Complicating the political utility and theatrics of relief was a profound
cultural and racial distrust of the newly acquired peoples.[33] Puerto Rico
had a population in 1898 of about 960,000, of which over 400,000 were
considered indigent. Davis and many of his subaltern officers believed the
Puerto Rican poor to be lazy, ignorant, and uninterested in their political
future or welfare. The causes of these characteristics were variously ascribed to Spanish misrule, Catholic superstitions, poor diet, or the defects
of racial interbreeding, and had been so defined in the writings of travelers and observers since the eighteenth century. The Puerto Rican *jíbaro* or
peasant acquired a reputation among some native intellectuals and foreign observers as vagrant, lazy, and violent, with a taste for drinking and
cockfighting, but in the early nineteenth century the *jíbaro* image had also
been adopted as a true and positive expression of the island's essence and
independent character by Liberals and those who hoped for independence. Thus discussions in the writings of Spanish and Puerto Rican authors about the peasantry's character in Puerto Rico by the time of the

American occupation were often carefully ambivalent, praising the rustic simplicity of "the good country folk," but warning that they were easily led astray into indolence and bad habits.[34] Later, in the twentieth century, Puerto Rican elites would elaborate the positive *jíbaro* myth even further and transform the peasant into the quintessential islander. Many U.S. military and private observers, however, had little sympathy for the rural peasantry and would have agreed with Davis that "a more discouraging outlook for a people who are classed as civilized it would be difficult to conceive."[35] Major John Van Hoff, Davis's appointee as president of the Charity Board and the director of the relief effort, fully shared these opinions and saw the U.S. mission as a version of the "white man's burden." He wrote to Davis, "we will keep them alive; we will lead them slowly, gently toward the light, and finally in half a hundred years they will catch the first glimmering ray which will show them what our standards are and what we wish theirs to be." Such attitudes of "tutelary colonialism" perfectly fitted into the predominant social assistance philosophy of the period.[36] There was a general fear, expressed by both military and civilian authorities and widely held throughout society, that free distribution of food or clothing to the indigent would create a dependency among the indigent poor that would turn them into beggars, and since the Puerto Ricans were "a people whose every tendency is in that direction," it was a danger to be avoided at all costs. Public assistance, no matter what its cause, bore a stigma, and the only way for recipients to lessen its mark was to work. The motto of the Charity Board was, "No one shall die of starvation and no able-bodied man shall eat the bread of idleness." This fixation pervaded the correspondence of the Charity Board and the statements of General Davis and his staff.

The problem that Davis and the board faced, however, was that except for road building, the government could offer little work, and private capital for reconstruction or development was virtually nonexistent. The challenge for Davis and his advisors was to transform hurricane relief into a project of economic stimulus, and thereby satisfy the objectives of economic recovery and development while using the occasion of the storm to demonstrate the advantages of Puerto Rico's new relationship with the

United States. But those objectives were complicated by attitudes and prejudices of both the American officials in Puerto Rico and those in Washington. Ideologies of racial defects, colonialism, and class came together in the creation of disaster relief policy. Lest we think that these attitudes were held exclusively by the island's new overlords, it must be noted that the Puerto Rican planters and urban elites also shared them.[37] The planters self-interestedly argued that direct aid was counterproductive not only because it was collected by vagrants and those who were not so needy, but also because people who had enough to eat would not present themselves to work in the coffee harvest. As discussed above in chapter 5, under the previous Spanish colonial regime from 1849 to 1873 such thinking had led to coercive legislation that forced the free-holding peasantry and rural laborers into plantation work arrangements, the infamous *libreta* system that required all males over sixteen years old to present themselves for employment. This deep distrust of the laboring classes, now combined with the desire to morally uplift and to "Americanize" the Puerto Ricans, was undergirded by a dominant philosophy of relief on both sides of the Atlantic that held that the poor would become idle paupers unless properly motivated and controlled. This philosophy led to relief policies that in post–San Ciriaco Puerto Rico played directly to the interests of the dominant agricultural and commercial interests on the island.

Whatever the political benefit from an effective and generous relief effort, pressures mounted to make the war and the new colony profitable, but due to the hurricane's impact on agriculture, that objective was difficult to achieve. In Puerto Rico before San Ciriaco about 120,000 acres were under coffee cultivation. The coffee economy had boomed in the 1880s and by 1890 Puerto Rico had become the world's fourth largest exporter, but by the late 1890s some observers were concerned about the effects of an overemphasis on one crop and the dependency of Puerto Rico's economy on foreign markets for this one crop. The hurricane had arrived just as the harvest of 1899 began, stripping berries from the branches, felling the coffee trees, and uprooting the protective shade trees. Exports in 1899 fell to only 10 percent of the previous five-year average, and General Davis estimated that San Ciriaco caused the loss of $12 million in coffee revenue, to say nothing of loss in capital stock. Although by 1902 there was some recovery, the planter situation was bleak: no crop to export, no money to rebuild, the markets disrupted.[38] Owners of small and medium-size coffee estates were particularly affected. New coffee trees would need four to five years before they would be fully productive, and the large shade trees felled by the hurricane would take even longer to replace. Meanwhile, these planters would have no capital for rebuilding and replanting, and those who labored for them would be unemployed and hungry. General Davis believed the only hope for the industry was to concentrate the coffee estates in fewer hands and to mechanize production. Displaced workers would have to migrate. He said, "life will be horrible, it is true, but such are the conditions to be expected everywhere in the tropics where the population is dense."[39]

Puerto Rico had about 60,000 acres in sugar cultivation, or about half the amount in coffee, when the San Ciriaco hurricane struck the island. The concentration of land in fewer but better financed hands had already taken place in the sugar economy. Two-thirds of the 1899 sugar crop was lost to the storm, but in this case the deluge had reinvigorated the fields, and sugarcane quickly recovered. The damaged mills were mostly old-fashioned, and were now replaced by larger steam-driven central units. By 1900, there were 22 *centrales* operating in Puerto Rico, and sugar had become the new investment crop. Overall, the sugar economy on the coasts recovered much faster than coffee in the highlands, so the government relief effort ended there more quickly and fewer grants were made to sugar planters. What the sugar planters needed was capital, not labor.[40] "American capital for the regeneration of these sugar mills," said Eben Swift, a district officer in Humacao, "would do more good than a fleet of transport ships loaded with food." That capital eventually came from investors and banks in the United States, who by 1930 had invested over $120 million in the expanding sugar economy.

In the minds of the U.S. administrators on the island, the issue of Puerto Rico's economic health could not be separated from the immediate problem of providing relief, and that concern in turn depended on their vision of the Puerto Ricans as a people. Swift had, in fact, very little sympathy for the laboring population, and believed that only widows, children, the elderly, and the infirm should be fed. As for the rest, "the whole barefoot population is indigent—that is, they are idle, shiftless, without ambition, and will not work except under the prospect of starvation. This does not mean that they ought to be fed."[41] Curiously, one of the only signs of public disorder had been some petty stealing caused, said a quartermaster, by the "false idea that pervaded the country that the relief supplies were for the people and could be taken by whoever was able to get them." Clearly, the people had misunderstood the meaning of relief.[42]

General Davis saw the future of the island and the hope for its recovery in the agricultural sector. He was in general supportive of tax relief, loans, and other benefits, but at the same time he faced the need to provide food, housing, and clothing to the indigent, most of whom were rural laborers, and many of who would be displaced by the recovery. How to resolve these competing needs? At first the Charity Board tried to introduce the use of work cards that each laborer would be required to have a planter sign, but this proved too cumbersome. It was replaced by a system in which the ration of one pound of food a day per family member was supplied to the planters; workers would have to be under contract to them to receive any aid. The Charity Board realized that worker treatment by the planters would be less than tender, but they welcomed the requests for workers from the planters as the best system possible, and one in which the planters would provide control and reaffirm the principle of "no work, no relief." Within a year, planters had made 12,000 applications for relief, and over 32 million pounds of food had been distributed to 117,000 people in rural areas. The Charity Board had met its objectives, which had never been purely humanitarian. It had improved farms, employed laborers, fed thousands, and had, in Van Hoff's opinion, taught the Puerto Ricans the value of honest labor. Moreover, it had addressed the planter concern that the 35 to 50 cents a day paid to coffee workers was too high and made Puerto Rico uncompetitive with Brazil and Central America. With the traditional links of patronage and dependency severely damaged by the post-storm conditions, the planters were fearful that post-hurricane relief would make the workers less willing to work for the old wages and drive up labor costs.[43] Davis put their minds at ease when he told his advisory board, and by extension the planters, that "The aid given by the people of the United States will be so applied as not to make paupers of the peaceful and worthy inhabitants of this Island nor to disturb the industrial and commercial business of communities."[44]

REACTION AND PERCEPTION IN PUERTO RICO

The administrative and humanitarian challenges for the United States were difficult, but far less so than for the island's inhabitants. The journalist José Elías Levis wrote in his novel *Estercolero* that after the hurricane of August 8 "misery had become desperation," and that "now the people wept for its past and its present."[45] The last decades of Spanish rule had seen an increase in the landless population and a worsening in public health, resulting in higher mortality rates. Landless workers migrated into the cities, or left for Cuba and the Dominican Republic. Rural unrest by underemployed or exploited laborers in the countryside was matched by strikes of a labor movement in the cities. All of this had been exacerbated by the war and its aftermath during which a guerilla campaign had been carried out against those who remained loyal to Spain, and sometimes by rural workers against planters as relations of dependency broke down. After Spain's sale of Puerto Rico in December 1898 as part of the negotiations ending the war, the U.S. military moved to suppress the violence.

All this served as a complex background for a reaction to the storm, which now created a new set of circumstances. Despite the destitution of a quarter of the island's population and the breakdown of municipal control in many areas, there was virtually no looting after the storm, and even the retributions against pro-Spanish individuals came to an end. To some extent the military occupation and the government's efforts to enforce control over the subject population had imposed order. As relief supplies and rebuilding efforts began, some workers sought to demand better wages or complained about the volunteers who were being mobilized to unload ships, but Davis refused to negotiate over wages and, in fact, ordered food withheld from workers and their families if they refused to accept his terms. With so many rural laborers unemployed, workers in general had little leverage in negotiations and were squeezed by rising food and housing costs and by the government's desire to hold wages down. Labor actions and strikes diminished following the storm, which seemed like one more unwanted tragedy heaped on the previous miseries of the island.

For much of the population survival was the immediate concern. Puerto Rico was already a food importer before the storm. Only about 100,000 acres or about a third of the land cultivated was devoted to foodstuffs, the rest used mostly for sugar, tobacco, and coffee. The hurricane made a bad situation impossible and had the potential to turn a calamity into catastrophe. Davis acted quickly, distributing rations and ordering the planting of "products of rapid harvest," but even so, hunger was a real problem; large numbers of rural workers faced with starvation and the loss of homes had little hope. Thousands moved to the towns and cities, occupying plazas and street corners, seeking shelter and food. Malnutrition, exposure, and poor sanitation caused chronic illnesses to worsen and hospital facilities were overwhelmed. Some people simply chose to leave, emigrating elsewhere in the Caribbean, or contracted to build a railway in Ecuador, or signed up to work the new sugar fields in Hawaii, transported under miserable conditions "to die of sadness in faraway countries after watering with tears" their lands of exile.[46]

During the storm, those affected had turned to their traditional protections and beliefs for comfort and explanation. After the storm had passed, observers sought to explain the disaster in more political terms, finding connections between the storm and the political and cultural transformations of the time. In Havana, the nationalist *Diario de la Marina* looked at its sister island and noted that Puerto Rico's former prosperity had been disturbed by "radical and sudden modifications in the local customs," and that the island now had lost even the autonomy that it had enjoyed under Spain. The *Diario* drew a providential lesson: the cyclone "is the just wrath of God toward the American occupation."[47] Not surprisingly, Don Juan Perpiña y Pibernat, dean of the diocese of Puerto Rico and a supporter of Spain, who was exercising episcopal authority in the absence of a bishop, read a different message in the hurricane. In his description of it, he wrote that anyone not blinded by atheism, materialism, or naturalism could see that this storm was God's punishment for the island's sins, which included secularism and adulation of the Americans by Spain's "ungrateful and denaturalized sons," who, after receiving language, religion, good customs, and wise laws, had abandoned the motherland. Don Juan admitted that there had been plenty of sins prior to the war, but the worst had taken place since the arrival of the Americans and the change of nationality. Chastisement for some was opportunity for others: the newly arrived Protestants on the island saw the change of sovereignty as confirmation of their superiority and used the opportunity to provide social assistance to gain adherents and fulfill their mission. Seen from afar, there were other interpretative uses to be made of the storm. The Jamaican press used the promptness of the American relief efforts in Puerto Rico to criticize the tardy nature of the British response to West Indian calamities.

The Jamaican observation was not without merit. For various reasons, the overall relief effort had been impressive, and Davis and Congress could point to it as a demonstration of American efficacy and humanitarianism. The fact of military occupation and the bureaucratic infrastructure it provided was certainly responsible to some extent, and sometimes in surprising ways. One was an important medical breakthrough; the treatment and control of hookworm, facilitated by the hurricane. Major Bailey K. Ashford had arrived in 1898 as an army physician with the Eleventh Infantry and was soon treating an outbreak of typhus among the troops in a hospital in Ponce. During the San Ciriaco hurricane, Ashford took a leading role in providing medical assistance to victims of the storm, many of whom were brought into tent housing managed by the military government in Ponce. It was during that period that Ashford observed that almost three-quarters of his 4,500 patients suffered from anemia, and had hemoglobin counts of less than fifty percent. This was a condition usually ascribed to dietary deficiencies of a peasantry that lived on plantains, rice, beans, and root crops. But dietary changes produced no improvement. Ashford, after further research, discovered an almost universal presence of hookworm parasites (*Ancylostoma duodenale*) in his mostly barefoot patients. He brought his finding to the attention of his superiors, and with Puerto Rican physicians began an extensive campaign of treatment.[48] He eventually married a Puerto Rican woman and settled in Puerto Rico. In his biography, he later wrote that the fabled lethargy of the island's *jíbaros*, the "laziness" that observers had commented upon for a century, had, in fact, a treatable medical cause. San Ciriaco and the political structure of the island at that time had created the conditions for Ashford's diagnosis. The eradication of hookworm, like the parallel U.S. program against yellow fever in Cuba, undoubtedly served American commercial and economic goals, and particularly helped to improve the supply of healthy laborers, besides lowering the mortality rate. Its success, and the personal popularity of Ashford on the island, like the relief effort in general, also served to demonstrate the advantages of the change in sovereignty.[49]

As the disruption of the storm began to diminish and the reality of the new political system became increasingly apparent, opinion about the relief effort, the objectives of the American government, and Puerto Rico's relationship with the United States became more negative. During the recovery from the storm, Congress had returned to Puerto Rico two million dollars in tax revenues, the amount the United States had collected from the tariffs it had levied against goods imported from Puerto Rico since the occupation. The advisory board and Coll y Toste thought that money was best used to repair buildings, but the planters and merchants argued that since it was commerce in agricultural goods that had generated these funds, they should be reinvested in agriculture, which would also put many people back to work. What the planters wanted was the creation of agricultural banks or municipal funds where they could seek capital. Two million dollars, in any case, was far below their needs, and the planters saw the return of this amount not as an act of magnanimous charity, but simply as justice, returning to Puerto Rico what never should have been taken in the first place.[50]

By May 1900, Puerto Rico was no longer under military government and General Davis had been replaced by Charles Allen, the first U.S. civilian governor. The temporary quiescence of the labor movement had ended, and now there were a number of small actions and strikes for higher wages. Dockworkers, bakers, masons, carpenters, and printers had all organized and were increasingly vocal in their demands. In 1906 a major strike erupted among sugarcane cutters. Opponents to these demands ascribed the workers' new belligerence to the leadership of "socialist" organizers like Santiago Iglesias Pantín, or to the fact that investment of American capital on the island had stimulated worker cupidity. Employers reacted by threatening to import West Indians or workers from St. Thomas, and they complained that if there was really so much misery and unemployment on the island, workers should be satisfied with the traditional wages. But by 1900 the moment of worker resignation had passed.

Some critics of the relief effort linked it to these subsequent problems. Eugenio Astol, writing in a San Juan newspaper under the pseudonym Glouster, expressed traditional planter attitudes toward rural workers by claiming that relief had made them vagrants and had lowered the morality of "our honored rural people."[51] Political criticisms also appeared in the press claiming that the funds had been awarded according to party affiliation, and that the Charity Board had been a "complete disaster." From the side of the rural workers, a different kind of criticism arose. The provision of food by planters as compensation for labor, as Davis and the Relief Board had insisted upon, had mostly benefited the planters.[52] The handful of rice and beans or piece of codfish was not equivalent to the value of the labor being performed. The newspaper *La Nueva Bandeira* of Mayagüez asked ironically about the program: "What charity, Oh God, what charity?"[53] The rural workers sang their own comments on the Americans and the storm.[54]

> The American said that he came to save us;
> but it seems that what he said was in vain.
> Although he sends red beans and crackers for the hurricane,
> those who give it out keep the best for themselves,
> and that's why we have to leave.[55]

The occupation and the hurricane had combined to create a singular set of circumstances with long-term political and economic implications. Measures taken by the United States in order to support the planter class after the war, such as the suspension of foreclosures on rural properties, had produced the unexpected consequence of freezing the rural credit market. After San Ciriaco, when capital was sorely needed for rebuilding it was in short supply. Davis had sought to help the coffee planters after the storm, but in some ways, the hurricane's destruction of coffee agriculture reinforced the American interest in, and demand for, Puerto Rican sugar. The hurricane had given the United States an opportunity to demonstrate efficiency and benevolence in a time of crisis. It did this by reinforcing the planter control of rural labor, although it also restructured the nature of that control by strengthening the hold of large planters and pursuing commercial policies more favorable to sugar producers. Those planters in need were thankful for government assistance, at least at first, but within a year criticism of the relief system and of its manipulation by the government for political purposes had emerged as Puerto Ricans perceived the political strategies and social philosophies that motivated it.

In January 1900, Congress carried out hearings on the future status of Puerto Rico. The shadow of San Ciriaco shaded the discussions. The first witness called was General Davis, who in his testimony stated: "It is doubtful if any land or district populated by nearly a million souls has, in modern times, been so devastated or overwhelmed as was Puerto Rico in one day of August last."[56] Other witnesses continued to bring the conditions created by the storm into the discussion of what political arrangement was best for the relationship of the island to the United States. Some argued for the extension of free trade and other economic measures, given the conditions on the island caused by the hurricane and the war. Major Ames, arguing for the establishment of an agricultural bank, told the committee that Puerto Rico needed nothing from the United States, and that its condition as a pauper was due only to the war and the hurricane. Given an opportunity, it would support itself. In opposition, those against granting open trade or other benefits to the island's products mixed political, cultural, and economic arguments. One opponent dismissed the descriptions of the hurricane's "horrors," pointing out the island had suffered from storms under Spain as well, and that American farmers were also in danger of similar disasters. He warned, "The Latin race, after years of the rule of despotism, suddenly given too much power, is a troublesome if not a dangerous factor with which to deal. The extension of too much sympathy can readily be lost."[57] Herbert Myrick, representative of beet sugar interests in the United States, argued that the United States should help Puerto Rico after the hurricane, but should not violate its principles of government in doing so by allowing importation without taxation.[58] Another trade protectionist pointed out that the war in the Philippines was still being fought and the humanitarianism shown to Puerto Rico would ultimately produce costs to be borne by American taxpayers in another colony.

The Organic Act of April 1900, known as the Foraker Act, established the political and commercial relations between the United States and its new dependency Puerto Rico, and created the form of civilian government that would function on the island under a presidentially appointed governor. This law reflected the prejudices and ambitions of various interests in the United States and Puerto Rico. The island became "an unincorporated territory" of the United States, and certain rights were recognized; but citizenship was not granted to the inhabitants, and the island had less political autonomy than it did in its final days under Spain. Conditions had been created for the expansion of the island's sugar economy with American capital. Puerto Rico's incorporation into the U.S. tariff and financial structure had protected the interests of sugar and tobacco growers in the United States, but negatively altered the island's relationship to its other markets. San Ciriaco did not determine the decision to place Puerto Rico in a dependent status, but it had created a context that made that decision easier.

The United States was now facing, for the first time, the problems of being a colonial power, and those in Washington debated how the federal government should respond to the effects of bad weather on a new, if distant, tropical possession. Who was liable for damages from natural catastrophes? What branches of government or institutions should assume responsibility if any for the relief, and what were the implications of action or inaction? Just four months after the passage of the Foraker Act, the United States would have to confront a disaster of comparative scale on its own shores, the single most destructive natural event in the nation's history: the deadly Galveston hurricane and flood of September 8, 1900.

WASN'T THAT A MIGHTY STORM? GALVESTON, 1900

The hurricane that struck Galveston, Texas, on September 8, 1900 has long been considered the single most deadly natural calamity in the history of the United States.[59] The identified dead numbered 4,263, but general esti-mates for loss of life from the storm and subsequent flooding are usually placed at 6,000 for the city, and perhaps 10–12,000 if the rest of the island on which the city was located and the nearby mainland are included.

The Gulf Coast had a long experience with tropical storms and hurri-canes, and Galveston itself had been battered by eleven hurricanes during the nineteenth century. Three storms in 1871 had done considerable dam-age. In 1875 another storm struck the city as well as Indianola, Galveston's Gulf Coast rival located 150 miles south. Damage to Indianola was enough that many people sought to relocate the town, but opposition from the Morgan Steamship Company prevented the move. Then in August 1886 the most violent hurricane ever to strike the United States, with winds over 150 miles per hour and a sea surge of 15 feet, destroyed Indianola, and the site was abandoned.

Galveston, on the other hand, although the city was located on a sandy, flat island with an elevation no higher than eight feet above sea level, had weathered that 1886 storm well. The city's location at the mouth of seventeen-mile-wide Galveston Bay made it the best natural port between New Orleans and Veracruz, Mexico. That fact made Galveston's locational risks seem worthwhile, and there was a certain trusting confidence that the city had some natural protection, although since the 1850s there had been warnings from mariners and engineers about the low-lying city's vulnerability to storm damage.

Positioned on a sandy island twenty-seven miles long and, at its wid-est, three miles wide, Galveston lay about two miles from the marshy coast where today four major wildlife refuges are located. Sandbars and shallow water surrounded the island, thus leading some of its residents to deem it a "cove of safety" protected from the potential dangers of hurri-cane winds and storm-driven water from the Gulf.[60] Suggestions to build a seawall to protect the city from the open sea had been debated by the city council and rejected. In fact, Isaac Cline, the head of the U.S. Weather Bu-reau in Galveston and a locally respected, highly trained, and skilled pro-fessional, was a firm believer that the island was relatively protected by the shallow waters and that a seawall was unnecessary, underscoring this belief in an article published in 1891. His confidence, as well as his statements that usual Caribbean hurricanes would be pulled north before reaching the Gulf Coast, created a false sense of security on the island. We know now that his belief about the protection from the sea offered by the shallow water misunderstood the difference between wind-driven waves that would be diminished by the shallow depth and a storm surge that would not. A storm surge is essentially a great dome of water some fifty miles in extent that is pulled ashore where the eye of a tropical storm crosses land. The height of the surge is inversely proportional to the depth of the seabed, thus the shallow waters off Galveston actually increased the city's vulnerability.[61]

Galveston had become a port when Mexico gained its independence from Spain, and it was incorporated into the short-lived Republic of Texas in 1839. Because of its location on the Gulf of Mexico, it became a major port for the export of cotton and an important terminal in the slave trade. During the Civil War the port was the scene of a major battle because of its importance to the Confederacy. After the war it flourished as a commercial center. It had a religiously and racially diverse population that included of Mexicans, European immigrants, and African Americans. By 1900 Galveston was a wealthy city, with a population of 37,000 and a privileged position as the best American port on the Gulf.

The story of the Galveston hurricane has been told in many forms— popular accounts, academic studies, oral testimony, a folksong-spiritual, novels, plays, autobiographies, and documentary films. There is no need to recount all the details here, but the issues of the tracking of the storm and the politics of prediction, the role of various levels of government in response, and the impact of social divisions on the relief effort all merit comment.

The storm first came to notice on August 27 as a tropical depression east of the Windwards. It entered the Caribbean and passed over Antigua as a tropical depression and then crossed over the Dominican Republic and southwestern Cuba on September 5 and passed to the west of Key West. Disastrously, the U.S. Weather Bureau, now with observation stations in the Caribbean and anxious to demonstrate its capacities, predicted that the storm would continue to move northward, and issued warnings for the southern Atlantic seaboard. By this time, the storm had probably gained hurricane force, with winds just over 73 miles per hour. Over the heated waters of the Gulf, it grew in size and intensity, and a ship caught in the storm in the Gulf reported on September 7 that winds had reached 100 miles per hour. The storm, blocked by high pressure over the southeastern United States, was, in fact, not moving north but west, as some Cuban meteorologists had warned. It swept over the Texas coast. At Galveston wind gusts reached 120 miles per hour, and some reports even suggest stronger gusts. During the storm passage over the city the barometer fell to 27.64. The fifteen-foot storm surge on September 8 was greater than any that Galveston had been experienced in previous hurricanes, and the city was completely unprepared. Flooding was general. Once it had battered Galveston and crossed the Texas mainland, the storm passed over Oklahoma and Kansas, continuing north and then curving east over the Great Lakes, where it still maintained winds of up to 50 miles per hour. It finally disappeared off the coast of Newfoundland.

The storm damage on Galveston Island was horrendous: the four bridges to the mainland were swept away, about a third of all buildings were destroyed, and the flooding from the surge killed thousands in a twenty-four-hour period. Damage in the Galveston area was estimated at the time at $40 million, which adjusted to 2014 values would be over $2 billion, making the Galveston storm one of the most costly in the history of the United States.[62]

The loss of life was horrific and very rapid, with most of the mortality due to drowning. Railroad barges were used to haul away the corpses. When burials at sea resulted in bodies washing ashore, ghastly funeral pyres were made to dispose of the remains.[63] They continued to burn for three months. Survivors and members of the burial detail (see fig. 6.2) would remember the debris, the mud and slime after the storm, and the piles of burning bodies for the rest of their lives.[64]

After the storm had passed over Galveston, the survivors and the nation's press raised the question of responsibility. Galveston had resident meteorologists. Isaac Cline had been there heading the Weather Bureau since 1889, and his younger brother Joseph, also a meteorologist, had joined him a few years later. Isaac had noticed the heavy rains that preceded the storm, a drop in barometric pressure, and the rising of the sea

FIGURE 6.2 A Galveston burial detail (Courtesy of Library of Congress Photographic Collection)

despite contrary winds. Tragically, he had been wrong in his professional evaluation of the city's vulnerability, and he paid a high price when his wife and unborn child died in the storm. He later claimed that as the storm struck he had ridden along the shoreline to give warnings to the residents, but his statements about that effort were never confirmed, and so a shadow of guilt hung over him. But there were other men higher in the Weather Bureau administration who had also been wrong about this storm, and they also now came under public scrutiny.

In 1900, Cuba was under U.S. military occupation following the Spanish-American War. The U.S. Weather Bureau had been developing a chain of observation posts through the 1890s, and by 1900 it had posts in much of the Caribbean. Although the sharing of weather information was part of an international and global program, there were still jealousies, personal ambitions, and competitive pettiness involved in the dissemination of weather information. The U.S. Weather Bureau had recently gone through a financial crisis and was sensitive about criticism of its training and methods. Under its director, Willis Moore, it had demanded more or less exclusive control of weather advisories in the United States. The Havana weather station was in 1900 under the control of William Stockman, an official with close ties to the military who shared some of the tutelary colonialist attitudes and negative opinions of the inhabitants of the islands, as did the other officers of the occupation forces in Puerto Rico, Cuba, and the Philippines.[65] Those attitudes clearly affected his willingness to listen to the opinions of the Cuban hurricane watchers.

By this date, Cuban meteorology was well developed, and the scientific heirs of Andrés Poëy and Padre Vines were certainly as proficient in prediction as the U.S. Weather Bureau. The Observatory of Belén had tracked the storm and wanted to issue warnings for the Gulf Coast, but Moore and Stockman had moved to keep "alarmists" and "cranks" from unduly affecting commerce or causing panic. They felt that the Cubans were too emotional and interpretative, and not wedded closely enough to mathematical readings: their reports could not be trusted. Fearing the competition of Belén, the Weather Bureau banned the telegraph messages on weather prediction coming from Havana. Cubans were predictably outraged, and the Weather Bureau was unprepared for the virulence of their complaint, but the ban held.

To what extent this attempt to monopolize the technology of information and to insist on the exclusive authority of government in the disaster was the cause of the disaster remains in debate, but even after the hurricane struck Galveston, the representative of the Weather Bureau in Havana still refused to believe that the Cubans had correctly warned of the track of the storm. In the aftermath of the hurricane and the Weather Bureau's considerable embarrassment, there was a cover-up in Washington at the Weather Bureau that sought to discredit the Cubans. As Raymond Arsenault has observed, this failure of the Weather Bureau to work cooperatively with its Cuban counterparts "had profound consequences, inhibiting scientific advancement and threatening public safety for at least a generation."[66]

In Galveston itself survival, security, and recovery were the immediate concerns. There were 20,000 to 30,000 people in need and over 10,000 homeless and hungry. Water and food were in short supply, and disease was an immediate threat. Moreover, there was fear of crime. Survivors armed themselves against possible looters with firearms, kitchen knives, and whatever they could find. Lloyd Fayling, a man with some experience in suppressing the Chicago Pullman strike and service in the Spanish-American War, organized a city militia or vigilante group until martial law was declared and the Texas state militia took over and disarmed all citizens.[67]

A relief committee composed of leading citizens was immediately created in the town. It was all male and all white. As was typical of the period, people made donations and charitable funds were created all over the country, but the total of contributions in money and supplies did not even reach $1.25 million, far below the $40 million damage estimate at the time. Volunteers began to work with the relief subcommittees in each ward, but the task was overwhelming and complex. There were many accounts of terrible damage and death, including the demise of almost all the children and nuns of a Catholic orphanage and the loss of a train swept into the bay from a trestle bridge. There were also tales of heroic actions and selfless social service. Singled out in the latter regard were Father James Kirwin, a Catholic priest who served on the Relief Committee, directed burial and burning of the dead, and drew up the martial law order, and his friend Rabbi Henry Cohen, also on the Relief Committee, who gave special attention to the hospitals, and whose undamaged B'nai Israel temple was made available to four Protestant congregations for services after the storm.[68] These tales of courage and selfless sacrifice and cooperation were the stories residents told to each other as part of the necessary response of community rebuilding.

The disaster was a challenge to national and state government. Since all communications had been cut, Washington acted slowly, and while Congress did not appropriate money for the relief, the federal government did eventually send a military contingent to provide a large number of campaign tents to shelter the thousands of homeless. Puerto Rico after San Ciriaco was occupied by the U.S. military and directly under the Department of War, and a major relief effort there served a national political objective. But Congress did not assume direct responsibility for the relief of Galveston. To some extent the constitutional taxing and spending clause had long been defined in a narrow "Madisonian" fashion, and aid in response to calamities had been left to the individual states or to private charities.[69] But that policy was not a rule, and Congress had historically granted relief or provided financial aid when it seemed to be for "the general welfare." In that way, it granted assistance for a variety of "disasters;" at first to individuals, and, after 1794, to collectives or classes of people, for losses suffered from fire or flood, pirate depredations, the War of 1812, or Indian attacks. Between 1860 and 1930 there were ninety such relief bills, some, like the bill establishing the post–Civil War Freedmen's Bureau, involving large expenditures. [70] Such actions had usually raised bitter debates about the role that "contributing negligence" or "moral innocence" of the claimants should play in congressional action. Congress remained wary of setting precedents, and denials of claims were usually justified by the desire to avoid them, rather than by specific constitutional objections.[71]

One reason Congress did not assume a more direct role in the case of the Galveston disaster was that in 1900 the U.S. federal government was able to turn directly to an institution to coordinate the relief efforts. The American Red Cross had been established in 1881 by Clara Barton after her contact with the Swiss-inspired International Red Cross in Europe. The Red Cross had acquired its first real hurricane relief experience in the very active U.S. hurricane seasons of the 1890s, especially in its 1893 efforts at relief in the South Carolina Sea Islands, where thousands of the mostly black, Gullah-speaking inhabitants had been killed and the precarious infrastructure of the region swept away. The humanitarian effort in that disaster had been tempered by the same social objectives and philosophy that were later apparent in the relief efforts following the San Ciriaco hurricane in Puerto Rico. Barton herself wrote that beside humanitarian aid to the indigent, the Red Cross objective was "to preserve them as well from habits of begging and pauperism; to teach them self-dependence, economy, and thrifts; how to provide for themselves and against future want, and help to fit them for the citizenship, which wisely or unwisely we have endowed them with."[72] An economic depression at the time and the fact that the victims were mostly African Americans had diminished Congress's desire to intervene directly. The relief effort thus had depended on large-scale private contributions, much of it raised in northern states, but the emphasis on helping the vulnerable and poor black population had been resented by white South Carolinians as unfair and punitive.[73] There was considerable competition among various humanitarian relief organizations, but in June 1900 Congress incorporated Barton's Red Cross and thus gave it a singular official standing, partly in recognition of the work done by Barton's Red Cross hospitals and orphanages in Cuba in 1898. Thus when the hurricane struck Galveston only a few months later, there was a government-sponsored institution ready to act. At age 78, Barton even went in person to visit the stricken area.[74]

The Red Cross worked with the local relief committees, bringing women into the administrative structures, to aid in fund raising and in distribution of goods. The usual mistrust of the poor and the notion that it was necessary to morally educate them through relief was very much complicated in Galveston by the issue of race, as it had been in after the 1893 Sea Islands storm. In Galveston, there were sensationalist and exaggerated reports in the press about scavenging, looting, and the desecration of bodies (see fig. 6.3a). Lurid descriptions of blacks cutting off of ears and fingers in a search for earrings, rings, and other valuables led to vigilante shootings. A 1902 account of disasters in general dedicated a chapter to Galveston filled with unsubstantiated stories of gangs of black "thugs," "ghouls," and "vampires" involved in these crimes, and of blacks from Houston and New Orleans hurrying to Galveston to join in the pillaging (fig. 6.3b).[75] Such reports, along with others that blacks refused to work or to cooperate in rescue efforts, demonstrated the depth of racial animosities. These attitudes led to the imposition of martial law and the deployment of the Texas militia to impose order. Black men were forced into cleanup crews to collect the rotting bodies at the point of a bayonet. Perhaps even worse were measures taken by the city's Relief Council to round up in an internment camp all women who were homeless or unemployed (mostly black women) and then release them only upon their acceptance of positions as maids and cooks. African Americans were accused in local and some of the national press of gaming the relief system and refusing to work; of childish, cowardly, or drunken behavior, a lack of initiative in rescue efforts, and an absence of community spirit in general.

The issue of race or of social disparity in situations of natural disaster was clearly underlined in the Galveston recovery. If providing for the "common good" was a responsibility of government, but was dependent

FIGURE 6.3 Popular images of the aftermath of the Galveston storm. (*top*) Shooting looters and vampires. (*bottom*) Survivors securing supplies. (From John Coulter, ed., *The Complete Story of the Galveston Horror*, Chicago: J.H. More, 1900; courtesy of the Beinecke Library, Yale University)

on the victims' situation resulting from an act of God and for which they bore no moral responsibility, then demonstrating that African Americans were morally corrupt and unconcerned for the "common good" was a way of diminishing or negating any claim they might have to share in relief. John Coulter's *Complete Story of the Galveston Horror* portrayed the criminality of blacks and Mexicans defiling bodies, but depicted the looting of stores by "starving survivors" as justifiable acts of necessity. He pointed out that as long as black women could get relief food for nothing, they would not work in white homes engaged in cleanup and rebuilding. The best solution was to limit their access to relief. It was the same message that had long been told in the Greater Caribbean.[76] Overall, the Red Cross proved to be much more sympathetic to the African American population of the city than the local government, providing an adequate share of relief, forming a black Red Cross auxiliary unit, and to some extent serving as a broker between them and the municipal relief organizations.[77]

The eventual recovery of Galveston was in large part due to its postdisaster response to the hazard of the hurricanes because of its geographical location. Much of the recovery was a result of effective civil engineering. A decision to build a three-mile-long seawall to protect the city from another storm surge was initiated in 1902, the first stone of the project laid with a blessing from Father Kirwin and the first section of the wall completed in 1905. The financing of the project was done with a city bond. The whole level of the city was raised by filling with dredged sand under repaired and reconstructed buildings, with many areas raised 15–17 feet above the previous level. Over 2,000 buildings were raised in this way. In addition, in the relief effort over 400 new homes were constructed and thousands of people provided accommodation. The experiences in Galveston made it clear that the technology of civil engineering should be used in response to natural hazard, but this application of technology raised all the usual questions: who would direct the application, who would benefit from it, and who would pay for it?

With these questions in mind, the nations and colonies of the Circum-Caribbean, always threatened not only by hurricanes but by a daunting variety of other natural disasters, entered the twentieth century. A major earthquake rocked Kingston, Jamaica in 1907 and killed over 2,000 in the falling buildings and resulting fires, and in May 1902 Mount Soufrière on the British Windward island of St. Vincent and Mount Pelée on French Martinique both erupted. In each case, the human and economic disasters that resulted raised questions about government responsibilities before and after the event, and about the importance of social organization in contributing to the human role in creating disaster. Both the French Antilles and the British Windward Islands had experienced hurricane blows in the 1890s, but the spectacular nature of these volcanic eruptions, and their potential to bring instant death to so many people, focused governmental attention and provoked worldwide humanitarian and political response in a way that hurricanes rarely did. The Martinique eruption was horrific, producing a rapidly moving pyroclastic cloud of burning gasses that enveloped the nearby port of St. Pierre, and killing some 30,000 people in a matter of minutes.[78] France immediately sent relief to its stricken territory, and aid and sympathy poured in from Caribbean neighbors, from other French colonies, and from the crowned rulers of England, Japan, Norway, and Germany. Sentiments of humanitarian sympathy and solidarity were expressed by many. Lord Roseberry, Duke of Argyll, wrote to the London correspondent of a Paris newspaper: "Such calamities affect all our human race, so they unite nations. I earnestly hope that it may be so."[79] A humanitarian impulse and a sense of common danger seemed, at least momentarily, to turn a cataclysmic event into a common experience that could overcome various kinds of social divisions and conflicts.

But in 1902 not everyone was impressed by these expressions or horror and sympathy. A week after the eruption, the *Leipziger Volkszeitung* published an inflammatory article in reaction to the tragedy of St. Pierre, and even more so, to the expressions of sympathy for its inhabitants. Written by the thirty-one-year-old Social Democrat Rosa Luxemburg, a Polish-Jewish activist who was a major thinker of the Left in prewar Germany, the article portrayed Mount Pelée as a dangerous but greathearted giant who had given warnings that human arrogance had ignored.[80] Just as before the great political eruptions of 1789 in Paris and 1848 in Vienna, governments had ignored the rumblings of their people and sought to maintain order and peace at all costs. Natural and political calamity had a common origin in human error and arrogance.

Luxemburg had yet another point to make in this essay. The erasure of rivalries and jealousies outlined by Lord Roseberry, the sentiments expressed for all the survivors on the stricken island as human beings without attention to the former distinctions between black and white, rich and poor, field hands and plantation owners, was, she believed, dishonest and misleading. "France weeps over the tiny island's forty thousand corpses and the whole world hastens to dry the tears of the Mother Republic," but where was the concern for the thousands in Madagascar swept away by French cannons when native peoples refused to accept the colonial yoke? Luxemburg's target was colonialism and social injustice, and she was enraged at the crocodile tears of the Tsar, the Kaiser, and the Americans who had on their hands the blood of colonial wars in Poland, the Philippines, China, and Africa. Nor was France to be exempted from indictment for its suppression at home of the 1871 uprising in Paris where "no volcano erupted, no lava stream poured down. Your cannons, Mother Republic, were turned on the tight packed crowd, screams of pain rent the air—over twenty thousand corpses covered the pavements of Paris." Luxemburg had no patience for the tears and condolences expressed by "benevolent murderers" or "weeping carnivores" who condemned Mount Pelée. She predicted a day when another kind of volcano would sweep colonialism—and capitalism—away. "And only on its ruins will the nations come together in true humanity, which will know but one deadly foe—blind dead nature."

This essay, seeming so modern and current, written, like Joseph Conrad's *Heart of Darkness*, in 1902 at the height of European colonial expansion, unintentionally brings to mind the sermons of the eighteenth century. Those warnings and exhortations had seen the hand of a punishing God in the visitations of natural disaster. Although divine providence is absent in Luxemburg's denunciation, it is still human error and sin that have made the natural world dangerous; but here the sin originates not in personal ethical or moral weakness, but rather in a communal failure born in the oppression of the weak by the powerful and of the colonized by the colonizers. Luxemburg's political manifesto, through its use of the volcano as a metaphor, understood the anthropogenic dimension of disasters and sensed the comparability of natural and human events in their effect on human suffering. It also expressed a view of nature as an enemy beyond human control, yet one that a united humanity could confront. Such ideas became central to the ways in which the twentieth century would deal with nature and with the ways in which disaster would be defined.

CHAPTER 7

Memories of Disaster in a Decade of Storms

Temporal, temporal, allá viene el The storm, the storm, here comes the
temporal, storm,
¿Que será de mi Borinken cuando What will become of my Puerto Rico
llegue el temporal? when the storm arrives?
—*Puerto Rican plena about the 1928 San Felipe hurricane*

They was talkin' bout a storm in the islands
Run, come see Jerusalem.
—*Bahamian calypso about the 1929 hurricane*

Cada vez que me acuerdo del ciclón Each time I remember the
hurricane,
se me enferma el corazón it makes me sick to the heart
—*"El Trío y el ciclón" by the Cuban Trío Matamoros*
about the 1930 San Zenón hurricane in
the Dominican Republic

During the first two decades of the twentieth century, while much of
the Atlantic world was sliding into World War I and then recovering
from it, the Caribbean was relatively spared by the great storms. Of course
there were hurricanes throughtout these years, but after the roaring years
of the 1890s culminating in the particularly heavy year of 1899, the year of
San Ciriaco, the frequency of hurricanes diminished until the mid 1920s

when a new cycle of more frequent storms began. Modern studies have suggested that the years just before or after an El Niño event in the Pacific often witness enhanced hurricane activity in the North Atlantic and Caribbean. The decade of the mid-1920s to mid-1930s was such a period of intense hurricane activity—in fact, it was the period of maximum hurricane activity in the last five centuries. The years witnessed anomalous events such as a November Category 5 hurricane that battered Cuba in 1932, and the 1933 hurricane season, in which there were three hurricanes simultaneously in the Caribbean.[1] This meteorological situation occurred during a period of intense and complex social and political activity in the societies of the region. In the United States, the flourishing of laissez-faire capitalism and the era of Prohibition was followed by the market crash of 1929, the Depression, and the New Deal. In the Hispanic Caribbean, there was a "dance of the millions" boom for the sugar producers of the region, followed by the crisis and depression of their industry, a situation that encouraged numerous strikes and the formation of labor unions. This unrest contributed in Cuba and the Dominican Republic to the rise of personalist *caudillos*, leaders whose appeal depended on their charisma and extended personal relationships rather than on a consistent political ideology, and it led in Puerto Rico to the emergence and repression of nationalism. Similar economic stresses in the British West Indies and French Antilles provoked the flourishing of transnational cultural movements like Garveyism and the anti-colonialist intellectual movements led by figures like the Martinican Aimé Cesaire.[2] All of this was accompanied by the intense ideological debates of the era, the critique of capitalism, the rise of fascism, and the diffusion of socialism in various local and international forms. Finally, this era in the North Atlantic was greatly influenced by the growing hegemony of the Unites States, its military and political interventions in the region, and its position as a principal market and as a source of credit. Response to natural disasters of the type that these tropical storms represented was a challenge and an opportunity to all of the societies of the region, sometimes revealing the weaknesses and social divisions of existing regimes, and sometimes providing models and stimuli for broader social transformations.

"RUN, COME SEE JERUSALEM": THE BAHAMAS
AND THE BRITISH CARIBBEAN

Throughout much of the British West Indies the period following the end of World War I was been a time of social unrest in the face of economic contraction. The creation of trade unions and political parties to advocate for better working conditions reflected the difficult situation in many colonies. The price of sugar was falling even before 1929, and lacking the subsidies and trade privileges in the U.S. markets enjoyed by Cuba and Puerto Rico, conditions in the British and French colonies, where many people worked at least seasonally in sugar, had worsened. Labor migration provided some relief, by offering employment elsewhere, but as the sugar market collapsed Cuba, Puerto Rico, and the United States also began to dry up as alternative places to find work. Living conditions worsened and incomes declined.

Colonial administrators and members of the creole elites continued to see the misery in the West Indian colonies at least in part due to the work habits and attitudes of the population, and set policy accordingly. Even after storms, charitable impulses of island governors were continually constrained by fears that aid would set a bad precedent.[3] It was an argument officials in the colonies made repeatedly. Only with the greatest difficulty could the governor of Jamaica convince his council to provide relief for Jamaican migrant workers when a 1932 hurricane struck the Cuban Isle of Pines, where they provided most of the labor to pick the citrus crops. Another storm that hit the Isle of Pines the following year (July 2, 1933) again left workers from Jamaica and the Cayman Islands destitute and stranded; again the council in Jamaica was reluctant to spend scarce resources on relief.[4]

One of the few British West Indies colonies that experienced some growth in this period was the Bahamas. The 700 low-lying islands and cays of the Bahamas, about thirty of which were settled, had always been vulnerable because of their location on a principal track of the storms, a fact that had contributed to the early Spanish decision to leave them unsettled once slaving had decimated their native populations. By the twentieth century, as a British colony, the Bahamas had survived with some plantations of cotton and sugar, but the colony was more dependent on sisal manufacture, fishing, ship salvage, and sponging. Bahamian sponges were highly prized in the world market, and an area off of Andros Island, with its crystalline waters and a great barrier reef, was home to one of the world's greatest concentrations of sponges. Exports per year, mostly in the hands of resident Greek middlemen, reached over a million and a half tons by 1910.[5]

The Bahamas had another advantage in its proximity to the United States. Only fifty miles separated Freeport, its second largest city, from the Florida coast, and that fact had long made trade, and especially contraband, a profitable island activity. Prohibition, which officially began with the Volstead Act of 1919, was a godsend to the islands' economy, as bootlegging, smuggling, and a tourism that involved "cruisin' down to Nassau by the sea, where we all get drunk on gin and Bacardi" became major economic activities.[6] The revenue from liquor sales in the period 1920–30 never fell below £500,000 annually, and in 1923 reached over £1 million.[7] Hotel development, the beginning of air connections to the United States, and an increasing integration into the U.S. economy characterized much of Bahamian life at least in Nassau, but the contraband trade affected many settlements on small outer islands and cays as well. The Bahamas was a good example of the extensive effects of the growing influence of the United States in the region after 1898.

But while the links of legal and illegal commerce to the United States softened the impact of the weakened European economy on the Bahamas, the islands could not avoid the reality of their location on the principal pathways of the Atlantic hurricanes. As we discussed in chapter 5, the Bahamas had suffered a terrific blow in 1866 when the eye of a major hurricane passed directly over Nassau, ruining almost every building in town and sinking virtually every ship in the harbor.

In the twentieth century, the Bahamas were struck by hurricanes on an average of every 2.3 years, and during the decade from 1926 to 1935, there was no area of the North Atlantic more threatened by the storms. Three hurricanes struck the islands in rapid succession in 1926. The "Great Nassau hurricane" came up the Leeward chain and passed over Nassau (July 26) as a Category 4 storm and then reached Florida as a Category 2 before weakening over Georgia and Alabama. This storm killed 268 people in the Bahamas, causing considerable damage to property and crops. Clearing and repair work had already begun when the second storm ripped through the islands before it made a direct hit on Miami (The Great Miami Hurricane) on September 17, then crossing Lake Okeechobee, the Florida Panhandle, and on into the southern United States. The third storm formed in the western Caribbean in October before striking Cuba (October 19) and subsequently the northern Bahamas and Bermuda. These storms revealed the Bahamas' vulnerability and the need for preparatory measures like a warning service and a building code. In fact, the government responded to the1926 storms with a building code with basic minimum requirements in construction and roofing, making the Bahamas one of the first Caribbean countries to establish such policies. On the other hand, a radio broadcast system covering the Bahamas was not in place until 1935, and thus without a better system of alarm, the outer islands of the colony remained vulnerable.

In 1928 the Bahamas suffered another hit from a September storm. This major hurricane had first struck Guadeloupe, causing much property damage and over a thousand fatalities. It then moved through the Leewards and brushed the Bahamas (September 16) before striking a devastating blow on Puerto Rico and then Florida. The storm had winds of a Category 4 hurricane as it passed through the Bahamas, but the warning system had functioned well and there was no loss of life on the islands, although boats and people were lost at sea. Ironically, however, as we will discuss shortly, many Bahamians lost their lives to this storm when it struck Lake Okeechobee in central Florida, where they were working as migrant agricultural laborers.

In the following year, 1929, a year in fact of slight hurricane activity in the North Atlantic, the Bahamas had the misfortune to be battered again. The "Great Andros hurricane" caused considerable property damage to homes, killed about fifty people, and sunk or grounded a number of ships. Three of ships, the *Ethel*, *Myrtle*, and *Pretoria*, were memorialized in singer "Blind Blake" Higgs's "Run, Come See Jerusalem." The song would become a folk classic (later sung by Pete Seeger and the Weavers in the 1950s), a monument set to music, a form of disaster remembrance found in various cultures of the region that allowed generations to pass the story along. Worst of all, the slow passage of the 1929 storm over the islands resulted in a very heavy impact on property, food supplies, and the sponge fishery, which was already showing signs of overexploitation.

Changes in the economic conditions in the Bahamas and the repeated visits from the hurricanes increased social and political discontent. More storms followed in 1932, 1933, and 1935.[8] The hurricanes damaged the Bahamian economy, but the end of Prohibition in 1933 had an even more devastating effect by diminishing the island's appeal for American tourists. Worsening economic conditions led to discontent. The British government had treated the Bahamas as far less troublesome and volatile than the agricultural colonies where the crisis of sugar and other crops had generated social unrest and an active labor movement, but by the mid-1930s those kinds of tensions had also appeared in the Bahamas.[9] The social and political relations in the colony were defined by a division of society between a white commercial elite, centered on Bay Street in Nassau and catering to a developing tourist and service industry, and a black and colored working and professional class. All the prejudices of class and race that grew from that division became increasingly obvious. The Bay Street interests obtained legislation in 1928 that basically excluded the arrival of migrants from other Caribbean islands who might cause trouble, and the assembly also made the arrival of Chinese and Jews difficult. There were attempts at worker organization in the 1930s, and eventually pressures did build for a minimum wage law and for use of the secret ballot in elections, but discontent festered. The growth of Nassau as a tourist destination increased its attraction for Bahamians in the outer islands faced with both the repeated stress of the storms and singular calamities like a strange fungus blight in 1938 that essentially wiped out a sponge fishery already badly damaged by the 1935 hurricane. [10]

The Bahamas in the 1920s and 1930s provided an ample example of the intersection and overall impact of environmental phenomena and socioeconomic conditions in the region, although its proximity to the United States in the era of Prohibition and then in the post-Depression economy created singular opportunities for tourism, contraband, and eventually for tax evasion and money laundering. Still, even in these peculiar circumstances the relationship between natural phenomena that produced hardship and penury, on the one hand, and economic cycles or conditions that had similar results, on the other, was made clear even to governors and an assembly that were usually far more favorable to the Bay Street interests than to the average Bahamian worker or outer island inhabitant. Both local government and imperial government felt impelled to respond.

While the Bahamas had a peculiar situation due to its location and the numerous hurricane strikes in this period, in some ways it was typical if somewhat less violent in terms of the working class unrest that swept through the British Caribbean in these years. The worldwide Depression and the weakening of prices for sugar and other West Indian exports in the United States and Europe created considerable unemployment and economic hardship for the working classes in the region. These conditions combined with a demand for political rights like universal suffrage and with a growing sense of nationalism. Beginning in 1934–35, sugar workers on St. Kitts, Demerara, and Jamaica, oil workers in Trinidad, and coal workers in St. Lucia all participated in strikes or public actions. In some places conditions were exacerbated by environmental shocks. British Honduras had been devastated by a hurricane in 1931 that killed a thousand people and destroyed much of the housing in Belize Town, where the governor's wife had generously opened the Government House to storm victims, but had carefully accommodated them by status and ethnicity: whites in the drawing room, natives in the pantry. Exports from British Honduras were already in decline, and the hurricane made a bad situation even worse. Malnutrition and poor health conditions added to the misery, and popular protests resulted, most effectively in the creation of the Labourers and Unemployed Association (LUA).[11] Here and elsewhere in the British Caribbean colonies, women, who were bearing the brunt of the economic conditions, were often in the forefront of militancy.

In the late 1930s, these conditions and the lack of an adequate welfare system throughout the region resulted in a chain of strikes and actions across the colonies. These actions often brought together portions of the middle class and working class, and sometimes, as in the case of Trinidad and Guyana, even bridged the usual divisions between black and the East Indian workers who had been brought into the colonies following emancipation. The British government responded with promises of reform. A commission under Lord Moyne (1938–39) did not recommend either independence or universal suffrage, which many had demanded, but did respond with suggestions for reform, including a federation of the colonies. The Colonial Development and Welfare Act of 1940 created a board and appropriated funds to carry out needed changes, but the beginning of World War II delayed any real action until 1945. The war did not slow the impetus for action, and during the 1940s trade unions and new political parties emerged to express popular demands.[12]

PUERTO RICO AND FLORIDA 1928: DISASTER AND SOVEREIGNTY ACROSS FRONTIERS

Because the great tropical storms had no respect for international boundaries or cultural divisions, they offer excellent vantage points to examine the influences of policy, culture, and politics on results close in time. A tremendous storm in 1928 that swept through the Caribbean, devastating Guadeloupe and St. Kitts on September 12, crossed Puerto Rico on September 13 and Nassau (as discussed above) on September 16; it then struck the Florida coast near West Palm Beach on September 17 before delivering a murderous blow to the areas around Lake Okeechobee. This storm thus provides an excellent occasion to see how national and local conditions shaped responses. As we have seen, hurricanes were no novelty on Puerto Rico, but the fury of this one was memorable.[13] No one who lived through the San Felipe hurricane forgot it. Winds reached 150 miles per hour, the strongest ever recorded on the island. Property damage was calculated at $80 million and over three hundred people officially (perhaps as many as fifteen hundred in reality) lost their lives as a direct result of the storm—a number that might have been much higher were it not for the lessons learned and precautions taken after the hurricane of 1899. Horace Towner, governor of Puerto Rico, later reported that the rainfall, up to 20 inches in 48 hours in the mountains, was the heaviest ever reported in Puerto Rico. The island was transformed, he said, from "a luxuriant flowered paradise" to something like "war-devastated areas of France or Belgium." [14]

The devastation was enormous. A third of the sugar crop was destroyed at a loss of over $17 million. Almost the entire coffee crop, valued at $10 million, was lost, and even worse, about half the coffee trees and sixty percent of the shade trees were destroyed. It would take five years to bring them back, and during those years the coffee planters would have little income. Rich, mountain-grown Puerto Rican coffee had been a major product in the late nineteenth century, amounting to almost sixty percent of the island's exports. But after the U.S. occupation, Puerto Rico lost its principal markets in Cuba and Spain, and it had no favorable status in the U.S. market. The 1928 hurricane was a *coup de grace*. Puerto Rico was never again a major exporter of coffee. Sugar, on the other hand, had flourished since the American occupation of the island. With a protected market in the United States and the infusion of large amounts of American capital in land and technology, production was ten times greater by 1930 than it had been in 1900. By that date, there was four times as much land in sugar as in coffee. Sugar had received a blow from the storm as well, especially since a change had been made in the variety of cane that was being used, substituting varieties that were richer in sucrose content but, unlike the strong *cristalina* cane used in Cuba, more susceptible to wind damage.[15] Still, the large American companies had been well insured and it seemed as though the industry would recover.

Meanwhile, however, over 500,000 people were left homeless and hungry. The mortality rate spiked sharply, and there was also a threat of epidemic disease and hunger. Overall, the island had been devastated. No better icon of the storm exists than the image of a palm tree in Utuado transfixed by a ten-foot-long two-by-four plank driven by the force of the wind to form a cross, symbolic of the island's Calvary (fig. 7.1).

Before it reached Puerto Rico, the storm had battered the British West Indian island of Dominica and French-speaking Guadeloupe and then had followed a northwest track, ripping into the Virgin Islands and leaving devastation and death in its wake. But the great storm was not done, its deadly course respecting no cultural or political frontiers. Now, after traversing Puerto Rico, and then passing north over the Bahamas, it slammed into West Palm Beach on September 17, 1928. It then moved west and north, skirting the Everglades and passing over Lake Okeechobee,

Figure 7.1 A symbol of Puerto Rico's Calvary after the San Felipe hurricane (Photograph provided by National Oceanic and Atmospheric Administration photographic collections.)

where thousands of Bahamian migrant laborers brought in to work the new fields perished in the rising waters and bursting dikes.

The San Felipe or Okeechobee storm brought, or created, challenges and opportunities, but these had varied along its path, and through those differing impacts and the responses to them we can derive some idea of differing social and political structures and hopes along its path. In two of these societies, Puerto Rico and the United States mainland, leadership had developed visions of an ideal future, and in both places those leaders were willing to use the disaster as a tool to make that future a reality. By 1928, the American National Red Cross was fully functioning, having cut its disaster teeth in Beaufort County, South Carolina after the Sea Islands hurricane of 1893, and in the Galveston disaster of 1900, to say nothing of the Johnstown, Pennsylvania flood of 1889 or the San Francisco earthquake of 1906. It not only became a major actor in both Florida and Puerto Rico in 1928 as the chief agency by which the government responded to natural disasters, but its reports and efforts in both areas also provide considerable information on the storm's impact and on the nature of reconstruction envisioned. The Red Cross had been nationalized in 1900, its status shifting from independent charitable relief organization to, essentially, a branch of the government, although still staffed by private individuals and financed by private contributions. This curious arrangement allowed Congress to maintain a fiction that disaster relief was still a local, religious, or private concern, but it also permitted the Red Cross to insist at times that it, and not government, would determine what was, and what was not, a "natural disaster," and thus what was the Red Cross's responsibility.[16]

Puerto Rico had been politically transformed since the San Ciriaco storm of 1899, when the island was still under U.S. military occupation. Military control had ended in 1900 as the Foraker Act became the political constitution. In 1917, Puerto Ricans acquired U.S. citizenship (Jones Law) just prior to the entry of the United States into World War I, but that arrangement came with the price of certain restrictions on the island's commerce and what it could manufacture.[17] The island continued to be governed by appointees by Washington whose cabinets were approved by the U.S. Senate. During the late 1920s, both sugar and coffee experienced contracting markets, and during that difficult decade political life intensified as labor unions began to form and become active and various political parties sought policy alternatives. One result was the emergence of both a Socialist Party and a pro-independence Nationalist Party whose presence forced the more conservative parties, formerly rivals, into electoral coalitions. These political objectives provided the context in which government response to natural disaster would be made.

Puerto Rico set to work to respond to the storm, and some in the governing class saw the crisis as an opportunity for change. While the mortality caused directly by the San Felipe storm itself had been kept relatively low, the hurricane left homeless about a third of the 1.5 million people living on the island. Most of the $85 million loss had been to privately owned properties. There were those in the political class of the island who saw the precarious condition of the island as an opportunity to restructure the society by creating a countryside populated with industrious small farmers living in neat cottages, the transformation of the overly independent or even "lazy" *jíbaro* into a hardy and orderly work force. Natalio Bayonet Díaz, former member of the House of Representatives, urged the governor to call on Puerto Ricans to shoulder the burden of the recovery and not depend on foreign aid. He warned that rural-to-urban migration had to be prevented at all costs and that only children and women either tending families or unable to work should be able to receive free food. Over 40,000 homes had to be rebuilt to house about 250,000 (rural) people left homeless by the storm, but that task also offered opportunities for reform. Bayonet Díaz argued that building new, orderly residences would be a necessary improvement, "solving once and for all the problem of hygienic dwelling for our laboring men, and causing to disappear from the countryside the wretched sight of the peasant shack (*bohío*) which is a stigma upon our civilization."[18] But one could not give the poor and destitute something for nothing. The rebuilding was to be done under the supervision of the relief agencies and municipal committees by the country people themselves, their labor paid for ten percent in cash and ninety percent in food.

Such social engineering also emerged in a plan for relief developed by island leaders representing the sugar growers and supported by Guillermo Esteves, the commissioner of the interior for Puerto Rico. This plan divided the affected population into three categories: small owners, the urban working poor, and the *arrimados*, those working on the big coffee estates who themselves could be divided into two groups, those who lived by cultivating a small plot and those who lived in small barracks as employees without any land. Esteves sought to convince the Red Cross that the social divisions or categories within the population had to be treated differently, and that "the good qualities of the Puerto Rican small farmer recognized by all" should be stimulated. The small proprietors were of "good moral character" and could be trusted to rebuild and improve their land and did not need to be supervised.[19] The other groups had to be treated more cautiously. Above all, he and the plan opposed the moving of *arrimados* from the coffee farms to small towns, and instead, he advocated the building of houses and distribution of small plots to the workers, but only after the haciendas had recovered, for if not, then there would be no work for them and the Red Cross would be forced to bear the burden. Esteves claimed, "these arrimados love the land they till and they are the seed from which future farmers will sprout," but his admiration for them had limitations. Since the resources of the landowners had to be used to replant their lands, the money for rebuilding for the workers should be given to the landowners, who could provide the rural laborers with shelter and work. It was a plan that responded to the specificities of the island's society, but that once again would place authority and resources in the hands of the planter class.[20]

These proposals on the island itself reproduced and paralleled similar if less well-informed arguments made in Washington. There, politicians expressed concerns about the cost of hurricane aid and doubted the desire or ability of Puerto Ricans to meet their own problems. A congressional committee was created to investigate conditions in Puerto Rico. The committee, headed by the Spanish-speaking Republican senator Hiram Bingham of Connecticut,[21] reported that this was the worst disaster the island had ever faced. The report and Bingham's call for aid in the form of an interest-free loan, as well as the testimony given by Governor Towner of Puerto Rico, were challenged by midwestern senators and congressmen who either believed Puerto Ricans should pay their own way, or were insistent that only the most destitute should receive relief. Uninformed about the nature or character of the nationalist movement, but concerned about rumors of disloyalty, they raised objections that "unworthy" people might receive aid. Governor Towner insisted that the coffee planters who most needed the loan were white, dependable, and loyal. Aid in the form of a loan with interest was extended to the island.[22] Rebuilding would begin, but at a price.

While those in authority in Washington and in San Juan sought to use the disaster to institute programs based on social differences, the people of the island later remembered the storm in terms of solidarity, of schools dismissed early, neighbors praying the rosary together, and practicing the *comelona*—a communal sharing of food. Sixty years later, one survivor would remember that in the period of recovery, "everyone felt [part of] Puerto Rico. There were no racial, political, or economic differences. We were one soul and one body."[23]

In Florida, too, there was a desire to rebuild for the future. The 1928 storm had followed close on the heels of a major hurricane that had killed 200 people in Miami on September 20, 1926. In the 1926 storm the city, damaged by the winds and a tremendous storm surge of thirteen feet in Biscayne Bay, suffered over $1 billion in losses, and reports, although downplayed by the local press hoping to project an image of the state as free of such dangers, indicated that two-thirds of the city had suffered damages. This disaster had taken place in the midst of a feverish land boom as developers sought to turn Dade County and especially Miami into an important urban center. Dredging of the mangroves and landfill had created conditions for the land boom as real estate values soared. The population had more than doubled between 1920 and 1926, to 100,000, as a frenzy of building had expanded to Miami Beach and the barrier islands of the bay.[24] The ecological effects of this transformation had received little consideration, and developers ignored the possible vulnerabilities of the real estate that had been recovered by dredging and filling.[25]

The 1926 hurricane hit Miami directly, and many of the new residents who had never experienced a hurricane before were caught in the open by the wind after they had left protected areas when the calm as the eye of the storm passed over them. The storm also caused considerable flooding and deaths in central Florida in the small farming communities around Lake Okeechobee, the great but shallow lake that fed the Everglades. These agricultural towns on the lakeshore and the rivers that fed the lake were clearly vulnerable, but the government of the state had refused to raise taxes to build barriers or dams to protect them.

The 1928 hurricane was a large Category 4 storm when it reached the Florida coast about 75 miles north of Miami. In the hurricane's aftermath real estate owners and developers in West Palm Beach and Boca Raton clamored for favorable government loans and aid, but in truth, the power of the storm had not been suffered equally. The 4,000 or so Bahamian and other West Indian workers brought in for the harvest and residing at Belle

Glade and other small communities near Lake Okeechobee had received a warning only twelve hours before the storm struck, and they had borne the brunt of the storm when the dikes could not contain the surge on the lake. The official report of deaths was set at under 2,000, but in reality was much higher.[26] The bodies were collected and burned on the lakeshore, the smoke drifting over the area. For months afterwards bodies continued to appear in the lake or slowly disappear into the Everglades.

In the racially differentiated world of Florida in the 1920s it was to be expected that in the effort to relieve and rebuild, differences of color would play a role. Burials were racially separated. In West Palm Beach, 69 white victims were buried in a mass grave at Woodlawn Cemetery, while 674 African Americans were interred in an unmarked mass grave at the pauper's cemetery, a site shared at various times with a "dump, sewage plant, and a street extension."[27] Only later were commemorative plaques placed at the sites; and in 1976 a monument with bronze sculptures of a fleeing family was finally raised at Belle Glade. Immediate attention after the storm went to property losses in Delray and Palm Beach, not to the un-named bodies swept away by the waters or burned in communal pyres near Okeechobee.[28]

There were complaints. The Red Cross, under considerable pressure, created a Colored Advisory Committee that had among its tasks the refu-tation of "rumors" that aid was not being apportioned equally to African Americans and whites. And there were problems. The poor had lost homes that were heavily mortgaged and faced foreclosure. If the Red Cross re-constructed them, then, it argued, the lenders, not the homeless, would profit. So such homes were not rebuilt. The Red Cross was defensive in the face of African American criticism of this decision. In its final report, it argued: "The Committee, knowing that its people are receiving their full pro-rata of relief, cannot but be embarrassed when ungrounded com-plaints are aired by 'chronic kickers.'" Meanwhile, state government shrugged its collective shoulders and saw the disaster as simply a quirk of nature for which it bore no direct responsibility.[29]

Such unpleasantness could not be allowed to stop progress. Local busi-ness interests, developers, state government, and the Florida press down-played the effects of the storm and any disruption it may have caused.

These had been boom times for south Florida, and local and state governments were committed to ordered growth, agricultural expansion, and urban development. In March 1929, before the director of the Red Cross left Florida, the West Palm Beach Chamber of Commerce arranged for him to make an overflight of the area. From the air he could see, the Red Cross report noted, "Cities, towns and villages had been set in order; cleared streets were lined with replanted parkings; agricultural lands were drained and covered with a most luxuriant growth of vegetation that seemed to have sprung up almost overnight; fields were again separated by ribbon-like drainage and irrigation canals; the whole countryside was dotted with reconstructed homes, the new unpainted lumber glittering brightly in the morning sun."[30] The storm had not been allowed to alter the road to Florida's progress. Both there and in Puerto Rico, the storm had been a disaster, made so by actions and decisions that long preceded the arrival of the winds.

Historian Raymond Arsenault has argued that the hurricanes in Galveston (1900), Miami (1926), and southern Florida (1928) and the extensive Mississippi flooding of 1927 (and we might add Puerto Rico in 1928) had a tremendous impact on how American attitudes were changing toward natural disaster and toward government's responsibility to warn and protect, and to then provide relief to victims. Legislation like the Mississippi Flood Control Act (1928) and the creation of the Hoover Dike on Lake Okeechobee as part of the Rivers and Harbors Act (1930) as well as demands for a better organized and more efficient Weather Bureau were evidence of these changes. Even more might have been done immediately, but the stock market crash of 1929 and the Depression moved energy in other directions. The financial disaster and the crisis of capitalism and liberal democracy it seemed to represent had wide-ranging international repercussions and effects. Among these were a change in the attitudes of governments toward relief and protection of their populations and a change in governmental style and rhetoric in terms of representing the interests and desires of the public.

Here we must shift our gaze back to Europe. Disaster of any kind evoked images of the horrors of the Great War, and since the conclusion of

World War I, the League of Nations in Geneva had been embarked on a campaign of limiting the potential for conflicts and violence. Among its efforts was the creation of a commission in 1923 in order to organize an international federation for the mutual assistance of populations struck by calamities. Giovanni Ciracolo, an Italian politician and president of the Italian Red Cross, presided over the commission. Ciracolo was aided by the French jurist and humanitarian activist René Cassin, who in 1968 would receive the Nobel Peace Prize for his work on the Declaration of Human Rights.[31] The core idea of Ciracolo was that relief to disaster victims should be given as a right, not as charity. It was, in fact, an obligation for the international community. Opposition to this concept came from those who thought that such an idea would be too expensive, or that it would hinder the work of the Red Cross, or, as the Americans argued, it should remain a matter for private charities. Nevertheless, the committee moved forward, and in 1927 the League of Nations approved the statutes for the International Union of Aid (UIS), which began to function in 1932. Its long-terms effects were limited, but the concept that aid was a right and not a matter charity, and that people had a right to expect assistance from their community, was changing the attitude of governments toward their populations. The rate of change, of course varied between nations, but there were similarities in policy and discourse that made the 1930s a watershed in the responses of governments to natural disasters.

San Zenón: Disaster and Dictatorship

Hurricanes and other natural disasters have always presented creative opportunities for governments, but rarely have the results been more obvious and more lasting than in the Dominican Republic, which saw the establishment of a brutal authoritarian regime following the 1930 San Zenón hurricane. That nation had experienced some stability in the 1880s under a modernizing authoritarian presidency buoyed by an expanding sugar economy, but overspending and financial problems eventually led to a period of turbulent politics, a default on the nation's foreign debt, and an occupation by the United States from 1916 to 1924. Effective civilian government returned to the island, and the United States withdrew but continued to control the Dominican customs income. President Horacio Vásquez's attempt to extend his eligibility beyond the limit of one term in the next election led to a political uprising. The government fell, and in new elections in May 1930, the commander of the armed forces, Rafael Trujillo, who was not reluctant to use the army to intimidate and suppress his opposition, was elected. Trujillo won with over ninety percent of the vote, since he was the only candidate.

Beneath this tale of political change was the story of sugar. That industry had boomed during World War I as competition from beet sugar producers in Europe had been eliminated. Large U.S. companies had bought up many of the centralized mills and much of the land, but the end of the war and a rise in competition from beet sugar producers had caused sugar prices to plummet, and the stock market crash of 1929 had been a disaster for both sugar and the country as a whole. In some ways, Trujillo's rise was a product of the nation's fiscal problems as much as its political turmoil.[32]

Trujillo had entered the military in 1919, after the U.S. occupation had created a National Guard to keep order and then gave it exclusive military power. Using his ties to U.S. Marine Corps officers as a member of the National Guard as well as his access to business opportunities, and personal relations, Trujillo had risen rapidly in what became the National Army. Now, as president, he was able to employ his control of the military as a political tool, along with a mixture of personal ties, populist rhetoric, a profound streak of megalomania, and a considerable ability to play off competing international interests against each other. He successfully mobilized the press, the universities, the Church, and the schools in support of his rule, and remained in power from 1930 until his assassination in 1961.

During the political unrest of the 1920s, the Dominican Republic had not escaped the effects of the hurricanes. In 1921 the eastern area of Higuey had suffered serious property losses in the "Magdalena hurricane," named in honor of an elderly woman swept into a well by the wind, but who miraculously survived without injury.[33] Then in 1926 and 1928, as the number of hurricanes increased, the same area was struck again.[34]

It was on September 3, 1930, only a few weeks after Trujillo took office, that the country was again struck by a devastating hurricane, but this time the capital city of Santo Domingo suffered an almost direct hit.[35] A Cape Verdean storm, the hurricane entered the Caribbean north of Barbados, moved westward, passing south of Puerto Rico, and, gathering force, then struck Santo Domingo with winds as high as 150 miles per hour and pressure dropping to 27.6 inches (933 millibars), which would have made it at least a Category 4 storm by contemporary standards, although some wind reports suggest that it reached Category 5 status. Crossing all of the Dominican Republic and Haiti, it then past just to the south of Cuba before it made a U-turn, battering western Cuba and then moving diagonally to the northwest as it crossed central Florida from the west to east coasts, and eventually ended as an organized storm in the Atlantic around the latitude of North Carolina. The major impact, however, had been in the Dominican Republic, where estimates of fatalities were as high as 8,000 people, making it one of the deadliest Atlantic hurricanes. Santo Domingo, which bore the brunt of the storm, had a population of about 50,000 when the storm hit, so that the reported 4,000 dead and 19,000 injured came close to half the population. Property damage was estimated at $40 million.

Trujillo, faced with the devastation and death, with thousands killed and thousands more left homeless and starving, seized the moment immediately. Acting with military efficiency and using the National Army forces trained by the U.S. Marine Corps, he proclaimed martial law, mobilizing the troops to help in relief work and to suppress any looting or violence. The hurricane was thus providing cover for Trujillo's campaign to disarm the country that had begun with his election.[36] On September 5, he issued a manifesto emphasizing that he had gone out into the streets during the storm and that his heart had been "wounded as a citizen and as a leader" by what he had seen. This claim about his personal involvement and presence on the streets during the storm and its aftermath was often repeated by the press and by his hagiographic biographers,[37] becoming an urban legend designed to show Trujillo's selflessness and his paternal care for the people (fig. 7.2). As Trujillo stated in his manifesto, "the people had not been, and would not ever be, abandoned by the government." With

FIGURE 7.2 General Trujillo and San Zenón victims (Photograph from *La Nueva Patria Dominicana*, Santo Domingo, 1935; Yale Photographic Services)

the help of all Dominicans and with aid from foreign nations, he would spare no effort; the country's congress had ceded to him all powers in order to facilitate the recovery of the city and the country. The manifesto, filled with populist language and emphasizing that he too had "drunk his own tears" in the midst of the devastation, essentially announced a governmental coup that had been developing since the election. The hurricane provided a useful emergency for that end. "I am, thus, identified with the people to suffer with them and to decisively help them to rebuild their homes from the ruins."[38] Three days later, on September 8, a second manifesto claimed that normalcy had been reestablished in the city and that now everyone was expected to get back to work. Leisure should not be added to the nation's misfortunes. Reconstruction was to be a common cause. Fatalism and despair were to be combated, and none would be allowed to remain passive. A vagrancy law in early November allowed the government to arrest anyone who was idle and put them to work without a trial.

Meanwhile, the city remained on edge. Hundreds camped out in parks and on the streets: the injured, the homeless, the hungry, and the sick. Social boundaries were in disarray as the poor and homeless sometimes gathered in upper-class neighborhoods, and there was a pervading sense of insecurity. Exactly a month after the storm, unidentified persons spread a rumor in the poorer neighborhoods of San Carlos and Villa Francisca that another hurricane was approaching that would hit the city at 4 a.m the following morning and would produce an accompanying earthquake. Panic spread, and people sought shelter in the churches and government buildings.[39] Ramón Lugo Lovatón, a journalist for *Listín Diario*, a major newspaper, wrote at the time of such rumors: "the new beast of legends and creations came to the city and sowed the seeds of panic everywhere."[40]

Strong and decisive leadership seemed to be what was needed, and Trujillo was prepared to provide it. The government's commitment to responsibility for the welfare of the country in a time of crisis became a regular part of Trujillo's discourse. A proclamation of September 12 reemphasized "the immediate mercy of the government that will not abandon for a minute its readiness to sustain the people so that they can support the terrible test to which destiny has subjected them." Lugo Lovatón, who chronicled the aftermath of the hurricane in a way favorable to Trujillo, used the occasion of his proclamation to underline the opportunities that the disaster had created: "every tragedy is at the same time, grave and cradle, goal and starting point, destination and pathway"[41] He did not say at the time that San Zenón had created a pathway to dictatorship. Not since the Marquis of Pombal had rebuilt Lisbon following the great earthquake of 1755 had a political figure been more adroit in using a natural disaster to consolidate their power.

Trujillo created committees for relief, sanitation, and other needs, fixed prices, and prohibited migration to the city. The dead were buried in mass graves or cremated. Local committees were organized in each city district for relief and reconstruction. Soup kitchens were set up in churches and neighborhood pharmacies. Trujillo organized a Dominican Red Cross chapter and also allowed the U.S. Red Cross to bring in rations and relief workers. In fact, Trujillo asked the U.S. embassy to allow one of his old Marine contacts, Major Tom Watson, to coordinate the relief operation.[42] A great international humanitarian effort quickly began to offer help. Dutch and British sailors from ships bringing relief supplies were brought on shore to help direct efforts. Planes arrived from Miami. The U.S. governor of Puerto Rico, Theodore Roosevelt Jr. rushed to send aid, as did the governments of Dutch Curaçao, Venezuela, and other Latin American nations. Cuban president Gerardo Machado, who in 1927 had manipulated his own reelection, dispatched a medical team of Cuban doctors, nurses, and a squad of soldiers to help with sanitation problems, and the archbishop of Haiti arrived with aid from that neighboring nation.[43] The threat of disease and the "lamentable sanitary situation" led to a vaccination campaign in the country under Aristides Fiallo Cabral, Trujillo's secretary of health, who later reported that the project had taken all the "clarities of my thought and all the energies of my spirit." Cabral claimed that the low barometric pressure during the storm had produced chemical changes that led to dysentery, typhoid fever, and influenza.[44] Despite such questionable medical theories, the project was carried out efficiently in the city, using foreign medical teams.

The order prohibiting migration to the city made relief to the urban victims easier, helped to prevent looting, and controlled the spread of disease, but over time, as rebuilding progressed and relocations took place, it was clear that a policy of moving the poor to neighborhoods outside the central city was also afoot. The old colonial buildings of stone and the major churches in the center of the city had survived the storm with slight damage. Residential areas had fared less well. While some upper-class neighborhoods were vocal in demanding attention, the worst-hit areas were poorer neighborhoods on the city's margins, like La Mina and Villa Francisca.

The rebuilding of the city allowed for the imposition of new building codes, the clearing away of the old wooden structures, and the construction of sturdier cement or cement block buildings; the result was a new social organization that was reflected in the "modernist" urban layout of the rebuilt city.[45] Old prejudices about rural "shacks" and the backwardness of rural peasant culture underlay an effort to exclude the lower classes from the heart of the city center, from the colonial zone of historic buildings, and from the *malecón* (breakwater) along the sea front. The new, modern city rising from the ruins of the San Zenón hurricane became a symbol of the reconstruction of a new and progressive nation, the "*patria nueva."* Now there were broad avenues and new modern buildings, including a luxury hotel with ballrooms and auditoriums that could serve the regime's ceremonial needs.[46] Trujillo urged progress and basked in its accomplishment.

At the same time that Trujillo was enacting these measures in response to the hurricane, he was also imposing a repressive political regime. Chronologies of the period based on daily news reports show that in September and October 1930, the disarming of the population, the exile or arrest of political opponents, the house arrest of the sisters of political rival General Cipriano Bencosme, and then the general's eventual capture and death, and plans for a single-party political system, were all simultaneously under way. The trappings of totalitarian rule were beginning to emerge: the image of the leader in all public venues, statues and streets named for the leader or his relatives, a constant stream of self-promoting honors and distinctions, a bought or bullied press that acted like a Greek chorus. The sycophantic congress even nominated Trujillo for a Nobel Peace Prize.

While much of the regime bore the stamp of the autocratic governments of the period, the traditional practices of Dominican politics were also employed to solidify power. Throughout late 1930 and during the following years, Rafael Vidal, Trujillo's secretary of state, received thousands of letters from people seeking personal help, favors, or positions, most of them promising political loyalty or fealty, and some even creatively composing *boleros* in honor of Trujillo. Many used the hurricane to highlight their need for help or favors.[47] The traditional personal ties were being mobilized in the creation of the new city and the foundation of the "New Fatherland." Through it all, Trujillo continued with a discourse of care for the people and charity as the motive of government. He stated in the fall of 1930: "By temperament and education, I consider charity is an uplifting virtue, and [it is] essential in men and is a salvational practice in the destiny of peoples."[48]

If one of the regime's slogans was "God in heaven, Trujillo on earth," people had not forgotten to seek divine protection during the storm; nor did Trujillo lose the opportunity to consolidate his ties to the Church after its blow. People had turned to the traditional protections of prayer and contrition. Prayers and rogations had been made during the storm. At 6

FIGURE 7.3 Dedication of the San Zenón monument (Photograph from *La Nueva Patria Dominicana*, Santo Domingo, 1935; Yale Photographic Services)

o'clock in the evening of October 2, one month after the storm, all the church bells of Santo Domingo were ordered to chime. On the following day, there was a burial service and procession accompanied by a military band, followed by the blessing and erection of a large granite cross in "memory of the victims who fell in the horrible hurricane."[49] Later in October, Trujillo convinced the archbishop of Santo Domingo to have the much-venerated Virgin of Altagracia brought from Higuey to the city on a visit of consolation for the victims, and the Church became centrally involved in the establishment of emergency kitchens for those left homeless. On September 3, 1931, one year after the storm, the archbishop celebrated a commemorative mass at the basilica of Santa Barbara in honor of the victims. This tradition continued over the next few years. Trujillo, who later in the 1940s would emulate Franco's emphasis on Hispanism and traditional Catholicism, intuitively recognized the utility of commemoration, and a statue to the memory of the victims was placed in the city (fig. 7.3). It was the first of a number of monuments to hurricane victims of the decade throughout the Greater Caribbean, as governments began to express more concern for their citizens as part of a populist discourse. In the case of Trujillo's rebuilt capital, however, the monument did not last long.

As the new city arose, megalomania overrode religious strategy.[50] The plaza was renamed the Parque Ramfis in honor of Trujillo's youngest son, and the memorial to the victims of the hurricane was replaced with an obelisque honoring the dictator's child.

But if Trujillo made the city's rebuilding a project to demonstrate his effectiveness and solidify his image and power, he was not frivolous or unaware of other forces that he needed to appease. From the very beginning of the rebuilding, he recognized that the cooperation of the United States was essential to his success. President Herbert Hoover had immediately authorized a loan of $3 million to the Dominican Republic, but Trujillo declined to accept it, and he made it clear in a public announcement that under no conditions would payment on the nation's existing debt be suspended, thus easing financial pressures from Washington. At a state dinner held on October 8 for Hoover's representative, Eliott Wadsworth, Trujillo made clear his appreciation of foreign aid, but emphasized that the work ethic of the Dominican people would be the key to recovery; and he stated that the painful hurricane was not the sole cause of the "vast and well-conceived Economic Plan" that he had launched to stimulate a national resurgence.[51]

The climax of Trujillo's seizure of the San Zenón disaster came in 1936 when the city of Santo Domingo, the oldest European settlement in the Americas, was renamed. On December 14, 1935, the Dominican senate petitioned for the city to be renamed Ciudad Trujillo and for a bronze plaque to be placed on an historical monument reading: "President Trujillo will not abandon his People, the People will not abandon Trujillo." On January 11, 1936 the vote was taken and, after a desultory debate, the change approved. The city's resurrection had become indelibly linked to Trujillo and to the story that he and his admirers and lackeys had crafted. The hurricane of San Zenón had served its political purpose.

Trujillo's commemorations of the victims of San Zenón had allowed him to continually reinforce the memory of how in the midst of a natural disaster he had stepped forward to save the nation, rescue a city, and console his people. By 1934, September 3 had been made into a Day of National Mourning, a commemoration of even broader meaning designed to keep the memory of Trujillo's great achievement alive. In September 1936 the Day of National Mourning was converted into "The Day of the Poor," a day in which thousands of food parcels, clothes, and money were distributed to the poor, with Trujillo's wife, María de los Angeles, serving as chief executive of the events. The relationship of government to disaster, born from the emergency response to the hurricane and the concept that government bore responsibility to those who had suffered calamity, had been transformed from a response to a particular crisis to a permanent contract between government and the disadvantaged. The transformation of September 3 in the civic calendar of the Dominican Republic had made the connection apparent, but, in fact, Trujillo had simply made clear an ideological and political trend that was taking place in much of Europe and the Americas.

THE DEPRESSION, THE STATE, AND LOVE
IN A TIME OF HURRICANES

The crash of 1929 and the crisis of the world economy had profound effects throughout the Greater Caribbean region. Trujillo was simply one example of the rise to power of a number of regimes in the region, some of them authoritarian, but almost all of them employing a populist or nationalist rhetoric much like that of the new authoritarian regimes that emerged in the 1930s in southern Europe and Germany. The degree of authoritarianism and populism varied among them and over time, but Batista in Cuba, Ubico in Guatemala, and Somoza in Nicaragua, to say nothing of Vargas in Brazil and Cárdenas in Mexico, all in some way reflected the crisis of capitalist economies and a search for alternatives, their policies often couched in a language of unity between the government and its people.[52] The United States often did not approve of all their policies or rhetoric, but was willing to accept these regimes to protect its own interests and to maintain regional stability. Moreover, the United States was itself in the midst of a political transformation that resulted in the election of Franklin D. Roosevelt in 1932, and the beginnings of the "New Deal."

Meanwhile, natural disasters continued to hammer the region. The early 1930s were particularly bad. Both 1932 and 1933 had multiple Category 5 hurricanes, a situation that has happened only six times between 1920 and the present.[53] In fact, the period 1930–35 emerges as one of maximum hurricane activity in the Caribbean and North Atlantic, perhaps the most active in the last five hundred years.[54] This intensification of storms bracketed an El Niño event in the Pacific in 1932, which also was a principal cause of the great "Dust Bowl" drought in the southwestern United States. What is interesting in this period of challenge and political change was a general tendency for governments to assume a greater role in direct response to calamity, and to express an interest and concern for individual misery and hardship that could then be transformed into a communal response.

The calamities were at times horrendous. In 1932 a late October storm passed through the Lesser Antilles and then curved northeast. It smashed into the Cayman Islands as a Category 4 hurricane and then on November 9, in the space of a few hours, it crossed Camaguey province in eastern Cuba from Santa Cruz del Sur to Nuevitas. Camaguey province had been one of the areas that witnessed sugar expansion after 1900 and Santa Cruz del Sur had for a while been a major port for lumber and wood, as forests were cleared and harvested. Between 1912 and 1923 a railroad had been built linking Santa Cruz del Sur with Puerto Principe and Camaguey, with concessions made to U.S. and British companies. A course change of the storm to the northeast had left little time for warning, so as seawater began to flood the streets along the Santa Cruz oceanfront many people sought refuge in the trains along the railroad tracks. The high winds and the sea surge of over twenty feet essentially eliminated the town; all the buildings were destroyed, and 2,870 people were identified as dead, but estimates of dead and missing were over 4,000. Damage was estimated at $40 million at the time. This was the greatest single natural disaster in Cuba's history. Much of the loss of life was ascribed to the refusal of the American-owned railroad company to send a locomotive to evacuate the townspeople unless it received a deposit of $500. The journalist Santiago González Palacios, who covered the disaster for the Havana newspaper *El Mundo*, wrote: "Never in my life have I seen so much grief, so much desolation, so many dead, so much sadness." The director of the Havana National Observatory, José Carlos Millas, one of the impressive lineage of Cuban meteorologists who held that position, penned an excellent report of the hurricane. His text rose above the normal physical and scientific descriptions that characterized most such reports:

> On the morning of Wednesday, November 9, 1932, a Cuban town disappeared. It was a noble, industrious town that played an important role in the first turbulent years of the history of our fatherland and then later knew how to maintain its virtues so that battles of a different type never detracted in the least from its noble tradition. This town was Santa Cruz del Sur.[55]

The town was rebuilt at a different location, and a monument was constructed in the cemetery for those lost on November 9. The event is still commemorated each year. The tragedy seared the national memory, poems and short stories were written about it, and those who survived, the *cicloneros*, bore witness to the disaster. The destruction and death of Santa Cruz del Sur eventually became part of a nationalist, and later socialist, critique of the failure of capitalism, or even a tale of its role in the creation of natural catastrophe. The memorial to the victims took on a meaning beyond that of remembrance of communal sorrow.[56] But even more than such obvious political uses, the Santa Cruz del Sur memorial, like that raised by Trujillo for the San Zenón victims three years before and that for storm victims in the Florida Keys three years later, reflected a growing concern for the victims of natural disaster, and an implied recognition that whatever God's intent or Nature's accidents, governments could do something in the face of such dangers.

While Cuba was dealing with this tragedy, Puerto Rico was also trying to cope with repeated hurricane blows. The San Felipe storm of 1928 was followed by a lesser hurricane (San Nicolás) in 1931 and then by another major storm, San Ciprián, in 1932. The San Nicolás hurricane had skirted the north coast of Puerto Rico, killing only two people and causing extensive rural damage, but the San Ciprián hurricane of September 1932, while less intense than the San Felipe storm, killed over 250 people, left half a million people homeless, and caused considerable damage, estimated at the time at over $30 million. The close succession of the three storms provides an opportunity to examine the ways in which the U.S. government and local island authorities dealt with the challenges they presented, San Felipe taking place before the financial crisis of 1929, and the other two storms shortly after it. Here the reactions of government, the intercession of nongovernmental institutions, and the expectations of the inhabitants of the island and of those who had an interest in its well-being, created a dialogue of intention and expectation that involved the humblest residents on the island, the political elite, and representatives of the federal government, which itself was in the midst of a debate about the "welfare state" and the measures that President Roosevelt would institute after 1933.[57] In that dialogue we can observe the contradictions born from a shift in perception and expectation about responsibility after a calamity. Previous emphasis on the role of charitable, community, and local institutions was now being supplanted by an expectation that national or imperial governments had a major obligation. In the historiography of the United States, considerable attention has been given to the effect of disaster relief in the United States in preparing the intellectual and moral justifications of the welfare state. The considerable role and actions of the federal government in Puerto Rico have not, however, played a central part in that discussion, although the increasing role of governmental agencies in dealing with catastrophe on the island had the effect of raising popular expectations about the government's responsibility in such situations, sometimes even in areas of life quite far from its traditional roles.

As we have seen, during the nineteenth century Puerto Ricans and Cubans had usually depended on *ad hoc* charity *juntas* or charitable auctions and subscriptions locally or in Spain itself to raise funds for the relief of such disasters; the inadequacy of these responses had eventually contributed to a critical attitude toward the Spanish government's inefficiency. After the Spanish-American War, Puerto Rican expectations of direct government involvement by the United States had been conditioned by the enormous relief effort following the San Ciriaco hurricane of August 1899 that had devastated the island shortly after the U.S. occupation. Policy advisors in Washington had seen that storm as an opportunity to demonstrate to the Puerto Ricans the advantages of being part of a modern and "progressive" nation, and so an enormous private and public relief effort was mounted that had the effect of reinforcing the political and economic dominance of the planter class on the island, but which by its efficiency had raised expectations of government involvement across class lines.[58] Similar governmental actions had reinforced those expectations following the San Felipe storm of 1928. The U.S. Congress had assigned $2 million for Puerto Rico's relief, and Governor Towner had effectively used the army, prison inmates, the National Guard, police, and schoolteachers in various capacities. Most importantly, the American Red Cross was now operating, and it took a major role in the response.[59] As Governor Towner wrote:

> It is unnecessary to say that which is so well known throughout the world that the American Red Cross is the best organization of national and international relief. . . . [it] is an American organization. The people of Puerto Rico are made up of American citizens. We can be sure that it will give to our people every kind of help in its hour of need.[60]

Towner made the Red Cross the central agency for the organization of relief efforts, but also mobilized direct aid from Washington. The congressional delegation headed by Senator Bingham had made favorable recommendations and eventually over $6 million was voted in congress for the island's recovery. [61] This response, directed by the Department of War, the Department of Insular Affairs, and a newly created Porto Rican Relief Commission, made clear the primary obligation of the federal government for the well-being of the island's population, and Puerto Ricans increasingly shared that sense of state responsibility for disaster relief.

The tremendous and relatively effective efforts made after the San Felipe hurricane to provide housing and to distribute food, clothing, and medical aid, and the effectiveness of the island government in obtaining support from Washington, set the stage for the next crisis. The hurricane of San Ciprián struck the island on the night of September 26, 1932. The island's governor at the time, Texas lawyer John Beverley, had served a term as interim governor in 1929, a position he assumed while serving as attorney general on the island. He knew the island, and unlike other governors, he spoke Spanish.[62] He moved with some alacrity to respond to the crisis, mobilizing his staff, especially his executive secretary, J. Saldaña, to handle the organization and mobilization of government response, and eventually using radio broadcasts to stimulate cooperation in the relief and rebuilding efforts.

The situation in Puerto Rico after the storm was grave. Most losses were uninsured. In the 1928 hurricane only ten percent of the damaged property had been insured, and crop insurance, mostly with Lloyd's of London, had only amounted to $2 million. In 1932, losses were estimated at $3 million, but between the two storms insurance companies had seen almost all their premium income for the preceding twenty years eliminated. The insurance companies found adjustment of hurricane claims in the tropics to be "no picnic," as a report on the insurance industry prepared by E. J. Werder for the governor lamented, and he insisted that this was work only for men of good health and strong constitutions. The record of constant losses would make future insurance rates impossible for many property owners and might even discourage the industry as a whole. The governor's office and an interdepartmental committee prepared reports on how best to insure the island's property and crops against future losses, but as. Werder noted in his report, the poor, not the companies, were the ones at the greatest risk:

> The great number of buildings occupied by the poorer class of people are of such a flimsy construction that they constitute a risk unacceptable to insurance companies. For these people, who are most in need and who lose, if struck by a hurricane, all their possessions, no insurance is available and they are hit the hardest without the possibility of protecting themselves by insurance, even if they are willing and able to pay the premium.[63]

After the storm, communications and letters of support poured into the governor's offices in San Juan. Various foreign governments expressed their sympathy and condolences. In Berlin, the German government sent an official to the U.S. *chargé des affaire* to express sympathy; in Oslo the government of Norway did likewise. Small relief contributions began to arrive from private individuals and corporations: the Rice Millers Association, U.S. Steel, Kolynos Toothpaste of New Haven, Colgate Palmolive, the Puerto Rican community of Hawaii, the workers and management of Ingenio Barahona in the Dominican Republic, the crew and passengers of the Spanish ship *Sebastián El Cano*.[64] A check for $290 arrived from Port-au-Prince, sent by Haitian and foreign contributors. Lecturer and comedian Will Rogers did a charitable performance in New York and turned over $475 to the Sisters of Notre Dame for the relief effort. But in truth, such efforts fell far below needs and expectations. As the vice chair of the Puerto Rican Hurricane Relief Committee in New York admitted to Governor Beverley, "it seems the Depression amongst our people here has made it unusually difficult to secure contributions," and while there had been a huge committee formed, in fact, only a few cooperated or gave of their time. The committee could send less than $2,000 to the island.[65]

Governor Beverley expressed his appreciation and sought to highlight the islanders' self-sufficiency by emphasizing their own efforts to bear the burdens of the recovery. At the same time, he astutely took the opportunity to emphasize that the island's prosperity would depend on the purchasing of Puerto Rico's sugar, tobacco, and needlework, and said he hoped for "consideration and even preference" from the "citizens on the continent."[66] His objective was to demonstrate that Puerto Ricans were morally guiltless for their situation and thus deserving of help. This had long been a key to the justification of disaster relief.

The Depression made the normal dependence on charitable agencies and contributions insecure. On October 4, 1932, former governor of the island Horace Towner, who had been in office during the San Felipe storm of 1928, wrote to Governor Beverly from Iowa that "The anxiety and sorrow through which we passed in 1928 is still very vivid in my mind, and how the feeling that in some way, at whatever cost, the suffering must be relieved, was with us at every hour." Towner hoped that the Red Cross would have profited from its earlier experience in 1928, but he was concerned that the economic situation of the Depression might undercut any relief efforts. As he put it, "I hope the mainland agencies that were helpful before will not be less so this time because of conditions."[67]

Of course, local authorities of the over 50 affected municipalities immediately turned to the island government. The mayor of Culebra, for example, wrote to Governor Beverley that only five houses in the town were standing and that not a school or hospital was serviceable, there was no communication by telegraph, and all the ships on Culebra had been sunk.[68] With such reports flooding the governor's office in the Fortaleza, Beverley asked for and received the loan of an airplane from Pan American Airways in order to view the damage himself. Beverley spent about two and a half hours in the air. He reported that half the houses in Bayamón had been destroyed, and in the Central Juanita the sugarcane fields had been leveled. Isabela, Añasco, and Arecibo had all suffered, especially the rural houses, as was to be expected.[69] In San Juan the governor worked closely with local authorities like Jesús Benítez Castaño, the administrator of the capital, who had cooperated with Beverley after the smaller storm of 1931 and who had been supportive of the insular government against those who had been critical.[70] In Ponce, the mayor, Guillermo Vivas Valdivieso wrote to Beverley and in a demanding and perhaps ironic tone said that "knowing the humanitarian features that adorn the people and government of the United States and its solvent economic situation, it would not be impossible get what we are asking for without being asked to pay interest." He then closed with an insistence on the obligation of the United States to its Puerto Rican citizens: "what nature has destroyed in one day is the labor of thirty years under the beautiful American flag that governs us with such skill that it cannot allow its American citizens to suffer the horrors of this immense disaster [*desgracia*]."[71]

There were others who saw the government's response and Governor Beverley's leadership as entirely insufficient. That line of criticism was made clear in a frank and passionate letter from San Juan lawyer J. Valldejulí Rodríguez to Beverley sent three days following the storm.[72] Valldejulí expressed shock at the "passivity of the government" in the face of this tragedy, and dismay at not seeing a single agent of the government providing relief to the homeless and hungry. He claimed that the previous governor, Theodore Roosevelt Jr. would have done a far better job in responding. In comparison with the "dynamic and paternal" response to the recent San Zenón hurricane of 1930 in the neighboring island nation of the Dominican Republic, the governor's response in Puerto Rico had been a "disgrace": the homeless and hungry were in the streets, no government agents were to be seen, the Red Cross had done nothing, and Washington remained uninformed about the extent of the damage. Valldejulí felt no compunction in insisting on a better reaction: he was "a member of this community that has the right to demand from you more attention and more service, since we are the ones who with our money support on our shoulders the government that you pretend to direct."[73] A reckoning was immanent: "The time will come when you will explain to the country the reason for this unjustifiable and bloody dereliction." Valldejulí's complaints, whether justified or not, revealed that there was no doubt in his mind that the government bore the principal responsibility to confront the emergency and that disaster relief was essentially a matter of public policy.

In Puerto Rico, the storms were, and of course had always been, a regular if intermittent aspect of island life with a differential impact on social classes and on urban and rural dwellers. Victor Clark, in his *Porto Rico and Its Problems* (1930), searched for what he believed to be the resignation to misfortune of the rural peasantry of the island. He believed that its origins might lay in slavery or feudalism or poverty, but suspected that "the terrific impact of periodic storms that carry all away with them and make human effort and ingenuity seem like naught" explained the "passive helplessness of the rural community."[74] This perception was repeated in the wake of San Ciprián. A social worker wrote from Barceloneta, where there was extensive unemployment, the sugar *central* had closed, malaria was rampant, and building materials were in short supply: "I have noted a great loss of optimism among the inhabitants. They have realized that the frequent hurricanes are a real inevitable calamity and have become aware of the fruitlessness of their efforts to build and repair their homes and to plant their farms anew."[75] These seeming attitudes of resignation or frustration in the face of this recurrent phenomenon were no longer principally explained by reference to divine punishment or warnings. In a sense, they had been secularized over time, as municipal government and charitable institutions and impulses had played a primary role in relief, but the presence of a strong central government now seemed to offer an alternative to local and community structures that had traditionally confronted the storms.

In the midst of the catastrophe, local administration, institutions, and many private citizens turned to the insular government for relief, seeking direct intervention. A widow with five daughters wrote that her deceased husband was a veteran and that after the great storm she had received none of his veteran's benefits nor any help from the Red Cross. She pleaded for help from the governor's office. Asunción Cruz, an elderly woman from Cidra, signed her letter to the governor with a cross and her thumbprint. Her little farm of five acres had been ruined, her husband was ill, and she was caring for a small child. She asked for a loan of $300–$400 to plant food crops in order to live and put a roof over her family's head. Her simple request, however, demonstrated a certain sophistication in her appreciation of the general difficulty of depending on charity from neighbors who were in similar circumstances, or the current difficulty of depending on the federal government, "whose financial situation is not very strong, we could say, and does not have sufficient resources to confront public disasters." [76] Sometimes the letters were in the form of complaints. The Methodist minister in Camuy complained that the government had used his church to house the sick and poor for a few days, but they had stayed for much longer, while the Catholic church had not been required to provide the same service, and the Red Cross had been uncooperative in relieving the situation. He suspected that there was "political favoritism" in the relief.[77] He, like many others, now saw the governor's office as the logical place to resolve any issue occasioned by the storm.

Increasingly those in authority felt the need, or sensed the usefulness, of paying attention to appeals for help, and sometimes to an unexpected degree. It is in this context that the handwritten letter dated September 30, 1932, from Carmen Campos, a woman in Mexico, to Governor Beverley is both informative and touching.[78] Having read about the storm, she pleaded with the governor to deliver her letter to Francisco Galán Miranda, who she feared had been killed or injured. "You, Mr. Governor, are the only one who can tell me about the whereabouts of that family, I plead with you a million times."

This direct and somewhat personal request from Señorita Campos was passed by Governor Beverley to his executive secretary, E. J. Saldaña, who, along with all his other responsibilities in the wake of the storm, was asked to contact the police to find the whereabouts and condition of Francisco Galán. Saldaña responded to the inquiry on October 14 that Galán was alive and had suffered no injury in the hurricane. This letter was received gratefully by Carmen Campos. In fact, she received it with such enthusiasm and hope that she then typed a long and plaintive response to Saldaña explaining that the real reason for her interest in Francisco Galán was a love affair that had gone wrong. She provided the details and of her long wait for letters that never came after Galán had stopped writing to her, and she poured out her disappointment and frustration to Saldaña.

Here in the midst of the government's preoccupations with the relief efforts, the demands of logistics, the threat to public health, and the reconstruction of the city, Saldaña did not let the matter stand. Instead, he called Galán to his office and required him to write a letter to Carmen explaining himself. Unfortunately, that missive is not to be found in the archives, but Saldaña could not resist the opportunity in the midst of his many duties to offer his own advice to Carmen: "Permit me to suggest that you forget this señor Galán, and the fact that you have had a relationship with him, as we must forget dreams because they lack any real substance. Galán [which means 'gallant'] could have been a 'gallant' and done it very well in his better days, but now he is a sun that is consumed in his own light because the twilight has arrived. . . . it is not worthwhile to carry in our soul a vain illusion." Finally, Saldaña offered this counsel: "We cannot waste our life looking at the grey distances of a limitless horizon when so many and such beautiful things, so worthy of our immediate attention, are all around us." Such avuncular advice, expressed so poetically, was not the usual response of government, but it now had been integrated into the assumption of state responsibility in the face of natural catastrophes and a growing sense of dialog between the general population and those in authority.

Federal response to natural disaster provided a prelude and a parallel for the New Deal institutions and programs introduced in Puerto Rico after 1933.[79] The continuing poverty of the island was exacerbated by the losses to the great storms, and the U.S. government also saw in the provision of emergency relief a way to undercut the troublesome nationalist movement that had emerged on the island. The image of a Puerto Rico made miserable by poverty and a lack of "progress" and in need of a program of recovery was made even more dramatic by the conditions caused by the hurricanes of 1928–32. They appeared to demand direct government intervention, and such intervention seemed to be welcomed and even expected by large segments of the island's population. The voices proclaiming the connection between structurally produced persistent poverty and the misery caused by natural disaster were becoming louder and more convincing, whether, as in the case of Trujillo, they made their point in Spanish, or, like the liberal Wisconsin senator Robert La Follette Jr., who became a principal congressional advocate for the New Deal, they did so in English.

In San Juan and Washington, Rio de Janeiro and Santo Domingo, leaders in the 1930s were reading their mail, speaking to the public, and claiming with ever more emphasis to govern on its behalf. Much has been made of President Franklin Delano Roosevelt's attention to private correspondence that came to the White House in the 1930s, and the care with which it was read and answered.[80] Response to personal hardship in disasters and in hard times played an important role in government's handling of that mail and in the efforts made through Roosevelt's radio broadcasts to demonstrate a sensibility to the needs of the nation's people. But, the United States was not alone in this regard. The state's role in public welfare was no longer in doubt, as we have seen in the Dominican Republic and Puerto Rico. Responses to disaster also gave those governments an opportunity to demonstrate concern.

FROM CATASTROPHE TO WELFARE

Hurricanes, like other potentially destructive or dangerous natural phenomena, had since the eighteenth century increasingly moved governments to make decisions and seek ways to respond to crises. Exceptional events called for exceptional measures. Subjects and then citizens expected the ruler or the state in the face of calamity to prevent, protect, provide, or relieve as much as it could given the vagaries of nature or the designs of God. Political theorists have called this development the rise of the "catastrophic state."[81] Over time, disasters came to be seen not primarily as divine judgments of human sin, but as natural phenomena that the state could manage. As the twentieth century advanced and the threats of war, disease, and economic disaster intensified with the advances of technology, communication, and science, both governments and peoples began to call for an expanded role of government and the creation of a "providential state," that is, a government that cared and provided for its citizens not just in emergencies, but in ordinary times. This was to be a secularized state that had assumed the responsibilities and functions of a "catastrophic" state.[82] This aid, although a moral obligation of government, was, however, to be provided not based primarily on morally determined distinctions between who was deserving and who was not, but because it was necessary for social and political cohesion. It was thus in the public interest. Such help implied the state's authority to regulate its inhabitants for what it perceived to be the common good. By the 1920s, this conception of government was growing, and the world financial crisis and the Depression blurred the distinctions between the emergencies created by fire, natural disaster, war, and epidemic and the "normal" state of hunger, unemployment, and misery created by market forces and economic cycles.

For a number of years the legal scholar Michele Landis Dauber has been arguing that the origins of the "New Deal" and the welfare state in the United States are to be found the often debated but hoary congressional tradition of governmental response to calamity and natural disaster.[83] Congress repeatedly if inconsistently responded to calamities both foreign and domestic, "in charity for the visitations of Providence," but, as we have seen, it often did so over the objections of congressmen who believed such actions should be limited to state governments, institutional charities, or private initiatives.[84] That restrictive view was sometimes brought into debates, but precedents of congressional spending for the "common good," or "general welfare," or which, like the relief sent to Caracas after the 1812 earthquake, could be seen as part of the government's foreign policy, generally held sway.[85] After 1929, traditional Republican attempts to limit such expenditures, or to emphasize local and private responsibility for such humanitarian aid, broke down in the face of the Depression, unemployment, and drought. This resulted in the birth of what Dauber called "The Sympathetic State."

Throughout this period of changing governmental responsibility, debates continued on how to distinguish those who were blameless victims and those whose personal decisions and failure to work or save were at the heart of their misfortune. Dauber's work, through a careful reading of congressional debates and the speeches of FDR, Robert La Follette Jr., and other New Deal politicians, has shown their continual emphasis of the parallels between disaster relief and welfare in general situations of adversity. Dauber argues: "In fact, disaster relief was the defining feature of countless histories of the welfare state told in order to show how the New Deal was consistent with this precedent for federal assistance and was thus legitimate."[86] In a similar fashion, opponents of the New Deal in the 1930s argued (as critics of government assistance of various kinds have argued since) that often recipients of such aid were not blameless victims, and that helping them created dependency. Moreover, society could simply not afford to offer such aid. There were just too many such claims. Finally, these opponents held that the federal government is constitutionally restricted in its power to spend funds in this way.

La Follette and others argued that the distinction between an "act of God" and a failure of leadership or an economic collapse made no difference in terms of the misery and harm they produced, and it mattered little to the sufferers the cause of their calamity. In these debates, some congressmen had noted European developments in the direction of aid to economic sufferers; but also part of the discussion was the recent response to the San Felipe hurricane in Puerto Rico in 1928 and the fact that the Red Cross had received a direct congressional appropriation for that crisis. In 1932, however, facing the Depression, the Red Cross was reluctant to become involved in the same way, and it now sought to distinguish between "natural disasters" and long-term crises like droughts or famines in which policy decisions seemed to have been at fault and which therefore did not qualify for Red Cross intervention. But such distinctions were becoming ever more difficult to make or defend in the face of the world economic crisis.

It is also possible that the political and cultural contexts of the late nineteenth and early twentieth centuries had contributed to a different perception of calamity and of government responsibility to respond to it. First, imperialism and colonial conditions had in their own way prepared the ground for this shift in governmental attitudes toward disaster response. The justifications of "the white man's burden" or the *"mission civilisatrice"* had always emphasized the natural dependency of the subject peoples and their need for help due to their own incapacities. Since they could not help themselves, they needed the humanitarian aid and direction of the imperial power, which had essentially entered into a contract to selflessly provide this help. To do otherwise would call into question the very moral basis on which empire depended. The British and French Antilles, given their history of European settlement, were treated somewhat differently than other imperial outposts, but the composition and character of their post-emancipation populations were such that a similar attitude existed to some degree amongst their administrators. There was always a reluctance to help the "lazy natives" or to promote dependency, the reports of disaster relief from the British and French colonies are laden with this language of paternal care and responsibility. This same language also appears in communications of American agents regarding their new insular possessions of Puerto Rico and the Philippines after 1898. Providing for these colonial, dependent populations in the face of recurrent natural disasters created a precedent for how dependent populations in the homelands might also be treated when they were in need and unable to help themselves.

Roosevelt's election in 1932 led to the creation of institutions and programs designed to build up infrastructure that would make populations less susceptible to natural disasters while at the same time providing employment for the jobless. In addition, institutions were created to facilitate government response to crises and disasters of various kinds. Some, like the Tennessee Valley Authority (TVA), specifically aimed at reducing ecological threats; others, like the Civilian Conservation Corps (CCC) and the Works Progress Administration (WPA), were used in government programs to ameliorate environmental conditions like flooding or soil deterioration. A rich literature has developed on this process, some of which traces the origins of governmental environmentalism to the New Deal programs.[87] But despite the benign purpose of such programs, these activities, whatever their intentions, sometimes produced negative results and new risks.

"WHO "MURDERED THE VETS?"
THE LABOR DAY HURRICANE OF 1935

The government's intervention in the economic crisis of the Depression and the recurrence of natural disaster came at great cost. The venue was once again Florida—this time the Florida Keys, the string of islands and cays extending southward from the southern tip of the peninsula.[88] Long an attraction to yachtsmen and fishermen, the sparsely populated island chain had been caught up in the frantic real estate boom, and when Henry Flagler, a developer, entrepreneur, and railroad builder, took up the construction of a railroad linking Miami to Key West, he was able to do so with the support of state government. The railroad, a tremendous feat of engineering, was built between 1905 and 1912, at a cost of almost $50 million and also at the expense of perhaps a thousand lives, many of them lost in hurricanes that swept through the Keys in the first decade of the century.

By 1935 the Depression was in full swing and unemployment was a central issue. Unemployed veterans from World War I who had been promised bonuses by Congress, which had overridden a 1924 veto by President Coolidge to assure this entitlement, were now seeking an early payment of their claims. In these hard times they could not wait to collect, and so in a number of cities, but most importantly, Washington, DC, they protested and demonstrated. This so-called "Bonus Army" of 17,000 veterans and thousands of family members camped in the Anacostia flats outside central Washington in order to pressure Congress to fulfill its promises to them and to find them employment. In July 1932, President Hoover ended their demonstration with violence, using troops commanded by General Douglas MacArthur and armed with gas and bayonets, and supported by cavalry and tanks, to break up their encampments. The confrontation and the death of two veterans shot during earlier demonstrations by the police produced a political scandal that contributed to Roosevelt's election, even though he had opposed the Bonus Army's tactics.

But as of 1934, the Bonus Army was still demanding employment. By that time the Roosevelt administration had created agencies like the Civilian Conservation Corps (CCC) and the Federal Emergency Relief Administration (FERA) that could offer employment in infrastructure building. Some 4,200 veterans were assigned to work camps in South Carolina and Florida. Among them was a group of some 600 veterans, many suffering from physical and psychological problems, assigned to help build a highway that would link the Keys to Miami and open the area to tourism and development. The Roosevelt administration had wanted to find work for these men who had "lived through the war, but had found peace too much for them."[89] It had treated the veterans better than did the Hoover administration, but it also wanted to get the rough and tumble demonstrators off the Washington streets.[90] The six hundred or so sent to the Florida Keys lived in flimsy housing in camps in the middle islands, particularly Lower Matacumbe Key, and for about $1.00 a day they labored into the summer months. Anyone who knew Florida and had lived through the storms of 1926 and 1928 knew that these workers were very vulnerable. On Labor Day, September 2, 1935, many of them were in the wrong place at the wrong time.

The hurricane that hit the Keys on that day was a small but deadly storm. It was the first recorded Category 5 storm to ever strike the U.S. mainland, and although the storm's diameter of about 10 miles was small, barometer readings in the keys of less than 27 inches were the lowest ever recorded in the United States up to that time and sustained winds of over 200 miles per hour were reported. The U.S. Weather Service, which had come under considerable criticism because of the Galveston disaster and the 1928 Okeechobee hurricane, had been reorganized earlier in 1935 and was on guard to avoid further disasters. It was already concerned about the workers' vulnerability and had developed a plan for evacuating them by train if the occasion arose. As the storm rolled through the Bahamas at the end of August it strengthened in the shallow waters to hurricane status. The Weather Bureau put up warnings for south Florida on September 1, but the storm appeared to be staying to the south and heading for the Gulf, and further reports mislocated the storm and miscalculated its speed. Hurricane specialist Kerry Emanuel believes that the small size of the hurricane made it particularly difficult to track with the technology of the period.

The supervisors of the veterans were reluctant to act while the warnings were still indefinite. By the time the error was realized, it was too late. The emergency evacuation train could not be arranged quickly enough, and the storm hit with devastating effect, with high winds and a storm surge of 15 to 20 feet breaking over areas that were mostly less than ten feet above sea level. The train that was finally sent was swept from the tracks, and the tracks themselves washed away, along with buildings, trees, and everything else. Nothing was left standing on Lower Matacumbe and surrounding areas. The official death count was 423 dead, of which 259 were veterans, but almost every subsequent researcher has said that figure is far too low. The only good fortune the veterans enjoyed was that it was Labor Day. Some 350 of them had gone to Miami or Key West for holiday demonstrations, and another 91 of the hard-drinking and tough men had the good luck to be in jail at the time.

The ensuing scandal was enormous. State and federal officials mouthed the "act of God" and "divine providence" excuses as was to be expected, but many observers found fault with decisions made by individuals and agencies of the local, state, and federal government. Fingers were pointed in every direction: the Weather Bureau, FERA, the Florida state government, and President Roosevelt himself. Congressional hearings did not clarify the situation. Ernest Hemingway, a long-time visitor of the Florida Keys attracted there by the marlin fishing, had ridden out the storm in his home at Key West. He was now commissioned to write an article about the disaster for the leftist magazine *The New Masses*, and he used that opportunity to accuse the government of deliberate negligence or worse. His "Who Murdered the Vets?" was a scathing and sarcastic denunciation of all involved, and a sympathetic defense of the veterans from the Bonus Army who had been placed in harm's way because their presence in Washington had been an embarrassment.[91] While Hemingway's charge may have been true, there were many who believed that the failures of the Weather Bureau or of the veteran's supervisors had certainly been unintentional and were not due to neglect.

Hemingway's critique was strident but effective. Why was the warning so late in coming? Why five days after the storm had the Red Cross been so ineffective? The civilians on the Keys were there of their own free will, and they knew the risk; but the veterans had been sent there and were left exposed: "they never had a chance for their lives." Hemingway saw the vets for what they were: "some were good guys and others put their checks in the Postal Savings and then came over to cadge drinks when better men were drunk; some liked to fight and others liked to walk around the town; and they were all what you get after a war." Hemingway addressed the victims: "You're dead now, brother, but who left you there in the hurricane months on the Keys where a thousand men died before you in the hurricane months when they were building the road that's now washed out? Who left you there? And what's the punishment for man-slaughter now?"

The poor and vulnerable had always suffered the most from natural disasters, whether overworked slaves in the nineteenth century or under-employed veterans in the 1935 hurricane in the Florida Keys. Heming-way's article provoked debate. Congress held hearings, but no one was ever punished for the disaster. Still, there was much empathy for the vic-tims, and a sense of shame for their plight and for the failure of govern-ment to protect them. Hemingway's article, as heated and as tendentious as it was, reflected a broad sympathy for disaster victims, and a growing belief that government had responsibilities to their people on such dread-ful occasions.

Hemingway was, in fact, building on a long tradition that had made hurricanes and other natural disasters an evocative theme of the litera-tures of the Greater Caribbean. Joel Chandler Harris, author of the Uncle Remus tales, and a man with an eye and an ear for personal and regional detail, had written a series of articles for *Scribner's Magazine* on the Caro-lina Sea Island hurricane of 1893 with wonderful line drawings of the people and places discussed. Harlem Renaissance writer Zora Neale Hur-ston's *Their Eyes Were Watching God* (1937) brought the misery of the 1928 Okeechobee hurricane and its impact on poor black families to the atten-tion of many people, and Marjorie Kinnan Rawling's Pulitzer Prize–win-ning *The Yearling* (1938) wove a hurricane into a tale of a boy's coming of age in the woods of northern Florida. This literature emphasized the plight and the fortitude of common people facing disaster. In the Hispanic Carib-bean as in much of Latin America this was the age of social realist novels

Figure 7.4 Dedication of the Islamorada memorial, 1937 (Courtesy of the State Archives of Florida Photographic Collection)

that made peasants, sugarcane cutters, indigenous communities, and the disadvantaged in general into the sympathetic subjects and protagonists of history, a role that easily accommodated the victims of natural disasters. In poetry, prose, and song and now in bronze and marble, the victims and disasters were remembered and described.

The dead veterans were buried in a mass grave with military honors. A priest, a rabbi, and a minister presided at the ceremony, and there were representatives from the veterans of the nation's past wars, and a flyover by the National Guard. President Roosevelt wrote to Colonel George Ijams of the Veteran's Administration to express regrets because of his inability to attend the ceremony and his grief at the "tragic death of these defenders of the nation." Wreaths from many veterans' organizations were placed at the grave. Most touchingly, the German War Veterans in the Miami area sent a wreath along with the old imperial flag of Germany; Ijams, himself a veteran of "the Great War," called it "a most graceful gesture." The national anthem was played and taps was sounded. When asked if all this pomp was excessive for the dead veterans in comparison to the civilian dead, Colonel Ijams later testified: "This was for all of them," all who had perished in the Keys.[92]

The storm of 1935 had indiscriminately killed veterans and civilians, and it had made their common claim on the government a reality. At Islamorada in the Florida Keys in November 1937, a monument to the victims of the Labor Day hurricane was dedicated (fig. 7.4). The monument had been designed by the Federal Art Project and built by the Works Projects Administration (WPA), two New Deal programs. An audience of 5,000 people attended the ceremony to watch Faye Marie Parker, a nine-year-old survivor of the storm, unveil the monument with its sculpted bending palms and waves and the accompanying plaque that read: "Dedicated to the Memory of the Civilians and War Veterans whose lives were lost in the Hurricane of September second 1935."[93]

In the Florida Keys, as in the memorials raised for the 1928 Okeechobee victims and for those of the 1930 San Zenón hurricane in the Dominican Republic, sites of memory were being created that in many ways treated the victims like those fallen in battle. In the age when popular music was being widely disseminated on the radio and composers were seeking increasingly to use folk themes to create national consciousness, *plenas*, calypso songs, and boleros were also commemorating the disaster of the storms. The direct ties between natural disaster and nation now had representations in marble and music. In the United States, and in much of the Greater Caribbean, the relationship between the state and natural disasters in general, and hurricanes in particular, would never be the same.

CHAPTER 8

Public Storms, Communal Action, and Private Grief

> Hurricanes and things like that are nothing
> compared to what a revolution can do.
> —*Fidel Castro, after Hurricane Flora (1963)*

> Humans caused the disaster just as humans made sure
> the governments of Nicaragua and Honduras were
> incapable of responding to the catastrophe.
> —*Alexander Cockburn and Jeffrey St. Clair on*
> *Hurricane Mitch (1998)*

> Hell of a job, Brownie.
> —*President Bush after Hurricane Katrina (2005)*

In September 1944, a tremendous hurricane first sighted northwest of Puerto Rico moved up the coast of the United States, battering shipping and shores from Cape Hatteras to Rhode Island. Only forty-six people on shore lost their lives directly from the storm, but among its victims at sea were two Coast Guard vessels and a Navy destroyer, which sank with the loss of 248 men. The damage on shore and to shipping was extensive, calculated at $100 million at the time (or over $1.2 billion in today's currency), but the storm had been less dangerous than the 1938 New England hurricane.[1] Still, the image of one of the nation's great warships, sunk in wartime by a storm, and of the nation's great cities like Philadelphia, Boston, and New York under siege by wind and wave, captured the attention of the United States at a time just when the fortunes of war seemed to be turning in favor of the allies. People wondered at the time if the same energy and ingenuity that had been invested in the war effort could be turned to the conquest of nature. In fact, it was during the September 1944 hurricane that military aircraft made the first planned flight to penetrate a hurricane in order to make observations. Technology had now become available to make a renewed attempt to contest the storms.

In many ways World War II transformed the study of hurricanes, providing the ability to observe and track storms, and the potential to predict their movement. During the war, meteorology had played an important role for all the participants, from the Japanese preparations for the attack on Pearl Harbor to the timing of the D-day invasion. For the United States alone, the planning and success of the Normandy landings in 1944 and the bad weather that proved so costly to the Allied campaign during the battle of the Bulge both drove home the importance of weather observation and prediction. Hurricanes proved to be both a logistical and operational challenge. At one point a hurricane in Texas had interrupted the production of much needed aviation fuel, and perhaps most famously, two Pacific hurricanes (typhoons) wreaked havoc on large American fleets in 1944 and 1945, embarrassing their commander, Admiral "Bull" Halsey, and causing tremendous loss of life and destruction to aircraft and ships.[2]

All of this weather impact on the war effort resulted in the investment of personnel and resources by the government and the military. In 1943, the first aircraft flew into the eye of a hurricane off the Texas Gulf coast as the result of a "bar bet," to be followed by the organized flight of 1944, and eventually, by the 1950s, these "Hurricane Hunter" aircraft were making regular observation flights. Meanwhile the development of radio waves to track enemy planes and ships (which came to be known during the war as radar) now allowed for weather observation at a distance, since rain, hail, and clouds could also be observed with this technology. The technical and scientific advances of meteorology made during the war were increasingly applied to civilian uses as air travel became common and weather observation gained in its technical proficiency in the postwar period.

The advances continued. High-altitude weather balloons were also introduced to capture information on wind currents, and then in the 1950s, the use of satellites for high-altitude observation of tropical weather became a major meteorological breakthrough.[3] The first weather satellite, Tiros I, was launched in 1960, and while the effectiveness of early weather satellites was limited, by the mid-1960s their technological capabilities had become much improved. Eventually, U.S. technology enabled other nations to make their own weather observation advances. In 1977, the first European meteorological satellite was placed into orbit from the United States. The satellites now gave scientists the ability to conduct observations over very broad expanses of the oceans.

Increased observations and knowledge led to growing convictions that hurricanes and other weather phenomena might be controlled or managed. This belief led to *Project Cirrus,* a 1947–52 program of cloud-seeding with dry ice. If successful, this technique would lessen the effect of rising hot air within a hurricane, and in theory could lower its wind speeds and damage potential, or in some cases, change its trajectory. The seeding of a 1947 storm that ended up hitting Savannah raised considerable complaints in the press about these procedures. In 1954 President Dwight D. Eisenhower appointed a commission to inquire into the hurricane modification project, and their findings were only reservedly positive. When subsequent hurricane seedings proved ineffective, the project was eventually supplanted by *Project Stormfury,* a program run by the National Hurricane Center between 1961 and 1983.

Whatever the scientific value of such attempts at weather modification, these hurricane projects and those to increase or decrease rainfall were always politically controversial, since changing the course of a hurricane or changing areas of rainfall might save one area from injury, but place another in danger. Fidel Castro claimed the United States was carrying out environmental warfare by trying to divert rainfall from Cuba to ruin its agriculture. There were Pentagon attempts to increase rainfall over the Ho Chi Minh supply trail during the Vietnam War, and some countries complained that weather manipulation was being carried out with economic and political objectives as much as environmental ones.[4] Conspiracy theories abounded, and to many observers it seemed as though human hubris had gone too far. Even those people whose point of reference was not theological or conspiratorial feared that such programs seemed to fit exactly the sociological warnings that we had moved into age of what came to be called "risk society." It seemed that technological advances, rather than eliminating risks, had now become the major producers of them. The atomic power meltdowns, the creation of resistant strains of bacteria, or the capricious tampering with nature without a clear vision of the effects of human intervention, had, because of their potential to create disasters, become the problem rather than the solution.[5]

In the midst of these concerns, the second half of the twentieth century was a period in which vulnerability to catastrophic storms was increasing. While new technologies had enhanced prediction and seemed to lower fatalities, at least for wealthier countries and more affluent sectors of populations, demographic growth, land development, and loose building restrictions were increasing the cost of damages. Between 1950 and 1994, thirteen major hurricane strikes were responsible for $33 billion in damages or 62 percent of all insured losses to floods, droughts, and other natural calamities.[6] As governments began to recognize this pattern, the urgency of responding became clear.

TECHNOLOGY, METEOROLOGY, AND MANAGEMENT

In the 1950s and 1960s, the technological advances in the study of the atmosphere were accompanied by an increasing administrative organization of weather observation and prediction in general, and of hurricane control and warning in particular. The Miami Weather Bureau became the National Hurricane Center in 1955, and a National Hurricane Research Laboratory was created in 1956 after a string of hurricanes struck the northeastern United States in the immediately preceding years. In 1970, the National Oceanic and Atmospheric Administration (NOAA) was created, and the National Weather Bureau was renamed the National Weather Service.[7] In 1979, the first federal organization for disaster relief was created. The Federal Emergency Management Agency (FEMA) became the principal agency for handling all disasters. All of these steps implied a growing recognition of government's direct involvement in the prediction of and preparation for natural hazards that had the potential to cause catastrophic damage.

None of these developments were free from the influences of Cold War challenges and ideology, and that too was a problem. In the United States, as early as 1950 the United States Civil Defense Agency assumed control over potential natural and other disasters, particularly atomic attack. Thus, the preparedness for hurricanes and the impact of other natural phenomena was often subordinated to political, military, or what today would be called "security" concerns. FEMA, which eventually became a dumping ground for innumerable political appointments with no particular experience with natural disaster preparation or response,[8] spent far more on preparing for nuclear attacks than on natural disasters, and its abysmal failure to respond adequately to Hurricane Hugo in 1989 or to various droughts, floods, and earthquakes was noteworthy in its disregard for the victims, especially the poorest of them. What was becoming apparent in the United States was a growing political and ideological division between those who saw disaster relief in many ways as an extension of the political transformations of the 1930s, and thus an essential governmental responsibility and a right that citizens as part of the political community could expect, and those who continued to view risk as individual responsibility that could best be handled by communal charities, through the marketplace of the insurance industry, or as a matter for local or state governments.

During the postwar era, the advances in prediction combined with the powerful diffusion of radio and television created an increasing public interest in the weather report. In the North Atlantic, the naming of storms, first using the military alphabetic code (Abel, Baker, Charlie, etc.) begun in 1950, was feminized by the use of women's names in 1953, with all the predictable accompanying journalistic metaphors and negative references to supposed female characteristics. The practice had broad popular appeal and made the storms easier to track for the press and public.[9] Eventually, in 1979, the gender bias was questioned and a new alphabetic series using both masculine and feminine names drawn from four different languages was introduced. The creation of the Saffir-Simpson scale in the 1970s, ranking storms by their wind force, also contributed to growing public interest in the storms by making it easy for the average citizen to compare their destructive potential. Weather casters began to appear as semi-celebrity personalities, not only in the United States, but in Puerto Rico, Jamaica, and Martinique as well. In Miami and San Juan, local newspapers published special supplements annually on hurricane lore, complete with maps showing latitude and longitude so that readers could track the season's storms.

Since the United States had emerged from World War II as the predominant power and had the equipment, materials, military organization, and financial resources to invest in these programs, it led the way in the Greater Caribbean region.[10] There were, however, a number of large collaborative programs, such as Global Atmospheric Research, which that involved over 60 nations and included comprehensive and detailed observations of tropical atmosphere. In 1977, under the auspices of the World Meteorological Organization, for the first time a Hurricane Committee, created in Mexico and involving thirty or so international specialists, met in order to discuss regional operations.[11]

For the most part, however, in the decades immediately following the war, attention in the Caribbean region was directed to the financial challenges produced by the war's end, and by the questions of governance and constitutional status, which in many places meant either decolonization or integration with the former metropoles. The result was considerable regional variation in terms of capacity to confront hurricanes and other disasters and a disparity in available resources to do so. The French Antilles became departments of France in 1948, and while differences in law and style with the metropolis never disappeared fully, in terms of the weather Martinique, Guadeloupe, and St. Martin fell under the jurisdiction of the French National Meteorological Association. Puerto Rico remained under American tutelage, but in 1948, the people of Puerto Rico were for the first time able to elect their own governor, Luís Muñoz Marín; and in 1952 he negotiated the Free Associated State or Commonwealth arrangement with the United States. The island continued to be integrated into the United States weather establishment and was an active participant in its institutions. Cuba, with its well-developed meteorological tradition, maintained its own weather service, as did the Dominican Republic, although their different political histories during the late twentieth century produced quite different outcomes in terms of their governments' ability to deal with natural hazards. Both, however, sought to join regional efforts at hurricane prediction and response. Of the British colonies, Jamaica (1962), Trinidad and Tobago (1962), and Barbados (1966) became independent, while others chose associated statehood in 1967. Although many of the islands of the Commonwealth developed local institutions to deal with natural disasters, they made attempts to join with other states of the Caribbean for regional cooperation. In 1984, a Pan-Caribbean Project for Disaster was created with help from the United Nations Disaster Relief Organization and the governments of Canada, the Netherlands, and the United States, but a more independent Caribbean organization (CDERA) was created by the Caribbean Community (CARICOM) in 1991 following the damages of Hurricane Hugo in 1989. The new organization sought to improve the preparation for hurricanes and reduce damages and deaths, but with scant resources, improvement was difficult through the 1990s, even though some foreign aid was available. In 2005, the organization's name was changed to the Caribbean Disaster Emergency Management Agency (CDEMA), and its activities have grown as the agency has matured.[12]

These problems of political definition, status, and future were never far distant from the global context, which by the 1950s had evolved into the ideological and political rivalries of the Cold War. The hurricane seasons now brought the great storms into a new political context that forced governments to respond with an increased concern for material and ideological impacts.

Finally, it is also important to note the demographic shifts taking place throughout the region. The population of the island Caribbean almost tripled, from 15 to 42 million, between 1945 and 2010, most (90 percent) living in the Greater Antilles. Rates of growth in Puerto Rico, the Dominican Republic, Haiti, and Jamaica were impressive, but there were also high rates of growth in some of the small islands as well. High population densities led to large-scale out-migration and to concentration in urban areas.[13] These shifts implied changes in the impact of the recurring tropical storms. These changes were also visible in the continental rimland of the Caribbean: in Mexico, where the population rose from 28 million in 1950 to 116 million in 2013, and in Central America, a region that was also subject to hurricanes. During this period new technologies of prediction and better communication systems tended to decrease the number of fatalities from hurricanes, but urban growth, population concentration, and the development of tourism in coastal areas increased the levels of property damage and loss.

COLD WAR DISASTERS: A REFORMER, AND A REVOLUTION

Puerto Rico had passed through a period of reform and reconstruction in the 1930s as an extension of the New Deal. During this time new political forces had emerged, including a progressive pro-independence Popular Democratic Party or *Populares* under Luís Muñoz Marín, a U.S-educated son of a distinguished politician and an important figure in the island's legislature in the 1930s. The presence of U.S. bases made Puerto Rico a part of the U.S. war effort in World War II, and many Puerto Ricans served in the armed forces, but sentiments for independence and nationalism remained strong in the face of continuing poverty on the island. Objections to the dependent relationship generated academic denunciations, labor unrest, and political activity. Not surprisingly, artists and poets appropriated the metaphor of the hurricane to describe the vulnerability of Puerto Rico, as well as the island's tension with the United States. The poet Luis Pales Mattos saw the sensuality of his island's African culture as a weapon and as a symbol of its opposition to its dependency.[14]

> Rumor of wind and water . . .
> the Island is dancing on the sea
> moving this way and that—
> shake it, shake it
> in the hurricane
>
> . . .
>
> to piss off Uncle Sam.

The *Populares* had originally been a pro-independence party, but Muñoz Marín's objectives changed, and as party leader he moved the party toward a position advocating more autonomy and development in collaboration with the United States. In 1948, under Muñoz Marin's urging as president of the Puerto Rican Senate, the government launched Operation Bootstrap, a program of social and economic reform offering a number of social programs and instituting a minimum wage and aiming at transforming the island's economic base from agriculture to industry. Also in that year, the United States granted Puerto Rico the right to elect their own governor, and voters elected Muñoz Marín. A poet and intellectual with broad political background and experience who had come to political maturity in the reformist and populist era of the 1930s, Muñoz Marín was, in the words of historian Francisco Scarano, "a *caudillo* of the masses and a man of state like few in his era."[15] Reelected three times, he dominated Puerto Rican political life until his decision not to run again in 1964, and he remained active into the next decade.

On taking office in 1949, Muñoz Marín initiated a program of legal, economic, and social change. This included constitutional reform and a program of industrialization, as well as various programs of social welfare, but it also included an abandonment of his former stance on nationalism and independence. In 1952, under his leadership, Puerto Rico declared itself a "Free Associated State" or Commonwealth, integrated in many ways with the United States, but clearly dependent on and subordinate to it. The pro-independence party, having failed in the electoral process, now moved to more radical action, including several shootouts in Puerto Rico and an attack on the U.S. Congress, all of which was met by Muñoz Marín and by federal agencies with severe limits on freedom of speech and expression, arbitrary arrests, and active repression. As the Cold War intensified, both local conditions on the island and political and ideological concerns of the United States contributed to these actions of repression. In the United States there was some desire to grant independence to the island and to simply abandon it as a troublesome and expensive investment, but Muñoz Marín sought U.S. allies to prevent that move and to strengthen Washington's commitment to the island's improvement.

It was in this context that Hurricane Betsy struck the island on August 12, 1956, the feast day of Santa Clara. This was a major storm, the first to strike the island since 1932, and like the majority of the most damaging Puerto Rican hurricanes, it traversed the island from the southeast to the northwest. There had already been rumors that a storm must be on the horizon, since 1956 was to be an electoral year, and in the past hurricanes had often come in politically sensitive years.[16] Puerto Rico, in the midst of the progressive reforms, was meteorologically ready. The Weather Bureau was well staffed and directed, and for the first time Hurricane Hunter aircraft were available and radar was in use. A professor of meteorology from the University of Puerto Rico, Dr. Clay McDonnell, kept the island's public aware of the storm's progress on television which was just beginning to arrive; his heavily accented Spanish in no way diminishing his popularity. The "public storm" had arrived on the island.

The storm started as a small Cape Verdean tropical depression; crossing the Atlantic, it was first announced in Puerto Rico on August 10 when it was still about 800 miles to the southeast. As it approached the island, it was moving at about twenty miles per hour and was fourteen miles in diameter. It struck with disastrous results, killing 16, injuring 244, leaving many families homeless, and causing over $40 million in damages. Overall, the various branches of government—Civil Defense, the Weather Bureau, the Red Cross, and the National Guard—and the information services of radio, press, and telephone all acted well, or at least that was the message that the governor later sought to convey to the population.[17]

Muñoz Marín knew how to mobilize a government—and he did so. Apparently, looking at how his predecessor Governor Beverley had responded to the San Ciprián storm in 1932, Muñoz Marín immediately made a tour of the affected areas, and then two days after the hurricane had passed, he went on radio to address the country.[18] Noting the scenes of destruction and temporary disorder, he emphasized his pride in the capacity of his compatriots to meet adversity: "After these days, I feel once again justified in the pride I feel to be part of this people and honored by its generous confidence. It gives one pleasure to serve a people who knows how to take care of itself, to honor a people that knows how to honor itself." Describing the challenges of lack of water, food, electricity, and housing, Muñoz Marín lauded the efforts to rebuild and recover. "Poor people, good people without more resources than those of their daily life," none sought help and all sought to help themselves. Only those who could not help themselves asked for aid, and he responded to them positively.

"The government feels compelled to do this not only as its duty as a democratic government, but because of the disinterested attitude, the self-effort and bravery before adversity that our people are demonstrating." This was a discourse that recalled the old medieval emphasis on the "deserving poor" as the rightful objects of welfare, but it was also an argument directed at the federal government as Muñoz Marín sought to assure Washington that Puerto Rico could care for itself and would not become more of a burden on the federal government than it was already.[19] He was convincing. Four days later President Eisenhower declared Puerto Rico a disaster area and appropriated millions for relief. Washington saw in Muñoz Marín a way to assure the stability of Puerto Rico and to use it as a democratic model for the rest of the region.[20] Help was forthcoming.

The months following the storm were filled with the problems of recovery and administering the aid. Appeals for damages poured into San Juan. Teodoro Moscoso, a leading figure in Muñoz Marín's government, prepared a report to guide the governor's response, but there were many problems that confronted the governor. A banker from Aibonito complained that his town was the "ugly duckling" and treated like an orphan even during the storm, and that the mayor and some of those in his administration were drunks or dishonest. The mayor of Utuado wrote a lengthy letter reporting over a thousand houses damaged and almost $2 million in losses. The homeless in Utuado could not rent houses, since there were none available, and if there were, no one would rent them to the indigent. Even worse, he complained that the local representative of the Red Cross had politicized the awarding of aid and destroyed the faith of the people in that "noble" institution.[21]

The tradition had continued after disasters to appeal directly to the governor, and Muñoz Marín was enough of a populist to encourage this practice, although the banker Leoncio Rivera Rodríguez wrote to him that many people suspected that he was not receiving the personal letters, and was thus unaware of the problems of recovery.[22] Poorer citizens, however, were not disillusioned and continued to write seeking his personal intervention in their situation. To a woman from Orocovis who had lost her home, Muñoz revealed his political thinking and placed it in a positive and populist light:

Doña Rosa, . . . your affection toward me in [leads] you to say that I am the father of the poor. I do not think in that way. I am more your friend and companion in the efforts that we are making, and that we will continue to make to better the conditions in the life of our people. In those efforts, your friend salutes you.[23]

The activities of rebuilding after Santa Clara fit comfortably in Muñoz Marín's program of improvement, and President Eisenhower's declaration of Puerto Rico as a disaster zone provided his administration an opportunity to emphasize that the United States would continue to play a positive role in the island's development as a showcase for a Latin America that seemed threatened by leftist tendencies. The Republican Party platform of 1956 both pledged the continuing support of Puerto Rico in its political growth and economic development "in accordance with the wishes of its people and the fundamental principle of self-determination," and celebrated the fall of the "communist regime of Guatemala" and its liberation from an imagined Kremlin control.

The hurricanes of this period provided both political challenges and opportunities. Eisenhower's approach and emphasis in responding to natural disasters was for the federal government to take limited action:

Federal government . . . should be kept always—when it is humanly possible—as a partner, to participate in a helpful way, but to keep the maximum of responsibility and direction of operations in the local scene . . . so that working all together we can, in the true American tradition, get something done without surrendering any of those great values for which this nation was founded—our private privileges and rights under the Constitution of America.[24]

How that principle could guide national policy in the face of local preferences, interests, and obstructions provides much of the background to the history of disaster preparation and response in recent times.[25]

The hurricane season of 1963 passed relatively unnoticed in the United States. A strong east coast area of high pressure during July and August forced storms forming in the Atlantic and moving westward to curve back into the Atlantic before reaching the U.S. coast, but in September conditions further south made the Caribbean region more favorable to cyclonic activity. For the first time in two years, a September hurricane, Cindy, made landfall in Louisiana and Texas, killing three people and causing $12 million in property damage. But this paled in comparison to the blow that Haiti and Cuba received later that month from Hurricane Flora, when 7–8,000 people died. Behind the great 1780 hurricane, Flora became the second deadliest hurricane in the region's history.[26] But Hurricane Flora's importance went far beyond the tally of dead and injured victims and destroyed crops and property, because by 1963 the Greater Caribbean had been fully drawn into the politics and maneuvering of the Cold War, and the impact of this storm revealed both the political dimensions of disasters and the opportunities that they could create. The success of Fidel Castro's Cuban Revolution in 1959 and Cuba's move toward socialism in the years immediately thereafter was the backdrop for Hurricane Flora and the political and humanitarian responses to its impact.

Flora had first been sighted by satellite observation on September 26 at a latitude 11.5°N, but not until September 30 did Hurricane Hunter aircraft enter the storm to make observations and record barometer readings. Flora's position was uncommonly close to the coast of South America. The San Juan Weather Bureau issued a hurricane warning, but the island of Tobago had only two hours to prepare before the storm, with winds at 90–100 miles per hour, struck on September 30, resulting in seventeen fatalities and $30 million in crop and property damages. Nearby Trinidad received heavy rain and winds gusting to 70 miles per hour, but its mountains on the north coast offered some protection. The storm then began to curve northward as it passed through the southern Caribbean. By October 3 as it approached the southern peninsula of Haiti its gusts had reached 200 miles per hour and the pressure had dropped to 27.64 inches (936 millibars). The hurricane delivered a ferocious blow to the island. The rain fell incessantly for three days, perhaps as much as 75 inches. The winds, flash flooding, and storm surge caused terrible damage. Over 100,000 were left homeless; deaths were estimated at 5,000, and damage at $125–180 million.

Virtually no pre-storm measures had been taken to mitigate the blow. Haiti at this time was under the control of François "Papa Doc" Duvalier, who had been elected to office in 1957 and had immediately begun to institute a regime of random violence and brutal dictatorship. During the storm, Duvalier's henchman and director of the Haitian Red Cross, Dr. Jacques Fourcand, had prohibited any radio weather broadcasts warning of the storm in order to "reduce panic," a decision that resulted in a lack of preparation and the sinking or destruction of scores of small boats.[27] The result was a disaster of tremendous proportions. Aid from the United States and other nations began to flow in immediately. The Duvalier regime was not shaken by the crisis: less than a year after Flora, Duvalier proclaimed himself president for life. He would continue to implacably suppress all opposition.

The brutality of the Duvalier regime was well known in the United States. Nevertheless, by 1961 about half of Haiti's budget was provided by U.S. aid to the regime and the Haitian armed forces. Duvalier's thugs, the *Tontons Makoutes*, were armed by the United States as well. President John F. Kennedy's administration understood the risks in supporting this regime, and saw the contradiction that Haiti's poverty, illiteracy, and violation of human and political rights under Duvalier presented to the Alliance for Progress's policy toward the region; but the fear of communism, brought to a head by the Cuban Revolution, forestalled any attempt to destabilize the Duvalier regime.[28] Moreover, the assassination of Trujillo in the neighboring Dominican Republic in 1961 had made the United States nervous about increasing regional instability. In January 1962, the United States, anxious to expel Cuba from the Organization of American States, got Haiti to cast the deciding vote in return for the promise of aid and a tacit recognition of Duvalier's legitimacy. Duvalier, using his opposition to communism as a cover, brutally suppressed any resistance to his regime, declared himself eligible for reelection, and staged a rigged election in 1961. His assumption of a life-term presidency in 1964 was done over the objections of the United States. While there were those in the Kennedy and Johnson administrations who wanted to undermine his regime, Duvalier's stubborn skills and the brutal stability he imposed won him the tacit recognition and support of the United States.

The contrast of Haiti's disaster with the situation in the neighboring Dominican Republic was striking. The Dominican Republic had just been visited by Hurricane Edith (September 26–27), which, while only a Category 1 storm when it reached the island, had brought heavy rains.[29] The Dominicans then escaped the worst impact of Flora, but suffered moderate winds, heavy rains, and severe flooding, and eventually forty fatalities. Bridges were destroyed, roads cut, and $60 million in losses were estimated, including about fifteen percent of the cacao harvest. The relief effort in the Barahona area was inefficient and corrupt, and residents complained that the clothing, medicine, and food sent by the Red Cross were being stolen or sold.[30] Still, the tracking of the storm had been fully announced, and some preventative measures had been effectively taken. This was notable, since the country was at that moment under the control of a military junta.

The junta came to power in September 25, 1963, deposing the president, Juan Bosch. Bosch, who had been elected only seven months before, was trying to enact a series of liberal reforms that had provoked the military, the Church, and powerful economic interests. Rumors about CIA involvement in the coup circulated widely in the press. John Bartlow Martin, the U.S. ambassador at the time, denied it, although his memoir reveals that Washington thought that Bosch's problems were of his own making and was not willing to do much to bolster his government. Two years later, when a popular uprising broke out to bring Bosch back from exile, U.S. troops intervened to prevent his return.[31] Martin later remembered that on the night of the coup, heavy rains preceding Hurricane Edith had drenched the capital city, and no crowd had gathered on the streets to defend the presidency that night, nor on the following day as the hurricane reached the city. He later justified the U.S. failure to support Bosch by arguing that the United States could not defend a government that its own people had been unwilling to support, but he mused on the inclemency of the weather as a factor in their failure to respond.[32]

The differences between the responses to natural disasters in Haiti and the Dominican Republic and between their results were nothing new. The island the two countries share had from 1850 to 2007 been subject to periodic earthquakes and 69 hurricanes. The risks have continued, and in 2010 Haiti suffered the shock of a 7.7 quake that killed 314,000 people.[33] Haiti, with a smaller size, denser population, and lower per capita income, has been more vulnerable to the effects of tropical cyclones and earthquakes, a situation made worse by its government's disregard for disaster preparedness and mitigation and its lack of resources to invest in the infrastructure to lessen vulnerability. San Zenón had taught Trujillo the transformative power of a disaster. He used that power. It was rumored that he also superstitiously feared the hurricane season for the rest of his life, and there is evidence that at one point in 1955, he briefly considered funding a research center for controlling and dispersing hurricanes.[34] Moreover, he took an interest (admittedly self-interested) in certain conservation policies, and occasionally spoke in terms of environmental protection. Duvalier had no interest in such details, and subsequent governments in Haiti, including that of his dictator son Jean-Claude Duvalier (in power 1971–86), faced with the meteorological and geophysical hazards of the country's location, lacked either the will or the resources to take adequate steps to respond to the threats.[35]

After flattening much of Haiti's southern peninsula, Hurricane Flora proceeded to the northwest, reaching the coast of Cuba's Oriente province between Guantanamo and Santiago de Cuba on October 4. Moving very slowly, it dumped enormous amounts of rain over the eastern end of the island as it took a peculiar route, affected by high pressure over the east coast of the United States that weakened the storm's forward force and caused it to "drift." Making a loop over Santa Cruz, on October 7–8 the storm crossed back over the same parts of Oriente province that it had visited on October 5–6. For five days the winds and rains hammered the area before Flora eventually moved off through the Bahamas. The rainfall amounts in Cuba were spectacular, most places reporting anywhere from 40 to almost 80 inches over the five days. Santiago reported over 100 inches, the highest amount of rainfall ever recorded for a single event in Cuba. The Salado, Bayamo, Cautillo, and Contramestre rivers all overflowed. The Cauto, Cuba's largest river, at one point was said to have swelled to fifty miles across, a distance wider than the mouth of the Amazon.[36] Oriente and Camaguey provinces bore the brunt of the storm; thousands of acres were flooded, crops were destroyed, and whole communities were inundated or washed away. The strange loop in the storm track, the torrents of rain, and the destruction recalled an older Cuban cyclone, the "five-day hurricane" of 1910, another October storm coming out of the southern Caribbean and moving northeastward as they often do. That one had battered western Cuba, made a tight loop and recrossed Pinar del Río, destroyed Casilda and Batabanó, and breached the waterfront wall of the *malecón* in Havana, which suffered flooding. It killed at least a hundred people and probably many more in the countryside, and had been Cuba's most destructive storm on record. Flora's damage was worse.

The Cuban Revolution ousted the Batista government in January 1959, and its leader, Fidel Castro, was consolidating his regime and embarking on a socialist path during the early 1960s. He had defeated the invasion force of exiles at the Bay of Pigs (April 1961) and had weathered the stand-off between the Soviet Union and the United States during the Missile Crisis (October 1962), but the settlement of that confrontation, made without much Cuban participation, had been something of an embarrassment to Castro.

Hurricane Flora came at as auspicious moment. It was the first real natural disaster faced by the Castro government, and it was a challenge that Castro needed to confront successfully in order to legitimate the new order and his leadership. The Cuban response to Flora differed markedly from that of its neighbors. All of the institutions of the regime were mobilized for the relief effort—the militias, the army, and the defense committees, as well as the Red Cross and police. Principal leaders of the revolution played important roles in these efforts, not only Fidel Castro, who visited the affected zones, spoke with victims, and directed operations from an amphibious vehicle as can be seen in figure 8.1, but also his brother Raúl, and men like Juan Almeida Bosque, a revolutionary commander and Fidel's companion from the early days, who took a leading role in the mobilization of relief. Bosque's memoir of these events, *Contra el agua y el viento* (1985), mixed his eyewitness observations and hortatory comments with the usual justifications of the revolution and condemnations of the previous regime as well as of Cuba's present enemies. The book was awarded the prestigious Casa de Las Américas prize of 1985 perhaps more for its message and for the author's career than for its literary merits, but Almeida's writing at times catches the scale of the disaster and the dimen-

FIGURE 8.1 Fidel Castro commands the response to Hurricane Flora (Available on-line at XXX)

sions of its challenge with personal observations that bring those days in October 1963 to life. He uses the "tak, tak, tak" of the helicopter blades as a background rhythm to the accounts of heroism, sacrifice, and loss, and he then compares that sound to the *clavateo*, the sound of pounding in nails that he remembered when he and his father were boarding up their home as the 1944 hurricane approached Havana.[37] That had been the storm that lived in Cuban popular memory and remained the point of reference for the evaluation of Hurricane Flora's impact.

The relief effort was impressive: helicopters, trucks, tanks, and amphibious landing craft brought in food and supplies and helped to evacuate thousands. The number of evacuees was estimated at 175,000. Photographs of a helmeted Fidel and other leaders filled the press, as did stories of his personal accessibility to the victims. The loss of 1,200 people was bad enough, but without the relief operations, the results could have been far worse. During the whole operation an explanatory discourse began to grow that soon became the central core of Flora's meaning to the revolution, and the way in which that meaning would be employed thereafter. In late October, before the calculation of damage and deaths had been completed, Castro offered a speech shaped by two themes that came to dominate the tale of Flora: the sense of community and common purpose created by the revolution, and the ability of the revolution to confront and overcome natural disasters. Comparing the heroism of the rescuers to the defenders at the Bay of Pigs, Castro claimed that the feeling of solidarity produced by their efforts would by itself justify the revolution. "What happened there was the opposite of selfishness, of everybody interested in only saving themselves and solving their own problems. There everybody helped everybody else. . . . They were in a battle with nature, and their determination, courage, stoicism, and calmness—even of those who lost everything—was impressive." This was a view that, as we have seen, some eighteenth-century Caribbean travelers like Moreau de St.-Méry or colonial officials like Governor Lyon of Barbados would have shared. Modern observers, too, have noted in other circumstances that the feeling of communal solidarity and common purpose often emerges from disaster.[38] Castro, however, saw this attitude as the result of the Cuban character and the principles of the revolution.

Castro's then made his final point, this time echoing Bolívar's challenge to the 1812 Caracas earthquake: "A revolution is a force stronger than nature. Hurricanes and things like that are nothing compared to what a revolution can do. A revolution has forces much greater than those of natural phenomena and cataclysms." He promised to build dams and reservoirs on the rivers in order to turn future torrential rains into a benefit for agriculture. "We will do something to compensate those who have suffered losses and to help the families. We will wage a veritable war with nature; protect our country against such misery and pain; and turn what is now a center of desolation, devastation, and death into a center of incalculable wealth for our country. . . . This is what our response should be, one of honor."[39]

These same messages were conveyed on film by Santiago Álvarez in a twenty-two-minute documentary entitled *Ciclón*. Using newsreel footage from TV cameramen, the army, and the Cuban Film Board (ICAIC), with music but no dialogue, this powerful film, Álvarez's first major effort, conveyed the horror of the disaster and the efforts of the rescuers. The helicopters in the film symbolized the ability of technology to overcome nature. Álvarez's striking and simple black-and-white documentary became a kind of *Triumph of the Will*, visually celebrating Castro and the regime.[40]

The Cuban campaign to recover from Flora became a transformational moment. Two years later, Che Guevara, in his famous letter to the Uruguayan journalist Carlos Quijano, recognized the peoples' heroism and solidarity during Hurricane Flora, and claimed that "the need to transform it into everyday practice is one of our fundamental tasks."[41] In other words, the sense of community produced by natural catastrophe should become the spirit of everyday life. Fidel himself returned to these themes in 1966 in a long speech in Havana, given as another hurricane threatened the island. In this pronouncement he spoke again of the model of collaboration in the face of natural disaster. In a country where fatalism before nature predominated and where in the past *"ciclonear"* (to hang out and drink) had become a common way to describe preparations for a hurricane, Castro now reminded his countrymen that among them were more don Quijotes than Sancho Panzas; and that in 1868 at the beginning of the Ten Years' War against Spain, at the Bay of Pigs, and in battling Flora, Cubans had demonstrated the qualities of sacrifice and bravery needed for the future. The "new man," a new spirit, and government action could overcome "the adversities that nature has imposed on us." The response to Flora had prepared the path: "if another Flora passes over the Oriente province, we are sure that the number of victims will be incomparably fewer, because if on that occasion thanks to an immense effort innumerable lives were saved, this time for many hours before absolutely no one will be left in the places to which the water can reach them." The speech continued in this fashion, emphasizing the steps taken to diversify the economy to meet the threat of hurricanes and claiming that neither natural disasters nor blockade or attacks would deter the revolution.[42]

Castro had, in fact, begun even before Flora to improve the nation's infrastructure to meet the environmental threat. Serious droughts from 1960 to 1962 moved his government to create an Institute of Hydraulic

Resources in August 1962. He later explained: "Do you know who raised our hydraulic consciousness? It was the last two years of drought." Castro's attitudes toward the recovery from Flora and eventually toward the government's responsibility in the face of natural disasters must be set in the political context of the moment. The political reorganization of the country was in full swing when Flora struck. Rationing of food had begun in Cuba even before the devastation caused by Flora, but the storm and the U.S. embargo were subsequently used to justify the practice. The revolution had passed an agrarian reform in 1959 that had nationalized large estates and companies, and in October 1963 the second agrarian reform nationalized another 11,000 farms and turned more land over to less efficient state-run enterprises.[43]

On October 30, Castro made a television address that emphasized the need for austerity due to the disaster and to U.S. harassment. Some of his claims about the United States were justified. The CIA had continued to run operations bringing men and materials into Cuba, and Cuba had repelled a ship, the *Rex*, used by the CIA for its operations. Castro claimed that the attempt to use the distraction of the hurricane as a cover for these actions was disgraceful and that the Red Cross was acting as an arm of the U.S. State Department and was not to be trusted.[44] The CIA, for its part, drew up a report on the effects of the storm, predicting that the sugar crop would suffer and that Castro would need aid, but that there would be little immediate discontent during the recovery.[45] In fact, the sugar crop did not suffer badly, but Flora did stop the move to diversify agriculture away from sugar production, which had been one of Castro's objectives.[46]

Meanwhile, Castro had also appealed to President Kennedy to lift economic restrictions on Cuba, given the emergency conditions created by the storm. *The New York Times* wrote that "politics should have no place in the face of such suffering," and that the United States should assume its "humanitarian duty" and offer aid through "unofficial channels" to the victims in both Cuba and Haiti, whatever the nature of their governments. "We have no quarrel with the Cuban people. That goes for the Haitians too."[47] As we now know, back channels had been opened between Castro and Kennedy about some form of *modus vivendi*, but these were abruptly derailed by Kennedy's assassination in November 1963.[48]

Castro's response to Hurricane Flora consolidated his leadership in Cuba, but also disheartened those in exile who opposed him, and even made some question the effectiveness of their opposition. On October 23, José Miró Cardona, a leading figure among the exile opponents to the Castro regime, wrote to the Cuban poet Pablo Le-Riverend in Miami:

> Flora has demonstrated (with how much pain and at what cost) that the acts of sabotage by themselves, isolated and without continuity and unlinked to a military plan that meets the situation, will lead the people to desperation and provoke retaliation and delay the moment of liberation. No one could do damage more efficiently than Flora. . . . and still Fidel is there.[49]

The Cuban response to Flora became part of the revolution's mythology and a model for the regime's response to future natural disasters. Further legislation in 1966, 1976, and 1994 solidified Cuba's system of civil defense. Castro became committed to avoiding past mistakes and to devoting considerable resources to preparation for natural disasters through education and popular mobilization. Cuba's record on reducing loss of life was impressive. Between 1996 and 2002 six hurricanes struck the island, causing loss and damage to over 240,000 homes. Over 2.3 million people were evacuated during those storms, and only sixteen lives were lost.[50] When in 1991 Hurricane Michelle (Category 4), the most serious storm threat to Cuba since the great storm of 1944, struck the island, only five people died. In 2005, Hurricane Dennis, another Category 4 storm, destroyed 30,000 acres of banana trees and left 2.5 million people without electricity, but the government's evacuation of 1.5 million or 13 percent of the Cuban population kept loss of life to sixteen people.[51] These results were obtained by a combination of a national emergency plan, organizational mobilization, required annual civil practice and simulation drills (the *Meteoro* program), and active international cooperation by the Cuban Institute for Meteorology, which also took on the responsibility for national advisory warnings. Steps as simple as trimming tree limbs, making sure of stockpiles of water, keeping hospitals open, and allowing people to evacuate their pets as well as themselves contributed, and continue to contribute, to the success of the Cuban response. Expectations on the island were raised. A poor performance in response to a 1985 hurricane led to sarcastic references in Cuba to the department of *mentirologia* (lying) rather than *meteorologia* and the dismissal of its director.

Cuban policies for disaster preparedness and mitigation became a model celebrated by the United Nations and the International Federation of the Red Cross and Red Crescent Societies, especially since Cuba is not a wealthy country and has limited resources to invest in these measures.[52] But the celebration of its accomplishment in reducing loss of life has not been without technical and ideological criticism. Some observers have criticized the top-down nature of the Cuban mobilization and the lack of local influence on national planning, while others have pointed out the failures in providing adequate housing that have been made worse by hurricane damage. Some critics are simply made uncomfortable by the state's ability to require evacuations, enforce restrictions on occupation of areas deemed to be of high risk, and demand involuntary mobilizations during the period of recovery.[53] The exchange of liberty for effectiveness is thought by some to be too costly.

Cuba's record on environmental issues in general was has remained mixed into the twenty-first century. The difficulty of balancing economic development and growth with environmental concerns remained a sensitive issue. Dr. José Oro, former director general of Cuba's Department of Natural Resources, remarked in 1992, "we have the industrial production of Honduras and the pollution of East Germany."[54] But by the mid-1990s, Castro was becoming aware that the rise of the oceans, global warming, and an increase in the size and frequency of hurricanes all had a particular importance for island nations. His statements increasingly expressed a "green" rhetoric in which he criticized the concept of perpetual growth and called for a more equitable distribution of wealth.[55] Meanwhile, Cuba had become a model for many Caribbean nations because its multidimensional approach and emphasis on disaster preparation and mitigation had proven so effective.

Global Warming and the Hurricane Debate

While there remains an intense debate over the principal causes for it, we know now that there is much variability in the annual frequency and intensity of tropical storms in the world. The "historical meteorologists" like Andrés Poëy in the nineteenth century and David Ludlum and José Carlos Millás in the twentieth century, who combed archives, ships logs, and old newspapers, had gathered a great deal of information about the storms back to the arrival of Columbus. They intuitively understood that establishing the historical record of the storms might reveal patterns that could lead to accurate prediction, but the scientific usefulness and accuracy of these historical reports and accounts was often questionable. With the use of aircraft reconnaissance, satellite observation (beginning in 1966), and the creation of institutions like NOAA, however, recorded data not only significantly increased in volume, but became much better, more accurate, and far more consistent.[56] Thus meteorologists can speak with some confidence about the characteristics of the great storms from about 1950 to the present, and their patterns of occurrence, if not about the causes of their variability over time.

Of the eighty or so hurricanes or typhoons that develop in all the world's oceans each year, the Atlantic produces about ten tropical storms, of which about six on average become hurricanes (defined as having sustained winds over 74 miles per hour). There is, however, considerable annual variability, and periods of greater or lesser activity. The periods of the mid-1920s to mid-1930s and the mid-1940s to the mid-1960s were very active in the North Atlantic with numerous hurricane landfalls in the United States. Florida, as we have seen, suffered heavy blows: Miami in 1926, Okeechobee in 1928, and the Keys in 1935. That state alone experienced 11 hurricanes from 1944 to 1950, suffering considerable economic losses as a result. During the period 1970–95 there seems to have been a marked decline in the number of hurricanes in the North Atlantic, with an average of only 1.5 major hurricanes (Category 3 and above) a year, compared to four a year for the previous period 1940–70.[57] But beginning in 1995, the number of Atlantic hurricanes, especially powerful Category 3 and above, rose dramatically. There were sixteen storms of that intensity between 1975 and 1989, but twenty-five in the following period of 1990 to 2004; as one study has demonstrated, the frequency of hurricanes did not increase between 1975 and 2005, but the proportion reaching Category 4 or 5 status doubled.[58]

Two concerns arise from this data, one meteorological and one historical. Why the variability? Is it simply part of a natural cycle, or is it today the result human activity? Modern scientific thinking has emphasized that hurricanes become more frequent when sea temperatures rise and vertical wind shear (higher altitude wind) decreases. During El Niño events, the tropical Atlantic usually has an increase in stratospheric winds, and that stronger wind shear inhibits the rising column of moisture from warm waters, which keeps tropical storms from reaching hurricane status.

Some studies have suggested that the recent warming of the Atlantic has been part of a climatic change—global warming—due primarily to carbon emissions into the atmosphere, that is, to human activity, but others have suggested that there is a periodic warming and cooling (the Atlantic Multidecadal Oscillation), which explains the current rise in hurricane frequency, or at least casts doubt on the anthropogenic nature of global warming. While the opponents of the global warming theory who favor the theory of naturally occurring cycles admit that there is plenty of evidence of the increase in hurricane numbers and intensity since the mid-1990s, they argue that such rises have also taken place in the past, and that the accurate scientific record is simply not long enough to draw any conclusions about the cause of the present conditions.

In some ways this debate is the product of the nineteenth century's turn away from explanations that viewed human sin and moral failure as the cause of natural disasters and toward natural explanations of geophysical and atmospheric phenomena. But whereas observers in the nineteenth century replaced divine anger with the laws of nature as the primary or at least secondary cause of hurricanes, the late-twentieth-century understanding of ecology and environment once again has placed human actions and failures at the heart of explanations of destructive natural phenomena.

By the 1980s, the scientific sides of the dispute were being clearly drawn.[59] Many of those who depended on a strong empiricist methodology and believed that human-caused global warming was not the root cause were, like Christopher Landsea and Roger Pielke Jr., students of William Gray, a meteorologist at Colorado State University. Beginning in the 1980s, Gray had gained notoriety as a hurricane *savant* because of his annual predictions of the number and type of hurricanes. On the opposing side were meteorologists like Kerry Emanuel of the Massachusetts Institute of Technology who had no doubt about anthropogenic causes of global warming and their effects on tropical cyclones. These differences led to a vigorous, and at times unseemly, debate among meteorologists, an argument that at its core was about methodologies and the relative utility of inductive versus deductive reasoning. It was a scientific disagreement between those who depend on observation, and who thus claimed that the record is simply not long or complete enough to warrant any firm conclusion, and those who, using computer-generated theoretical models, have concluded that human effects have indeed altered the atmosphere and increased the risks from hurricanes.[60] By the 1990s, however, the question had become increasingly politicized, as those who wanted no restrictions on the use of fossil fuels and carbon emissions favored the Gray position, and those who hoped to slow or eliminate human effects of global warming based their arguments on the work of Emanuel and a growing number of other scientists.[61]

In this battle over the existence of anthropogenic global warming, hurricane frequency and intensity became a focal point where the effects of global warming seemed to have an immediate and easily perceived impact. Thus, when hurricane damage in the United States alone reached about $42 billion in 2004, and over $100 billion in the Atlantic community in 2005, the topic of hurricanes became a matter of increasing public and political interest as well as the center of scientific controversy.[62] In the wake of the disaster of Hurricane Katrina in 2005, the controversy and disagreements became even more important and more public as competing papers argued over gaps in the data, statistical techniques, and overall interpretations.

Not only did political interests seize on scientific evidence to support their positions, but the scientists themselves also began to make policy suggestions on the basis of their findings. In a carefully argued paper in 2003, Roger Pielke Jr., Christopher Landsea, and others reasoned that the scientific evidence cannot substantiate the relative impact of global warming on hurricanes because the data before 1850 is spotty and incomplete, and because in a time frame of only five centuries it is difficult to make comparative statements about geophysical or atmospheric conditions across millennia. To those who argue that losses in life and property have greatly increased as a result of mega-storms, Roger Pielke Jr. and his associates presented evidence showing that when "normalized," or adjusted to include demographic changes and inflation, losses in life and property to hurricanes do not display a significant increase for recent decades, and that the average loss per hurricane between 1900 and 1950 was not statistically less than between 1951 and 2000. Their argument emphasizes that both changes in environment such as global warming and changes in society (demographics, settlement patterns, migration, building codes, etc.) affect hurricane impacts, and that given the present state of scientific knowledge about hurricanes and the influence of climatic change on them, a concentration on "political, institutional, and intellectual" aspects, that is, limiting population densities near the seacoast, or strictly enforcing building codes, has a better chance of lowering vulnerability to hurricanes than does the hope of reducing hurricane frequency or intensity by energy policy.[63] While their point is well taken, given the political realities in twenty-first-century American politics, the goals of ending poverty and enforcing limits on population growth or development seem even less likely to be achieved than limitations on use of fossil fuels. Scientific debate on this issue had become exacerbated by an alignment of political forces with the two positions: one side committed to an expansion of the use of fossil fuels and industrial growth with limited environmental restrictions, and therefore dubious about claims of global warming; and the other side desirous of finding alternate sources of energy and enforcing strict environmental codes to slow the levels of pollution and the melting of the Arctic icecaps and the rise of sea levels.

Societies and Storms at the Century's End

In historical terms, the last decade of the twentieth century and first decades of the twenty-first century have witnessed a profound political and ideological divergence on how best to deal with this problem of climate change in the long and short term. The questions of whether global warming exists how best to deal with it raise many issues about the nature of economic development and the responsibility of governments in the long term. But there has also arisen a position on the short-term management of disaster preparation and recovery, which has reverted from the tendency, growing since the late eighteenth century, for national governments to take a more active role in confronting such disasters. In the United States, during the 24 years from 1969 to 1993, the Democrats controlled the White House only four years (President Carter, 1977–81); during this period the predominant philosophy of disaster management placed great emphasis on local and regional organizations, and community and faith-based groups, with government contracting for services. President Ronald Reagan good-naturedly summed up this philosophy in a 1984 letter to a South Carolina seventh grader who had appealed directly to the president for federal relief aid when his mother told him his room was a "disaster." Reagan responded that funds were low, that his administration believed that many things could be done better by volunteers at the local level, and that he had already sponsored a Private Sector Initiative. The boy's request seemed like an excellent candidate for such action and for volunteerism.[64] The spirit of the president's note was humorous, but the underlying principle was serious. Those same strategies were also advocated by various governmental agencies and by regional and international organizations like the World Bank and the Organization of American States in which the United States participated.

What the period from the 1970s to the mid-1990s made clear, however, was that even during El Niño events that produced periods of lower cyclonic activity, hurricanes still occur and can sometimes achieve great intensity with deadly effects. Hurricane Camille (U.S. South, 1969) Hurricane David (Dominican Republic and Haiti, 1979), Hurricane Gilbert

(Jamaica, 1988), and Hurricane Hugo (Puerto Rico and Florida, 1989) all provided evidence of that fact. Those storms forced governments and societies to respond, but if we take a wide-angle view of the period, it would seem that a lower frequency of hurricane-generated disasters during this period coincided with diminished governmental concern and with reduced fiscal appropriations to meet their potential threat. In the United States it was during these "years of fracture," as historian Daniel Rodgers has called this period, that a profound debate over the nature of society and of social responsibility and inclusion took place. In reaction to the Johnson administration's "Great Society" expansion of civil rights and welfare provisions, and to the world economic crisis of the mid-1970s, a vigorous critique of government expenditure on the "underclass" developed which often warned of the moral hazards of creating dependencies by promoting programs of social assistance.[65] Such language had been long applied in various ways to the poor and to victims of disaster, but the warnings and caveats took on a new power during the 1970s and 1980s and resonated with governments throughout the world that wished to promote market-driven, neoliberal economic policies, and in the face of calamities, wished to return responsibility to state or local authorities, to charitable institutions, to churches, or to the victims themselves and their communities. The debates in the United States over these issues were often reflected in the way in which other nations of the region responded to similar challenges, and in the way U.S. cooperation with or aid to those nations was provided.

Of course, the social, economic, and political contexts always made a difference in the degree of vulnerability to hurricanes and the nature of response. Hurricane Gilbert, which battered Jamaica in 1988, provides a case in point. That storm caught Jamaica in the midst of a turbulent period during which that island was seeking to define its political character. The island was a parliamentary democracy and the prime minister served as the head of government, although the country remained part of the British Commonwealth and the ruler of Great Britain was head of state. In 1972, Michael Manley, son of a well-known Jamaican politician and former premier, took the reins of government, improved relations with socialist Cuba, helped establish a Caribbean common market, and instituted a series of labor, land, and economic reforms. Opposition to him both from the United States, which feared this turn toward the left, and within Jamaica, from the more conservative parties, led to much violence during his successful campaign for reelection in 1976. In 1980, his program in deep financial difficulties, Manley was defeated by the more conservative Edward Seaga, head of the Jamaica Labor Party, a successful businessman and politician with a reputation for efficient management.[66] Seaga set into motion social and economic programs based on austerity, privatization, and diversification of the economy. He also pursued a foreign policy much less threatening to the United States. In fact, in 1981, he was the first foreign head of state received in Washington after the election of Ronald Reagan as president, and he worked closely with him thereafter. The economy of Jamaica, like that of many other countries of Latin America and the Caribbean, had stagnated or struggled through much of the 1970s and early 1980s, but from 1986 to 1989 under Seaga's leadership it grew about 4.5 percent a year. Hurricane Gilbert cut that trend short, destroying 70 percent of the coffee crop and most of the banana and cocoa exports for the year, and also ruining much of the privately grown foodstuffs on which Jamaicans depended.

The storm had moved rapidly through the Caribbean, and then traversed the whole island of Jamaica from east to west before proceeding to strike the Yucatan peninsula and then the Mexican state of Nuevo León. Over Jamaica it had been a serious storm, with gusts at times over 130 miles per hour, an eye fifteen miles in diameter, and a pressure that fell at one point to 26.22 inches (888 millibars), the lowest ever recorded in the Western Hemisphere to that date.[67] The city of Kingston and its 750,000 people (out of Jamaica's 2.3 million) took a direct hit; and the geographers David Baker and David Miller point out that the passage across the island was made during the daytime so almost everyone on the island observed its traverse and the damage that it caused.[68] The storm dumped much of its rain over the sea, but on the island, most rain fell after the winds had already defoliated and uprooted large numbers of trees; the resulting severe erosion and mudslides caused almost $20 million in damage to roads. Overall, island damage was estimated at about $1 billion, a figure in excess of the country's annual foreign earnings at the time. A Jamaican Office of Disaster Preparedness had been created in 1980 and a Disaster Plan had been in place since 1983, but the dimensions of the crisis simply overwhelmed it.[69] Some places had no potable water, electricity, telephone communication, or housing for three months. Over 400,000 people had been evacuated during the storm, and their relocation created a burden on the government. The banana crop was totally lost, the sugar crop reduced by 17 percent, and food supplies lost. Not only was agriculture disrupted and damaged, but tourism—already an important island industry—was also affected, with about 80 percent of the hotels on Jamaica's north coast suffering losses.

Specialists on disaster management emphasize that it is much more efficient to spend money on preparation and mitigation before a hurricane than on post-disaster relief. Such expenditure for a risk that may or may not happen is always a gamble, though, and poorer countries often find it particularly difficult to invest scarce resources in the possibility of disaster. That economic situation has characterized much of the island Caribbean, but a cultural interpretation has also been offered to explain the lack of adequate preparation for the storms. [70] Author Mark Kurlansky has suggested that Jamaicans, like other peoples of the Caribbean, have always been great survivors, but are not great planners. Since traditionally there was not much that could be done to prepare for a hurricane, people did little. Most effort and imagination went into post-disaster survival, but in truth, as in most of the small Caribbean nations, it was difficult for Jamaica to appropriate sufficient funds to prepare for an emergency of this magnitude. In 1986 there was no separate emergency fund. In fact, none was created until 1995, and it has usually been insufficiently funded. In June 2013, the Jamaican Office of Disaster Preparedness and Emergency Management reported its funding was dangerously inadequate.[71] Thus Jamaica, like other islands, had tended to concentrate on relief in the post-disaster period rather than on mitigation and preparation.

For the Jamaican population in 1988 that strategy meant that facing the storm became a personal or family challenge for survival (fig. 8.2). The storm was quickly personified as "Gilbert," who one victim called "badder dan all of dem. Him mash down everyt'ing and gone."[72] The storm was quickly integrated into popular culture. At least ten recordings were

FIGURE 8.2 Jamaican survivors getting water after Hurricane Gilbert (Photograph in public domain at Wikipedia Commons)

issued with songs about the storm, varying in tone from the suggestive and comic reggae "Gilbert, One Hellva Blow Job," to Gregory Isaac's "What a Disaster." The Jamaica *Gleaner* wrote that Gilbert provided "the lesson that affluence and poverty have common cause when it comes to nature," but the storm in fact underlined the social disparities and inequalities in Jamaican society. The chorus of Lloyd Lovindeer's "Wild Gilbert," a song that sold 30,000 records, made fun of the satellite TV dishes that had blown away from the homes of the wealthy, while applauding the looting done by the youth: "You see mi fridge, Gilbert gimme; yuh see my color TV, Gilbert gimme, Yuh see my new stereo, Gilbert gimme."[73] Lovindeer's lyric even took up the old problematic providentialist interpretations, but with a Jamaican twist. A Rastafarian might celebrate the storm as Jah's punishment for the sins of nonbelievers, to "tear off dem roof and bruk dem window," but "Natty Deadlocks" could not explain why his shack had also lost its roof to Gilbert.[74] A different "Wild Gilbert" by Bananaman told Jamaicans that "starting all over again is gonna be rough," and then emphasized how Jamaicans had to come together as a nation to overcome the disaster. It was the same theme that Castro had developed following Hurricane Flora; and, in fact, communal cooperation and solidarity has been shown by many post-disaster studies to be more common than the often-feared breakdown of public order.[75]

But there had been breakdown of public order and then widespread corruption and theft during the rebuilding process, and more conservative observers were far less sympathetic to it than Lovindeer's lyrics had been. An official inquiry commissioned by the governor general, the Queen's representative on the island, did not deny the poor living conditions or poverty and violence on the island as causes of social breakdown, but it laid the real blame on a "corruption that insinuates itself into every woof of the nation's tapestry, shredding its fabric like a rotting thread. Our citizens slither stealthily through the eye of a hollowing Hurricane to filch and pilfer. . . . like rodent brigades. . . . like scavengers picking at a lifeless corpse."[76] This was a condemnation of the looting and of political action. The author, Sole Commissioner Errington George Green, complained: "We organize demonstrations and marches for every cause, real or imagined, purposing to pounce on every unshuttered business premises, to smash and loot and vanish with our ill-gotten gain."

Hurricane Gilbert influenced the next election. For a while some observers like the *New York Times* writers thought that the storm and Seaga's ability to distribute aid to the victims might change the dynamic of the campaign and would overcome the negative opinion that had grown against his austerity programs and cool manner.[77] The economy had recovered, but unemployment remained at 20 percent, and by 1989 Seaga's popularity had declined. Manley won the election and returned to the prime minister's office, this time with a rhetoric and program far less radical and far friendlier to the United States.

Hurricane Gilbert had been a major storm in a period of lower hurricane frequency, but by the mid-1990s the level of hurricane activity began to increase again. Between 1995 and 1999 there were sixty-five named storms, forty-one hurricanes and twenty of them above Category 3.[78] The year 1999 alone produced an extraordinary five Category 4 hurricanes. Nations and peoples throughout the Greater Caribbean were faced with a level of potential hazard unlike their previous experience, a challenge that placed tremendous burdens on governments and budgets and highlighted the underlying social disparities and ideological differences in those societies.

One of the most disastrous storms of the period struck the Caribbean rimlands of Central America. This was a region always prone to natural disasters because of its geophysical characteristics, its location, and its history. Susceptible to earthquakes and volcanic activity, and like Mexico located between the Caribbean and the eastern Pacific, two active centers of hurricane formation, Central America had long struggled to confront these environmental challenges. Further, in the twentieth century Honduras, El Salvador, and Nicaragua were among the poorest nations of Latin America, and their governments had a poor record of concern for the environmental effects of mining, cattle raising, and forms of agriculture that had led to deforestation, overuse of soils, clear cutting, close cropping, and erosion. All of this increased their vulnerability to serious damage from the passage of hurricanes. Added to that vulnerability was a political history in the late twentieth century involving authoritarian militarism (El Salvador, Honduras, Guatemala) and personalist dictatorship (Nicaragua), and only Costa Rica maintained a functioning participatory democracy.

More immediately, during the 1980s, Central America had become a major battlefield in the Cold War. The Reagan administration sponsored a strong United States military presence in the region primarily to oppose the Sandinista Revolution in Nicaragua, offering funding and support to the *contra* military resistance against that regime. The United States also maintained foreign and aid policies to isolate and oppose the Sandinista government and contain the spread of its social programs and its leftist sympathies to the rest of the region, all of which shaped the political history of the region. Political instability, decades of civil war, and violence were piled upon endemic poverty. The paths for development and growth—export agriculture, sweatshop industries, and urbanization—that seemed to provide an escape from that poverty rested upon an unstable ecological balance that made much of the region increasingly susceptible to natural hazards.[79] That vulnerability had increased during the period after 1987 when peace began to return to the region.

Hurricane Mitch of 1998, a late October storm, was the second deadliest storm in the history of the Caribbean. At various moments it reached Category 5 status, with winds up to 180 miles per hour and a barometric pressure of 26.72 inches (905 millibars). Like Hurricane Flora in 1963, its potential for harm was a result not only of its intensity, but of the erratic track that it followed, moving ashore over the Caribbean coast of Honduras on October 29 and then meandering over the isthmus until it turned eastward again, passing over Guatemala, Belize, and the Yucatan peninsula by November 3 before striking Florida on November 5 as a tropical storm. For most of the time it was over Central America, its winds were not particularly dangerous, but it affected almost all of Central America and it dumped an enormous amount of rain over Honduras and Nicaragua. The eye of the storm, in fact, never passed over Nicaragua, but the effects of the rainfall nevertheless were devastating. In some places, amounts equaled the expected yearly totals. In Polostega, Nicaragua, near the Pacific coast for example, 80 inches of rain fell in October 1998, while the average for that month during the preceding ten years was less than 16 inches.[80] The storm killed at least 6,000 people in Honduras and 3,000 in Nicaragua; estimates of the dead and missing for the areas it affected in Central America, Yucatan, and Florida were as high as 19,000 people. Most of the deaths were due to flooding and landslides rather than to wind.

Hurricane Mitch left two and a half million people homeless and eventually caused between $6.5 and $8.5 billion in damages.[81] Honduras suffered damage to sixty percent of its infrastructure. The storm destroyed or damaged 285,000 homes, and affected eighty-one towns and cities.[82] In Nicaragua, the northern departments suffered the worst effects, and in Chinandega there was a "disaster within the disaster" when the heavy rains caused a tremendous landslide on the slopes of the Casita volcano that killed 2,500 people in the towns of El Porvenir and Rolando Rodrí-guez.[83] For months after the storm, parts of Honduras and Nicaragua suffered from threats to health, a lack of food, population dislocation, and lack of materials for rebuilding. In Honduras alone, a quarter of the public schools were destroyed and 25,000 children left without a school to attend.[84]

Mitch seemed to represent a new generation of superstorm and was thought by many to be a harbinger of disasters to come, but some meteorologists, as cited by the conservative Cato Institute, believed that it was not the characteristics of the storm that explained its devastating effects, but the nature and vulnerability of the societies over which it passed.[85] In Honduras and Nicaragua, the key to the destruction seemed to lie in ecological vulnerabilities. Deforested areas and agricultural zones where no attention had been given to environmental concerns were the areas that suffered the worst loss of life and physical damage; and the situation was even worse in areas characterized by rural poverty where peasants had lost lands to the expansion of large-scale export agriculture that had been taking place since the 1950s. In Honduras about sixty percent of the economy in 1998 was controlled by U.S. interests; the United States had become the principal market and principal lender to the country in the 1980s, just at the moment when the Reagan administration decided to make Honduras an alternative model as well as a bastion and a forward base against the Sandinista government that in 1979 had come to power in neighboring Nicaragua. The motivation for this U.S. "Caribbean Basin Initiative" was to be economic expansion through agricultural diversification, foreign and domestic investment, and the promotion of a series of "structural adjustments" which were essentially what came to be called "neoliberal" policies, promoting the full operation of market forces by limiting all forms of government intervention and regulation of the economy.[86] This was, in fact, the second stage of a neoliberalism: no longer seeking to find ways in which laissez-faire economics could be advanced by a strong state as in the 1950s, but now emphasizing economic "freedom" to be attained by deregulation, privatization, and an unrestrained market.[87] Adopted as a political and economic stance by Ronald Reagan, and in Great Britain by Margaret Thatcher, the emphasis on reduced government spending and involvement in the marketplace was a radical form of individualism and an attack on various forms of collective or "communal" action that had come to be associated with any government expenditure or activity. Due to the example and political influence of the United States and other western economies, these ideas had broad global impacts, among them, reducing the ability of governments to respond to various kinds of disaster.

As the *Contra* War slowed in the late 1980s and the amounts of U.S. money flowing to the country decreased, the economic situation of Honduras worsened. A new government in 1989, following a neoliberal program, secured loans from the World Bank and the International Monetary Fund, both of which supported the structural adjustments of privatization, less regulation of trade, and currency devaluation. Even though in the 1990s the economy of Honduras had a growth rate of 3.2 percent a year, it was unable to keep pace with its population, which was growing 3.3 percent annually.[88] Social services and incomes declined, and inequalities grew to the point that 70 percent of the population lived below the poverty level. The country had one of the lowest per capita GDPs in all of Latin America, just slightly below that of neighboring Nicaragua.

Nicaragua had gone through a turbulent decade after 1979 when the Sandinistas won the presidency and instituted a series of social and economic changes accompanied by a socialist revolutionary rhetoric. The attempted reforms, civil unrest, and guerilla opposition, financed to some extent by the CIA, along with a U.S. embargo on trade contributed to an economic decline during the decade. By 1990, a war-weary population had had enough and voted out the Sandinistas. The following years saw a shift back toward austerity, fewer social programs, and a reduction of spending, accomplished with the support of and pressure from the IMF and World Bank, but little progress toward economic stability was made, and droughts, a tidal wave, and other natural phenomena also created further economic strains. In a way, despite their differing political histories, by 1998 Honduras and Nicaragua faced similar problems of economic weakness, social inequality, and environmental vulnerability that made them particularly susceptible to natural disaster.[89] Hurricane Mitch was the disaster that was waiting to happen.

The governments of Nicaragua and Honduras failed to respond adequately to the warning of an approaching hurricane. President Alemán of Nicaragua, anxious to separate himself from the Sandinistas, refused at first to declare a state of emergency or to mount a major effort of evacuation, steps he felt the Sandinistas would have taken if they had been in power. When a National Emergency Committee finally declared an emergency on October 30, it was already too late. In the post-disaster stage there were complaints on all sides: graft and corruption in distribution of funds and resources, favoritism given to areas controlled by members of Alemán's Liberal Party, denial of appeals from Sandinista mayors, cronyism, and incompetence. The Nicaraguan Civil Defense, in existence since 1972 and reinforced in 1992, should have provided leadership, but during the civil war and the struggle against the *contras* it had mostly been involved with national security issues and then had been weakened by budget reductions and cutbacks. While the Catholic Church, other charities, and various NGOs were all active in providing relief in the aftermath of Hurricane Mitch, coordination and cooperation between them was poor.

In Honduras, the government was simply overwhelmed. Its emergency management agency (COPECO) was understaffed and sadly short of helicopters, so short, in fact, that some regions could not be given emergency help. Aid distribution was very slow and insufficient; when President Flores turned over distribution of aid to the Catholic and evangelical churches its delivery improved, but problems remained. In a curious way, much of the process of "structural adjustment" that weakened central governments had dovetailed with the rapidly growing development of disaster management as a field of study, and with an international boom of institutions and agencies to administer and direct relief and reconstruction. A predominant concept in the literature produced by these institutions and which guided their actions was an emphasis on community, local, individual, and private response as the most efficient and effective way to manage disasters, but that emphasis diminished the potential of central governments to meet the crises, to coordinate efforts, or to effectively plan and respond on a national level.

In Honduras, however, the decentralized approach to disaster response did not go uncontested. The country had a long tradition of centralized and authoritarian government, and it now reemerged with the crisis. President Flores declared a state of emergency, suspended the legislature, and ruled by decree. On November 3, civil rights were suspended and a curfew imposed. A Plan for Reconstruction was centrally prepared, with no local or outside participation, and a special cabinet created to enact the plan. The reconstruction would be done by contracts, but there was no competitive bidding, and many contracts went to cronies, friends. and family members of the political elite. The president opposed appeals from municipal governments to be involved in the planning and to receive five percent of the national budget, as was required by law. Through the next two years this situation created tensions between the central government and the institutions of civil society as well as external international donors. These institutions and the donors were seeking to promote more civil participation in government and to insure that reconstruction included not just construction of buildings and roads, but the rebuilding of civil society as well. Their criticism of corruption and continued pressure on the government eventually led to improvements and a more open political process during reconstruction, but the change was incomplete and the remedies inadequate.[90]

The world community had responded well to the disaster in Honduras, pledging $9 billion for reconstruction. The United States sent $300 million immediately and pledged another $1 billion, and institutions like the World Bank and the Inter-American Development Bank also made commitments toward reconstruction, debt relief, and development. First Lady Hilary Clinton and Tipper Gore, wife of the vice president, made a goodwill visit to the region to express American concern, and American military personnel, helicopters, and other equipment were fully involved in the relief effort, as were teams from over a dozen other nations. A Cuban offer of help was turned down by Honduras for ideological reasons.

For some institutions Hurricane Mitch provided an opportunity to intensify the process of neoliberal transformation. The Inter-American Development Bank, in a perceptive assessment of the effect of the storm on Central America, saw Hurricane Mitch as a "call to action to find new schemes of development in a form that would reduce vulnerability of the society to future natural phenomena and that would strengthen democracy and the perspectives of future economic development." The bank proposed debt relief and funds to aid with rural poverty, and celebrated progress already made in "the privatization of state-owned communications, electric power enterprises, railways, mail, ports, and airports."[91] It urged more such changes. In many ways, the underlying conception here was a preliminary effort at "disaster capitalism," the use of the shock of disastrous situations to dismantle state participation in the economy and to implant structural changes in the form of laissez-faire capitalism.[92] As the Guatemalan foreign minister said in 1999, "destruction carries with it an opportunity for foreign investment."[93] Radical journalist Alexander Cockburn and his coauthor Jeffrey St. Clair summed up a critique of the process and its role in the creation of this disaster in particular: "Humans caused the disaster just as humans made sure the governments of Nicaragua and Honduras were incapable of responding to the catastrophe. After a decade of 'structural adjustment,' imposed by the World Bank, the International Monetary Fund, and USAID, these governments are hollow shells, mutilated by enforced cutbacks." Cockburn wondered what a government could do when it had no money for gasoline to evacuate people, no buses, no vaccines, few staff, no capacity to stockpile water and food. The government had not failed; it had atrophied. "The Honduras government didn't put the country on alert. It simply hoped the hurricane would go away. After structural adjustment that's about all it could do."[94] Nature had provided the elements for a potential disaster; human actions and decisions had produced it.[95]

Hurricane Mitch was a Central American tragedy, but such events were now internationalized by the role of governments, international organizations, and nongovernmental agencies in the financing of relief and reconstruction as well as in humanitarian aid. Here and throughout the Greater Caribbean region, the models, strategies, interests, and influence of the United States in disaster management were always present. Moreover, the danger of reducing the explanation of disaster to an accident of nature or an act of God rather than a result of failed policies, misguided decisions, greed, indifference, or worse was always present.

FEMA AND THE POLITICS OF AMERICAN DISASTER MANAGEMENT

As we have seen, the United States government had slowly assumed a more direct role in disaster relief from the days of the early republic when grants were made to individuals or communities who had suffered some loss or calamity. Much of the change took place in the 1930s, when President Roosevelt and his supporters had seen the transition from federal disaster aid to the social programs of the New Deal as a logical extension of government's responsibilities. The Flood Control Act of 1936 had been an important step in the increasing federal involvement in disaster response. Just as the post–World War II era witnessed scientific and technical advances in the study of the weather in general and hurricanes in particular, the same period was one of increasing action by the government to play a role in disaster relief as an aspect of both domestic and foreign policy. It was not until 1950 that the Disaster Relief Act granted the president the power to declare a disaster area, enabling the distribution of aid and the mobilization of various government agencies and resources to meet the needs of the victims. Subsequent legislation like the National Flood Insurance Act of 1968 and the Disaster Relief Act of 1974 sought to make federal relief funding dependent on compliance with building codes, the acquisition of insurance coverage, and general efforts to decrease vulnerability.[96] Still, the predominant paradigm in American disaster response was for local, state, and federal governments to bear responsibilities in that same order, each level only calling on the next when its own resources were incapable of adequate action. The tension between these two visions of government responsibility, top down or bottom up, a tension that had existed in the country from the days of Jefferson and Hamilton, grew more intense as the twentieth century drew to a close. Moreover, during the 1950s and 1960s, disaster preparation, response, and management often conflated natural hazards and the threat of enemy attack or nuclear war. Thus while disaster responsibilities often were shared by a variety of governmental institutions or agencies, they were generally under the control of the Department of Defense, whose attention was usually fixed on military matters.

Failures of coordination in responding to events like Hurricane Agnes in 1972 and then the meltdown at the Three Mile Island nuclear plant in 1979 resulted in President Carter's creation of the Federal Emergency Management Agency (FEMA) as an attempt to improve national and local administration of disaster. This change in the structure of governmental response to disaster took place at roughly the same moment that a new field of action and study—disaster management—emerged in the academic areas of sociology, psychology, geography, and economics as well as among members of nongovernmental agencies, international and humanitarian charitable organizations, and various international organizations such as the United Nations and the World Bank. Managing and coping with disasters in technical and administrative terms was becoming an industry. Parallel to this development was the growing importance and professionalization of the National Hurricane Center and of the whole organization of meteorology in the United States and internationally.

While the United States faced a variety of disasters in these years in the last half of the twentieth century, from blizzards, floods, and tornados to the atomic accident at Three Mile Island, hurricanes were a recurrent natural hazard. Throughout this era in the United States, the storms were well-known and frequent visitors. While studies have shown that their long-term impact on the national economy of a large country like the United States was negligible, the diffusion of television and of weather reporting made regional disasters into events that captured national attention.[97] Moreover, the concentration of the storms in the southeastern portion of the country tended to reveal the racial and political tensions that dominated the nation's attention in the second half of the century, in some ways continuing the social and economic themes that had dominated the history of the Greater Caribbean since the sixteenth century.

Two major storms of the 1960s provide good examples (see fig. 9.1). Hurricane Betsy (September 9, 1965), a large storm that killed fifty people in New Orleans and breeched one of the levees protecting the city, provoked an outcry from the large African American population of that city. Some of them believed that the levee had been dynamited in the Lower Ninth Ward, where the population was almost 90 percent black, in order to save other, predominantly white neighborhoods.[98] It was an accusation with some traction, since during the 1927 Mississippi floods levees had, in fact, been dynamited in poorer parishes to alleviate flooding in New Orleans.[99] Hurricane Betsy struck Louisiana just as the federal Civil Rights Act of 1964 was being implemented. This legislation, designed to end segregation in various public spaces and institutions and to expand the franchise, had met with heated secessionist rhetoric and a good deal of stubborn recalcitrance from public officials. A personal visit to the area by President Johnson and congressional action to provide relief soon had local officials praising Washington for the help that the city and state had received, but throughout the recovery period, the African American residents of New Orleans remained suspicious that they had not been treated fairly. Five years later, Hurricane Camille (August 17–20, 1969) swept in a great arc through the southeast, affecting Mississippi, Tennessee, Kentucky, West Virginia, and Virginia. A Category 5 storm when it slammed into the Mississippi coast, its winds reached 190 miles per hour, causing a storm surge of 24 feet, and eventually spinning off about 100 tornadoes as it tore down houses and trailer parks in its path. It became a tropical depression, moving eastward through the mountains of West Virginia and then passed through Virginia into the Atlantic.[100] Historian Mark Smith noted that years thereafter those who had lived where the storm passed could not hear the sound of a chainsaw without recalling the months of clearing away debris with that tool following the storm. Damage at the time was estimated at $1.4 billion (about $9 billion in 2013 dollars) and about 5,000 homes were destroyed or badly damaged. Mississippi and Virginia were particularly hurt by the storm, and 153 people died in Virginia from flooding.

The nature of local and federal response in those states was conspicuously influenced by the civil rights revolution taking place in those years, and by the political strategies of national political parties. Recently elected President Nixon, whose Republican "Southern Strategy" of moving slowly on the civil rights legislation had brought him the support of the South, took charge of the relief effort, mobilizing the Office of Emergency Preparedness to coordinate military and civilian efforts. While that office was generally effective, there were complaints from African Americans that policies of segregation determined much of the delivery of relief, as it had the efforts at evacuation before the storm struck.

The intersection of hurricane relief, race, and politics came at a time when Mississippi schools were, at least theoretically, in the process of desegregation. The schools had been due to be integrated by August 1969. The Nixon administration dragged its feet, but Leon Panetta, assistant to the Secretary of the Department of Health, Education, and Welfare, along with other officials of the department, insisted on enforcing the civil rights legislation and tried to tie federal assistance directly to compliance with the Civil Rights Act of 1964: no integration, no materials or funds for repair of schools.[101] Nixon, under considerable pressure from southern congressional allies, was able to slow the process of integrating the schools, but he was not willing to prevent desegregation. Almost invariably in the post-disaster recuperation there were complaints about the maintenance of racial and class differences in the receipt of aid and about the disadvantages of the poor in securing grants or loans in order to recover or rebuild.

Hurricanes Hugo (1989) and Andrew (1992) were major storms that caused considerable property damage and loss of life. Each was the costliest disaster to have occurred in the United States up to that time, and even when adjusted for inflation or "normalized" by adjustments for population and economic growth, they remain among the United States' costliest hurricanes. Hugo was a Category 4 storm as it moved through the Leewards and over St. Croix. It threatened a direct hit on San Juan with winds as high as 120 miles per hour, but as it crossed the tropical park on El Yunque mountain the storm was deflected and the city spared somewhat. For years after, votive candles were placed in thanks by visitors to El Yunque. Nevertheless, Hugo left $1 billion in damage on the island in its wake. The hurricane then moved northwest, striking the South Carolina coast and causing storm tides of over 20 feet from Charleston to Myrtle Beach. It caused 21 deaths and left $7 billion in damages, a figure due in part to the inadequacy of building codes that was revealed by the storm. While there were complaints from affected areas of South Carolina about the slow and ineffective actions taken by FEMA and the Red Cross to provide help after the storm, there also emerged a contrary train of argument that would grow in popularity in the following decades. A conservative think tank framed the problem from a libertarian perspective. Why should the government, any government, be involved at all? [102] Taxpayers not affected had no responsibility to those who suffered losses, and those who did suffer them could depend on the open insurance market to protect their interests. Forced evacuations and curfews were limitations on freedom. Laws against raising prices on essentials in the aftermath of the storm led to shortages that the free market would have avoided. The unrestrained market and the right to property was the best solution for all. The "professional foes of humanity—the environmentalists," who wished to limit construction on the beaches and who had promoted state laws to that effect, had to be stopped, and FEMA should simply be abolished. This position, which was argued by the American economist Murray Rothbard and his Ludwig von Mises Institute, a conservative libertarian think tank that promotes the anti-statist economics of the "Austrian School," was a somewhat extreme version of a neoliberal view, and it had elements that resonated on the right of the American political spectrum. Rothbard made his position clear. He called disaster relief an aspect of the "welfare state."[103]

Only three years later Hurricane Andrew came through the Bahamas and struck Dade County in southern Florida (August 24, 1992), with sustained winds of 145 miles per hour and gusts of 170 miles per hour. Although the storm was relatively small in size, the winds and a barometric pressure that fell to 27.19 inches (922 mb) caused a storm surge of over 17 feet and horrendous damage to communities south of Miami before it crossed Florida, eventually striking Gulf oil rigs and the Louisiana and Mississippi shoreline as a Category 3 hurricane. Insurance payouts amounted to $15 billion and total damage was estimated at $26 billion. So many claims were made that eleven insurance companies failed, and the Florida legislature had to create a special fund to provide residents with adequate coverage. Even today, Hurricane Andrew remains the fourth costliest storm to have struck the United States.[104]

In many ways Andrew was a transformational storm. It revealed administrative and infrastructure weaknesses at every level. Both the federal and state responses were deficient. Tied up in bureaucratic red tape, three days after the storm had hit and after Florida's governor, Democrat Lawton Chiles, had asked Republican president George H.W. Bush for federal intervention, the Dade County director of Emergency Operations could still ask publicly, "Where the hell is the cavalry on this one?" About 180,000 people had been made homeless, and FEMA, under the leadership of an inexperienced director, was ineffective and slow to respond.[105] One meteorologist later stated: "FEMA was prepared to do essentially nothing, and that's what it did for days."[106] Local pressure mounted and President George H.W. Bush authorized the dispatch of troops to aid in the relief effort and to stop some looting that had taken place in south Florida. Eventually $290 million was distributed in federal aid and $746 million spent on infrastructure rebuilding, but despite this action there had also been failures at the local level. The insurance industry in south Florida was overwhelmed and incapable of satisfying the over 600,000 claims.[107] The building codes had not been followed, and too much development of low-lying and beachfront property had been allowed, which had then created high-risk vulnerability in many areas.

There were political ramifications. Although in the elections of 1992 President Bush carried Florida again by a slim margin, and many incumbents in local government were returned to office, nationally the failure of FEMA and the lackluster performance in responding to Hurricane Andrew contributed to the victory of President William (Bill) Clinton and the Democrats' gain of thirty-one seats in the House of Representatives. President Clinton appointed James Lee Witt, a man with experience in disaster management, as director of FEMA, and raised that position to the cabinet level. Recognizing, as many studies have shown, that a dollar spent in mitigation and preparedness yields at least four times that amount in terms of the costs of recovery, FEMA initiated Project Impact, designed to aid communities to prepare for disasters.[108]

But after the election of George W. Bush in 2000, FEMA was placed under the leadership of Joe Allbaugh, his former campaign manager, who dismantled the project as "an oversized entitlement program," and essentially removed FEMA from any role in preparedness. Its budget had already been reduced when, after the terrorist attacks of September 11, 2001, FEMA was then subsumed within the new Department of Homeland Security. Its primary focus was shifted to anti-terrorist activities and its function in preparing for natural disasters was all but eliminated; and suggestions were made that its functions might be less politicized and more efficient if turned over to the private sector.[109]

This was the neoliberal remedy that looked to the market as the best solution to the challenges of public policy, and it came at a time when governments were forced to face simultaneously risks of different kinds, natural hazards and, increasingly, man-made ones. The German sociologist Ulrich Beck has argued that modernity and technology did not eliminate risks, but had made them a central aspect of everyday existence, the "risk society" of the modern world. Beck did not devote much attention, however, to how a society might prioritize the various risks it faced, or deal with them simultaneously. After 2001, the United States, traumatized and made vengeful by the terrorist attack on New York and the Pentagon, opted to wage a war on terror as its primary response to the risks it faced. The decision to concentrate on terrorism subordinated other hazards in terms of budget and political objectives. The immediate hazard of the recurring hurricanes was downgraded, especially in terms of long-range projects and responses. The even longer range possibility of global warming as an anthropogenic hazard, which fit so well into Beck's scheme, was either ignored or simply denied by a large segment of the political right, and not even market-based solutions were politically feasible to address it.

On August 30, 2005, the day after Hurricane Katrina destroyed New Orleans in what became the worst natural disaster in the nation's history, journalist Eric Holderman in the pages of the *Washington Post* noted the downgrading and transformation of FEMA and the danger that this had created for the country. New terrorist attacks were certainly a possibility, he said, but "hurricanes, tornadoes, earthquakes, volcanoes, tsunamis, floods, windstorms, fires and flu were destined to be a national concern on a weekly or daily basis. "They are coming for sure, sooner or later, even as we are, to an unconscionable degree, weakening our ability to respond to them."[110]

CHAPTER 9

Ancient Storms in a New Century

We wasn't in a war but every day was Iraq
Made you ride through my city in a boat,
like a third world country that ain't got no hope.
—*BJ Willis, Katrina survivor*

If it keeps on raining, the levee's gonna break.
Some people still sleepin', and some people wide awake.
—*Bob Dylan, "The Levee's Gonna Break"*

Hurricane Katrina, which battered Louisiana and Mississippi and inundated the city of New Orleans in 2005, was no anomaly. The most expensive disaster in the history of the United States (estimates between $81 and 125 billion) and with 1,833 directly caused fatalities (the most deadly storm since the 1928 Okeechobee hurricane), it was the logical outcome of a long history of encounters between changing social and political concerns and the challenges presented by the geophysical conditions in the islands and rimlands of the Greater Caribbean. The themes that make up the narrative of Katrina's tragic passage are the same that had characterized the history of the great storms for centuries: local perceptions and actions, political and religious ideologies and convictions, differing concepts of government responsibilities, conflicts of authority, community solidarities, social and racial divisions, selflessness and sacrifice, greed and corruption.[1] But Hurricane Katrina also came at a moment when new concerns about human impact on the environment and on the intensity and frequency of hurricanes were a subject of scientific and political debate. No hurricane or its aftermath in the history of the Greater Caribbean has ever received as much attention, analysis, and governmental investigation as Katrina. In these concluding pages, my objective is not to repeat those detailed inquiries and studies, but to place Katrina within the long and still evolving history of the impact of hurricanes on the peoples of the North Atlantic region. Hurricane Katrina also forces us to examine the present controversies about the environmental conditions that affect the frequency and intensity of the storms, and the appropriate social, economic, and political ways that best meet the hurricanes and their underlying climatic causes. "Katrina" has become shorthand for all that is unnatural about natural disasters.

New Orleans is perhaps historically and socially one of the most "Caribbean" cities of the North American rimlands, with a history of imperial confrontations and changes of sovereignty, cultural and linguistic fusions, and a long history of a significant African American presence. It has also, since its founding, been in constant danger of flooding. The original trading post, built by the French in 1718 on slightly elevated ground between the Mississippi River and Lake Ponchartrain, had always been susceptible to inundations, either from the river, or from hurricane-caused storm surges on the lake. The United States purchased Louisiana from Napoleon in 1803, and as steam navigation opened the river to commerce, New Orleans flourished despite its environmental vulnerabilities. Before 1871, the town had flooded thirty-eight times and the levees built from New Orleans northward along the river toward Baton Rouge were never sufficient to eliminate the threat. In fact, as the levees upstream got higher and stronger, the problems downstream got worse. Eventually Congress created a Mississippi River Commission in 1879 to control both commerce and water management. Now the Army Corps of Engineers rather than local governments or private individuals built dikes and levees and dredged new channels, and although there was another bad flood in 1927 that killed 500 people, flooding thereafter diminished and an excellent drainage system was constructed.[2] The creation of a National Flood Insurance Program (1968) and the Federal Emergency Management Agency (1979) pointed to the increasing centralization of disaster response.

The city's growth and its location on land that was poorly drained, swampy, and in danger of flooding from both the river and the lake created a constant concern for public health, civil engineering, and water management. A large segment of the city's population lived below sea level. New Orleans survived in a tense relationship with its environment under normal conditions, but it also was particularly vulnerable to hurricanes. Past experience suggested that these were sure to come.[3] Of the 323 hurricanes that struck the United States mainland between 1851 and 2004, 49 crossed Louisiana, and of these, 18 were Category 3 storms or above. This placed Louisiana only third behind Florida and Texas as the state most likely to be hit by a major storm.[4] The tension between environmental vulnerability and government action was apparent when primary response fell to parish or local government, to the state, or to private individuals, and it was also a concern as the role of central government grew.

During the late twentieth century New Orleans' vulnerability to storms had also increased because of environmental and social transformations. The wetlands and marshes at the mouth of the Mississippi and to the west of the city that had provided a buffer against storm surges had shrunk considerably because of canal construction and dredging to facilitate shipping on the river, and because of energy development in the search for petroleum. The desire for economic advantage and "progress" lay behind these developments, and the Corps of Engineers was a generally willing and active participant in the plans; ecological results such as the increasing saltwater penetration of the coastal wetlands when canals were built or channels widened were either ignored or downplayed.[5] By 2000 about 25,000 acres of wetlands were being lost annually.

As the regional ecology changed, so too did the city's social composition. In 1950, the city was 70 percent white and 30 percent African American; by 1980 the ratio had changed to 50 percent white, 50 percent African American; and by 2005 whites, Hispanics, and Asians together made up 33 percent and African Americans 67 percent of the urban population.[6] When Hurricane Katrina struck the city, about a quarter of the city's population was living below the poverty line, and the median household income ($30,711) was a third below the national average ($46,242). Despite the promoted image of Mardi Gras, jazz, and "Let the good times roll" living, the city was residentially segregated, divided between its business community and the rest of the population who lived with high levels of poverty, crime, illiteracy, and unemployment. The burdens of race weighed heavily on the city and the state of Louisiana, second poorest in the country. New Orleans contained a large population with few resources that was exceptionally vulnerable to catastrophe.[7] In its poorer areas like the Lower Ninth Ward, African Americans outnumbered whites about four to one. The Lower Ninth Ward was the area most devastated when the levees broke during Hurricane Katrina.

The fear of a major hurricane over New Orleans had long existed and was often discussed. City officials, journalists, and academics had all given cautionary warnings in the last decades of the twentieth century, and hurricanes Betsy (1965) and Camille (1969; fig. 9.1) had both come close enough to offer a clear warning of the hazard of a hurricane strike and potential flooding of a geographically vulnerable urban center with a large population of poor citizens. Concerns were serious enough that in the post-9/11 planning undertaken by various governmental agencies in the United States, FEMA compiled a list of possible disaster scenarios, which included a hurricane strike and flooding in New Orleans that called for planning and preparation. To that end, in 2004 a coordinated "practice drill" named Hurricane Pam was organized. Much was accomplished by the drill, but a lack of federal funding eliminated a follow-up symposium to address deficiencies or problems that the exercise had identified, and chief among these was the fact that a large segment of the population, perhaps as many as 100,000, did not have the means to evacuate their homes if the need arose. Discussions to have church groups responsible for their evacuation were unsuccessful, and no adequate plan for their removal was in place when Hurricane Katrina struck the city.

The 2005 hurricane season was a record breaker. A decade before, the 1995 season had been extraordinary, with its nineteen named storms, twice the average number. Eleven of them became hurricanes and five of them reached Category 5 level, but many of those storms had stayed out to the east in the Atlantic. The year 2005 was different. There were seven major hurricanes and they exacted a heavy toll throughout the region:

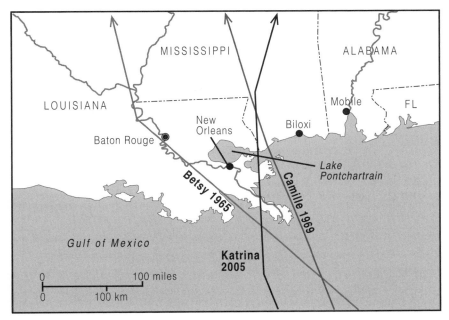

FIGURE 9.1 Hurricane tracks over New Orleans (Map by Santiago Muñoz Arbalaez, based on Cliff Duplechin in *World Watch Magazine*, Sept.–Oct. 2007.)

3,913 deaths and almost $160 billion in damages. Mexico, Florida, Cuba, the Bahamas, and the U.S. Gulf Coast from Alabama to Texas all suffered strikes, some of them from more than one storm. Hurricanes Rita and Wilma, both Category 5 hurricanes, both came ashore in the United States but did not cause as much destruction as Katrina, which was only a Category 3 storm when it struck the Gulf Coast.

Hurricane Katrina, the eleventh storm of the season, formed near the Bahamas in mid-August. At its birth it gave little sign that it would be one of the most dangerous storms of the season. It crossed south Florida (August 25) as a minimal hurricane, but then quickly gathered strength over the Gulf, becoming a Category 5 hurricane. Its central pressure of 26.59 inches (902 millibars) was the third lowest ever recorded in the United States.[8] It was a slow-moving but "wet" storm, and even though original estimates of its track placed its landfall further to the east on the Gulf Coast, New Orleans did have a few days warning before the storm arrived. The meteorologists and the Weather Service had done their job.[9] The mayor, Ray Nagin, had tried to warn the city and to set emergency plans in motion—"This is the real deal"—but he delayed a compulsory evacuation of hospitals and hotels, hoping not to disrupt the tourist industry and because he was reluctant to create future legal problems with affected businesses and services. Finally, on the night of August 27 he ordered an evacuation. Despite his delay, emergency warnings by the governor, Kathleen Blanco, and by President George W. Bush had already been made.

Katrina came ashore near the mouth of the Mississippi as a Category 3 hurricane late on August 28, but the storm surge of 32.8 feet that it produced along the coasts of Mississippi, Alabama, and Louisiana was of Category 5 dimensions. Damage along those coasts was catastrophic. New Orleans was overwhelmed. A levee on Lake Ponchartrain could not contain the surge, and then some levees on the canals in the city were breached. Large parts of the city, eventually about eighty percent of New Orleans, were under water. The city had become a creole Atlantis. Waters mixed with household fluids, wreckage and refuse filled the streets, and people ascended to their rooftops or waded through the rising fetid waters. This was the storm that New Orleans had feared for a centuries.

The physical blow of the storm had been heavy, but the disaster was only beginning. Washington was slow to realize the seriousness of the situation, the mayor had failed to mobilize all of the city's buses to get people out, and FEMA, responsible for the disaster plan, seemed to be inattentive, ineffective, or incompetent. Promised supplies of water and food, planned for in the Hurricane Pam exercise, had not been stockpiled in sufficient quantities in the havens of last resort. FEMA's leadership had little experience in disaster relief, and its operations were tied up in red tape that slowed or interfered with simple commonsense procedures. Horror stories abounded: doctors were turned away from aiding victims because they did not have state licenses; buses were not mobilized because they lacked air-conditioning or toilets; bus drivers were not allowed to serve until they had the required sexual harassment training; the governor's request for national aid was delayed for five days because it had not been made in writing. To make matters worse, FEMA itself had been sub-

FIGURE 9.2 Hurricane Katrina survivor and child (United Press International, photographer: Jeremy L. Grisham)

ordinated to the Department of Homeland Security and some of its funding and some of its funding diverted to anti-terrorist activities. Its political and security goals had taken precedence over its mission to respond to natural disasters.[10] Despite FEMA's attempt to prohibit photos of the dead and other negative images, television coverage made this a most public storm, and the nation watched aghast at the scenes of people, most of them black, pleading for rescue from rooftops or attic windows, wading through flooded streets, or hanging on to anything that could float (fig. 9.2).

Worst of all was the situation at the refuges of last resort, the Convention Center and especially the Superdome, where some 25,000 people had sought shelter. Inadequate preparations had been made there, and now thousands of people who could not leave the city gathered in unbearable conditions with little food, water, sanitation, or medical attention. It appeared that the system of disaster preparation and relief had completely broken down as a result of mismanagement, unclear lines of authority, poor communication, and in some cases, indifference or incompetence. Particularly irritating during the immediate recovery were bureaucratic self-congratulations about the relief effort, and dismissals of the reports of horrible conditions and deaths as "rumors."

Eleanor Thornton, who walked through the flooded streets to get to the Convention Center, saw the conditions from the inside. She noted kids with guns looted from Wal-Mart terrorizing people in the Convention Center, and said that there were bad and good people in any situation, but her worst criticism was reserved for the government.

> They treated us as badly as you could treat your fellow human beings. I don't care who you are, what color, where you're from of what's your background. I wouldn't treat a dog like that. The United States blows up Baghdad, and the'll drop them food. (My brother is serving in Iraq). But they didn't do it for us. They didn't bring food for the convention center until the fifth day after the storm. I would love to know how they sleep at night.[11]

In fact, about eighty percent of the city's population had been evacuated, but the majority of those who remained and who were in dire need of help were the poor, the elderly, and mostly, African Americans. The planners knew that these people did not have the ability to leave on their own, but no plan was in place for them. The images of their misery and vulnerability that appeared each day in television coverage drove home a message of social and racial inequalities as an underlying theme in the breakdown of public policy.[12]

Many volumes have been devoted to the details of the failures in the preparations before and the relief efforts after Hurricane Katrina. Three themes help to place Hurricane Katrina within the context of the long story of hurricanes in the formation of the Greater Caribbean. First was the importance of location. The ability of New Orleans to evacuate the majority of its citizens and find them refuge as far away as Houston, Atlanta, and Memphis demonstrated the great advantage that larger islands or continental rimlands always had in the shadow of catastrophic storms. A small island like Barbados, Martinique, or Antigua often had no unaffected area after the passage of a major hurricane, and thus had less opportunity to find refuge for its population or accessible sources of food or supplies thereafter. Big islands like Cuba or Jamaica were better able to absorb the blows internally; and still better was the capacity of Mexico or the United States to do so. Much of the history of Katrina in New Orleans was by necessity a story of diaspora.

Social order or disorder was a second theme central to the story of Katrina and integral to the history of hurricanes in general. The possibility of the breakdown of social order following a natural disaster and the alternative development of community solidarities influenced the actions of those in authority and the public in general. In the New Orleans of Katrina in 2005, as in Barbados in 1831 or Galveston in 1900, reports and rumors of lawless behavior, looting, and defiance of authority quickly spread, reports that not only often turned out to be greatly exaggerated, but also were heavily tinged with racialized images and overtones. In New Orleans, about a third of the police had deserted their positions during the storm, and others from neighboring communities actually fired on victims trying to escape by foot over a bridge leading out of the flooded city into a predominantly white suburb. Journalistic accounts of shots fired at rescue helicopters, or of gang rapes and murders at the Superdome, were exaggerated or simply untrue, and the press made little effort to distinguish "looting" from efforts to survive by people in need of water, milk, bread, and toilet paper.[13] Those in authority feared, as after a damaging hurricane they always did, the breakdown of social order. They called for a military presence, but in both Mississippi and Louisiana the governors were reluctant to relinquish control of the state National Guard to federal authority. Louisiana governor Blanco wanted federal troops to control a hostile populace. Although Secretary of Defense Donald Rumsfeld had intentionally delayed their deployment, battle-hardened U.S. regular army troops arrived in New Orleans, but it was only because their commanding officer, General Russel Honoré, ordered them to remember that their mission was to help the victims in relief and recovery that they lowered their weapons.[14]

Somewhat lost in the exaggerated narrative of social breakdown were the stories of community solidarities and humanitarian responses. Scores of rural residents from the lands and bayous outside the city, most of them white, appeared voluntarily in small boats to help in the poorly prepared rescue efforts, forming what was later called the "Cajun flotilla." Doctors, nurses, builders, and social workers from nearby states and from across the country volunteered their services. Foreign governments offered help. Canadian Mounties did extraordinary service, and even Cuba's Fidel Castro and Venezuela's Hugo Chavez extended offers of aid, which, of course, were turned down. Private voluntary contributions poured into the Red Cross, an institution with its own record of failures in this crisis. Even in the breakdown of order in the Superdome, the disaster had not reduced people to a state of nature, each against all, but had formed groups for protection, and a kind of informal communal government had emerged.[15] When troops finally arrived there expecting to find hundreds of bodies, only six were found, four of them having died from natural causes and one from a suicide. What the aftermath of Katrina, like many other posthurricane situations, had demonstrated was that actions of self-help, community solidarities, and humanitarian action were at least equal to those of social breakdown, even though law enforcement often found that difficult to grasp.[16]

Those evacuated sometimes experienced what they felt was discriminatory behavior, or were met with bureaucratic indifference, but others were impressed by the generosity and care extended to them. BJ Willis, who had been living a "gangsta" life of despair amidst the poverty and crime of the city, rapped: "We wasn't in a war but every day was Iraq / Made you ride through my city in a boat / like a third world country that ain't got no hope." His experience in Katrina, the images he viewed of children and the elderly dying, and of National Guard troops with shoot-to-kill orders, were burned into his mind; but his positive experience in Memphis, where he had been relocated, and attempts by his family to survive moved him to try to overcome all this trauma by seeking to live a more moral life. "I got a lot ahead of me and I ain't going to let none of that discourage me."[17] In the recovery period, residents expressed frustration at their abandonment and sarcasm at the claims of government, quipping, "Want to call FEMA? The number is 1–800-HAHA," or wearing post-Katrina T-shirts: "FEMA = a new four-letter F word," or "FEMA = Fix Everything, My Ass."[18]

The role of government in natural disasters was a third theme in the long history of hurricanes that Katrina underlined. The failures of the government response to Hurricane Katrina threw into sharp contrast the alternative ideological positions that had developed since the 1980s about the best way for societies to confront disasters. We have already noted transnational differences in the case of Hurricane Mitch in Central America and Gilbert in Jamaica. The differences of approach were really extensions of a broad international debate about the very nature and objectives of government itself, but because of deeply held traditional beliefs about the limited nature of government in the United States, and because of the influence of the United States over the Greater Caribbean and the world economy, the calamity of Katrina seemed to offer a singular opportunity to evaluate the competing models for government response.

Explanations of the storm and criticism of the apparent failure of government came from many directions. Some observers held the indifference or incompetence of the Bush White House directly responsible, but others believed that the underlying explanation was that both the attention and the resources of the United States had been diverted by the trauma of the terrorist attack of 9/11 and the war in Iraq; money was now being spent on preparations for such uncommon events, rather than on the much more usual threat of natural disasters like hurricanes.[19] The levee maintenance budget had been seriously cut in 2005, and National Guard troops later complained that their best equipment had gone to Iraq and was unavailable for the rescue efforts. In Katrina, the United States had shown itself lacking in the resources to cope with a recurring natural hazard on its own territory. Many other critics, however, suggested that the inadequate governmental response resulted from a concept of limited government structured primarily by a belief in laissez-faire capitalism and dependence on market-driven solutions. The disaster was in the concept of government, not in the execution of its policies. Under Republican administrations, the government of the United States had become a "noninterventionist state"[20] with a much-reduced concept of the public sector. This implied that government's abandonment of its primary role in social welfare, education, and disaster relief and its concession of these responsibilities within a market framework to private institutions, individuals, or local authorities, was the principal origin of the Katrina catastrophe. Defenders of this theory of government laid the blame on the victims for their own plight. Talk show host Bill O'Reilly suggested that those who had not evacuated were drug addicts unwilling to leave their suppliers, while Pennsylvania senator Rick Santorum, later a Republican presidential hopeful, at first said that people who had failed to evacuate the city should be penalized in some way.[21] One Louisiana congressman, Robert Baker from Baton Rogue, son of a Methodist minister, saw a divine purpose in the destruction: "We finally cleaned up public housing in New Orleans. We couldn't do it, but God did."[22]

From the opposite perspective, a large number of academic studies and journalistic commentaries saw Katrina as a "neoliberal deluge," and the process of recovery, which included the dismissal of 4,000 schoolteachers and a reduction of publicly supported housing by half, as an excellent example of "shock capitalism," the use of a disaster to carry out drastic structural changes by eliminating any constraints on the operation of a free market economy.[23] Just as the storm had differentially affected populations based on their gender, race, and income, so too, the reconstruction of the city tended to be faster and more advantageous for wealthier and whiter citizens. Liberal critics also pointed out that the economic and social costs of "corporate looting" in the form of "crony" capitalism, no-bid contracts, expensive subcontracting, and backroom arrangements were far higher than were the costs of looting food and electronics by the poor after the storm.

Hurricane Katrina provided a lesson, but how that lesson was perceived very much depended on one's prior ideological position. Liberal economist Paul Krugman, in a widely cited 2007 *New York Times* column, "Katrina All the Time," saw the storm as a revealing example of the inherent flaws of neoliberalism and governmental abandonment of the idea of a public good. He warned that this policy would be the future of the Bush administration. Conversely, some conservative commentators like the economists at the Von Mises Institute saw the helplessness of the city's poor simply as evidence of the evils and dependencies created by the welfare state.[24] Still others, without any consideration of recent budget cuts and diminished resources, found in the failure of government a confirmation that its involvement in anything was destined to be deficient. More serious conservative economists and policy planners drew the lesson that wealthier populations and nations were better able to confront disasters, and so unbridled capitalism, strong property rights, and individual freedoms were the best insurance against the recurrence of such catastrophes. Although the Bush administration, embarrassed by its failures in response to Katrina and under considerable political criticism, pledged large amounts of money to rebuilding the city, congressional Republicans quickly responded that other states were not responsible for Louisiana's problems, or that disaster relief funding would be too costly for the government and should be left to the free market.

In fact, the insurance industry learned quickly to adjust. Over a million insured homeowners made claims after Katrina, and eventually insurers paid over $40 billion and federal flood insurance covered another $15.7 billion. After the hurricanes of the late 1990s and then Katrina, the insurance industry realized that it was greatly exposed and had badly underestimated its potential losses. It had made great profits in the low hurricane years of the 1970s and 1980s, but in a changing environment by the 1990s it was an industry in trouble.[25] A new financial instrument appeared—catastrophe bonds—a kind of roulette based on disaster prediction. While Katrina proved to be a costly lesson, the industry, now dependent on scientific information, increasingly believed that climate change was real and that the risk of natural disaster warranted higher premiums. In the face of consumer complaints about those rates and the reluctance of some companies to offer catastrophe insurance, state governments have stepped in to help subsidize catastrophe insurance, a situation that helps wealthy homeowners who want to build close to the beaches, but that encourages such risky behavior by spreading its cost across the whole of society. Market solutions to the new environmental challenges have created their own conundrums.

A market-driven neoliberal response is not the only possible model for the avoidance of, or recovery from, natural disaster. The failure of the United States to respond adequately to the challenge of Katrina seemed to stand in marked contrast with the success of socialist Cuba in dealing with the threat of hurricanes. The measures begun by Cuba in Hurricane Flora in 1963, and then its excellent record thereafter in terms of reducing fatalities, became a model that many nations admired. In 2004 during Hurricane Ivan, Cuba was able to evacuate about ten percent of the nation's population without suffering a single fatality.[26] In the following year, Hurricane Dennis, a Category 4 storm and the most serious since Flora, struck the island, destroying or damaging 120,000 houses and leaving two and a half million without power. Some 1.5 million people, or over thirteen percent of the population, were moved to safety, and only sixteen people died in Cuba from that storm.[27] These impressive achievements in evacuation have been ascribed to policies like preparatory lists of elderly, sick, and infirm residents, provisions for evacuation of pets, and moving local doctors with the rest of the population in order to maintain medical care. A consistent plan for the integration of effort by many institutions with clear lines of authority was in place.

The contrast between Cuba and the United States was stark, but if we widen our perspective, it is clear that this difference is not simply a result of differences between capitalism and socialism. Vietnam is also a socialist nation, yet it has a relatively poor record of fatalities from hurricanes, while Japan, a capitalist country, has an excellent record, one, in fact, much better than that of the United States.[28] Relative national wealth and the ability to invest in mitigation and preparation is an important factor to be sure, but as Canadian sociologist Robert Brym has argued, the decisive factor is not the wealth or the ideological basis of a nation's economy, but "the collective will to take responsibility for helping fellow citizens in need, a will that is typically expressed through government policy." Brym concludes: "Compared to other rich countries that collective will is weak in the United States." But in truth, national attitudes about governmental disaster relief and other exercises of social responsibility remain deeply divided and heatedly contested in the United States, and those differences also influence the conflicting perceptions of the ecological and environmental arguments associated with the effect of global warming on the future of hurricanes.[29]

The smaller nations of the Caribbean looked for their own possible response to the risk of disasters, viewing natural hazards, and especially the increasing risk of hurricane activity in the first decades of the new century, as a particularly challenging threat.[30] One estimate placed the number of deaths in Latin America due to natural phenomena at 4,724,502 for the period 1991–2005. In the particular case of the Caribbean, the Small Island Developing States (SIDS) lack the resources of the United States to respond to disasters, but they too are confronted by the same hazards. International banking and financial institutions have sought to offer strategies for coping. A 2013 study by the International Monetary Fund noted that the Caribbean is one of the world's most disaster-prone regions, having suffered 187 natural disasters in the previous sixty years.[31] In Jamaica and the Bahamas, the probability of a hurricane in any given year is over 20 percent, and for much of the eastern Caribbean the probability is over 10 percent. Given the economic situation in the islands and their dependence on agriculture and tourism, they are particularly susceptible to natural disasters. The IMF study predicted that natural disasters would lower growth rates by 1–5 percent, and that burden combined with growing debt would produce a downward economic spiral. The IMF suggested the standard measures of reduced borrowing for social programs, reduction of the public sector, debt reduction and "growth-enhancing structural reforms." A main objective here is "to replace public sector demand with self-financing private sector demand." The report makes no mention of the possibility that this neoliberal solution might impact the ability of these island nations to respond to the very risks that had made them so vulnerable in the first place.

HURRICANE SANDY AND THE FUTURE

In the midst of the scientific controversy about the effect of climate change on the intensity and frequency of cyclonic storms and the ideological debates about the nature and role of government in preparing and protecting its citizens from calamity, the old questions about the primary causes of hurricanes have never disappeared. Natural causes, divine intervention, sin, and human error are still part of the debate.

Since the Atlantic hurricane season comes each year between June and November, it is no surprise that every four years there is a possibility that one or more of these storms will have a direct effect on an American presidential election. Such was the case in 2012, when Hurricane Sandy swept across the Greater Antilles, striking Jamaica, Cuba, Haiti, and the Dominican Republic, and then moved up the east coast of the United States to batter New Jersey, New York, and coastal New England. A storm of enormous size, the superstorm boasted a diameter of 1,100 miles. Sandy killed 286 people, and caused over $68 billion in damages along its track from Kingston, Jamaica to Quebec. Only a Category 2 hurricane with winds at 80 miles per hour when it struck New Jersey, the damage it caused still made it second in the United States only to Hurricane Katrina in terms of property and infrastructure loss. The images of Democratic president Barack Obama and Republican New Jersey governor Chris Christie walking the beaches of New Jersey and actively collaborating in the recovery and response became iconic at a moment when political gridlock had become the usual situation in Washington (fig. 9.3). In the election held the following month, Obama was swept into office by a large margin. Christie's popularity in the polls soared thereafter, and within a year he was already positioning himself for a run at the presidency, although a subsequent scandal involving his aides, partisan manipulation of Hurricane Sandy relief funds, and a large state deficit had diminished some of his luster by 2014. The cooperation of Obama and Christie during Hurricane Sandy was not the only reason for their popularity, but most observers agreed, and some exit polls confirmed, that it had definitely been an important factor in Obama's reelection and Christie's popularity. It was a demonstration that government can effectively provide help in time of crisis—or at least, as Paul Krugman argued provocatively, when those in authority do not hold government in contempt.[32]

Although the great controversies about natural disasters now center on science and political ideology, hurricanes like Katrina and Sandy still elicit providential interpretations, usually but not always from religious leaders or communities of believers. Not surprisingly, evangelical ministers saw Katrina as punishment for the sexual permissiveness in New Orleans, for gay rights, abortion, and a variety of other sins, but even the city's mayor, Ray Nagin, said in his reelection campaign that God had punished New Orleans for the war in Iraq, and in a later speech claimed that God wanted New Orleans to be an African American city.[33]

FIGURE 9.3 President Obama and Governor Christie after Hurricane Sandy (Reuters, photographer: Larry Downing)

Hurricane Sandy, coming on the eve of a presidential election, might also have elicited providential interpretations, but the voices that have always seen the hand of God in such events and even presumed to know God's will and the cause of his particular displeasure were, in this case, reticent; in fact, the silence on the evangelical right was deafening. A few sought to use the storm to justify their own particular opposition to abortion, or gay marriage, or gun control, but except for popular evangelist Pat Robertson, who saw the storm as God's design to keep Republican candidate Mitt Romney, a Mormon, out of the White House, most evangelical leaders remained quiet about God's intention in unleashing Hurricane Sandy. Given the positive outcome of Obama's handling of the storm in terms of the election results, none of the most popular evangelical ministers were moved to put forward an interpretation that God had sent the storm to show that the continual denigration of Obama had been unjust, or that opposition to his policies to help society's disadvantaged was against Christian teachings. Such interpretations of signs might have been possible, but providentialism was, as it has usually been, employed to support existing political convictions rather than as a catalyst for new interpretations or changes of heart.

But while both Obama and Christie had profited politically from their efforts to provide assistance to the victims of this storm, the underlying political and scientific questions that hurricanes provoke remained in contention: How might the hazard of natural phenomena best be confronted? To what extent were governments responsible to provide protection or relief from calamity? To what extent is climatic change occurring, and if it is, what needs to be done to lessen its impact on environments and societies? Hurricane Sandy provided an example of the complex and sometimes contradictory relationship of these questions. Governor Christie ardently sought federal help for the post-Sandy recovery of his state and was criticized by fellow Republican politicians for a "big government" approach and dependence on Washington. But on the question of global warming and its possible effects on the risk of natural disasters, he was and, at the time of this writing, remains as skeptical as his Republican colleagues, and on a number occasions voiced his doubts about climate change, or at least emphasized that such arcane questions are less important to him than immediate problem solving.[34]

But to separate the issue into a matter of words versus deeds is too facile. During Hurricane Sandy, the New Jersey Transit Corporation, despite the fact that it had an emergency plan in place to move its trains to high ground in case of a hurricane, failed to do so, instead leaving them in the low-lying Meadowlands, where the storm caused a loss of a quarter of rolling stock and over $150 million in damages. Governor Christie and New Jersey Transit officials believed that their pre-storm calculations based on past experience had been correct, and explained their miscalculation as a result of the severity of the storm that no one could have predicted. But New York's Metropolitan Transportation Authority (MTA), faced with the same problem, suffered far fewer losses and recovered far more quickly from the storm. In New York, Governor Andrew Cuomo and the MTA had, as a result of earlier storms and problems, come to believe that if climate change was indeed a reality, the past was no longer a reliable guide for the future. Cuomo and the MTA had taken the new risk seriously. At a press conference on October 30, the day after Hurricane Sandy hit the region, Cuomo stated, "Climate change is a reality. Extreme weather is a reality. It is a reality that we are vulnerable and if we are going to do our job as elected officials we are going to need to make modifications necessary so we don't incur this type of damage."[35] He, too, avoided the highly charged political question of what caused climate change and what should be done about it.

In this particular instance, however, accepting the possibility that climate change was a reality had produced a positive result for New York, while Christie's doubts and ambivalence about it, and the doubts of the transit officials he appointed, resulted in a disaster for neighboring New Jersey. Both the Federal Transportation Agency and a 2011 internal New Jersey report had warned of catastrophic results from a high storm surge, and the National Weather Service had given early projections warning that Sandy was a major storm. At least twenty-four hours before Sandy struck New Jersey, the Weather Service estimated a 15-foot storm surge, but little attention was given by New Jersey officials to that possibility, and the result in New Jersey was a transportation disaster.

Hurricane Sandy gave evidence that the practical solutions and responses to the risks of natural phenomena like hurricanes cannot be separated from the scientific controversies and political debates that surround them, and that a leader or a nation that tries to do so increases the vulnerability of all those at risk. The fact that the funding of FEMA had been so reduced that shoreline maps of possible areas of flooding in New York and New Jersey prior to Sandy were fifteen or twenty years out of date revealed how a lack of attention to the larger questions of climate change contributed to the creation of disaster.[36]

In October 2013, after being reelected as governor of New Jersey, Christie's victory speech referred to the "spirit of hurricane Sandy," the sense of community and cooperation that the hurricane had produced, in terms very much like those used by Fidel Castro in the days following Hurricane Flora in 1963. Castro's experience, however, had made him sensitive to the challenges of environmental change and to the political advantages of strong government action in response to natural disasters. It remains unclear whether Christie, a Republican, who was looking ahead to a run for the presidency in 2016, had learned the same lesson, and whether he could make that message appealing to his supporters and his political party, the leadership of which continued either to deny mounting scientific evidence of anthropogenic climate change, or suggested that if climate change did exist, the problem was better confronted and vulnerability more effectively reduced by changing social patterns rather than trying to change the climate by reducing carbon emissions. This was a position that some meteorologists like Pielke and Landsea had advocated, and it intersected nicely with an ideological position that emphasized an unrestrained free market and the continued use of fossil fuels.[37] Since poor people and poor countries always suffer the most from natural disasters, they argued that the best protection against the rise of sea level or "hypercanes" was to eliminate poverty and raise economic levels. When in May 2014 Senator Marco Rubio of Florida, representative of a state considered to be particularly vulnerable to a rise in sea level and to the effects of large hurricanes, questioned the prevailing scientific opinion about the anthropogenic causes of global warming, and stated that nothing could be effectively done to alter climate change that would not be economically damaging to the United States, he was stating in simple terms the outline of an ideological position that had been widely adopted since the 1980s, not only in the United States, but within the Greater Caribbean and in the rest of the world. [38] The extent to which that position had made vulnerabilities worse by weakening both financial support for the public sector and investments in infrastructure, or by diminishing or dismantling the central authority of national states or regional organizations, has become a crucial issue of political debate. In a way, the hurricanes and how societies deal with them have become symbolic of competing worldviews.

Now, each new year, when in June the sea begins to warm and the stars of the ancient Carib constellation of the heron's canoe rise again in the Caribbean night sky, the hurricanes will return. The peoples of the North Atlantic will need to confront the storms and the old questions they raise: How best can their threat be met? Who is responsible to do so? And what role do God, nature, and humankind have in their origins and effects? In this new century, these ancient questions must be raised and answered with more urgency than ever before.

Abbreviations

༄༅༅༅

ARCHIVES

AGI	Archivo General de Indias (Seville)
AGPR	Archivo General de Puerto Rico
AGNRD	Archivo General de la Nación de la Republica Dominicana
AHN	Archivo Historico Nacional (Madrid)
AHMP	Archivo Municipal de Ponce
AHMCH	Archivo Historico del Museo de la Ciudad de la Habana
AHMC	Archivo Historico Municipal de Caguas
ANOM	Archive National d'Outre-Mer (Aix-en-Provence)
BNM	Biblioteca Nacional (Madrid)
FMM	Fundación Luís Muñoz Marín (San Juan)
JA	Jamaica Archives (Spanish Town)
USNA	National Archives (Washington, DC)
NAGB	National Archive Great Britain
NAH	Nationaal Archief Den Haag (The Hague)
NLJ	National Library of Jamaica (Kingston)
RC	Rigsarkivet (Copenhagen)
ZAM	Zeeuws Archief (Middleburg)

PUBLICATIONS

CCSD	*Cartas del Cabildo de la Ciudad de Santo Domingo en el siglo XVI*
CES	Cuba: *Economia y sociedad*
CSPC	*Calendar of State Papers: Colonial*
EPR	*Episcopológio de Puerto Rico*

Notes

◌◌◌◌

PREFACE

1. Fernand Braudel, *The Mediterranean and the Mediterranean World in the Age of Philip II*, 2 vols. (New York: Harper & Row, 1976). The book was written originally while Braudel was a prisoner of war without access to his notes. It was first published in 1949. The first revised French edition was published in 1966. For an alternate view of Mediterranean history emphasizing change over time and human agency over geographical constraints, see David Abulafia, *The Great Sea: A Human History of the Mediterranean* (New York: Oxford University Press, 2011), xxv–xxviii.

2. Benjamín Vicuña Mackenna, *El clima de Chile: Ensayo histórico* (Buenos Aires: Editorial Francisco de Aguirre, 1970).

3. N.A.T. [Neville] Hall, *Slave Society in the Danish West Indies: St. Thomas, St. John and St. Croix*, ed. B. W. Higman (Mona, Jamaica: University of the West Indies Press, 1992), 1.

4. General overviews that have provided summaries of meteorological information that have proven useful to me are Roger A. Pielke, *The Hurricane* (London: Routledge, 1990); Paul V. Kislow, *Hurricanes: Background, History and Bibliography* (New York: Nova Science Publishers, 2008); Patrick J. Fitzpatrick, *Natural Disasters: Hurricanes—A Reference Handbook*, Contemporary World Issues (Santa Barbara, CA: ABC-CLIO, 1999); Richard J. Murnane and Kam-biu Liu, *Hurricanes and Typhoons: Past, Present, and Future* (New York: Columbia University Press, 2004); James B. Elsner and A. Birol Kara, *Hurricanes of the North Atlantic: Climate and Society* (New York: Oxford University Press, 1999). A tremendous amount of information on past and present storms is now available on the website of the National Oceanic and Atmospheric Administration (NOAA) and its National Hurricane Center. See www.noa.gov/index and www.nhc.noaa.gov. Most important in historical terms is the HURDAT or Atlantic Basin Hurricane database, which gathers information on historical storms from 1850 to the twentieth century.

5. On the field of environmental history I have found particularly helpful the essays by John McNeill ("Observations on the Nature and Culture of Environmental History," *History and Theory* 42, no. 4 (2003): 5–43) and José Augusto Pádua ("As bases teóricas da história ambiental," *Estudos Avançados* 24, no. 68 (Jan. 2010): 81–101).

6. A model study of the impact of disease in the region is John Robert McNeill, *Mosquito Empires: Ecology and War in the Greater Caribbean, 1620–1914*, New Approaches to the Americas (New York: Cambridge University Press, 2010).

7. John Fowler, *A General Account of the Calamities Occasioned by the Late Tremendous Hurricanes and Earthquakes in the West-India Islands, Foreign as Well as Domestic: With the Petitions to, and Resolutions of, the House of Commons, in Behalf of the Sufferers at Jamaica*

and Barbados: Also a List of the Committee Appointed to Manage the Subscriptions of the Benevolent Public, Towards Their Further Relief (London: J. Stockdale and W. Richardson, 1781), i.

8. I first began to develop this idea in Stuart B. Schwartz, "Virginia and the Atlantic World," in *The Atlantic World and Virginia, 1550–1624,* ed. Peter C. Mancall (Williamsburg, VA: Omohundro Institute of Early American History and Culture, 2004), 558–70. For more general views of the Atlantic history concept, see Jack P. Greene and Philip D. Morgan, eds., *Atlantic History: A Critical Appraisal* (Oxford: Oxford University Press, 2009).

9. The early modern era is dealt with in Bernard Bailyn, *Atlantic History: Concept and Contours* (Cambridge, MA: Harvard University Press, 2005). Two major Atlantic history texts essentially end in 1900: see Douglas R. Egerton, *The Atlantic World: A History, 1400–1888* (Wheeling, IL: Harlan Davidson, 2007); Thomas Benjamin, *The Atlantic World: Europeans, Africans, Indians and Their Shared History, 1400–1900* (Cambridge: Cambridge University Press, 2009). John K. Thornton, *A Cultural History of the Atlantic World, 1250–1820* (Cambridge: Cambridge University Press, 2012), ends in the early nineteenth century. One essay on Ireland and liberation theology in the twentieth century is included in Jorge Cañizares-Esguerra and Erik R Seeman, *The Atlantic in Global History, 1500–2000* (Upper Saddle River, NJ: Pearson Prentice Hall, 2007).

10. On the Bermuda High and its effects, see Ivor Van Heerden and Mike Bryan, *The Storm: What Went Wrong and Why during Hurricane Katrina—The Inside Story from One Louisiana Scientist* (New York: Viking, 2006), 18–19.

11. Jill S. M. Coleman and Steven A. LaVoie, "Paleotempestology: Reconstructing Atlantic Tropical Cyclone Tracks in the Pre-HURDAT Era," in *Modern Climatology,* ed. Shih-Yu Simon Wang (N.p.: InTech, 2012), http://www.intechopen.com/books/modern-climatology/paleotempestology-reconstructing-atlantic-tropical-cyclone-tracks-in-the-pre-hurdat-era.

12. For example, see James W. Wiley and Joseph M. Wunderle, "The Effects of Hurricanes on Birds, with Special Reference to Caribbean Islands," *Bird Conservation International* 3, no. 4 (1993): 319–49; Emery R. Boose, Mayra I. Serrano, and David R. Foster, "Landscape and Regional Impacts of Hurricanes in Puerto Rico," *Ecological Monographs* 74, no. 2 (May 2004): 335–52.

13. Barometer readings of atmospheric pressure are usually given in millibars (metric) or in inches. At sea level average pressure is 1013 millibars, or 29.92 inches. Lowest recorded pressure (excluding tornadoes) has been 870 millibars, or 25.70 inches.

14. The Fujita scale, which predicts the effects of tornado wind speed on buildings, has sometimes been used in descriptions of hurricane damage.

15. Pitirim Aleksandrovič Sorokin, *Man and Society in Calamity: The Effects of War, Revolution, Famine, Pestilence upon Human Mind, Behavior, Social Organization and Cultural Life* (Westport, CT: Greenwood Press, 1968). A grand tradition in the social sciences study of disaster developed with outstanding books like Kai Erikson, *Everything in Its Path: Destruction of Community in the Buffalo Creek Flood* (New York: Simon and Schuster, 1976); Michael Barkun, *Disaster and the Millennium* (Syracuse, NY: Syracuse University Press, 1986); Barbara Bode, *No Bells to Toll: Destruction and Creation in the Andes* (New York: Scribner, 1989); E. L. Jones, *The European Miracle: Environments, Economies, and Geopolitics in the History of Europe and Asia,* 2nd ed. (Cambridge: Cambridge University Press, 1987); Theodore Steinberg, *Acts of God: The Unnatural History of Natural Disaster in America* (New York: Oxford University Press, 2000); these are among the works that I have found particularly useful as I designed this project.

16. Matthew Mulcahy, *Hurricanes and Society in the British Greater Caribbean, 1624–1783* (Baltimore: Johns Hopkins University Press, 2006); Charles F. Walker, *Shaky Colonialism: The 1746 Earthquake-Tsunami in Lima, Peru, and Its Long Aftermath* (Durham, NC: Duke University Press, 2008); Geoffrey Parker, *Global Crisis: War, Climate Change and Catastrophe in the Seventeenth Century* (New Haven: Yale University Press, 2013); Louis A. Pérez, *Winds of Change: Hurricanes and the Transformation of Nineteenth Century Cuba* (Chapel Hill: University of North Carolina Press, 2001); Sherry Johnson, *Climate and Catastrophe in Cuba and the Atlantic World in the Age of Revolution* (Chapel Hill: University of North Carolina Press, 2011); Erik Larson, *Isaac's Storm: a Man, a Time, and the Deadliest Hurricane in History* (New York: Crown Publishers, 1999); Raymond Arsenault, "The Public Storm: Hurricanes and the State in Twentieth-Century America," in *American Public Life and the Historical Imagination*, ed. Wendy Gamber, Michael Grossberg, and Hendrik Hartog (Notre Dame, IN: University of Notre Dame Press, 2003), 262–92; Ulrich Beck, *Risk Society: Towards a New Modernity* (London: Sage Publications, 1992).

CHAPTER 1. STORMS AND GODS IN A SPANISH SEA

1. J. Omar Ruiz Gordillo, "Fundaciones urbanas en México: La Veracruz en el siglo XVI," *Altepetl. Revista de Geografía Histórica—Social y Estudios Regionales* 5–6 (2012) (http://www.uv.mx/altepetl/No5/anteriores/alt02/arts/funcaiones%20urbanas.pdf).

2. AGI, Patronato 181. On the role of Veracruz in the Spanish mercantile system, see Pierre Chaunu, "Veracruz en la segunda mitad del siglo XVI y primera mitad del siglo XVII," *Historia Mexicana* 9, no. 4 (1960): 521–57.

3. Virginia García Acosta, Juan Manuel Pérez Zevallos, and América Molina del Villar, *Desastres agrícolas en México: Catálogo Histórico*, Sección de Obras de Ciencia y Tecnología (Mexico City: Centro de Investigaciones y Estudios Superiores en Antropología Social, Fondo de Cultura Económica, 2003), 108–9.

4. This overall chronology is presented in François Walter, *Catastrophes: Une histoire culturelle, XVIe–XXIe siècles*, Univers Historique (Paris: Seuil, 2008).

5. Monica Juneja and Franz Mauelshagen, "Disasters and Pre-industrial Societies Historiographic Trends and Comparative Perspectives," *Medieval History Journal* 10, no. 1–2 (Oct. 2007): 1–31.

6. François Walter, "Pour une histoire culturelle des risques naturels," in *Les cultures du risque: XVIe–XXIe siècles*, ed. François Walter, Bernardino Fantini, and Pascal Delvaux (Geneva: Presses d'histoire suisse, 2006), 6–28; Jean Delumeau, *Rassurer et protéger: Le sentiment de sécurité dans l'Occident d'autrefois* (Paris: Fayard, 1989), 179–210.

7. García Acosta, Pérez Zevallos, and Molina del Villar, *Desastres agrícolas en México*, I, 109.

8. See Héctor Cuevas Fernández and Mário Navarrete Hernández, "Los hurracanes en la época prehispánica y en el siglo XVI," in *Inundaciones 2005 en el estado Veracruz* (Xalapa, Veracruz: Universidad Veracruzana, 2006), ed. Adalberto Tejeda Martínez and Carlos Welsh Rodríguez, 39–49. See also Herman W. Konrad, "Fallout of the Wars of the Chacs: The Impact of Hurricanes and Implications for Prehispanic Quintana Roo Maya Processes," in *Status, Structure, and Stratification: Current Archaeological Reconstructions: Proceedings of the Sixteenth Annual Conference*, ed. Marc Thompson, Maria Teresa Garcia, and F. J Kense (Calgary: University of Calgary, Archaeological Association, 1985), 321–30.

9. Román Piña Chán and Patricia Castillo Peña, *Tajín: La ciudad del dios Huracán* (Mexico City: Fondo de Cultura Económica, 1999), 46.

10. Konrad, "Fallout of the Wars of the Chacs," 334. On the hurricanes of Yucatan in the nineteenth and twentieth centuries, see Emery R. Boose et al., "Geographical and Historical Variation in Hurricanes across the Yucatán Peninsula," in *The Lowland Maya Area: Three Millennia at the Human-Wildland Interface*, ed. Arturo Gómez-Pompa et al. (Binghamton, NY: Food Products Press, 2003), 495–516.

11. On the complicated history of Columbus's journal, see Robert H. Fuson, *The Log of Christopher Columbus* (Camden, ME: International Marine Publishing Company, 1991), 1–13. Fuson's edition and translation, like all others, depend on an edited abstract made by Father Bartolomé de Las Casas sometime between 1527 and 1539, based on a copy of the original. A link to Carib languages is suggested by Douglas Taylor, "Spanish Huracán and Its Congeners," *International Journal of American Linguistics* 22 (1956): 275–76.

12. Sebastián de Covarrubias, *Tesoro de la lengua castellana o española*, ed. Martín de Riquer (Barcelona: S.A. Horta, 1943), 706. I believe this entry is one of the additions of Benito Remigo Noydens from the edition of 1674.

13. Irving Rouse, *The Tainos: Rise and Decline of the People Who Greeted Columbus* (New Haven, CT: Yale University Press, 1992).

14. Fernando Ortiz, *El huracán, su mitología y sus símbolos* (Mexico City: Fondo de Cultura Económica, 1947).

15. The bishop of Santo Domingo noted in 1531 noted that "in these months the Caribs are likely to come [to Puerto Rico] because there are more advantages to be had than in other months" (*suelen venir los caribes por haber mas bonanzas que en otros meses del año*). See AGI (Archivo General de Indias [Seville]), Santo Domingo (SD) 93, ramo 1, doc. 2.

16. Sebastián Robiou Lamarche, *Caribes: Creencias y rituales* (San Juan, PR: Editorial Punto y Coma, 2009), 182–92.

17. Ibid., 190. See Jacques Bouton, *Relation de l'establissement des Francois depuis l'an 1635: En l'isle de la Martinique, l'vne des Antilles de l'Amerique. Des mœurs des sauvages, de la situation, & des autres singularitez de l'isle* (Paris: Sebastien Cramoisy, 1640).

18. The Saffir-Simpson scale has been used since 1973 to distinguish the intensity of hurricanes in the Western Hemisphere. It uses five categories of wind speed: 1 (74–95 mph), 2 (96–110 mph), 3 (111–129 mph), 4 (130–156 mph), 5 (157+ mph).

19. Antonio de Herrera Tordesillas, *Descripción de las Indias occidentales* (Madrid, 1601), dec. 1, lib. 2, cap. 15.

20. The original account appears in Bartolomé de las Casas, *Historia de las Indias*, ed. Lewis Hanke (Mexico City: Fondo de Cultura Económica, 1951). It has been analyzed in meteorological terms by David McWilliams Ludlum, *Early American Hurricanes, 1492–1870*, The History of American Weather, no. 1 (Boston: American Meteorological Society, 1963), 6–7. It is also discussed in cultural terms by Peter Hulme, *Colonial Encounters: Europe and the Native Caribbean, 1492–1797* (New York: Methuen, 1986), 94–95.

21. Craig Martin, "Experience of the New World and Aristotelian Revisions of the Earth's Climates during the Renaissance," *History of Meteorology* 3 (2006): 1–15.

22. John H. Elliott, *The Old World and the New 1492–1650*, The Wiles Lectures 1969 (Cambridge: University Press, 1970); Jorge Cañizares-Esguerra, "New World, New Stars: Patriotic Astrology and the Invention of Indian and Creole Bodies in Colonial Spanish America, 1600–1650," *American Historical Review* 104, no. 1 (Feb. 1999): 33–68; Anthony Grafton, *New Worlds, Ancient Texts: The Power of Tradition and the Shock of Discovery* (Cambridge, MA: Belknap Press of Harvard University Press, 1992).

23. Martín Gelabertó Vilagrán, "Tempestades y conjuros de las fuerzas naturales:

Aspectos magico-religiosos de la cultura en la alta edad moderna," *Pedralbes: Revista d'historia moderna* 9 (1989): 193–99. An excellent analysis of the dialogue between learned and popular culture in the understanding of comets is presented in Sara Schechner, *Comets, Popular Culture, and the Birth of Modern Cosmology* (Princeton, NJ: Princeton University Press, 1997). See also Jorge Cañizares-Esguerra, *Puritan Conquistadors: Iberianizing the Atlantic, 1550–1700* (Stanford, CA: Stanford University Press, 2006), 120–77.

24. This observation is made by Antonello Gerbi, *Nature in the New World: From Christopher Columbus to Gonzalo Fernandez de Oviedo* (Pittsburgh: University of Pittsburgh Press, 1985), 121–23. Gerbi notes that the expeditions of Yañez Pinzon (1501), Ojeda (1505), Velázquez (1518), and Magellan (1519) were not asked to submit reports. On a more general relative lack of European curiosity, see Elliott, *The Old World and the New 1492–1650*.

25. Rómulo D. Carbia, *La crónica oficial de Las Indias occidentales* (La Plata: Argentina, 1934); cited in Gerbi, *Nature in the New World*, 120.

26. James Scott, *Seeing like a State: How Certain Schemes to Improve the Human Condition Have Failed* (New Haven: Yale University Press, 1998).

27. I have not entered here into the question of making this knowledge the exclusive property of Spain. That question has been taken up by a number of authors. See, for example, Alison Sandman, "Controlling Knowledge: Navigation, Cartography, and Secrecy in the Early Modern Spanish Atlantic," in *Science and Empire in the Atlantic World*, ed. James Delbourgo and Nicholas Dew (New York: Routledge, 2008), 31–52. A good specific example of the effect of restricting useful information was the publication ban of Juan Escalante de Mendoza, *Itinerario de navegación de los mares y tierras occidentales* (1575) because of its specific description of the best sailing routes to the Indies. Despite the prohibition, it circulated widely in manuscript. It contained a section on hurricanes.

28. This utilitarian aspect of knowledge gathering in Spanish science of the period is emphasized by Antonio Barrera-Osorio, *Experiencing Nature: The Spanish American Empire and the Early Scientific Revolution* (Austin: University of Texas Press, 2006). For a general discussion of the development of Spanish cosmography, see María M. Portuondo, *Secret Science: Spanish Cosmography and the New World* (Chicago: University of Chicago Press, 2009).

29. Enciso's work also appeared in editions of 1530 and 1546. See the discussion in Gerbi, *Nature in the New World*.

30. Pérez de Oliva discusses early hurricanes but does not use that word and instead employs *torbellino*, a term from European experience: Fernán Pérez de Oliva, *Historia de la invención de las Indias*, ed. José Juan Arrom (Mexico City: Siglo Veintiuno, 1991).

31. Casas, *Historia de las Indias*, chapter 69, "De las más terribles tormentas que se cree haber en todas los mares del mundo son las que por estos mares destas islas y tierra firme suele hacer."

32. Gonzalo Fernández de Oviedo y Valdes, *De la natural hystoria de las Indias* (Toledo: Remon de Petras, 1526). The first part of the *Historia general* was published in 1535, and the second part was finished in 1541, but not published until 1557.

33. Oviedo, *Historia general*, 1:168–69; 3:10; 6:3.

34. Gonzalo Fernández de Oviedo y Valdés, *Natural History of the West Indies*, North Carolina. University, Studies in the Romance Languages and Literature, no. 32 (Chapel Hill: University of North Carolina Press, 1959), 37; Gonzalo Fernández de Oviedo y

Valdés, *Sumario de la natural historia de Las Indias*, Biblioteca Americana. Serie de Cronistas de Indias 13 (Mexico City: Fondo de Cultura Económica, 1950), 130.

35. It appears in Oviedo *Natural History;* Las Casas, *Historia de las Indias;* and López Medel, *De los Tres elementos.*

36. Francisco del Paso y Troncoso and Silvio Arturo Zavala, *Epistolario de Nueva España, 1505–1818* (México City: Antigua Librería Robredo, de J. Porrúa e Hijos, 1939), 36–40.

37. I am following here the important work done by Martín Gelabertó Vilagrán in "Tempestades y conjuros de las fuerzas naturales."

38. Fernández de Oviedo y Valdés, *Natural History of the West Indies*, 37.

39. Diego de Landa, *Relación de Las Cosas de Yucatán*, ed. Héctor Pérez Martínez, 7th. ed (Mexico City: Editorial P. Robredo, 1938), chapter 10, p. 23. My thanks to Matthew Restall for this translation.

40. "las cosas que están por venir ya sabéis, señor, que solo Dios nuestro Señor las sabe, y no las puede saber ninguna criatura, si no es quien su Divina bondad las revela." See Juan de Escalante de Mendoza, *Itinerario de navegación de los mares y tierras orientales 1575* (Madrid: Museo Naval, 1985), 140.

41. Strangely, the 1590 work of the Jesuit José de Acosta, although much influenced by classical ideas of meteorology and geography, makes no mention of hurricanes. Acosta applied Aristotle's ideas that winds are the exhalations of the earth's humidity to explain the winds of the New World. See José de Acosta, *Natural and Moral History of the Indies*, ed. Jane E. Mangan, trans. Frances López-Morillas (Durham, NC: Duke University Press, 2002).

42. Historian Berta Ares believes that when Juan de Ovando became *visitador* of the Council of the Indies and began gathering geographical information that López Medel probably prepared his manuscript. There was little place in his work for monstrosities or marvels, and he emphasized the "rational" nature of the New World. He believed that "natural man" was closer to God, and that Indians fell into that category. See Tomás López Medel, *De los tres elementos: Tratado sobre la naturaleza y el hombre del Nuevo Mundo,* Berta Ares Queija, ed. (Madrid: Quinto Centenario and Alianza, 1990), xxxii–xxxiii.

43. "concurso y contraste de diversos y contraries vientos."

44. For example, on the impact of hurricanes on Yucatan, see Herman W. Konrad, "Caribbean Tropical Storms: Ecological Implications for Pre-Hispanic and Contemporary Maya Subsistence on the Yucatan Peninsula," *Revista de la Universidad Autónoma de Yucatán* 18, no. 224 (2003): 99–126; Virginia García Acosta, "Huracanes y/o desastres en Yucatán," *Revista de La Universidad Autónoma de Yucatán* 17, no. 223 (2002): 3–15.

45. López Medel, *De los tres elementos*, 33.

46. Particularly useful in regard to these issues in Spain are Martín Gelabertó Vilagrán, "Astrología, religión y pronóstico en el renacimiento," *Historia y Vida* 305 (August 1993): 68–75; and "Supersticiones y augurios climáticos en la España de la Edad Moderna," *Historia y Vida* 296 (Nov. 1996): 23–28. Most important is his "La palabra del predicador: Contrarreforma y superstición en Cataluña (siglos XVII y XVIII)" (dissertation, University of Barcelona, 2003), published as Martí Gelabertó, *La palabra del predicador: Contrarreforma y superstición en Cataluña, siglos XVII–XVIII*, Colección Hispania 17 (Lleida: Editorial Milenio, 2005).

47. Ernest Germana, "Astrology, Religion and Politics in Counter-Reformation Rome," in *Science, Culture, and Popular Belief in Renaissance Europe*, ed. Stephen Pumfrey,

Paolo L. Rossi, and Maurice Slawinski (Manchester, Manchester University Press, 1991), 249.

48. Carmen Gonzalo de Andrés, "La predicción del tiempo en el Siglo de Oro español," Revista del Aficionado de Meteorología (n.d.), http://www.tiempo.com/ram /167/la-prediccion-del-tiempo-en-el-siglo-de-oro-espanol-s-xvi–xvii.

49. Julio Ismael Martínez Betancourt, "Predicciones climáticas y el conocimiento popular tradicional del campesino cubano," Cautauro: Revista Cubana de Antropología 12, no. 22 (2010): 121–30; V. Cubilla, "Las cabañuelas y la Estación Climatológica Agricola," Revista INRA 5 (1961): 60–63.

50. Christopher Columbus, The "Libro de las profecías" of Christopher Columbus, ed. Delno C. West and August Kling (Gainesville: University of Florida Press, 1991), 106–7.

51. The statement is drawn from the prefatory letter of Columbus to Ferdinand and Isabella in his book of prophecies. See ibid., 107.

52. Franz Mauelshagen, "Disaster and Political Culture in Germany since 1500," in Natural Disasters, Cultural Responses: Case Studies toward a Global Environmental History, ed. Christof Mauch and Christian Pfister, The German Historical Institute Studies in International Environmental History (Lanham, MD: Lexington Books, 2009), 60.

53. I refer here to the argument of Jean Delumeau, Sin and Fear: The Emergence of a Western Guilt Culture, 13th–18th Centuries (New York: St. Martin's Press, 1990).

54. Bartolomé de las Casas, Apologética historia sumaria, ed. Vidal Abril Castelló, vols. 6–8 of Obras Completas / Bartolomé de Las Casas (Madrid: Alianza, 1992).

55. AGI, SD legajo 2.

56. Relación verdadera, en que se dà quenta del horrible Huracàn que sobrevino à la Isla, y Puerto de Santo Domingo de los Españoles el dia quinze de Agosto de 1680 (Madrid: Lucas Antonio de Bedmar, 1681).

57. See Alain Corbin, Village Bells: Sound and Meaning in the Nineteenth-Century French Countryside, European Perspectives (New York: Columbia University Press, 1998).

58. See Teodoro Vidal, El control de La naturaleza: Mediante la palabra en la tradición Puertorriqueña (San Juan: Ediciones Alba, 2008), 17–25.

59. Ibid.

60. Ortiz, El huracán, 54. In the seventeenth century Father Labat, like many of his contemporary commentators, believed that thunder dissipated the wind, but his position changed after a hurricane he experienced in 1695.

61. For example, Fray Iñigo Abbad reported that the threatening sky over the town of Aguada on the northwestern coast of Puerto Rico in 1772 led the population to seek divine mercy with two days of public rogations in the hermitage of Our Lady of Espinal. See Rafael W. Ramírez de Arellano, "Los huracanes de Puerto Rico," Boletin de La Universidad de Puerto Rico 3, no. 2 (Dec. 1932): 21. In Cuba, the survivors of the San Evaristo hurricane of 1837 recalled many years later their prayer, promises, and the removal of the saints' images from the churches to ask for the "clemency of heaven." See José Martínez Fortún y Foyo, Entry for 1837, Anales y efemérides de San Juan de los Remedios, vol. 1, part 1 (1492–1849). This text is fully available at http://www.cubangenclub .org/clist.php?nm=76.

62. Damián López de Haro, ed., Sínodo de San Juan de Puerto Rico de 1645 (Madrid: Centro de Estudios Históricos del CSIC, 1986), 73.

63. My mother-in-law, Divina Arroyo de Jordán, informed me that in Cabo Rojo when she was a girl in the 1920s her grandmother spoke of the burning of blessed

palms as a defense against storms. The use of ashes to make crosses in homes as protection against storms was recounted by Ortiz, *El huracán*, 79.

64. *"San Lorenzo, San Lorenzo, amarra el perro y suelta el viento."* Vidal, *El control de la naturaleza*, 41.

65. The term *cordonazo* ("lashing") is used for hurricanes on the Pacific coast of Mexico. The oldest Spanish building in the Americas is the "casa de cordon," in Santo Domingo. Begun in 1503, it served as residence for Francisco de Garay, a supporter of Columbus who later became governor of Jamaica. The knotted Franciscan cord that adorns its entry was a common decorative element in Isabelline Gothic architecture of the fifteenth century in Spain, but its presence on this building has never been adequately explained, and since the city suffered three hurricanes during the period of construction, its presence as a symbolic protection is certainly possible.

66. I have drawn this material from Ortiz, *El huracán*, 78–81.

67. "Santa Barbara, doncella, líbranos de rayos y centellas, como libraste a Jonás del vientre de la ballena." "San Isidro, labrador, quita el agua y pon el sol." Vidal, *El control de la naturaleza*, 31, 56. Vidal gives excellent examples collected in rural Puerto Rico from elderly informants.

68. Francisco Moscoso, *Juicio al gobernador: Episodios coloniales de Puerto Rico, 1550* (Hato Rey: Universidad de Puerto Rico, Decanato de Estudios Graduados e Investigación, Publicaciones Puertorriqueñas Editores, 1998), 134.

69. The work is cited and discussed in Hulme, *Colonial Encounters*, 100–101. See also Peter Hulme, "Hurricanes in the Caribbees: The Constitution of the Discourse of English Colonialism," in *1642: Literature and Power in the Seventeenth Century: Proceedings of the Essex Conference on the Sociology of Literature, July 1980*, ed. Francis Barker and Jay Bernstein (Colchester: University of Essex, 1981), 55–83.

70. Moreau de Jonnes, *Histoire physique des Antilles Francaise* (Paris, 1822), as cited in Ramírez de Arellano, "Los huracanes de Puerto Rico," 9–10.

71. "Captain Langford's Observations of his own Experience upon hurricanes and their Prognostiks," *Philosophical Transactions of the Royal Society* 20 (1698): 407, cited in Mulcahy, *Hurricanes and Society*, 51.

72. Iñigo Abbad y Lasierra, *Historia geográfica, civil y natural de l a Isla de San Juan Bautista de Puerto Rico*, 3rd edition (San Juan: Ediciones de la Universidad de Puerto Rico, 1970), 530.

73. Jean Baptiste Labat, *Nouveau Voyage aux Isles de l'Amerique* (La Haye: P. Husson, 1724), 165–66.

74. Ramírez de Arellano, "Los huracanes de Puerto Rico," 10.

75. López Medel, *De los tres elementos*, 32. Similar statements were made by Desiderio Herrera y Cabrera, *Memoria sobre los huracanes en la Isla de Cuba* (Havana: Impr. de Barcina, 1847).

76. Crab Jack reported: "Crabs is mighty queer critters, and the best barometers ye ever seen. Where there's a storm coming crabs goes for deep water and buried 'emselves in the mud, an' they don't come back afore the storms over." Lisa Waller Rogers, *The Great Storm: The Hurricane Diary of J. T. King, Galveston, Texas, 1900* (Lubbock: Texas Tech University Press, 2001), 30–32. See also David G. McComb, *Galveston: a History* (Austin: University of Texas Press, 1986), 123.

77. Ortiz, *El huracán*, 54.

78. "unas tormentas que llaman huracanes, las mayores que en el mar se conocen. . . ." Juan López de Velasco, *Geografía y descripción universal de las Indias* (Madrid: Estab. tip. de Fortanet, 1894), 60.

79. See also Escalante de Mendoza, *Itinerario de navegación*.

80. The etymology of the term has been examined by Hulme, *Colonial Encounters*, 101–2. See also Mulcahy, *Hurricanes and Society*.

81. *Noticias de Madrid*, 1621–22.

82. Craig Martin, *Renaissance Meteorology: Pomponazzi to Descartes* (Baltimore: Johns Hopkins University Press, 2011), 26.

83. A study of the Caribbean from 1982 to 1992 suggests that the passage of a low-pressure cell from a hurricane's eye was followed by seismic activity within ten days and within a thousand miles of the storm's path, and that seismic activity increases during the months of September and October, which suggests that atmospheric change triggers seismic activity. See Karen Fay O'Loughlin and James F. Lander, *Caribbean Tsunamis: A 500-Year History from 1498–1998* (Dordrecht: Kluwer Academic Publishers, 2004), 75–79. A similar relationship but caused by seismic stress brought about by displacement of soils was suggested in 2010 by University of Miami geophysicist Shimon Wdowinski. See http://rsmas.miami.edu/users/swdowinski/highlights.html.

84. "tumulto de rigurosos truenos y relampagos con grandíssimos terremotos de huracanes de ayre . . ." See *Espantoso huracan que vino sobre la Villa de Çafra, que fue servido Dios . . . sucediesse por nuestros grandes pecados, para que sea escarmiento a tantas maldades como cada dia cometemos contra su divina Magestad: dase cuenta de la grande ruyna que uvo de personas y haziendas, en este . . . terremoto 1624*. (Seville: Juan de Cabrera, 1624).

85. Waldo Ross, *Nuestro imaginario cultural: Simbólica literaría hispanoamericana*, Autores, Textos y Temas 11 (Barcelona: Anthropos, 1992), 117. Neither the term *terremoto* nor the word *huracán* appear in Sebastián Covarrubias Orozco, *Tesoro de la lingua castellana o español* (Madrid, 1611).

86. Robert Hermann Schomburgk, *The History of Barbados* (London: Brown, Green and Longmans, 1848), 47–48.

87. Gov. Dalling to Lord George Germaine, 12 Jan. 1781, in John Fowler, *A General Account of the Calamities Occasioned by the Late Tremendous Hurricanes and Earthquakes in the West-India Islands*, 5–7. See Edward Long, *The History of Jamaica* (London: T. Lowndes, 1774).

88. Bryan Edwards, *The History, Civil and Commercial, of the British Colonies in the West Indies* (5 vols., London: T. Miller, 1819), 4:273–74.

89. Schomburgk, *The History of Barbados*, 37.

90. Parker, *Global Crisis*, 14–15.

91. Johnson, *Climate and Catastrophe in Cuba*, 4. Johnson's argument is based to a large extent on Joëlle L. Gergis and Anthony M. Fowler, "A History of ENSO Events since A.D. 1525: Implications for Future Climate Change," *Climatic Change* 92, no. 3–4 (Feb. 2009): 343–87; and César N. Caviedes, "Five Hundred Years of Hurricanes in the Caribbean: Their Relationship with Global Climatic Variabilities," *GeoJournal* 23, no. 4 (1 Apr. 1991): 301–10.

92. John Davy, *The West Indies, Before and Since Slave Emancipation, Comprising the Windward and Leeward Islands' Military Command* (London: W. & F. G. Cash, 1854), 213.; John Poyntz, *The Present Prospect of the Famous and Fertile Island of Tobago: With a Description of the Situation, Growth, Fertility and Manufacture of the Said Island. To Which Is Added, Proposals for the Encouragement of All Those That Are Minded to Settle There* (London: G. Larkin, 1683). While hurricanes are infrequent at that latitude, they are not unknown. Tobago suffered heavy damage in 1847. See *Tobago Hurricane of 1847: Papers Relative to the Hurricane in Tobago Presented to Both Houses of Parliament by Command of Her Majesty*

Queen Victoria, on April 11, 1848, Historical Documents of Trinidad and Tobago, no. 3 (Port of Spain: Government Printery, 1966).

93. AGI, SD 93, doc. 47 (10 Oct. 1600).

94. José Luis Sáez, "Una carta anua de la residencia de Santo Domingo (23 Octubre 1695)," *Archivum Historicum Societatis Iesu* 62, no. 124 (1993): 281–312.

95. Augustín Udías, "Earthquakes as God's Punishment in 17th-and 18th-century Spain," in *Geology and Religion: a History of Harmony and Hostility,* ed. Martina Kölbl-Ebert, Geological Society Special Publication no. 310 (London: Geological Society, 2009), 41–48.

96. Bernard Lavalle, "Miedos terranales, angustias escatológicas y pánicos en tiempos de terremotos a comienzos del siglo XVII en el Perú," in *Una historia de los usos del miedo,* ed. Pilar Gonzalbo, Anne Staples, and Valentina Torres Septién (Mexico City: Colegio de México: Universidad Iberoamericana, 2009), 103–127; Walker, *Shaky Colonialism*; Jaime Valenzuela Márquez, "El terremoto de 1647: Experiencia apocalíptica y representaciones religiosas en Santiago colonial," in *Historias Urbanas: Homenaje a Armando de Ramón,* ed. Jaime Valenzuela Márquez (Santiago: Ediciones Universidad Catolica de Chile, 2007), 27–65.

97. Juan Solórzano Pereira, *De indiarum iure,* C. Baciero et al. (Madrid: Consejo Superior de Investigaciones Científicas, 2001), 259–65.

98. The phrase "moral cosmos" is Bob Scribner's. It is cited and discussed in Alexandra Walsham, *Providence in Early Modern England* (Oxford: Oxford University Press, 1999).

99. AGN, Inquisición, v. 710, expediente 68, fs. 469–82. My thanks to María Jordán Arroyo for this reference.

100. Carla Rahn Phillips, *Six Galleons for the King of Spain: Imperial Defense in the Early Seventeenth Century* (Baltimore: Johns Hopkins University Press, 1986), 161. The association of Our Lady of Mount Carmel with storms comes from the Old Testament story of the prophet Elijah, whose victory over the prophets of Baal on Mount Carmel brings a cloud that ends a drought in Israel.

CHAPTER 2. MELANCHOLY OCCASIONS: HURRICANES IN A COLONIAL WORLD

1. The Cabeza de Vaca account notes his experience with hurricanes and storms beginning with the hurricane he experienced in the port of Trinidad, Cuba. The definitive edition is Rolena Adorno and Patrick Charles Pautz, *Alvar Núñez Cabeza de Vaca: His Account, His Life, and the Expedition of Pánfilo de Narváez* (Lincoln: University of Nebraska Press, 1999).

2. On the confusing and contradictory reports of the 1530 hurricanes in Puerto Rico, see José Carlos Millás, *Hurricanes of the Caribbean and Adjacent Regions, 1492–1800* (Miami, FL: Academy of the Arts and Sciences of the Americas, 1968), 60–62.

3. See, for example, William Stapleton to Lords of Trade, 16 July 1683, *Calendar of State Papers: Colonial (CSPC),* vol. 11 (1681–85), 452–62, http://www.british-history.ac.uk/report.aspx?compid=69878

4. *CSPC,* Aug. 1612, vol. 1 (1574–1660), 14, http://www.british-history.ac.uk/report.aspx?compid=68941&strquery=.

5. John T. McGrath, *The French in Early Florida: In the Eye of the Hurricane* (Gainesville: University Press of Florida, 2000), 20–21.

6. Millás, *Hurricanes of the Caribbean and Adjacent Regions,* 130–31.

7. See for example the report of Lic. Hurtado on the hurricane in Santo Domingo of

1552 that "burned" all the trees and crops and left the island cut off from commerce. AGI, SD 49, ramo 23, no. 145, printed in Genaro Rodríguez Morel, *Cartas de la real audiencia de Santo Domingo (1547–1575)* (Santo Domingo: Archivo General de la Nación, 2011), 189.

8. Phillips, *Six Galleons for the King of Spain*, 11–13. Overviews of the transatlantic fleet system are provided by Alfredo Castillero Calvo, "La carrera, el monopolio y las ferias del trópico," in *Historia general de América Latina* (Madrid and París: Editorial Trotta, Ediciones UNESCO, 1999), 3:75–124; Murdo MacLeod, "Spain and America: The Atlantic Trade, 1492–1720," in *The Cambridge History of Latin America*, ed. Leslie Bethell (Cambridge and New York: Cambridge University Press, 1984), 1: 341–88.

9. Levi Marrero, *Cuba: Economia y sociedad* (CES), 2:149.

10. See Oscar Cruz Barney, *El combate a la piratería en Indias, 1555–1700* (Mexico City: Oxford University Press, 1999).

11. Antonio Domínguez Ortiz, *Política y hacienda de Felipe IV* (Madrid: Editorial de Derecho Financiero, 1960).

12. Alejandro de la Fuente, César García del Pino, and Bernardo Iglesias Delgado, "Havana and the Fleet System: Trade and Growth in the Periphery of the Spanish Empire, 1550–1610," *Colonial Latin American Review* 5, no. 1 (1996): 95–115. See also Alejandro de la Fuente, *Havana and the Atlantic in the Sixteenth Century* (Chapel Hill: University of North Carolina Press, 2008), 51–81.

13. AGI, SD 49, ramo xvi, n. 97, printed in Rodríguez Morel, *Cartas de la real audiencia de Santo Domingo*, 448–49.

14. Marrero, CES, 3:246.

15. AGI, leg. 179 v.

16. AGI, Santo Domingo leg. 173, ff. 1161–64, cited in *EPR* 3:212–13. Bishop Padilla stated, "only those of us who have seen it can understand its gravity." See AGI, SD 173, f. 1127.

17. Abbad y Lasierra, *Historia geográfica, civil y natural de La Isla de San Juan Bautista de Puerto Rico*. Cited in Fernando Ortiz Fernández, *El Huracán*,6; Long, *The History of Jamaica*, 3:22. A similar argument is presented in Davy, *The West Indies, Before and Since Slave Emancipation*, 63. Robert Schomburgk later argued that if the hurricanes were a divine gift, given the terror they cause "it is a sharp and afflictive remedy." See Schomburgk, *The History of Barbados*, 45.

18. M.L.E. Moreau de Saint-Méry, *A Topographical and Political Description of the Spanish Part of Saint-Domingo* 2 vols. (Philadelphia, 1796), 1:30.

19. Hilary McDonald Beckles, "The 'Hub of Empire': The Caribbean and Britain in the Seventeenth Century," in *The Oxford History of the British Empire*, ed. William Roger Louis et al. (Oxford: Oxford University Press, 1998), 1:218–40.

20. B. W. Higman, *A Concise History of the Caribbean* (New York: Cambridge University Press, 2011), 118–20; J. H. Parry and Philip Manderson Sherlock, *A Short History of the West Indies* (London: Macmillan, 1968), 55–80.

21. Cardinal-duc de Richelieu, Armand Jean du Plessis (1585–1642), served as principal minister of France. He was succeeded by Cardinal Jules Mazarin (1602–1661).

22. This story is told in detail in Philip P. Boucher, *France and the American Tropics to 1700: Tropics of Discontent?* (Baltimore: Johns Hopkins University Press, 2008), 66–87. See also, Michel Devèze, *Antilles, Guyanes, La Mer des Caraïbes, de 1492 à 1789*, Regards sur l'histoire; 29: II, *Histoire générale* (Paris: SEDES, 1977), 224–46.

23. Unless otherwise noted, I have used the terms "Leeward" and "Windward" as they are commonly used in English based on the British administrative divisions. The

use of the terms can be confusing. Geographically, first the Spaniards and then the other Europeans divided the Lesser Antilles into two groups of islands: the meridional chain extending from the Virgin Islands south to Trinidad, which were called "Islands to the Windward" ("Islas de Barlovento" or "Iles au Vent"), and the islands from Margarita westward to Aruba along the South American coast, which were called "Islands to the Leeward" ("Islas de Sotavento" or "Iles sous le Vent"). The Windward group, directly affected by the northeasterly trade winds, tended to be more humid, the Leeward group, more arid. The British, however, divided their islands in the meridional Antilles into two administrative units: the islands from Guadeloupe to the north, which they called the Leeward Islands, and those from Martinique to the south, which they called the Windward Islands. Dominica, which lies between Guadeloupe and Martinique, was originally in the Leeward group, but in 1940 it became part of the Windward group. Administratively, Barbados, Trinidad, and Tobago were not part of the British Windward islands. The British administrative division is now commonly used in a geographic sense for grouping the islands. See the discussion in Helmut Blume, *The Caribbean Islands* (London: Longman, 1974), 5–6.

24. Anne Pérotin-Dumon, "French, English, and Dutch in the Lesser Antilles: From Privateering to Planting (1550–1650)," in *General History of the Caribbean*, ed. P. C. Emmer et al. (London: Macmillan Caribbean; UNESCO Pub, 1997), 2:114–59.

25. Wim Klooster, "Other Netherlands beyond the Sea," in *Negotiated Empires: Centers and Peripheries in the Americas, 1500–1820*, ed. Christine Daniels and Michael V. Kennedy (New York: Routledge, 2002), 171–91; Linda M. Rupert, *Creolization and Contraband: Curaçao in the Early Modern Atlantic World* (Athens: University of Georgia Press, 2012).

26. J. Franklin Jameson, "St. Eustatius in the American Revolution," *American Historical Review* 8, no. 4 (July 1903): 683–708.

27. Hall's book provides excellent studies of slave society in the Danish islands.

28. David Eltis, *The Rise of African Slavery in the Americas* (Cambridge: Cambridge University Press, 2000), 24. See also Ignacio Pérez Tostado, "Desarrollo politico y económico de Las Antillas británicas, siglos XV–XVIII," in *Historia de Las Antillas*, ed. Consuelo Naranjo Orovio, Ana Crespo Solana, and Ma Dolores González-Ripoll Navarro (Madrid: Consejo Superior de Investigaciones Científicas; Doce Calles, 2009), 185–214.

29. Boucher, *France and the American Tropics to 1700*, 20–21.

30. Abénon, "Ouragans et cyclones à La Guadeloupe au XVIII siècle," 163–71.

31. François Roger Robert, 1 Feb. 1700 (ANOM[Archive National d'Outre-Mer (Aix-en-Provence)], Col C8A 12 F 87).

32. Charles Mesnier, controleur de la marine à Martinique, 23 Sept. 1713 (ANOM, Col. C8A, 19F, 485).

33. Mulcahy, *Hurricanes and Society*, 10–34.

34. Joannes de Laet, *Nieuvve wereldt, ofte, Beschrijvinghe van West-Indien wt veelderhande schriften ende aen-teeckeninghen van verscheyden natien* (Leiden: Isaack Elzeviet, 1625).

35. Dierick Ruiter, *Toortse der Zee-vaert: Om te beseylen de custen gheleghen bezuyden den Tropicus Cancri, als Brasilien, West-Indien, Guinea, en Angola, etc.* (Vlissingen: Marten Abrahamsz van der Nolck, 1623), 156.

36. ZA Middleburg, 1580.1 State Publications, 1590–1695, *"Vrydom voor de gene die met hare Persoonen Huysgesinnen en Gevolgh near SURINAME gaen"* (Freedom for those people who will go to Suriname on their own, or with their families and entourage).

Similar arguments were made to promote Tobago, Trinidad, and even, for a while, Barbados.

37. Geeraert Brandt, *Het leven en bedryf van den Heere Michiel de Ruiter . . .* (Amsterdam: Wolfgang, Waasberge, Boom, Van Someren en Goethals, 1687).

38. Labat, *Nouveau voyage aux Isles de l'Amerique*, 165–66. See Jean-Pierre Sainton and Raymond Boutin, eds., *Histoire et civilisation de La Caraïbe: Guadeloupe, Martinique, Petites Antilles: La construction des sociétés antillaises des origines au temps présent, structures et dynamiques*, vol. 1 (Paris: Editions Maisonneuve et Larose, 2004), 41–42.

39. Guillaume Thomas François Raynal, *Histoire philosophique et politique des établissements et du commerce des européens dans les deux indes*, J. Justamond, trans. (Dublin, 1776), 5:24–28.

40. Gabriel Debien, *Lettres de colons* (Laval: Madiot, 1965), 56, 64.

41. Ibid., 234.

42. William Smith, *A Natural History of Nevis, and the Rest of the English Leeward Charibee Islands in America* (London: J. Bentham, 1745), 243.

43. William Beckford, *A Descriptive Account of the Island of Jamaica*, 2 vols. (London, T. and J. Egerton, 1790), 355.

44. NAGB, CO, 156/52, Gov. Payne to Earl of Hillsborough, 5 Sept. 1772.

45. See, for example, Henry Laurens, *The Papers of Henry Laurens*, vol. 1, ed. Philip M. Hamer et al., 16 vols. (Columbia: University of South Carolina Press, 1968).

46. Richard Pares, "The London Sugar Market, 1740–1769," *Economic History Review* 9, no. 2 (1956): 254–70, especially p. 264.

47. Gov. Atkins to Lords of Trade (July 4/14, 1676). CSP, West Indies 9, fs. 419–25/ Colonial Office 1/37, no. 22.

48. Lt. Gov. Stede to Lords of Trade (18 Sept. 1687), *NAGB*, CO 1/68, no. 53.

49. William Dickson, *Letters on Slavery . . . to Which Are Added Addresses to the Whites, and to the Free Negroes of Barbadoes* (London, 1789), 40; George Frere, *A Short History of Barbados, from Its First Discovery and Settlement, to the End of the Year 1767* (London: J. Dodsley, 1768), 33. J. R. Ward ("The British West Indies in the Age of Abolition, 1748–1815," in *The Oxford History of the British Empire*, ed. William Roger Louis et al., Oxford: Oxford University Press, 1998, vol. 2, *The Eighteenth Century*, table 19.2, 433) claims that Barbados had 50,000 whites and 70,000 slaves in the 1670s, but Russell R. Menard (*Sweet Negotiations* Charlottesville: University of Virginia Press, 2006, 25), gives lower figures of 22,400 whites and 40,400 slaves for 1670.

50. Natalie Zacek, *Settler Society in the English Leeward Islands, 1670–1776* (New York: Cambridge University Press, 2010), 20.

51. Marco Meniketti, "Sugar Mills, Technology, and Environmental Change: A Case Study of Colonial Agro-Industrial Development in the Caribbean," *IA: The Journal of the Society for Industrial Archeology* 32, no. 1 (Jan. 2006): 53–80.

52. Tony Williams, *Hurricane of Independence: The Untold Story of the Deadly Storm at the Deciding Moment of the American Revolution* (Naperville, IL: Sourcebooks, 2008), 68–69. See also Rhys Isaac, *Landon Carter's Uneasy Kingdom: Revolution and Rebellion on a Virginia Plantation* (Oxford: Oxford University Press, 2004).

53. Anonymous, *An Account of the Late Dreadful Hurricane, Which Happened on the 31st of August, 1772. Also the Damage Done on That Day in the Islands of St. Christopher and Nevis, Attempted to be ascertained. by the Editor* (St. Christopher: Thomas Howe, 1772).

54. Lowell J. Ragatz, *The Fall of the Planter Class in the British Caribbean, 1763–1833: A Study in Social and Economic History* (New York: Century Co., 1928), 18–21, presents a generally negative view of religious life in the British West Indies.

55. Ibid., 20–21.

56. Anonymous, *An Account of the Late Dreadful Hurricane,* 1.

57. Bohun, for example believed that Jamaica, Cuba, and Hispaniola were not affected by hurricanes.

58. Mulcahy, *Hurricanes and Society,* 10–32.

59. *Cartas del Cabildo de la Ciudad de Santo Domingo en el siglo XVII* (CCSD, XVII) (27 Oct. 1630): 300.

60. AHMCH (Archivo Historico del Museo de la Ciudad de la Habana), *Acuerdos* of the *cabildo* of Havana. The years 1550–78 have been published as *Actas capitulares del Ayuntamiento de la Habana,* vol. 1584–1599 (Havana: Municipio de la Habana, 1937). See also Marrero, CES, 2:109–11.

61. Marrero, CES, 3:246.

62. See, for example, the request for funds to repair a rampart damaged by a hurricane of 1551 in Puerto Rico, in *Catalogo de Cartas y peticiones del cabildo de San Juan (CCPCSJ),* doc. 29 (1551).

63. Ramírez de Arellano, "Los huracanes de Puerto Rico," 12–13.

64. AGI, SD 2280, libro 1, fs. 77–78v. At the same time, Blas de Villasanti was granted a two-year grace period for the payment of debts because of the damages three hurricanes caused to his sugar mill (*ingenio*). See AGI, SD 2280, lib. 1, f. 76v–77v.

65. "de su voluntad no han de pagar blanca en su vida." AGI, SD 49, ramo xvi, no. 97, in Rodríguez Morel, *Cartas de la real audiencia de Santo Domingo,* 448–49. In 1552 the council complained again about hurricane losses. See CCSD XVI (5 December 1551), 1:221–25.

66. AGI, SD leg. 164, no. 8 (1534).

67. Alvaro Huerga, *Ataques de los Caribes a Puerto Rico en el siglo XVI,* Historia Documental de Puerto Rico vol. 16 (San Juan: Academia Puertorriqueña de la Historia; Centro de Estudios Avanzados de Puerto Rico y el Caribe; Fundación Puertorriqueña de las Humanidades, 2006), 82–83.

68. CCSD XVI, Cabildo to King Charles I, 22 June 1555, 233–36.

69. Ibid.

70. CCSD XVIII (20 Aug. 1592), 193.

71. AGI Santo Domingo leg. 184 (Nov. 1615).

72. CCPCSJ, doc. 180 (12 Nov. 1615), doc. 182 (7 March 1616).

73. Reduction in the *almojarifazgo, diezmo, and chancellería. See* CCPCSJ, doc. 194 (25 Sept. 1625). See also Enriqueta Vila Vilar, *Historia de Puerto Rico (1600–1650)* (Seville: Escuela de Estudios Hispano-Americanos, 1974), 38–40.

74. "Que todo cuanta falta se desculpa con la tormenta y viene a ser tormenta para mí porque en virtud de este me falta de los diezmos," Salvador Arana Soto, *Historia de nuestras calamidades* (San Juan, 1968), 100.

75. Memorial of Bishop of San Juan to the Audiencia of Santo Domingo: EPR, 3 113n.

76. Juan Luis Vives, *Tratado del socorro de los pobres* (Valencia: Impr. Hijo de F. Vives Mora, 1942). The role of the state in social welfare is discussed in Domingo de Soto, *Deliberación en la causa de los pobres (1545)* (Madrid: Instituto de Estudios Políticos, 1965). See the general discussion in Robert Jütte, *Poverty and Deviance in Early Modern Europe,* New Approaches to European History 4 (Cambridge: Cambridge University Press, 1994).

77. On the general development of royal responsibility and response to calamity in

France, see Jean Delumeau and Yves Lequin, eds., *Les malheurs des temps: Histoire des fléaux et des calamités en France* (Paris: Larousse, 1987).

78. ANOM, Col A25, F259 n. 185 (30 March 1741); n. 66 (9 Nov. 1728).

79. ANOM, *Ordonnance* (18 Aug. 1766), Col C8A 68F 57; ANOM, Col. C8B 12 n. 205.

80. Queen to Gov. Parke, 4 Sept. 1708, *CSPC* 24, no. 127: 91.

81. Gov. Stapleton to Lords of Trade, 13 Feb. 1684, *CSPC* 1; Merchants of Nevis, 9 Nov. 1708, *CSPC* 24, no. 187: 140–41; Council of Trade to Gov. Parke, 25 Nov. 1708, *CSPC* 24, no. 209: 153–55.

82. Jonathan Mercantini, "The Great Carolina Hurricane of 1952," *South Carolina Historical Magazine* 103, no. 4 (2002): 351–65. On the 1740 fire in Charleston, see Matthew Mulcahy, "The 'Great Fire' of 1740 and the Politics of Disaster Relief in Colonial Charleston," *South Carolina Historical Magazine*, 99 (April 1998), 135–57.

83. Jonathan I. Israel, *The Dutch Republic: Its Rise, Greatness and Fall, 1477–1806*, The Oxford History of Early Modern Europe (Oxford: Clarendon Press, 1995), 353–60.

84. St. Eustatius was also badly damaged. A letter from L. J. Benners and son (7 Oct. 1772) reported: "At present, one sees grief and misery among the citizens." ZAM, Middelburgsche Commercie Compagnie, n. 57 Correspondence, Saint Eustatius 1746–1773.

85. Request of George Hassell et al., NAH, West Indies, no. 1.05.06 (inventory n. 1151). Saba, although a Dutch island at the time, had been held at times by both France and England. Its white population was predominantly British. The petition was written in English and most of the signers had English surnames.

86. Gov. Willem Hendrik Rink and Council, St. Martin (21 Aug. 1792), NAH, St. Eustatius, St. Maarten, Saba, n. 1.05.13.01 (inventory no. 295).

87. H. Th. Rolandus, in a letter to the editor of the *Algemeen Handelsblad* (Amsterdam, 13 Dec. 1898), in response to a hurricane that had struck Curaçao, suggested the creation of a national fund and asked for support, but the fund was apparently not created at that time.

88. Edwards, *The History, Civil and Commercial, of the British Colonies in the West Indies*, 2:303.

89. Moreau de Saint-Méry, *A Topographical and Political Description*, 31–32.

CHAPTER 3. WAR, REFORM, AND DISASTER

1. McNeill, *Mosquito Empires*, 18–20.

2. Millás, *Hurricanes of the Caribbean and Adjacent Regions*, 176.

3. A "muddy compromise between Paris and Venice": Shannon Lee Dawdy, *Building the Devil's Empire: French Colonial New Orleans* (Chicago: University of Chicago Press, 2008), 82.

4. Jefferson T. Dillman, "From Paradise to Tropics: Landscape in the British West Indies to 1800" (Ph.D. dissertation, University of Texas at Arlington, 2011, ProQuest/UMI, AAT 3495001), 257.

5. Reinaldo Funes Monzote, *From Rainforest to Cane Field in Cuba: An Environmental History since 1492* (Chapel Hill: University of North Carolina Press, 2008), 20–45. See also Manuel Moreno Fraginals, *El Ingenio: Complejo económico social cubano del azúcar* (Havana: Editorial de Ciencias Sociales, 1978), 1:157–66.

6. Armand Nicolas, *Histoire de La Martinique*, vol. 1 (Paris: L'Harmattan, 1996), 115.

7. William Beckford, *A Descriptive Account of the Island of Jamaica: With Remarks Upon the Cultivation of the Sugar-cane, Throughout the Different Seasons of the Year, and Chiefly*

Considered in a Picturesque Point of View; Also Observations and Reflections Upon What Would Probably Be the Consequences of an Abolition of the Slave-trade, and of the Emancipation of the Slaves (London: T. and J. Egerton, 1790), 1:x–xi.

8. Matthew Mulcahy presents evidence that contemporaries in the West Indies believed that forest clearing improved health conditions and opened areas to a cleansing by the winds. Mulcahy, *Hurricanes and Society*, 27–28.

9. See the discussion in the chapter "Climate, Conservation, and Carib Resistance: The British and the Forests of the Eastern Caribbean, 1760–1800," in Richard Grove, *Green Imperialism: Colonial Expansion, Tropical Island Edens, and the Origins of Environmentalism, 1600–1860* (Cambridge: Cambridge University Press, 1995), 264–305.

10. John J. McCusker and Russell R. Menard, eds., *The Economy of British America, 1607–1789*, Needs and Opportunities for Study Series (Chapel Hill: University of North Carolina Press, 1985), 153–54.

11. McNeill, *Mosquito Empires*, 129–33; Karen Fay O'Loughlin and James F. Lander, *Caribbean Tsunamis: A 500-Year History from 1498–1998* (Dordrecht: Kluwer Academic Publishers, 2003).

12. Steve Pincus and James Robinson, "Wars and State-Making Reconsidered: The Rise of the Interventionist State" (unpublished paper, 2012); Charles Tilly, *Coercion, Capital, and European States, AD 990–1992*, Studies in Social Discontinuity (Cambridge, MA: Blackwell, 1992).

13. Allan J. Kuethe and Kenneth J. Andrien, *War and Reform in the Eighteenth–Century Spanish Atlantic World, 1713–1796* (Cambridge: Cambridge University Press, 2014).

14. For the general history I am drawing on Jan Golinski, *British Weather and the Climate of Enlightenment* (Chicago: University of Chicago Press, 2007), 80–91; Vladimir Janković, *Reading the Skies: a Cultural History of English Weather, 1650–1820* (Chicago: University of Chicago Press, 2001). See also M. Chenoweth, J. M. Vaquero, R. García-Herrera, and D. Wheeler, "A Pioneer in Tropical Meteorology: William Sharpe's Barbados Weather Journal, April–August 1680," *Bulletin of the American Meteorological Society* 88, no. 12 (Dec. 2007): 1957–64.

15. Chenoweth et al., "A Pioneer in Tropical Meteorology," 1963.

16. Jean-Baptiste Thibault de Chanvalon, *Voyage à La Martinique: Contenant diverses observations sur la physique, l'histoire naturelle, l'agriculture, les moeurs, & les usages de cette isle, faites en 1751 & dans les années suivantes: Lu à l'Académie Royale Des Sciences de Paris en 1761* (Paris: J. B. Bauche, 1763), 135.

17. See the discussion in James E. McClellan, *Colonialism and Science: Saint Domingue in the Old Regime* (Chicago: University of Chicago Press, 2010), 166–67.

18. Oldendorp, C.G.A. *Oldendorp's History of the Mission of the Evangelical Brethren on the Caribbean Islands of St. Thomas, St. Croix, and St. John*, ed. Johann Jakob Bossart, trans. Arnold R. Highfield and Vladimir Barac (Ann Arbor, MI: Karoma Publishers, 1987), 41–49.

19. N. Díaz-Argüelles García, "El Observatorio fisico-meteorico de La Habana," *Anuario—Centro de Estudios de Historia y Organizacion de la Ciencia* no. 1 (1988): 218–47. See also the observations on climate in Alexander von Humboldt, *Ensayo político sobre La Isla de Cuba*, ed. Miguel Angel Puig-Samper, Consuelo Naranjo Orovio, and Armando García González (Madrid: Ediciones Doce Calles, 1998), 149–65. This edition also provides a useful summary of the Enlightenment origins of science in Cuba (pp. 47–57).

20. Jean-Baptiste Thibault de Chanvalon, *Voyage à La Martinique*, 94. For a critique of pro-slavery and racialist ideas within Enlightenment thought, see Louis Sala-Molins,

Les misères des lumières: Sous la raison, l'outrage (Paris: Homnisphères, 2008); Laurent Estève, *Montesquieu, Rousseau, Diderot: Du genre humain au bois d'ébène: Les silences du droit naturel* (Paris: UNESCO, 2002). These intellectual tendencies are placed alongside the political thought of slaves and free people of color in Laurent Dubois, "An Enslaved Enlightenment: Rethinking the Intellectual History of the French Atlantic," *Social History* 31, no. 1 (2006): 1–14.

21. Trevor G. Burnard, *Mastery, Tyranny, and Desire: Thomas Thistlewood and His Slaves in the Anglo-Jamaican World* (Chapel Hill: University of North Carolina Press, 2004), 101–36; Michael Chenoweth, *The 18th Century Climate of Jamaica Derived from the Journals of Thomas Thistlewood, 1750–1786* (Philadelphia: American Philosophical Society, 2003).

22. For the development of pro-slavery ideology, see Gordon K. Lewis, *Main Currents in Caribbean Thought: The Historical Evolution of Caribbean Society in Its Ideological Aspects, 1492–1900* (Baltimore: Johns Hopkins University Press, 1983), 94–170.

23. The phase is cited in E. L. Jones, *The European Miracle*, xix.

24. Governor Russell to Lords of Trade, 24 Oct. 1694, CSPC 14, no. 446, p. 385.

25. See Johnson, *Climate and Catastrophe in Cuba and the Atlantic World*, 72–73.

26. Pierre J. Pannet, *Report on the Execrable Conspiracy Carried Out by the Amina Negroes on the Danish Island of St. Jan in America, 1733*, ed. Aimery Caron and Arnold R. Highfield (Christiansted, St. Croix: Antilles Press, 1984).

27. RC (Rigsarkivet [Danish National Archives]), *Generalguvernementet 1716–1882. Plakatbøger* [General Government 1716–1882. Public notices.] (2 Sept. 1772). Similar measures were taken by the governor on St. Croix after a hurricane in 1785 when the destruction of slave provision grounds moved the government to remove all taxes on food imports (27 Aug. 1785).

28. Anonymous, *An Account of the Late Dreadful Hurricane which happened on the 31st of August, 1772* (St. Christopher, 1772).

29. Ibid., 2.

30. Ibid., 15.

31. Ibid., 40.

32. Ibid., 50–51.

33. Marrero, CES, vol. 8, 107.

34. Elias Regnault, *Histoire des Antilles et des colonies françaises, espagnoles, anglaises, danoises et suédoises* (Paris: Firmin Didot Frères, 1849), 33.

35. Abbad y Lasierra, *Historia geográfica*, as cited by Ortiz, *El huracán*, 61. Guillaume Thomas François Raynal, *Histoire philosophique et politique des établissements et du commerce des européens dans les deux Indes* (Amsterdam, 1772). 5:24–28. For a similar English observation, see Edward Long's statement: "Hurricanes, however destructive therefore they may be in some respects, they fertilize the earth, purge the atmosphere from malignant vapors, and bring with them a bountiful season." Long, *The History of Jamaica*, 3:622.

36. AGI, SD 2417, no. 129. See also AHN (Archivo Historico Nacional [Madrid]), Ultramar 1067, exp. 56 (25 Sept. 1815). There is controversy over the dating on the hurricanes of 1815 and 1816. See Luis A. Salivia, *Historia de los temporales de Puerto Rico y Las Antillas, 1492 a 1970*, 2nd ed. (San Juan: Editorial Edil, 1972), 147–51. I believe that AGI, SD 2417, no. 129 confirms that there were hurricanes on 30 August 1815 and 19 February 1816.

37. Arturo Morales Carrión, *Puerto Rico y la lucha por la hegemonía en El Caribe: Colonialismo y contrabando, siglos XVI–XVIII*, Colección Caribeña (San Juan: Centro de Inves-

tigaciones Históricas, Editorial de la Universidad de Puerto Rico, 1995), 93–154; Fernando Picó, *Historia general de Puerto Rico* (Río Piedras, PR: Ediciones Huracán, 1986), 98–114; Francisco A. Scarano, *Puerto Rico: Cinco siglos de historia* (San Juan: McGraw-Hill, 1993), 267–96.

38. Acta (22 Oct. 1738), Aída R. Caro Costas and Viola Vidal de Rodríguez, eds., *Actas del Cabildo de San Juan Bautista de Puerto Rico* (San Juan: Municipio de San Juan, 1949), no. 95, 143–45. See the discussion in Luis E. González Vales, "El Cabildo de San Juan Bautista de Puerto Rico en el siglo XVIII y la defensa de los derechos de los vecinos," *Revista Chilena de Historia del Derecho* 16 (1990): 205–18.

39. Acta (22 Oct. 1738), *Actas del Cabildo de San Juan Bautista de Puerto Rico*, no. 95, 44.

40. Ibid.

41. Acta (16 Jan. 1739), *Actas del Cabildo de San Juan Bautista de Puerto Rico*, no. 100, 151–52.

42. Ramírez de Arellano, "Los huracanes de Puerto Rico," 18–19.

43. A classic account is Enrique Florescano, *Precios del maíz y crisis agrícolas en México (1708–1810); Ensayo sobre el movimiento de los precios y sus consecuencias económicas y sociales*, Centro de Estudios Históricos New Series 4 (Mexico City: El Colegio de México, 1969). See also the evidence in García Acosta, Pérez Zevallos, and Molina del Villar, *Desastres agrícolas en México*, 317–71.

44. Johnson, *Climate and Catastrophe in Cuba and the Atlantic World*, 2–3. For an alternate chronology of the Little Ice Age, see Brian M. Fagan, *The Little Ice Age: How Climate Made History, 1300–1850* (New York: Basic Books, 2000).

45. AGI, leg. 1136 (16 Oct. 1768); AGI, leg. 1137, Negocios de Habana.

46. An excellent and detailed examination of these storms and their effects appears in Johnson, *Climate and Catastrophe in Cuba and the Atlantic World*, 110–22.

47. Mulcahy, *Hurricanes and Society*, 141–64.

48. John Frederic Schlegel, *A Short Account of the Effects of the Late Hurricane in the West Indies: As Far as Relates to the Missions of the Brethren in the Islands of St. Croix and St. Christopher* (n.p., 1785), 3.

49. Matthew Mulcahy, "The 'Great Fire' of 1740," 135–57. Charitable subscriptions by the London Society of West India Merchants raised after various fires in West Indian cities are listed in Ragatz, *The Fall of the Planter Class in the British Caribbean*, 15.

50. Gov. Ulrick Wilhelm Röepstorff to the crown (2 Sept. 1772), RC, Generalguvernementet 1716–1882, Plakatbøger; Vestindiske Regering (St. Croix, 27 Aug. 1785).

51. Anne Pérotin-Dumon, *Être patriote sous les tropiques: La Guadeloupe, la colonisation et la révolution (1789–1794)* (Basse-Terre: Société d'Histoire de la Guadeloupe, 1985), 39.

52. Grégory Quenet, *Les tremblements de terre en France aux XVIIe et XVIIIe siècles: La naissance d'un risque* (Seyssel: Champ Vallon, 2005), 228–50.

53. Ibid.

54. Ibid. See also René Favier, "La monachie d'Ancien Régime et l'indemnisation des catastrophes naturelles à la fin du XVIII siècle," in *Les pouvoirs publics face aux risques naturels dans l'histoire*, ed. René Favier (Grenoble: CNRS—Maison Sciences de l'Homme-Alpes, 2002), 71–104.

55. Favier, "La monachie d'Ancien Régime," 72.

56. ANOM, Col. C8A 19F 420; ANOM, Col. C8A 19F, 485.

57. Pritchard, *In Search of Empire*, 79.

58. Anne Pérotin-Dumon, *La ville aux iles, la ville dans l'île: Basse-Terre et Pointe-à-Pitre, Guadeloupe, 1650–1820* (Paris: Karthala, 2000), 153.

59. Abénon, "Ouragans et cyclones à La Guadeloupe au XVIIIe siècle," 168–71.

60. Beckford, *A Descriptive Account of the Island of Jamaica*, 90.

61. I based this overview on Millás, *Hurricanes of the Caribbean and Adjacent Regions*, 253–60; Ludlum, *Early American Hurricanes*, 70–72. See also Edward N. Rappaport and José Fernandez-Partagás, "History of the Deadliest Atlantic Tropical Cyclones since the Discovery of the New World," in *Hurricanes: Climate and Socioeconomic Impacts*, ed. Henry F. Diaz and Roger S. Pulwarty (New York: Springer, 1997), 93–108.

62. The letter is quoted in Ludlum, *Early American Hurricanes*, 69.

63. Ibid., 70. Published originally in *The Gentleman's Magazine*, vol. 50 (1780), 621–23; *Annual Register*, 1780, 292–98.

64. Mulcahy, *Hurricanes and Society*, 108–14.

65. "Relation de l'Ouragan du 10 octubre 1780 par William Matthew Burt," ANOM, Col. C8B 15 N 44.

66. NAH, St. Eustatius, St. Maarten en Saba, 1.05.13.01 inventory number 550, Memorial, journal, ledger and outgoing mail of Beaujon and Son, 1780–87. Millás reports the heavy loss of life and ship losses at St. Eustatius, but the Beaujon letter, dated 13 November 1780, ends: "In short, one writes, one hears nothing but disasters, accidents, and damage, caused by this woesome hurricane. How good has God been to us on this little rock, and how much do we owe Him to be thankful in our hearts! The products begin slowly to arrive again and the shipping begins to get going. . . ." Millás, *Hurricanes of the Caribbean and Adjacent Regions*, 257.

67. Letter from St. Eustatia, 20 Oct. 1780, printed in Fowler, *A General Account of the Calamities Occasioned by the Late Tremendous Hurricanes and Earthquakes in the West-India Islands*, 71–73.

68. The attack on St. Eustatius resulted in a scandal, since Admiral George Rodney and the military commander, General George Vaughn, were accused of personally profiting from the sack of the island. A joint Dutch-French expedition retook the island in 1781. See J. Franklin Jameson, "St. Eustatius in the American Revolution," *American Historical Review* 8, no. 4 (July 1903), 683–708.

69. See Cipriano de Utrera, *Santo Domingo: Dilucidaciones históricas, I–II* (Santo Domingo, DR: Secretaría de Estado de Educación, Bellas Artes y Cultos, 1995), 1:432; Salivia, *Historia de los temporales de Puerto Rico y Las Antillas*, 113–15.

70. Supplement to *Royal Gazette* (7–14 Oct. 1780). Simon Taylor, Jamaican plantation owner, wrote to Chaloner Arcedeckne (14 Dec. 1786) that he was planting yams and cassava in order to avoid dependence on plantains, but he complained that storms were so frequent that it was impossible to build up a stock of even those more resistant crops. In the following year (1 May 1787) he complained that breadfruit that had been brought from the Pacific would probably not survive the hurricanes. Excerpts of this correspondence are available at http://blog.soton.ac.uk/slaveryandrevolution.

71. Gov. Dalling to Lord George Germain, 20 Oct. 1780, Jamaica Archives, 1B/5/18.

72. Edwards, *The History, Civil and Commercial, of the British Colonies in the West Indies*, 234–35.

73. David Beck Ryden, "Producing a Peculiar Commodity: Jamaican Sugar Production, Slave Life, and Planter Profits on the Eve of Abolition, 1750–1807" (Ph.D. dissertation, University of Minnesota, 1999), 193–99.

74. The problematic relationship of the planters to imperial government and their relative loss of influence after the loss of the continental colonies are noted in Trevor Burnard, "Harvest Years? Reconfigurations of Empire in Jamaica, 1756–1807," *Journal of Imperial and Commonwealth History* 40, no. 4 (2012): 533–55.

75. Fowler, *A General Account of the Calamities Occasioned by the Late Tremendous Hurricanes and Earthquakes in the West-India Islands*.

76. ANOM, Col. C8A 79 F 10. By late December 1780 the Intendant Peynier reported that 1,600 barrels of flour and 1,200 of salted meat had been distributed to the three islands, half of it as a gift and the rest to be repaid by the following July. See ANOM, Col. C8A 79 F 173.

77. Félix Renouard Sainte-Croix, *Statistique de la Martinique* (Paris, 1822), vol. 1. 96, 120–21.

78. ANOM, Col. C8B 15 N66.

79. AGI, leg. 1127 negociado de la Habana. Petition to rebuild the jail and municipal hall with tax moneys and to excuse clergy from tax obligations were denied.

80. Johnson, *Climate and Catastrophe in Cuba and the Atlantic World*, 150–53.

81. Ludlum, *Early American Hurricanes*, 68; Gilbert C. Din and John E. Harkins, *The New Orleans Cabildo: Colonial Louisiana's First City Government, 1769–1803* (Baton Rouge: Louisiana State University Press, 1996), 95.

82. For example, *Actas del cabildo de San Juan Bautista de Puerto Rico* (20 June 1783), n. 1273; AGI, SD 2304 (20 Sept. 1784); AGI, SD 2305 (6 Sept. 1785); AGI, SD 2308 (24 Aug. 1786).

83. AGI, SD 2308 (26 April 1788).

84. Thomas Thistlewood sold his share to a bookkeeper for about £140. See Burnard, *Mastery, Tyranny, and Desire*, 65.

85. Details of these complaints are provided in Kamau Braithwaite, *The Development of Creole Society in Jamaica, 1770–1820* (Kingston, Jamaica: Ian Randle, 2006), 149–50.

86. An excellent summary of the petitions and the problems they generated is provided in Mulcahy, *Hurricanes and Society*, 180–88.

87. A fuller discussion appears in Melanie J. Newton, *The Children of Africa in the Colonies: Free People of Color in Barbados in the Age of Emancipation* (Baton Rouge: Louisiana State University Press, 2008), 95–96.

88. The best analysis of the hurricanes' relation to slavery is Mulcahy, *Hurricanes and Society*, 97–105. Mulcahy has also distilled this information in Matthew Mulcahy, "Hurricanes, Slavery, and Social Disorder in the British Greater Caribbean" (paper presented at the Third Biennial Allen Morris Conference on the History of Florida and the Atlantic World, Florida State University, 2003).

89. See Andrew Jackson O'Shaughnessy, *An Empire Divided: The American Revolution and the British Caribbean* (Philadelphia: University of Pennsylvania Press, 2000).

90. Richard B. Sheridan, "The Crisis of Slave Subsistence in the British West Indies during and after the American Revolution," *William and Mary Quarterly*, Third Series, 33, no. 4 (Oct. 1976): 615–41.

91. O'Shaughnessy, *An Empire Divided*, 173.

92. Burnard, *Mastery, Tyranny, and Desire*, 5.

93. Beckford, *A Descriptive Account of the Island of Jamaica*, 1:115, 138–40.

94. Mulcahy, *Hurricanes and Society*, 107–15.

95. Robert E. Luster, *The Amelioration of the Slaves in the British Empire, 1790–1833* (New York: P. Lang, 1995), 3–4. Historian William Beckford, who had lived in Jamaica for 15 years, was an important advocate of amelioration as the best path for slaves. His *A Descriptive Account of the Island of Jamaica* (2 vols in 1).; London, 1790) was actually written while he was imprisoned for having posted security for a friend who suffered heavy losses after the 1780 hurricane.

96. Hector Macneill, *Observations on the Treatment of the Negroes, in the Island of Ja-*

maica Including Some Account of Their Temper and Character: With Remarks on the Importation of Slaves from the Coast of Africa: in a Letter to a Physician in England (London: G.G.J. and J. Robinson, 1788), 38–39.

97. Ibid., 39–40.

98. Dickson, *Letters on Slavery*, 96, 162.

99. The story seems to originate as an entry for January 1816 in Matthew G. Lewis, *Journal of a West India proprietor, kept during a residence in the island of Jamaica* (London: John Murray, 1834). It was expanded in Theodora Elizabeth Lynch, *The Wonders of the West Indies* (London: Seeley, Jackson, & Halliday, 1856).

100. Fowler, *A General Account of the Calamities Occasioned by the Late Tremendous Hurricanes and Earthquakes in the West-India Islands*, i–ii. Cf. Richard B. Sheridan, "The Formation of Caribbean Plantation Society, 1689–1748," in *The Oxford History of the British Empire*, ed. William Roger Louis et al. (Oxford: Oxford University Press, 1998), 2:404–5.

101. Particularly interesting in this regard is J. L. Carstens's description of the whites of Danish St. Thomas made in the 1740s, where all the usual negative characteristics ascribed to the creoles of the British colonies also appear. See J. L. Carstens and Arnold R. Highfield, *J. L. Carstens' St. Thomas in Early Danish Times: A General Description of All the Danish, American or West Indian Islands* (St. Croix: Virgin Islands Humanities Council, 1997), 54–57.

102. Michel-René Hilliard d'Auberteuil, *Considérations sur l'état présent de la colonie française de Saint-Domingue* (Paris: Grangé, 1776). See Doris Lorraine Garraway, *The Libertine Colony: Creolization in the Early French Caribbean* (Durham, NC: Duke University Press, 2005), 28–29; Madeleine Dobie, *Trading Places: Colonization and Slavery in Eighteenth-century French Culture* (Ithaca, NY: Cornell University Press, 2010), 222–23; Pierre Pluchon and Lucien-René Abénon, *Histoire des Antilles et de la Guyane* (Toulouse: Privat, 1982), 215–18. On Hilliard d'Auberteuil's caustic pen and curious ideas about racial engineering, see William Max Nelson, "Making Men: Enlightenment Ideas of Racial Engineering," *American Historical Review* 115, no. 5 (2010): 1364–94.

103. Leslie, *New History*, 40–41.

104. BL YU Thistlewood Papers, Diary, 1780, box 6.

105. Burnard, *Mastery, Tyranny, and Desire*, 65–66. An excellent discussion of planter mentality is presented in O'Shaughnessy, *An Empire Divided*, 3–33.

106. Jean-Baptiste Leblond, *Voyage aux Antilles, et a l'Amérique Méridionale* (Paris: A. Bertrand, 1813), 60–61.

CHAPTER 4. CALAMITY, SLAVERY, COMMUNITY, AND REVOLUTION

1. David Patrick Geggus, "Slavery, War, and Revolution in the Greater Caribbean, 1789–1815," in *A Turbulent Time: The French Revolution and the Greater Caribbean*, ed. David Patrick Geggus and David Barry Gaspar (Bloomington: Indiana University Press, 1997), 1–51. An excellent overview of the political and social changes in the period is presented in Higman, *A Concise History of the Caribbean*, 141–58.

2. Coleman and LaVoie, "Paleotempestology."

3. Roger A. Pielke Jr. and Christopher N. Landsea, "La Niña, El Niño and Atlantic Hurricane Damages in the United States," *Bulletin of the American Meteorological Society* 80, no. 10 (Oct. 1999): 2027–33.

4. Richard H. Grove, "The Great El Niño of 1789–93 and Its Global Consequences Reconstructing an Extreme Climate Event in World Environmental History," *Medieval History Journal* 10, no. 1–2 (Oct. 2007): 75–98.

5. Fagan, *The Little Ice Age*, 167–80.

6. Considerable detail on these debates is provided by Mulcahy, *Hurricanes and Society*, 176–88.

7. The document is published in full in Sidney Daney de Marcillac, *Histoire de la Martinique, depuis la colonisation jusqu'en 1815* (Fort-Royal: Impr. de E. Ruelle, 1846), vol. 4, 42–47.

8. Lt. General Claude Charles de Marillac, Vicomte de Damas, 16 Aug. 1788, ANOM, Co C8A 88 F 99.

9. ANOM, Guadeloupe 2/87, Correspondance sur l'ouragan de 1825. See also Félix-Hilaire Fortuné, *Cyclones et autres cataclysmes aux Antilles* (Fort-de-France: Editions La Masure, 1986).

10. Hugh Thomas, *Cuba: The Pursuit of Freedom* (New York: Harper & Row, 1971), 72–92; Franklin W. Knight, *Slave Society in Cuba during the Nineteenth Century* (Madison: University of Wisconsin Press, 1970), 3–25; Pérez, *Winds of Change*, 38–43.

11. Moreno Fraginals, *El Ingenio*, vol. 3; 43.

12. Ramírez de Arellano makes no mention of the hurricane of August 1793, which struck St. Thomas and St. Eustatius but probably also caused considerable damage in Puerto Rico. Ramírez de Arellano, "Los huracanes de Puerto Rico." On August 26, the *cabildo* of San Juan discussed the shortage of flour and "the great necessity that can result after the plantains that have fallen in the hurricane have been eaten." See ACCSJ, 26 Aug. 1793, no. 1609.

13. Scarano, *Puerto Rico*, 382–87.

14. Johnson, *Climate and Catastrophe in Cuba and the Atlantic World*, 168–75. Johnson developed this story in detail in Sherry Johnson, "El Niño and Environmental Crisis: Reinterpreting American Rebellions in the 1790s" (paper presented at the Third Allen Morris Biennial Conference, Tallahassee: Florida State University, 2004).

15. "Enfrente tenemos las ricas y bellas islas españolas que nunca serán más que enemigas." Bolívar to Santander (23 Dec. 1823), cited in José Luciano Franco, *La batalla por el dominio del Caribe y el Golfo de Mexico* (Havana: Instituto de Historia, Academia de Ciencias, 1964), 320.

16. AHN, Ultramar 2007, no. 2 (22 Oct. 1824).

17. AGPR (Archivo General de Puerto Rico), Gobierno español, caja 185 (circular of 5 Aug. 1825). A *cuerda* equals 0.97 acres.

18. "Estado que manifiesta los estragos sufridos en la isla . . . la noche del 26 al 27 de julio de 1825," AGR, FGEPR, asuntos politicos y civiles, caja 185.

19. AGPR, Gobierno español, asuntos políticos y civiles, caja 185, circular nos. 123, 124. See also Ramírez de Arellano, "Los huracanes de Puerto Rico," 26–27.

20. AGPR, Gobierno español 185 (8 Nov. and 23 Nov. 1825), assuntos políticos y civiles, caja 185.

21. AGPR, Gobierno español, caja 118 (5 Aug. 1825).

22. United States of America, Congress, *Abridgment of the Debates of Congress from 1789 to 1856: Nov.7, 1808–March 3, 1813*. vol. 4, *Relief for Caracas* (New York: D. Appleton, 1857), 531–32. On the general question of U.S. relations with the independence movements in Latin America, see Caitlin Fitz, "The Hemispheric Dimension of Early U.S. Nationalism: The War of 1812 and Spanish American Independence," *Journal of American History* (forthcoming).

23. Michele Landis Dauber, "The Real Third Rail of American Politics," in *Catastrophe: Law, Politics, and the Humanitarian Impulse*, ed. Austin Sarat and Javier Lezaun (Amherst: University of Massachusetts Press, 2009), 60–82. See also Jack M. Balkin, "Disaster

Relief and the Constitution: A History of 'Strict Construction,'" *Balkinization*, 31 Aug. 2005, http://balkin.blogspot.com/2005/08/disaster-relief-and-constitution.html.

24. Robert L. Paquette and Stanley L. Engerman, "Crisscrossing Empires: Ships, Sailors, and Resistance in the Lesser Antilles in the Eighteenth Century," in *The Lesser Antilles in the Age of European Expansion* (Gainesville: University Press of Florida, 1996), 128–43. On the Spanish search for freedom of conscience in the English colonies, see Stuart B. Schwartz, *All Can Be Saved: Religious Tolerance and Salvation in the Iberian Atlantic World* (New Haven: Yale University Press, 2008), 225–34.

25. ANOM Col. C8B 15 N 44.

26. AHN, Ultramar 1067, exp. 56.

27. AGPR, Gobierno español, municipalidades, Fajardo, caja 450.

28. Johnson, *Climate and Catastrophe in Cuba and the Atlantic World*, 150.

29. The pistols can be seen in Paul Pialoux, *Le Marquis de Bouillé: Un soldat entre deux mondes* (Brioude: Edition Almanach de Brioude, 1977), 167. The story bears remarkable similarity to Benjamin Franklin's account of the *Elizabeth* out of Jamaica, driven by a storm to seek refuge at Havana in 1746, and surrendered there with its cargo by its captain. The Governor of Cuba refused to take as a prize of war a ship driven to seek asylum from a storm, saying, "We, though enemies, being Men are bound as such by the laws of Humanity to afford relief to men who ask it of us." The incident is discussed in Michael J. Drexler, "Hurricanes and Revolutions," in Martin Brückner, ed., *Early American Cartographies*, Omohundro Institute of Early American History and Culture (Chapel Hill: University of North Carolina Press, 2011), 441–66. The Bouillé story circulated widely and was sometimes contrasted to the actions of one British officer who imprisoned a boatload of French seamen that survived the loss of their ship to a hurricane. See George Stewart, *Progress of Glasgow: A Sketch of the Commercial and Industrial Increase of the City during the Last Century* (Glasgow: J. Baird, 1883), 85–87.

30. From John Poyer, *History of Barbados* (London: J. Mawman, 1808), 454. Cited in *Account of the Fatal Hurricane, by Which Barbados Suffered in August 1831* (Bridgetown: Printed for Samuel Hyde, 1831), 7.

31. AGPR, Gobierno español, caja 185 (26 Feb. 1826).

32. Anne-Marie Mercier-Faivre and Chantal Thomas, eds., *L'invention de la catastrophe au XVIII siècle* (Geneva: Droz, 2008), 7–15.

33. Cañizares-Esguerra, *Puritan Conquistadors*, 126.

34. Walter, "Pour une histoire culturelle des risques naturels." Unlike Walter, Cañizares-Esguerra emphasizes the similarities of Catholic and Protestant conceptions of nature and providential intervention: Cañizares-Esguerra, *Puritan Conquistadors*, 144–47. See also Kathleen Murphy, "Prodigies and Portents: Providentialism in the Eighteenth- Century Chesapeake," *Maryland Historical Magazine* 97, no. 4 (Jan. 2002): 397–421.

35. Edwards, *The History, Civil and Commercial, of the British Colonies in the West Indies*, 52.

36. "The Advantages of Religion to Societies," in John Tillotson, *The Works of the Most Reverend Dr. John Tillotson* (Edinburgh: W. Ruddiman & Co., 1772), 35–36.

37. Jonathan Israel emphasizes that by the eighteenth century the most accepted explanation of the divine origin of catastrophe was that some disasters were messages from God and some were not. Jonathan I. Israel, *Democratic Enlightenment: Philosophy, Revolution, and Human Rights 1750–1790* (New York: Oxford University Press, 2011), 40–54. It was believed that an angry God usually provided a warning like monstrous

births before causing destruction. See David D. Hall, *Worlds of Wonder, Days of Judgment: Popular Religious Belief in Early New England* (New York: Knopf, 1989), 76–78.

38. Mulcahy, *Hurricanes and Society*, 48. This theme is also developed in Nicholas M. Beasley, *Christian Ritual and the Creation of British Slave Societies, 1650–1780* (Athens: University of Georgia Press, 2009), 49. The English tradition of fast sermons on important occasions is discussed in Ian Kenneth Steele, *The English Atlantic, 1675–1740: An Exploration of Communication and Community* (New York: Oxford University Press, 1986). Steele provides additional bibliography on this theme.

39. Davy, *The West Indies, Before and Since Slave Emancipation*, 277.

40. NAH, St. Eustatius, St. Maarten, en Saba, 1.05.13.01, 13 July 1749.

41. Ibid., 11 July 1793, no. 295. Register of placards, publications, notifications, and edicts.

42. *Gazette Officiale de la Guadeloupe*, 31 July 1825, 42.

43. Waldemar Christian Westergaard, *The Danish West Indies under Company Rule (1671–1754) with a Supplementary Chapter 1755–1917* (New York: The Macmillan Company, 1917), 6. C.G.A. Oldendorp, the Moravian missionary, reported in the eighteenth century that the day of repentance and prayer was actually July 25, not June 25. See Oldendorp, *C.G.A. Oldendorp's History of the Mission*, 45.

44. Cited in Westergaard, *The Danish West Indies*, 6.

45. Walter, "Pour une histoire culturelle des risques naturels."

46. Benjamin Cohen Carillon at different times in the 1840s served as leader of the Jewish congregation in Jamaica as well as that of St. Thomas. Judah M. Cohen, *Through the Sands of Time: A History of the Jewish Community of St. Thomas, U.S. Virgin Islands* (Hanover, NH: Brandeis University Press, 2004), 57–58.

47. AGPR, Letter of Francisco Valderrama, 16 Apr. 1812, Fondo General, Asuntos políticos y civiles, Cónsules Santo Domingo, 1796–1858, caja 34 (16 April 1812).

48. Pablo Rodriguez, "1812: El terremoto que interrumpió una revolución," in *Una historia de los usos del miedo*, ed. Pilar Gonzalbo, Anne Staples, and Valentina Torres Septién (Mexico City: Colegio de México; Universidad Iberoamericana, 2009), 247–73. I have followed his argument closely. See also the major contribution of Rogelio Altez, *El desastre de 1812 en Venezuela: Sismos, vulnerabilidades y una patria no tan boba* (Caracas: Fundación Empresas Polar, 2006).

49. James Ramsay, *Essay on the Treatment and Conversions of African Slaves in the British Sugar Colonies* (London: James Phillips, 1784). See also Frank Wesley Pittman, "Fetishism, Witchcraft, and Christianity among the Slaves," *Journal of Negro History* 11, no. 4 (1926): 650–68; Ortiz, *El huracán*, 78–80.

50. Edward Bartlett Rugemer, *The Problem of Emancipation: The Caribbean Roots of the American Civil War* (Baton Rouge: Louisiana State University Press, 2008), 17–66. See the overview in Franklin W. Knight, "The Disintegration of the Caribbean Slave Systems, 1772–1886," in *General History of the Caribbean*, ed. Franklin Knight, vol. 3 (London: UNESCO, 1997), 322–45.

51. Robert L. Paquette, Stanley L. Engerman, and David Barry Gaspar, "Ameliorating Slavery: The Leeward Islands Slave Act of 1798," in *The Lesser Antilles in the Age of European Expansion* (Gainesville: University Press of Florida, 1996), 241–58.

52. Michael Craton, *Sinews of Empire: A Short History of British Slavery* (New York: Anchor Press, 1974), 266. Eric Williams, *Capitalism and Slavery* (1944) was the classic formulation the argument that the attack on slavery was carried out by humanitarians and capitalists as a joint effort. A debate still rages over this issue. See the excellent summary of the main points under dispute in Dale Tomich, "Econocide? From Abolition to

Emancipation in the British and French Caribbean," in Stephan Palmié and Francisco A. Scarano, *The Caribbean: A History of the Region and Its People* (Chicago: University of Chicago Press, 2011), 303–16.

53. Claude Levy, "Barbados: The Last Years of Slavery 1823–1833," *Journal of Negro History* 44, no. 4 (Oct. 1959): 308–45.

54. Schomburgk, *The History of Barbados*, 434.

55. F.W.N. Bayley, *Four Years' Residence in the West Indies, in the Years 1826, 1827, 1828, 1829* (London: W. Kidd, 1831), 696.

56. *Account of the Fatal Hurricane, by Which Barbados Suffered in August 1831*, 29.

57. S. D. Smith, "Storm Hazard and Slavery: The Impact of the 1831 Great Caribbean Hurricane on St Vincent," *Environment and History* 18, no. 1 (Feb. 2012): 97–123; *Account of the Fatal Hurricane, by Which Barbados Suffered in August 1831*.

58. Ludlum, *Early American Hurricanes*, 140–43.

59. Charles Shephard, *An Historical Account of the Island of Saint Vincent* (London: W. Nicol, 1831), 211. Cited in Ragatz, *The Fall of the Planter Class*, 375.

60. J. R. Ward, *British West Indian Slavery, 1750–1834: The Process of Amelioration* (Oxford: Oxford University Press, 1988); Luster, *The Amelioration of the Slaves in the British Empire, 1790–1833*.

61. Cited in Smith, "Storm Hazard and Slavery," 113.

62. Princeton University Library, Papers of Bearded Hall Estate, 1740–1831, box 1, folder 18.

63. Schomburgk, *The History of Barbados*, 439; Claude Levy, *Emancipation, Sugar, and Federalism: Barbados and the West Indies, 1833–1876* (Gainesville: University Presses of Florida, 1980), 25–33.

64. Ragatz, *The Fall of the Planter Class*, 408.

65. *Account of the Fatal Hurricane, by Which Barbados Suffered in August 1831*, 66–67.

66. Ibid., 77.

67. Ibid., 116–21.

68. Ibid., 120.

69. Schomburgk, *The History of Barbados*, 440. The sum of £100,000 was voted in the House of Commons on 29 February 1832 for Barbados, St. Vincent, and St. Lucia. The money was originally to be directed to the indigent. A subsequent dispute arose when some of these funds were designated for rebuilding of damaged churches. By 1835 many of the damaged estates and sugar mills had been rebuilt, helped by the good sugar crops of 1832 and 1833. In 1835 the commissioners assigned remaining funds to compensate owners who had lost slaves in the 1831 hurricane, and therefore were not able to collect compensation for them as a result of emancipation in 1834.

70. This and subsequent quotations from the governor's speech are found in Schomburgk, *The History of Barbados*, 442–43. See also *Account of the Fatal Hurricane, by Which Barbados Suffered in August 1831*, 142–43, 146.

71. Barkun, *Disaster and the Millennium*, 163.

72. Summaries of the governor's message and the assembly's response are provided in Schomburgk, *The History of Barbados*, 443–44. See also Levy, "Barbados," 323–27.

73. O. Nigel Bolland, "The Politics of Freedom in the British Caribbean," in *The Meaning of Freedom: Economics, Politics, and Culture after Slavery*, ed. Frank McGlynn and Seymour Drescher (Pittsburgh: University of Pittsburgh Press, 1992), 113–46.

74. Ludlum, *Early American Hurricanes*, 140–41; David Ludlum, "The Espy-Redfield Dispute," *Weatherwise* 22, no. 6 (1969): 224–61.

75. Ludlum, *Early American Hurricanes, 1492–1870*; Fitzpatrick, *Natural Disasters: Hurricanes*, 117–18. An excellent summary of these advances in meteorology is given in Bob Sheets and Jack Williams, *Hurricane Watch: Forecasting the Deadliest Storms on Earth* (New York: Vintage, 2001). I have used it as the basis of my summary. See also Chris Mooney, *Storm World: Hurricanes, Politics, and the Battle over Global Warming* (Orlando, FL: Harcourt, 2007), 15–30.

76. I am following the explanation of Sheets and Williams, *Hurricane Watch*, 38–39.

77. Sterling Library, Yale University, William Redfield Meteorological mss, box 2.

78. K. G. Beauchamp, *History of Telegraphy* (London: Institution of Electrical Engineers, 2001), 51–57.

79. Jorma Ahvenainen, *The History of the Caribbean Telegraphs before the First World War* (Helsinki: Suomalainen Tiedeakatemia, 1996), 200–201, emphasizes that until the end of World War I the cable companies barely broke even in the Caribbean.

80. *Account of the Fatal Hurricane, by Which Barbados Suffered in August 1831*, 146.

81. A summary of the work of the observatory at the Colegio de Belén is presented in Walter M. Drum, *The Pioneer Forecasters of Hurricanes* (Havana: Observatory of Belén, 1905). See also Mercedes Valero González, "El observatorio del Colegio de Belén en el siglo XIX," in *Anuario: Centro de Estudios de Historia y Organización de la Ciencia* (Havana: Centro de Estudios de Historia y Organización de la Ciencia, 1988), 200–17; Díaz-Argüelles García, "El Observatorio fisico-meteorico de La Habana." On Jesuit interest in astronomy and meteorology in general see, Agustín Udías Vallina, *Searching the Heavens and the Earth: The History of Jesuit Observatories* (Dordrecht: Kluwer Academic Publishers, 2003).

CHAPTER 5. FREEDOM, SOVEREIGNTY, AND DISASTERS

1. This summary is based on Stanley L. Engerman and Herbert Klein, "The Transition from Slave to Free Labor: Notes on a Comparative Economic Model," in *Between Slavery and Free Labor: The Spanish-Speaking Caribbean in the Nineteenth Century*, ed. Manuel Moreno Fraginals, Frank Moya Pons, and Stanley L. Engerman (Baltimore: Johns Hopkins University Press, 1985), 255–69. I have not mentioned here the process in the areas of the British West Indies outside the normal hurricane tracks, particularly Trinidad and British Guiana. Both of these areas had expanding sugar sectors prior to the 1830s, but despite efforts to force emancipated slaves to remain at work, the availability of lands made this impossible. The result was a drop in production until the 1870s, when the importation of indentured laborers, particularly from India, allowed for considerable recovery of the plantation economy.

2. James L. Dietz, *Economic History of Puerto Rico: Institutional Change and Capitalist Development* (Princeton, NJ: Princeton University Press, 1986), 19.

3. Ibid.

4. Francisco A. Scarano, "Azúcar y esclavitud en Puerto Rico: La formación de la economía de haciendas en Ponce, 1815–1849," in *Azucar y esclavitud*, ed. Andrés Ramos Mattei (San Juan: University of Puerto Rico, 1982), 13–52; Francisco A. Scarano, *Sugar and Slavery in Puerto Rico: The Plantation Economy of Ponce, 1800–1850* (Madison: University of Wisconsin Press, 1984); Luis A. Figueroa, *Sugar, Slavery, and Freedom in Nineteenth-Century Puerto Rico* (Chapel Hill: University of North Carolina Press, 2005).

5. The complaint of "lack of workers" (*falta de brazos*) was constant in the nineteenth century. From the 1830s there had been a series of laws aimed at forcing peasants and free rural workers into labor arrangements. The most famous of these was the law of 1849 requiring work cards, but it was really part of a continuing policy of labor compul-

sion. See Gervasio Luis García, "Economía y trabajo en el Puerto Rico del siglo XIX," *Historia Mexicana* 38, no. 4 (April, 1989): 855–78; Fernando Picó, *Libertad y servidumbre en el Puerto Rico del siglo xix* (Río Piedras, PR: Ediciones Huracán, 1982).

6. Pérez, *Winds of Change*, 39–55. I am following in this section Pérez's excellent and detailed study of the 1844 and 1846 hurricanes and their effects. In addition, an important source is *Huracán de 1846: Reseña de sus estragos en la isla de Cuba* (Havana: Oficina del Faro Industrial, 1846). This latter work is a compendium of materials and reports that appeared in the periodical *El Faro Industrial*.

7. Luis Martínez-Fernández, "Political Change in the Spanish Caribbean during the United States Civil War and Its Aftermath, 1861–1878," *Caribbean Studies* 27, no. 1/2 (Jan. 1994): 37–64.

8. Christopher Schmidt-Nowara, "National Economy and Atlantic Slavery: Protectionism and Resistance to Abolitionism in Spain and the Antilles, 1854–1874," *Hispanic American Historical Review* 78, no. 4 (Nov. 1998): 603–29.

9. See José Fernández Partagás, "Impact on Hurricane History of a Revised Lowest Pressure at Havana (Cuba) During the October 11, 1846 Hurricane" (unpublished paper, 1993), http://www.aoml.noaa.gov/hrd/Landsea/Partagas/impacthurrhist .pdf.

10. Pérez, *Winds of Change*, 73.

11. "Consagrarse pues con nuevo ánimo, com más brios á reparar las desgracias y empuñar nuevamente el arado para obligar á la madre comun á darnos con mano pródiga lo que nos robó la furiosa tempestad, es lo que dicta la prudencia, el único partido que en este momento nos queda." The full letter appears reprinted in Ramírez de Arellano, "Los huracanes de Puerto Rico," 29–33. The author states that the letter is in his private collection.

12. Ibid.

13. Mariano Esteban de Vega, "La asistencia liberal en la España de la Restauración," *Revista de la historia de la economía y de la empresa*, no. 4 (2010): 49–61.

14. *Huracan de 1846*, 71. In 1851, the Spanish government suspended the paper, published since 1842, because of the annexationist discourse of then-editor John Thrasher.

15. "Nuestras autoridades superiors tomaron las medidas que el caso exijia" in ibid., 12. See also the extended discussion and cited sources in Pérez, *Winds of Change*, 112–22.

16. Pérez, *Winds of Change*, 138.

17. James Patterson Smith, "The Liberals, Race, and Political Reform in the British West Indies, 1866–1874," *Journal of Negro History* 79, no. 2 (April 1994): 131–46.

18. Ibid., 141.

19. See the discussion in Bonham C. Richardson, *Economy and Environment in the Caribbean: Barbados and the Windwards in the Late 1800s* (Gainesville: University Press of Florida, 1997), 1–20.

20. Cited by Bridget Brereton, *An Introduction to the History of Trinidad and Tobago* (Oxford: Heinemann Educational Publishers, 1996), 27. For a general "official history," see Henry Iles Woodcock, *A History of Tobago* (Printed for the author, 1867).

21. Curiously, Lt. Gov. Graeme believed that the island had never before been visited by a hurricane. He reported as much in his letter of 14 October 1847 to the Governor at Trinidad. See *Tobago Hurricane of 1847*, 3.

22. Bridget Brereton, "Family Strategies, Gender and the Shift to Wage Labour in the British Caribbean," in *The Colonial Caribbean in Transition: Essays on Post-Emancipation*

Social and Cultural History, ed. Bridget Brereton and Kevin A. Yelvington (Gainesville: University Press of Florida, 1999), 87.

23. Ibid., 14–15. *"An Act for the summary punishment of Persons detected in stealing or pilfering Goods, Lumber, & Co., exposed or scattered by the late Hurricane."*

24. Henry Iles Woodcock, *A History of Tobago*, 110–13. Woodcock notes that only about £20,000 was actually loaned and that payments were delayed on two occasions in part because of the economic depression in the colonies.

25. Woodcock celebrated the "energy and perseverance" of "individuals of all classes" in restoring prosperity, along with the prompt liberality of the Home Government. Ibid., 109.

26. Engerman and Klein, "The Transition from Slave to Free Labor," 266.

27. I have drawn on three studies of the Irish potato famine. See John Kelley, *The Graves Are Walking: The Great Famine and the Saga of the Irish People* (New York: Henry Holt and Co., 2012); Cormac Ó Gráda, Richard Paping, and Eric Vanhaute, eds., *When the Potato Failed: Causes and Effects of the Last European Subsistence Crisis, 1845–1850* (Turnhout: Brepols, 2007); Ciarán Ó Murchadha, *The Great Famine: Ireland's Agony, 1845–52* (London: Continuum International Publishing Group, 2011).

28. *Report on the Bahamas' Hurricane of October 1866: With a Description of the City of Nassau, N.P.* (Nassau: Printed at the "Nassau Guardian" by E. C. Moseley, 1868), 9.

29. Public statement (9 Nov. 1866) published in ibid., 29.

30. Arthur Rumbold to Governor Hill of Antigua (12 Nov. 1867), reprinted in *Sainte Thomae Tiende* (4 Dec. 1867), reprinted in Roy A. Watlington and Shirley H. Lincoln, *Disaster and Disruption in 1867: Hurricane, Earthquake, and Tsunami in the Danish West Indies* (St. Thomas: Eastern Caribbean Center, University of the Virgin Islands, 1997), 23–25.

31. Terencia K. Joseph, "The Storm before the Calm: The 1898 Hurricane and Official Responses, Saint Lucia" (paper presented at the Annual Conference of the Association of Caribbean Historians, San Juan, Puerto Rico, 2011). This paper is based to a large extent on a close reading of the St. Lucia newspaper *The Voice*. I thank Prof. Joseph for her permission to cite this study and the sources cited therein.

32. Ibid., 20. Joseph cites Peter Adrien, *Metayage, Capitalism and Peasant Development in St. Lucia, 1840–1957* (Mona, Jamaica: Consortium Graduate School of Social Sciences, University of the West Indies, 1996), 37. Adrien shows almost a tripling of peasant freeholds between 1853 and 1896.

33. *The Voice*, 8 Dec. 1898, cited in Joseph, "The Storm before the Calm," 20. On the generally depressed economic conditions of the Windwards in this period, see Richardson, *Economy and Environment in the Caribbean*, 50–67.

34. This brief summary draws on Gert Oostindie and Inge Klinkers, *Decolonising the Caribbean: Dutch Policies in a Comparative Perspective* (Amsterdam: Amsterdam University Press, 2003), 29–32, 57–62.

35. Han Jordaan and To van der Lee, "The Hurricane of 1819," in *Building Up the Future from the Past: Studies on the Architecture and Historic Monuments in the Dutch Caribbean*, ed. Henry E. Coomans, Michael A. Newton, and Maritza Coomans-Eustatia (Zutphen, Netherlands: Walburg Pers, 1990), 99–108.

36. Ibid., 104–5.

37. Guadeloupe: 1809 (3 hurricanes), 1821, 1824, 1825, 1833, 1846, 1865, 1888, 1889 1893, 1899. Martinique: 1804, 1806, 1809, 1816, 1817, 1825 (3), 1834, 1837, 1846, 1855, 1872, 1875, 1891, as well as a series of tropical storms, 1883, 1886, 1888, 1889, 1894, 1896.

38. Henri Monet, *La Martinique* (Paris: A. Savine, 1892), 12. For his listing of Martinique's hurricanes, see pp. 205–40.

39. Ibid., 373.

40. "Relativo a la suscripción voluntaria," AGPR, Fondo Municipal, San Juan, leg. 34, exp. 8; AHMP (Archivo Municipal de Ponce), s-282, exp. 3.

41. *St. Thomae Tiende*, 7 Dec. 1867; Extra Money Bill to the Budget of the Municipality of St. Croix in U.S. Consular dispatches, St. Thomas, 1868.

42. Anna Brickhouse, "'L'Ouragan de Flammes' ('The Hurricane of Flames'): New Orleans and Transamerican Catastrophe, 1866/2005," *American Quarterly* 59, no. 4 (2007): 1097–1127.

43. These statements in the *New York Times*, 8 Apr. 1866, 5, are similar to those in the journal of an English eyewitness. The *Times* account, however, unlike that of Burgess, fails to mention the presence of the Haitian president and his ministers in the streets during the fire, or the positive attitude of survivors afterwards. There was no evidence for the supposed arson, and other reports suggested that the fire started in a theater. See George Burgess, *Last Journal of the Rt. Rev. George Burgess, D.D., Bishop of Maine, from December 27, 1865, to April 20, 1866* (Boston: E. P. Dutton and Co., 1866), entry for 19 and 20 March 1866.

44. John Bassett Moore, "Doc. 551," in *A Digest of International Law: 56th Congress, House of Representatives*, vol. 1 (Washington, DC: Government Printing Office, 1906), 601–10. The classic study on the eventual sale of the islands to the United States is Charles Callan Tansill, *The Purchase of the Danish West Indies* (Baltimore: Johns Hopkins Press, 1932). See also Erik Overgaard Pedersen, *The Attempted Sale of the Danish West Indies to the United States of America, 1865–1870* (Frankfurt: Haag & Herchen, 1997). Seward was also apparently concerned that the Danes might sell the islands to Austria to be included in Emperor Maximilian's throne in Mexico. Halvdan Koht, "The Origin of Seward's Plan to Purchase the Danish West Indies," *American Historical Review*, 50, no. 4 (July 1945): 762–67.

45. USNA, Consular Dispatches, St. Thomas, Admiral Porter to Sec. of State William Seward (31 Oct. 1867), Roll 8, vol. 8. See also the report of Consul A. B. Simmons to Secretary of State Seward of the same date.

46. Gordon K. Lewis, "An Introductory Note to the Study of the Virgin Islands," *Caribbean Studies* 8, no. 2 (July 1968): 5–21.

47. *St Thomas Tiende*, editorial, 14 Dec. 1867, reprinted along with the Royal Order of 18 Jan. 1832 in Watlington and Lincoln, *Disaster and Disruption in 1867*, 109–10.

48. James Parton, *The Danish Islands: Are We Bound in Honor to Pay for Them?* (Boston: Fields, Osgood, & Co., 1869).

49. Bret Harte, "St. Thomas: A Geographical Survey," in *The Heathen Chinee: Poems and Parodies.* (London: Richard Edward King, 1888).

50. Accounts of hurricanes for 1867 do not include this *temporal*, but extensive documentary evidence shows that this must have been a storm of major dimensions that preceded the San Narciso hurricane of 29 October 1867. Many reports for municipalities are found in AGPR, Obras Publicas 159.

51. AGPR, Obras Publicas 159, letters of 17 Sept. and 17 Oct. 1867.

52. Carlos de Rojas to Inspector General of Public Works, 24 Oct. 1867, AGPR, Obras Públicas 159.

53. The *escudo* was equivalent to half a peso. The *escudo* coins circulated in Spain in the 1850s and 1860s as part of a monetary reform but circulated less in Cuba and Puerto Rico. Ramírez de Arellano, "Los huracanes de Puerto Rico," 37. The governor required

reports from every district. The report from the Isabela district is a good example. Of losses totaling 110,373 *escudos*, crops in the field totaled 54,568 and products like sugar, rum, molasses, and cotton, 44,794. See AGPR, Fondo Documental Municipal, Isabela, caja 109, exp. 1684; exp. 1686 gives the listing of losses in each neighborhood made by the owners themselves.

54. AGPR, FMSJ, leg. 34, exp. 11, "Relación de los edificios que sufrieron deterioros con motivo de los temblores de 1867." Exp. 9 and 10 include discussions of the San Juan municipal council in response to the disasters that reveal a preoccupation with the possibility of infectious disease due to the many unburied bodies in the aftermath of the storm and the earthquakes (25 November 1867). It was also suggested that ships coming from St. Thomas should be carefully watched and perhaps quarantined.

55. AHN, Ultamar 379, exp. 10 (10 Oct. 1867).

56. AHN, Ultramar 379, exp. 10 (20 Oct. 1867): "podian llevar a esta pacifica y tranquila sociedad hasta el bordo de principios en que jamas se ha visto ni en que VE puede consenter que nunca se encuentre."

57. "malestar general data del antiguo," José Lianhes to Gobierno Superior Civil (Nov. 1867), AHN, Ultramar, leg. 379, exp. 10.

58. Ibid.

59. "la mayoria de los habitantes crea en la immoralidad de una Administración mirada como estrangera y enemiga." AHN, Ultramar 379, Miguel de Campos to Ingen. encargado del Negociado de Obras Públicas del Ministerio de Ultramar (9 April 1868).

60. Louis van Housel, "An Earthquake Experience," *Scribner's Monthly*, 15 (1878), excerpted in Watlington and Lincoln, *Disaster and Disruption in 1867*, 41–62. Van Housel notes, "A small Spanish man-of-war, the name of which I regret to say I cannot recall, deserves special mention." He then proceeds to describe its actions in rescuing the drowning.

61. Vicente Fontán y Mera, *La memorable noche de San Narciso y los temblores de tierra* (San Juan: Imprenta del Comercio, 1868), 40.

62. AGPR, Obras Publicas 159, unsigned report, Lares, 14 Nov. 1867: "De ahí la ruina de muchos, la disanimación de otros y el terror y espanto de todos."

63. Laird W. Bergad, "Toward Puerto Rico's Grito de Lares: Coffee, Social Stratification, and Class Conflicts, 1828–1868," *Hispanic American Historical Review* 60, no. 4 (Nov. 1980): 617–42.

64. For the general context of the Lares rebellion, see Olga Jiménez de Wagenheim, *Puerto Rico's Revolt for Independence: El Grito de Lares* (Boulder: Westview Press, 1985); Francisco Moscoso, *La Revolución puertorriqueña de 1868: El grito de Lares* (Puerto Rico: Instituto de Cultura Puertorriqueña, 2003).

65. Francisco Moscoso, *Clases, revolución y libertad: Estudios sobre el Grito de Lares de 1868* (Río Piedras [Puerto Rico]: Editorial Edil, Inc., 2006).

66. Ibid., 45–46.

67. José Pérez Moris and Luis Cueto y González Quijano, *Historia de la insurección de Lares* (Barcelona: Establecimiento Tip. de Narciso Ramirez y C., 1872), 298.

68. BNM, Ms. 20.128, "Proclama de Betances a los puertoriqueños," 109–10.

69. Pérez Moris and Cueto y González Quijano, *Historia de la insurección de Lares*, 74–76.

70. Ibid., 50, 56.

71. "Todavia tiembla la isla y se estremece Puerto Rico de ver a sus hijos insensibles a la servidumbre," Betances to Pedro Lovera, Santo Domingo, 18 April 1868, in *Ramón*

Emeterio Betances: Obras completas, ed. Félix Ojeda Reyes and Paul Estrade, vol. 5, Escritos politicos: Correspondencia relativa a Puerto Rico (forthcoming).

72. *New York Times*, 23 Nov. 1868, 5.

73. Caviedes, "Five Hundred Years of Hurricanes in the Caribbean."

74. Pérez, *Winds of Change*, 134.

75. AGPR, Gob. Español, political/civil, leg. 118 (10 Dec. 1967).

76. "*tantas y tantas calamidades públicas.*" *Memoria en que se da cuenta de los trabajos de la Junta General de Socorros para Cuba y Filipinas* (Madrid: Manuel Tello, 1884), 5.

77. AGPR, Obras Públicas, leg. 159, "Relación de las suscripciones de los empleados de la Inspección General de Obras Públicas." Contributions ranged from 44 to 12 *escudos*.

78. *El hurácan de Vuelta-Abajo: Curiosa recopilacion de todo lo que de mas notable ha publicado la prensa con motivo de aquella tremenda catástrofe* (Havana: Impr. La Idea, 1882), 16.

79. AGPR, Fondo Municipal, San Juan 34, exp. 9 (9 Nov. 1867).

80. AHMP, s-282, exp. 2.

81. AGPR, Fondo Municipal, Manatí, leg. 62, registro 1754.

82. AHMC, Calamidades, caja 13, exp. 3.

83. AHMP, s-282, exp. 5.

84. *El huracán de Vuelta-Abajo*, 7.

85. Ibid.

86. Fontán y Mera, *La memorable noche de San Narciso y los temblores de tierra*, 47–48.

87. *El huracán de Vuelta-Abajo*, 18–19; AGPR, Obras Públicas 159 (11 Oct. 1867).

88. *El huracán de Vuelta-Abajo*, 13–14.

89. Ibid.

90. Manuel Fernandez de Castro, *Estudio sobre los huracanes ocurridos en la isla de Cuba durante el mes de octubre de 1870* (Madrid: Lapuente, 1871), 48. "Ni los torrentas de agua que han derramado sobre Cuba los huracanes de 1870 han bastado para lavar la sangre que la inunda ni apagar el incendio que la devora."

91. José Carlos Millás y Hernández, "Genesis y marcha de los huracanes antillanos," in *Astronomy, Meteorology, and Seismology: Proceedings of the Second Pan-American Scientific Congress*, ed. Robert Simpson Woodward (Washington, DC: Government Printing Office, 1917), 42–55.

92. this work first appeared in the previous year in the *Annales hydrographiques*. The Andrés Poëy papers are today located in the Museo Montané in the Faculty of Biology at the University of Havana.

93. AHN, Ultramar 374, exp. 2. His treatise, "Descripcion del huracan de 13 de septiembre de 1876," is available online though the Portal de Archivos Españoles, PARES.

94. Raymond Arsenault, "The Public Storm: Hurricanes and the State in Twentieth-Century America," in *American Public Life and the Historical Imagination*, ed. Wendy Gamber, Michael Grossberg, and Hendrik Hartog (Notre Dame, IN: University of Notre Dame Press, 2003), 267–68.

95. Yrj Kaukiainen, "Shrinking the World: Improvements in the Speed of Information Transmission, c. 1820–1870," *European Review of Economic History*, 5, no. 1 (2001): 1–28.

96. John A. Britton, "International Communications and International Crises in Latin America, 1867–1881," *The Latin Americanist* 52, no. 1 (2008): 131–54.

97. In an 1952 essay entitled "Presencia de la naturaleza," Alejo Carpentier criticizes Goethe's famous reference to an "amiable Nature" that in Europe is "dominated and quieted" by man, reminding him and us that "America still lives under the telluric sign

of the great storms and the great floods." See Alejo Carpentier, *Letra y solfa: Literatura, poética. Selección de crónicas de Alejo Carpentier* (Havana: Letra Cubanas, 2001). Reprinted in Jorge Ángel Pérez, ed., *La danza del huracán* (Havana: Letras Cubanas, 2002), 9–10. On the question of technology, colonialism, and the control of Nature there is an extensive literature: for an introduction, see Michael Adas, *Machines as the Measure of Men: Science, Technology, and Ideologies of Western Dominance* (Ithaca, NY: Cornell University Press, 1989); Stuart George McCook, *States of Nature: Science, Agriculture, and Environment in the Spanish Caribbean, 1760–1940* (Austin: University of Texas Press, 2002).

98. *El huracan de Vuelta-Abajo*, 16.

99. Walter, "Pour une histoire culturelle des risques naturels," 1–18.

100. This point is nicely made in Mack Holt's review of Jean Delumeau, *Rassurer et protéger: Le sentiment de sécurité dans l'Occident d'autrefois* (*Journal of Social History* 24, no. 4 (July 1991): 851–53).

101. Steve Pincus and James Robinson argue that by the end of the eighteenth century, over 30 percent of British state expenditures were aimed at various forms of social amelioration. Pincus and Robinson, "Wars and State-Making Reconsidered: The Rise of the Interventionist State."

102. François Lebrun, "La protection du monarque (1660–1800)," in *Les malheurs des temps: Histoire des fléaux et des calamites en France,* ed. Jean Delumeau and Yves Lequin (Paris: Larousse, 1987), 321–22.

103. This point is made cogently in Jonathan Levy, "Risk as We Know It," *Chronicle of Higher Education,* 10 Sept. 2012, http://chronicle.com/article/Risk-as-We-Know-It /134148/.

104. There is an extensive and provocative literature on the rise of "Risk Society," in which science and technology itself have become the major threat of disaster since the middle of the twentieth century. The starting point is Ulrich Beck, *Risk Society: Towards a New Modernity* (London: Sage Publications, 1992). See the critique in Jean Baptiste Fressoz, "Beck Back in the 19th Century: Towards a Genealogy of Risk Society," *History and Technology*, 23, no. 4 (Dec. 2007): 333–50. A parallel approach has been made by François Ewald, *Histoire de l'état providence: Les origines de la solidarité* (Paris: Grasset, 1996). The use of the concept to describe early modern times is made by a number of contributors to François Walter, Bernardino Fantini, and Pascal Delvaux, eds., *Les cultures du risque: XVIe–XXIe siècles* (Geneva: Presses d'Histoire Suisse, 2006). See also Jonathan Levy, *Freaks of Fortune: The Emerging World of Capitalism and Risk in America* (Cambridge, MA: Harvard University Press, 2012).

CHAPTER 6. NATURE AND POLITICS AT THE CENTURY'S TURN

1. Paul N. Edwards, "Meteorology as Infrastructural Globalism," *Osiris* 21: 1 (2006): 229–50. See also Frederik Nebeker, *Calculating the Weather: Meteorology in the 20th Century* (San Diego: Academic Press, 1995), 11–15.

2. J. M. Walker, *History of the Meteorological Office* (Cambridge: Cambridge University Press, 2012), 3–8.

3. NOAA's National Weather Service, "Evolution of the National Weather Service," http://www.nws.noaa.gov/pa/history/timeline.php.

4. Arsenault, "The Public Storm," 267–69.

5. James Francis Warren, "Scientific Superman: Father José Algué, Jesuit Meteorology in the Philippines under American Rule," in *The Colonial Crucible Empire in the Making of the Modern American State*, ed. Alfred W. McCoy and Francisco A. Scarano (Madison: University of Wisconsin Press, 2009), 508–22.

6. Nebeker, *Calculating the Weather*, 1–3.

7. Ibid., 269. See also David Longshore, *Encyclopedia of Hurricanes, Typhoons, and Cyclones* (New York: Facts on File, 1998), 409–10.

8. I am drawing here on my earlier article and the extensive sources cited therein: Stuart B. Schwartz, "The Hurricane of San Ciriaco: Disaster, Politics, and Society in Puerto Rico, 1899–1901," *Hispanic American Historical Review* 72, no. 3 (Aug. 1992): 303–34.

9. On conditions in Ponce during the storm, we have the observations of Dr. Ashford, who was stationed in the town in 1899. See Bailey K. Ashford, *A Soldier in Science: The Autobiography of Bailey K. Ashford, Colonel M.C., U.S.A.* (San Juan: Editorial de la Universidad de Puerto Rico, 1998), 39.

10. HURDAT information presented in http://www.aoml.noaa.gov/hrd/hurdat. The storm became a hurricane on August 5, and over the course of its existence it was downgraded to a tropical storm and then upgraded again to hurricane status.

11. AHMP, Calamidades, Caja S-282, exp. 2. In the days immediately following the storm it was not referred to as the San Ciriaco hurricane but rather as the "ciclon de 8 de agosto." See Salivia, *Historia de los temporales de Puerto Rico y las Antillas*, 255–77.

12. "Ponce Wrecked by Hurricane," *New York Times*, 12 Aug. 1899.

13. José López Pelaez and his wife were the great-grandparents of Judge Jose A. Cabranes, of the U.S. Court of Appeals, Second Circuit, who graciously provided me this family anecdote. Personal correspondence, 23 June 2012.

14. Salivia places the figure at 3,369 deaths, or 2,183 more than the total of all previously recorded hurricanes on the island. The mortality rate was 43.2/1000, whereas in the preceding years it was 29.7/1000. Salivia, *Historia de los temporales de Puerto Rico y Las Antillas*, 255. See also *Report of the Military Governor*, no. 4088, 219.

15. See for example, Vicente Toledo Rohena, "El recuerdo devastador de San Ciriaco," in the supplement "Huracanes y seguridad," *El Vocero*, 10 July 2000, S5.

16. The remarkable product of this inventory taking can be seen in works such as Henry K. Carroll, *Report on the Island of Puerto Rico*, Treasury Dept. doc. 2118 (Washington, DC, 1899); War Department, *Report on the Census of Porto Rico, 1899* (Washington, DC, 1900); *Puerto Rico al tomar posesión de ella los Estados Unidos* (San Juan: Imprenta de "La Corespondencia," 1899).

17. A brief but comprehensive overview is provided in Luis Martínez-Fernández, "Puerto Rico in the Whirlwind of 1898: Conflict, Continuity, and Change," *OAH Magazine of History* 12, no. 3 (April 1998): 24–29.

18. Hoff's wife Lavinia was made head of the Woman's Relief Society, which distributed clothing throughout the island. Davis always mentioned her positively in his reports. See *Report of the Military Governor of Porto Rico*, 56th Cong., 2nd session, H. doc. N. 4088, 759–61.

19. Ibid., 45–53.

20. For example, AGPR, Fondo Documental Municipal, Fajardo, caja 282. For a full accounting see "Estadistica de los daños causados por el huracán del 8 de agosto de 1899," in Ramón Aráez y Fernando, *Historia del ciclón del día de San Ciriaco* (San Juan: Imprenta Heraldo Español, 1905), 340.

21. After the U.S. occupation the United States government set the exchange rate for the Puerto Rican peso at 60 percent of the U.S. dollar, an exchange rate considerably lower than the historical parity between the two currencies. Ostensibly this was done to promote Puerto Rican exports to the U.S. market, but it also had the effect of lower-

ing the price of land on the island, which made it cheaper for American investors. My thanks to Professor Francisco Scarano for this information.

22. *Boletín Mercantil de Puerto Rico* 61 (Sept. 1899): 1.

23. Carmen Centeno-Añeses, "Huellas de San Ciriaco en la literature puertorriquña de comienzos de siglo," in *La Llegada del Cíclope: Percepciones de San Ciríaco a cien años de su visita*, ed. Raquel Rosario Rivera (San Juan: Fundación Puertorriqueña de las Humanidades, 2000), 89–97.

24. In the 1890s, a young generation of non-elite writers had emerged with the growth of journalism and with the development of the labor movement. The San Ciriaco storm appears as an important element in Eladio Ayala Moura, *El hijo de Carmen, o, Aventuras de un obrero novela original* (Ponce, PR: Tip. Pasarell, 1909); José Elías Levis Bernard, *Estercolero* (San Juan: La Editorial Universidad de Puerto Rico, 2008); José Elías Levis Bernard, *Mancha de lodo; novela.* (Mayaguez: Imp. El Progreso, 1903); Matías González García, *Gestación; novela de carater social y economico.* (San Juan, 1938).

25. AGPR, Fondo Documental Municipal, San Juan, leg. 34, exp.28; AGPR Fondo Fortaleza, 1899, caja 28, exp. 5125.

26. *El Diario de Puerto Rico*, 9 Aug. 1900, 2.

27. "Report of the Governor," *2nd Annual Report (May 1, 1901–July 1, 1902)* (Washington, DC, 1902); AGPR, Fondo Documental Municipal. Lares, *Actas del ayuntamento*, 12 Aug., 23 Oct., 13 Nov. 1899, caja 45, 112–14.

28. *New York Times*, 12 Aug. 1899, 2.

29. Ibid., 1–2. The direct appeal to U.S. governors for relief of Puerto Rico from Secretary of State Root is reported in *New York Times*, 15 Aug. 1899, 5.

30. "Help for Puerto Ricans," *New York Times*, 11 Aug. 1899, 3.

31. Peter Steven Gannon, "The Ideology of Americanization in Puerto Rico, 1898–1909: Conquest and Disestablishment" (Ph.D. dissertation, New York University, 1979); Edward J. Berbusse, *The United States in Puerto Rico, 1898–1900* (Chapel Hill: University of North Carolina Press, 1966), 103–105.

32. See, for example, *New York Times*, 11, 12, and 15 Aug. 1899.

33. See, for example, Cathy Duke, "The Idea of Race: The Cultural Impact of American Intervention in Cuba, 1898–1912," in *Politics, Society, and Culture in the Caribbean: Selected Papers of the XIV Conference of Caribbean Historians*, ed. Blanca Silvestrini (Río Piedras: Universidad de Puerto Rico, 1983), 85–110.

34. Francisco A. Scarano, "The Jíbaro Masquerade and the Subaltern Politics of Creole Identity Formation in Puerto Rico, 1745–1823," *American Historical Review* 101, no. 5 (Dec. 1996): 1398–1431; Lillian Guerra, *Popular Expression and National Identity in Puerto Rico the Struggle for Self, Community, and Nation* (Gainesville: University Press of Florida, 1998), 53–55.

35. *Report of the Military Governor*, no. 4088, 775; Gannon, "The Ideology of Americanization in Puerto Rico, 1898–1909," 150–56; María Dolores Luque de Sánchez, *La ocupación norteamericana y la Ley Foraker: La opinion publica Puertorriqueña, 1898–1904* (Río Piedras: Editorial Universitaria, Universidad de Puerto Rico, 1977), 90–93.

36. Van Hoff to Davis (undated but probably late Aug. 1899), reprinted in *Report of the Military Governor*, no. 4088, 780. The phrase "social assistance philosophy" is from Julian Go, *American Empire and the Politics of Meaning: Elite Political Cultures in the Philippines and Puerto Rico During U.S. Colonialism* (Durham, NC: Duke University Press, 2008), 25.

37. Teresita Martínez de Carrera, "The Attitudes of Influential Groups of Colonial Society Toward the Rural Working Population in Nineteenth-Century Puerto Rico,

1860–73," *Journal of Caribbean History* 12 (1979): 35–54; Scarano, "The Jíbaro Masquerade," 1420–25.

38. Testimony of Gen. Davis, *Hearings before the Committee on Pacific Islands and Puerto Rico* (Senate Bill 22640, 56TH Cong., 1ST sess., Senate doc. 147, n. 3851), 30–32.

39. *Report of the Military Governor*, no. 4088, 192.

40. An excellent overview of the coffee economy is provided by Francisco A. Scarano, *Puerto Rico: Cinco Siglos de Historia* (San Juan: McGraw-Hill, 1993), 460–76.

41. Swift to Charity Board, 18 Sept. 1899, *Report of the Military Governor*, n. 4088, p. 720.

42. Major Cruse to Major Van Hoff, 18 July 1900, *Report of the Military Governor*, n. 4088, 709–12.

43. Go, *American Empire and the Politics of Meaning*, 55–92.

44. AGPR, Fondo Fortaleza, caja 28 (28 Aug. 1899).

45. The remarks are cited in the editorial essay in José Elías Levis Bernard, *Estercolero*, ed. Carmen Centeno Añeses (San Juan: La Editorial de la Universidad de Puerto Rico, 2008), 137–51. José Elías Levis Bernard, a journalist and artist from Aguadilla of French Jewish background, had published his first novel *El Estecolero* in 1899, but after the hurricane, he rewrote it and published *Estecolero* in 1901, making the disaster of the hurricane a major element in the novel and dedicating the book to the widows of the poor and the orphans created by the storm. There are two excellent modern editions. See José Elías Levis Bernard and Estelle Irizarry, *Las novelas: El estercolero (1899); Estercolero (1901)* (San Juan: Ediciones Puerto, 2008) and the above cited edition by Carmen Centeno Añeses, José Elías Levis Bernard, *Estercolero* (San Juan: La Editorial de la Universidad de Puerto Rico, 2008).

46. The statement is from the Liberal journalist Manuel Fernández Juncos, as cited in Irene Fernández Aponte, "La dislocalización poblacional y el éxodo migratorio como resultado del huracán de San Ciriaco," in *La llegada del Cíclope: percepciones de San Ciríaco a cien años de su visita*, ed. Raquel Rosario Rivera (San Juan: Fundación Puertorriqueña de las Humanidades, 2000), 113–21.

47. *Diario de la Marina* (Havana) as cited in *New York Times*, 15 Aug. 1899, 4.

48. Henry J. Nichols, "Fact and Fancy about the Hookworm," *Medical Record* no. 80 (1911): 322–24. See also Ileana M. Rodríguez-Silva, *Silencing Race: Disentangling Blackness, Colonialism, and National Identities in Puerto Rico* (New York: Palgrave Macmillan, 2012), 206–7. Considerable detail of the conditions in the field hospital following the hurricane is provided in Ashford, *A Soldier in Science*.

49. Cf. Mariola Espinosa, "A Fever for Empire: U.S. Disease Eradication in Cuba as Colonial Public Health," in *The Colonial Crucible Empire in the Making of the Modern American State*, ed. Alfred W. McCoy and Francisco A. Scarano (Madison: University of Wisconsin Press, 2009), 288–96.

50. "Pro patria," *El Diario de Puerto Rico*, 3 April 1900.

51. *El Diario de Puerto Rico*, 19 May 1900.

52. Schwartz, "The Hurricane of San Ciriaco," 328–33, discusses the criticism and provides a quantitative analysis of the regional distribution of relief funds.

53. *La Nueva Bandera* (Mayagüez), quoted in *El Diario de Puerto Rico*, 16 May 1900.

54. This *canción* "La invasion Yanqui" appears in María Cadilla de Martínez, *La poesía popular en Puerto Rico* (San Juan: Sociedad Histórica de Puerto Rico, 1999), 322. It is cited and discussed in José G. Amador, "'Redeeming the Tropics': Public Health and National Identity in Cuba, Puerto Rico, and Brazil, 1890–1940" (Ph.D. dissertation, University of Michigan, 2008), 112–15.

55. "El Americano dijo que venía por salvarnos; / pero asina me parece que lo que dijo fué en vano. / Aunque manda coloradas y galletas pa el ciclón / se quedan con lo major los que el mantengo reparten, / y asina para otra parte tendremos que dir rodando."

56. "Document 14," in *Industrial and Other Conditions of the Island of Puerto Rico, and the Form of Government Which Should Be Adopted for It: Hearings before the Committee on Pacific Islands and Puerto Rico of the United States Senate on Senate Bill 2264, to Provide a Government for the Island of Puerto Rico, and for Other Purposes* (Washington, DC: U.S. Government Printing Office, 1900), 34.

57. Ibid., testimony of Henry Oxnard, 150–53.

58. Ibid., testimony of Herbert Myrick, 164–65.

59. John D Cox, *Storm Watchers: The Turbulent History of Weather Prediction from Franklin's Kite to El Niño* (Hoboken, NJ: Wiley, 2002), 120–22.

60. McComb, *Galveston*, 29–30, 120–22.

61. Neil Frank, "The Great Galveston Disaster of 1900," in *Hurricane! Coping with Disaster: Progress and Challenges since Galveston, 1900*, ed. Robert H Simpson, Richard A. Anthes, and Michael Garstang (Washington, DC: American Geophysical Union, 2003), 129–40. An excellent discussion of the meteorological aspects of the Galveston storm is presented in Kerry A. Emanuel, *Divine Wind: The History and Science of Hurricanes* (Oxford; New York: Oxford University Press, 2005), 83–92.

62. The Miami storm of 1926 has been estimated at $157 billion and New Orleans' Katrina at $81 billion.

63. Casey Edward Greene and Shelly Henley Kelly, *Through a Night of Horrors: Voices from the 1900 Galveston Storm* (College Station: Texas A&M University Press, 2000), 133.

64. Ibid., 133.

65. Larson, *Isaac's Storm*, 104–8.

66. Arsenault, "The Public Storm," 270.

67. Greene and Kelly, *Through a Night of Horrors*, 75–93.

68. Henry Cohen II, *Kindler of Souls: Rabbi Henry Cohen of Texas* (Austin: University of Texas Press, 2007). On Kirwin, see accounts in Clarence Ousley, *Galveston in Nineteen Hundred: The Authorized and Official Record of the Proud City of the Southwest as It Was before and after the Hurricane of September 8, and a Logical Forecast of Its Future* (Atlanta: W.C. Chase, 1900).

69. Michele Landis Dauber, "Let Me Next Time Be 'Tried by Fire': Disaster Relief and the Origins of the American Welfare State 1789–1874," *Northwestern University Law Review* 92 (1997–1998): 967–1034.

70. Michele Landis Dauber, *The Sympathetic State*, Stanford Public Law Working Paper No. 77 (Stanford, CA: Stanford University, Jan. 2004), 5–6.

71. Dauber, "Let Me Next Time Be 'Tried by Fire,'" 981–83.

72. Clara Barton, *The Red Cross in Peace and War* (Washington, DC: American Historical Press, 1899), 198.

73. Bill Marscher and Fran Marscher, *The Great Sea Island Storm of 1893* (Macon, GA: Mercer University Press, 2004).

74. Elizabeth Hayes Turner, "Clara Barton and the Formation of Public Policy in Galveston" (paper presented at Philanthropy and the City: A Historical Overview, City University of New York: Rockefeller Archive Center and Russell Sage Foundation, 2000).

75. John Coulter ed., *The Complete Story of the Galveston Horror* (Chicago: E. E. Sprague, 1900), 133–216.

76. Ibid., 216–18.

77. Hayes Turner, "Clara Barton and the Formation of Public Policy in Galveston," 11. Turner provides considerable evidence drawn from Galveston newspapers such as *The Daily News* and the *News*. See also Melanie Gilbert, *Race and the Media in Natural Disasters: The Media's Portrayal of African Americans in the Galveston Storm of 1900 and in Hurricane Katrina*, Research Paper 211 (Southern Illinois University, 1 May 2011), http://opensiuc.lib.siu.edu/gs_rp/211.

78. The spectacular nature of the Martinique eruption has produced a large number of popular and academic studies. See Solange Contour, *Saint-Pierre, Martinique*, 2 vols. (Paris: Editions Caribéennes, 1989); William A Garesché, *The Complete Story of the Martinique and St. Vincent Horrors* (Chicago: Monarch Book Co., 1902); Angelo Heilprin, *Mont Pelée and the Tragedy of Martinique: A Study of the Great Catastrophes of 1902, with Observations and Experiences in the Field* (Philadelphia: J. B. Lippincott, 1903); Alwyn Scarth, *La Catastrophe: The Eruption of Mount Pelée, the Worst Volcanic Eruption of the Twentieth Century* (Oxford: Oxford University Press, 2002); Ernest Zebrowski, *The Last Days of St. Pierre: The Volcanic Disaster That Claimed Thirty Thousand Lives* (New Brunswick, NJ: Rutgers University Press, 2002).

79. Garesché, *The Complete Story*, 118–20.

80. Available online at http://www.icl-fi.org/print/english/wv/953/martinique.htm

CHAPTER 7. MEMORIES OF DISASTER IN A DECADE OF STORMS

1. Caviedes, "Five Hundred Years of Hurricanes in the Caribbean," 304–8.

2. A succinct outline of this period in the Caribbean is presented by O. Nigel Bolland, "Labor Protest, Rebellions and the Rise of Nationalism during Depression and War," in *The Caribbean: A History of the Region and Its Peoples*, ed. Stephan Palmié and Francisco A. Scarano (Chicago: University of Chicago Press, 2011), 459–74.

3. NLJ, ms. 931.

4. JA, 1B/5/77/208 Gov. Ransford Slater's Log.

5. Wayne Neely, *Great Bahamian Hurricanes of 1926: The Story of Three of the Greatest Hurricanes to Ever Affect the Bahamas* (Bloomington, IN: iUniverse, 2009), 86–88.

6. Ibid., 81–93. The song lyric comes from "Mammy Don't Want No Peas, No Rice," by Blind Blake.

7. Michael Craton and Gail Saunders, *Islanders in the Stream: A History of the Bahamian People*, vol. 2: *From the Ending of Slavery to the Twenty-First Century* (Athens: University of Georgia Press, 1992), 2:237–42.

8. Bahamian historian Wayne Neely has written a number of books on the Bahamian hurricanes in general and on individual storms that, although somewhat repetitive, provide much valuable material on local conditions. See, for example, Neely, *Great Bahamian Hurricanes of 1926*; Neely, *The Great Bahamas Hurricane of 1929* (Nassau: Media Publications, 2005).

9. Richardson, *Economy and Environment in the Caribbean*, 18–67.

10. Craton and Saunders, *Islanders in the Stream*, 2:268–76.

11. Anne S. Macpherson, *From Colony to Nation: Women Activists and the Gendering of Politics in Belize, 1912–1982* (Lincoln: University of Nebraska Press, 2007), 115–20.

12. Bridget Brereton and Kevin A. Yelvington, *The Colonial Caribbean in Transition: Essays on Post-Emancipation Social and Cultural History* (Gainesville: University Press of Florida, 1999), 10–15; O. Nigel Bolland, *On the March: Labour Rebellions in the British Caribbean, 1934–39* (Kingston, Jamaica: Ian Randle Publishers, 1995); O. Nigel Bolland,

Colonialism and Resistance in Belize: Essays in Historical Sociology (Kingston, Jamaica: University of the West Indies Press, 2003).

13. I have published some of the material in the following paragraphs as part of Stuart B. Schwartz, "Hurricanes and the Shaping of Circum-Caribbean Societies," *Florida Historical Quarterly* 83, no. 4 (April 2005): 381–409.

14. Horace A. Towner, *Twenty-ninth Annual Report of the Governor of Porto Rico* (Washington, DC: Government Printing Office, 1930), 1–3.

15. Puerto Rico had shifted to BH 10–12 and SC 12–4 because they had a higher sucrose content and were more resistant to disease. About eighty percent of Puerto Rican cane was of these varieties by the late 1920s. The Cubans continued to use the less brittle *cristalina* variety. "Testimony of Carlos Chardón, Commissioner of Agriculture," in *Relief of Porto Rico: Joint Hearings before the Committee on Territories and Insular Possessions, United States Senate and the Committee on Insular Affairs, House of Representatives, Seventieth Congress, 2nd Session on S.J. Res. 172 and H.J. Res. 333, a Bill for the Relief of Porto Rico, December 10 and 11, 1928* (Washington, DC: Government Printing Office, 1929), 64.

16. Thomas Reynolds, "American Red Cross Disaster Services, 1930–47" (Ph.D. dissertation, Columbia University, 1954); Jonathan C. Bergman, "The Shape of Disaster and the Universe of Relief: A Social History of Disaster Relief and The 'Hurricane of '38,' Suffolk County, Long Island, New York, 1938–41" (Ph.D. dissertation, State University of New York at Buffalo, 2008), 35–36.

17. Dietz, *Economic History of Puerto Rico*, 90–91.

18. Bayonet Díaz to Governor of Puerto Rico, 25 Sept. 1928, AGPR, Obras publicas, leg. 166. Much information is also provided in Emilio del Toro, *Final Report of the Insular Executive Committee of Supervision and Relief* (San Juan, 1929) and in *Report on Damage by the Storm of September 13, 1928: Island of Puerto Rico* (San Juan, 1928). These reports were made by appraisers of the Federal Land Bank of Baltimore, Porto Rico Branch.

19. Guillermo Esteves to Governor, 15 Oct. 1928, AGPR, Obras publicas, leg. 166 and leg. 207.

20. Guillermo Esteves to Red Cross Constitutive Committee, 31 Oct. 1928, AGPR, Obras publicas, leg. 160 and leg. 166.

21. Bingham was a former Yale professor and "discoverer" of Machu Picchu.

22. An excellent review of these discussions and debate is found in Ronald Fernandez, *The Disenchanted Island: Puerto Rico and the United States in the Twentieth Century* (Westport, CT: Praeger, 1996), 98–101.

23. Carmen Chiesa de Pérez, "El huracán de San Felipe," *El Mundo*, 16 Sept. 1990, 4.

24. "Great Miami Hurricane of 1926," http://www.srh.noaa.gov/mfl/?n=miami hurricane1926.

25. An excellent summary of hurricane impact on Florida during the period of its rapid development in the 1920 and 1930s is presented in Steinberg, *Acts of God*, 48–68.

26. Arsenault, "The Public Storm," 272.

27. Deborah Sharp, "Storm's Path Remains Scarred after Seventy-Five Years," *USA Today*, 5 Sept. 2003, 4A.

28. , Steinberg presents a review of these events based on newspapers and periodicals of the period. Steinberg, *Acts of God*, 55–60. See also Lawrence E. Will, *Okeechobee Hurricane and the Hoover Dike* (St. Petersburg, FL: Great Outdoors Pub. Co., 1961); Robert Mykle, *Killer 'Cane: The Deadly Hurricane of 1928* (New York: Cooper Square Press, 2002), 5–10. Excellent use of interviews and statements from survivors is made by Eliot Kleinberg, *Black Cloud: The Great Florida Hurricane of 1928* (New York: Carroll & Graf Publishers, 2003).

29. Steinberg, *Acts of God*, 54–61. See also Will, *Okeechobee Hurricane and the Hoover Dike*.

30. American Red Cross, *The West Indies Hurricane Disaster* (Washington, DC, 1928); Schwartz, "Hurricanes and the Shaping of Circum-Caribbean Societies," 407–9.

31. Antoine Prost and Jay Winter, *René Cassin and Human Rights: From the Great War to the Universal Declaration* (Cambridge: Cambridge University Press, 2013) 157–60. My thanks to Jay Winter for allowing me to see the pre-publication proofs of this book.

32. Emilio Rodríguez Demorizi, *Cronología de Trujillo*, vol. 1 (Ciudad Trujillo: Impresora Dominicana, 1955), 28–45; Fernando A. Infante, *La era de Trujillo: Cronología histórica, 1930–1961* (Santo Domingo, DR: Editora Collado, 2007), 48–53.

33. As in Cuba and Puerto Rico, in the Dominican Republic the tradition is to name hurricanes by the saint's day on which they occur, but the Dominicans also have a custom of naming storms according to individuals associated with them usually because of some mishap or miracle: the 1921 hurricane of Magdalena; the 1834 hurricane of Padre Ruiz (who was being buried in the cathedral when the storm struck); the 1894 hurricane of Lilís (the nickname of General Hereaux, who ruled the country at that time).

34. Vetilio Alfau Durán, "Los principals huracanes habidos en Santo Domingo," in *Vetilio Alfau Durán en el Listín diario: Escritos*, ed. Arístides Incháustegui and Blanca Delgado Malagón (Santo Domingo, DR: Secretaría de Estado de Educación, Bellas Artes y Cultos, 1994), 15–25.

35. The San Zenón hurricane's role in the consolidation of the Trujillo regime has been the subject of a number of excellent modern studies. A succinct overview is presented in Frank Moya Pons, *El ciclón de San Zenón y la "patria nueva": Reconstrucción de una ciudad como reconstrucción nacional* (Santo Domingo, DR: Academia Dominicana de la Historia, 2007). The cultural and social effects of Trujillo's post-storm program are emphasized in Lauren Derby, *The Dictator's Seduction: Politics and the Popular Imagination in the Era of Trujillo* (Durham, NC: Duke University Press, 2009), 66–108. The diplomatic aspects in relation to the United States are covered in Eric Roorda, *The Dictator Next Door: The Good Neighbor Policy and the Trujillo Regime in the Dominican Republic, 1930–1945* (Durham, NC: Duke University Press, 1998), 55–62. The literary impact and uses of the San Zenón hurricane are analyzed in Mark D. Anderson, *Disaster Writing: The Cultural Politics of Catastrophe in Latin America* (Charlottesville: University of Virginia Press, 2011), 29–55. For a somewhat similar political use of natural disaster, see Mark Alan Healey, *The Ruins of the New Argentina: Peronism and the Remaking of San Juan After the 1944 Earthquake* (Durham, NC: Duke University Press, 2011).

36. Infante, *La era de Trujillo*, 59.

37. Ramón Lugo Lovatón, *Escombros: Huracán del 1930* (Ciudad Trujillo, DR: Ed. del Caribe, 1955). The book is a collection of articles published originally during the recovery from the hurricane.

38. Rafael Leónidas Trujillo Molina, *Discursos, mensajes y proclamas* (Santiago, DR: Editorial El Diario, 1946), 22–23.

39. Infante, *La era de Trujillo*, 58.

40. "la nueva bestia de las leyendas y invenciones llegó a la ciudad, y la sembró entera de semillas del pánico." Lugo Lovatón, *Escombros*, 93.

41. "toda tragedia es a la vez sepulcro y cuna, meta y partida, descanso y sendero." Ibid., 13.

42. Roorda, *The Dictator Next Door*, 56–58. Roorda discusses the tensions between the diplomatic corps who were distrustful and suspicious of Trujillo and the Naval and

Marine officers who supported him. Trujillo's request for Watson was treated as an opportunity for the embassy to get some leverage with the new government.

43. After his fall in 1933, Machado was protected by Trujillo, who refused to extradite him to Cuba on humanitarian grounds. Machado eventually moved to the United States. See his letter of thanks to Trujillo of 16 Jan. 1934, Gerardo Machado Papers, University of Miami Libraries.

44. Aristides Fiallo Cabral, *Memoria del Secretario de Estado de Sanidad, 1930 (Santo Domingo, 1931)*, 5–6.

45. Derby, *The Dictator's Seduction*, 80–81.

46. Ibid.

47. Curro Pérez to Vidal, 1 Oct. 1930, AGNRD, Fondo Polítíco, leg. D351, exp. 5.

48. AGNRD, Presidencia, 1.25, LD 620 (Calendario político de Trujillo, 1930–40).

49. AGNRD, Presidencia, 1.25 LD 620. Archbishop of Santo Domingo to Rafael Vidal, 30 Sept. 1930.

50. Derby, *The Dictator's Seduction*, 80–88. Derby concentrates on the city's rebuilding and the social implications of the project.

51. Trujillo Molina, *Discursos, mensajes y proclamas*, 67–72.

52. Fulgencio Batista (1933–44, 1952–59), Jorge Ubico (1931–49), Anastacio Somoza (1934–56), Lázaro Cárdenas (1934–40), Getulio Vargas (1930–45, 1951–54). See Eric Paul Roorda, "Genocide Next Door: The Good Neighbor Policy, the Trujillo Regime, and the Haitian Massacre of 1937," *Diplomatic History* 20, no. 3 (1996): 301–19. The post-1929 economic crisis also produced other responses such as the French Popular Front government and, in some ways, the Vichy regime that succeeded it. See Philip Nord, France's New Deal (Princeton, NJ: Princeton University Press, 2010), 19–39.

53. Seasons counting multiple Category 5 hurricanes (with winds in excess of 157 miles per hour) are 1932, 1933, 1960, 1961, 2005, and 2007.

54. Caviedes, "Five Hundred Years of Hurricanes in the Caribbean," 301–10.

55. José Carlos Millás, *Memoria del huracán de Camaguey de 1932* (Havana: Seoane y Fernández, 1933), 6.

56. In 2005, Santa Cruz del Sur was struck by another Category 5 storm but no lives were lost. This was celebrated by Raúl Castro as evidence of the effectiveness of a socialist government in dealing with natural disaster, and his brother Fidel Castro wrote, "a stong and energetic Civil Defense protects our population and offers it more security from catastrophes than does the United States."Destaca Raúl Castro preservación de vidas durante huracán," *La Crónica de Hoy*, 17 Feb. 2013, http://www.cronica.com.mx /notas/2008/397131.html; Fidel Castro, *Reflexiones de Fidel*, vol. 8 (Havana: Oficina de Publicaciones del Consejo de Estado, 2007), 69.

57. Michele Dauber, "Fate, Responsibility, and 'Natural' Disaster Relief: Narrating the American Welfare State," *Law and Society Review* 33 (1999): 257–318; Dauber, "The Real Third Rail of American Politics." On the New Deal in Puerto Rico, see Manuel R. Rodriguez, *A New Deal for the Tropics: Puerto Rico during the Depression Era, 1932–1935* (Princeton, NJ: Markus Wiener Publishers, 2010).

58. I have provided considerable detail in Schwartz, "The Hurricane of San Ciriaco," 327–34.

59. Foster Rhea Dulles, *The American Red Cross: A History* (New York: Harper & Brothers, 1950).

60. *Boletin administrativo n. 323. Proclama del gobernador de Puerto Rico* (24 Sept. 1928), AGPR, Obras Publicas 166. The activities of the Red Cross in the San Felipe hurricane

were summarized in American Red Cross, *El ciclón que azotó a Puerto Rico septiembre 13, 1928* (San Juan, 1929).

61. Towner, *Twenty-ninth Annual Report of the Governor of Porto Rico*, 3–4.

62. The John R. Beverley papers are housed in the Briscoe Center for American History at the University of Texas (Austin).

63. AGPR, "Tropical Storms and Hurricane Insurance," Of. Gob., caja 1846, 27/15. See also "A Plan for the Protection of the Agriculture of Puerto Rico," report by S. M. Thomson prepared by the Interdepartmental Committee on Puerto Rico.

64. AGPR, Of. Gob., caja 1845; War Dept. to Governor of Puerto Rico (14 Oct. 1932).

65. Frank Antonsanti to Gov. Beverley (22 Nov. 1932), AGPR, Of. Gob., caja 1845.

66. AGPR, Of. Gob., caja 1845 (Sept. 1932). (This letter of Gov. Beverley is made on stationery with the letterhead of the Puerto Rican American Tobacco Company.)

67. Towner to Beverley, 4 Oct. 1932, AGPR, Of. Gob. 27/6.

68. AGPR, Of. Gob., Caja 1845.

69. AGPR, Of. Gob. 27/2.

70. AGPR, Of. Gob. 27/6.

71. Vivas Valdivieso to Gov. Beverley (15 Sep. 1928), AHMP, caja S-282, Newspaper files, *El Aguila de Puerto Rico* (15 Sept. 1928).

72. AGPR, Of. Gob. 255.2 27/6.

73. AGPR, Of. Gob. 255.2 (29 Sept. 1932).

74. Victor S. Clark and Brookings Institution, *Porto Rico and Its Problems* (Washington, DC: Brookings Institution, 1930), xxi.

75. M. Moure de Carmona to Governor, Oct. 1932, AGPR, Of. Gob. Caja 1845.

76. AGPR, Of. Gob. 1845, Asunción Cruz to Gov. Beverley, Caguas, 14 Oct. 1932.

77. J.P. Santana to Gov. Beverley, undated (1932), AGPR, Of. Gob. 1845

78. This letter, along with the related correspondence, is found in AGPR, Of. Gob., Cajas 1845 and 1846.

79. Gordon K. Lewis, *Puerto Rico: Freedom and Power in the Caribbean* (New York: Monthly Review Press, 1963), 68–87.

80. Dauber, *The Sympathetic State*, 185–224. Dauber makes a quantitative analysis of the letters sent to Eleanor Roosevelt.

81. Adi Ophir, "The Two-State Solution: Providence and Catastrophe," *Journal of Homeland Security and Emergency Management* 4, no. 1 (21 March 2007): 1–44.

82. I am using the phrase here only to refer to the growing state response to natural disasters or other emergencies, and not in the sense implied by Ophir that the catastrophic state, which rules by exceptions and the need to discriminate among its inhabitants, is, in effect, the totalitarian state. See ibid., 25–26.

83. For example, Dauber, "Fate, Responsibility, and 'Natural' Disaster Relief"; Dauber, "The Real Third Rail of American Politics"; Dauber, *The Sympathetic State*.

84. Dauber, "The Real Third Rail of American Politics," 65. Opponents of federal involvement in disaster relief always argued that these measures were outside the constitutional responsibility of the federal government and that exceptions were not strictly "relief" and should not constitute a precedent.

85. Leland R. Johnson et al., *Situation Desperate: U.S. Army Engineer Disaster Relief Operations, Origins to 1950* (Alexandria, VA: Office of History, U.S. Army Corps of Engineers, 2011), 17–18.

86. Dauber, "Fate, Responsibility, and 'Natural' Disaster Relief," 273.

87. For example, David B. Woolner and Harry L. Henderson, *FDR and the Environment* (New York: Palgrave Macmillan, 2005); Neil M. Maher, *Nature's New Deal: The Ci-*

vilian Conservation Corps and the Roots of the American Environmental Movement (Oxford: Oxford University Press, 2008).

88. I have based my discussion on part of the extensive literature on this storm. See Thomas Neil Knowles, *Category 5: The 1935 Labor Day Hurricane* (Gainesville: University Press of Florida, 2009); John M. Williams and Iver W. Duedall, *Florida Hurricanes and Tropical Storms, 1871–2001* (Gainesville: University of Florida Press, 2002); Willie Drye, *Storm of the Century: The Labor Day Hurricane of 1935* (Washington, DC: National Geographic Society, 2002); Les Standiford and Henry Morrison Flagler, *Last Train to Paradise: Henry Flagler and the Spectacular Rise and Fall of the Railroad That Crossed the Ocean* (New York: Crown Publishers, 2002); Gary Dean Best, *FDR and the Bonus Marchers, 1933–35* (Westport, CT: Praeger, 1992). I have also used Emanuel, *Divine Wind*. For a concise outline of events, I have also drawn upon Steinberg, *Acts of God*, 48–65. For useful detail, see Jerry Wilkerson, "The Florida Keys Memorial," *Keys Historeum*, 2 Aug. 2013, http://www.keyshistory.org/hurrmemorial.html. Excellent use of the government investigations of the disaster are made in Seiler Christine Kay, "The Veteran Killer: The Florida Emergency Relief Administration and the Labor Day Hurricane of 1935" (Ph.D. dissertation, Florida State University, 2003).

89. Thomas Hibben, Chief Engineer of FERA used this phrase. Cited in Kay, "The Veteran Killer."

90. *Florida Hurricane Disaster. Hearings before the Committee on World War Veterans' Legislation, House of Representatives, Seventy-fourth Congress, Second Session, on H.R. 9486, a Bill for the Relief of Widows, Children and Dependent Parents of World War Veterans Who Died as the Result of the Florida Hurricane at Windley Island and Matecumbe Keys, September 2, 1935* (Washington, DC: Government Printing Office, 1936).

91. David S. Heidler and Jeanne T. Heidler present a detailed and quite critical analysis of how this article fit into Hemingway's biography and how it reflects his inconsistent and somewhat confused political perceptions. See David S. Heidler and Jeanne T. Heidler, " 'You're Dead Now, Brother': Hemingway and the 1935 Labor Day Hurricane," *David S. and Jeanne T. Heidler American Historians*, 1 Sept. 2010, http://djheidler.com/~djheid5/Blog/~%281%29~Hurricane.htm.

92. Colonel Ijams's testimony appears in *Florida Hurricane Disaster. Hearings before the Committee on World War Veterans' Legislation, House of Representatives, . . . September 2, 1935*, 375–87.

93. Wilkerson, "The Florida Keys Memorial."

CHAPTER 8. PUBLIC STORMS, COMMUNAL ACTION, AND PRIVATE GRIEF

1. "1944—Great Atlantic Hurricane," *Hurricane: Science and Society*, n.d., http://www.hurricanescience.org/history/storms/1940s/GreatAtlantic/.

2. Sheets and Williams, *Hurricane Watch*, 125–42. A number of this important generation of hurricane scientists and students like Bob Sheets himself and the historian David Ludlum had been trained in the military during or following World War II.

3. Chapter 5 ("The 1950s") of Sheets and Williams, *Hurricane Watch*, provides a useful and detailed narrative of the scientific, technological, and institutional advances of the postwar period. See also the useful narrative summary in Arsenault, "The Public Storm," 275–83.

4. James Rodger Fleming deals with the general scientific and ethical issues that climate manipulation raises. See Fleming, *Fixing the Sky: The Checkered History of Weather and Climate Control* (New York: Columbia University Press, 2010).

5. Fleming also presents the long history of human attempts to modify the environ-

ment and the usual disregard for moral implications or unexpected physical consequences.

6. Stanley A. Chagnon, "Factors affecting temporal fluctuations in damaging storm activity in the United States based on insurance loss data," *Meteorological Applications* 6, no. 1 (1999):1–10; Roger Pielke Jr., Joel Gratz, Christopher Landsea, et al., "Normalized Hurricane Damage in the United States, 1900–2005," *Natural Hazards Review* 9, no. 1 (2008): 29–42.

7. I have relied here on Fitzpatrick, *Natural Disasters: Hurricanes*, 71–96.

8. Steinberg, *Acts of God*, 185–87.

9. Naming practices vary according to the world region. At present the Atlantic uses six lists of 21 male and female names that are repeated after six years. Names of particularly memorable storms are sometimes retired and replaced. If more than 21 storms appear in a year, the letters of the Greek alphabet are used.

10. Many of the early Hurricane Hunter flights were made with World War II aircraft like the B-29 that were available for conversion to civilian purposes in the 1950s.

11. The International Meteorological Organization had been founded in 1873. See Fortuné, *Cyclones et autres cataclysmes aux Antilles*.

12. The key study of this organization is Denise D. P. Thompson, "Building Effectiveness in Multi-State Disaster Management Systems: The Case of the Caribbean Disaster and Emergency Response Agency" (Ph.D. dissertation, Pennsylvania State University, 2010). See also www.cderma.org and "Caribbean Disaster Emergency Management Agency," *Wikipedia, the Free Encyclopedia*, http://en.wikipedia.org/w/index.php?title=Caribbean_Disaster_Emergency_Management_Agency&oldid=565071598.

13. Higman, *A Concise History of the Caribbean*, 275–79.

14. Luis Pales Matos, "La plena de menéalo," reprinted in *La Revista de Centro de Estudios Avanzados de Puerto Rico y el Caribe* 2 (1986): 81–82.

> Bochinche de viento y agua . . .
> Sobre el mar
> Está la Antilla bailando
> —de aquí payá, de ayá pacá
> Menéalo, menéalo
> En el huracán
> . . .
> ¡Pará que rabie el Tío Sam!

15. Scarano, *Puerto Rico*, 779.

16. Salivia, *Historia de los temporales de Puerto Rico y Las Antillas, 1492 a 1970*, 332; Edwin Miner Solá, *Historia de los huracanes en Puerto Rico* (San Juan,: First Book, 1995), 40–42.

17. Salivia, *Historia de los temporales* 321–30. I have followed his account closely.

18. A document ("Resumen de los datos. . . .") exists in the files of the FMM, section V, series 16, dated 13 Sept. 1956 (the day after the hurricane), which summarizes newspaper accounts in *La Democracia* and *El Mundo* of the government's response to the 1932 storm.

19. "Mensaje radial del gobernador del ELA (14 Aug. 1956), FMM, section V, series 16, subsection 29.

20. A. W. Maldonado, *Luis Muñoz Marín: Puerto Rico's Democratic Revolution* (San Juan: Editorial Universidad de Puerto Rico, 2006), 335.

21. Ermelindo Santiago to Luís Muñoz Marín, FMM, Section V, series 16, subsection 29.

22. FMM, Section V, series 16, subsection 29, Rivera Rodriguez to Muñoz Marín (15 Aug. 1956).

23. Ibid., Muñoz Marín to Rosa Rodrigues Rivera (14 Sept. 1956).

24. Dwight D. Eisenhower, "Remarks on Drought and Other Natural Disasters. McConnell Air Force Base, Wichita, Kansas," ed. John T. Wooley and Gerhardt Peters, *The American Presidency Project*, 15 Jan. 1957, http://www.presidency.ucsb.edu/wc/?pid=10823#axzz2hCN1AmZM.

25. Rudolph Homère Victor, "Cette nuit là les portes del'enfer s'étaient en'ouvertes," *Mr. Météo: Toutes les infos météos*, 31 May 2013, http://mrmeteo.info/site/2013/05/31/cette-nuit-la-les-portes-de-lenfer-setaient-entrouvertes/.

26. Gordon E. Dunn, "The Hurricane Season of 1963," *Monthly Weather Review* 92, no. 3 (1965): 128–37.

27. Laurent Dubois, *Haiti: The Aftershocks of History* (New York: Metropolitan Books, 2012), 335–50.

28. Ibid., 335–36.

29. Hurricane Edith had caused considerable damage in St. Lucia and Dominica, and in Martinique, it killed ten people, injured fifty, and caused $40 million in damages. The storm had weakened over the Lesser Antilles before it reached Santo Domingo. See Dunn, "The Hurricane Season of 1963," 132–33.

30. "nunca se repartieron ni nadie las ha visto," AGNRD, Fondo Presidencial 13288, 20157–28.

31. There is an excellent political memoir of this period by the U.S. ambassador. See John Bartlow Martin, *Overtaken by Events: The Dominican Crisis from the Fall of Trujillo to the Civil War* (New York: Doubleday, 1966), especially 546–90.

32. Ibid., 585.

33. Christian Webersik and Christian Klose, "Environmental Change and Political Instability in Haiti and the Dominican Republic: Explaining the Divide," paper presented to the Conference on Computer Supported Cooperative Work Workshop, 16–17 Dec. 2010, http://file.no/files/projects/workinggroup/webersik_CSCW_WG_3_workshop_dec10.pdf.

34. The rumor about Trujillo's fear of hurricanes is noted in Martin, *Overtaken*, 585. Trujillo was in contact with Joseph O'Brien, a New York engineer, who had created a New York Waterway Research Society and who wanted to create the Franklin Science Center. O'Brien had a theory that the energy in hurricanes and the electrical and magnetic energy developed by the earth were related and that concern with air pressure variables was misguided. O'Brien's real interest was the creation of a canal from the East coast to the Great Lakes and from Lake Superior to Hudson's Bay, but he sought Trujillo's financial support as well for the hurricane study. See O'Brien to Trujillo (14 Sept. 1955), AGNRD, Fondo Presidencial, caja 13288, 20157–28.

35. Denis Watson, "Menaces hydrométéorologiques et risques géophysiques en Haiti," *Revue de La Société Haïtienne d'Histoire, de Géographie et de Géologie* nos. 241–44 (2011): 31–66. Haiti suffered at least 20 major natural disasters in the twentieth century. Denis's article concentrates on events in the last decade, but his observations are applicable to the previous century as well.

36. Osviel Castro Medel, "Ciclón Flora en Cuba: El lazo mortal," 4 Oct. 2010, http://osvielcastro.wordpress.com/2010/10/04/ciclon-flora-en-cuba-el-lazo-mortal-i/.

37. Juan Almeida Bosque, *Contra el agua y el viento* (Havana: Ediciones Verde Olivo, 2002), 24–25.

38. See Rebecca Solnit, *A Paradise Built in Hell: The Extraordinary Communities That Arise in Disasters* (New York: Viking, 2009).

39. Julio García Luis, "Hurricane Flora (October 4, 1963)," in *Cuban Revolution Reader: a Documentary History of 40 Key Moments of the Cuban Revolution* (Melbourne: Ocean Press 2001), 129–33. See also Castro's important speech "Informe sobre el paso del ciclón Flora por las provincias de Camagüey y Oriente por la cadena Nacional de Radio y Televisión (21 Oct. 1963)," in *Obra revolucionaria* 27 (1963): 7–25.

40. Michael Chanan, *Cuban Cinema* (Minneapolis: University of Minnesota Press, 2004), 22.

41. Che Guevara, "Socialism and Man in Cuba," in *Manifesto: Three Classic Essays on How to Change the World* (Melbourne: Ocean, 2005).

42. Fidel Castro, "Discurso pronunciado en la conmemoración del VI aniversario de los CDR" (Plaza de la Revolución, Havana, 28 Sept. 1966), http://www.cuba.cu /gobierno/discursos/1966/esp/f280966e.html.

43. See Fidel Castro, "Discurso en el acto por la conmemoración del Instituto Nacional de Recursos Hidráulicos" (10 Aug. 1963), *Obra revolucionaria,* 21 (1963), 29–40. Thomas, *Cuba,* 1479.

44. Maurice Halperin, *The Rise and Decline of Fidel Castro: An Essay in Contemporary History.* (Berkeley: University of California Press, 1972), 285–86.

45. "The Effects of Hurricane Flora on Cuba," Special National Intelligence Estimate, 85–3-63 (15 Nov. 1963), LBJ Library, Case NLJ 94–29, doc. 5.

46. Cuban sugar production actually rose between 1962 and 1965. The figures in thousands of tons are: 1962, 51.6; 1963, 52.6; 1964, 60.1; 1965, 65.1. Thomas, *Cuba,* Appendix 3, 1560–64. On the effects of Flora on agricultural policy in Cuba, see Amelia Estrada, "'Y Vino Dos Veces': Hurricane Flora and Revolutionary Cuba at the Crossroads" (paper presented at the American Historical Association Annual Meeting, San Francisco, 2002).

47. "Cuba, Haiti, and Flora," editorial, *The New York Times,* 8 Oct. 1963.

48. President Kennedy insisted that the contacts be kept secret. A list of relevant documents about the initiation of a dialogue between Cuba and the United States on improving relations can be found at the web page National Security Archive, George Washington University, http://www2.gwu.edu/ñsarchiv/index.html.

49. Miró Cardona to Pablo Le-Riverend, San Juan, 23 Oct. 1963, Cuban Heritage Collection, University of Miami Libraries, box 26, folder 2. (My thanks to Michael Bustamante for this reference.)

50. Martha Thompson and Izaskun Gaviria, *Cuba Weathering the Storm: Lessons in Risk Reduction from Cuba* (Boston: Oxfam America, 2004), 8–9. See also José Carlos Lezcano, "Aspectos esenciales sobre la mitigación de los desastres naturales en Cuba," in *Cuba in Transition* (Miami: Association for the Study of the Cuban Economy, 1995), 5:399–406; José Alvarez, *The Potential Correlation between Natural Disasters and Cuba's Agricultural Performance* (Gainesville: Department of Food and Resource Economics, Florida Cooperative Extension Service, University of Florida, 2004), http://edis.ifas .ufl.edu/fe490.

51. Robert J. Brym, *Sociology as a Life or Death Issue* (Toronto: Pearson, 2008), 67.

52. Such criticism appears in Holly Sims and Kevin Vogelmann, "Popular Mobilization and Disaster Management in Cuba," *Public Administration and Development* 22, no. 5 (2002): 389–400. See also Thompson and Gaviria, *Cuba Weathering the Storm.*

53. Keyser and Smith present a positive view of the Cuban disaster mitigation system, while B. E. Aguirre recognizes Cuba's success in preparation for disasters, but criticizes its failures in post-disaster reconstruction. See Jonathan Keyser and Wayne Smith, *Disaster Relief Management in Cuba*, Center for International Policy, 18 May 2009, http://www.ciponline.org/research/html/disaster-relief-management-in-cuba; B. E. Aguirre, "Cuba's Disaster Management Model: Should It Be Emulated?" *International Journal of Mass Emergencies and Disasters* 23, no. 3 (2005): 55–71. Much of Aguirre's critique seems to lie on the nature of the Cuban political system as such and on "the long political dictatorship of Mr. Castro." See also Sergio Díaz-Briquets, "The Enduring Cuban Housing Crisis: The Impact of Hurricanes," Papers and Proceedings of the Fifth Annual Meeting of the Association for the Study of the Cuban Economy (ASCE), 429–41, http://www.ascecuba.org/publications/proceedings/volume19/.

54. Quoted in Sergio Diaz-Briquets and Jorge F Pérez-López, *Conquering Nature: The Environmental Legacy of Socialism in Cuba* (Pittsburgh, PA: University of Pittsburgh Press, 2000), 1–23. Much of their criticism is political in nature.

55. See, for example, the 1994 interview given by Castro in Barbados following the UN Global Conference on that island. Latin American Network Information Center, Castro Speech Data Base. See also Fidel Castro, *Fidel Castro: My Life*, ed. Ignacio Ramonet (New York: Scribner, 2008), 355–56, 396–400.

56. This was especially true after NOAA's creation of HURDAT (Atlantic Basin Hurricane Data Base), which now includes data from 1851 to the present.

57. Johan Nyberg et al., "Low Atlantic Hurricane Activity in the 1970s and 1980s Compared to the Past 270 Years," *Nature*, 447, no. 7145 (7 June 2007): 698–701. See also "Hurricanes: The Greatest Storms on Earth," http://earthobservatory.nasa.gov/Features/Hurricanes/hurricanes_3.php.

58. Roger A. Pielke Jr. et al., "Hurricanes and Global Warming," *Bulletin of the American Meteorological Society* 86, no. 11 (Nov. 2005): 1571–75; P. J. Webster et al., "Changes in Tropical Cyclone Number, Duration, and Intensity in a Warming Environment," *Science* 309, no. 5742 (16 Sept. 2005): 1844–46. See also J. Marshall Shepherd and Thomas Knutson, "The Current Debate on the Linkage between Global Warming and Hurricanes," *Geography Compass* 1:1 (2007): 1–24; Thomas R. Knutson et al., "Tropical Cyclones and Climate Change," *Nature Geoscience*, 3, no. 3 (March 2010): 157–63.

59. Mooney, *Storm World*.

60. The controversy of hurricane climatology has been ably presented in ibid.

61. Knutson et al., "Tropical Cyclones and Climate Change."

62. Shepherd and Knutson, "The Current Debate on the Linkage between Global Warming and Hurricanes."

63. Roger A. Pielke Jr. et al., "Hurricane Vulnerability in Latin America and the Caribbean: Normalized Damage and Loss Potentials," *Natural Hazards Review* 4, no. 3 (2003): 101–14.

64. Ronald Reagan, *Reagan: a Life in Letters*, ed. Martin Anderson, Annelise Anderson, and Kiron K. Skinner (New York: Free Press, 2003), 664.

65. Daniel T. Rodgers, *Age of Fracture* (Cambridge, MA: Belknap Press of Harvard University Press, 2011), 180–202, http://site.ebrary.com/id/10456081.

66. Mark Kurlansky, *A Continent of Islands: Searching for the Caribbean Destiny* (Reading, MA: Addison-Wesley, 1992), 34–40.

67. David Barker and David Miller, "Hurricane Gilbert: Anthropomorphising a Natural Disaster," *Area* 22, no. 2 (June 1, 1990): 107–16. The current record low pressure of 26.05 inches (882 mb) is held by hurricane Wilma (2005).

68. Ibid., 108.

69. Kevin J. Grove, "From Emergency Management to Managing Emergence: A Genealogy of Disaster Management in Jamaica," *Annals of the Association of American Geographers* 103, no. 3 (2013): 570–88.

70. World Bank and United Nations, *Natural Hazards, Unnatural Disaster: The Economics of Effective Prevention* (Washington, DC: World Bank, 2010), 16–18.

71. ODPEM, http://www.odpem.org.jm/ArticleDetails/tabid/226.

72. Mr. Needham quoted in *Daily Gleaner*, 18 Sept. 1988, excerpted in Barker and Miller, "Hurricane Gilbert," 114.

73. Kurlansky, *A Continent of Islands*, 35–36.

74. The lyrics of "Wild Gilbert" are available at www.elyrics.net/read/l/lloyd-lovindeer.

75. Solnit, *A Paradise*, 267–304.

76. JA, 1B/38/1/14, Errington George Green, Sole Commissioner, "Report of the Commission of Enquiry (27 February 1993)," chapter 1.

77. Laura Tanna, "On Development and Losing Elections," *Jamaica Gleaner Online*, 14 March 2010, http://jamaica-gleaner.com/gleaner/20100314/arts/arts4.html.

78. Walter J. Fraser, *Lowcountry Hurricanes: Three Centuries of Storms at Sea and Ashore* (Athens: University of Georgia Press, 2006), 247.

79. An excellent—if critical—political overview of U.S. policy in this era is provided in Greg Grandin, *Empire's Workshop: Latin America, the United States, and the Rise of the New Imperialism*, The American Empire Project (New York: Owl Books, 2007).

80. Sébastien Hardy, "Risque naturel et vulnérabilité: Un analyse de la catastrophe de Posoltega (30 octobre 1998)," in *Nicaragua, dans l'oeil du cyclone*, ed. Joël Delhom and Alain Musset (Paris: Institut des Hautes Etudes de l'Amérique Latine, 2000), 41–52.

81. Pielke Jr. et al., "Hurricane Vulnerability in Latin America."

82. Manuel Torres, *Huracán Mitch, 1998–2003: Retrato social de una tragedia natural* (Tegucigalpa: Centro de Documentación de Honduras, 2004), 1.

83. Alain Musset, "Entre cyclones et tremblement de terre: Le Nicaragua face au risqué naturel," in *Nicaragua, dans l'oeil du cyclone*, ed. Joel Delhom and Alain Musset (Paris: Institut des Hautes Etudes de l'Amérique Latine, 2000), 34–35.

84. An excellent summary of the effects of Hurricane Mitch based on UN reports is Marisa Olivo Ensor and Bradley E. Ensor, "Hurricane Mitch: Root Causes and Responses to the Disaster," in *The Legacy of Hurricane Mitch: Lessons from Post-Disaster Reconstruction in Honduras*, ed. Marisa Olivo Ensor (Tucson: University of Arizona Press, 2009), 22–46.

85. The conservative Cato Institute think tank argued that such claims of "hypercanes" were unproven and alarmist, a result of "White House huckstering" by the Clinton administration. See Patrick J. Michaels, "Mitch, That Sun of a Gun," *Cato Institute*, 15 Dec. 1998, http://www.cato.org/publications/commentary/mitch-sun-gun.

86. Ensor and Ensor, "Hurricane Mitch," 32–33, 42.

87. Daniel Steadman Jones, *Masters of the Universe: Hayek, Friedman and the Birth of Neoliberal Politics* (Princeton, NJ: Princeton University Press, 2012), 297–329.

88. Torres, *Huracán Mitch*, 27–30.

89. *Hurricane Mitch and Nicaragua*, Special Publication 38 (Boulder, CO: Natural Hazards Research and Applications Information Center Institute of Behavioral Science University of Colorado, n.d.), 4–6, http://www.colorado.edu/hazards/publications/sp/sp38/part4.html.

90. Vilma Elisa Fuentes, "Post-Disaster Reconstruction," in *The Legacy of Hurricane*

Mitch: Lessons from Post-disaster Reconstruction in Honduras, ed. Marisa Olivo Ensor (Tucson: University of Arizona Press, 2009), 100–28; Catherine Ambler, "The Distribution of Emergency Relief in Post Hurricane Mitch Nicaragua" (B.A. thesis, Williams College, 2003).

91. Consultative Group for the Reconstruction and Transformation of Central America, "Central America after Hurricane Mitch: The Challenge of Turning a Disaster into an Opportunity," *Inter-American Development Bank*, n.d.

92. Naomi Klein, *The Shock Doctrine: The Rise of Disaster Capitalism* (New York: Metropolitan Books/Henry Holt, 2007), 501.

93. Cited in ibid. The statement was made at a meeting of the World Economic Forum in 1999.

94. Alexander Cockburn and Jeffrey St. Clair, "The Politics of Hurricane Mitch," *Counterpunch*, 15 June 1999, http://www.counterpunch.org/1999/06/15/the-politics -of-hurricane-mitch/.

95. This is the basic argument for Steinberg, *Acts of God*, 201.

96. Bruce B. Clary, "The Evolution and Structure of Natural Hazard Policies," *Public Administration Review* 45 (1985): 20–28.

97. On the diminished impact of hurricanes on the GDP of the United States, see Roger M. Vogel, "Natural Disaster and U.S. Economic Growth: 1952–2009," *International Journal of Humanities and Social Science* 1:14 (2011): 46–50; Arsenault, "The Public Storm," 278–82. Disaster impact on small island nations tends to be much greater. See Economic Commission for Latin America and the Caribbean, "Caribbean Small States, Vulnerability and Development," 2005, http://www.eclac.cl/cgi-bin/getProd.asp?xml =/publicaciones/xml/8/23558/P23558.xml&xsl=/portofspain/tpl-i/p9f.xsl&base =/portofspain/tpl/top-bottom.xsl.

98. Andy Horowitz, "Help: Hurricane Betsy and the Politics of Disaster in New Orleans' Lower Ninth Ward, 1965–1967" (unpublished paper).

99. John Barry, *Rising Tide: The Great Mississippi Flood of 1927 and How It Changed America* (New York: Simon and Schuster, 1997).

100. The basic facts of the storm are recounted in Mark M. Smith, *Camille: 1969 Histories of a Hurricane* (Athens: University of Georgia Press, 2011), 17–35.

101. This was a position much like that taken in 1867 by Senator Charles Sumner, who wanted no federal funds sent to flooded towns along the Mississippi River until the loyalty to the Union of Mississippi and other southern states was assured by their adherence to republican principles, including the voting franchise and free public schools for all. Panetta was a Republican at this time. He became a Democrat in 1971, later serving in Congress.

102. On the problems of disaster management before and after Hugo, see Roy Popkin and Claire Rubin, *Disaster Recovery after Hurricane Hugo in South Carolina* (Washington, DC: Center for International Science, Technology, and Public Policy, George Washington University, 1990), www.colorado.edu/hazards/publications/wp/wp69.pdf.

103. Murray Newton Rothbard, "Government and Hurricane Hugo: A Deadly Combination," in *Making Economic Sense* (Auburn, AL: Ludwig von Mises Institute, 1995), http://www.mises.org/econsense/ch26.asp.

104. Lynee McChristian, *Hurricane Andrew and Insurance: The Enduring Impact of an Historic Storm* (New York: Insurance Information Institute, Aug. 2012), http://www .insuringflorida.org/assets/docs/pdf/paper_HurricaneAndrew_final.pdf.

105. The story of FEMA's mismanagement and concentration on plans for taking over the government in case of attack is detailed in Christopher Cooper and Robert

Block, *Disaster: Hurricane Katrina and the Failure of Homeland Security* (New York: Times Books, 2006), 45–66.

106. Van Heerden and Bryan, *The Storm*, 138–40.

107. "Hurricane Andrew 20th Anniversary Is a Reminder to Prepare for Emergencies," *Federal Emergency Management Agency*, 22 Aug. 2012, http://www.fema.gov /news-release/2012/08/22/hurricane-andrew-20th-anniversary-reminder-prepare -emergencies. On the effect of Hurricane Andrew on local politics, see David K. Twigg, *The Politics of Disaster: Tracking the Impact of Hurricane Andrew* (Gainesville: University Press of Florida, 2012).

108. James Surowiecki, "Disaster Economics," *The New Yorker*, 3 Dec. 2012 (http:// www.newyorker.com/talk/financial/2012/12/03/121203ta_talk_surowiecki). Estimates of savings are sometimes higher.

109. Van Heerden and Bryan, *The Storm*, 139; Cooper and Block, *Disaster*, 86–87. An article critical of the political use of disaster relief through FEMA by two economists demonstrated that Presidents Reagan, George H.W. Bush, Clinton, and George W. Bush all declared more disasters in reelection years than in any other year of their incumbency. The authors suggested the advantages of the private sector taking over the administration of disaster relief. Thomas A. Garrett and Russell S. Sobel, "The Political Economy of FEMA Disaster Payments," *Economic Inquiry* 41, no. 3 (2003): 496–509.

110. Eric Holdeman, "Destroying FEMA," *Washington Post*, 30 Aug. 2005, sec. Opinions (http://www.washingtonpost.com/wp-dyn/content/article/2005/08/29 /AR2005082901445.html).

CHAPTER 9. ANCIENT STORMS IN A NEW CENTURY

1. The literature on Hurricane Katrina is overwhelming. A keyword search in the Yale University library database yields 1,074 items excluding the periodical literature and scholarly articles, principally books and government reports. I have found useful overviews in Cooper and Block, *Disaster*; Van Heerden and Bryan, *The Storm*; Michael Eric Dyson, *Come Hell or High Water: Hurricane Katrina and the Color of Disaster* (New York: Basic Civitas Books, 2006); William R. Freudenburg et al., *Catastrophe in the Making: The Engineering of Katrina and the Disasters of Tomorrow* (Washington, DC: Island Press/Shearwater Books, 2009); Ronald J. Daniels, Donald F. Kettl, and Howard Kunreuther, *On Risk and Disaster: Lessons from Hurricane Katrina* (Philadelphia: University of Pennsylvania Press, 2006); Robert J. Brym, "Hurricane Katrina and the Myth of Natural Disasters," in *Sociology as a Life or Death Issue* (Toronto: Pearson, 2008), 53–80.

2. Roger D. Congleton, *The Story of Katrina: New Orleans and the Political Economy of Catastrophe*, SSRN Scholarly Paper (Rochester, NY: Social Science Research Network, 2006), http://papers.ssrn.com/abstract=908046; Craig E Colten, *An Unnatural Metropolis: Wresting New Orleans from Nature* (Baton Rouge: Louisiana State University Press, 2005).

3. Colten, *An Unnatural Metropolis*, 14–15.

4. NOAA Technological Memorandum NWS TPC-4 "The Deadliest, Costliest, and Most Intense United States Hurricanes from 1851–2004," cited in Congleton, *The Story of Katrina*, 12.

5. On the negative effects of the work of the Corps of Engineers and the program of engineered water systems, see Freudenburg et al., *Catastrophe in the Making*, 91–135.

6. Richard Campanella, "An Ethnic Geography of New Orleans," *Journal of American History*, 94, no. 3 (Dec. 2007): 704–15.

7. Elizabeth Fussell, "Constructing New Orleans, Constructing Race: A Population History of New Orleans," *Journal of American History* 94, no. 3 (Dec. 2007): 846–55.

8. Ewen McCallum and Julian Heming, "Hurricane Katrina: An Environmental Perspective," *Philosophical Transactions of the Royal Society A: Mathematical, Physical and Engineering Sciences* 364, no. 1845 (15 Aug. 2006): 2099–15.

9. Van Heerden and Bryan, *The Storm*, 21–32.

10. Romain Huret, "L'ouragan Katrina et l'Etat federal américain: Une hypothèse de recherche," *Nuevo Mundo Mundos Nuevos. Nouveaux mondes mondes nouveaux* (8 May 2007), http://nuevomundo.revues.org/3928.

11. D'Ann R. Penner and Keith C. Ferdinand, *Overcoming Katrina: African American Voices from the Crescent City and Beyond* (New York: Palgrave Macmillan, 2009), 137.

12. William F. Shughart II, "Katrinanomics: The Politics and Economics of Disaster Relief," *Public Choice* 127, no. 1/2 (April 2006): 31–53. Shughart argues that the Katrina disaster was evidence of "American dependency on the public sector." He agrees that there were institutional failures during Katrina, but presents an argument that government is always ineffective, that spending on infrastructure will not boost the economy, and that the fact that FedEx and Wal-Mart did a better job in meeting the challenge than did FEMA demonstrates that free market economics is the best solution to natural disasters. He goes so far as to suggest that federal or state aid to victims for rebuilding creates a "moral hazard" of dependency that only encourages worse disasters in the future. He also claims that there was no evidence of racial bias in the response failures, and that imposing minimum wage standards in the rebuilding process disadvantaged minority contractors.

13. Congleton, *The Story of Katrina*, 18–19; Erik Auf der Heide, "Common Misconceptions about Disasters: Panic, the 'Disaster Syndrome' and Looting," in *The First 72 Hours: A Community Approach to Disaster Preparedness*, ed. Margaret O'Leary (New York: iUniverse, 2004), 340–80.

14. Dyson, *Come Hell or High Water*, 14–15. Cf. Cooper and Block, *Disaster*, 206–61; Paul Krugman, "A Katrina Mystery Explained," *New York Times Blog: The Conscience of a Liberal*, 17 May 2009, http://krugman.blogs.nytimes.com/2009/05/17/a-katrina-mystery-explained/.

15. Penner and Ferdinand, *Overcoming Katrina*.

16. Auf der Heide, "Common Misconceptions about Disasters."

17. Penner and Ferdinand, *Overcoming Katrina*, 204–10.

18. Maura Fitzgerald, *What Was Found: New Orleans after the Storm* (2007). A class project done at Yale University and now on deposit in the Beinecke Library at Yale University.

19. Eric Steiger, "L'ouragan Katrina: Les leçons d'un échec: Les faiblesses du dispositif de sécurité intérieure des Etats-Unis," *La Revue Géopolitique*, 1 Jan. 2008, http://www.diploweb.com/L-ouragan-Katrina-les-lecons-d-un.html.

20. This phrase is used by Romain Huret, "La fin de l'État Providence? Un bilan de la politique sociale de George W. Bush," *Vingtième Siècle* no. 97 (Jan. 2008): 105–16. See also his "L'ouragan Katrina."

21. Henry A. Giroux, "Reading Hurricane Katrina: Race, Class, and the Biopolitics of Disposability," *College Literature* 33, no. 3 (July 2006): 171–96. Santorum subsequently retracted his remarks.

22. *Huffington Post*, 12 Sept. 2005.

23. Klein, *The Shock Doctrine*.

24. Cf. Paul Krugman, "Katrina All the Time," *New York Times*, 31 Aug. 2007, sec. Opinion (http://www.nytimes.com/2007/08/31/opinion/31krugman.html); Robert Tracinski, "Katrina y el estado de beneficencia," *TIADaily.com*, 2 Sept. 2005 (http://www.contra-mundum.org/castellano/tracinski/Katr_EdoBenef.pdf).

25. Michael Lewis, "In Nature's Casino," *New York Times*, 26 Aug. 2007.

26. Vicki Bier, "Hurricane Katrina as a Bureaucratic Disaster," in *On Risk and Disaster: Lessons from Hurricane Katrina*, ed. Ronald J Daniels, Donald F Kettl, and Howard Kunreuther (Philadelphia:University of Pennsylvania Press, 2006), 243–55; Tracinski, "Katrina y el estado de beneficencia."

27. Brym, "Hurricane Katrina and the Myth of Natural Disasters."

28. Ibid., 62–64. Brym presents data from 1980–2000 that demonstrates high or low vulnerability to hurricane fatalities for 34 countries based on deaths relative to population at risk. During that period, Australia, New Zealand, Cuba, Japan, Mexico, and China all had vulnerabilities lower than expected, while Vietnam, Bangladesh, Honduras, Nicaragua, and India had higher than expected hurricane fatalities. The United States had an average of 222 hurricane-related deaths per year, while Japan (a country with more people exposed to that hazard) had 39. Cuba had an average of only 3 deaths per year during this period.

29. Ibid., 62–64. Matthew Kahn argues that wealth is the key element in reducing fatalities and thus, he implies, further capitalist development is the best protection against an increase in natural disasters due to global warming. Matthew E. Kahn, "The Death Toll from Natural Disasters: The Role of Income, Geography, and Institutions," *Review of Economics and Statistics* 87: 2 (May 2005): 271–84.

30. Economic Commission for Latin America and the Caribbean, "Caribbean Small States, Vulnerability and Development" (Nov. 2005), http://www.eclac.cl/cgi-bin/getProd.asp?xml=/publicaciones/xml/8/23558/P23558.xml&xsl=/portofspain/tpl-i/p9f.xsl&base=/portofspain/tpl/top-bottom.xsl.

31. The IMF definition of a natural disaster is that it kills at least 10 people and affects at least 100, or that a state of emergency had been declared. See *Caribbean Small States: Challenges of High Debt and Low Growth* (Washington, DC: International Monetary Fund, 20 Feb. 2013).

32. Krugman, "Sandy versus Katrina," *New York Times*, 4 Nov. 2012, sec. Opinion (http://www.nytimes.com/2012/11/05/opinion/krugman-sandy-versus-katrina.html).

33. Brett Martel, "Storms Payback from God," *Washington Post*, 17 Jan. 2006.

34. Rebecca Leber, "Chris Christie Denies Climate Change Has Anything to Do with Hurricane Sandy," Climate Progress, 21 May 2013, http://thinkprogress.org/climate/2013/05/21/2039811/christie-climate-change-sandy/.

35. Patricia Levi, "Hurricane Sandy Climate Change: Andrew Cuomo Rightly Raises Global Warming Issue," *PolicyMic*, 2 Nov. 2012, http://www.policymic.com/articles/17930/hurricane-sandy-climate-change-andrew-cuomo-rightly-raises-global-warming-issue.

36. Eleanor Randolph, "What if the Flood Maps Are Just Plain Wrong?" *New York Times*, 6 Dec. 2013, Opinion page.

37. Pielke Jr. et al., "Hurricane Vulnerability in Latin America," 112.

38. Emmarie Huettiman, "Rubio on a Presidential Bid, and Climate Change," *New York Times*, 12 May 2014.

Bibliography of Works Consulted

ↄ◎ⓒↄ

PUBLISHED WORKS

"1944—Great Atlantic Hurricane." *Hurricane: Science and Society*, n.d. http://www
.hurricanescience.org/history/storms/1940s/GreatAtlantic/.

Abbad y Lasierra, Iñigo. *Historia geográfica, civil y natural de la Isla de San Juan Bautista de
Puerto Rico*, 3rd ed. San Juan: Ediciones de la Universidad de Puerto Rico, 1970.

———. *Historia geográfica, civil y natural de la Isla de San Juan Bautista de Puerto Rico*, edited by Jose Julian de Acosta y Calbo and Gervasio Garcia. San Juan: Doce Calles,
2002.

Abénon, Lucien-René. *La Guadeloupe de 1671 à 1759: Étude politique, économique et sociale.*
Paris: L'Harmattan, 1987.

———. "Ouragans et cyclones à la Guadeloupe au XVIIIe siècle: Le problème alimen-
taire." In *Les catastrophes naturelles aux Antilles: D'une Soufrière à une autre*, edited by
Alain Yacou, 163–71. Paris: Editions Karthala, 1999.

Abulafia, David. *The Great Sea: A Human History of the Mediterranean.* New York: Oxford
University Press, 2011.

Account of the Fatal Hurricane, by which Barbados Suffered in August 1831. Bridgetown:
Printed for Samuel Hyde, 1831.

Acevedo Vázquez, Juan. "1899: Los Cagüeños en San Ciriaco." *Caguas* (December 1999):
39–41.

Acosta, José de. *Natural and Moral History of the Indies*, edited by Jane E. Mangan; translated by Frances López-Morillas. Durham, NC: Duke University Press, 2002.

Actas capitulares del Ayuntamiento de la Habana. Vol. 1584–1599. Havana: Municipio de la
Habana, 1937.

Adas, Michael. *Machines as the Measure of Men: Science, Technology, and Ideologies of Western Dominance.* Ithaca, NY: Cornell University Press, 1989.

Adorno, Rolena, and Patrick Charles Pautz. *Alvar Núñez Cabeza de Vaca: His Account,
His Life, and the Expedition of Pánfilo de Narváez.* Lincoln: University of Nebraska
Press, 1999.

Adrien, Peter. *Metayage, Capitalism and Peasant Development in St. Lucia, 1840–1957.*
Mona, Jamaica: Consortium Graduate School of Social Sciences, University of the
West Indies, 1996.

Aguilera, Jesús. "Los huracanes del Caribe (1875–1980)." *Tierra Firme* 2, no. 7 (1984):
371–80.

Aguirre, B. E. "Cuba's Disaster Management Model: Should It Be Emulated?" *International Journal of Mass Emergencies and Disasters* 23, no. 3 (2005): 55–71.

Ahvenainen, Jorma. *The History of the Caribbean Telegraphs before the First World War.*
Helsinki: Suomalainen Tiedeakatemia, 1996.

Alegría, Ricardo E., ed. *Documentos históricos de Puerto Rico*. 5 vols. San Juan: Centro de Estudios Avanzados de Puerto Rico y el Caribe, 2009.

Alfau Durán, Vetilio. "Los principals huracanes habidos en Santo Domingo." In *Vetilio Alfau Durán en el Listín diario: Escritos*, edited by Arístides Incháustegui and Blanca Delgado Malagón. Santo Domingo, DR: Secretaría de Estado de Educación, Bellas Artes y Cultos, 1994.

Almeida Bosque, Juan. *Contra el agua y el viento*. Havana: Ediciones Verde Olivo, 2002.

Altez, Rogelio. *El desastre de 1812 en Venezuela: Sismos, vulnerabilidades y una patria no tan boba*. Caracas: Fundación Empresas Polar, 2006.

———. *Si la naturaleza se opone: Terremotos, historia y sociedad en Venezuela*. Caracas: Editorial Alfa, 2010.

Alvarez, José. *The Potential Correlation between Natural Disasters and Cuba's Agricultural Performance*. Gainesville: Department of Food and Resource Economics, Florida Cooperative Extension Service, University of Florida, 2004. http://edis.ifas.ufl.edu/fe490.

Ambler, Catherine. "The Distribution of Emergency Relief in Post Hurricane Mitch Nicaragua." B.A. thesis, Williams College, 2003.

American Red Cross. *El ciclón que azotó a Puerto Rico septiembre 13, 1928*. San Juan, 1929.

———. *The West Indies Hurricane Disaster*. Washington, DC, 1928.

Anderson, Mark D. *Disaster Writing: The Cultural Politics of Catastrophe in Latin America*. Charlottesville: University of Virginia Press, 2011.

Andrews, Kenneth R. *The Spanish Caribbean: Trade and Plunder, 1530–1630*. New Haven: Yale University Press, 1978.

Ángel Pérez, Jorge, ed. *La danza del huracán*. Havana: Letras Cubanas, 2002.

Anonymous. *An Account of the Late Dreadful Hurricane, Which Happened on the 31st of August, 1772. Also the Damage Done on That Day in the Islands of St. Christopher and Nevis, Attempted to Be Ascertained. By the Editor*. St. Christopher: Thomas Howe, 1772.

Aponte, Irene Fernández. "La dislocalización poblacional y el éxodo migratorio como resultado del huracán de San Ciriaco." In *La llegada del Cíclope: Percepciones de San Ciríaco a cien años de su visita*, edited by Raquel Rosario Rivera, 113–21. San Juan: Fundación Puertorriqueña de las Humanidades, 2000.

Aráez y Fernando, Ramón. *Historia del ciclón del día de San Ciriaco*. San Juan: Imprenta Heraldo Español, 1905.

Arana Soto, Salvador. *Historia de nuestras calamidades*. San Juan [n.p.], 1968.

Arsenault, Raymond. "The Public Storm: Hurricanes and the State in Twentieth-Century America." In *American Public Life and the Historical Imagination*, edited by Wendy Gamber, Michael Grossberg, and Hendrik Hartog, 262–92. Notre Dame, IN: University of Notre Dame Press, 2003.

Ashford, Bailey K. *A Soldier in Science: The Autobiography of Bailey K. Ashford, Colonel M.C., U.S.A.* San Juan: Editorial de la Universidad de Puerto Rico, 1998.

Asselin de Beauville, Christian. "Les perturbations tropicales." In *Les catastrophes naturelles aux Antilles: D'une soufrière à une autre*, edited by Alain Yacou, 197–209. Paris: Editions Karthala, 1999.

Auf der Heide, Erik. "Common Misconceptions about Disasters: Panic, the 'Disaster Syndrome' and Looting." In *The First 72 Hours: A Community Approach to Disaster Preparedness*, edited by Margaret O'Leary, 340–80. New York: iUniverse, 2004.

Ayala Moura, Eladio. *El hijo de Carmen, o, Aventuras de un obrero novela original*. Ponce, PR: Tip. Pasarell, 1909.

Bacardí y Moreau, Emilio. *Crónicas de Santiago de Cuba*. Barcelona: Tip. de Carbonell y Esteva, 1908.

Bailyn, Bernard. *Atlantic History: Concept and Contours*. Cambridge, MA: Harvard University Press, 2005.

Balkin, Jack M. "Disaster Relief and the Constitution: A History of 'Strict Construction' " *Balkinization*, 31 August 2005. http://balkin.blogspot.com/2005/08/disaster-relief -and-constitution.html.

Barker, David, and David Miller. "Hurricane Gilbert: Anthropomorphising a Natural Disaster." *Area* 22, no. 2 (1 June 1990): 107–16.

Barkun, Michael. *Disaster and the Millennium*. Syracuse, NY: Syracuse University Press, 1986.

Barnes, Jay. *Florida's Hurricane History*. Chapel Hill: University of North Carolina Press, 1998.

Barrera-Osorio, Antonio. *Experiencing Nature: The Spanish American Empire and the Early Scientific Revolution*. Austin: University of Texas Press, 2006.

Barry, John, *Rising Tide: The Great Misssissippi Flood of 1927 and How It Changed America*. New York: Simon and Schuster, 1997.

Barton, Clara. *The Red Cross in Peace and War*. Washington, DC: American Historical Press, 1899.

Bayley, F.W.N. *Four Years' Residence in the West Indies, in the Years 1826, 1827, 1828, 1829*. London: W. Kidd, 1831.

Beasley, Nicholas M. *Christian Ritual and the Creation of British Slave Societies, 1650–1780*. Race in the Atlantic World, 1700–1900. Athens: University of Georgia Press, 2009.

Beauchamp, K. G. *History of Telegraphy*. London: Institution of Electrical Engineers, 2001.

Beck, Ulrich. *Risk Society: Towards a New Modernity*. London: Sage Publications, 1992.

Beckford, William. *A Descriptive Account of the Island of Jamaica: With Remarks Upon the Cultivation of the Sugar-cane, Throughout the Different Seasons of the Year, and Chiefly Considered in a Picturesque Point of View; Also Observations and Reflections Upon What Would Probably Be the Consequences of an Abolition of the Slave-trade, and of the Emancipation of the Slaves*. London: T. and J. Egerton, 1790.

Beckles, Hilary McDonald. "The 'Hub of Empire': The Caribbean and Britain in the Seventeenth Century." In *The Oxford History of the British Empire*, vol. 1: *The Origins of Empire. British Overseas Enterprise to the Close of the Seventeenth Century*, edited by Nicholas P. Canny, 218–40. Oxford: Oxford University Press, 1998.

Bell, Henry Hesketh Joudou, *Obeah: Witchcraft in the West Indies*. London: Sampson, Low, Marston, Searle and Rivington, 1889.

Benjamin, Thomas. *The Atlantic World: Europeans, Africans, Indians and Their Shared History, 1400–1900*. Cambridge: Cambridge University Press, 2009.

Berbusse, Edward J. *The United States in Puerto Rico, 1898–1900*. Chapel Hill: University of North Carolina Press, 1966.

Bergad, Laird W. "Toward Puerto Rico's Grito de Lares: Coffee, Social Stratification, and Class Conflicts, 1828–1868." *Hispanic American Historical Review* 60, no. 4 (November 1980): 617–642.

Best, Gary Dean. *FDR and the Bonus Marchers, 1933–35*. Westport, CT: Praeger, 1992.

Betances, Ramón Emeterio. "Todavia Tiembla La Isla y Se Estremece Puerto Rico de Ver a Sus Hijos Insensibles a La Servidumbre." Betances to Pedro Lovera (Santo Domingo, 18 April 1868). In *Ramón Emeterio Betances: Obras completas*, edited by Félix

Ojeda Reyes and Paul Estrade. Vol. 5, *Escritos politicos: Correspondencia relativa a Puerto Rico*. Forthcoming.

Bier, Vicki. "Hurricane Katrina as a Bureaucratic Nightmare." In *On Risk and Disaster: Lessons from Hurricane Katrina*, edited by Ronald J. Daniels, Donald F. Kettl, and Howard Kunreuther, 243–55. Philadelphia: University of Pennsylvania Press, 2006.

Bixel, Patricia Bellis, and Elizabeth Hayes Turner. *Galveston and the 1900 Storm: Catastrophe and Catalyst*. Austin: University of Texas Press, 2000.

Blume, Helmut. *The Caribbean Islands*. London: Longman, 1974.

Bode, Barbara. *No Bells to Toll: Destruction and Creation in the Andes*. New York: Scribner, 1989.

Bolland, O. Nigel. *Colonialism and Resistance in Belize: Essays in Historical Sociology*. Kingston, Jamaica: University of the West Indies Press, 2003.

———. "Labor Protest, Rebellions and the Rise of Nationalism during Depression and War." In *The Caribbean: A History of the Region and Its Peoples*, edited by Stephan Palmié and Francisco A. Scarano, 459–74. Chicago: University of Chicago Press, 2011.

———. *On the March: Labour Rebellions in the British Caribbean, 1934–39*. Kingston, Jamaica: Ian Randle Publishers, 1995.

———. "The Politics of Freedom in the British Caribbean." In *The Meaning of Freedom: Economics, Politics, and Culture after Slavery*, edited by Frank McGlynn and Seymour Drescher, 113–46. Pittsburgh: University of Pittsburgh Press, 1992.

Boose, Emery R., David R. Foster, Audrey Barker Plotkin, and Brian Hall. "Geographical and Historical Variation in Hurricanes across the Yucatán Peninsula." In *The Lowland Maya Area: Three Millennia at the Human-Wildland Interface*, edited by Arturo Gómez-Pompa, Scott Ferdick, Juan Jiménez-Osornio, and Michael Allen, 495–516. Binghamton, NY: Food Products Press, 2003.

Boose, Emery R., Mayra I. Serrano, and David R. Foster. "Landscape and Regional Impacts of Hurricanes in Puerto Rico." *Ecological Monographs* 74, no. 2 (May 2004): 335–52.

Booy, Theodoor de. "The Virgin Islands of the United States." *Geographical Review* 4, no. 5 (November 1917): 359–73.

Boucher, Philip P. *France and the American Tropics to 1700: Tropics of Discontent?* Baltimore: Johns Hopkins University Press, 2008.

———. "The 'Frontier Era' of the French Caribbean, 1620s–1690s." In *Negotiated Empires: Centers and Peripheries in the Americas, 1500–1820*, edited by Christine Daniels and Michael V. Kennedy, 207–34. New York: Routledge, 2002.

Bouton, Jacques. *Relation de l'establissement des Francois depuis l'an 1635: En l'isle de la Martinique, l'vne des Antilles de l'Amerique. Des mœurs des sauuages, de la situation, & des autres singularitez de l'isle*. Paris: Chez Sebastien Cramoisy, 1640.

Bouza Suárez, Alejandro. "Algunos hechos asociados al desarrollo de la beneficencia en Cuba hasta el siglo XVIII." *Revista Cubana de Salud Publica* 26, no. 1 (2000): 63–67.

Bowden, Martyn J. *Hurricane in Paradise: Perception and Reality of the Hurricane Hazard in the Virgin Islands*. St. Thomas: Island Resources Foundation, 1974.

Braithwaite, Kamau. *The Development of Creole Society in Jamaica, 1770–1820*. Kingston, Jamaica: Ian Randle, 2006.

Brandt, Geeraert. *Het leven en bedryf van den Heere Michiel de Ruiter . . .* Amsterdam: Wolfgang, Waasberge, Boom, Van Someren en Goethals, 1687.

Braudel, Fernand. *La Méditerranée et le monde méditeranéen à l'époque de Philippe II*. Revised and expanded 2nd ed. Paris: A. Colin, 1966.

———. *The Mediterranean and the Mediterranean World in the Age of Philip II*. 2 vols. New York: Harper & Row, 1976.

Brereton, Bridget. "Family Strategies, Gender and the Shift to Wage Labour in the British Caribbean." In *The Colonial Caribbean in Transition: Essays on Post-Emancipation Social and Cultural History*, edited by Bridget Brereton and Kevin A. Yelvington, 77–107. Gainesville: University Press of Florida, 1999.

———. *An Introduction to the History of Trinidad and Tobago*. Oxford: Heinemann Educational Publishers, 1996.

Brereton, Bridget, and Kevin A. Yelvington. *The Colonial Caribbean in Transition Essays on Postemancipation Social and Cultural History*. Gainesville: University Press of Florida, 1999.

Brickhouse, Anna. " 'L'Ouragan de Flammes' ('The Hurricane of Flames'): New Orleans and Transamerican Catastrophe, 1866/2005." *American Quarterly* 59, no. 4 (2007): 1097–1127.

Britton, John A. "International Communications and International Crises in Latin America, 1867–1881." *The Latin Americanist* 52, no. 1 (2008): 131–54.

Brym, Robert J. *Sociology as a Life or Death Issue*. Toronto: Pearson, 2008.

Burgess, George. *Last Journal of the Rt. Rev. George Burgess, D.D., Bishop of Maine, from December 27, 1865, to April 20, 1866*. Boston: E. P. Dutton and Co., 1866.

Burnard, Trevor G. "Harvest Years? Reconfigurations of Empire in Jamaica, 1756–1807." *Journal of Imperial and Commonwealth History* 40, no. 4 (2012): 533–55.

———. *Mastery, Tyranny, and Desire: Thomas Thistlewood and His Slaves in the Anglo-Jamaican World*. Chapel Hill: University of North Carolina Press, 2004.

Byrd, Alexander X. *Captives and Voyagers: Black Migrants across the Eighteenth-Century British Atlantic World*. Antislavery, Abolition, and the Atlantic World. Baton Rouge: Louisiana State University Press, 2008.

Cadilla de Martínez, María. *La poesía popular en Puerto Rico*. San Juan: Sociedad Histórica de Puerto Rico, 1999.

Campanella, Richard. "An Ethnic Geography of New Orleans." *Journal of American History* 94, no. 3 (December 2007): 704–15.

Cañizares-Esguerra, Jorge. "Iberian Science in the Renaissance: Ignored How Much Longer?" *Perspectives on Science* 12, no. 1 (March 2004): 86–124.

———. *Nature, Empire, and Nation: Explorations of the History of Science in the Iberian World*. Stanford, CA: Stanford University Press, 2006.

———."New World, New Stars: Patriotic Astrology and the Invention of Indian and Creole Bodies in Colonial Spanish America, 1600–1650." *American Historical Review* 104, no. 1 (February 1999): 33–68.

———. *Puritan Conquistadors: Iberianizing the Atlantic, 1550–1700*. Stanford, CA: Stanford University Press, 2006.

Cañizares-Esguerra, Jorge, and Erik R Seeman. *The Atlantic in Global History, 1500–2000*. Upper Saddle River, NJ: Pearson Prentice Hall, 2007.

Carbia, Rómulo D. *La crónica oficial de las Indias occidentales*. La Plata: República Argentina, 1934.

Cárdenas Ruiz, Manuel, *Crónicas francesas de los indios caribes*. Río Piedras: Editorial Universidad de Puerto Rico and Centro de Estudios Avanzados de Puerto Rico y el Caribe, 1981.

"Caribbean Disaster Emergency Management Agency." *Wikipedia, the Free Encyclopedia*, http://en.wikipedia.org/w/index.php?title=Caribbean_Disaster_Emergency _Management_Agency&oldid=565071598.

Caro Costas, Aída R., and Viola Vidal de Rodríguez, eds. *Actas del Cabildo de San Juan Bautista de Puerto Rico*. San Juan: Municipio de San Juan, 1949.

Carpentier, Alejo. *Letra y Solfa: Literatura, Poética. Selección de crónicas de Alejo Carpentier*. Havana: Letra Cubanas, 2001.

Carroll, Henry K., *Report on the Island of Puerto Rico*, Treasury Dept. doc. 2118 (Washington, DC, 1899).

Carstens, J. L., and Arnold R. Highfield. *J. L. Carstens' St. Thomas in Early Danish Times: A General Description of All the Danish, American or West Indian Islands*. St. Croix: Virgin Islands Humanities Council, 1997.

Casas, Bartolomé de las. *Apologética historia Sumaria*. Edited by Vidal Abril Castelló. Vols. 6–8 of *Obras Completas / Bartolomé de Las Casas*. Madrid: Alianza, 1992.

———. *Historia de las Indias*. Edited by Lewis Hanke. Mexico City: Fondo de Cultura Económica, 1951.

Castillero Calvo, Alfredo. "La carrera, el monopolio y las ferias del trópico." In *Historia General de América Latina*, edited by Alfredo Castillero Calvo and Allan J. Kuethe. Vol. 3, part 1: *Consolidación del orden colonial*, 75–124. Madrid: Editorial Trotta, Ediciones UNESCO, 1999.

Castro, Fidel. "Discurso en el acto por la conmemoración del Instituto Nacional de Recursos Hidráulicos" (10 Aug. 1963), *Obra revolucionaria*, 21 (1963), 29–40.

———. "Discurso pronunciado en la conmemoración del VI aniversario de los CDR." Plaza de la Revolución, Havana, Cuba, 28 September 1966. http://www.cuba.cu /gobierno/discursos/1966/esp/f280966e.html.

———. *Fidel Castro: My Life*. Edited by Ignacio Ramonet. New York: Scribner, 2008.

———. *Reflexiones de Fidel*. Vol. 8. Havana: Oficina de Publicaciones del Consejo de Estado, 2007.

Castro Herrera, Guillermo, and Reinaldo Funes Monzote. *Naturaleza en declive: Miradas a la historia ambiental de América Latina y el Caribe*. Valencia: Centro Francisco Tomás y Valiente UNED Alzira-Valencia Fundación Instituto de Historia Social, 2008.

Castro Medel, Osviel. "Ciclón Flora en Cuba: El lazo mortal." http://osvielcastro .wordpress.com/2010/10/04/ciclon-flora-en-cuba-el-lazo-mortal-i/ (4 Oct. 2010).

Caviedes, César N. "Five Hundred Years of Hurricanes in the Caribbean: Their Relationship with Global Climatic Variabilities." *GeoJournal* 23, no. 4 (April 1991): 301–10.

Centeno-Añeses, Carmen. "Huellas de San Ciriaco en la literature puertorriqueña de comienzos de siglo." In *La llegada del Cíclope: percepciones de San Ciríaco a cien años de su visita*, edited by Raquel Rosario Rivera, 89–97. San Juan: Fundación Puertorriqueña de las Humanidades, 2000.

Chagnon, Stanley A. "Factors Affecting Temporal Fluctuations in Damaging Storm Activity in the United States Based on Insurance Loss Data." *Meteorological Applications* 6, no. 1 (1999):1–10.

Chanan, Michael. *Cuban Cinema*. Minneapolis: University of Minnesota Press, 2004.

Chanvalon, Jean-Baptiste Thibault de. *Voyage a La Martinique: Contenant Diverses Observations Sur La Physique, L'histoire Naturelle, L'agriculture, Les Moeurs, & Les Usages de Cette Isle, Faites En 1751 & Dans Les Années Suivantes: Lu à l'Académie Royale Des Sciences de Paris En 1761*. Paris: Chez Cl. J. B. Bauche, 1763.

Chaunu, Pierre. "Veracruz en la segunda mitad del siglo XVI y primera mitad del siglo XVII." *Historia Mexicana* 9, no. 4 (1960): 521–57.

Chenoweth, M[ichael], J. M. Vaquero, R. García-Herrera, and D. Wheeler. "A Pioneer in

Tropical Meteorology: William Sharpe's Barbados Weather Journal, April–August 1680." *Bulletin of the American Meteorological Society* 88, no. 12 (Dec. 2007): 1957–64.

———. *The 18th Century Climate of Jamaica Derived from the Journals of Thomas Thistlewood, 1750–1786.* Philadelphia: American Philosophical Society, 2003.

Clark, Victor S, and Brookings Institution. *Porto Rico and Its Problems.* Washington, DC: Brookings Institution, 1930.

Clary, Bruce B. "The Evolution and Structure of Natural Hazard Policies." *Public Administration Review* 45 (January 1985): 20–28.

Cline, Isaac Monroe. *Tropical Cyclones, Comprising an Exhaustive Study . . . of . . . Features Observed and Recorded in Sixteen Tropical Cyclones Which Have Moved in on Gulf and South Atlantic Coasts During the Twenty-Five Years, 1900 to 1924 Inclusive.* New York: Macmillan Company, 1926.

Cockburn, Alexander, and Jeffrey St. Clair. "The Politics of Hurricane Mitch." *Counterpunch*, 15 June 1999. http://www.counterpunch.org/1999/06/15/the-politics-of-hurricane-mitch/.

Cohen Henry, II. *Kindler of Souls: Rabbi Henry Cohen of Texas.* Austin: University of Texas Press, 2007.

Cohen, Judah M. *Through the Sands of Time: A History of the Jewish Community of St. Thomas, U.S. Virgin Islands.* Hanover, NH: Brandeis University Press, 2004.

Coleman, Jill S. M., and Steven A. LaVoie. "Paleotempestology: Reconstructing Atlantic Tropical Cyclone Tracks in the Pre-HURDAT Era." In *Modern Climatology*, edited by Shih-Yu Simon Wang. N.p.: InTech, 2012. http://www.intechopen.com/books/modern-climatology/paleotempestology-reconstructing-atlantic-tropical-cyclone-tracks-in-the-pre-hurdat-era.

Colten, Craig E. *An Unnatural Metropolis: Wresting New Orleans from Nature.* Baton Rouge: Louisiana State University Press, 2005.

Columbus, Christopher. *The "Libro de las profecías" of Christopher Columbus.* Edited by Delno C. West and August Kling. Gainesville: University of Florida Press, 1991.

Congleton, Roger D. *The Story of Katrina: New Orleans and the Political Economy of Catastrophe.* SSRN Scholarly Paper. Rochester, NY: Social Science Research Network, January 6, 2006. http://papers.ssrn.com/abstract=908046.

Consultative Group for the Reconstruction and Transformation of Central America. "Central America after Hurricane Mitch: The Challenge of Turning a Disaster into an Opportunity." *Inter-American Development Bank*, n.d.

Contour, Solange. *Saint-Pierre, Martinique.* 2 vols. Paris: Editions Caribéennes, 1989.

Cooper, Christopher, and Robert Block. *Disaster: Hurricane Katrina and the Failure of Homeland Security.* New York: Times Books, 2006.

Corbin, Alain. *Village Bells: Sound and Meaning in the Nineteenth-century French Countryside.* European Perspectives. New York: Columbia University Press, 1998.

John Coulter, ed. *The Complete Story of the Galveston Horror.* Chicago: E. E. Sprague, 1900.

Covarrubias Orozco, Sebastián de. *Tesoro de la lengua castellana, o española.* Madrid: L. Sanchez, 1611.

———. *Tesoro de la lengua castellana, o española.* Madrid: Sanchez, 1873. http://archive.org/details/tesorodelalengua00covauoft.

———. *Tesoro de la lengua castellana o española*, edited by Martín de Riquer. Barcelona: S.A. Horta, 1943.

Cox, John D. *Storm Watchers: The Turbulent History of Weather Prediction from Franklin's Kite to El Niño.* Hoboken, NJ: Wiley, 2002.

Crabb, John. *A Poem Upon the Late Storm and Hurricane. With an Hymn. Dedicated to the Queen. By John Crabb, A.M. Late Fellow of Exeter College in Oxford*. London: printed for John Wyat, at the Rose, in S. Paul's Church-Yard, 1704.

Craton, Michael. *Sinews of Empire: A Short History of British Slavery*. New York: Anchor Press, 1974.

Craton, Michael, and Gail Saunders. *Islanders in the Stream: A History of the Bahamian People*. Vol. 2: *From the Ending of Slavery to the Twenty-First Century*. Athens: University of Georgia Press, 1992.

Cruz Barney, Oscar. *El combate a la piratería en Indias, 1555–1700*. Mexico City: Oxford University Press, 1999.

Cubilla, V. "Las cabañuelas y la Estación Climatológica Agricola." *Revista INRA* 5 (1961): 60–63.

Cuevas Fernández, Héctor, and Mário Navarrete Hernández. "Los huracanes en la época prehispánica y en el siglo XVI." In *Inundaciones 2005 en el estado Veracruz*, edited by Adalberto Tejeda Martínez and Carlos Welsh Rodríguez. Xalapa, Veracruz: Universidad Veracruzana, 2006. 39–49.

Daney de Marcillac, Sidney. *Histoire de la Martinique, depuis la colonisation jusqu'en 1815*. Vol. 4. Fort-Royal: Impr. de E. Ruelle, 1846.

Daniels, Ronald J., Donald F. Kettl, and Howard Kunreuther. *On Risk and Disaster: Lessons from Hurricane Katrina*. Philadelphia: University of Pennsylvania Press, 2006.

Dauber, Michele Landis. "Fate, Responsibility, and 'Natural' Disaster Relief: Narrating the American Welfare State." *Law and Society Review* 33 (1999): 257–318.

———. "Let Me Next Time Be 'Tried by Fire': Disaster Relief and the Origins of the American Welfare State 1789–1874." *Northwestern University Law Review* 92 (1997–98): 967–1034.

———. "The Real Third Rail of American Politics." In *Catastrophe: Law, Politics, and the Humanitarian Impulse*, edited by Austin Sarat and Javier Lezaun, 60–82. Amherst: University of Massachusetts Press, 2009.

———. *The Sympathetic State*. Stanford Public Law Working Paper No. 77. Stanford, CA: Stanford University, January 2004. http://papers.ssrn.com/sol3/papers.cfm?abstract_id=486245.

Davy, John. *The West Indies, Before and Since Slave Emancipation, Comprising the Windward and Leeward Islands' Military Command*. London: W. & F. G. Cash, 1854.

Dawdy, Shannon Lee. *Building the Devil's Empire: French Colonial New Orleans*. Chicago: University of Chicago Press, 2008.

De la Fuente, Alejandro. *Havana and the Atlantic in the Sixteenth Century*. Chapel Hill: University of North Carolina Press, 2008.

De la Fuente, Alejandro, César García del Pino, and Bernardo Iglesias Delgado. "Havana and the Fleet System: Trade and Growth in the Periphery of the Spanish Empire, 1550–1610." *Colonial Latin American Review* 5, no. 1 (1996): 95–115.

Debien, Gabriel. *Lettres de colons*. Laval: Madiot, 1965.

Delhom, Joël, and Alain Musset, eds. *Nicaragua, dans l'oeil du cyclone*. Travaux and Mémoires de l'Institut Des Hautes Études de l'Amérique Latine no. 69. Paris: Institut des Hautes Etudes de l'Amérique Latine (IHEAL), 2000.

Delumeau, Jean. *Rassurer et protéger: Le sentiment de sécurité dans l'Occident d'autrefois*. Paris: Fayard, 1989.

———. *Sin and Fear: The Emergence of a Western Guilt Culture, 13th-18th Centuries*. New York: St. Martin's Press, 1990.

Delumeau, Jean, and Yves Lequin, eds. *Les malheurs des temps: Histoire des fléaux et des calamités en France*. Paris: Larousse, 1987.

Denis, Watson. "Menaces hydrométéorologiques et risques géophysiques en Haiti." *Revue de La Société Haïtienne d'Histoire, de Géographie et de Géologie* nos. 241–44 (2011): 31–66.

Derby, Lauren. *The Dictator's Seduction: Politics and the Popular Imagination in the Era of Trujillo*. Durham, NC: Duke University Press, 2009.

"Destaca Raúl Castro preservación de vidas durante huracán." *La Crónica de Hoy*, 17 February 2013. http://www.cronica.com.mx/notas/2008/397131.html.

Devèze, Michel. *Antilles, Guyanes, La Mer Des Caraïbes, de 1492 à 1789*. Paris: SEDES, 1977.

Diaz, Henry, and Pulwarty, Roger, eds. *Hurricanes: Climate and Socioeconomic Impacts*. Berlin: Springer, 1997.

Díaz-Argüelles García, N. "El Observatorio Fisico-Meteorico de La Habana." *Anuario—Centro de Estudios de Historia y Organizacion de la Ciencia* no. 1 (1988): 218–47.

Díaz-Briquets, Sergio. "The Enduring Cuban Housing Crisis: The Impact of Hurricanes." Papers and Proceedings of the Fifth Annual Meeting of the Association for the Study of the Cuban Economy (ASCE), 429–41. http://www.ascecuba.org/publications/proceedings/volume19.

Diaz-Briquets, Sergio, and Jorge F Pérez-López. *Conquering Nature: The Environmental Legacy of Socialism in Cuba*. Pittsburgh, PA: University of Pittsburgh Press, 2000.

Díaz Hernández, Luis Edgardo. *Temblores y terremotos de Puerto Rico*. 3rd ed. Ponce, PR, 1990.

Dickson, William. *Letters on Slavery . . . to Which Are Added Addresses to the Whites, and to the Free Negroes of Barbadoes*. London, 1789.

Dietz, James L. *Economic History of Puerto Rico: Institutional Change and Capitalist Development*. Princeton, NJ: Princeton University Press, 1986.

Din, Gilbert C., and John E. Harkins. *The New Orleans Cabildo: Colonial Louisiana's First City Government, 1769–1803*. Baton Rouge: Louisiana State University Press, 1996.

Dobie, Madeleine. *Trading Places: Colonization and Slavery in Eighteenth-century French Culture*. Ithaca, NY: Cornell University Press, 2010.

"Document 14." In *Industrial and Other Conditions of the Island of Puerto Rico, and the Form of Government Which Should Be Adopted for It: Hearings before the Committee on Pacific Islands and Puerto Rico of the United States Senate on Senate Bill 2264, to Provide a Government for the Island of Puerto Rico, and for Other Purposes*. Washington, DC: Government Printing Office, 1900.

Domínguez Ortiz, Antonio. *Política y Hacienda de Felipe IV*. Madrid: Editorial de Derecho Financiero, 1960.

Drexler, Michael J., "Hurricanes and Revolutions." In *Early American Cartographies*, edited by Martin Brückner, 441–66. Omohundro Institute of Early American History and Culture. Chapel Hill: University of North Carolina Press, 2011.

Drum, Walter M. *The Pioneer Forecasters of Hurricanes*. Havana: Observatory of Belén, 1905.

Drye, Willie. *Storm of the Century: The Labor Day Hurricane of 1935*. Washington, DC: National Geographic Society, 2002.

Du Tertre, Jean Baptiste. *Histoire générale des Antilles habitées par les françois: Divisées en deux tomes, et enrichie de cartes & de figures*. Paris: Chez Thomas Iolly, 1667.

Dubois, Laurent. "An Enslaved Enlightenment: Rethinking the Intellectual History of the French Atlantic." *Social History* 31, no. 1 (2006): 1–14.

———. *Haiti: The Aftershocks of History*. New York: Metropolitan Books, 2012.

Duke, Cathy. "The Idea of Race: The Cultural Impact of American Intervention in Cuba, 1898–1912." In *Politics, Society, and Culture in the Caribbean: Selected Papers of the XIV Conference of Caribbean Historians*, edited by Blanca Silvestrini, 85–110. Universidad de Puerto Rico, 1983.

Dulles, Foster Rhea. *The American Red Cross: A History*. New York: Harper & Brothers, 1950.

Dunn, Gordon E. "The Hurricane Season of 1963." *Monthly Weather Review* 92, no. 3 (1965): 128–37.

Dyson, Michael Eric. *Come Hell or High Water: Hurricane Katrina and the Color of Disaster*. New York: Basic Civitas Books, 2006.

Economic Commission for Latin America and the Caribbean. "Caribbean Small States, Vulnerability and Development." November 2005. http://www.eclac.cl/cgi-bin/getProd.asp?xml=/publicaciones/xml/8/23558/P23558.xml&xsl=/portofspain/tpl-i/p9f.xsl&base=/portofspain/tpl/top-bottom.xsl.

Edwards, Bryan. *The History, Civil and Commercial, of the British Colonies in the West Indies*. 5 vols. London: T. Miller, 1819.

———. *Thoughts on the Late Proceedings of Government, Respecting the Trade of the West India Islands with the United States of North America*. 2nd ed. London: Printed for T. Cadell, 1784.

Edwards, Paul N. "Meteorology as Infrastructural Globalism." *Osiris* 21, no. 1 (2006): 229–50.

Egerton, Douglas R. *The Atlantic World: A History, 1400–1888*. Wheeling, IL: Harlan Davidson, 2007.

Eisenhower, Dwight D. "Remarks on Drought and Other Natural Disasters. McConnell Air Force Base, Wichita, Kansas." Edited by John T. Woolley and Gerhardt Peters. *The American Presidency Project*, 15 January 1957. http://www.presidency.ucsb.edu/ws/?pid=10823#axzz2hCNlAmZM.

El hurácan de Vuelta-Abajo: Curiosa recopilacion de todo lo que de mas notable ha publicado la prensa con motivo de aquella tremenda catástrofe. Havana: Impr. La Idea, 1882.

Elliott, John Huxtable. *The Old World and the New 1492–1650*. Wiles Lectures 1969. Cambridge: Cambridge University Press, 1970.

Elsner, James B., and A. Birol Kara. *Hurricanes of the North Atlantic: Climate and Society*. New York: Oxford University Press, 1999.

Eltis, David. *The Rise of African Slavery in the Americas*. Cambridge: Cambridge University Press, 2000.

Emanuel, Kerry A. *Divine Wind: The History and Science of Hurricanes*. Oxford; New York: Oxford University Press, 2005.

Engerman, Stanley L., and Herbert Klein. "The Transition from Slave to Free Labor: Notes on a Comparative Economic Model." In *Between Slavery and Free Labor: The Spanish-speaking Caribbean in the Nineteenth Century*, edited by Manuel Moreno Fraginals, Frank Moya Pons, and Stanley L. Engerman, 255–69. Baltimore: Johns Hopkins University Press, 1985.

Ensor, Marisa Olivo, and Bradley E. Ensor. "Hurricane Mitch: Root Causes and Responses to the Disaster." In *The Legacy of Hurricane Mitch: Lessons from Post-Disaster Reconstruction in Honduras*, edited by Marisa Olivo Ensor, 22–46. Tucson: University of Arizona Press, 2009.

Erikson, Kai. *Everything in Its Path: Destruction of Community in the Buffalo Creek Flood*. New York: Simon and Schuster, 1976.

Escalante de Mendoza, Juan de. *Itinerario de navegación de los mares y tierras occidentales 1575*. Madrid: Museo Naval, 1985.

Espantoso huracan que vino sobre la Villa de Çafra, que fue servido Dios . . . sucediesse por nuestros grandes pecados, para que sea escarmiento a tantas maldades como cada dia cometemos contra su divina Magestad : dase cuenta de la grande ruyna que uvo de personas y haziendas, en este . . . terremoto 1624. Seville: Juan de Cabrera, 1624.

Espinosa, Mariola. "A Fever for Empire: U.S. Disease Eradication in Cuba as Colonial Public Health." In *The Colonial Crucible Empire in the Making of the Modern American State*, edited by Alfred W McCoy and Francisco A Scarano, 288–96. Madison: University of Wisconsin Press, 2009.

Estève, Laurent. *Montesquieu, Rousseau, Diderot: Du genre humain au bois d'ébène: Les silences du droit naturel*. Mémoire Des Peuples. Paris: UNESCO, 2002.

Ewald, François. *Histoire de l'état providence: Les origines de la solidarité*. Paris: Grasset, 1996.

Fagan, Brian M. *The Little Ice Age: How Climate Made History, 1300–1850*. New York: Basic Books, 2000.

Favier, René. "La monachie d'Ancien Régime et l'indemnisation des catastrophes naturelles à la fin du XVIII siècle." In *Les pouvoirs publics face aux risques naturels dans l'histoire*, edited by René Favier, 71–104. Grenoble: CNRS—Maison Sciences de l'Homme-Alpes, 2002.

Fernandez de Castro, Manuel. *Estudio sobre los huracanes ocurridos en la isla de Cuba durante el mes de octubre de 1870*. Madrid: Lapuente, 1871.

Fernández de Oviedo y Valdés, Gonzalo. *De la natural hystoria de las Indias*. Toledo: Remon de Petras, 1526.

———. *Natural History of the West Indies*. North Carolina University Studies in the Romance Languages and Literature no. 32. Chapel Hill: University of North Carolina Press, 1959.

———. *Sumario de la natural historia de las Indias*. Biblioteca Americana. Serie de Cronistas de Indias 13. Mexico City: Fondo de Cultura Económica, 1950.

Fernandez, Ronald. *The Disenchanted Island: Puerto Rico and the United States in the Twentieth Century*. Westport, CT: Praeger, 1996.

Figueroa, Luis A. *Sugar, Slavery, and Freedom in Nineteenth-Century Puerto Rico*. Chapel Hill: University of North Carolina Press, 2005.

Fitz, Caitlin. "The Hemispheric Dimension of Early U.S. Nationalism: The War of 1812 and Spanish American Independence." *Journal of American History* (forthcoming).

Fitzpatrick, Patrick J. *Natural Disasters: Hurricanes—A Reference Handbook*. Contemporary World Issues. Santa Barbara, CA: ABC-CLIO, 1999.

Fleming, James Rodger. *Fixing the Sky: The Checkered History of Weather and Climate Control*. New York: Columbia University Press, 2010.

Florescano, Enrique. *Precios del maíz y crisis agrícolas en México (1708–1810): Ensayo sobre el movimiento de los precios y sus consecuencias económicas y sociales*. Centro de Estudios Históricos. New Series 4. Mexico City: El Colegio de México, 1969.

Florida Hurricane Disaster. Hearings before the Committee on World War Veterans' Legislation, House of Representatives, Seventy-fourth Congress, Second Session, on H.R. 9486, a Bill for the Relief of Widows, Children and Dependent Parents of World War Veterans Who Died as the Result of the Florida Hurricane at Windley Island and Matecumbe Keys, September 2, 1935. Washington, DC: Government Printing Office, 1936.

Fontán y Mera, Vicente. *La memorable noche de San Narciso y los temblores de tierra*. San Juan: Imprenta del Comercio, 1868.

Fortuné, Félix-Hilaire. _Cyclones et autres cataclysmes aux Antilles._ Fort-de-France [Martinique]: Editions La Masure, 1986.

Fowler, John. _A General Account of the Calamities Occasioned by the Late Tremendous Hurricanes and Earthquakes in the West-India Islands, Foreign as Well as Domestic: With the Petitions to, and Resolutions of, the House of Commons, in Behalf of the Sufferers at Jamaica and Barbados: Also a List of the Committee Appointed to Manage the Subscriptions of the Benevolent Public, Towards Their Further Relief._ London: J. Stockdale and W. Richardson, 1781.

Franco, José Luciano. _La batalla por el dominio del Caribe y el Golfo de Mexico._ 2 vols. Havana: Instituto de Historia, Academia de Ciencias, 1964.

Frank, Neil. "The Great Galveston Disaster of 1900." In _Hurricane! Coping with Disaster: Progress and Challenges since Galveston, 1900,_ edited by Robert H. Simpson, Richard A. Anthes, and Michael Garstang, 129–40. Washington, DC: American Geophysical Union, 2003.

Fraser, Walter J. _Lowcountry Hurricanes: Three Centuries of Storms at Sea and Ashore._ Athens: University of Georgia Press, 2006.

Frere, George. _A Short History of Barbados, from Its First Discovery and Settlement, to the End of the Year 1767._ London: J. Dodsley, 1768.

Fressoz, Jean-Baptiste. "Beck Back in the 19th Century: Towards a Genealogy of Risk Society." _History and Technology_ 23, no. 4 (December 2007): 333–50.

Freudenburg, William R., Robert Gramling, Shirley Bradway Laska, and Kai Erikson. _Catastrophe in the Making: The Engineering of Katrina and the Disasters of Tomorrow._ Washington, DC: Island Press/Shearwater Books, 2009.

Fuentes, Vilma Elisa. "Post-Disaster Reconstruction." In _The Legacy of Hurricane Mitch: Lessons from Post-Disaster Reconstruction in Honduras,_ edited by Marisa Olivo Ensor, 100–128. Tucson: University of Arizona Press, 2009.

Funes Monzote, Reinaldo. _From Rainforest to Cane Field in Cuba: An Environmental History since 1492._ Chapel Hill: University of North Carolina Press, 2008.

Fuson, Robert H. _The Log of Christopher Columbus._ Camden, ME: International Marine Publishing Company, 1991.

Fussell, Elizabeth. "Constructing New Orleans, Constructing Race: A Population History of New Orleans." _Journal of American History_ 94, no. 3 (December 2007): 846–55.

García, Gervasio Luis. "Economía y trabajo en el Puerto Rico del siglo XIX." _Historia Mexicana_ 38, no. 4 (April 1989): 855–78.

García Acosta, Virginia. "Huracanes y/o desastres en Yucatán." _Revista de la Universidad Autónoma de Yucatán_ 17, no. 223 (2002): 3–15.

———."La perspectiva histórica en la antropología del riesgo y del desastre: Acercamientos metodológicos." _Relaciones: Estudios de Historia y Sociedad_ 25, no. 97 (2004): 125–42.

García Acosta, Virginia, Juan Manuel Pérez Zevallos, and América Molina del Villar. _Desastres agrícolas en México: Catálogo histórico._ Sección de Obras de Ciencia y Tecnología. Mexico City: Centro de Investigaciones y Estudios Superiores en Antropología Social/Fondo de Cultura Económica, 2003.

García Luis, Julio, "Hurricane Flora (October 4, 1963)." In _Cuban Revolution Reader: A Documentary History of 40 Key Moments of the Cuban Revolution,_ 129–33. Melbourne: Ocean Press, 2001.

Garesché, William A. _The Complete Story of the Martinique and St. Vincent Horrors._ Chicago: Monarch Book Co., 1902.

Garraway, Doris Lorraine. *The Libertine Colony: Creolization in the Early French Caribbean.* Durham, NC: Duke University Press, 2005.

Garrett, Thomas A., and Russell S. Sobel. "The Political Economy of FEMA Disaster Payments." *Economic Inquiry* 41, no. 3 (2003): 496–509.

Geggus, David Patrick. "Slavery, War, and Revolution in the Greater Caribbean, 1789–1815." In *A Turbulent Time: The French Revolution and the Greater Caribbean,* edited by David Patrick Geggus and David Barry Gaspar, 1–51. Bloomington: Indiana University Press, 1997.

Gelabertó, Martí. *La palabra del predicador: Contrarreforma y superstición en Cataluña, siglos XVII–XVIII.* Colección Hispania 17. Lleida: Editorial Milenio, 2005.

Gerbi, Antonello. *Nature in the New World: From Christopher Columbus to Gonzalo Fernandez De Oviedo.* Pittsburgh, PA: University of Pittsburgh Press, 1985.

Gergis, Joëlle L., and Anthony M. Fowler. "A History of ENSO Events since A.D. 1525: Implications for Future Climate Change." *Climatic Change* 92, no. 3–4 (February 2009): 343–87.

Germana, Ernest. "Astrology, Religion and Politics in Counter-Reformation Rome." In *Science, Culture, and Popular Belief in Renaissance Europe,* edited by Stephen Pumfrey, Paolo L. Rossi, and Maurice Slawinski. Manchester: Manchester University Press, 1991.

Giroux, Henry A. "Reading Hurricane Katrina: Race, Class, and the Biopolitics of Disposability." *College Literature* 33, no. 3 (July 2006): 171–96.

Glantz, Michael H. *Currents of Change: El Niño's Impact on Climate and Society.* Cambridge: Cambridge University Press, 1996.

Go, Julian. *American Empire and the Politics of Meaning: Elite Political Cultures in the Philippines and Puerto Rico during U.S. Colonialism.* Durham, NC: Duke University Press, 2008.

Gøbel, Erik. *A Guide to Sources for the History of the Danish West Indies (U.S. Virgin Islands), 1671–1917.* Administrationshistoriske Studier; Studies in Danish Administrative History, vol. 15. Odense: University Press of Southern Denmark, 2002.

Golinski, Jan. *British Weather and the Climate of Enlightenment.* Chicago: University of Chicago Press, 2007.

González Vales, Luis E. "El Cabildo de San Juan Bautista de Puerto Rico en el siglo XVIII y La defensa de los derechos de los vecinos." *Revista Chilena de Historia del Derecho* 16 (1990): 205–18.

Gonzalo de Andrés, Carmen. "La predicción del tiempo en el Siglo de Oro español." *Revista del Aficionado de Meteorología* (n.d.). http://www.tiempo.com/ram/167/la-prediccion-del-tiempo-en-el-siglo-de-oro-espanol-s-xvi-xvii/.

Goveia, Elsa V. *A Study on the Historiography of the British West Indies to the End of the Nineteenth Century.* Washington, DC: Howard University Press, 1980.

Grafton, Anthony. *New Worlds, Ancient Texts: The Power of Tradition and the Shock of Discovery.* Cambridge, MA: Belknap Press of Harvard University Press, 1992.

Grandin, Greg. *Empire's Workshop: Latin America, the United States, and the Rise of the New Imperialism.* The American Empire Project. New York: Owl Books, 2007.

"Great Miami Hurricane of 1926." http://www.srh.noaa.gov/mfl/?n=miami hurricane1926.

Greene, Casey Edward, and Shelly Henley Kelly. *Through a Night of Horrors: Voices from the 1900 Galveston Storm.* College Station: Texas A&M University Press, 2000.

Greene, Jack P., and Philip D. Morgan, eds. *Atlantic History: A Critical Appraisal.* Oxford:

Oxford University Press, 2009. http://search.ebscohost.com/login.aspx?direct=true &scope=site&db=nlebk&db=nlabk&AN=257648.

Grove, Kevin J. "From Emergency Management to Managing Emergence: A Genealogy of Disaster Management in Jamaica." *Annals of the Association of American Geographers* 103, no. 3 (2013): 570–88.

Grove, Richard H. "The Great El Niño of 1789–93 and Its Global Consequences Reconstructing an Extreme Climate Event in World Environmental History." *Medieval History Journal* 10, no. 1–2 (October 2007): 75–98.

———. *Green Imperialism: Colonial Expansion, Tropical Island Edens, and the Origins of Environmentalism, 1600–1860.* Cambridge: Cambridge University Press, 1995.

Guerra, Lillian. *Popular Expression and National Identity in Puerto Rico: The Struggle for Self, Community, and Nation.* Gainesville: University Press of Florida, 1998.

Guevara, Che. "Socialism and Man in Cuba." In *Manifesto: Three Classic Essays on How to Change the World.* Melbourne: Ocean, 2005.

Hall, David D. *Worlds of Wonder, Days of Judgment: Popular Religious Belief in Early New England.* New York: Knopf, 1989.

Hall, Neville. *Slave Society in the Danish West Indies: St. Thomas, St. John, and St. Croix.* Johns Hopkins Studies in Atlantic History and Culture. Baltimore: Johns Hopkins University Press, 1992.

———. *Slave Society in the Danish West Indies: St. Thomas, St. John and St Croix.* Edited by B. W. Higman. Mona, Jamaica: University of the West Indies Press, 1992.

Hall, Richard, Sr., and Richard Hall, Jr., eds. *Acts, Passed in the Island of Barbados. From 1643, to 1762, Inclusive; Carefully Revised, Innumerable Errors Corrected: And the Whole Compared and Examined, with the Original Acts, in the Secretary's Office.* London: Printed for R. Hall, 1764.

Halperin, Maurice. *The Rise and Decline of Fidel Castro: An Essay in Contemporary History.* Berkeley: University of California Press, 1972.

Hardy, Sébastien. "Risque naturel et vulnérabilité: Un analyse de la catastrophe de Posoltega (30 octobre 1998)." In *Nicaragua, dans l'oeil du cyclone,* edited by Joël Delhom and Alain Musset, 41–52. Paris: Institut des Hautes Etudes de l'Amérique Latine, 2000.

Harte, Bret. "St. Thomas: A Geographical Survey." In *The Heathen Chinee: Poems and Parodies.* London: Richard Edward King, 1888.

Hayes Turner, Elizabeth. "Clara Barton and the Formation of Public Policy in Galveston." Paper presented at Philanthropy and the City: A Historical Overview. City University of New York: Rockefeller Archive Center and Russell Sage Foundation, 2000. http://www.rockarch.org/publications/conferences/turner.pdf.

Healey, Mark Alan. *The Ruins of the New Argentina: Peronism and the Remaking of San Juan after the 1944 Earthquake.* Durham, NC: Duke University Press, 2011.

Heidler, David S., and Jeanne T. Heidler. "'You're Dead Now, Brother': Hemingway and the 1935 Labor Day Hurricane." *David S. and Jeanne T. Heidler American Historians,* September 1, 2010. http://djheidler.com/~djheid5/Blog/~%281%29~Hurricane .htm.

Heilprin, Angelo. *Mont Pelée and the Tragedy of Martinique: A Study of the Great Catastrophes of 1902, with Observations and Experiences in the Field.* Philadelphia: J.B. Lippincott Company, 1903.

Heninger, S. K. *A Handbook of Renaissance Meteorology, with Particular Reference to Elizabethan and Jacobean Literature.* New York: Greenwood Press, 1968.

Herrera Tordesillas, Antonio de. *Descripción de las Indias occidentales.* Madrid, 1601.

Herrera y Cabrera, Desiderio. *Memoria sobre los huracanes en la isla de Cuba.* Havana: Impr. de Barcina, 1847.

Higman, B. W. *A Concise History of the Caribbean.* Cambridge Concise Histories. New York: Cambridge University Press, 2011.

Hilliard d'Auberteuil, Michel-René. *Considérations sur l'état présent de la colonie française de Saint-Domingue.* Paris: Grangé, 1776.

Holdeman, Eric. "Destroying FEMA." *Washington Post,* 30 August 2005. http://www.washingtonpost.com/wp-dyn/content/article/2005/08/29/AR2005082901445.html.

Holt, Mack P. "Review of *Rassurer et protéger: Le sentiment de sécurité dans l'Occident d'autrefois* by Jean Delumeau." *Journal of Social History* 24, no. 4 (July 1991): 851–53.

Huettiman, Emmarie. "Rubio on a Presidential Bid, and Climate Change," *The New York Times,* 12 May 2014.

Huerga, Alvaro. *Ataques de los Caribes a Puerto Rico en siglo XVI.* Historia Documental de Puerto Rico, vol. 16. San Juan: Academia Puertorriqueña de la Historia; Centro de Estudios Avanzados de Puerto Rico y el Caribe; Fundación Puertorriqueña de las Humanidades, 2006.

Hulme, Peter. *Colonial Encounters: Europe and the Native Caribbean, 1492–1797.* New York: Methuen, 1986.

———. "Hurricanes in the Caribbees: The Constitution of the Discourse of English Colonialism." In *1642: Literature and Power in the Seventeenth Century: Proceedings of the Essex Conference on the Sociology of Literature, July 1980,* edited by Francis Barker and Jay Bernstein, 55–83. Colchester: University of Essex, 1981.

Humboldt, Alexander von. *Ensayo político sobre la isla de Cuba.* Edited by Miguel Angel Puig-Samper, Consuelo Naranjo Orovio, and Armando García González. Madrid: Ediciones Doce Calles, 1998.

Huracán de 1846: Reseña de sus estragos en la isla de Cuba. Havana: Oficina del Faro Industrial, 1846.

Huret, Romain. "La fin de l'État providence? Un bilan de la politique sociale de George W. Bush." *Vingtième Siècle* no. 97 (January 2008): 105–16.

———. "L'ouragan Katrina et l'Etat federal américain: Une hypothèse de recherche." *Nuevo Mundo Mundos Nuevos (Nouveaux mondes mondes nouveaux; New World New Worlds)* (8 May 2007).

"Hurricane Andrew 20th Anniversary Is a Reminder to Prepare for Emergencies." *Federal Emergency Management Agency,* 22 August 2012. http://www.fema.gov/news-release/2012/08/22/hurricane-andrew-20th-anniversary-reminder-prepare-emergencies.

Hurricane Mitch and Nicaragua. Special Publication 38. Boulder, CO: Natural Hazards Research and Applications Information Center Institute of Behavioral Science University of Colorado, n.d. http://www.colorado.edu/hazards/publications/sp/sp38/part4.html.

Infante, Fernando A. *La era de Trujillo: Cronología histórica, 1930–1961.* Santo Domingo: Editora Collado, 2007.

Ingram, K. E. *Sources of Jamaican History 1655–1838: A Bibliographical Survey with Particular Reference to Manuscript Sources.* Zug: Inter Documentation, 1976.

International Monetary Fund. "Caribbean Small States: Challenges of High Debt and Low Growth." Washington, DC, 20 February 2013. http://www.imf.org/external/np/pp/eng/2013/022013b.pdf.

Isaac, Rhys. *Landon Carter's Uneasy Kingdom: Revolution and Rebellion on a Virginia Plantation.* Oxford: Oxford University Press, 2004.

Israel, Jonathan I. *Democratic Enlightenment: Philosophy, Revolution, and Human Rights 1750–1790.* New York: Oxford University Press, 2011.

———. *The Dutch Republic: Its Rise, Greatness and Fall, 1477–1806.* The Oxford History of Early Modern Europe. Oxford: Clarendon Press, 1995.

Jameson, J. Franklin. "St. Eustatius in the American Revolution." *American Historical Review* 8, no. 4 (July 1903): 683–708.

Janković, Vladimir. *Reading the Skies: A Cultural History of English Weather, 1650–1820.* Chicago: University of Chicago Press, 2001.

Jennings, Gary. *The Killer Storms: Hurricanes, Typhoons, and Tornadoes.* Philadelphia: Lippincott, 1970.

Johns, Alessa. *Dreadful Visitations: Confronting Natural Catastrophe in the Age of Enlightenment.* New York: Routledge, 1999.

Johnson, Leland R., and United States, Army, and Corps of Engineers. *Situation Desperate: U.S. Army Engineer Disaster Relief Operations, Origins to 1950.* Alexandria, VA: Office of History, U.S. Army Corps of Engineers, 2011.

Johnson, Sherry. *Climate and Catastrophe in Cuba and the Atlantic World in the Age of Revolution.* Envisioning Cuba. Chapel Hill: University of North Carolina Press, 2011.

———. "Climate, Community, and Commerce among Florida, Cuba, and the Atlantic World, 1784–1800." *Florida Historical Quarterly* 80, no. 4 (April 2002): 455–82.

———. "El Niño, Environmental Crisis, and the Emergence of Alternative Markets in the Hispanic Caribbean, 1760s–70s." *William and Mary Quarterly* Third Series, 62, no. 3 (July 2005): 365–410.

Jones, E. L. *The European Miracle: Environments, Economies, and Geopolitics in the History of Europe and Asia.* 2nd ed. Cambridge: Cambridge University Press, 1987.

Jordaan, Han, and To van der Lee. "The Hurricane of 1819." In *Building Up the Future from the Past: Studies on the Architecture and Historic Monuments in the Dutch Caribbean,* edited by Henry E Coomans, Michael A Newton, and Maritza Coomans-Eustatia, 99–108. Zutphen, Netherlands: Walburg Pers, 1990.

Juneja, Monica, and Franz Mauelshagen. "Disasters and Pre-industrial Societies Historiographic Trends and Comparative Perspectives." *Medieval History Journal* 10, no. 1–2 (October 2007): 1–31.

Jütte, Robert. *Poverty and Deviance in Early Modern Europe.* New Approaches to European History 4. Cambridge: Cambridge University Press, 1994.

Kahn, Matthew E. "The Death Toll from Natural Disasters: The Role of Income, Geography, and Institutions." *Review of Economics and Statistics* 87, no. 2 (May 2005): 271–84.

Kaukiainen, Yrj. "Shrinking the World: Improvements in the Speed of Information Transmission, c. 1820–1870." *European Review of Economic History* 5, no. 1 (2001): 1–28.

Kelley, John. The Graves Are Walking: *The Great Famine and the Saga of the Irish People.* New York: Henry Holt and Co., 2012.

Keyser, Jonathan, and Wayne Smith. *Disaster Relief Management in Cuba.* Center for International Policy, 18 May 2009. http://www.ciponline.org/research/html/disaster-relief-management-in-cuba.

Kislow, Paul V. *Hurricanes: Background, History and Bibliography.* New York: Nova Science Publishers, 2008.

Klein, Naomi. *The Shock Doctrine: The Rise of Disaster Capitalism*. New York: Metropolitan Books/Henry Holt, 2007.

Kleinberg, Eliot. *Black Cloud: The Great Florida Hurricane of 1928*. New York: Carroll & Graf Publishers, 2003.

Klooster, Wim. "Other Netherlands beyond the Sea." In *Negotiated Empires: Centers and Peripheries in the Americas, 1500–1820*, edited by Christine Daniels and Michael V. Kennedy, 171–91. New York: Routledge, 2002.

Knight, Franklin W. "The Disintegration of the Caribbean Slave Systems, 1772–1886." In *General History of the Caribbean*, edited by Franklin Knight. Vol. 3. London: UNESCO, 1997.

———. *Slave Society in Cuba during the Nineteenth Century*. Madison: University of Wisconsin Press, 1970.

Knowles, Thomas Neil. *Category 5: The 1935 Labor Day Hurricane*. Gainesville: University Press of Florida, 2009.

Knutson, Thomas R., John L. McBride, Johnny Chan, Kerry Emanuel, Greg Holland, Chris Landsea, Isaac Held, James P. Kossin, A. K. Srivastava, and Masato Sugi. "Tropical Cyclones and Climate Change." *Nature Geoscience* 3, no. 3 (March 2010): 157–63.

Koht, Halvdan. "The Origin of Seward's Plan to Purchase the Danish West Indies." *American Historical Review* 50, no. 4 (July 1945): 762–67.

Konrad, Herman W. "Caribbean Tropical Storms: Ecological Implications for Pre-Hispanic and Contemporary Maya Subsistence on the Yucatan Peninsula." *Revista de la Universidad Autónoma de Yucatán* 18, no. 224 (2003): 99–126.

———. "Fallout of the Wars of the Chacs: The Impact of Hurricanes and Implications for Prehispanic Quintana Roo Maya Processes." In *Status, Structure, and Stratification: Current Archaeological Reconstructions: Proceedings of the Sixteenth Annual Conference*, edited by Marc Thompson, Maria Teresa Garcia, and F. J Kense, 321–30. Calgary, AB: University of Calgary, Archaeological Association, 1985.

Krugman, Paul. "Katrina All the Time." *The New York Times*, 31 August 2007, sec. Opinion. http://www.nytimes.com/2007/08/31/opinion/31krugman.html.

———. "A Katrina Mystery Explained." *New York Times Blog: The Conscience of a Liberal*, 17 May 2009. http://krugman.blogs.nytimes.com/2009/05/17/a-katrina-mystery -explained/.

———. "Sandy versus Katrina." *The New York Times*, 4 November 2012, sec. Opinion. http://www.nytimes.com/2012/11/05/opinion/krugman-sandy-versus-katrina .html.

Kuethe, Allan J., and Kenneth J. Andrien. *War and Reform in the Eighteenth-Century Spanish Atlantic World, 1713–1796*. Cambridge: Cambridge University Press, 2014.

Kurlansky, Mark. *A Continent of Islands: Searching for the Caribbean Destiny*. Reading, MA: Addison-Wesley, 1992.

Labat, Jean Baptiste. *Nouveau Voyage aux Isles de l'Amerique*. La Haye: P. Husson, 1724.

Laet, Joannes de. *Nieuwe wereldt, ofte, Beschrijvinghe van West-Indien wt veelderhande schriften ende aen-teeckeninghen van verscheyden natien*. Leiden: Isaack Elzeviet, 1625.

Landa, Diego de. *Relación de las cosas de Yucatán*. Edited by Héctor Pérez Martínez. 7th ed. Mexico City: Editorial P. Robredo, 1938.

Larson, Erik. *Isaac's Storm: A Man, a Time, and the Deadliest Hurricane in History*. New York: Crown Publishers, 1999.

Laurens, Henry. *The Papers of Henry Laurens*. Vol. 1. Edited by Philip M. Hamer et al. Columbia: University of South Carolina Press, 1968.

Lavalle, Bernard. "Miedos terranales, angustias escatológicas y pánicos en tiempos de terremotos a comienzos del siglo XVII en el Perú." In *Una historia de los usos del miedo*, edited by Pilar Gonzalbo, Anne Staples, and Valentina Torres Septién, 103–27. Mexico City: Colegio de México, Universidad Iberoamericana, 2009.

Leber, Rebecca. "Chris Christie Denies Climate Change Has Anything to Do with Hurricane Sandy." *Climate Progress*, 21 May 2013. http://thinkprogress.org/climate/2013/05/21/2039811/christie-climate-change-sandy/.

Leblond, Jean-Baptiste. *Voyage aux Antilles, et a l'Amérique Méridionale*. Paris: A. Bertrand, 1813.

Lebrun, François. "La protection du monarque (1660–1800)." In *Les malheurs des temps: Histoire des fléaux et des calamités en France*, edited by Jean Delumeau and Yves Lequin, 321–66. Paris: Larousse, 1987.

Légier, Emile. *La Martinique et la Guadeloupe. Considérations économiques sur l'avenir et la culture de la canne, la production du sucre et du rhum et les cultures secondaires dans les Antilles françaises. Notes de voyage. Avec une carte des Antilles et plusieurs figures dans le texte*. Paris, 1905.

Leslie, Charles. *A New History of Jamaica*. Dublin: Oli. Nelson, 1741.

Levi, Patricia. "Hurricane Sandy Climate Change: Andrew Cuomo Rightly Raises Global Warming Issue." *PolicyMic*, 2 Nov. 2012. http://www.policymic.com/articles/17930/hurricane-sandy-climate-change-andrew-cuomo-rightly-raises-global-warming-issue.

Levis Bernard, José Elías. *Estercolero*. San Juan: La Editorial Universidad de Puerto Rico, 2008.

———. *Mancha de lodo: Novela*. Mayaguez, PR: Imp. El Progreso, 1903.

Levis Bernard, José Elías, and Estelle Irizarry. *Las novelas: El estercolero (1899); Estercolero (1901)*. San Juan: Ediciones Puerto, 2008.

Levy, Claude. "Barbados: The Last Years of Slavery 1823–1833." *Journal of Negro History* 44, no. 4 (October 1959): 308–45.

———. *Emancipation, Sugar, and Federalism: Barbados and the West Indies, 1833–1876*. Gainesville: University Presses of Florida, 1980.

Levy, Jonathan. *Freaks of Fortune: The Emerging World of Capitalism and Risk in America*. Cambridge, MA: Harvard University Press, 2012.

———. "Risk As We Know It." *Chronicle of Higher Education*, 10 September 2012. http://chronicle.com/article/Risk-as-We-Know-It/134148/.

Lewis, Gordon K. "An Introductory Note to the Study of the Virgin Islands." *Caribbean Studies* 8, no. 2 (July 1968): 5–21.

———. *Main Currents in Caribbean Thought: The Historical Evolution of Caribbean Society in Its Ideological Aspects, 1492–1900*. Baltimore: Johns Hopkins University Press, 1983.

———. *Puerto Rico: Freedom and Power in the Caribbean*. New York: Monthly Review Press, 1963.

Lewis, Michael. "In Nature's Casino." *The New York Times*, 26 August 2007.

Lewis, Matthew G. *Journal of a West India proprietor, kept during a residence in the island of Jamaica*. London: John Murray, 1834.

Lezcano, José Carlos. "Aspectos esenciales sobre la mitigación de los desastres naturales en Cuba." In *Cuba in Transition*, 5:399–406. Miami: Association for the Study of the Cuban Economy, 1995.

Lobdell, Richard. "Economic Consequences of Hurricanes in the Caribbean." *Review of Latin American Studies* 3 (1990): 178–90.

Long, Edward. *The History of Jamaica*. London: T. Lowndes, 1774.

Longshore, David. *Encyclopedia of Hurricanes, Typhoons, and Cyclones*. New York: Facts on File, 1998.

López de Haro, Damián, ed. *Sínodo de San Juan de Puerto Rico de 1645*. Colección Tierra Nueva e Cielo Nuevo, 18. Sínodos Americanos, vol. 4. Madrid: Centro de Estudios Históricos del CSIC, 1986.

López de Velasco, Juan. *Geografía y descripción universal de las Indias*. Madrid: Estab. tip. de Fortanet, 1894.

López Medel, Tomás. *De los tres elementos: Tratado sobre la naturaleza y el hombre del Nuevo Mundo*. Edited by Berta Ares Queija. Series El Libro de Bolsillo, 1503. Madrid: Quinto Centenario and Alianza, 1990.

Ludlum, David McWilliams. *Early American Hurricanes, 1492–1870*. The History of American Weather, no. 1. Boston: American Meteorological Society, 1963.

———. "The Espy-Redfield Dispute." *Weatherwise* 22, no. 6 (1969): 224–61.

Lugo Lovatón, Ramón. *Escombros: Huracán del 1930*. Santo Domingo, DR: Ed. del Caribe, 1955.

Luque de Sánchez, María Dolores. *La ocupación norteamericana y la Ley Foraker: La opinion publica Puertorriqueña, 1898–1904*. Río Piedras: Editorial Universitaria, Universidad de Puerto Rico, 1977.

Luster, Robert E. *The Amelioration of the Slaves in the British Empire, 1790–1833*. New York: P. Lang, 1995.

Lynch, Theodora Elizabeth. *The Wonders of the West Indies*. London: Seeley, Jackson, & Halliday, 1856.

MacLeod, Murdo. "Spain and America: The Atlantic Trade, 1492–1720." In *The Cambridge History of Latin America*, edited by Leslie Bethell, 1:341–88. Cambridge and New York: Cambridge University Press, 1984.

Macneill, Hector. *Observations on the Treatment of the Negroes, in the Island of Jamaica Including Some Account of Their Temper and Character: With Remarks on the Importation of Slaves from the Coast of Africa: in a Letter to a Physician in England*. London: G.G.J. and J. Robinson, 1788.

Macpherson, Anne S. *From Colony to Nation: Women Activists and the Gendering of Politics in Belize, 1912–1982*. Lincoln: University of Nebraska Press, 2007.

Maher, Neil M. *Nature's New Deal: The Civilian Conservation Corps and the Roots of the American Environmental Movement*. Oxford: Oxford University Press, 2008.

Maldonado, A. W. *Luis Muñoz Marín: Puerto Rico's Democratic Revolution*. San Juan: Editorial Universidad de Puerto Rico, 2006.

Marrero, Levì. *Cuba: Economia y sociedad*. 15 vols. Río Piedras, PR: Editorial San Juan, 1972–92.

Marscher, Bill, and Fran Marscher. *The Great Sea Island Storm of 1893*. Macon, GA: Mercer University Press, 2004.

Martel, Brett. "Storms Payback from God." *Washington Post*, 17 Jan. 2006.

Martin, Craig. "Experience of the New World and Aristotelian Revisions of the Earth's Climates during the Renaissance." *History of Meteorology* 3 (2006): 1–15.

———.*Renaissance Meteorology: Pomponazzi to Descartes*. Baltimore: Johns Hopkins University Press, 2011.

Martin, John Bartlow. *Overtaken by Events: The Dominican Crisis from the Fall of Trujillo to the Civil War*. New York: Doubleday, 1966.

Martínez Betancourt, Julio Ismael. "Predicciones climáticas y el conocimiento popular tradicional del campesino cubano." *Cautauro: Revista Cubana de Antropología* 12, no. 22 (2010): 121–30.

Martínez de Carrera, Teresita. "The Attitudes of Influential Groups of Colonial Society toward the Rural Working Population in Nineteenth-Century Puerto Rico, 1860–73." *Journal of Caribbean History* 12 (1979): 35–54.

Martínez-Fernández, Luis. "Political Change in the Spanish Caribbean during the United States Civil War and Its Aftermath, 1861–1878." *Caribbean Studies* 27, no. 1/2 (January 1994): 37–64.

———. "Puerto Rico in the Whirlwind of 1898: Conflict, Continuity, and Change." *OAH Magazine of History* 12, no. 3 (April 1998): 24–29.

Martinez-Fortún y Foyo, José Andrés. *Anales y efemerides de San Juan de los Remedios y su jurisdicción* , vol. 1, part 1 (1492–1849). Havana: Impr. Pérez Sierra y Comp., 1930.

Matos, Luis Pales. "La plena de menéalo," reprinted in *La Revista de Centro de Estudios Avanzados de Puerto Rico y el Caribe* 2 (1986):81–82.

Mauch, Christof, and Christian Pfister, eds. *Natural Disasters, Cultural Responses: Case Studies toward a Global Environmental History*. The German Historical Institute Studies in International Environmental History. Lanham, MD: Lexington Books, 2009.

Mauelshagen, Franz. "Disaster and Political Culture in Germany since 1500." In *Natural Disasters, Cultural Responses: Case Studies toward a Global Environmental History*, edited by Christof Mauch and Christian Pfister. The German Historical Institute Studies in International Environmental History. Lanham, MD: Lexington Books, 2009.

McCallum, Ewen, and Julian Heming. "Hurricane Katrina: An Environmental Perspective." *Philosophical Transactions of the Royal Society A: Mathematical, Physical and Engineering Sciences* 364, no. 1845 (15 August 2006): 2099–2115.

McChristian, Lynee. *Hurricane Andrew and Insurance: The Enduring Impact of an Historic Storm*. New York: Insurance Information Institute, August 2012. http://www .insuringflorida.org/assets/docs/pdf/paper_HurricaneAndrew_final.pdf.

McClellan, James E. *Colonialism and Science: Saint Domingue in the Old Regime*. Chicago: University of Chicago Press, 2010.

McComb, David G. *Galveston: A History*. Austin: University of Texas Press, 1986.

McCook, Stuart George. *States of Nature: Science, Agriculture, and Environment in the Spanish Caribbean, 1760–1940*. Austin: University of Texas Press, 2002.

McCusker, John J., and Russell R. Menard, eds. *The Economy of British America, 1607–1789*. Needs and Opportunities for Study Series. Chapel Hill: University of North Carolina Press, 1985.

McGrath, John T. *The French in Early Florida: In the Eye of the Hurricane*. Gainesville: University Press of Florida, 2000.

McNeill, John Robert. *Mosquito Empires: Ecology and War in the Greater Caribbean, 1620–1914*. New Approaches to the Americas. New York: Cambridge University Press, 2010.

———. "Observations on the Nature and Culture of Environmental History." *History and Theory* 42, no. 4 (2003): 5–43.

Medrano Herrero, Pío. *Don Damián López De Haro y Don Diego de Torres y Vargas: Dos figuras del Puerto Rico Barroco*. Colección Dédalo. San Juan: Editorial Plaza Mayor, 1999.

Meilink-Roelofsz, M.A.P. "A Survey of Archives in the Netherlands Pertaining to the History of the Netherlands Antilles." *West-Indische Gids* 35 (1953): 1–38.

Memoria en que se da cuenta de los trabajos de la Junta General de Socorros para Cuba y Filipinas. Madrid: Manuel Tello, 1884.

Meniketti, Marco. "Sugar Mills, Technology, and Environmental Change: A Case Study of Colonial Agro-Industrial Development in the Caribbean." *IA: The Journal of the Society for Industrial Archeology* 32, no. 1 (January 2006): 53–80.

Mercantini, Jonathan. "The Great Carolina Hurricane of 1952." *The South Carolina Historical Magazine* 103, no. 4 (2002): 351–65.

Mercier-Faivre, Anne-Marie, and Chantal Thomas, eds., *L'invention de la catastrophe au XVIII siècle*. Geneva: Droz, 2008.

Michaels, Patrick J. "Mitch, That Sun of a Gun." Cato Institute, 15 December 1998. http://www.cato.org/publications/commentary/mitch-sun-gun.

Millás, José Carlos. "Genesis y marcha de los huracanes antillanos." In *Astronomy, Meteorology, and Seismology: Proceedings of the second Pan-American Scientific Congress*, edited by Robert Simpson Woodward, 42–55. Washington, DC: Government Printing Office, 1917.

————. *Hurricanes of the Caribbean and Adjacent Regions, 1492–1800*. Miami, FL: Academy of the Arts and Sciences of the Americas, 1968.

————. *Memoria del huracán de Camagüey de 1932*. Havana: Seoane y Fernández, 1933.

Miner Solá, Edwin. *Historia de los huracanes en Puerto Rico*. San Juan: First Book, 1995.

Monet, Henri. *La Martinique*. Paris: A. Savine, 1892.

Mooney, Chris. *Storm World: Hurricanes, Politics, and the Battle over Global Warming*. Orlando, FL: Harcourt, 2007.

Moore, John Bassett. "Doc. 551." In *A Digest of International Law: 56th Congress, House of Representatives*. Vol. 1. Washington, DC: Government Printing Office, 1906.

Morales Carrión, Arturo. *Puerto Rico and the Non Hispanic Caribbean: A Study in the Decline of Spanish Exclusivism*. 2nd ed. Río Piedras: University of Puerto Rico, 1971.

————. *Puerto Rico y la lucha por la hegemonía en el Caribe: Colonialismo y contrabando, siglos XVI–XVIII*. Colección Caribeña. San Juan: Centro de Investigaciones Históricas, Editorial de la Universidad de Puerto Rico, 1995.

Moreau de Saint-Méry, M.L.E. *A Topographical and Political Description of the Spanish Part of Saint-Domingo: Containing, General Observations on the Climate, Population, and Productions, on the Character and Manners of the Inhabitants, with an Account of the Several Branches of the Government: To Which Is Prefixed, a New, Correct, and Elegant Map of the Whole Island*. Philadelphia, 1796.

Moreno Fraginals, Manuel. *El Ingenio: Complejo económico social cubano del azúcar*. 3 volumes. Havana: Editorial de Ciencias Sociales, 1978.

Moscoso, Francisco. *Clases, revolución y libertad: Estudios sobre el Grito de Lares de 1868*. Río Piedras, PR: Editorial Edil, Inc., 2006.

————. *Juicio al gobernador: Episodios coloniales de Puerto Rico, 1550*. Hato Rey, PR: Universidad de Puerto Rico, Decanato de Estudios Graduados e Investigación: Publicaciones Puertorriqueñas Editores, 1998.

————. *La Revolución puertorriqueña de 1868: El Grito de Lares*. San Juan: Instituto de Cultura Puertorriqueña, 2003.

Moya Pons, Frank. *El ciclón de San Zenón y la "patria nueva": Reconstrucción de una ciudad como reconstrucción nacional*. Santo Domingo, DR: Academia Dominicana de la Historia, 2007.

Mulcahy, Matthew. "The 'Great Fire' of 1740 and the Politics of Disaster Relief in Colonial Charleston." *South Carolina Historical Magazine* 99, no. 2 (April 1998): 135–57.

————. *Hurricanes and Society in the British Greater Caribbean, 1624–1783*. Early America. Baltimore: Johns Hopkins University Press, 2006.

————. "The Port Royal Earthquake and the World of Wonders in Seventeenth-Century

Jamaica." *Early American Studies: An Interdisciplinary Journal* 6, no. 2 (2008): 391–421.

———. "A Tempestuous Spirit Called Hurricano: Hurricanes and Colonial Society in the British Greater Caribbean." In *American Disasters*, edited by Steven Biel, 11–38. New York: New York University Press, 2001.

———. "Urban Disasters and Imperial Relief in the British-Atlantic World, 1740–1780." In *Cities and Catastrophes: Coping with Emergency in European History—Villes et catastrophes: Réactions face à l'urgence dans l'histoire européenne*, edited by Geneviève Massard-Guilbaud, Harold L Platt, and Dieter Schott, 105–22. Frankfurt am Main: P. Lang, 2002.

Murnane, Richard J., and Kam-biu Liu. *Hurricanes and Typhoons: Past, Present, and Future*. New York: Columbia University Press, 2004.

Murphy, Kathleen. "Prodigies and Portents: Providentialism in the Eighteenth-Century Chesapeake." *Maryland Historical Magazine* 97, no. 4 (January 2002): 397–421.

Musset, Alain. "Entre cyclones et tremblement de terre: Le Nicaragua face au risqué naturel." In *Nicaragua, dans l'oeil du cyclone*, edited by Joël Delhom and Alain Musset, 34–35. Paris: Institut des Hautes Etudes de l'Amérique Latine, 2000.

Mykle, Robert. *Killer 'Cane: The Deadly Hurricane of 1928*. New York: Cooper Square Press, 2002.

Nebeker, Frederik. *Calculating the Weather: Meteorology in the 20th Century*. San Diego: Academic Press, 1995.

Neely, Wayne. *The Great Bahamas Hurricane of 1929*. Nassau: Media Enterprises, 2005.

———. *Great Bahamian Hurricanes of 1926: The Story of Three of the Greatest Hurricanes to Ever Affect the Bahamas*. Bloomington, IN: iUniverse, 2009.

Nelson, William Max. "Making Men: Enlightenment Ideas of Racial Engineering." *American Historical Review* 115, no. 5 (2010): 1364–94.

Newton, Melanie J. *The Children of Africa in the Colonies: Free People of Color in Barbados in the Age of Emancipation*. Baton Rouge: Louisiana State University Press, 2008.

Nichols, Henry J. "Fact and Fancy about the Hookworm." *Medical Record* no. 80 (1911): 322–24.

NOAA, National Weather Service. "Evolution of the National Weather Service." http://www.nws.noaa.gov/pa/history/timeline.php.

Nord, Philip. *France's New Deal*. Princeton: Princeton University Press, 2010.Nyberg, Johan, Björn A. Malmgren, Amos Winter, Mark R. Jury, K. Halimeda Kilbourne, and Terrence M. Quinn. "Low Atlantic Hurricane Activity in the 1970s and 1980s Compared to the Past 270 Years." *Nature* 447, no. 7145 (7 June 2007): 698–701.

Ó Gráda, Cormac, Richard Paping, and Eric Vanhaute, eds. *When the Potato Failed: Causes and Effects of the "Last" European Subsistence Crisis, 1845–1850*. Turnhout, Belgium: Brepols, 2007.O'Loughlin, Karen Fay, and James F. Lander. *Caribbean Tsunamis: A 500-Year History from 1498–1998*. Dordrecht: Kluwer Academic Publishers, 2003.

Ó Murchadha, Ciarán. *The Great Famine: Ireland's Agony, 1845–52*. London: Continuum International Publishing Group, 2011.

O'Shaughnessy, Andrew Jackson. *An Empire Divided: The American Revolution and the British Caribbean*. Philadelphia: University of Pennsylvania Press, 2000.

Oldendorp, C.G.A. *C.G.A. Oldendorp's History of the Mission of the Evangelical Brethren on the Caribbean Islands of St. Thomas, St. Croix, and St. John*. Edited by Johann Jakob Bossart. Translated by Arnold R. Highfield and Vladimir Barac. Ann Arbor, MI: Karoma Publishers, 1987.

Oliver-Smith, Anthony. "Anthropological Research on Hazards and Disasters." *Annual Review of Anthropology* 25 (January 1996): 303–28.

Olson, Richard Stuart, and A. Cooper Drury. "Un-therapeutic Communities: A Cross National Analysis of Post-Disaster Political Unrest." *International Journal of Mass Emergencies and Disasters* 15, no. 2 (1997): 221–38.

Olson, Richard Stuart, and Vincent T Gawronski. "Disasters as Critical Junctures? Managua, Nicaragua, 1972 and Mexico City, 1985." *International Journal of Mass Emergencies and Disasters* 21, no. 1 (2003): 5–35.

Oostindie, Gert, and Inge Klinkers. *Decolonising the Caribbean: Dutch Policies in a Comparative Perspective.* Amsterdam: Amsterdam University Press, 2003.

Ophir, Adi. "The Two-State Solution: Providence and Catastrophe." *Journal of Homeland Security and Emergency Management* 4, no. 1 (21 March 2007): 1–44.

Ortiz Fernández, Fernando. *El huracán, su mitología y sus símbolos.* Mexico City: Fondo de Cultura Económica, 1947.

Ousley, Clarence. *Galveston in Nineteen Hundred: The Authorized and Official Record of the Proud City of the Southwest as It Was before and after the Hurricane of September 8, and a Logical Forecast of Its Future.* Atlanta: W.C. Chase, 1900.

Pádua, José Augusto. "As bases teóricas da história ambiental." *Estudos Avançados* 24, no. 68 (January 2010): 81–101.

Pagney, Françoise. "Trois ouragans sur la Guadeloupe: Hugo (1989), Luis et Marilyn (1995) et l'activité touristique." In *Les catastrophes naturelles aux Antilles: D'une soufrière à une autre,* edited by Alain Yacou, 184–96. Paris: Editions Karthala, 1999.

Pannet, Pierre J. *Report on the Execrable Conspiracy Carried Out by the Amina Negroes on the Danish Island of St. Jan in America, 1733.* Edited by Aimery Caron and Arnold R. Highfield. Christiansted, St. Croix: Antilles Press, 1984.

Paquette, Robert L., and Stanley L. Engerman. "Crisscrossing Empires: Ships, Sailors, and Resistance in the Lesser Antilles in the Eighteenth Century." In *The Lesser Antilles in the Age of European Expansion,* 128–43. Gainesville: University Press of Florida, 1996.

Paquette, Robert L., Stanley L. Engerman, and David Barry Gaspar. "Ameliorating Slavery: The Leeward Islands Slave Act of 1798." In *The Lesser Antilles in the Age of European Expansion,* 241–58. Gainesville: University Press of Florida, 1996.

Pares, Richard. "The London Sugar Market, 1740–1769." *Economic History Review* 9, no. 2 (1956): 254–70.

Parker, Geoffrey. *Global Crisis: War, Climate Change and Catastrophe in the Seventeenth Century.* New Haven: Yale University Press, 2013.

Parry, J. H., and Philip Manderson Sherlock. *A Short History of the West Indies.* London: Macmillan, 1968.

Parton, James. *The Danish Islands: Are We Bound in Honor to Pay for Them?* Boston: Fields, Osgood, & Co., 1869.

Paso y Troncoso, Francisco del, and Silvio Arturo Zavala. *Epistolario de Nueva España, 1505–1818.* Mexico City: Antigua librería Robredo, de J. Porrúa e Hijos, 1939.

Pedersen, Erik Overgaard. *The Attempted Sale of the Danish West Indies to the United States of America, 1865–1870.* Frankfurt: Haag & Herchen, 1997.

Penner, D'Ann R., and Keith C. Ferdinand. *Overcoming Katrina: African American Voices from the Crescent City and Beyond.* New York: Palgrave Macmillan, 2009.

Pérez, Louis A., Jr. *Winds of Change: Hurricanes and the Transformation of Nineteenth Century Cuba.* Chapel Hill: University of North Carolina Press, 2001.

Pérez de Oliva, Fernán. *Historia de la invención de las Indias*. Edited by José Juan Arrom. Mexico City: Siglo Veintiuno, 1991.

Pérez Moris, José, and Luis Cueto y González Quijano. *Historia de la insurección de Lares*. Barcelona: Establecimiento Tip. de Narciso Ramirez y C., 1872.

Pérez Tostado, Ignacio. "Desarrollo politico y económico de Las Antillas Británicas, siglos XV–XVIII." In *Historia de Las Antillas*, edited by Consuelo Naranjo Orovio, Ana Crespo Solana, and Ma Dolores González-Ripoll Navarro, 185–214. Madrid: Consejo Superior de Investigaciones Científicas; Doce Calles, 2009.

Pérotin-Dumon, Anne. *Être patriote sous les tropiques: La Guadeloupe, la colonisation et la révolution (1789–1794)*. Basse-Terre: Société d'histoire de la Guadeloupe, 1985.

————. "French, English, and Dutch in the Lesser Antilles: From Privateering to Planting, (1550–1650)." In *General History of the Caribbean*, edited by P. C. Emmer, Germán Carrera Damas, Franklin W. Knight, and B. W. Higman, 2:114–59. London: Macmillan Caribbean; UNESCO, 1997.

————. *La ville aux iles, la ville dans l'île: Basse-Terre et Pointe-à-Pitre, Guadeloupe, 1650–1820*. Paris: Karthala, 2000.

Perpiña y Pibernat, Juan. *Sobre el ciclón del Glorioso San Ciriaco y compañeros mártires*. Puerto Rico: A. Lynn e Hijos de Pérez Movis, 1899.

Pfister, Christian, Rudolf Bralzdil, Ruldiger Glaser, eds. *Climatic Variability in Sixteenth-Century Europe and Its Social Dimension*. Dordrecht: Kluwer Academic Publishers, 1999.

Phillips, Carla Rahn. *Six Galleons for the King of Spain: Imperial Defense in the Early Seventeenth Century*. Baltimore: Johns Hopkins University Press, 1986.

Paul Pialoux, *Le Marquis de Bouillé: Un soldat entre deux mondes*. Brioude: Edition Almanach de Brioude, 1977.

Picó, Fernando. *Historia general de Puerto Rico*. Río Piedras, PR: Ediciones Huracán, 1986.

————. *Libertad y servidumbre en el Puerto Rico del siglo XIX*. Río Piedras, PR: Ediciones Huracán, 1982.

Pielke, Roger A. *The Hurricane*. London: Routledge, 1990.

Pielke, R[oger] A., Jr., J. Gratz, C. W. Landsea, D. Collins, M. A.Saunders, and R. Musulin. "Normalized Hurricane Damages in the United States: 1900–2005." *Natural Hazards Review* 9, no. 1 (2008): 29–42.

Pielke, Roger A., Jr., and Christopher N. Landsea. "La Niña, El Niño and Atlantic Hurricane Damages in the United States." *Bulletin of the American Meteorological Society* 80, no. 1.0 (October 1999): 2027–33.

Pielke, Roger A., Jr., Christopher Landsea, M. Mayfield, J. Laver, and R. Pasch. "Hurricanes and Global Warming." *Bulletin of the American Meteorological Society* 86, no. 11 (November 2005): 1571–75.

Pielke, Roger A., Jr., J. Rubiera, C. Landsea, M. Fernández, and R. Klein. "Hurricane Vulnerability in Latin America and the Caribbean: Normalized Damage and Loss Potentials." *Natural Hazards Review* 4, no. 3 (2003): 101–14.

Piña Chán, Román, and Patricia Castillo Peña. *Tajín: La ciudad del Dios Huracán*. Mexico City: Fondo de Cultura Económica, 1999.

Pittman, Frank Wesley, "Fetishism, Witchcraft, and Christianity among the Slaves." *Journal of Negro History* 11, no. 4 (1926): 650–68.

Pluchon, Pierre, and Lucien-René Abénon. *Histoire des Antilles et de la Guyane*. Toulouse: Privat, 1982.

Poëy y Aguirre, Andrés. *Bibliographie cyclonique: Catalogue comprenant 1,008 ouvrages, brochures et écrits qui ont paru jusqu'a ce jour sur les ouragans et les tempêtes cycloniques.* Paris: Imprimerie administrative de Paul Dupont, 1866.

Popkin, Roy, and Claire Rubin. *Disaster Recovery after Hurricane Hugo in South Carolina.* Washington, DC: Center for International Science, Technology, and Public Policy, George Washington University, 1990. www.colorado.edu/hazards/publications/wp/wp69.pdf.

Portuondo, María M. *Secret Science: Spanish Cosmography and the New World.* Chicago: University of Chicago Press, 2009.

Poyer, John. *History of Barbados.* London: J. Mawman, 1808.

Poyntz, John. *The Present Prospect of the Famous and Fertile Island of Tobago: With a Description of the Situation, Growth, Fertility and Manufacture of the Said Island. To Which Is Added, Proposals for the Encouragement of All Those That Are Minded to Settle There.* London: G. Larkin, 1683.

Pritchard, James S. *In Search of Empire: The French in the Americas, 1670–1730.* Cambridge: Cambridge University Press, 2004.

Prost, Antoine, and Jay Winter. *René Cassin and Human Rights: From the Great War to the Universal Declaration.* Cambridge: Cambridge University Press, 2013.

Quenet, Grégory. *Les tremblements de terre en France aux XVIIe et XVIIIe siècles: La naissance d'un risque.* Seyssel: Champ Vallon, 2005.

Ragatz, Lowell J. *The Fall of the Planter Class in the British Caribbean, 1763–1833: A Study in Social and Economic History.* New York: Century Co., 1928.

———. *A Guide for the Study of British Caribbean History, 1763–1834, including the Abolition and Emancipation Movements.* Annual Report, American Historical Association, 1930, vol. 3. Washington, DC: Government Printing Office, 1932.

Ramírez de Arellano, Rafael W. "Los huracanes de Puerto Rico." *Boletin de La Universidad de Puerto Rico* 3, no. 2 (December 1932): 7–76.

Ramsay, James. *Essay on the Treatment and Conversions of African Slaves in the British Sugar Colonies.* London: James Phillips, 1784.

Rappaport, Edward N., and José Fernandez-Partagás. "History of the Deadliest Atlantic Tropical Cyclones since the Discovery of the New World." In *Hurricanes: Climate and Socioeconomic Impacts,* edited by Henry F. Diaz and Roger S. Pulwarty, 93–108. New York: Springer, 1997.

Raynal, Guillaume Thomas François. *Histoire philosophique et politique des établissements et du commerce des européens dans les deux Indes.* Amsterdam: Berry, 1772.

———. *Histoire philosophique et politique des établissements et du commerce des européens dans les deux Indes.* J. Justamond, trans. Dublin, 1776.

Reagan, Ronald. *Reagan: A Life in Letters.* Edited by Martin Anderson, Annelise Anderson, and Kiron K. Skinner. New York: Free Press, 2003.

Real Díaz, José Joaquín, San Juan (PR) Cabildo, and Archivo General de Indias. *Catálogo de las cartas y peticiones del cabildo de San Juan Bautista de Puerto Rico en el Archivo General de Indias, siglos XVI–XVIII.* San Juan: Instituto de Cultura Puertorriqueña, 1968.

Regnault, Elias. *Histoire des Antilles et des colonies françaises, espagnoles, anglaises, danoises et suédoises.* L'univers. Histoire et Description de Tous les Peuples. Paris: Firmin Didot Frères, 1849.

Reilly, Benjamin. *Disaster and Human History: Case Studies in Nature, Society and Catastrophe.* Jefferson, NC: McFarland & Co., 2009.

Relación verdadera, en que se dà quenta del horrible Huracàn que sobrevino à la Isla, y Puerto de Santo Domingo de los Españoles el dia quinze de Agosto de 1680. Madrid: Lucas Antonio de Bedmar, 1681.

Report on the Bahamas' Hurricane of October 1866: With a Description of the City of Nassau, N.P. Nassau: Printed at the "Nassau Guardian" by E. C. Moseley, 1868.

Richardson, Bonham C. *Economy and Environment in the Caribbean Barbados and the Windwards in the Late 1800s.* Gainesville: University Press of Florida, 1997. http://search .ebscohost.com/login.aspx?direct=true&scope=site&db=nlebk&db=nlabk&AN =54117.

Robiou Lamarche, Sebastián. *Caribes: Creencias y rituales.* San Juan: Editorial Punto y Coma, 2009.

Rochefort, Charles de. *Histoire naturelle et morale des Iles Antilles de l'Amerique. Enrichie d'un grand nombre de belles figures en taille douce, des places & des raretez les plus considerables, qui y sont décrites. Avec un vocabulaire caraïbe.* 2nd ed. Rotterdam: A. Leers, 1665.

Rodgers, Daniel T. *Age of Fracture.* Cambridge, MA: Belknap Press of Harvard University Press, 2011. http://site.ebrary.com/id/10456081.

Rodríguez Demorizi, Emilio. *Cronología de Trujillo.* Vol. 1. Ciudad Trujillo: Impresora Dominicana, 1955.

Rodriguez, Manuel R. *A New Deal for the Tropics: Puerto Rico during the Depression Era, 1932–1935.* Princeton, NJ: Markus Wiener Publishers, 2010.

Rodriguez, Pablo. "1812: El terremoto que interrumpió una revolución." In *Una historia de los usos del miedo,* edited by Pilar Gonzalbo, Anne Staples, and Valentina Torres Septién, 247–273. Mexico City: Colegio de México, Universidad Iberoamericana, 2009.

Rodríguez Morel, Genaro. *Cartas de la real audiencia de Santo Domingo (1547–1575).* Santo Domingo, DR: Archivo General de la Nación, 2011.

———. *Cartas del cabildo de la ciudad de Santo Domingo en el siglo XVIII.* Santo Domingo, DR: Centro de Altos Estudios Humanísticos y del Idioma Español, 2007.

Rodríguez-Ramírez, M. E. "Cronología clasificada de los ciclones que han azotado a La Isla de Cuba desde 1800 hasta 1956." *Revista Cubana de Meteorología* 2, no. 4 (1956).

Rodríguez-Silva, Ileana M. *Silencing Race: Disentangling Blackness, Colonialism, and National Identities in Puerto Rico.* New York: Palgrave Macmillan, 2012.

Rogers, Lisa Waller. *The Great Storm: The Hurricane Diary of J. T. King, Galveston, Texas, 1900.* Lone Star Journals 2. Lubbock: Texas Tech University Press, 2001.

Roorda, Eric Paul. *The Dictator Next Door: The Good Neighbor Policy and the Trujillo Regime in the Dominican Republic, 1930–1945.* Durham, NC: Duke University Press, 1998.

———. "Genocide Next Door: The Good Neighbor Policy, the Trujillo Regime, and the Haitian Massacre of 1937." *Diplomatic History* 20, no. 3 (July 1996): 301–19.

Rosario Rivera, Raquel. *La llegada del cíclope: Percepciones de San Ciríaco a cien años de su visita.* San Juan: Fundación Puertorriqueña de las Humanidades, 2000.

Ross, Waldo. *Nuestro imaginario cultural: Simbólica literaría hispanoamericana.* Autores, Textos y Temas 11. Barcelona: Anthropos, 1992.

Rothbard, Murray Newton. "Government and Hurricane Hugo: A Deadly Combination." In *Making Economic Sense,* edited by Murray Newton Rothbard. Auburn, AL: Ludwig von Mises Institute, 1995. http://www.mises.org/econsense/ch26.asp.

Rouse, Irving. *The Tainos: Rise and Decline of the People Who Greeted Columbus.* New Haven: Yale University Press, 1992.

Rugemer, Edward Bartlett. *The Problem of Emancipation: The Caribbean Roots of the American Civil War.* Baton Rouge: Louisiana State University Press, 2008.

Ruiter, Dierick. *Toortse der Zee-vaert: Om te beseylen de custen gheleghen bezuyden den Tropi-*

cus Cancri, als Brasilien, West-Indien, Guinea, en Angola, etc. Vlissingen: Marten Abrahamsz van der Nolck, 1623.

Ruiz Gordillo, J. Omar. "Fundaciones urbanas en México: La Veracruz en siglo XVI."
Altepetl. Revista de Geografía Histórica—Social y Estudios Regionales 5–6 (2012). http://
www.uv.mx/altepetl/No5/anteriores/alt02/arts/funcaiones%20urbanas.pdf.

Rupert, Linda Marguerite. *Creolization and Contraband: Curaçao in the Early Modern Atlantic World*. Early American Places. Athens: University of Georgia Press, 2012.

Sáez, José Luis. "Una carta anua de La residencia de Santo Domingo (23 Octubre 1695)."
Archivum Historicum Societatis Iesu 62, no. 124 (1993): 281–312.

Sainte-Croix, Félix Renouard. *Statistique de la Martinique*. Vol. 2. Paris, 1822.

Sainton, Jean-Pierre, and Raymond Boutin, eds. *Histoire et civilisation de La Caraïbe: Guadeloupe, Martinique, Petites Antilles: La construction ses sociétés antillaises des origines au
temps présent, structures et dynamiques*. Vol. 1: *Le temps des genèses: Des origines à 1685*.
Paris: Editions Maisonneuve et Larose, 2004.

Sala-Molins, Louis. *Les misères des lumières: Sous la raison, l'outrage*. Collection Savoirs
Autonomes. Paris: Homnisphères, 2008.

Salivia, Luis A. *Historia de los temporales de Puerto Rico y Las Antillas, 1492 a 1970*. 2nd ed.
San Juan: Editorial Edil, 1972.

Sandman, Alison. "Controlling Knowledge: Navigation, Cartography, and Secrecy in
the Early Modern Spanish Atlantic." In *Science and Empire in the Atlantic World*, edited by James Delbourgo and Nicholas Dew, 31–52. New York: Routledge, 2008.

Sarasola, Simón. *Los huracanes en las Antillas*. 2nd ed. Madrid: B. del Amo, 1928.

Scarano, Francisco A. "Azúcar y esclavitud en Puerto Rico: La formación de la economía
de haciendas en Ponce, 1815–1849." In *Azucar y esclavitud*, edited by Andrés Ramos
Mattei, 13–52. San Juan: University of Puerto Rico, 1982.

———. "The Jíbaro Masquerade and the Subaltern Politics of Creole Identity Formation in Puerto Rico, 1745–1823." *American Historical Review* 101, no. 5 (December
1996): 1398–1431.

———. *Puerto Rico: Cinco siglos de historia*. San Juan: McGraw-Hill, 1993.

———. *Sugar and Slavery in Puerto Rico: The Plantation Economy of Ponce, 1800–1850*.
Madison: University of Wisconsin Press, 1984.

Scarth, Alwyn. *La Catastrophe: The Eruption of Mount Pelée, the Worst Volcanic Eruption of
the Twentieth Century*. Oxford: Oxford University Press, 2002.

Scatena, F. N., and M. C. Larsen. "Physical Aspects of Hurricane Hugo in Puerto Rico."
Biotropica 23, no. 4 (December 1991): 317–23.

Schechner, Sara. *Comets, Popular Culture, and the Birth of Modern Cosmology*. Princeton,
NJ: Princeton University Press, 1997.

Schlegel, John Frederic. *A Short Account of the Effects of the Late Hurricane in the West Indies: As Far as Relates to the Missions of the Brethren in the Islands of St. Croix and St.
Christopher*. N.p., 1785.

Schmidt-Nowara, Christopher. "National Economy and Atlantic Slavery: Protectionism and Resistance to Abolitionism in Spain and the Antilles, 1854–1874." *Hispanic
American Historical Review* 78, no. 4 (November 1998): 603–29.

Schomburgk, Robert Hermann. *The History of Barbados*. London: Brown, Green and
Longmans, 1848.

Schwartz, Stuart B. *All Can Be Saved: Religious Tolerance and Salvation in the Iberian Atlantic World*. New Haven: Yale University Press, 2008.

———. "The Hurricane of San Ciriaco: Disaster, Politics, and Society in Puerto Rico,
1899–1901." *Hispanic American Historical Review* 72, no. 3 (August 1992): 303–34.

————."Hurricanes and the Shaping of Circum-Caribbean Societies." *Florida Historical Quarterly* 83, no. 4 (April 2005): 381–409.

————."Virginia and the Atlantic World." In *The Atlantic World and Virginia, 1550–1624*, edited by Peter C. Mancall, 558–70. Williamsburg, VA: Omohundro Institute of Early American History and Culture, 2004.

Sheets, Bob, and Jack Williams. *Hurricane Watch: Forecasting the Deadliest Storms on Earth*. New York: Vintage, 2001.

Shephard, Charles. *An Historical Account of the Island of Saint Vincent*. London: W. Nicol, 1831.

Shepherd, J. Marshall, and Thomas Knutson. "The Current Debate on the Linkage between Global Warming and Hurricanes." *Geography Compass* 1, no. 1 (2007): 1–24.

Sheridan, Richard B. "The Crisis of Slave Subsistence in the British West Indies during and after the American Revolution." *William and Mary Quarterly* 3rd series, 33, no. 4 (October 1976): 615–41.

————. "The Formation of Caribbean Plantation Society, 1689–1748." In *The Oxford History of the British Empire*, vol. 2: *The Eighteenth Century*, edited by P. J. Marshall, 394–414. Oxford: Oxford University Press, 1998.

————. "The Jamaican Slave Insurrection Scare of 1776 and the American Revolution." *Journal of Negro History* 61, no. 3 (July 1976): 290–308.

Shughart, William F., II. "Katrinanomics: The Politics and Economics of Disaster Relief." *Public Choice* 127, no. 1/2 (April 2006): 31–53.

Sims, Holly, and Kevin Vogelmann. "Popular Mobilization and Disaster Management in Cuba." *Public Administration and Development* 22, no. 5 (2002): 389–400.

Smith, James Patterson. "The Liberals, Race, and Political Reform in the British West Indies, 1866–1874." *Journal of Negro History* 79, no. 2 (April 1994): 131–46.

Smith, Mark M. *Camille, 1969: Histories of a Hurricane*. Athens: University of Georgia Press, 2011.

Smith, S. D. "Storm Hazard and Slavery: The Impact of the 1831 Great Caribbean Hurricane on St Vincent." *Environment and History* 18, no. 1 (February 2012): 97–123.

Smith, William. *A Natural History of Nevis, and the Rest of the English Leeward Charibee Islands in America: With Many Other Observations on Nature and Art, Particularly, an Introduction to the Art of Decyphering in Eleven Letters from the Revd. Mr. Smith, Sometime Rector of St. John's at Nevis, and Now Rector of St. Mary's in Bedford, to the Revd. Mr. Mason, B.D. Woodwardian Professor, and Fellow of Trinity-College, in Cambridge*. Cambridge: Printed by J. Bentham . . . and sold by W. Thurlbourn in Cambridge, S. Birt . . . , C. Bathurst . . . , and J. Beecroft . . . , London, 1745.

Solnit, Rebecca. *A Paradise Built in Hell: The Extraordinary Communities That Arise in Disasters*. New York: Viking, 2009.

Sorokin, Pitirim Aleksandrovič. *Man and Society in Calamity: The Effects of War, Revolution, Famine, Pestilence upon Human Mind, Behavior, Social Organization and Cultural Life*. Westport, CT: Greenwood Press, 1968.

Soto, Domingo de. *Deliberación en la causa de los pobres (1545)*. Madrid: Instituto de Estudios Políticos, 1965.

Standiford, Les, and Henry Morrison Flagler. *Last Train to Paradise: Henry Flagler and the Spectacular Rise and Fall of the Railroad That Crossed the Ocean*. New York: Crown Publishers, 2002.

Steadman Jones, Daniel, *Masters of the Universe: Hayek, Friedman and the Birth of Neoliberal Politics*. Princeton, NJ: Princeton University Press, 2012.

Steele, Ian Kenneth. *The English Atlantic, 1675–1740: An Exploration of Communication and Community*. New York: Oxford University Press, 1986.

Steiger, Eric. "L'ouragan Katrina: Les leçons d'un échec: Les faiblesses du dispositif de sécurité intérieure des Etats-Unis." *Revue Géopolitique*, 1 January 2008. http://www.diploweb.com/L-ouragan-Katrina-les-lecons-d-un.html.

Steinberg, Theodore. *Acts of God: The Unnatural History of Natural Disaster in America*. New York: Oxford University Press, 2000.

Stewart, George. *Progress of Glasgow: A Sketch of the Commercial and Industrial Increase of the City during the Last Century*. Glasgow: J. Baird, 1883.

Surowiecki, James. "Disaster Economics." *The New Yorker*, 3 December 2012. http://www.newyorker.com/talk/financial/2012/12/03/121203ta_talk_surowiecki.

Tanna, Laura. "On Development and Losing Elections." *Jamaica Gleaner Online*, 14 March 2010, http://jamaica-gleaner.com/gleaner/20100314/arts/arts4.html.

Tannehill, Ivan Ray. *Hurricanes, Their Nature and History, Particularly Those of the West Indies and the Southern Coasts of the United States*. Princeton, NJ: Princeton University Press, 1938.

Tansill, Charles Callan. *The Purchase of the Danish West Indies*. Baltimore: Johns Hopkins Press, 1932.

Taylor, Charles Edwin. *Leaflets from the Danish West Indies: Descriptive of the Social, Political, and Commercial Condition of These Islands*. London: The author, 1888.

Taylor, Douglas. "Spanish Huracán and Its Congeners." *International Journal of American Linguistics* 22 (1956): 275–76.

Téfel, Reinaldo Antonio, et al. *El huracán que desnudo a Nicaragua*. Foro Democrático 5. Managua, Nicaragua: Foro Democrático, 1999.

"Testimony of Carlos Chardón, Commissioner of Agriculture." In *Relief of Porto Rico: Joint Hearings before the Committee on Territories and Insular Possessions, United States Senate and the Committee on Insular Affairs, House of Representatives, Seventieth Congress, 2nd Session on S.J. Res. 172 and H.J. Res. 333, a Bill for the Relief of Porto Rico, December 10 and 11, 1928*. Washington, DC: Government Printing Office, 1929.

Thomas, Hugh. *Cuba: The Pursuit of Freedom*. New York: Harper & Row, 1971.

Thompson, Martha, and Izaskun Gaviria. *Cuba Weathering the Storm: Lessons in Risk Reduction from Cuba*. Boston: Oxfam America, 2004.

Thornton, John K. *A Cultural History of the Atlantic World, 1250–1820*. Cambridge: Cambridge University Press, 2012.

Tillotson, John. *The Works of the Most Reverend Dr. John Tillotson*. Edinburgh: W. Ruddiman & Co., 1772.

Tilly, Charles. *Coercion, Capital, and European States, AD 990–1992*. Studies in Social Discontinuity. Cambridge, MA: Blackwell, 1992.

Tobago Hurricane of 1847: Papers Relative to the Hurricane in Tobago Presented to Both Houses of Parliament by Command of Her Majesty Queen Victoria, on April 11, 1848. Historical Documents of Trinidad and Tobago, no. 3. Port of Spain: Government Printery, 1966.

Tomich, Dale. "Econocide? From Abolition to Emancipation in the British and French Caribbean." In *The Caribbean: An Illustrated History*, edited by Stephan Palmié and Francisco Scarano. Chicago: University of Chicago Press: 2011, 303–16.

Torres, Manuel. *Huracán Mitch, 1998–2003: Retrato social de una tragedia natural*. Tegucigalpa: Centro de Documentación de Honduras, 2004.

Towner, Horace A. *Twenty-ninth Annual Report of the Governor of Porto Rico*. Washington, DC: Government Printing Office, 1930.

Tracinski, Robert. "Katrina y el estado de beneficencia." *TIADaily.com*, 2 September 2005. http://www.contra-mundum.org/castellano/tracinski/Katr_EdoBenef.pdf.

Trelles, Carlos M. *Biblioteca Científica Cubana*. Matanzas: Impr. de J. F. Oliver, 1918.

Trujillo Molina, Rafael Leónidas. *Discursos, mensajes y proclamas*. Santiago, DR: Editorial El Diario, 1946.

———. *La nueva patria dominicana: Recopilación de discursos, mensajes y memorias del generalísimo Rafael Leónidas Trujillo Molina*. Santo Domingo, 1934.

Twigg, David K. *The Politics of Disaster: Tracking the Impact of Hurricane Andrew*. Gainesville: University Press of Florida, 2012.

Udías Vallina, Augustín. "Earthquakes as God's Punishment in 17th- and 18th-Century Spain." In *Geology and Religion: A History of Harmony and Hostility*, edited by Martina Kölbl-Ebert, 41–48. Geological Society Special Publication no. 310. London: Geological Society, 2009.

———. *Searching the Heavens and the Earth: The History of Jesuit Observatories*. Dordrecht: Kluwer Academic Publishers, 2003.

United States of America, Congress. *Abridgment of the Debates of Congress, from 1789 to 1856: Nov. 7, 1808–March 3, 1813*. Volume 4, *Relief for Caracas*. New York: D. Appleton, 1857.

United States Earthquake Investigation Commission. *Los terremotos de Puerto Rico de 1918, con descripción de terremotos anteriores*. Edited by Harry Fielding Reid and Stephen Taber. San Juan: Negociado de Materiales, Imprenta, y Transporte, 1919.

Utrera, Cipriano de. *Santo Domingo: Dilucidaciones históricas*. Santo Domingo, DR: Secretaría de Estado de Educación, Bellas Artes y Cultos, 1995.

Valenzuela Márquez, Jaime. "El terremoto de 1647: Experiencia apocalíptica y representaciones religiosas en Santiago colonial." In *Historias urbanas: Homenaje a Armando de Ramón*, edited by Jaime Valenzuela Márquez, 27–65. Santiago: Ediciones Universidad Catolica de Chile, 2007.

Valero González, Mercedes. "El Observatorio del Colegio de Belén en el siglo XIX." *Anuario, Centro de Estudios de Historia y Organización de La Ciencia* (1988): 200–17.

Van Heerden, Ivor, and Mike Bryan. *The Storm: What Went Wrong and Why during Hurricane Katrina—The Inside Story from One Louisiana Scientist*. New York: Viking, 2006.

Vega, Mariano Esteban de. "La asistencia liberal en la España de la restauración." *Revista de la historia de la economía y de la empresa* no. 4 (2010): 49–61.

Victor, Rudolph Homère. "Cette nuit là les portes de l'enfer s'étaient entr'ouvertes." *Mr. Météo: Toutes Les Infos Météos*, 31 May 2013. http://mrmeteo.info/site/2013/05/31/cette-nuit-la-les-portes-de-lenfer-setaient-entrouvertes/.

Vicuña Mackenna, Benjamín. *El clima de Chile: Ensayo histórico*. Buenos Aires, Santiago de Chile: Editorial Francisco de Aguirre, 1970.

Vidal, Teodoro. *El control de la naturaleza: Mediante la palabra en la tradición puertorriqueña*. San Juan: Ediciones Alba, 2008.

Vila Vilar, Enriqueta. *Historia de Puerto Rico (1600–1650)*. Publicaciones de la Escuela de Estudios Hispano-Americanos de Sevilla, 223. Seville: Escuela de Estudios Hispano-Americanos, 1974.

Vilagrán, Martín Gelabertó. "Astrología, religión y pronóstico en el renacimiento." *Historia y Vida* 305 (August 1993): 68–75.

———. "Supersticiones y augurios climáticos en la España dela edad moderna." *Historia y Vida* 296 (November 1996): 23–28.

———. "Tempestades y conjuros de las fuerzas naturals: Aspectos magico-religiosos de la cultura en la alta edad moderna." *Pedralbes: Revista d'historia moderna* 9 (1989): 193–99.

Viñes, Benito. *Investigaciones relativas a la circulación y traslación ciclónica en los huracanes de las Antillas.* Facsimile ed. Miami: Editorial Cubana, 1993.

Vives, Juan Luis. *Tratado del socorro de los pobres.* Valencia: Impr. Hijo de F. Vives Mora, 1942.

Vogel, Roger M. "Natural Disaster and U.S. Economic Growth: 1952–2009." *International Journal of Humanities and Social Science* 1, no. 14 (2011): 46–50.

Wagenheim, Olga Jiménez de. *Puerto Rico's Revolt for Independence: El Grito de Lares.* Boulder, CO: Westview Press, 1985.

Walker, Charles F. *Shaky Colonialism: The 1746 Earthquake-Tsunami in Lima, Peru, and Its Long Aftermath.* Durham, NC: Duke University Press, 2008.

Walker, J. M. *History of the Meteorological Office.* Cambridge: Cambridge University Press, 2012.

Walsham, Alexandra. *Providence in Early Modern England.* Oxford: Oxford University Press, 1999.

Walter, François. *Catastrophes: Une histoire culturelle, XVIe–XXIe siècles.* Univers Historique. Paris: Seuil, 2008.

———. "Pour une histoire culturelle des risques naturels." In *Les cultures du risque: XVIe–XXIe siècle,* edited by François Walter, Bernardino Fantini, and Pascal Delvaux, 1–29. Travaux d'histoire suisse 3. Geneva: Presses d'Histoire Suisse, 2006.

Walter, François, Bernardino Fantini, and Pascal Delvaux. *Les cultures du risque: XVIe–XXIe siècle.* Presses d'histoire suisse, 2006.

Ward, J. R. *British West Indian Slavery, 1750–1834: The Process of Amelioration.* Oxford: Oxford University Press, 1988.

———. "The British West Indies in the Age of Abolition, 1748–1815." In *The Oxford History of the British Empire,* edited by William Roger Louis, Alaine M. Low, Nicholas P. Canny, and P. J. Marshall, vol. 2, *The Eighteenth Century,* 415–39. Oxford: Oxford University Press, 1998.

Warren, James Francis. "Scientific Superman: Father José Algué, Jesuit Meteorology in the Philippines under American Rule." In *The Colonial Crucible Empire in the Making of the Modern American State,* edited by Alfred W. McCoy and Francisco A. Scarano, 508–22. Madison: University of Wisconsin Press, 2009.

Watlington, Roy A., and Shirley H. Lincoln. *Disaster and Disruption in 1867: Hurricane, Earthquake, and Tsunami in the Danish West Indies.* St. Thomas: Eastern Caribbean Center, University of the Virgin Islands, 1997.

Watts, David. *The West Indies: Patterns of Development, Culture, and Environmental Change since 1492.* Cambridge Studies in Historical Geography 8. Cambridge; New York: Cambridge University Press, 1987.

Webster, P. J., G. J. Holland, J. A. Curry, and H.-R. Chang. "Changes in Tropical Cyclone Number, Duration, and Intensity in a Warming Environment." *Science* 309, no. 5742 (16 September 2005): 1844–46.

Westergaard, Waldemar Christian. *The Danish West Indies under Company Rule (1671–1754) with a Supplementary Chapter 1755–1917.* New York: Macmillan Company, 1917.

Wiley, James W., and Joseph M. Wunderle. "The Effects of Hurricanes on Birds, with Special Reference to Caribbean Islands." *Bird Conservation International* 3, no. 4 (1993): 319–49.

Wilkerson, Jerry. "The Florida Keys Memorial." *Keys Historeum,* 2 August 2013. http://www.keyshistory.org/hurrmemorial.html.

Will, Lawrence E. *Okeechobee Hurricane and the Hoover Dike*. St. Petersburg, FL: Great Outdoors Publishing Co., 1961.

Williams, Eric. *Capitalism and Slavery*. New York: Russell & Russell, 1944.

Williams, John M., and Iver W. Duedall. *Florida Hurricanes and Tropical Storms, 1871–2001*. Gainesville: University of Florida Press, 2002.

Williams, Tony. *Hurricane of Independence: The Untold Story of the Deadly Storm at the Deciding Moment of the American Revolution*. Naperville, IL: Sourcebooks, 2008.

Woodcock, Henry Iles. *A History of Tobago*. Printed for the author, 1867.

Woolner, David B., and Harry L. Henderson. *FDR and the Environment*. New York: Palgrave Macmillan, 2005.

World Bank and the United Nations, *Natural Hazards, Unnatural Disaster: The Economics of Effective Prevention*. Washington, DC: World Bank, 2010.

Worster, Donald, ed. *The Ends of the Earth: Perspectives on Modern Environmental History*. Studies in Environment and History. Cambridge: Cambridge University Press, 1988.

Zacek, Natalie. *Settler Society in the English Leeward Islands, 1670–1776*. New York: Cambridge University Press, 2010.

Zebrowski, Ernest. *The Last Days of St. Pierre: The Volcanic Disaster That Claimed Thirty Thousand Lives*. New Brunswick, NJ: Rutgers University Press, 2002.

PH.D DISSERTATIONS AND UNPUBLISHED PAPERS

Amador, José G. "'Redeeming the Tropics': Public Health and National Identity in Cuba, Puerto Rico, and Brazil, 1890–1940." Ph.D. dissertation, University of Michigan, 2008.

Bergman, Jonathan C. "The Shape of Disaster and the Universe of Relief: A Social History of Disaster Relief and the 'Hurricane of '38,' Suffolk County, Long Island, New York, 1938–1941." Ph.D. dissertation, State University of New York at Buffalo, 2008.

Chauleau, Liliane. "Les sources de l'histoire des Antilles françaises dans les archives: Leur repartition, leur intérèt pour la recherché historique." Paper presented to 28th International Conference of Caribbean Historians. Barbados, University of the West Indies, 1996.

Dillman, Jefferson T. "From Paradise to Tropics: Landscape in the British West Indies to 1800." Ph.D. dissertation, University of Texas at Arlington, 2011. ProQuest/UMI (AAT 3495001).

Estrada, Amelia. "'Y Vino Dos Veces': Hurricane Flora and Revolutionary Cuba at the Crossroads." Paper presented at the American Historical Association Annual Meeting, San Francisco, 3–6 January 2002.

Gannon, Peter Steven. "The Ideology of Americanization in Puerto Rico, 1898–1909: Conquest and Disestablishment." Ph.D. dissertation, New York University, 1979.

Gilbert, Melanie. *Race and the Media in Natural Disasters: The Media's Portrayal of African Americans in the Galveston Storm of 1900 and in Hurricane Katrina*. Research Paper 211. Southern Illinois University, 1 May 2011. http://opensiuc.lib.siu.edu/do/search/?q=author_lname%3A%22Gilbert%22%20author_fname%3A%22Melanie%22&start=0&context=585089.

Horowitz, Andy. "Help: Hurricane Betsy and the Politics of Disaster in New Orleans' Lower Ninth Ward, 1965–1967." Unpublished paper.

Johnson, Sherry. "El Niño and Environmental Crisis: Reinterpreting American Rebellions in the 1790s." Paper presented at the Third Allen Morris Biennial Conference, Florida State University, 2004.

Joseph, Terencia K. "The Storm before the Calm: The 1898 Hurricane and Official Responses, Saint Lucia." Paper presented at the Annual Conference of the Association of Caribbean Historians, San Juan, 2011.

Kay, Seiler Christine. "The Veteran Killer: The Florida Emergency Relief Administration and the Labor Day Hurricane of 1935." Ph.D. dissertation, Florida State University, 2003.

Mulcahy, Matthew. "Hurricanes, Slavery, and Social Disorder in the British Greater Caribbean." Paper presented at the Third Biennial Allen Morris Conference on the History of Florida and the Atlantic World. Florida State University, 2003.

Partagás, José Fernández. "Impact on Hurricane History of a Revised Lowest Pressure at Havana (Cuba) During the October 11, 1846 Hurricane." Unpublished paper, 1993. http://www.aoml.noaa.gov/hrd/Landsea/Partagas/impacthurrhist.pdf.

Pincus, Steve, and James Robinson. "Wars and State-Making Reconsidered: The Rise of the Interventionist State." Unpublished paper, 2012.

Reynolds, Thomas. "American Red Cross Disaster Services, 1930–47." Ph.D. dissertation, Columbia University, 1954.

Ryden, David Beck. "Producing a Peculiar Commodity: Jamaican Sugar Production, Slave Life, and Planter Profits on the Eve of Abolition, 1750–1807." Ph.D. dissertation, University of Minnesota, 1999.

Thompson, Denise D.P. "Building Effectiveness in Multi-State Disaster Management Systems: The Case of the Caribbean Disaster and Emergency Response Agency." Ph.D. dissertation, Pennsylvania State University, 2010.

Vilagrán, Martín Gelabertó. "La palabra del predicador: Contrarreforma y superstición en cataluña (siglos XVII y XVIII)." Dissertation, University of Barcelona, 2003.

Webersik, Christian, and Christian Klose. "Environmental Change and Political Instability in Haiti and the Dominican Republic: Explaining the Divide," paper presented to Conference on Computer Supported Cooperative Work Workshop, (16–17 Dec. 2010).

Index

 ᗡᏯᏯᗡ

Pages in italics indicate figures.